Android™ Boot Camp for Developers Using Java™

A Guide to Creating Your First Android Apps

Fourth Edition

Corinne Hoisington

Australia • Brazil • Canada • Mexico • Singapore • United Kingdom • United States

***Android Boot Camp for Developers Using Java: A Guide to Creating Your First Android Apps,* Fourth Edition**
Corinne Hoisington

SVP, Product: Cheryl Costantini

VP, Product: Thais Alencar

Senior Portfolio Product Director: Mark Santee

Portfolio Product Director: Rita Lombard

Portfolio Product Manager: Tran Pham

Product Assistant: Anh Nguyen

Learning Designer: Mary Convertino

Content Manager: Samantha Enders

Digital Project Manager: John Smigielski

Technical Editor: Danielle Shaw

Developmental Editor: Dan Seiter

VP, Product Marketing: Jason Sakos

Director, Product Marketing: Danae April

Product Marketing Manager: Mackenzie Paine

Content Acquisition Analyst: Ann Hoffman

Production Service: Straive

Designer: Erin Griffin

Cover Image Source: Martzin / Shutterstock.com / Source ID: 264538211

Library of Congress Control Number: 2023906016

ISBN: 978-0-357-88123-1

Cengage
200 Pier 4 Boulevard
Boston, MA 02210
USA

Printed in the United States of America
Print Number: 01 Print Year: 2023

Brief Contents

Contents

Chapter 3

Chapter 4

Explore! Icons and Decision-Making Components 111

Chapter 5

Investigate! Android Lists, Arrays, Switch Statements, and Web Browsers 153

Chapter 12

About the Author

Corinne Hoisington is a full-time professor of Information Systems Technology at Central Virginia Community College in Lynchburg, Virginia. She has more than 30 years of teaching experience. She travels over 250,000 miles a year delivering keynote addresses to college instructors, university professors, and K–12 educators in over 70 cities worldwide and to customers such as the Microsoft Corporation, Microsoft Canada International Events, Cengage Learning, ByteSpeed, National Geographic Abu Dhabi, Capital One International Bank, Executive LIVE in London and Johannesburg, and the international South by Southwest (SXSW) event in Austin, Texas. Professor Hoisington is the recipient of the Microsoft Most Valuable Professional award in Computer Programming. She has authored over 30 textbooks with Cengage Learning and National Geographic on topics such as Outlook 365, Office 365, Microsoft Windows, Android Boot Camp Java, Technology Now, and Visual Basic.

Conceptual Approach for the Instructor

Welcome to *Android Boot Camp for Developers Using Java: A Guide to Creating Your First Android Apps, Fourth Edition*. This book is designed for people who are either new to Java developing or have some programming experience and want to move into the exciting world of developing apps for Android mobile devices on a Windows or Mac computer. Google Android is quickly becoming the operating system of choice for mobile devices, including smartphones and tablets, with nearly three-quarters of the world's mobile devices running on the Android platform. To help you participate in the growing Android market, this book focuses on developing apps for Android devices.

The approach used in *Android Boot Camp for Developers Using Java* is straightforward. You review a completed Android app and identify why people use the app, and then analyze the tasks it performs and the problems it solves. You also learn about the programming logic, Java tools, and code syntax you can use to create the app. Next, a hands-on tutorial guides you through the steps of creating the Android app, including designing the user interface and writing the code. After each step, you can compare your work to an illustration that shows exactly how the interface should look or what the code should contain. Using the illustrations, you can avoid mistakes and finish the chapter with an appealing, real-world Android app.

The main tool used in *Android Boot Camp for Developers Using Java* is the standard one that developers use to create Android apps: Android Studio, a free, open-source integrated development environment. Android Studio includes an emulator for testing your apps, so you don't need a smartphone or tablet to run any of the apps covered in this book. You may choose to use all the chapters in the book or add several chapters to your traditional Java course. Instructions for downloading and setting up Android Studio are provided later in this preface.

The course objectives of this textbook are developed with each chapter:

Chapter 1 introduces the Android platform and describes the current market for Android apps. You create your first Android project using Android Studio and become familiar with the Android Studio interface and its tools. As programming tradition mandates, your first project is called Hello Android World, which you complete and then run in an emulator.

Chapter 2 focuses on the Android user interface. While developing an app for selecting and displaying healthy recipes, you follow a series of steps that you repeat every time you create an Android app. You learn how to develop a user interface using certain types of controls, select a screen layout, and write code that responds to a button event (such as a tap or click). While creating the chapter project, you develop an app that includes more than one screen and can switch from one screen to another. Finally, you learn how to correct errors in Java code.

In **Chapter 3**, you learn about user input, variables, and operations. You develop an Android app that allows users to enter the number of concert tickets they want to purchase and then tap or click a button to calculate the total cost of the tickets. To develop the app, you create a user interface using an Android theme and add controls to the interface, including text fields, buttons, and spinner controls. You also declare variables, use arithmetic operations to perform calculations, and then convert and format numeric data.

Chapter 4 discusses icons and decision-making controls. The sample app provides healthcare professionals with a mobile way to convert the weight of a patient from pounds to kilograms and from kilograms to pounds. You create this project using a custom application icon, learn how to fine-tune the layout of the user interface, and include radio buttons for user selections. You also learn how to program decisions using If statements, If Else statements, and logical operators.

In **Chapter 5**, you learn how to use lists, arrays, and web browsers in an Android app. You design and create an Android app that people can use as a traveler's guide to popular attractions in Chicago. To create the app, you work with lists, images, and the Switch decision structure. You also learn how to let users access a web browser while using an Android app.

Chapter 6 explains how to include audio such as music in Android apps. The sample app opens with a splash screen and then displays a second screen where users can select a song to play. To develop this app, you create and set up a splash screen, learn about the Activity life cycle, pause an Activity, and start, play, stop, and resume music playback.

Chapter 7 demonstrates how to use an Android layout tool called GridView, which shows thumbnail images in a scrolling grid. When the user taps or clicks a thumbnail, the app displays a larger image below the grid. You also learn how to use an array to manage the images.

In **Chapter 8**, you design a calendar program that includes a DatePicker control for selecting a date to book a reservation. Because this app is designed for a larger tablet interface, you also learn how to design an app for a tablet device and add an Android virtual device specifically designed for tablets.

In **Chapter 9**, you continue to explore Android apps designed for tablet devices. In this chapter, you create a multipane interface with a list of options in the left pane and details about the selected option in the right pane. Each pane displays a different layout and Activity. To create the multipane interface, you work with the Primary/Detail Flow template.

Chapter 10 explains how to create two types of animation. Using a frame-by-frame approach, you animate a series of images so that they play in sequence. Using a motion tween animation, you apply an animated effect to a single image.

Chapter 11 shows you how to create an Android app that requests data, stores it, and then modifies the data to produce a result throughout multiple activities. You learn about the ways Android apps can save persistent application data, and then use one—the SharedPreferences class—to store data for an electric car financing app.

In **Chapter 12**, you learn how to publish an Android app to the Google Play Store. Before publishing the app, you test it, prepare it for publication, create a package, digitally sign the app, and prepare promotional materials.

New to This Edition

The fourth edition of *Android Boot Camp for Developers Using Java* includes the following updated features:

- **Major updates**—Each chapter has been updated to reflect the latest methodology and coding techniques in Java coding.
- **Objectives**—Each chapter begins with a list of learning objectives that are numbered and mapped to the chapter's major headings and end-of-chapter questions. The objectives focus learning and serve as a useful study aid.
- **Quick Check questions**—Throughout each chapter, Quick Check questions test your knowledge of the key terms and new concepts from your reading.
- **Figures and tables**—The chapters contain a wealth of updated screenshots of the development environment to guide you as you create Android apps and learn about the Android marketplace. In addition, many updated tables are included to give you a quick summary of useful information.

Inclusivity and Diversity

Cengage is committed to providing educational content that is inclusive and welcoming to all learners. Research demonstrates that students who experience a sense of belonging in class more successfully make meaning out of, and find relevance in, what they encounter in learning content. To improve both the learning process and outcomes, our materials seek to affirm the fullness of human diversity with respect to ability, language, culture, gender, age, socioeconomic status, and other forms of human difference that students may bring to the classroom.

Across the computing industry, standard coding language such as "master" and "slave" is being retired in favor of language that is more inclusive, such as "primary/replica" or "leader/follower." Different software development and social media companies are adopting their own replacement language, and currently there is no shared standard. In addition, the terms "master" and "slave" remain deeply embedded in legacy code, and understanding this terminology remains necessary for new programmers. When required for understanding, Cengage will introduce the noninclusive term in the first instance but will then provide appropriate replacement terminology for the remainder of the discussion or example. We appreciate your feedback as we work to make our products more inclusive for all.

For more information about Cengage's commitment to inclusivity and diversity, please visit *www.cengage.com/inclusion-diversity*.

Features of the Text

- **Good to Know, On the Job, and Critical Thinking**—Good to Know notes offer tips about Android devices, Android apps, and the Android development tools. The On the Job features provide programming advice and practical solutions similar to those used by professionals in the information technology sector. The Critical Thinking features pose thought-provoking questions and provide answers related to programming and Java.
- **Step-by-step tutorials**—Starting in Chapter 1, you create complete, working Android apps by performing the steps in a series of hands-on tutorials that lead you through the development process in the newest version of Android.
- **Code syntax features**—Many new programming concepts or techniques are introduced with code syntax examples that highlight a type of statement or programming structure. The code is analyzed and explained thoroughly before you use it in the chapter project.
- **Summaries**—At the end of each chapter is a summary list that recaps the Android terms, programming concepts, and Java coding techniques covered in the chapter. The list provides a way to check your understanding of the chapter's main points.
- **Key terms**—Each chapter includes a list of new terms that are alphabetized for ease of reference. This feature is another useful way to review the chapter's major concepts. Definitions of these terms are included in a glossary at the end of the book.
- **Developer FAQs**—Each chapter contains many short-answer questions that help you review the key concepts in the chapter. These questions are aligned with the objectives listed at the beginning of the chapter.
- **Beyond the Book**—In addition to review questions, each chapter provides research topics and questions. You can search the web to find the answers to these questions and further your Android knowledge.
- **Case programming projects**—Except for Chapter 12, each chapter outlines realistic programming projects, including their purpose, algorithms, and conditions. For each project, you use the steps and techniques you learned in the chapter to create a running Android app on your own.
- **Quality**—Every chapter project and case programming project was tested using Windows 10/11 and macOS computers.

Ancillary Package

Additional instructor resources for this product are available online. Instructor assets include an Instructor Manual, Educator's Guide, PowerPoint® slides, and a test bank powered by Cognero®. Sign up or sign in at *www.cengage.com* to search for and access this product and its online resources.

Instructor Manual—The Instructor Manual follows the text chapter by chapter to assist in planning and organizing an effective, engaging course. The manual includes learning objectives, chapter overviews, lecture notes, ideas for classroom activities, and additional resources.

PowerPoint presentations—This text provides PowerPoint slides to accompany each chapter. Slides are included to guide classroom presentations and can be made available to students for chapter review or to print as classroom handouts.

Solution and Answer Guide (SAG)—Solutions and rationales to review questions, exercises, and projects are provided to assist with grading and student understanding.

Data files—Data files necessary to complete some of the steps and projects in the course are available.

Educator's Guide—The Educator's Guide provides an overview of the features of the text and resources available on the instructor resource site.

Complete list of learning objectives—A complete list of all objectives addressed in the textbook is available to help instructors plan and manage their course.

Test bank—Cengage Learning Testing Powered by Cognero is a flexible online system that allows you to author, edit, and manage test bank content from multiple Cengage Learning solutions, create multiple test versions in an instant, and deliver tests from your LMS, your classroom, or anywhere you want.

Acknowledgments

This book is the product of a wonderful team of professionals working toward a single goal: providing students with pertinent, engaging material to further their knowledge and careers. Thank you to the folks at Cengage—specifically, Content Manager Samantha Enders, Developmental Editor and wordsmith Dan Seiter, and Learning Designer Mary Convertino.

Writing a book is similar to entering a long-term relationship with an obsessive partner. Throughout the journey, life continues around you: teaching classes full time, presenting around the world, and celebrating family milestones. As the world continues, those closest to you allow you to focus on your reclusive writing by assisting with every other task. My husband, Timothy, is credited with taking part in my nomadic life and most of all for his love, following me to 95 countries, and patience. Special thanks to my six children, Tim, Brittany, Ryan, Daniel, Breanne, and Eric (and partners), for providing much-needed breaks filled with pride and laughter. And special thanks to the wee members of my family, my grandchildren Liam, Lochlan, Colin, Jackson, Reagan, Griffin, McKinley, and Naomi, who all make me smile like no others. I can't wait to see the world through your eyes.

Prelude! Installing the Android SDK with Android Studio

Setting Up the Android Environment

To begin developing Android applications, you must first set up the Android programming environment on your computer. This preface walks you through the installation and setup of a development environment on a Windows or Mac computer. The Android Software Development Kit (SDK) allows developers to create applications for the Android platform. The Android SDK includes Android Studio along with sample projects including source code, development tools, an emulator, and required libraries to build Android applications, which are written using the Java programming language.

Although installing the Android SDK with Android Studio is easy, you must follow the instructions here to correctly prepare for creating an Android application. Before writing your first application in Chapter 1, complete the following general steps to successfully install the Android SDK with Android Studio on your computer:

- Prepare your computer for the installation.
- Download and install the Android SDK and Android Studio integrated development environment (IDE).
- Set up the Android emulator.

Preparing Your Computer

The Android Software Development Kit is compatible with Windows 8.x (32-, 64-, or 128-bit), Windows 10/11 (32-, 64-, or 128-bit), macOS (Intel only), and Linux. At least 2 GB of RAM is required for all platforms. Java Development Kit (JDK) 8 must already be installed on the PC. To install the basic files needed to write an Android application, your hard drive needs at least 1 GB of available space. Android Studio is the officially recommended IDE of Android app development, replacing Eclipse.

Before getting started, confirm that the latest free Java updates for your computer have been installed. If necessary, go to *java.com* to install the latest Java updates and prepare for the Android installation. You cannot install Android Studio unless the Java updates are installed.

Note that this textbook was written using the Tiramisu version of Android Studio. You can either use the current version or download the Tiramisu version to your computer by going to *developer.android.com/studio/archive*.

Downloading the Android SDK with Android Studio

The preferred Java program development software for mobile applications is called the Android SDK, which includes Android Studio and additional tools. The Android SDK provides you with the API libraries and developer tools necessary to build, test, and debug apps for Android. The Android SDK with Android Studio is a free and open-source IDE. The AVD Manager provides a graphical user interface in which you can create and manage Android Virtual Devices (AVDs) that run in the Android emulator.

To download the Android SDK with Android Studio and then start Android Studio, complete the following steps. Note that the images shown in the figures may look different on your computer.

Step 1

- Use a browser to open the webpage **http://developer.android.com/sdk/**.

The Download page opens in the browser (Figure 1).

Figure 1 Android Studio download site

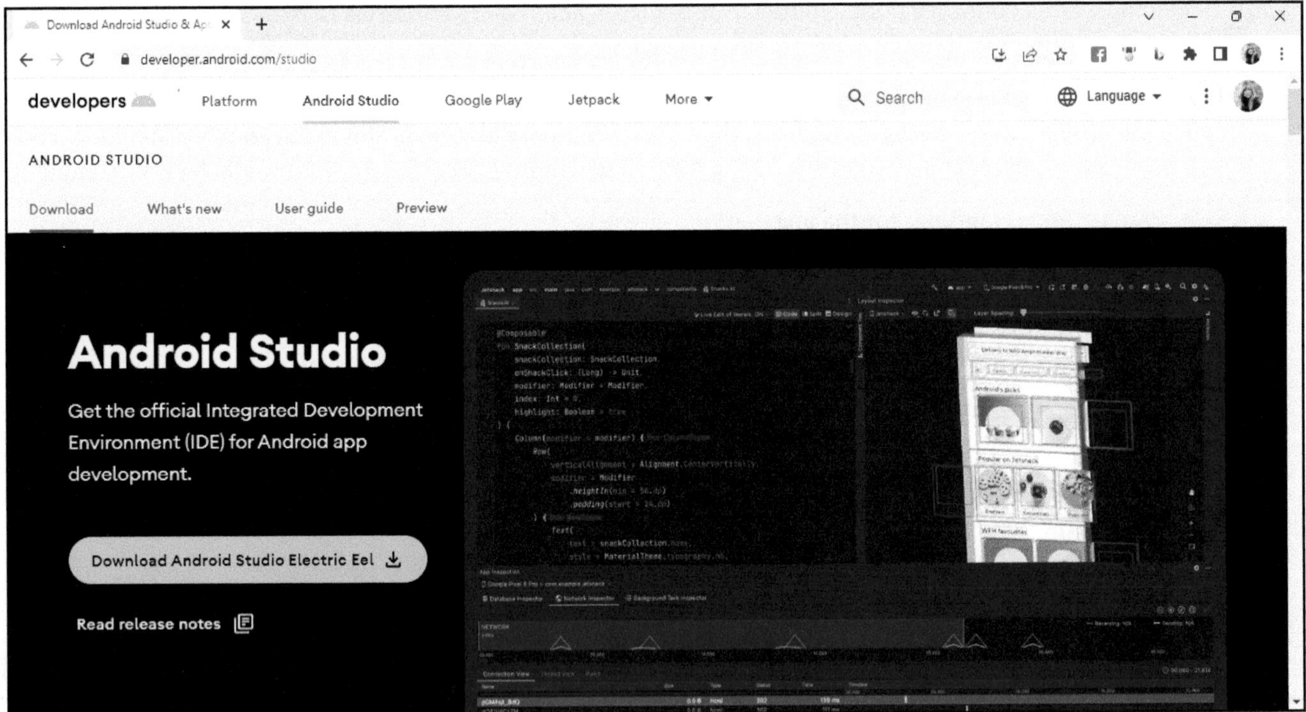

Step 2

- Click the Download Android Studio button to download the most recent version of Android Studio. If you are using a Mac, the button is named Download Android Studio for Mac.

The website detects whether you are installing the Android SDK on a computer running Windows or macOS. The latest Android system image for the emulator is included with this installation.

The Terms and Conditions webpage opens (Figure 2).

Figure 2 Terms and Conditions page of Android Studio

Download Android Studio Electric Eel | 2022.1.1 Patch 1

Before downloading, you must agree to the following terms and conditions.

Terms and Conditions

This is the Android Software Development Kit License Agreement

1. Introduction

1.1 The Android Software Development Kit (referred to in the License Agreement as the "SDK" and specifically including the Android system files, packaged APIs, and Google APIs add-ons) is licensed to you subject to the terms of the License Agreement. The License Agreement forms a legally binding contract between you and Google in relation to your use of the SDK. 1.2 "Android" means the Android software stack for devices, as made available under the Android Open Source Project, which is located at the following URL: https://source.android.com/, as updated from time to time. 1.3 A "compatible implementation" means any Android device that (i) complies with the Android Compatibility Definition document, which can be found at the Android compatibility website (https://source.android.com/compatibility) and which may be updated from time to time; and (ii) successfully passes the Android Compatibility Test Suite (CTS). 1.4 "Google" means Google LLC, organized under the laws of the State of Delaware, USA, and operating under the laws of the USA with principal place of business at 1600 Amphitheatre Parkway, Mountain View, CA 94043, USA.

2. Accepting this License Agreement

2.1 In order to use the SDK, you must first agree to the License Agreement. You may not use the SDK if you do not accept the License Agreement. 2.2 By clicking to accept and/or using this SDK, you hereby agree to the terms of the License Agreement. 2.3 You may not use the SDK and may not accept the License Agreement if you are a person barred from receiving the SDK under the laws of the United States or other countries, including the country in which you are resident or from which you use the SDK. 2.4 If you are agreeing to be bound by the License Agreement on behalf of your employer or other entity, you represent and warrant that you have full legal authority to bind your employer or such entity to the License Agreement. If you do not have the requisite authority, you may not accept the License Agreement or use the SDK on behalf of your employer or other entity.

Step 3

- Scroll down the page and then click the "I have read and agree with the above terms and conditions" check box.
- Click the Download Android Studio for Windows (or for Mac) button.
- Save the file on your computer.
- Navigate to the location of the downloaded file and then double-click the file to begin the setup.

The Android Studio Setup dialog box opens (Figure 3).

Figure 3 Android Studio Setup dialog box

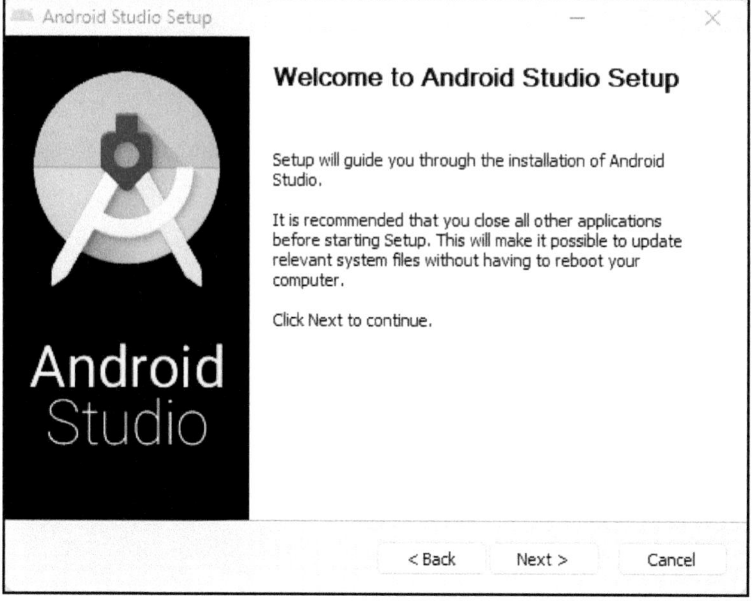

Step 4

- Click the Next button to continue. If you are using a Mac, drag the Android Studio icon to the Applications folder.
- Accept the default settings throughout the rest of the download and installation of Android Studio.
- By default, Android Studio opens after the installation of the program.

Android Studio starts. You may want to create a shortcut on the desktop to make it easier to start Android Studio. After successfully downloading Android Studio, you are ready to begin coding with various preinstalled emulators that test your newly built apps. This textbook uses the Resizable API 33 built-in emulator for testing smartphone apps.

Installing an Android Studio Emulator

The Android Studio Emulator simulates Android devices on your computer so that you can test your application on a variety of devices and Android API levels without needing to have each physical device. For example, you can test smartphones, tablets, smartwatches, and even Android TV devices. To install an emulator in the Android Studio SDK, complete the following steps.

Step 1

- Open Android Studio and click Tools on the menu.
- Click Device Manager to add an emulator.

Device Manager opens (Figure 4).

Figure 4 Device Manager

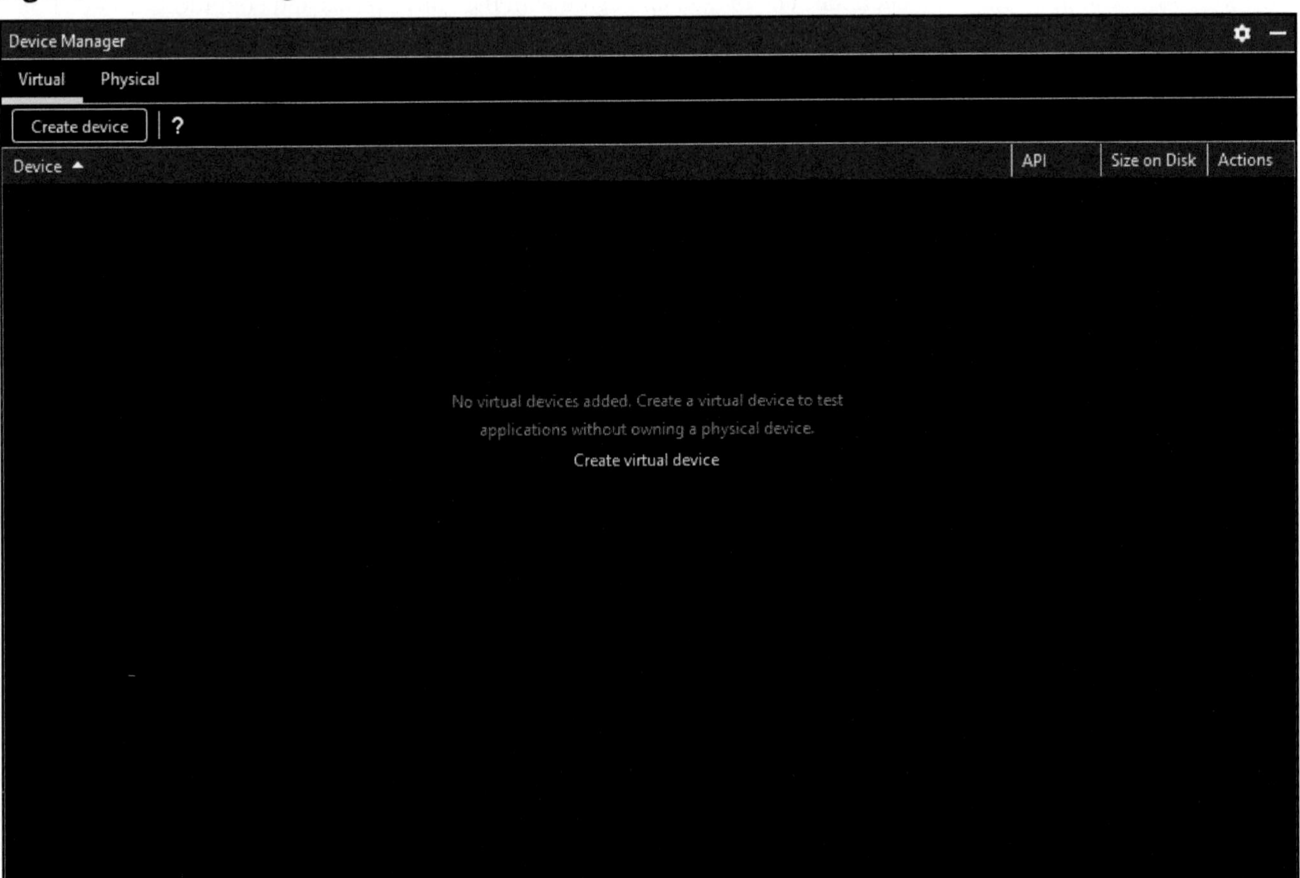

Step 2

- Click the Create virtual device button to select a virtual device.

The Virtual Device Configuration dialog box opens and allows you to select the hardware emulator you want (Figure 5).

Figure 5 Virtual Device Configuration dialog box

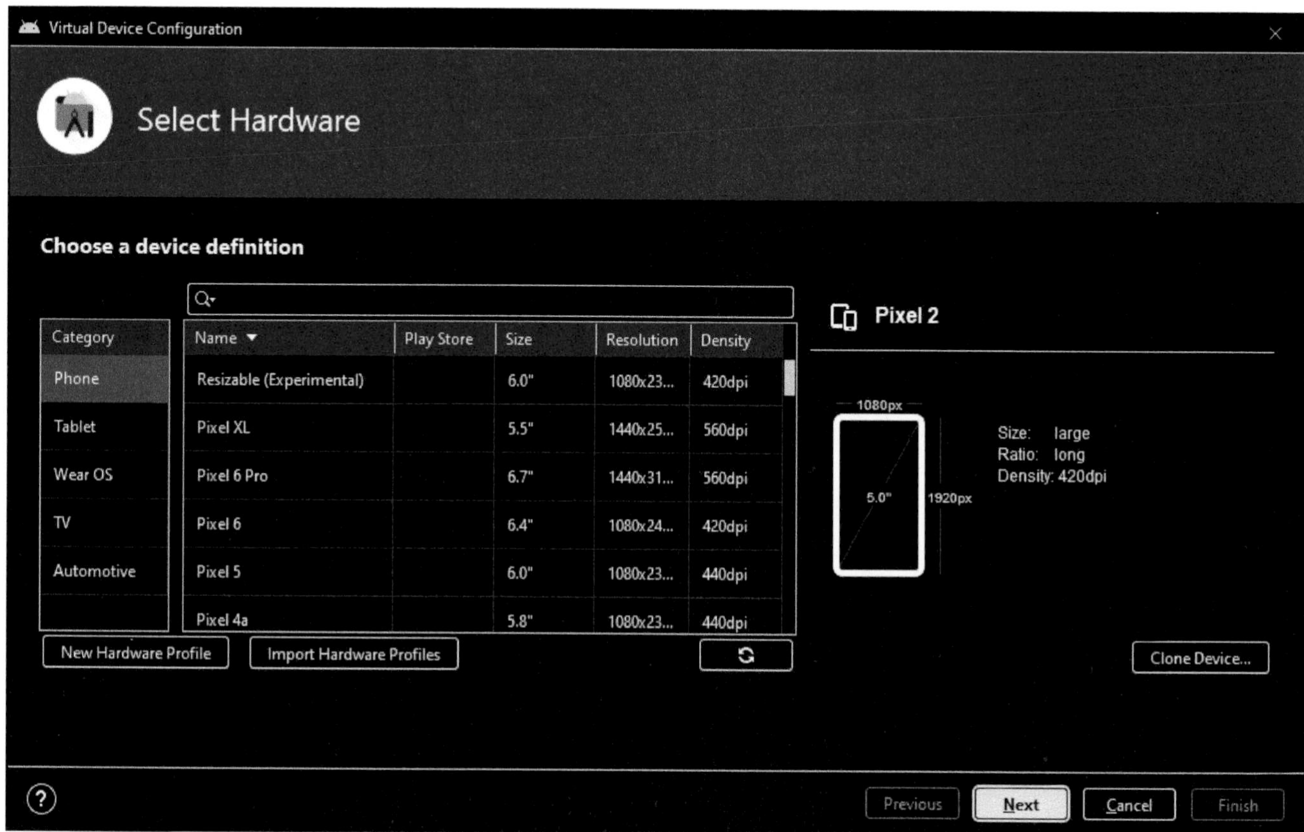

Step 3

- Click Resizable or another phone emulator based on your instructor's recommendation.
- Click the Next button and follow the prompts to complete the installation of your phone emulator.

The phone emulator is installed in Android Studio.

Chapter 1

Voilà! Meet the Android

Learning Objectives

At the completion of this chapter, you will be able to:

1.1 Describe the market for Android applications

1.2 Identify the role of the Android platform in the mobile market

1.3 Describe the features of the Android phone

1.4 Identify the languages used in Android development

1.5 Describe the role of Google Play in the marketplace

1.6 Understand the connection between Windows and Android

1.7 Create an Android project using Android Studio

1.8 Design the user interface layout within the virtual device

1.9 Execute an Android application on an emulator

1.10 Open a saved Android project in Android Studio

1.1 Understanding the Market for Android Applications

Welcome to the beginning of your journey in creating Android phone applications and developing for the mobile device market. Mobile computing has become the most popular way to make a personal connection to the Internet and view your email, social media, and webpages—all on your phone. Mobile phones and tablets comprise the fastest-growing category of any technology in the world. Mobile phone usage has quickly outgrown the simple expectations of voice calls and text messaging. An average data plan for a mobile device, often called a smartphone, typically includes browsing the web, playing popular games such as Call of Duty: Mobile or Among Us, taking photos, using business applications, reading a menu with a QR code, checking email, listening to music, recording live video, and mapping locations with GPS (global positioning system). According to Reviews.org, the average person spends 2 hours and 54 minutes a day on their phone.

When purchasing a smartphone, you can choose from two primary mobile operating systems (OSs), including iOS for the iPhone and Google Android. Recently, the Android phone has become the sales leader, outselling its competitors. According to Statista.com, the current number of smartphone users in the world today is 6.648 billion, which means 83.72 percent of the world's population owns a smartphone. The world's population downloads more than 112 billion apps and games from Google Play each month. Nearly 72 percent of the world's mobile devices run on the Android platform. About 28 percent of the world's mobile devices run on the iOS platform.

On the Job

Almost two-thirds of all U.S. households have canceled their landlines for the convenience of handling only one bill from a mobile carrier.

Quick Check

By far, what is the most popular smartphone operating system?

Answer: Android.

Creating mobile applications, called **apps**, for the Android phone market is an exciting new job opportunity. Whether you become a developer for a technology firm that creates professional apps for corporations or a hobbyist developer who creates games, niche programs, or savvy new applications, the Android marketplace provides a new means to earn income. Many retail and service products have their own mobile apps, such as Delta Airlines, Airbnb, Etsy, and Duolingo. An Android developer specializes in designing and creating apps for the Android marketplace. Android developers generally work in-house for a large organization, or an app development agency may employ them instead.

Good to Know

According to *Indeed*, an app developer is considered the top job in the technology field, earning a median salary of $91,513. Some of the highest-paying cities in the United States for application developers are Dallas, Austin, Atlanta, New York, and Houston, but many app developers work from anywhere as remote workers.

1.2 The Role of the Android in the Mobile Market

The Android phone platform is built on a free, open-source operating system primarily created by a company called Android, Inc. In 2005, Google obtained Android, Inc., to start a venture in the mobile phone market. Because Google intended the Android platform to be open source, the Android code was released under the Apache license, which permits anyone to download the full open-source Android code for free. Two years later, Google unveiled its first open-standards mobile device called the Android (**Figure 1-1**). In less than a decade, the Android phone market has grown into the world's best-selling phone platform.

Open-Source Platform

Android is the first open-source technology platform for mobile devices. Being an **open-source operating system** effectively means that no company or individual defines the features or direction of the development. Organizations and developers can extract, modify, and use the code for creating any app. The rapid success of the Android phone

Figure 1-1 Android phone

can be attributed to the collaboration of the **Open Handset Alliance**, an open-source business alliance of 80 firms that develop standards for mobile devices. The Open Handset Alliance is led by Google. Other members include companies such as Samsung, Sony, HTC, Texas Instruments, Kyocera, and LG. Google has produced its own phone, a modular device, under the name Project Ara. Competitors such as Apple, which produces the iPhone, do not have an open-source coding environment but instead work with proprietary operating systems. The strength of the open-source community lies in the developers' ability to share their source code. Even though the open-source Android software is free, many developers are paid to build and improve the platform. For example, proprietary software such as the Apple operating system is limited to company employees licensed to build a program within the organization. The Android open-source platform allows more freedom so people can collaborate and improve the source code.

Many phone manufacturers install the Android operating system on their brand-name mobile phones due to its open-source environment. The open-source structure means that manufacturers do not pay license fees or royalties; with a small amount of customization, each manufacturer can place the Android OS on its latest devices. This minimal overhead allows manufacturers to sell their phones in the retail market for the relatively low price of $300 or more. Low prices on Android mobile devices have increased their sales and popularity.

The open-source community also makes Android phones attractive for consumers. Android has a large community of developers writing apps that extend the functionality of the devices. Users, for example, can benefit from over 2.5 million apps available in the Android marketplace, many of which are free. Because the Android phone platform has become the leader in sales in the mobile market, the Android application market is expected to keep pace with growing app demand.

Good to Know | According to Simform, an average person has 40 apps installed on their phone. Of those 40 apps, 89 percent of a user's time is split among 18 apps.

Android Open-Source Devices

The open-source Android smartphones, tablets, and smartwatches are sold by a variety of companies under names you may recognize, such as Samsung, Google Pixel, Huawei, OnePlus, Motorola, and several others that sell only in regional markets (**Figure 1-2**).

Figure 1-2 Android devices

> **On the Job**
>
> The Android platform is the core of many home products. Use your voice to stream on a television with Chromecast and Google Home. Use Nest cameras to protect your property on the Android platform.

> **Good to Know**
>
> Google checks every Android application in the Google Play Store to confirm that the apps do not have malware or viruses.

Figure 1-3 Android Studio emulator

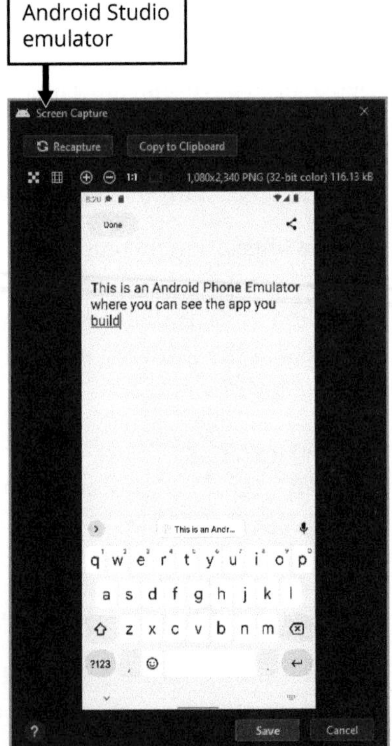

Android devices come in many shapes and sizes, as shown in Figure 1-2. The Android OS powers all types of mobile devices, including smartphones, foldable phones, tablets, watches, MP4 players, automobiles, and Internet TVs. Android devices are available with a variety of screen dimensions. Many devices support landscape mode, in which the width and height are spontaneously reversed depending on the orientation of the device. As you design Android apps, you must recognize that the screen size affects the layout of the user interface. To take full advantage of the capabilities of a particular device, you need to design user interfaces specifically for that device. For example, a smartphone and a tablet not only have a different physical screen size, they also have different screen resolutions and pixel densities, which change the development process.

As you develop an Android app, you can test the results on an **emulator**, which duplicates how the app looks and feels on a particular device. The Android emulator (**Figure 1-3**) mimics all the hardware and software features of a typical mobile device, except that it cannot place actual phone calls. You can change the Android emulators to simulate the layout of a smartphone with a 4.5-inch screen or a tablet with a larger screen, both with high-density graphics. Android automatically scales content to the screen size of the device you choose, but if you use low-quality graphics in an app, the result is often a poorly pixelated display. As a developer, you need to continue to update your app as the market shifts to different platforms and screen resolutions.

The Android phone market has many more hardware case and size options than the 5.4- to 6.8-inch screen options of an iPhone. Several Android phones, such as the Galaxy and Google Pixel, have screens that are 6 inches or larger and can fold vertically or flip horizontally. The different sizes and shapes are excellent for phone users who like to watch movies, play games, or view full webpages on their phone. In addition, many types of tablets run on the Android platform. Popular models of Android tablets include the Amazon Fire, Lenovo Tab, Onyx Boox Note Air, Amazon Kindle, and Alcatel Joy Tab. Android tablets are in direct competition with other tablets and slate computers, such as the iPad (various generations) and Windows tablets. The iPad tablet may have name recognition, but Android tablets dominate the market share.

1.3 Features of the Android Phone

As a developer, you must understand a phone's capabilities in order to use its full functionality. The Android platform offers a wide variety of features that apps can utilize. Some features vary by model. Most Android phones provide the features listed in **Table 1-1**.

Table 1-1 Android platform features

Feature	Description
3D graphics	The interface can support 3D graphics for a 3D interactive game experience or 3D image rendering.
Split screen	A split-screen, multiwindow feature displays more than one Android application at the same time. Watch a movie on the left side and hold a video call with your friends who are also watching the movie.
Dark mode	The Dark mode feature helps to save the phone's battery life. Blank white space consumes more power and drains the battery.
Facial recognition	Android provides this high-level feature for automatically identifying or verifying a person's face from a digital image or a video frame.
Front- and rear-facing camera	Android phones can use either a front- or rear-facing camera, allowing developers to create applications involving video calling.
Multiple language voice-to-text support	Android supports multiple human languages. Android provides a feature of converting text to speech in different languages. Text messages can be read aloud to help people who are visually impaired.
On-screen keyboard	The on-screen keyboard offers suggestions for spelling corrections as well as options for completing words you start typing. The on-screen keyboard also supports voice input.
Power management	Android identifies programs running in the background that are using memory and processor resources. You can close those apps to free up the phone's processor memory, extending the battery power. For optimized gaming, Android supports the use of a gyroscope, gravity and barometric sensors, linear acceleration, and rotation vectors, which provide game developers with highly sensitive and responsive controls.
Voice-based recognition	Android recognizes voice actions for calling, texting, and navigating with the phone.
Wi-Fi Internet tethering	Android supports tethering, which allows a phone to be used as a wireless or wired hotspot that other devices can use to connect to the Internet.

1.4 The Languages Used in Android Development

The coding language that is used to build most of the Android apps in the Google Play Store is called **Java**. Java is also the language most supported by Google. In addition, Java has a great online community for support in case problems develop with your code that you need help solving. A second language that you can use to code Android apps is named *Kotlin*. It was introduced as a secondary official Java language in 2017. Kotlin can interoperate with Java, and it runs on the Java Virtual Machine. Java is the most popular programming language in the world; it runs most web browsers, web applications, desktop applications, game development, and servers.

Java is a language and a platform originated by Sun Microsystems. Java is an **object-oriented programming language** patterned after the C++ language. Object-oriented programming encourages good software engineering practices such as code reuse. The official tool for Android application development, released in December 2014, is called **Android Studio**, an integrated development environment (IDE) for building and integrating application development tools and open-source projects. Android Studio IDE is exclusively dedicated to creating Android applications. Prior to Android Studio, Eclipse ADT was the primary Android development environment. Eclipse developed applications in many programming languages, including Java, C, C++, COBOL, Ada, and Python.

As shown in the preface of this book, the first step in setting up your Android programming environment is to download and install the free Android Studio IDE on your PC or Mac computer from the website *https://developer.android.com/studio*. The installation includes the Android **Software Development Kit (SDK)**, which runs in Android Studio, and the emulator downloaded in the Device Manager. The Android SDK includes a set of development tools that help you design the interface of the program, write the code, and test the program using a built-in Android handset emulator. Another language called **XML** (Extensible Markup Language) is used to assist in the layout of the Android emulator.

Quick Check

What are the two primary languages used to program Android phones?

Answer: Java and Kotlin.

Android Emulator

When you run your Android program, you can either display it on an actual Android device, such as your smartphone or smartwatch, or you can display the app on an emulator. The Android emulator lets you design, develop, prototype, and test Android applications without using a physical device. When you run an Android program in Android Studio, the emulator starts so you can test the program. You can then use the mouse to simulate touching the screen of the device. The emulator mimics almost every feature of a real Android handset except for the ability to place a voice phone call. A running emulator can play video and audio, render gaming animation, and store information. Multiple emulators are available within the Android SDK to target various devices and versions from early Android phones onward. Developers should test their apps on several versions to confirm the stability of a particular platform. Android Studio includes a live layout editing mode that previews an app's user interface across a range of devices (**Figure 1-4**).

Versions of Android

The first Android version, release 1.0, was introduced in September 2008. Each subsequent version adds new features and fixes any known bugs in the platform. Android has adopted a naming system for each version based on sugary treats and dessert items, as shown in **Table 1-2**. After the first version, dessert names were assigned in alphabetical order. When the revision level reached 10.0, Android started emphasizing revision numbers over names because it was difficult to identify a common dessert name starting with *Q*.

Figure 1-4 Android Studio running Java code

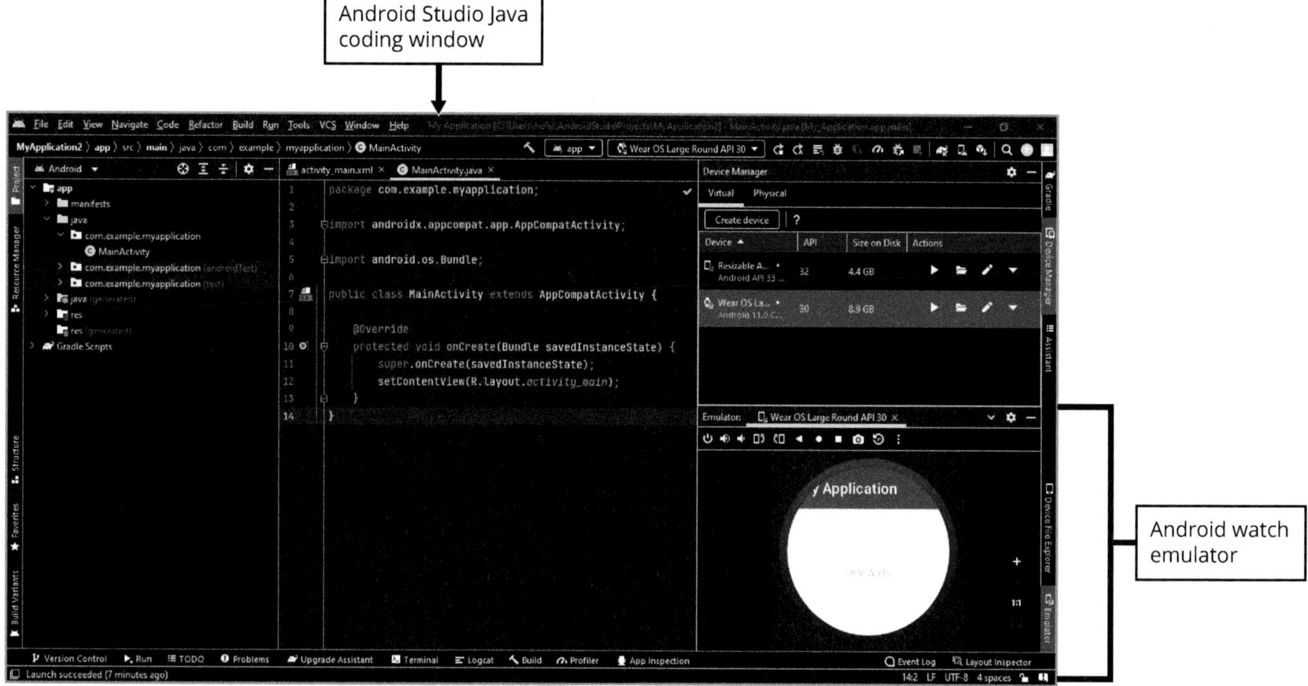

Table 1-2 Android version history

Version Name	Release Date
1.0 First version	September 2008
1.5 Cupcake	April 2009
1.6 Donut	September 2009
2.0 Éclair	October 2009
2.2 Froyo (Frozen Yogurt)	May 2010
2.3 Gingerbread	December 2010
3.0 Honeycomb	February 2011
4.0 Ice Cream Sandwich	May 2011
4.1 Jelly Bean	July 2012
4.4 Kit Kat	October 2013
5.0 Lollipop	November 2014
6.0 Marshmallow	October 2015
7.0 Nougat	August 2016
8.0 Oreo	August 2017
9.0 Pie	August 2018
Android 10.0 (internal name: Quince Tart)	September 2019
Android 11.0 (internal name: Red Velvet Cake)	September 2020
Android 12.0 (internal name: Snow Cone)	October 2021
Android 13.0 (internal name: Tiramisu)	October 2022

Critical Thinking

When creating an app, should I target the most current Android version only?

To support as many Android devices as possible, you should set the minimum development version to the lowest available version that allows your app to provide its core feature set.

1.5 Google Play in the Marketplace

The Android platform consists of the Android OS, the Android application development tools, and a marketplace for Android applications. After you write and test a program, you compile the app into an Android package file with the filename extension .apk. Programs written for the Android platform are sold and deployed through an online store called **Google Play** (*play.google.com*), which provides registration services and certifies that the program meets minimum standards of reliability, efficiency, and performance. Google Play requires that you sign an agreement and pay a one-time registration fee (currently $25). After registration, you can publish your app on Google Play, provided the app meets the minimum standards. You can also release updates as needed for your app. If your app is free, Google Play publishes your app at no cost. If you want to charge for your app, the standard split is 85 percent of sales for the developer and 15 percent for wireless carriers for the first $1 million of annual earnings from selling digital goods or services. For example, if you created an app for your city that featured all the top restaurants, hotels, attractions, and festivals and sold the app for $1.99, you would net $1.69 for each app sold. If you sell 5,000 copies of your app, you will earn almost $8,500. You can use Google Play to sell a wide range of content, including downloadable content such as media files or photos and virtual content such as game levels or potions (**Figure 1-5**). As an Android developer, you have the opportunity to develop apps for a fairly new market and easily distribute them to millions of Android mobile device owners. Developers can create Associated Developer Accounts (ADAs) on Google Play to sell their apps.

Figure 1-5 Google Play

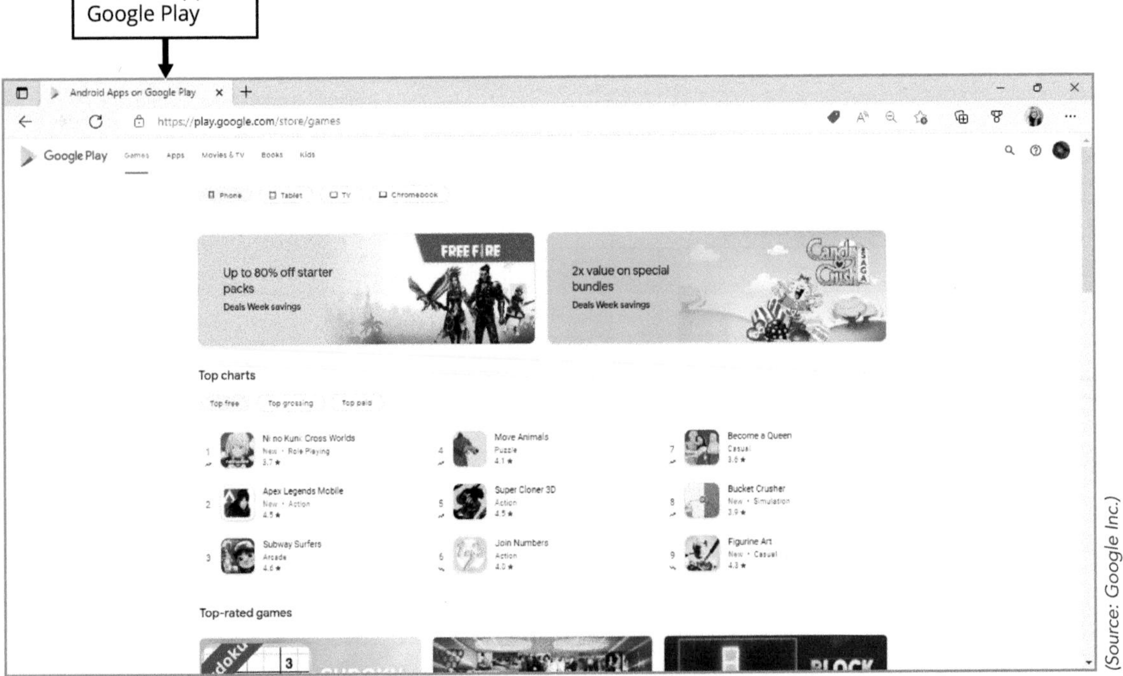

(Source: Google Inc.)

On the Job

The Apple iTunes App Store charges a $99 yearly registration fee to publish an app through the iPhone Dev Center. The iTunes App Store has a much more rigorous standards approval process than Google Play.

The online company Amazon also has a separate Appstore (*amazon.com/appstore*) where Android apps can be deployed and sold. The Amazon Appstore for Android is a category listed on Amazon.com. Customers can shop for apps from their PCs and mobile devices. The Amazon Appstore has an established marketing environment and search engine that displays a trusted storefront and creates app recommendations based on customers' past purchases. The Amazon Appstore has a "free developer program fee," which covers application processing and account management for the Amazon Appstore Developer Program. Amazon also pays developers 80 percent of the sale price of the app; in addition, you can post free apps. Amazon grants app developers 10 percent of their Appstore revenue in the form of a credit for AWS (Amazon Web Services).

Quick Check

If you sold your app in the Play Store 10,000 times for $3.99 each, how much would you earn as the developer?

Answer: You would earn $33,915. Wow!

1.6 The Connection between Windows and Android

Beginning with Windows 11, you can download Android apps to your PC from the Microsoft Store, as shown in **Figure 1-6**. Instead of running apps like TikTok or WhatsApp only on your phone, you can download Android apps directly to your Windows 11 PC, even if you do not own an Android phone. Likewise, Windows-based tablets and other touch devices have more apps available with the addition of Android apps. The Microsoft Store includes desktop apps, Windows 11 apps, and Android apps from the Amazon Appstore. Android apps provide entertainment and games, sophisticated productivity suites, social experiences, creativity tools, tools for unique hobbies, and developer tools to create virtualized environments. You can pin Android apps to your Start menu or taskbar and interact with

Figure 1-6 Using the Microsoft Store to download an Android app

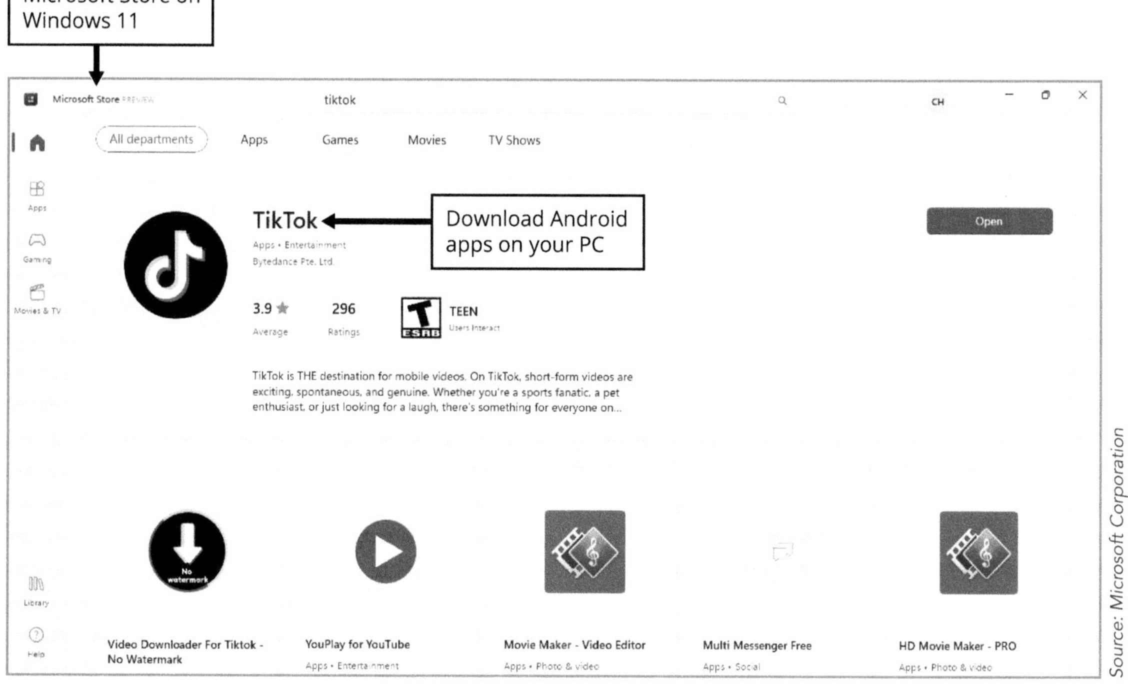

them via mouse, touch, or pen input. Enjoy using your Windows tablet to read your favorite book with the Kindle Android app or a digital comic series with the Comics Android app; you can swipe pages with the ease of a finger flick. If you are taking a foreign language this semester, you can download the Android app named Duolingo to your PC; just open the Microsoft Store, search for Duolingo, and run the app on your PC. You can do so without an Android smartphone.

Phone Link App

In addition to downloading Android apps to your PC, having an Android phone means that you can connect your phone to your computer using the Microsoft **Phone Link** app. By connecting an Android phone to your Windows 11 PC, you can send and receive text messages, see notifications, and instantly copy photos from your phone to share with others. If your instructor wanted to teach you to use a certain app in your class, they could display their Android phone on their PC and take you step by step through the process. The Phone Link app has four tabs, as shown in **Figure 1-7**.

Figure 1-7 Phone Link on Windows 11 with an Android phone

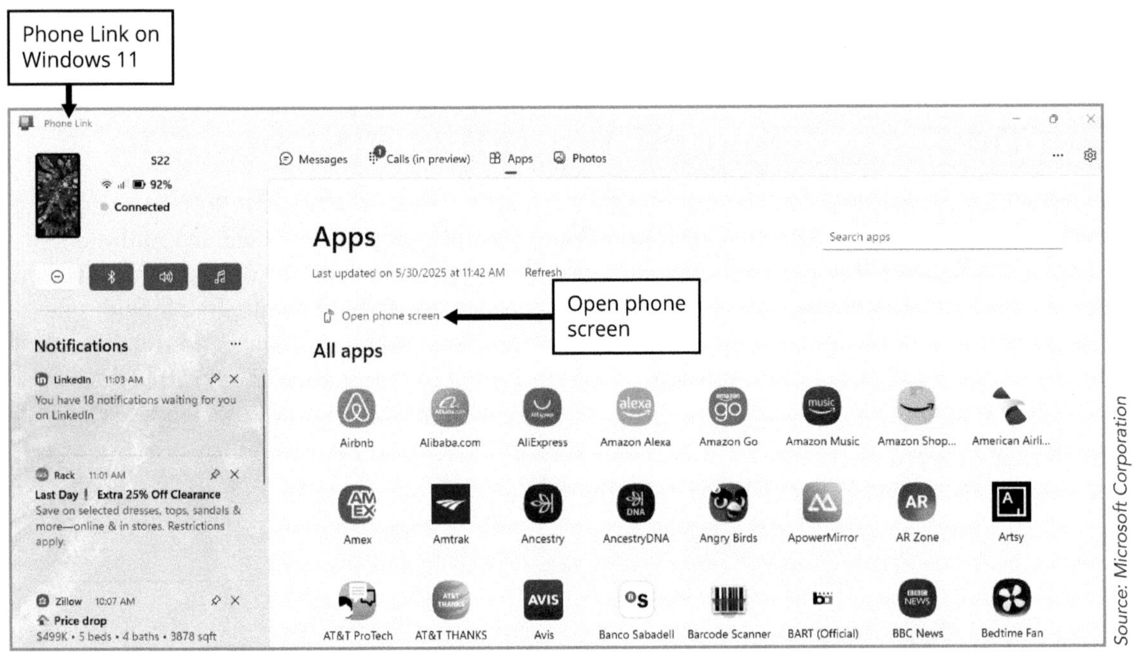

Source: Microsoft Corporation

If you have an Apple iPhone, you can connect it to a computer running Windows 11, but you will not get the same depth of experience that Android users do. Microsoft has stated that it wants to bring the iPhone's functionality to Windows, but Apple has not expressed much interest in sharing its proprietary products.

1.7 Creating an Android Project Using Android Studio

After installing Android Studio (*developer.android.com/studio*) as instructed in the preface of this book, the next step is to create your first Android application. As programming tradition mandates, your first program is called Hello Android World. The following sections introduce you to the elements of Android Studio and provide a detailed description of each step needed to create your first app. As stated in the preface, we will not use the standard Darcula theme; instead, we will use the File and Settings menu to change the theme of Android Studio to High Contrast, which will make it easier for everyone to view the screenshots in this textbook. If you have red-green color vision deficiency, you can adjust colors under the Theme settings.

Opening Android Studio to Create a New Project

To create a new Android project, you first open Android Studio. A message may appear that updates are available for Android Studio. As stated in the preface, this book uses the Tiramisu Android 13.0 version. Do not update or use a later version because the procedural steps in this book will not match the version. As you create your first project, you provide the following information:

- *Name*—This is the human-readable title for your application, which will appear on the Android device.
- *Package name*—This Java package namespace is where your source code will reside. The package name must be unique when posted in Google Play. The package name would be com.example.helloandroidworld in this example.
- *Save location*—This location indicates the directory on your hard drive or USB drive where you store the files related to the Android Studio project.
- *Minimum SDK*—This value specifies the minimum application programming interface (API) level required by your application.
- *Language*—Android Studio provides the coding environment for both the Java and Kotlin coding languages.

Creating the Hello Android World Project

Android Studio makes it easy to create Android apps for various form factors, such as smartphones, tablets, TV, and smartwatch devices. A **form factor** is the physical size and shape of a technology device; for example, smartphones and tablets are sold in various sizes or form factors. An Android project is equivalent to a single program or app using Java in Android Studio. The two most common projects are an Empty Activity or a Basic Project. An Empty Activity creates a code skeleton that allows you to quickly get started coding your app; a Basic Project has a more elaborate coding skeleton for more structured apps. In the first project, we will keep it simple with an Empty Activity to explain how to add code that will display text on the smartphone emulator. To create a new Android project, follow these steps:

Step 1

- Open the Android Studio program.

The Android Studio window opens, displaying the Welcome to Android Studio page (**Figure 1-8**). If you already have a project open, click File on the menu bar, click New, and then click New Project.

Step 2

- Click the New Project button on the Welcome to Android Studio window to open the New Project window.
- Click Phone and Tablet template, if not already selected, and drag the scroll bar down to view the Empty Activity template.
- Click the Empty Activity template.

The New Project window opens, displaying the form factor templates on the left and the project activities on the right (**Figure 1-9**). The Empty Activity is selected to allow you to create a limited skeleton of code that creates an app.

Step 3

- Click the Next button on the New Project window.
- On the New Project Empty Activity window, enter the Name **Hello Android World** for the name of the application. Notice the Package name and Save location changes after you change the name of the application.

Figure 1-8 Welcome to Android Studio window

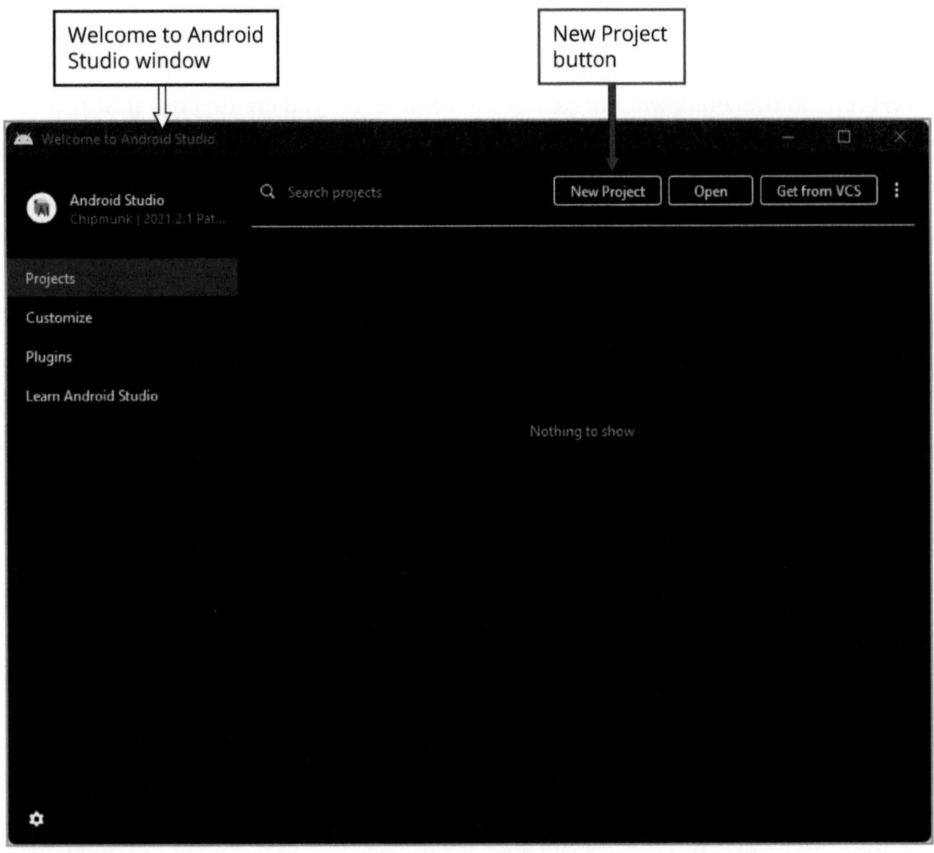

Figure 1-9 New Project window with Empty Activity

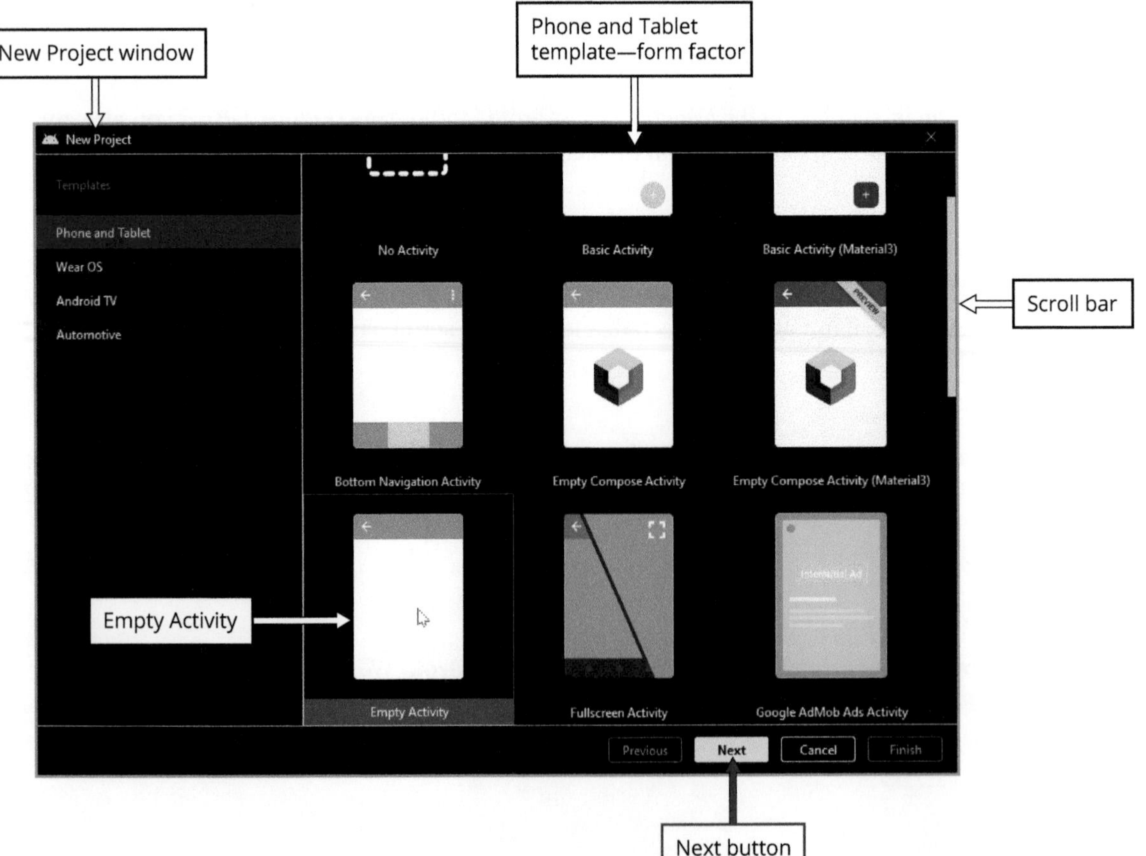

- Ask your instructor for the location or folder where you should save your project. Your instructor may ask that you save your work on a USB drive.
- Click the Language drop-down box and select Java as the coding language.
- Click the Minimum SDK box and select API 23: Android 6.0 (Marshmallow) as the minimum API on a device that can run this app. The **API version** is the version of an Android on which to preview your layout.

A new application named Hello Android World is configured to be saved to your preferred location and coded in the Java programming language with a minimum of API 23 (**Figure 1-10**). A workspace (or save location) is a directory where Android Studio stores the projects that you define. When you specify the workspace location, Android Studio creates files within this directory to manage the project.

Figure 1-10 Creating Empty Activity

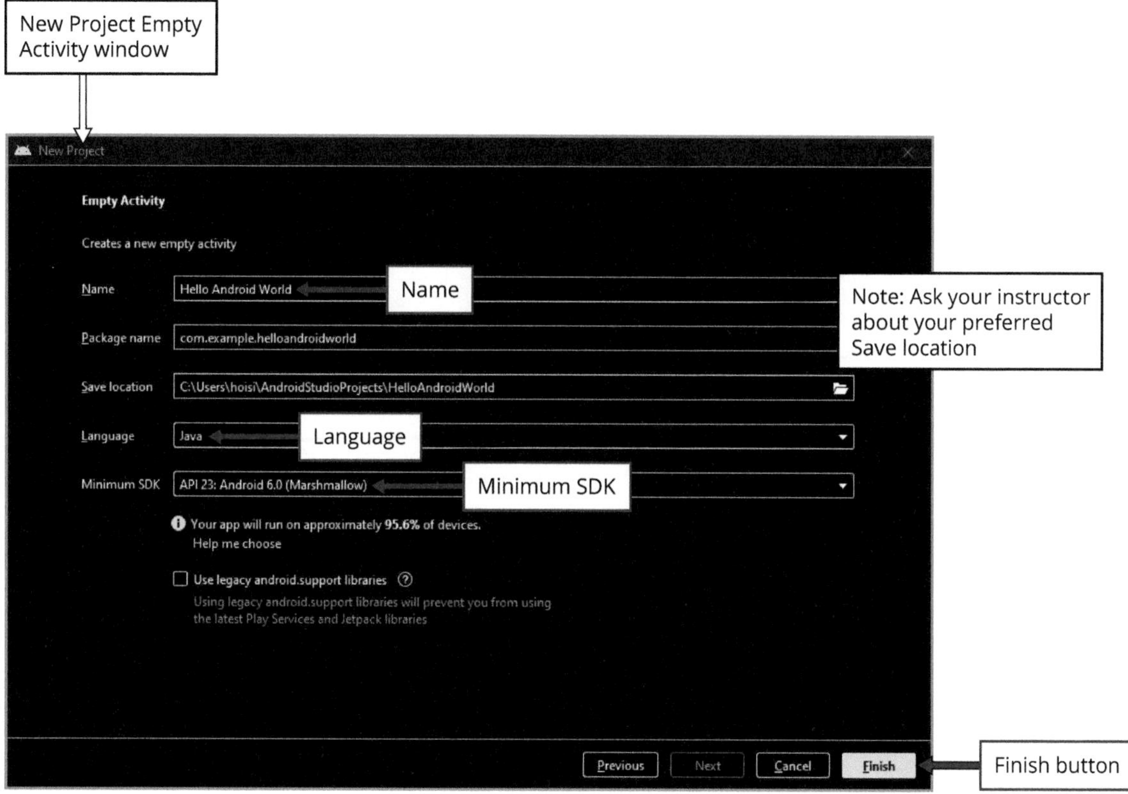

Good to Know

When you select the Minimum SDK option, you want to use the latest Android features and include as many Android smartphone devices that use various versions of the SDK as feasibly possible. The key tradeoff to consider is the percentage of Android devices you want to support versus the amount of work needed to maintain your app on each of the different versions that the devices run on. For example, if you choose to make your app compatible with many different versions of Android, you increase the effort that's required to maintain compatibility between the legacy and brand-new versions.

Step 4

- Click the Finish button on the New Project Empty Activity window.

The Android project files are created in your saved file location. The project Hello Android World appears in the left pane of Android Studio (**Figure 1-11**).

Figure 1-11 Android Studio project view

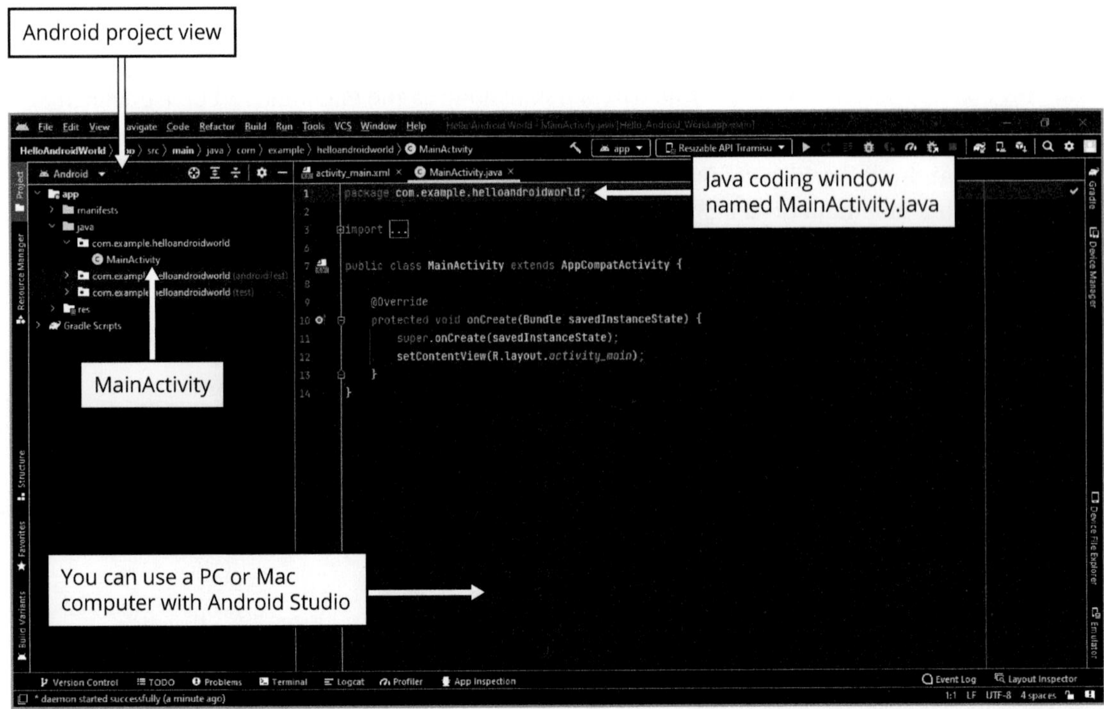

Building the User Interface

This first Android app will display the simple message, "Hello World – My First Android App." Beyond the tools and gadgets of the Android environment, what will stand out most is the user experience—how a user feels while using a particular device. Ensuring an intuitive user interface that does not detract from functionality is the key to successful usage. Android supports two ways of building the user interface of an application: through Java code and through XML layout files. The XML method is preferred because it allows you to design the user interface of an application without needing to write large amounts of code. Both methods and more details about building the user interface are covered in later chapters.

The Android Project View

The **Android project view** on the left side of the Android Studio program window contains the key source application folders for a project. As shown in Figure 1-11, the Android project view includes files in the following folders:

- The **manifests folder** includes the **AndroidManifest.xml** file, which contains all the information about the application that Android needs to run.
- The **java folder** includes the Java code source files for the project along with the code within the MainActivity.
- The **res folder** contains all the resources, such as images, music, and video files, that your application may need. The user interface named activity_main.xml is in a subfolder of the res folder named layout.

Quick Check

Which folder contains all the Java code?

Answer: The java folder.

1.8 The User Interface Layout within the Virtual Device

To assist you in designing the Android user interface, the Android SDK includes layout files called activity_main.xml in the res/layout folder of an Android app, as shown in **Figure 1-12** and in the left pane of the Android project view. When you double-click the activity_main.xml file, the **Layout Editor** opens. The Layout Editor contains the Palette, Component Tree, toolbar, **Design editor**, and Attributes pane. You can create a layout and then add widgets to the layout from the Palette. A **layout** is a container that can hold as many widgets as needed. The Android Studio **Palette** contains various widgets that can be dragged onto the emulator device screen in the Design layout. A **widget** is a single element, also called an object, such as a TextView, Button, or ImageView component from the Palette. By default, a TextView component or widget displays the text Hello World within the emulator. The Layout Editor displays the emulator as a phone and a blueprint of the layout. The **Attributes pane** to the right of the emulator contains the attributes and settings of the currently active Android app project or object. An **attribute** describes what an object can do; for example, if you change the text property of a TextView component, the updated text is displayed in the emulator. Upcoming chapters demonstrate many layouts, each with unique properties and characteristics.

Figure 1-12 Coding window in Android Studio

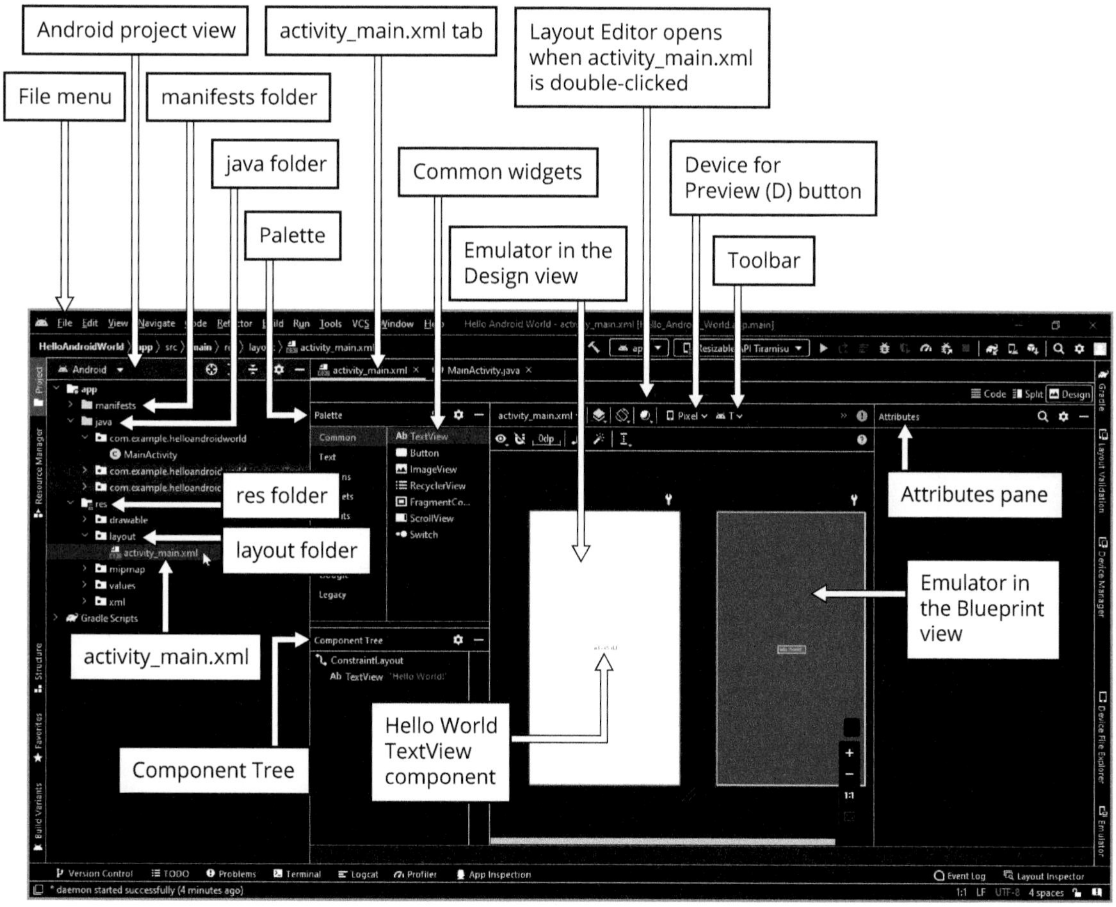

Instead of using only a smartphone to display the output of your app during the testing stages of development, Android Studio displays an emulator configuration called the **Android Virtual Device (AVD)** for design and layout purposes. Typically, developers test their apps on various virtual devices to provide a useful and accurate environment for every device that can download the apps. To change the virtual device and view the attributes, follow these steps:

Step 1

- Click the arrow (>) in front of the res folder to expand the folder.
- Click the arrow (>) in front of the layout folder to expand the folder.
- Double-click the activity_main.xml file to open the emulator design of the virtual device.

The activity_main.xml layout window opens; this window is called the Layout Editor (**Figure 1-13**).

Figure 1-13 Layout Editor for emulator layout design

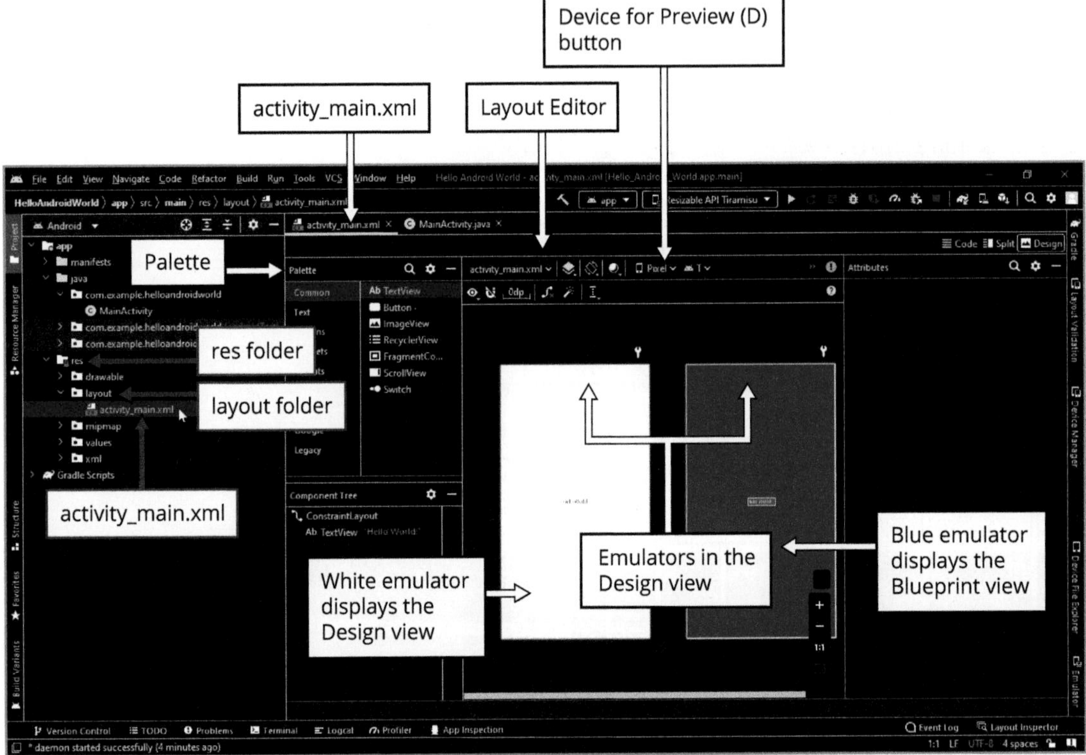

Good to Know When you view the Layout Editor, notice there are two emulators by default. The emulator screens within the Design editor display a white emulator called the Design view and a blue emulator called the Blueprint view. The Design editor displays a rendered preview of your layout. The Blueprint view only displays outlines of your layout. If we were to use these design terms in building a house, the design would be an actual picture of the finished home and the blueprint would show just the wall and roof outlines.

Step 2

- Click the Device for Preview (D) button (Pixel 5), which is on the toolbar directly to the right of the palette on the activity_main.xml tab in the Layout Editor.

The devices that can be used for previewing an app are listed below the Device for Preview button in the Layout Editor (**Figure 1-14**).

Figure 1-14 Device for Preview button

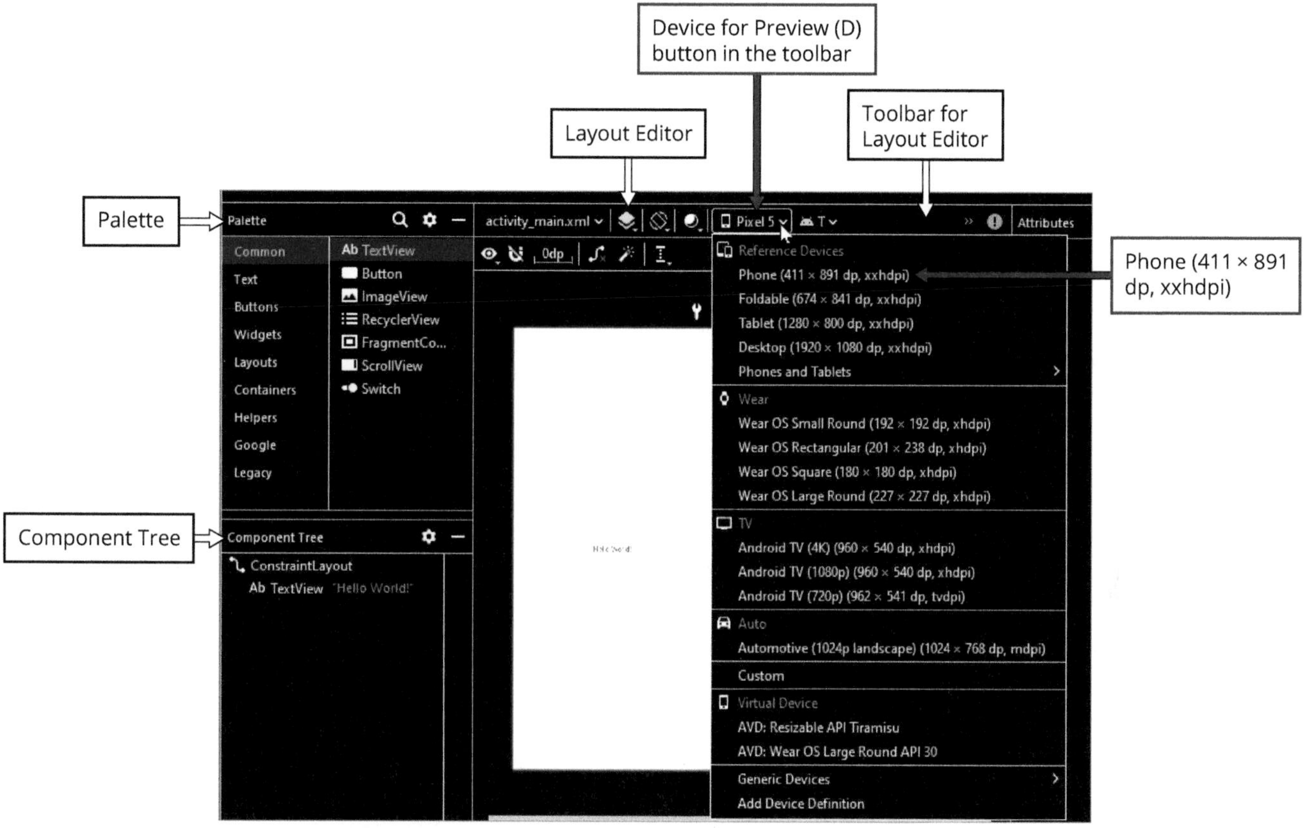

Step 3

- Click Phone (411 × 891 dp, xxhdpi). You can preview your app on any selected device in Android Studio during design, but to fully test the app, you must install any of the device emulators as a virtual device under the Device Manager. These emulators include smartphones, tablets, watches, and TVs.

The generic Phone emulator is displayed. Note that Android placed a default TextView component in the emulator (**Figure 1-15**).

Step 4

- In the emulator, select the default TextView component, which displays the text Hello World! in the Component Tree.

The default TextView component is selected and displayed in a blue selection box (**Figure 1-16**). The **Component Tree** displays the widgets in the order you placed each of them on the emulator; in this case, the TextView component displays the text Hello World!

Step 5

- Scroll down the Attributes pane to display the text attribute under the Common Attributes category.

The text attribute of the default TextView component is displayed (**Figure 1-17**). The text Hello World! is displayed in the Attributes pane.

Figure 1-15 Generic phone selected for Device for Preview

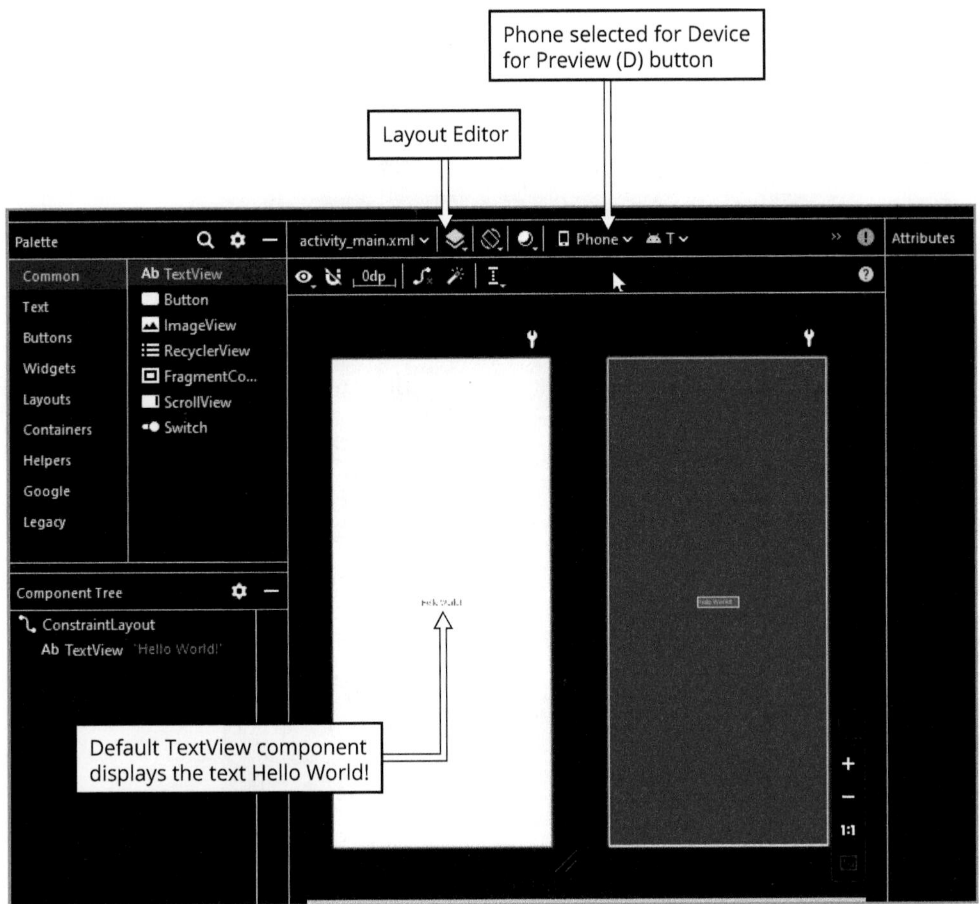

Figure 1-16 Design editor

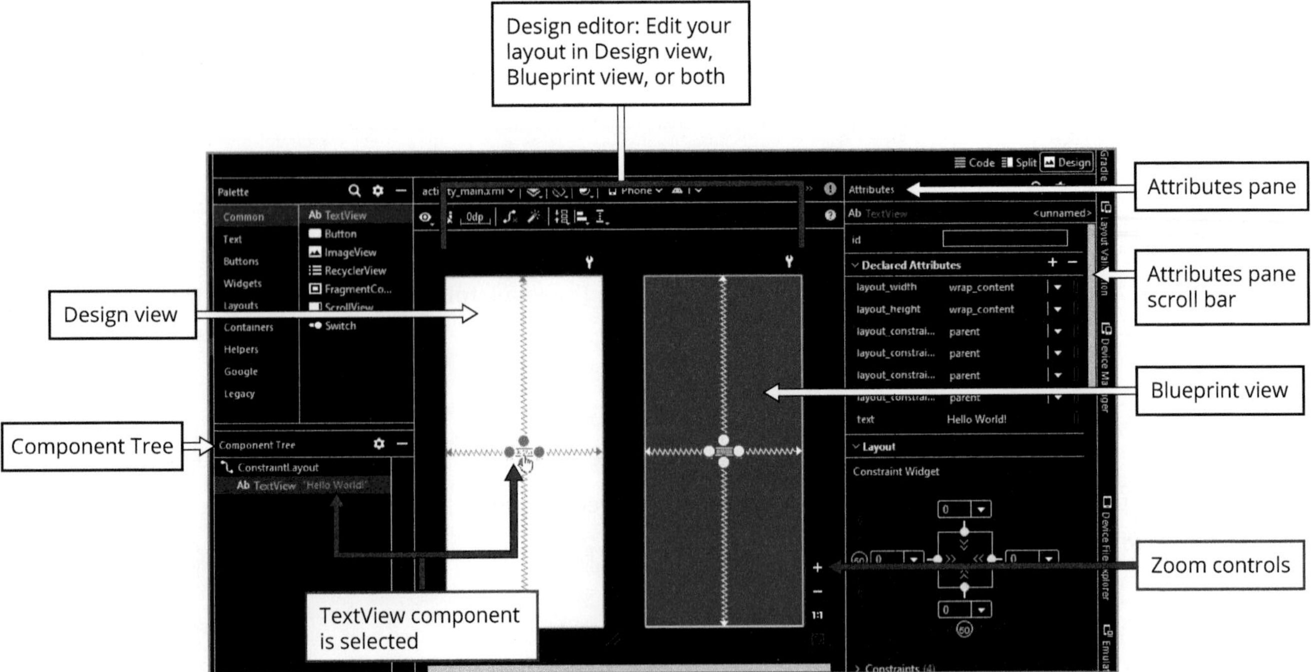

Figure 1-17 Attributes pane

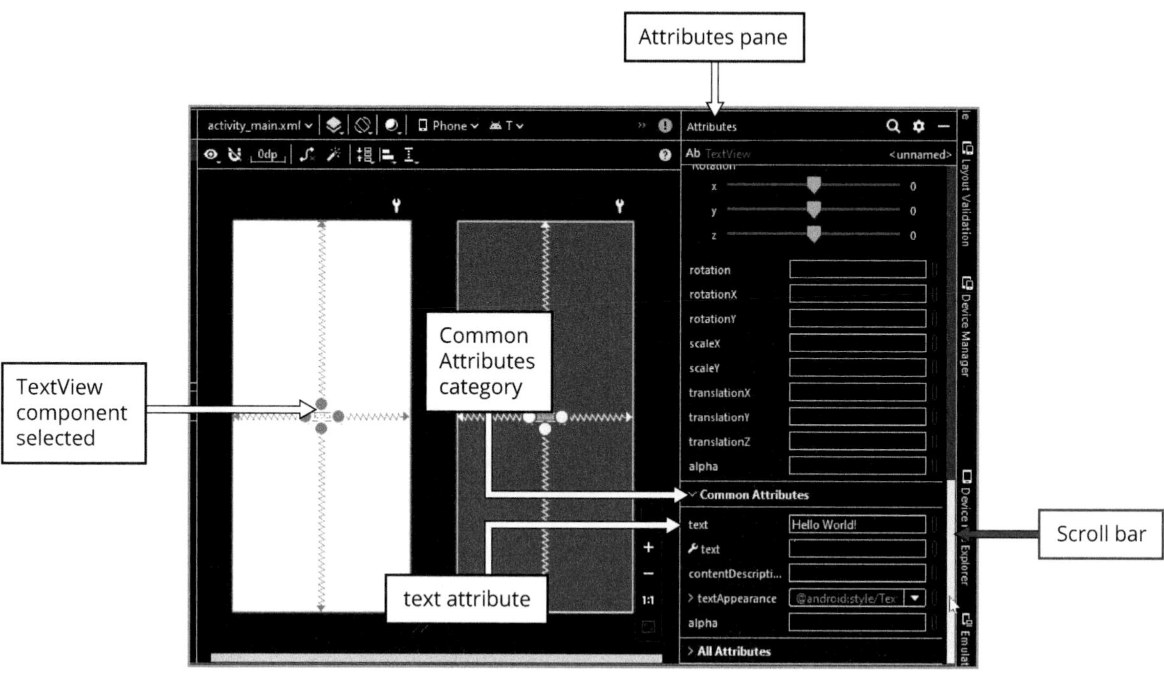

The TextView Component

By default, a TextView component or widget displaying the text Hello World! is placed on the emulator. In this first chapter, we will change the hard-coded value for the text attribute in the Attributes pane. In future chapters, we will update text by modifying resource files or changing the application XML source code. If the Hello Android World app was developed for multiple spoken languages such as Spanish and Japanese, the resource file could contain the translated text.

To change the text property in the TextView attribute within the emulator so that it displays the appropriate message, an id attribute or name is added for good programming practice. In this example, the id attribute is tvWelcome; the prefix *tv* means that the id is a TextView component. In the app, we will not add Java code to move, resize, or flash the TextView component, but in future chapters, naming the component will be important so we know the name of the object we intend to change. To change the text attribute and add the name (id) of the TextView component, follow these steps:

Step 1

- In the Attributes pane, delete Hello World! in the text attribute box.
- Type **Hello World – My First Android App** in the text attribute box.
- Click the Zoom button (+ sign) several times to increase the size of the emulator and view the text in the Design view.

The default value of the TextView component is changed to Hello World – My First Android App in the Attributes pane and in the Design view of the emulator (**Figure 1-18**). Note that your computer's resolution may differ, resulting in a different layout of your Android Studio window.

Step 2

- Scroll up in the Attributes pane to the first attribute named id and click the box to the right of the id attribute.
- Type **tvWelcome** to name the TextView component with the prefix *tv* and press the Enter key.

The default TextView component has been named tvWelcome in the id attribute box (**Figure 1-19**). Note that Java is a case-sensitive language, so type the component name in the same case.

Figure 1-18 Emulator with TextView control and text attribute

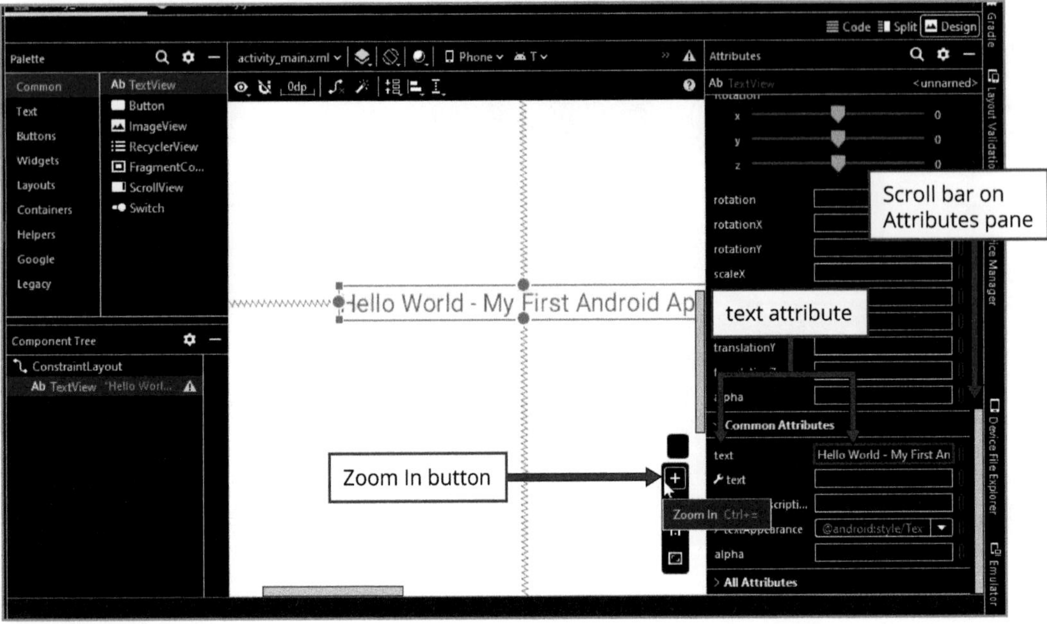

Figure 1-19 The id attribute

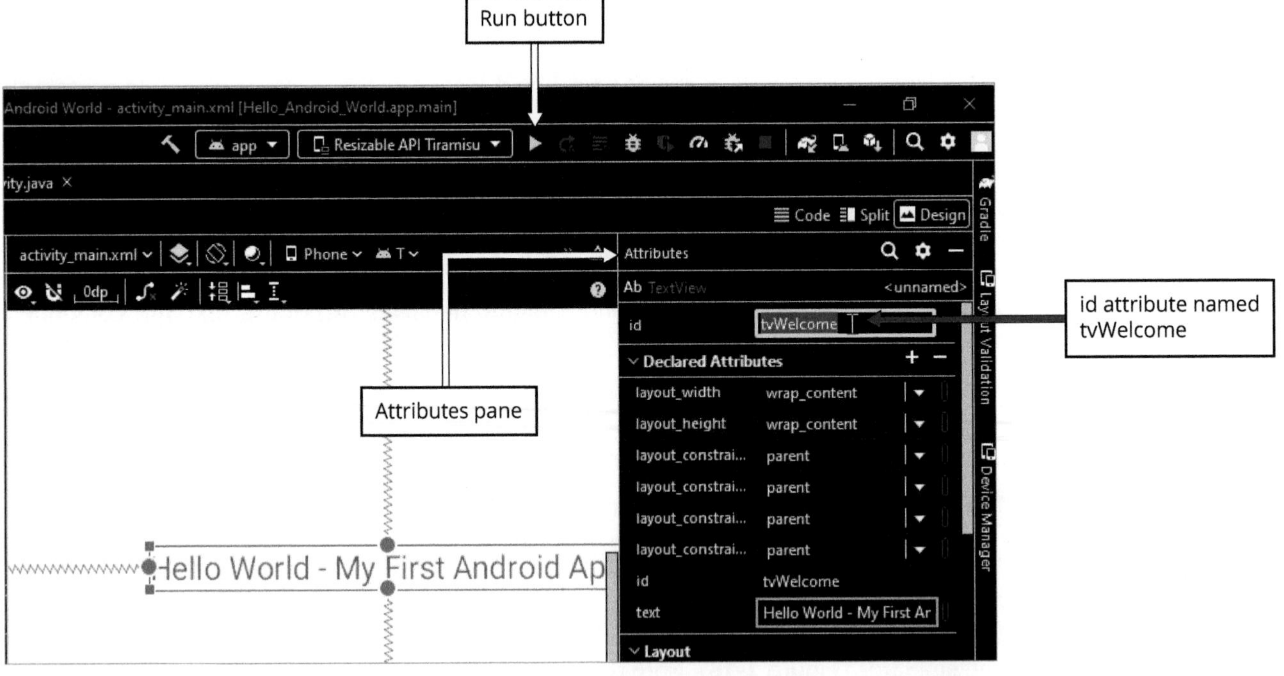

Critical Thinking

Can I change the text by directly typing in the strings.xml file?

Yes, you can modify the XML code, but as a beginner in Android development, the Attributes pane is simpler to use.

Good to Know | To deploy your app to an actual Android device instead of the emulator, plug in the device to your development machine with a USB cable. You may need to install the appropriate USB driver for your device if you are using a Windows operating system. In Android Studio, click Run on the toolbar and select Run.

1.9 Executing an Android Application on an Emulator

Time to see the finished result! Keep in mind that the Android emulator (virtual device) runs slowly. The emulator will first display the Android opening screen and then load the application. It can take a few seconds or more to display your finished results in the emulator, based on the speed of your computer. Even when the emulator is idling, it consumes a significant amount of CPU time, so you should close the emulator when you complete your testing. To run the application and automatically save the app, follow these steps:

Step 1

- Click the Run app button (the green arrow) on the toolbar.
- If you set up your emulator as specified in the preface, the app should open the Resizable API Tiramisu Emulator (or a recent emulator version) with your Welcome message displayed. If the Emulator is too large or too small, click the Zoom buttons to display the emulator properly.

The Emulator opens slowly and displays a welcome message: Hello World – My First Android App (**Figure 1-20**). When you run an application, the app is automatically saved to the file path specified when you created the app.

Figure 1-20 Hello Android World app displayed in emulator

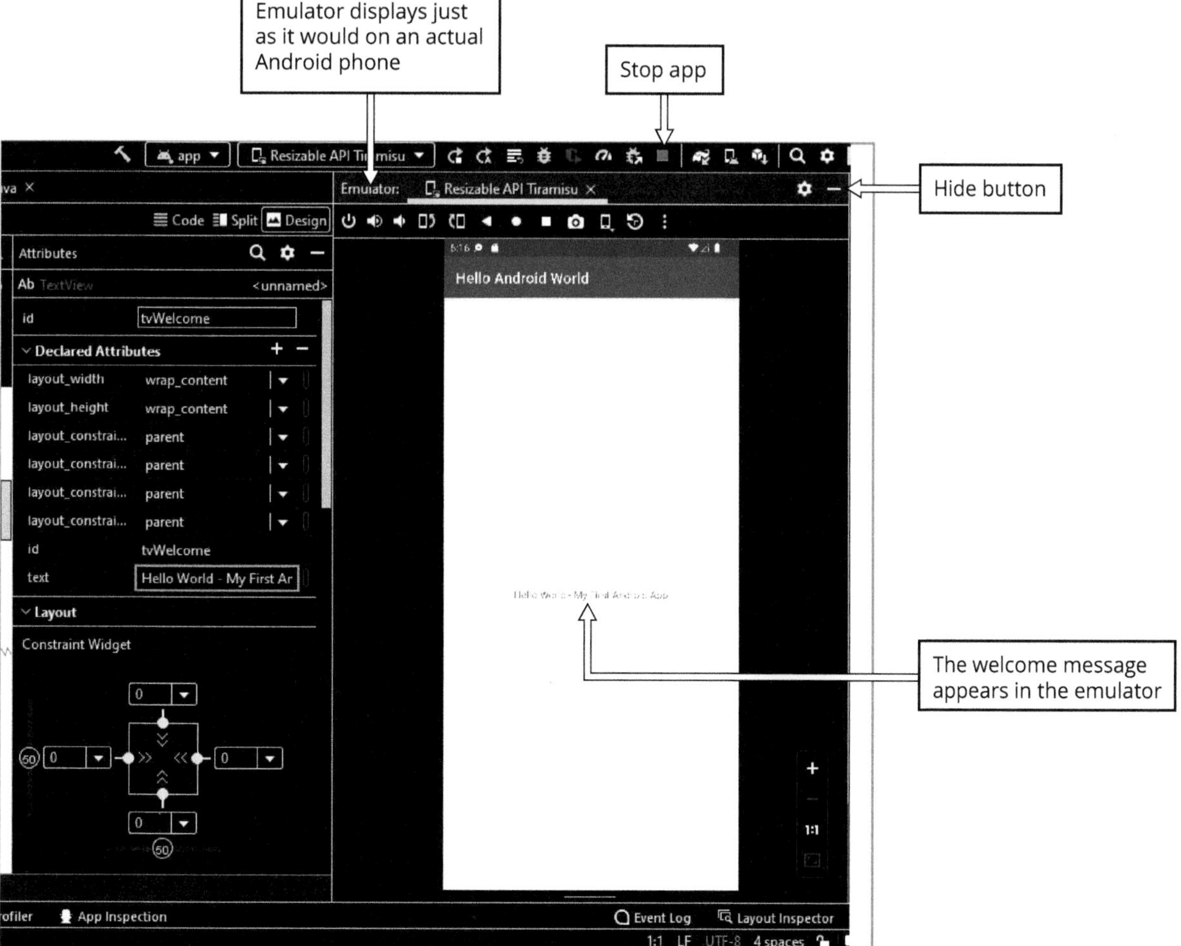

Step 2

- Click the Hide button to hide the Emulator.
- Click File on the menu bar and then click Close Project.
- Click the Terminate button to stop the emulator from running.

The emulated application window closes. The program is saved each time the program is run. Click Quit Android Studio if you are working on a Mac.

Good to Know | Shift+F10 is the Windows shortcut key combination for running your Android application in Android Studio. On a Mac, the shortcut keys are Command+Shift+F11.

1.10 Opening a Saved Android Project in Android Studio

After you save a project and close Android Studio, you might need to open the project and work on it again. To open a saved project, you can follow this step:

Step 1

- Open Android Studio.
- Click the Hello Android World project in the Recent Projects column. If the project is not listed in the Recent Projects column, click Open an existing Android Project in the Quick Start column, navigate to the path of the saved project, and click the OK button.

The program loads into Android Studio. You can now continue working on your user interface and code.

Wrap It Up—Chapter Summary

This chapter provided an overview of the Android open-source platform, which is positioned for fast innovation without the restraints of a proprietary system. With its rich feature set, the Android Studio environment allows you to develop useful, inventive Android apps for the platform with the largest market share for mobile devices. In the first chapter project, Hello Android World, you completed steps that start your journey to creating more interesting applications in future chapters.

- The Android operating system is released under a full open-source license for free.
- The Android OS powers all types of mobile devices, including smartphones, tablets, Internet TVs, Android wearable devices such as watches, and Google Glass.
- To write Android apps, you can use Android Studio, a dedicated development environment for building Android applications using Java, an object-oriented programming language.
- The Android emulator lets you design, develop, prototype, and test Android applications without using a physical device. When you run an Android program in Android Studio, the smartphone emulator starts so you can test the program as if it were running on a specified Android mobile device.

- The Android platform consists of the Android OS, the Android application development platform, and Google Play, a marketplace for Android applications.
- Android Studio using Java supports two ways of building the user interface of an application: through Java code and through XML layout files. The XML method is preferred, as it allows you to design the user interface of an application without needing to write large amounts of code.
- The Android project view on the left side of the Android Studio program window contains the folders for an Android project.
- To design a user interface for an Android app, you can create a layout, which is a container that displays widgets such as TextView, Button, and CheckBox components.
- The text and id properties of components can be changed using the Attributes pane.
- After you create an application, you can run it in the Android emulator to test the application and make sure it runs correctly.

Key Terms

Android project view
Android Studio
Android Virtual Device (AVD)
AndroidManifest.xml
API version
app
attribute
Attributes pane
Component Tree
Design editor
emulator
form factor
Google Play
Java
java folder
layout
Layout Editor
manifests folder
object-oriented programming language
Open Handset Alliance
open-source operating system
Palette
Phone Link
res folder
Software Development Kit (SDK)
widget
XML

Developer FAQs

1. What is the dessert name that starts with an "N" to identify an Android version? (1.4)
2. What is the one-time cost for a developer's account at Google Play? (1.5)
3. When you post an Android app at Google Play, what percentage of the app price does the developer keep? (1.5)
4. ______________ is the web address of Google Play. (1.5)
5. What share of the world's smartphone market is represented by Android? (1.1)
6. Java is the most popular coding language used to create Android apps. What other language is also used? (1.4)
7. In which subfolder is the activity_main.xml file stored? (1.7)
8. Name three widgets in the Palette mentioned in this chapter. (1.8, 1.9)
9. What is the name of the widget that was used in the Hello Android World app? (1.8, 1.9)
10. Which two key combinations can you press to run an Android app in Android Studio? (1.9)

11. Which Android version is Kit Kat? (1.4)
12. Using the alphabetical theme for Android version names, name three possible future names for the next versions of Android device operating systems. (1.4)
13. Which two attributes were changed in the Hello Android World app? (1.9)
14. What does SDK stand for? (1.4)
15. What does XML stand for? (1.4)

Beyond the Book

Search the web for answers to the following questions to further your Android knowledge.

1. Research a particular model of a popular Android smartphone or tablet device and write a paragraph on its features, specifications, price, and manufacturer.
2. Name five Android mobile device features not mentioned in Chapter 1.
3. Research and provide three advantages that a Windows 11 user has with Android smartphones and apps. Write and explain the advantages in full sentences.
4. Go to the Google Play website and take a screenshot of each of the following app categories: education, gaming, mapping, travel, and personal hobby. Place the screenshots in a word-processing document and label each one to identify them.
5. Create a timeline of the Android product from the past to present day.

Case Programming Projects

Complete one or more of the following case programming projects. Use the same steps and techniques taught within the chapter. Successful completion of these projects requires knowledge of all chapter learning objectives. Submit the program(s) you create to your instructor. The level of difficulty is indicated for each case programming project.

Case Project 1–1: Famous Technology Quotes App (Beginner)

Requirements Document

Application title:	Tech Quotes
Purpose:	In the Tech Quotes app, a technology quote of your choice is displayed.
Algorithms:	The opening screen displays the famous technology quote of the day. Find a quote online.
Conditions:	Please change the quote to one of your own and name the id tvQuote (**Figure 1-21**). Name the project TechQuotes, with your first name after the project name.

Figure 1-21 Tech Quotes app

Case Project 1–2: Android Dessert Names App (Intermediate)

Requirements Document

Application title: Dessert Names

Purpose: In the Dessert Names app, the Android version names (desserts) introduced in Chapter 1 are displayed.

Algorithms: The opening screen displays the dessert names of Android versions listed in this chapter.

Conditions: Please change the list to one of your own and name the id tvDessert (**Figure 1-22**). Name the project Dessert Versions, with your first name after the project name.

Figure 1-22 Dessert Names app

Case Project 1–3: Large Tech Companies (Advanced)

Requirements Document

Application title:	Top Tech Companies
Purpose:	In the Top Tech Companies app, the current top five technology companies in the world are displayed.
Algorithms:	The opening screen displays the top five world technology companies, separated by commas. Please research this topic and order the companies based on revenue. The current companies may not be in the same order shown in **Figure 1-23**.

Figure 1-23 Top Tech Companies app

Chapter 2

Simplify! The Android User Interface

Learning Objectives

At the completion of this chapter, you will be able to:

2.1 Develop a user interface using the TextView, ImageView, and Button components

2.2 Add text using the String table in the Translations Editor

2.3 Construct the user interface using a ConstraintLayout

2.4 Plan out program design

2.5 Create multiple Android activities

2.6 View activities in the Android Manifest file

2.7 Write code using the onCreate( ) method

2.8 Create a Button event handler

2.9 Code a Button event handler

2.10 Correct errors in code

2.11 Run the completed app in the emulator

Before a mobile app can be coded using Java, it must be designed. Designing a program can be compared with constructing a building. Before cement slabs are poured, steel beams put in place, and walls erected, architects and engineers must design the building to ensure that it will perform as required and be safe and reliable. Electricity and plumbing are added to make the building more functional. The same ideas hold true for a computer app developer. The walls of the app are the user interface design, which automatically creates Extensible Markup Language (XML) code behind the scenes as the supports for the emulator design. Next, Java code is added to perform the functions for which it was designed, much like the electricity and plumbing in your building.

2.1 Designing an Android App

To illustrate the process of designing and implementing an Android app, in this chapter you design and code the Easy Recipes app shown in **Figures 2-1** and **2-2**.

Figure 2-1 Easy Recipes Android app

Nadezhda Nesterova/Shutterstock.com

Figure 2-2 Second screen with recipe

Strawberry Sorbet Recipe

Ingredients

6 cups chopped strawberries

1 T. lemon juice

1 cup sugar

¼ cup cold water

Directions

Process until smooth in the blender. Freeze for 8 hours in a covered container.

The Android app in Figures 2-1 and 2-2 could be part of a larger app that is used to display Easy Recipes. The app begins by displaying the recipe name, which is Strawberry Sorbet Recipe, and an image illustrating the sorbet. If the user taps the VIEW RECIPE button, a second window opens and displays the full recipe, including the ingredients and preparation for making sorbet.

On the Job | If you own a data-plan phone, tablet, or slate device, download the free app called Tasty to get an idea of how this Easy Recipes app would function in a much larger application in the real world.

The Big Picture

To create the Easy Recipes application, you follow a set of steps that you repeat every time you create an Android application.

1. Create the user interface, also called an XML layout, for every screen in the application. In this app, you will create two screens.
2. Create a Java class, also called an Activity, for every screen in the application.
3. Code each Java class with the appropriate objects and actions as needed.
4. Test the application in the Android phone emulator.

Using the Android User Interface

Before writing any code for an Android application, you design the user interface as the space where interactions occur between people and the app; such interactions are called the user experience. An Android application can run on various form factors, such as a smartphone, smartwatch, tablet, wearable VR (virtual reality) glasses, televisions, robotics, cars, and many other devices. **Form factor** refers to the screen size, configuration, or physical layout of a device. For an Android application, the user interface is a window on the screen of any mobile device in which the user interacts with the program. The user interface is stored in the res/layout folder in the Android project view. The layout for the user interface is stored as XML code. Special Android-formatted XML code is extremely compact, which means the application uses less space and runs faster on the device. Using XML for layout also saves you time in developing your code; for example, if you develop the preceding recipe app for use in eight human languages, you could use the same Java code with eight unique XML layout files, one for each language. An easy way to think of XML is as a set of directions for where to place all your furniture in your room, except the pieces of furniture are the components and the room is your emulator screen. To open the layout of the user interface for the Easy Recipes app and begin the application, follow these steps:

Step 1

- Open the Android Studio program.
- In the Welcome to Android Studio window, scroll down and click the New Project button in the Phone and Tablet templates to create a new Android Studio project.

A new empty application is selected to create a new empty Android project (**Figure 2-3**).

Figure 2-3 Configuring your new project

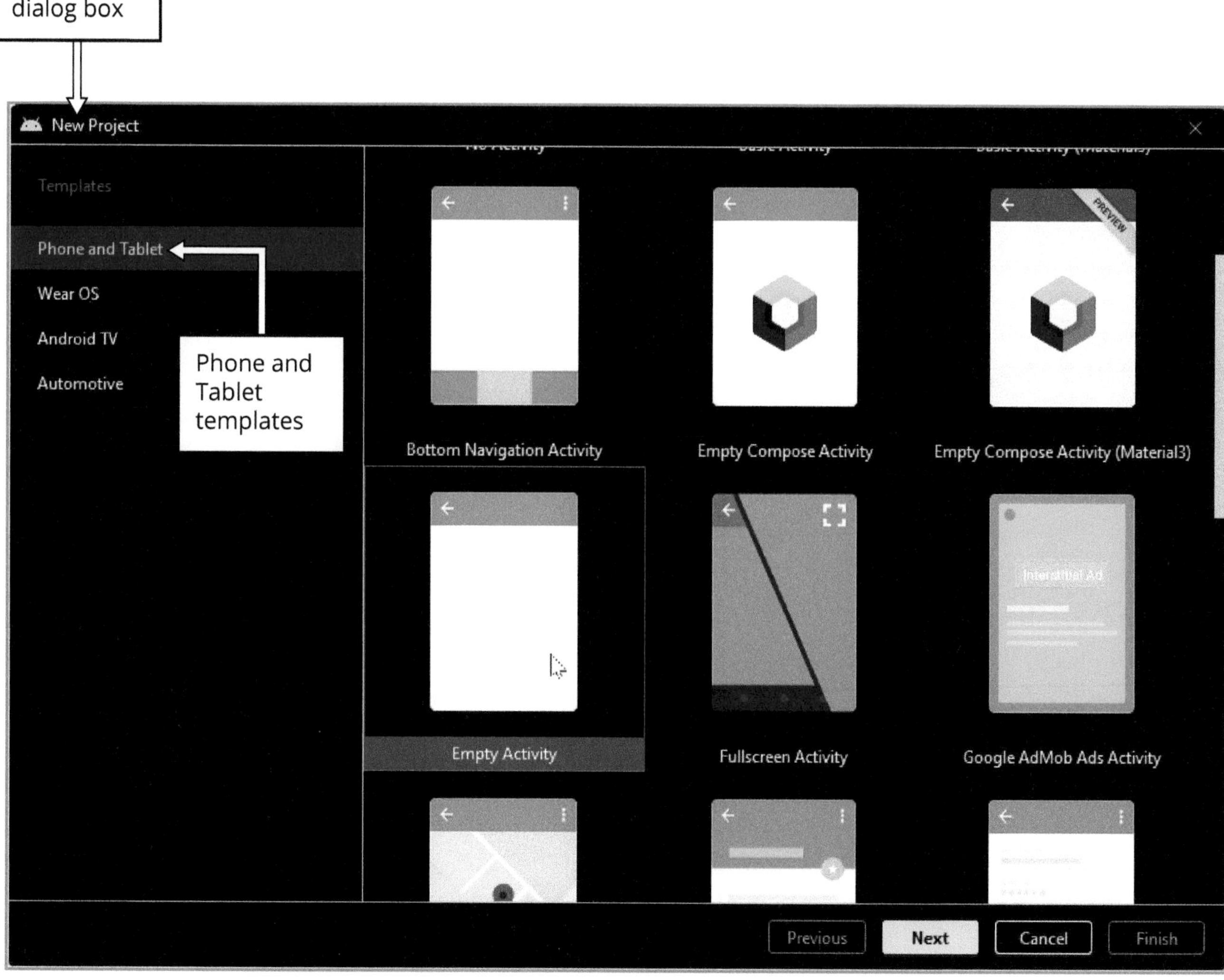

Step 2

- Click the Next button in the New Project window.
- Type **Easy Recipes** in the Name text box.
- If necessary, select Java in the Language text box.
- If necessary, select API 23: Android 6.0 (Marshmallow) as the Minimum SDK.

A new Java Android project named Easy Recipes is configured to save on your local computer (**Figure 2-4**).

Figure 2-4 Creating an empty activity for the Easy Recipes app

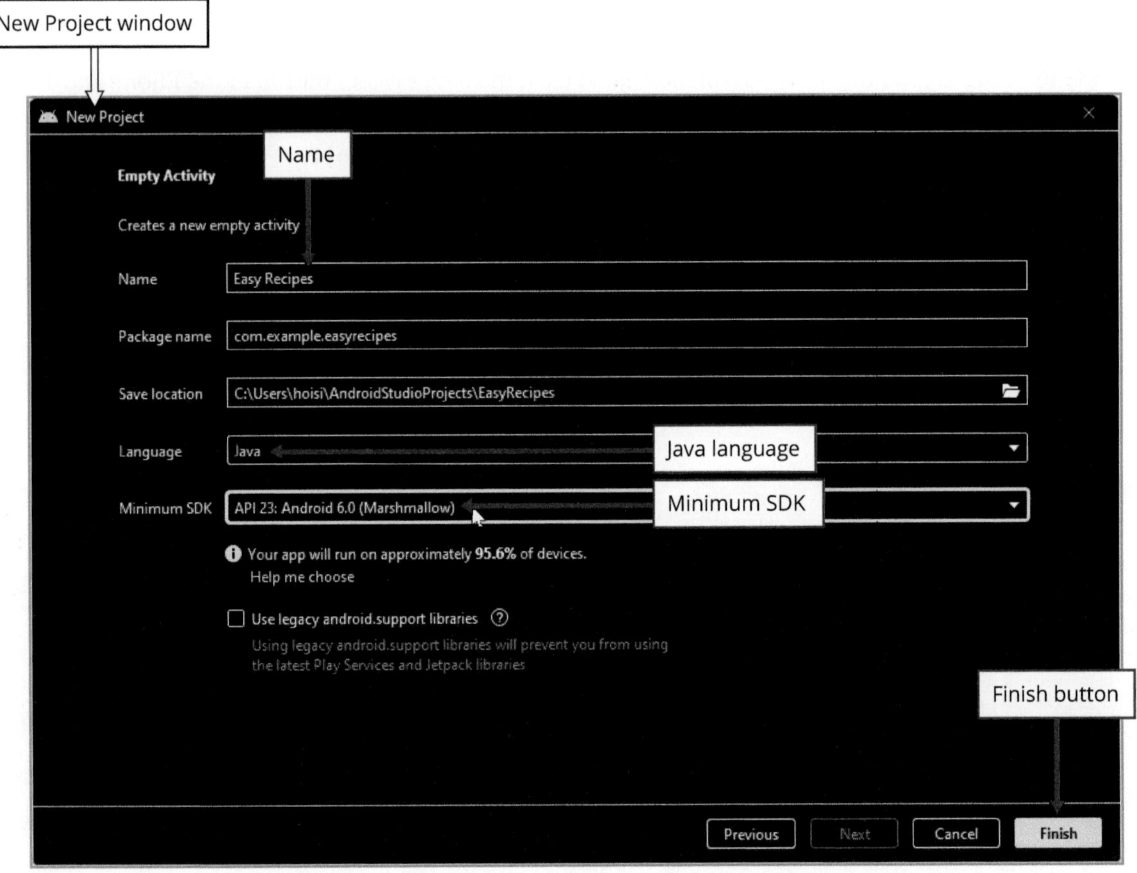

Step 3

- Click the Finish button on the New Project window.
- Click the arrow (>) in front of the res folder to expand the folder.
- Click the arrow (>) in front of the layout folder to expand the folder.
- Double-click the activity_main.xml file to open the emulator design of the virtual device.
- Click the Hello world! TextView component in the emulator. This component is displayed by default.

The activity_main.xml layout window opens the Layout Editor and the default Hello world! TextView is selected (**Figure 2-5**).

Figure 2-5 Android Studio open and ready for you to design the Easy Recipes app

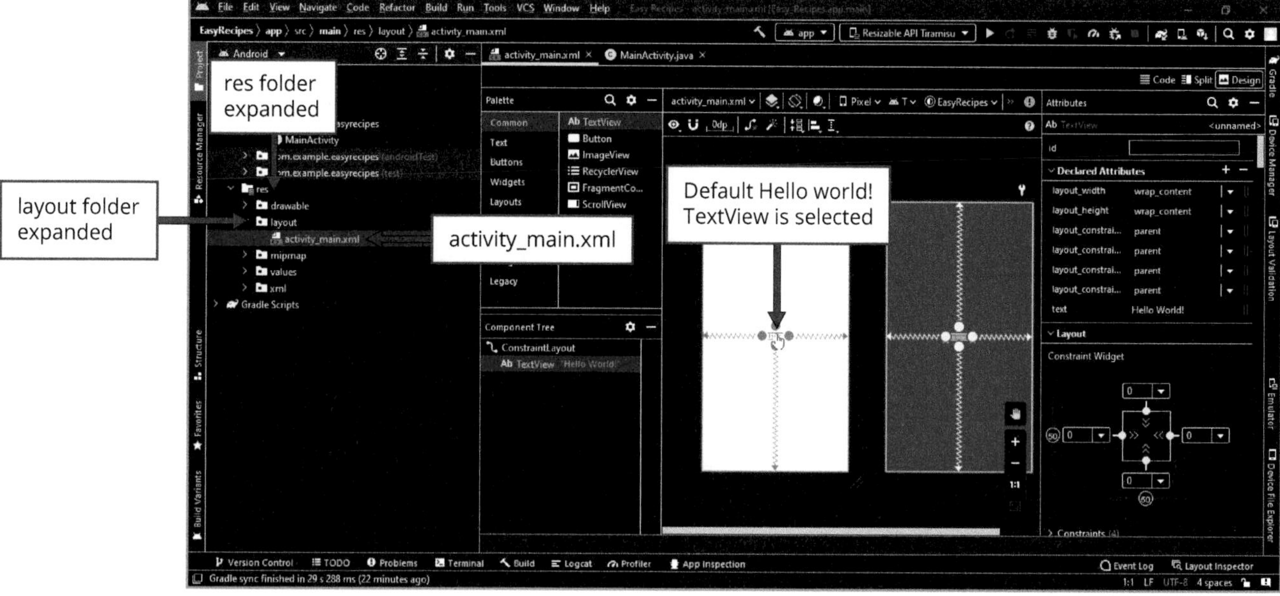

- Press the Delete key to delete the default TextView component.
- Click the Device for Preview (D) button, which is also known as the emulator button, and then click Phone for the Reference Devices.

The Android Easy Recipes project files are created, the Hello world! TextView widget is deleted, and the Phone device for preview is selected (**Figure 2-6**).

Figure 2-6 Deleting the default TextView component

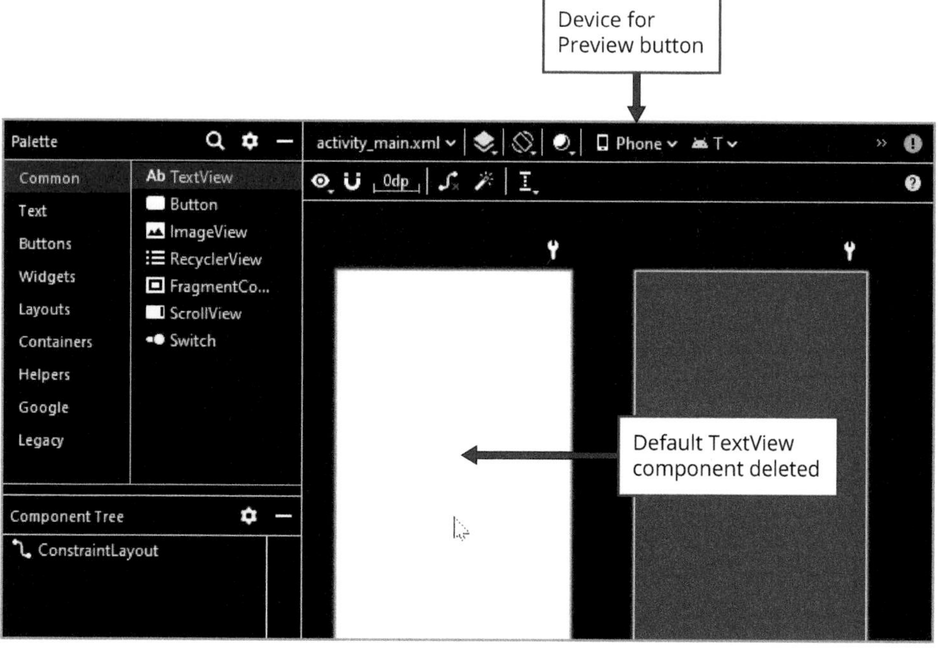

2.2 Adding Text Using the String Table in the Translations Editor

Earlier in this course, you added text directly to the Attributes pane in Android Studio. This approach, known as hard coding, is not optimal because when you publish the app, it cannot be translated to multiple languages and cultures for a worldwide audience. The **Translations Editor** in Android Studio can display the original text in the language in which it was programmed, but the language of the current locale can also be displayed, as well as culturally specific settings. Supporting multiple languages goes beyond using locale-specific languages and unique letters or characters. Some users speak a language that uses right-to-left (RTL) written scripts, such as Arabic or Hebrew.

Android Studio recommends that values such as text strings be stored in the form of resources within the res folder. The simplest way to update text is by modifying resource files instead of changing the application's XML source code. If the Hello Android World app from Chapter 1 was developed for multiple spoken languages such as Spanish and Chinese, the resource file could contain the translated text.

To change the text attribute in the TextView widget on the emulator to display the appropriate message, the resource file links to the Translations Editor to add text to the TextView component by changing the text in the strings.xml file. Instead of adding text directly in a TextView component's text attribute, you add it to the strings.xml file. Entering text in a single file offers significant advantages.

The String Table

For example, suppose you are hired to write an app and you enter text in the text attribute of each component. After testing the app, your customer decides to change all the text within the app. Now you must check for the original text component by component, file by file, including .xml and .java files, for all the text you have inserted and then replace it. As a time-saving alternative, Android provides the strings.xml file or **String table** inside the Resources folder. If your customer wants to change all the text within the app, you can go to a single file location to make the changes.

The string items that are displayed in the TextView component of the Easy Recipes app will not be typed directly in the Attributes pane, but instead in a string array in the res/values folder. A file named **strings.xml** is a default file that is part of every Android application and contains commonly used strings for an application. You enter text in this file using the String table because it can easily be changed without changing code. A **string** is a series of alphanumeric characters that can include spaces. Android loads text resources from the project's String table.

The String table can also be used for localization for the language read in a certain country or region. **Localization** is the use of the String table to change text based on the user's preferred language. For example, Android can select text in Spanish from the String table within the Translations Editor, based on the current device configuration and locale. The developer can add multiple translations in the Translations Editor.

Good to Know

This textbook recommends prefixes such as tv for TextView components, iv for ImageView components, and bt for Button components because prefixes reduce typing Java code, work better with auto-completion, and allow people who are viewing your code to quickly determine attribute types.

Every string is composed of a **key**, also called the **id attribute**, which is the name of a component, and a default value, which is the text associated with the component. In the Easy Recipes app, the first TextView component displays the text "Strawberry Sorbet Recipe." The name of the component is tvTitle, which is specified in its key, and the default value is Strawberry Sorbet Recipe. The second component on the opening screen is an ImageView component that displays an image of the finished recipe. To create an application that is accessible to those with visual disabilities, add **descriptions** to the user interface components that can be read out loud to your user by a speech-based accessibility service such as a screen reader. The description accessibility feature provides a person with visual disabilities an idea of what the picture displays. To display an on-screen description of the recipe image for accessibility purposes, add the description text to the String table using a key and default value pair. The Button component that displays the text "VIEW RECIPE" specifies btRecipe as its key and VIEW RECIPE as its default value.

To add the text for TextView, ImageView, and Button components to the strings.xml file for the opening screen, follow these steps. You will use tv, iv, and bt prefixes, respectively, to help identify the three components.

Step 1

- In the Android project view, expand the values folder within the res folder.
- Double-click the strings.xml file to display its default string resources.

The strings.xml tab is displayed, showing the string resources. Notice that the strings.xml file already contains one default string with the title of the Android app (**Figure 2-7**).

Figure 2-7 The strings.xml tab displaying XML code

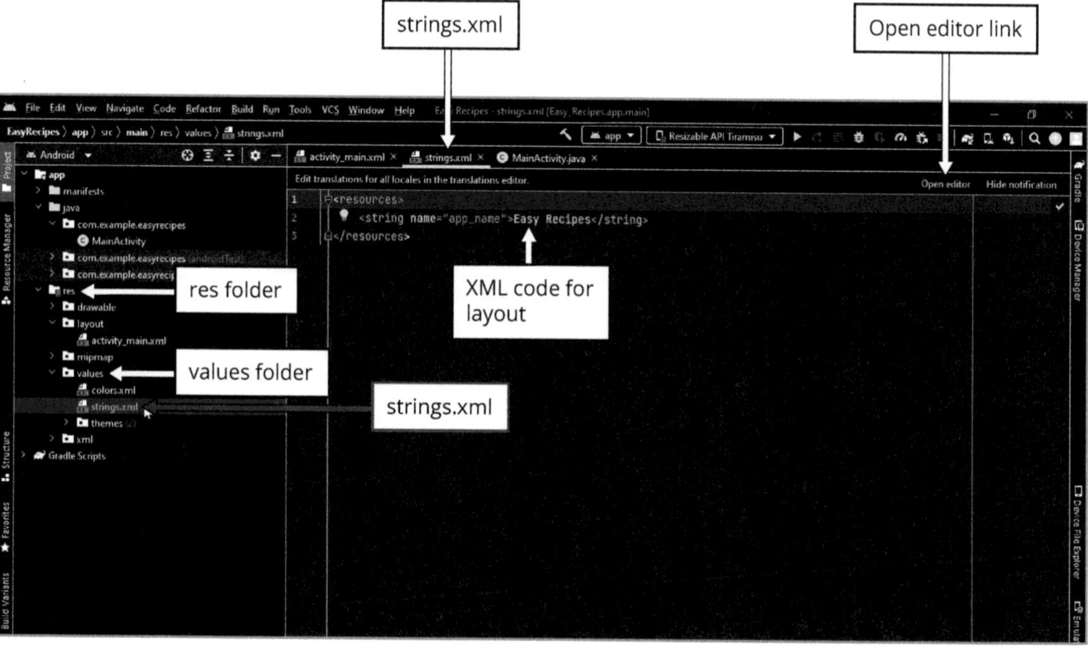

Step 2

- Click the Open editor link to display the String table in the Translations Editor tab.
- Click the Add Key (plus sign) button in the Translations Editor.
- In the Key text box, type **tvTitle** to name the string for the TextView component.
- In the Default Value text box, type **Strawberry Sorbet Recipe** to define the text to display.

The key and default value of the TextView component are entered using the Translations Editor's Add Key dialog box to add to the String table (**Figure 2-8**).

Figure 2-8 Add Key dialog box in the Translations Editor

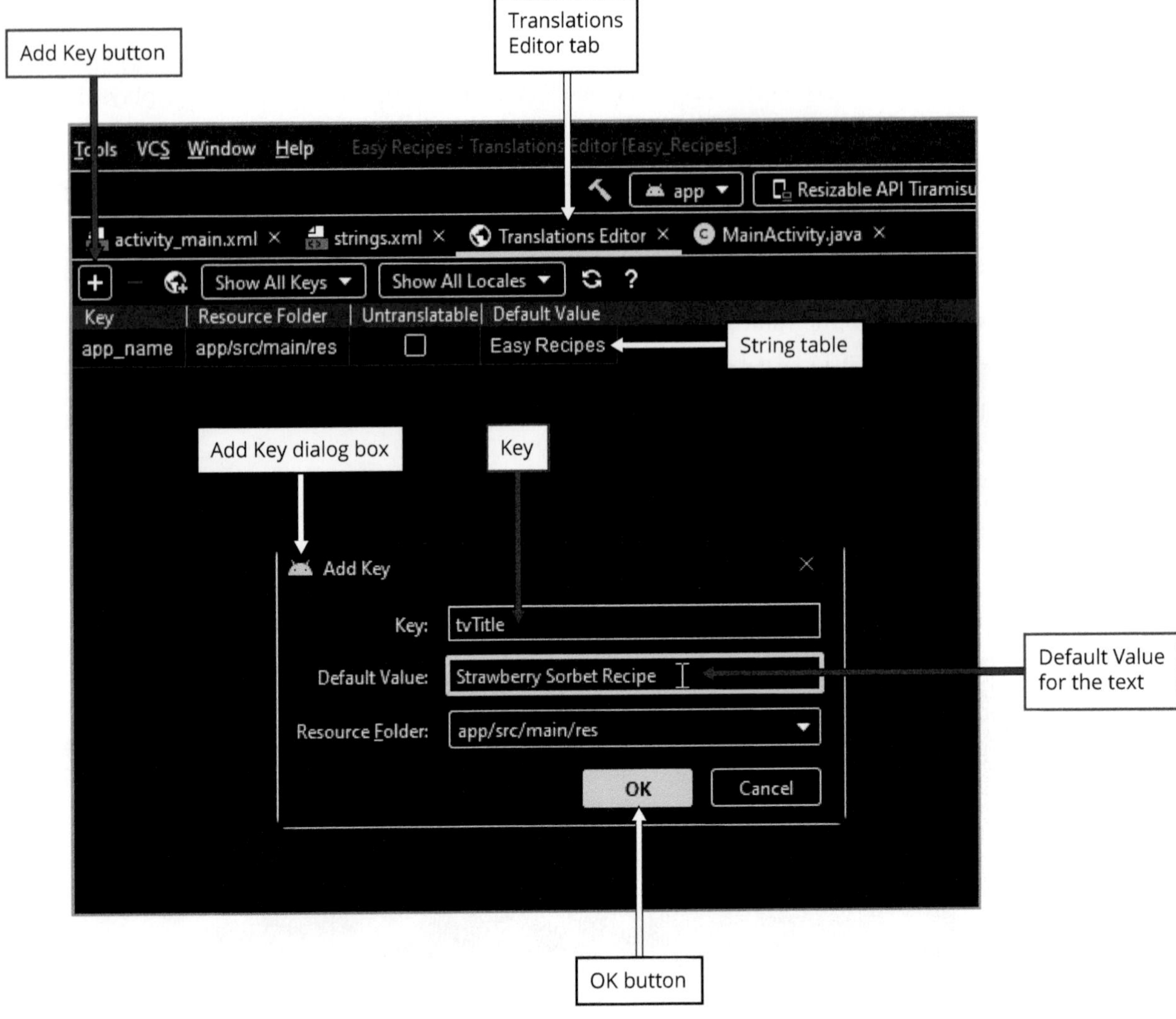

Step 3

- Click the OK button to add tvTitle to the String table.
- Click the Add Key (plus sign) button in the Translations Editor.
- In the Key text box, type **description** to name the string for the ImageView component. The screen reader will search for the description to read when the image is displayed for the user.
- In the Default Value text box, type **Recipe Image of Strawberry Sorbet** to explain the image that displays.

The key and default value of the ImageView description are entered in the dialog box (**Figure 2-9**).

Figure 2-9 Adding a string to the String table

Step 4

- Click the OK button.
- Click the Add Key (plus sign) button in the Translations Editor.
- In the Key text box, type **btRecipe** to name the string for the Button component.
- In the Default Value text box, type **View Recipe** to define the text.

The key and default value of the Button component are entered in the dialog box (**Figure 2-10**).

The second screen of the Easy Recipes app displays the ingredients and directions for preparing the sorbet recipe. Notice in Figures 2-1 and 2-2 that both screens display the same opening Strawberry Sorbet Recipe title using the tvTitle string twice. To add the rest of the text displayed on the second user interface, follow these steps:

Step 1

- Click the OK button to add the string for the Button component to the String table, and then click the Add Key (plus sign) button in the Translations Editor.
- In the Key text box, type **tvIngredients** to name the string for a TextView component to display on the second app screen.
- In the Default Value text box, type **Ingredients** to define the text, and then click the OK button to add the string to the String table.

Figure 2-10 Adding another string to the String table

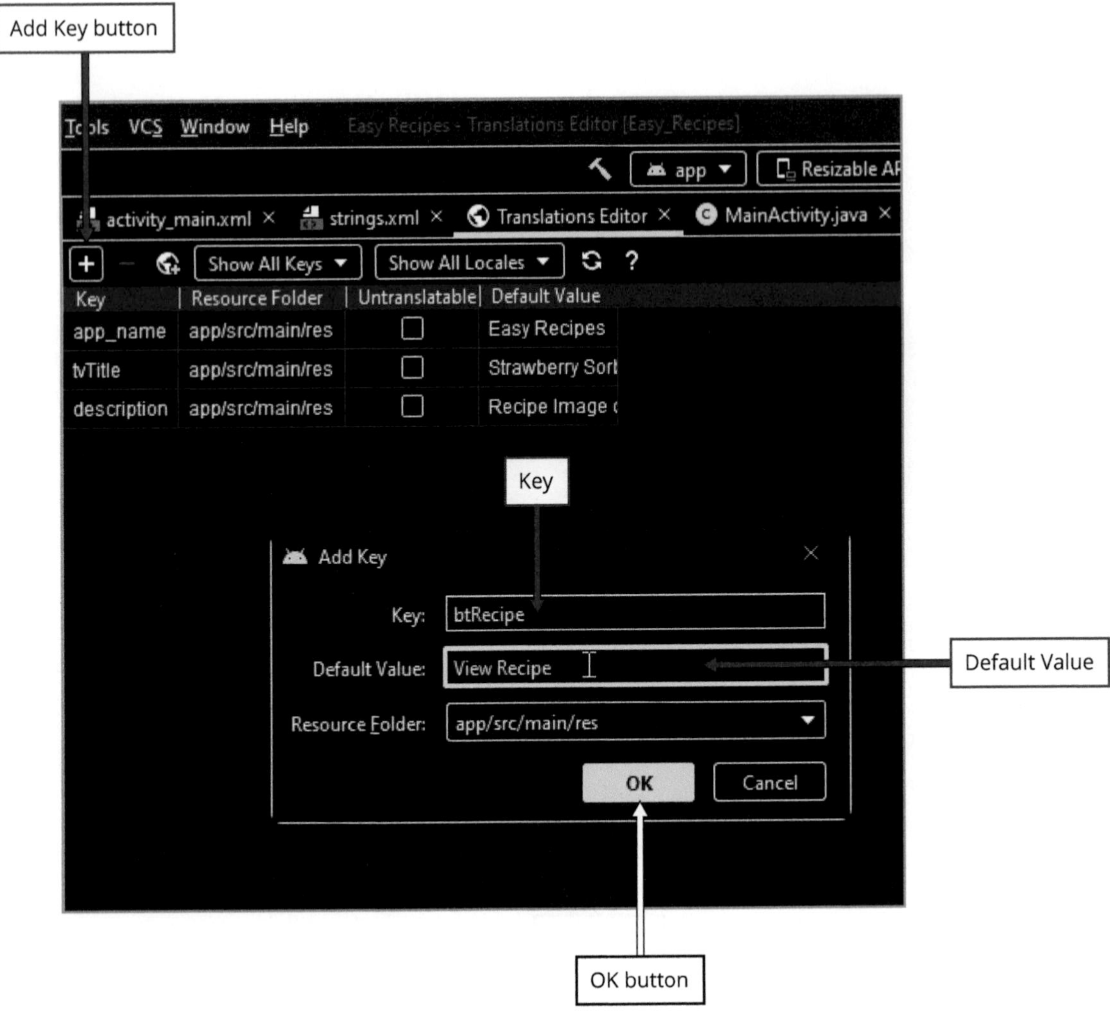

- Using the techniques taught in this step, add the strings shown in **Table 2-1** to the String table in the Translations Editor.

Table 2-1 Strings for the second screen in the Easy Recipes app

Key	Default Value
tvItem1	6 cups chopped strawberries
tvItem2	1 T. lemon juice
tvItem3	1 cup sugar
tvItem4	¼ cup cold water
tvDirections	Directions
tvMix	Process until smooth in the blender. Freeze for 8 hours in a covered container.

The text for the first and second user interfaces is added to the String table in the Translations Editor (**Figure 2-11**).

Step 2

- Close the Translations Editor tab.
- Close the strings.xml tab.
- Click the Save All button to save the Android project.

Figure 2-11 Completed String table on the Translations Editor tab

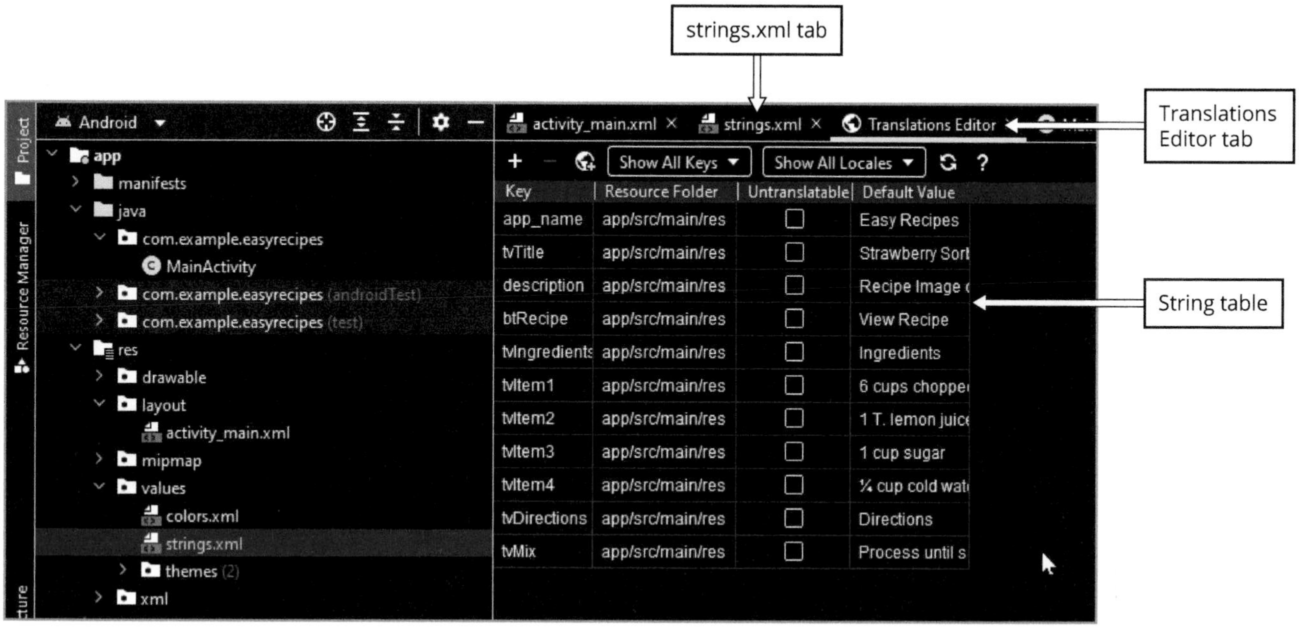

2.3 Constructing the User Interface with the ConstraintLayout

The Android user interface includes a layout resource designer called the **ConstraintLayout** in the Component Tree that organizes how components appear on the app's various screens with the help of the Layout Editor's visual tools. This layout provides more flexibility in positioning components than other layouts. Each component from the Palette can be placed on the emulator by dragging and dropping, but it is important to understand that if you simply drag a component into the Design Mode emulator, the component will not stay in that location when you run the app. To make the component stay in the correct location, you must use constraints. **Constraints** are the building blocks in an Android layout that attach or align a component to the screen, either by attaching it vertically and horizontally to the edges of the screen or aligning it with another component (or parent) on the screen. By using constraints, you can make your layout a **Responsive Design UI**. A Responsive Design UI is an approach that is based on the size of your screen, platform, and orientation. In other words, if you use a ConstraintLayout, your app can work on a phone of any size and automatically adjust, whether the phone has a vertical or horizontal orientation.

Constraint Handles

When you drag a component such as the TextView component, there are four circular dots on the edges called constraint handles, as shown in **Figure 2-12**. If you do not constrain a component, it will float to the top of the screen when the app is run. A constraint component must have at least two constraints—a vertical and a horizontal one. ConstraintLayout is a new layout for Android Studio; four handles on every component determine the start, end, top, and bottom of the control on the screen.

To constrain a component, click and drag a Constraint handle to the desired edge on two sides horizontally and vertically. If you drag all four Constraint handles to the four edges of the emulator screen (the top, bottom, left, and right), you can then drag the component anywhere on the screen and it will stay in that location when you run the app. If you do not use the Constraint handles properly, an error message will appear in the Component Tree.

Figure 2-12 The four circles are Constraint handles

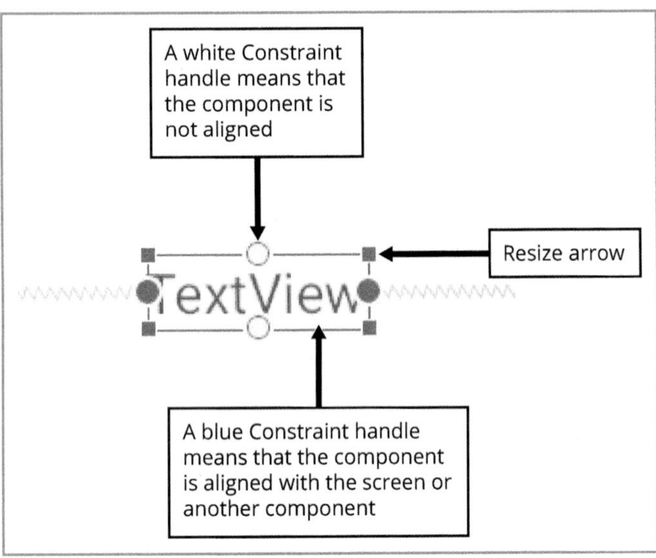

XML Code

After you move the Constraint handles in the Design view, Android Studio updates your layout resources as XML code in the res/layout resource directory for the Android application corresponding to the user interface template. To see the XML code, click the Code view in activity_main.xml, as shown in **Figure 2-13**. For example, consider a Button component with Constraint handles connected to the edge of the screen. You can place the Button so that it will be 30 percent from the left side of the screen on any device—this is called Horizontal bias in the XML code.

```
app:layout_constraintHorizontal_bias="0.30"
```

Figure 2-13 ConstraintLayout XML code

Other common layouts used in Android Studio are shown in **Table 2-2**.

Table 2-2 Common layouts in Android Studio

Layout Type	Best Use
LinearLayout	Used when different components, such as a TextView component and Buttons, are placed in a linear fashion that could be vertical (top to bottom) or horizontal (left to right).
RelativeLayout	As the name suggests, elements are placed relative to other components. If no relationship is defined, components go to the upper-left corner of the screen.
TableLayout	Used to divide the screen into rows and columns.
GridView	Used to display items in a two-dimensional, scrollable grid.

Good to Know

ConstraintLayout is the latest and most interesting layout in Android Studio. You also can use a combination of layouts, which means you can nest components within one another. The ConstraintLayout is the easiest of them all.

The Easy Recipes Opening User Interface

When the Easy Recipes app opens, the initial screen shown in Figure 2-1 displays a TextView component with the text "Strawberry Sorbet Recipe," an ImageView component with a picture of sorbet, and a Button component with the text "VIEW RECIPE." Notice that the components are aligned using ConstraintLayout, which allows you to place the components freely on the screen. You can modify a component's attributes using the Attributes pane. To change the attribute of a component, select the component first and then change the appropriate attribute, such as the text or size, in the Attributes pane. To view only the Design view (the white emulator) without the Blueprint view, you can click the Select Design Surface (B) button and select Design.

Android Text Attributes

The most popular text attributes change the displayed text, modify the size of the text, and change the alignment of the text. The **text attribute** uses text from a string resource to display within the component. The **textSize attribute** can use various units of measurement, as shown in **Table 2-3**. The preferred unit of measurement is often **sp**, which stands for "scaled-independent pixels," and the textSize attribute has a default setting of 14, which is too small for most devices. The reason for using this unit of measurement is that if a user has set up an Android phone to display a large font size for more clarity and easier visibility, the font in the app will be scaled to meet the user's size preference.

Table 2-3 Measurements used for the textSize attribute

Unit of Measure	Abbreviation	Example
Inches	in	"0.5in"
Millimeters	mm	"20mm"
Pixels	px	"100px"
Density-independent pixels	dp or dip	"100dp" or "100dip"
Scaled-independent pixels	sp	"10sp"

Quick Check

Why is it important to make the text larger on a smartphone than the default textSize attribute of 14sp?

Answer: The text will be too small to view on most devices without zooming in. Creating an accessible design means ensuring that you make your content as usable as possible for people who suffer from blindness, visual impairments, neurodiversity, and other problems.

On the opening screen of the Easy Recipes app, you can center the TextView component for the title, the ImageView component for the sorbet picture, and the Button component using the ConstraintLayout in the Component Tree.

The TextView component used to represent the title is named tvTitle. To name the TextView component, you use the id attribute. The prefix *tv* conveys information about the component—specifically, that you are using a TextView component. To place a centered TextView component on the emulator using the ConstraintLayout, follow these steps:

Step 1

- Click the Select Design Surface (B) button.

The options display for the Select Design Surface (**Figure 2-14**).

Figure 2-14 Display options for design surface

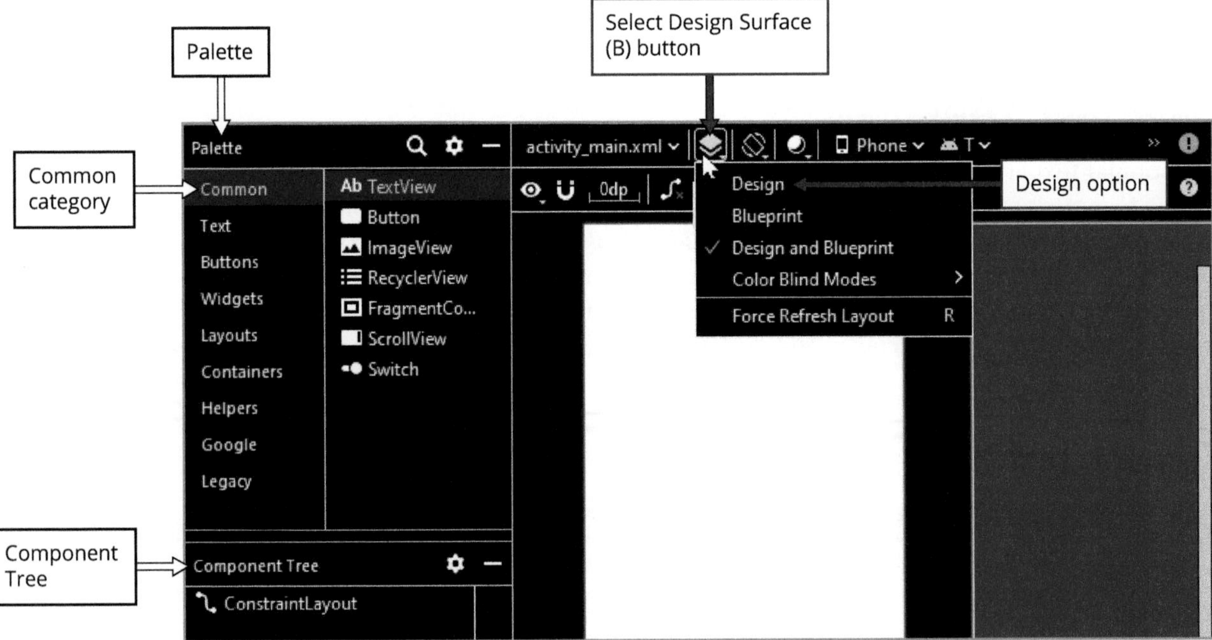

Step 2

- Click Design to display only the Design view of the emulator.
- In the Common category in the Palette, select the component named TextView. Drag the TextView component near the top center of the emulator.
- Drag the top Constraint handle to the top of the emulator screen and release the handle.

- Drag the bottom Constraint handle to the bottom of the emulator screen and then release the handle. You should now have all four constraints anchored to the edge of the screen; blue curly arrows should touch the top, bottom, left, and right sides of the emulator.
- Click the TextView component and move it back to the top center of the emulator.
- In the Attributes pane, under the Declared Attributes category, change the layout_constraintHorizontal_bias attribute to 0.50.
- Change the layout_constraintVertical_bias attribute to 0.20.

The TextView component is placed in the Design view emulator centered at 50 percent horizontally and 20 percent from the top vertically (**Figure 2-15**).

Figure 2-15 Constraint handles must be pulled to the edge of the emulator screen

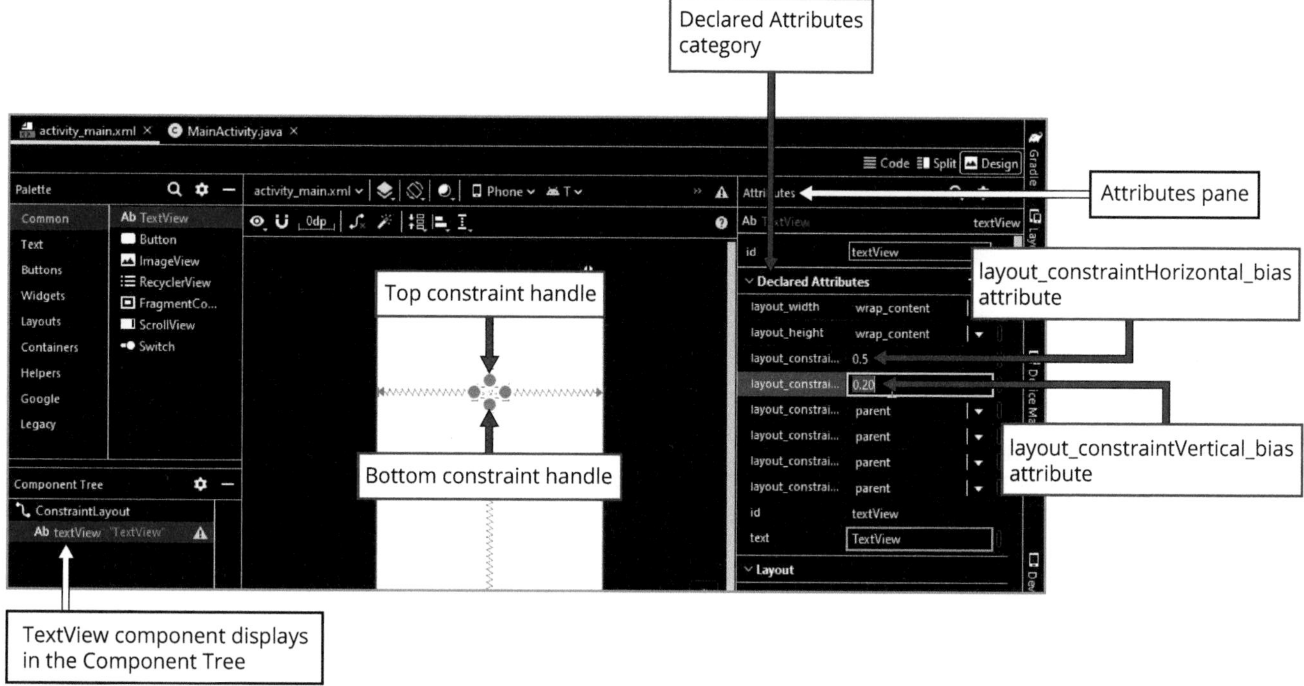

Good to Know

The yellow icon to the right of the TextView component in Figure 2-16 means that the component is currently hard-coded with the default text "TextView" in the text attribute. This warning symbol disappears after the text in the String table is associated with the TextView component.

Step 3

- Under the category of Declared Attributes, change the text attribute in the Attributes pane to **@string**.

The text attribute displays all the Translations Editor's String table keys that you typed in earlier (**Figure 2-16**).

Step 4

- Click @string/tvTitle from the drop-down list for the text attribute.
- Change the Zoom In + setting to 25 percent to view the text in the emulator.

The text resource tvTitle is selected from the strings.xml file (String table) and the text "Strawberry Sorbet Recipe" is displayed (**Figure 2-17**). Now the text attribute is no longer hard-coded and the error disappears.

Figure 2-16 The text attribute with @string used to display the String table

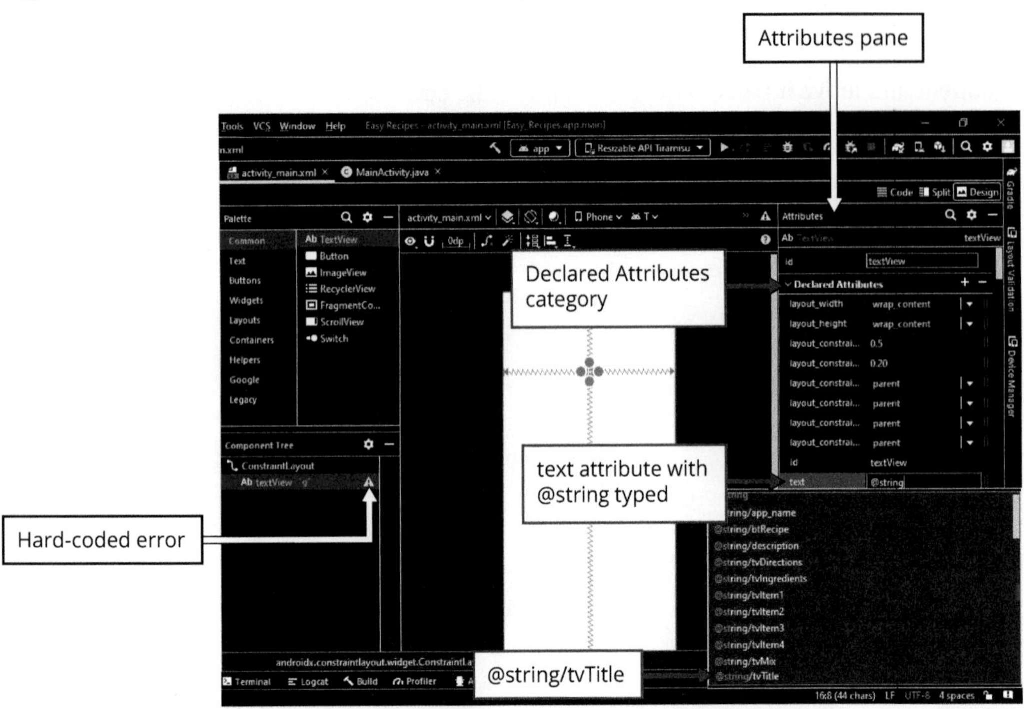

Figure 2-17 TextView text displayed in emulator after @string selected

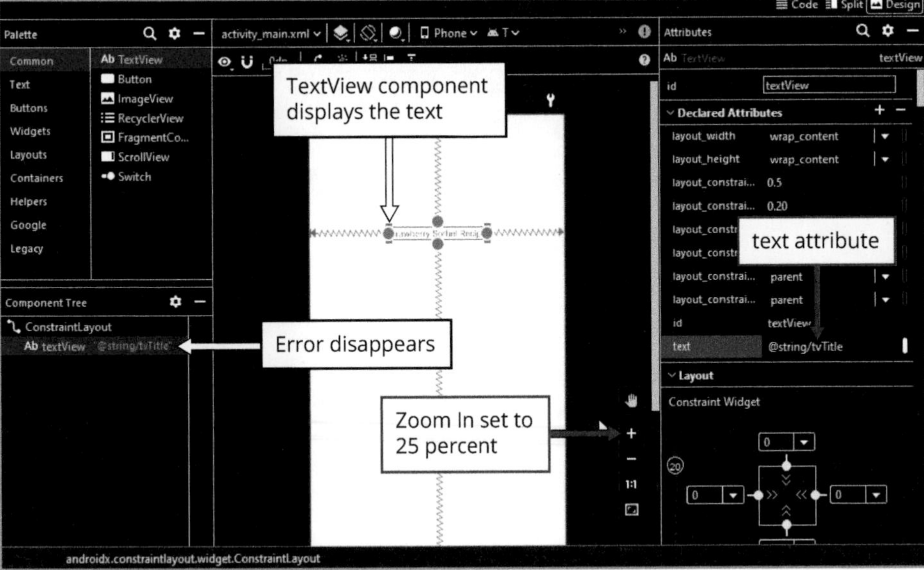

Step 5

- Scroll down the Attributes pane on the right side of the window to the textSize attribute under the All Attributes category.
- Click to the right of the textSize attribute, type **35sp** to represent the scaled-independent pixel size, and then press Enter.

The TextView component displays the text Strawberry Sorbet Recipe using a text size of 35sp (**Figure 2-18**). You want the text to be large enough to view on a smaller smartphone.

Figure 2-18 Updating the textSize of the TextView component

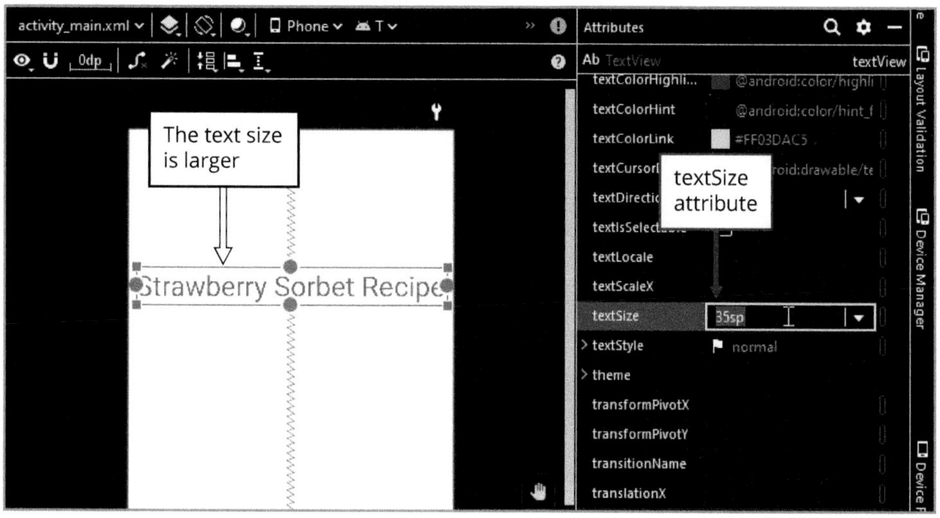

Good to Know | Throughout the book, note that Windows computers have an Enter key, but Mac computers use the Return key.

Good to Know | At the time of this writing, the top free Android apps were TikTok, Cash app, Instagram, WhatsApp Messenger, and Disney, in that order. Check to see if that is still true at the Google Play store.

Adding a File to the Resources Folder

In the Easy Recipes application, an image of strawberry sorbet is displayed in an ImageView component. Images provide a visually appealing way to convey information to your users without explicitly stating it. Before you can insert the ImageView component in the emulator, you must place the appropriate picture file in the resources folder. In the Android project view, the res (resource) folder contains a folder named *drawable*. The graphics used by the application can be stored in this folder. Android supports three types of graphic formats: .png (preferred), .jpg (acceptable), and .gif (discouraged).

Critical Thinking | **How can I convert an Android camera .jpg photo to the preferred .png file type?**

On a PC, Windows Paint can convert picture file types. On a Mac, Paintbrush is a similar program for image file type conversion. Open the image in the program and save it with the .png file extension.

Android categorizes device screens using two general properties: size and density. You should expect that your app will be installed on devices with screens that vary in both size and density. Android creates a Drawable resource for images when you save them in the res/drawable folder. To add an image to the res/drawable folder, you can drag and drop it into the folder from your computer. You should already have the student files for this text that your instructor gave you or that you downloaded from the book's webpage (*www.cengage.com*). To place a copy of the sorbet.png image into the res/drawable folder, follow these steps:

Step 1

- If necessary, copy the student files to your computer. Open the file folder that contains the file sorbet.png.
- To copy the sorbet.png file, click sorbet.png, then drag the file to the res/drawable folder in the Android project view.

A Move dialog box confirms the name and directory to which the image is being copied (**Figure 2-19**).

Figure 2-19 The sorbet.png file copied into the drawable folder within the res folder

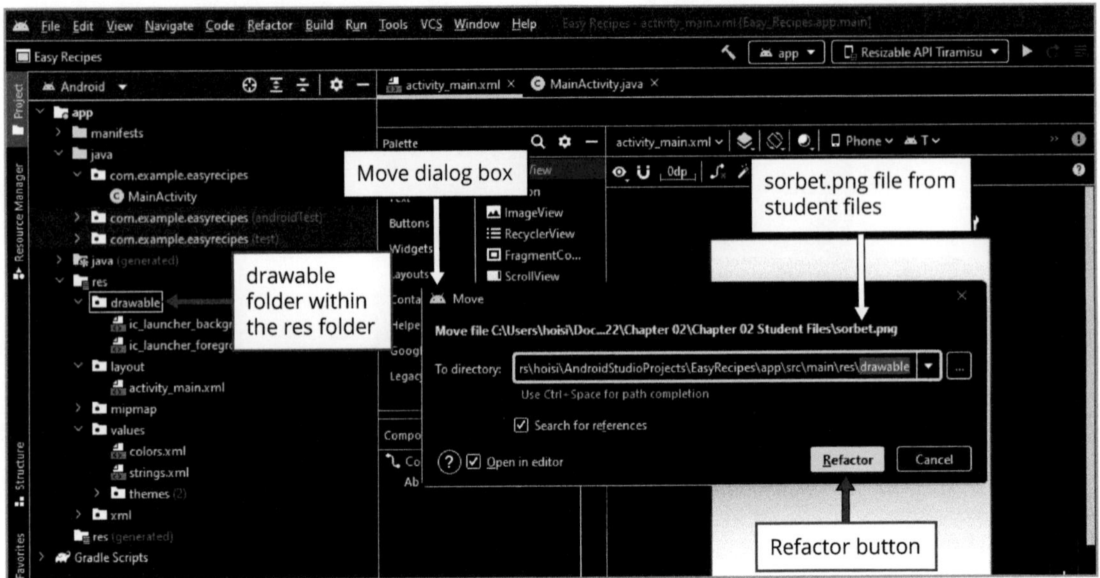

Step 2

- Click the Refactor button in the Move dialog box.

A copy of the sorbet.png file appears in the drawable folder and opens to confirm that you copied the correct image (**Figure 2-20**).

Figure 2-20 The sorbet image displays once copied into the drawable folder

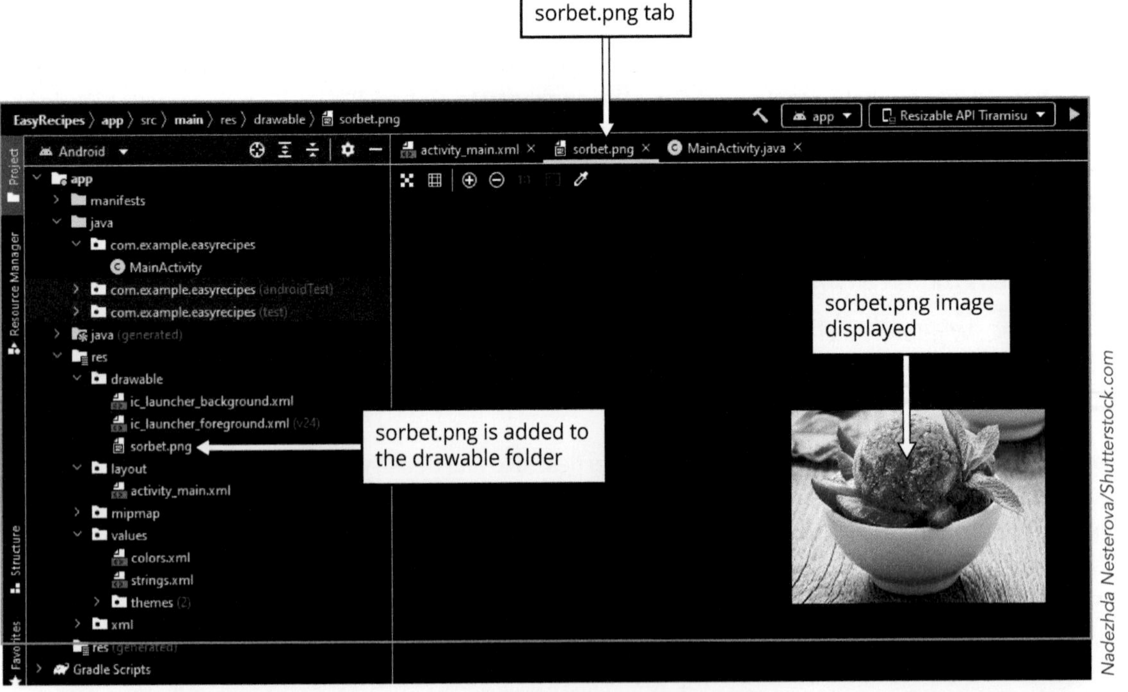

Good to Know An image or ImageView component has the proportions of the original image's width and height, known as the aspect ratio. For example, if you stretch an image to be larger, you want to keep its aspect ratio so that it does not appear distorted.

The ImageView Component

After an image is placed in a drawable resource folder, you can place an ImageView component in the emulator. An **ImageView component** can display an icon, a company logo, or a graphic on the Android screen. To add an ImageView component from the Widgets category of the Palette, follow these steps:

Step 1

- Close the sorbet.png tab.
- Click ImageView in the Common category in the Palette on the activity_main.xml tab.
- Drag an ImageView component to the center of the emulator until a pink image of a person is centered horizontally below the Strawberry Sorbet Recipe text, indicating the component is centered. Release the mouse button.

The ImageView component (the pink square placeholder) is centered in the emulator and the Pick a Resource dialog box opens (**Figure 2-21**).

Figure 2-21 Assigning the sorbet image to the ImageView component in the Pick a Resource dialog box

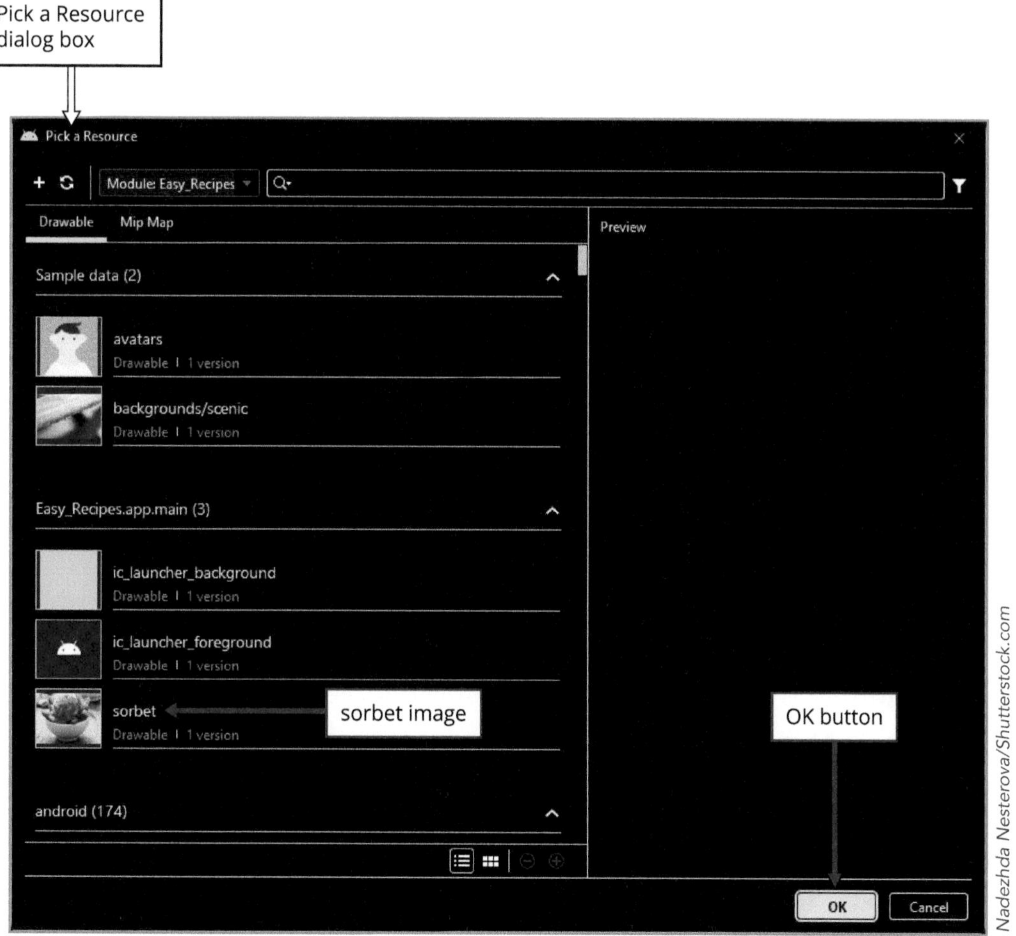

Step 2

- Click sorbet to select the sorbet.png image in the Pick a Resource dialog box.

The sorbet image is selected in the Pick a Resource dialog box (**Figure 2-22**).

Figure 2-22 Displaying the image to confirm that you have the correct resource

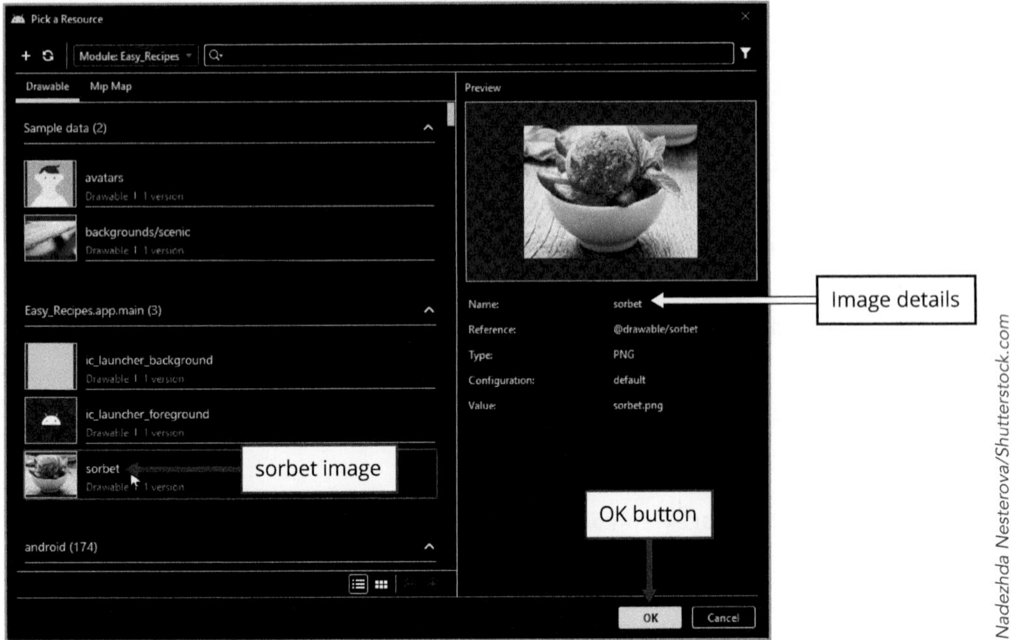

Step 3

- Click the OK button in the Pick a Resource dialog box.
- To keep the image below the text during runtime, drag the top Constraint handle of the ImageView component to the top of the emulator screen and then release the handle.
- Drag the bottom Constraint handle of the ImageView component to the bottom of the emulator screen and release the handle. You should now have all four constraints anchored to the edge of the screen; blue curly arrows should touch the top, bottom, left, and right sides of the emulator.
- Drag the ImageView component and move it back below the Strawberry Sorbet Recipe text.
- Type ivRecipe in the id text box of the Attributes pane to name the ImageView component.

The sorbet ImageView component named ivRecipe no longer displays an error after the constraints are set (**Figure 2-23**).

Step 4

- Scroll down the Attributes pane to display the contentDescription attribute in the All Attributes category.
- Type **@string** to display the String table text in the contentDescription attribute text box.

The description string resource from strings.xml is assigned to the contentDescription attribute, which will display a description of the ivRecipe ImageView component for accessibility purposes (**Figure 2-24**).

Step 5

- Click **@string/description** to set the text for the image's contentDescription.

The sorbet image contains a contentDescription attribute for the screen reader for accessibility purposes (**Figure 2-25**).

Figure 2-23 ImageView component with image displayed in the emulator and the id entered

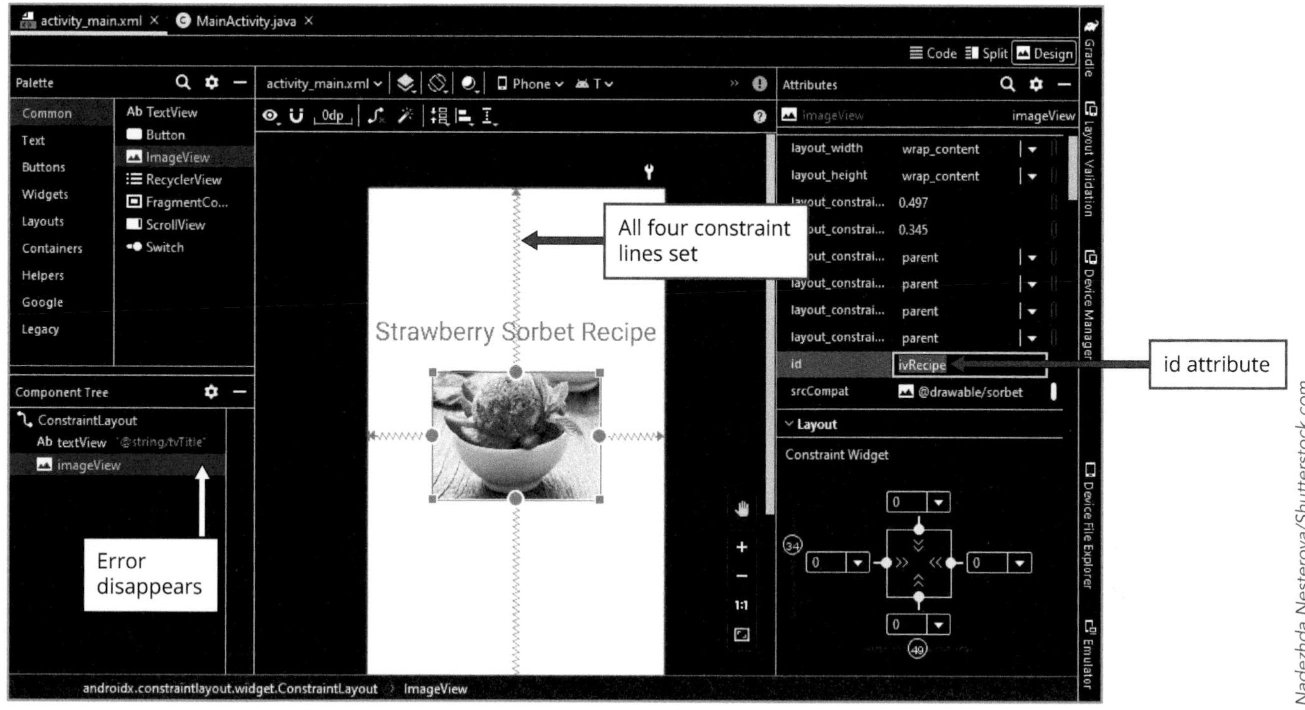

Nadezhda Nesterova/Shutterstock.com

Figure 2-24 The contentDescription set for accessibility

Figure 2-25 The contentDescription assigned from the String table

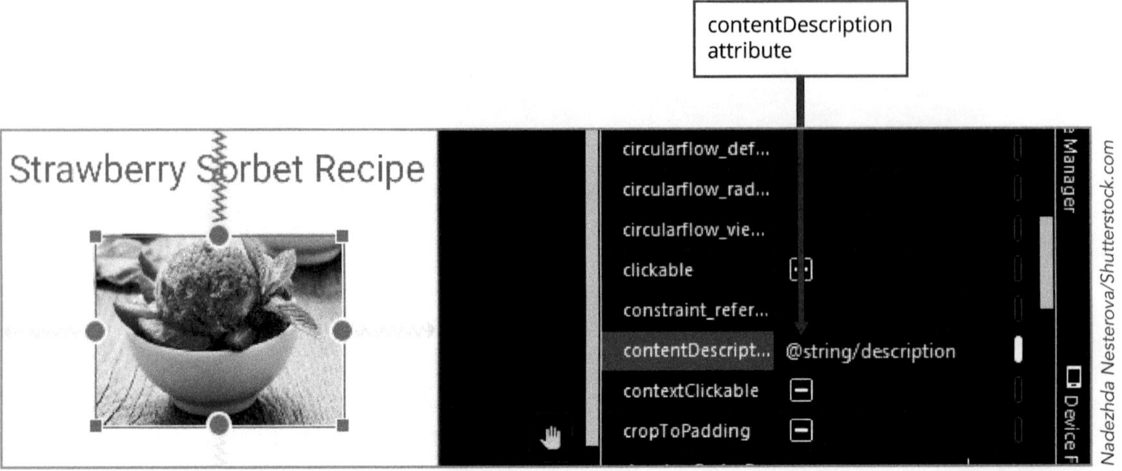

Quick Check

What is the purpose of a contentDescription attribute?

Answer: The contentDescription attribute describes the image for accessibility purposes within the screen reader.

On the Job

When you are selecting images for your app, consider using the advanced search features of Google or Bing to locate an open-source license graphic. An open-source license is a type of license for images that allows a picture to be used, modified, and shared under defined terms and conditions. If you reproduce, publish, or distribute a copyrighted image without permission or a valid license, you are committing a legal offense called copyright infringement.

Adding a Button Component

A Button component is commonly used in a graphical user interface. For example, you probably are familiar with the OK or Submit buttons used in many applications. Generally, buttons are used to cause an event to occur. The Android SDK includes four types of button components: Button, FloatingActionButton, ToggleButton, and ImageButton. The Button component is provided in the Buttons category in the Palette.

In the Easy Recipes app, the user taps a Button component to display the sorbet recipe on a second screen. To name the Button component, you use its id attribute. For example, use btRecipe as the id attribute for the Button component in the Easy Recipes app. The prefix *bt* represents a button in the code. The id btRecipe is used to code the Button component in Java. The component **backgroundTint** can be added to a Button component to set a background color such as red, yellow, and green. You can change the text color of a Button or TextView component by changing the **textColor** attribute. The color displays as a hexadecimal color name, such as FFFFFFFF to represent the color red. To add a Button component from the Buttons category of the Palette, follow these steps:

Step 1

- Drag the Button component to the emulator below the ImageView component and center it horizontally. Release the mouse button.
- To keep the Button below the image during runtime, drag the top Constraint handle of the Button component to the top of the emulator screen and then release the handle.

- Drag the bottom Constraint handle of the Button component to the bottom of the emulator screen and release the handle. You should now have all four constraints anchored to the edge of the screen; blue curly arrows should touch the top, bottom, left, and right sides of the emulator.
- Drag the Button component and move it back below the sorbet image.
- Click in the id component and type **btRecipe** in the id text box within the Attributes pane.

The Button component is named btRecipe and is centered below the sorbet image (**Figure 2-26**).

Figure 2-26 Button component placed on emulator and the id named

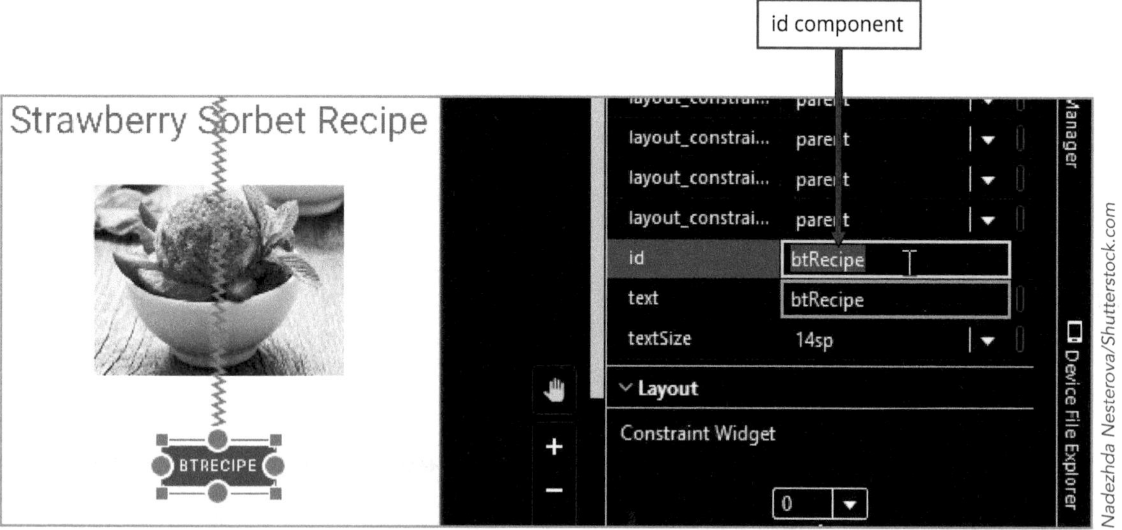

Nadezhda Nesterova/Shutterstock.com

Step 2

- In the Attributes pane, change the textSize attribute to **36sp** and press Enter.
- Type **@string** into the text attribute and select **@string/btRecipe** to change the text in the Button component.

The Button component displays the text VIEW RECIPE, which has the text size of 36sp (**Figure 2-27**).

Figure 2-27 Button displaying larger text

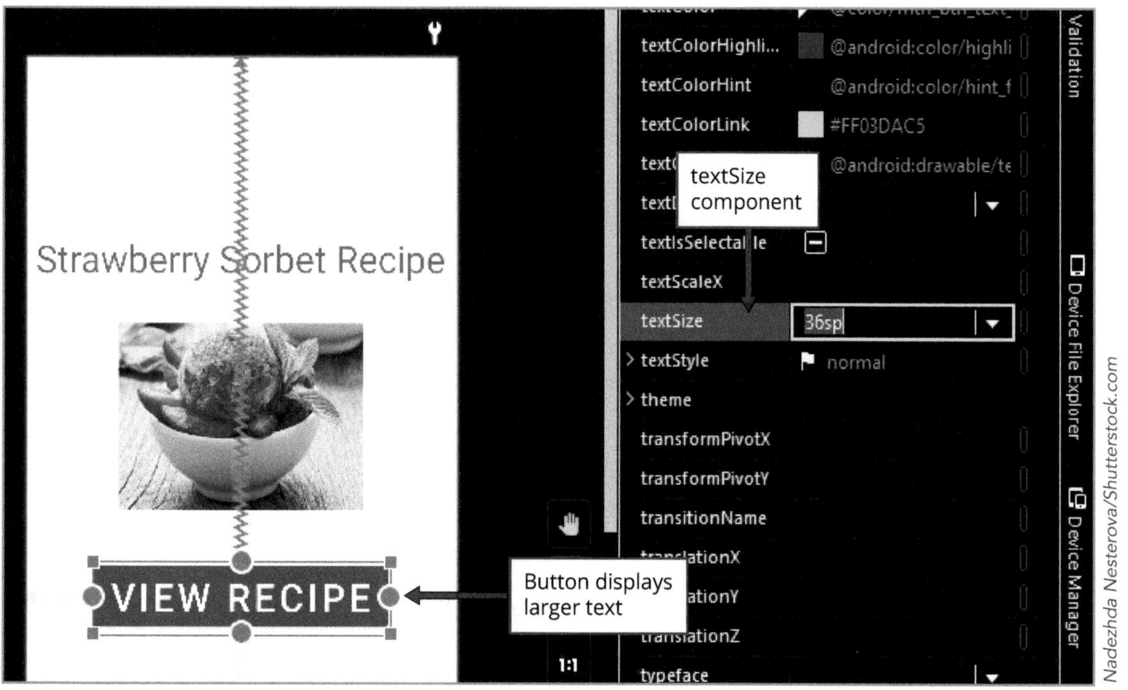

Nadezhda Nesterova/Shutterstock.com

Step 3

- In the Attributes pane, click the eyedropper symbol next to the backgroundTint component for the btRecipe Button.

When the eyedropper next to the backgroundTint component is selected, the color options are displayed (**Figure 2-28**).

Figure 2-28 Button with colors displayed for background tint color

Step 4

- Click the red color (the first under the Material 500 category) to select the hexadecimal color of #F44336, and then click the Button component on the emulator to close the Resources dialog box.

The red background displays on the Button component (**Figure 2-29**).

Figure 2-29 Button with changed backgroundTint attribute

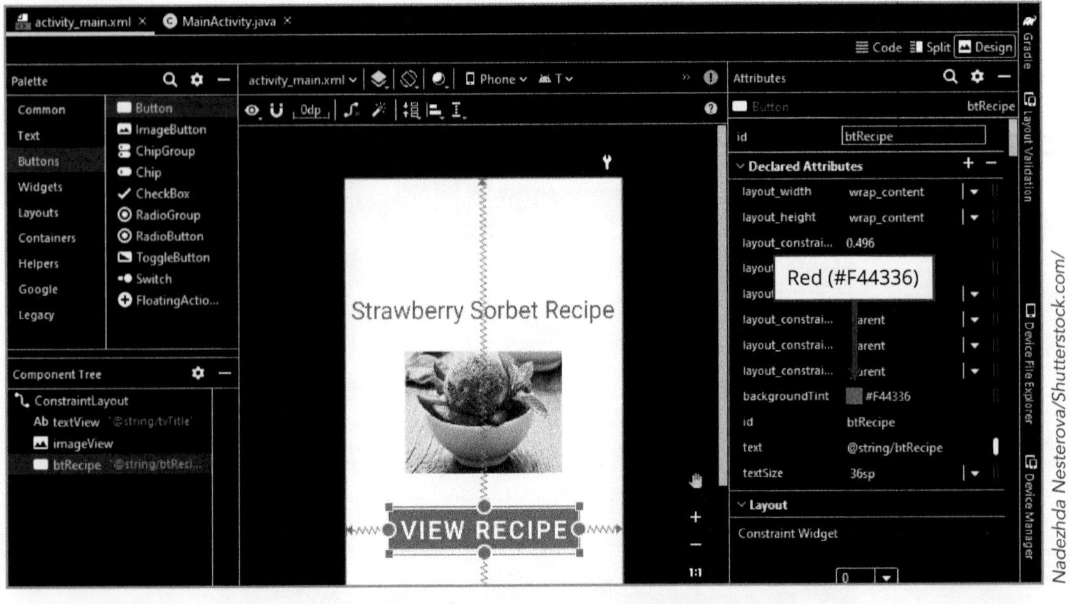

Quick Check

Which attributes would you change if you wanted a yellow button with black text on the button?

Answer: You would change backgroundTint and textColor.

2.4 Planning Out Program Design

As you acquire the skills necessary to design an Android user interface, you are ready to learn about the program development life cycle—a set of phases and steps that developers follow to design, create, and maintain an Android program. Following are the phases of the program development life cycle, which provide an overview of the major steps in developing an app.

1. *Gather and analyze the program requirements*—The developer must obtain the information that identifies the program requirements and then document these requirements.
2. *Design the user interface*—After the developer understands the program requirements, the next step is to design the user interface. The user interface provides the framework for the processing that occurs within the program.
3. *Design the program processing objects*—An Android app consists of one or more processing objects that perform the tasks required in the program. The developer must determine what processing objects are required and then determine the requirements of each object. Your design of the user interface plays an important part in keeping the overall Android experience consistent and enjoyable to use.
4. *Code the program*—After the processing objects have been designed, the objects must be implemented in program code. Program code consists of the instructions written using XML and Java code that ultimately can be executed.
5. *Test the program*—As the program is being coded, and after the coding is completed, the developer should test the program code to ensure that it is executing properly.

Good to Know

You can use comments to document your code. Comments are ignored by the Java compiler, but they make your code much easier to read and to explain to your colleagues. When you want to make a one-line comment, type two forward slashes (//), and then enter your comment. For example:

```
// This is a single-line comment
```

Another way to comment is to use block comments. For example:

```
/* This is a
block comment
*/
```

It is good programming practice to begin all sections of code with a brief comment describing its author and functional characteristics of the procedure (what it does). Such comments are not only for your own benefit but for the benefit of anyone else who examines the code. Comments are also helpful in defining the purpose of variables in your code.

Creating Activities

The Easy Recipes app displays two screens, as shown previously in Figures 2-1 and 2-2. The system requirement for this app is for the user to select a recipe name and then tap a button to display the recipe details. Screens in the Android environment are defined in layout files. Figure 2-29 shows the completed design for the first screen, which is defined in activity_main.xml. A second screen must be created and designed in a layout file named activity_recipe.xml. Each of the two screens is considered an Activity. An **Activity**, one of the core components of an Android application, is the point at which the application makes contact with your users. For example, an Activity might create a menu of websites, request a street address to display a map, or even show an exhibit of photographs from an art museum. An Activity is an important component of the life cycle of an Android app. You can construct activities by using XML layout files and a Java class.

2.5 Creating Multiple Android Activities

The src folder in the Android project view includes the MainActivity.java file. This file contains the MainActivity class that opens the activity_main.xml screen, which you designed for the app's user interface. In object-oriented terminology, a class describes a group of objects that establishes an introduction to each object's attributes. A **class** is simply a blueprint or a template for creating objects by defining its properties. Classes are the fundamental building blocks of a Java program. Classes are categories, and objects are items within each category. An **object** is a specific, concrete instance of a class.

When you create an object, you instantiate it. When you **instantiate**, you create an instance of the object by defining one particular variation of the object within a class, giving it a name, and locating it in the memory of the computer. Each class needs its own copy of an object. A class determines what data an object can hold and the way it can behave when using the data. For instance, imagine a set of design plans (**Figure 2-30**) for a Mini Cooper car that detail how the vehicle will be manufactured. These plans represent the class. Next, imagine that you order your own Mini Cooper car (i.e., instantiate your own copy) using the design plans and that you select one that is candy-apple red with a yellow racing stripe. A class can be instantiated countless times, but each instantiation creates a new and unique object, just like BMW can create thousands of Mini Cooper cars.

Figure 2-30 The class is the model of a Mini Cooper, and the instantiations are custom models of these four Mini Coopers with different colors and options

Vectorism7788/Shutterstock.com

Later in this chapter, Java code is added to the MainActivity class to recognize the action of tapping the Button component to open the recipe screen. Recall that each screen represents one single Activity. In addition, each Activity must have a matching Java class file within the java folder in Android Studio. A second Activity named Recipe.java creates a corresponding XML file named activity_recipe.xml that displays the layout for the second screen. The activity_recipe.xml layout file can then be designed as shown in Figure 2-2. It is a Java standard to begin a class name with an uppercase letter, include no spaces, and emphasize each new word with an initial uppercase letter. An XML layout filename typically starts with a lowercase letter using the same name as the class name.

Good to Know | Using an uppercase letter to begin a Java class name and starting each new word with an uppercase letter is known as **Pascal case**.

To add a second Java class with a second XML layout page to the application, follow these steps:

Step 1

- Close the activity_main.xml tab.
- In the Android project view, expand the java folder and the first com.example.easyrecipes package to view the MainActivity Java class.
- To create a second class, right-click the first com.example.easyrecipes folder, click New on the shortcut menu, and then click Activity.

The Activity shortcut menu is displayed to add a second activity (**Figure 2-31**).

Figure 2-31 Creating a second class in the app

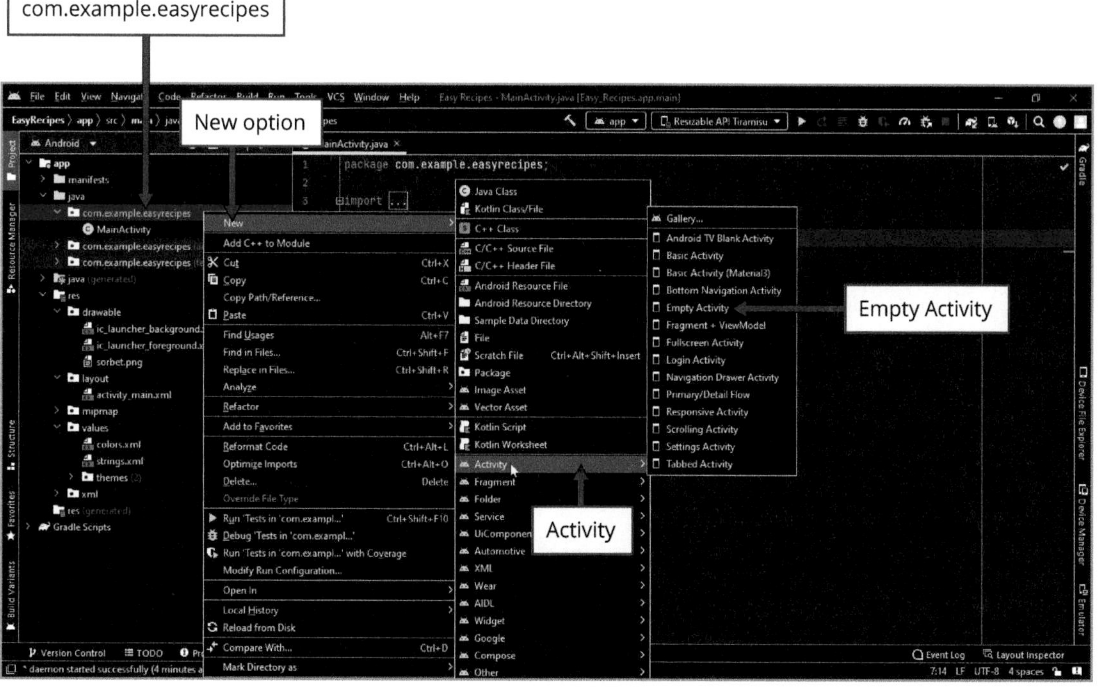

Step 2

- Click Empty Activity to create a second Activity class.
- In the Activity Name text box, type **Recipe** to create a second class.

A new class named Recipe is named with the second layout, activity_recipe, in the layout folder (**Figure 2-32**).

Figure 2-32 Creating the Recipe class

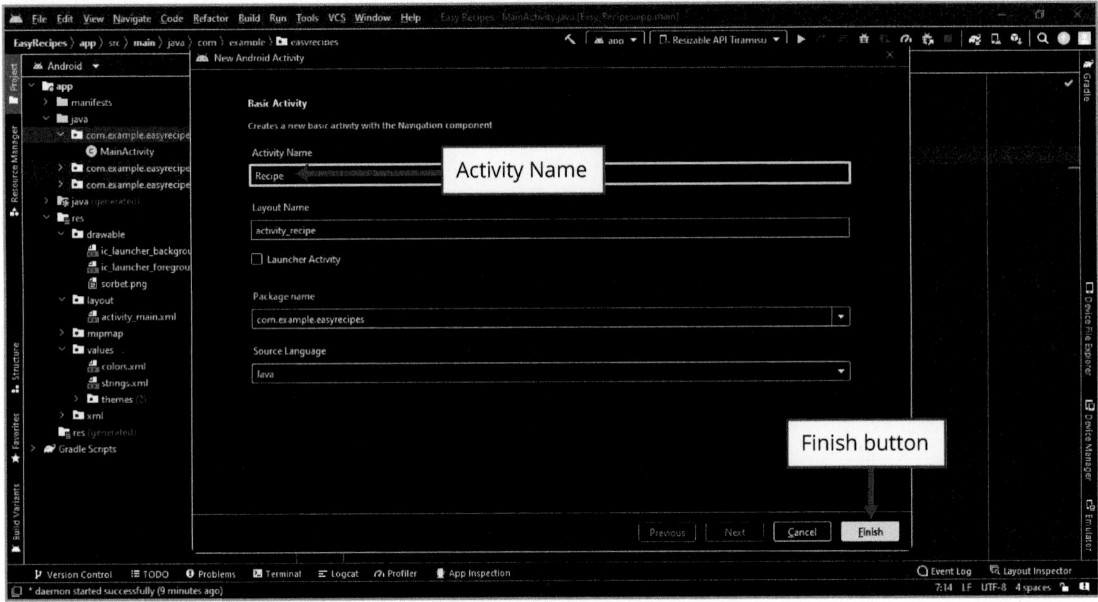

Step 3

- Click the Finish button to finish creating the Recipe class and XML layout for the second screen.
- Using the techniques taught earlier in the chapter, create the second user interface, activity_recipe.xml, with multiple TextView components.

The second user interface, activity_recipe.xml, is designed (**Figure 2-33**).

Figure 2-33 Designing the user interface for activity_recipe.xml

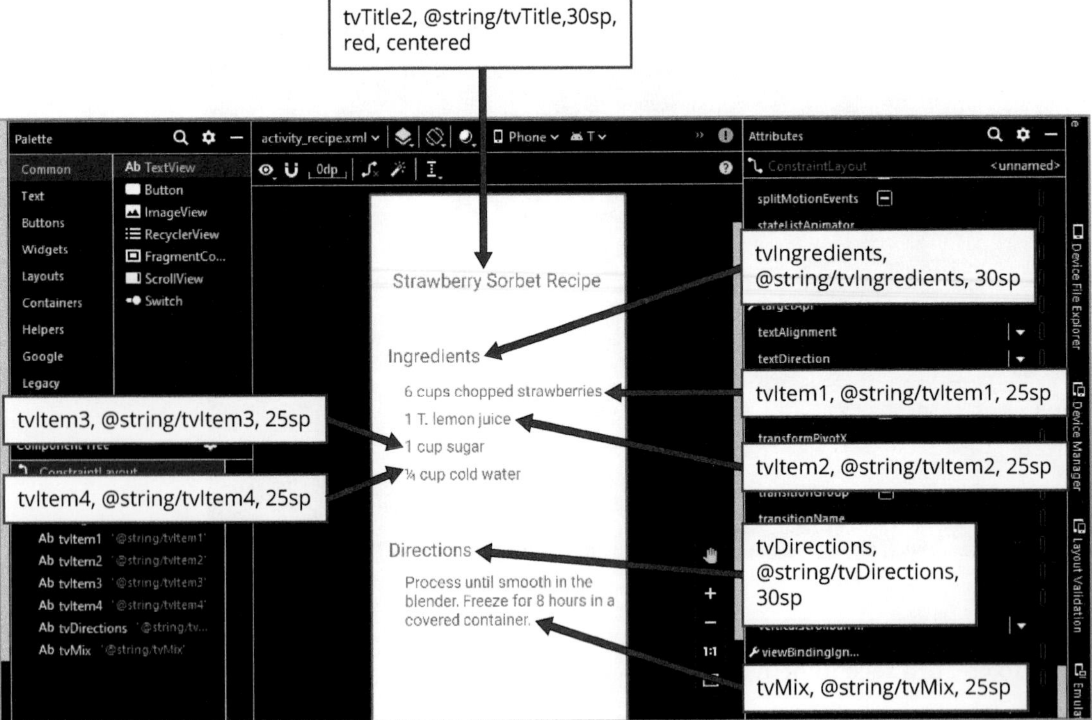

Step 4

- Close the activity_recipe.xml tab.
- Open the Recipe.java tab code window.

The newly created Recipe.java class is displayed (**Figure 2-34**).

Figure 2-34 New Recipe class in the Easy Recipes project

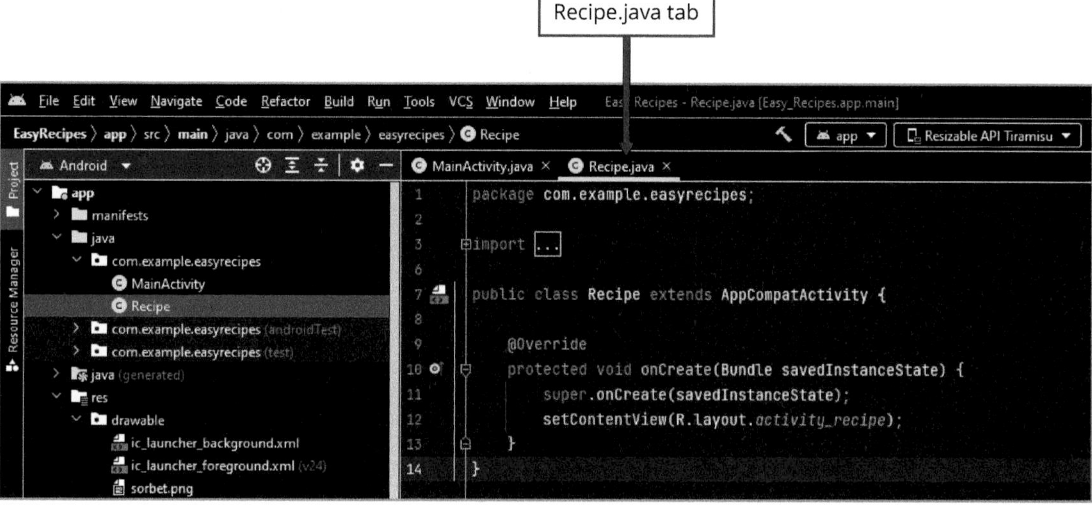

2.6 Viewing Activities in the Android Manifest File

An Android project consists of far more than the XML layout files that create the user interface emulator design. The other important components of any Android project are the Android Manifest file and the Java code in the Java classes. The **Android Manifest** file is necessary in every Android application, and the file must be named AndroidManifest .xml. The Android Manifest file provides essential information to the Android device, such as the name of your Java application, a listing of each activity, any permissions needed to access other Android functions (such as the use of the Internet, services, and broadcast receivers), and the minimum level of the Android API. This file lets the Android system know what components are used and under what conditions they can be launched. AndroidManifest.xml is like a project manager of a business process that determines which activities are scheduled, the permissions that are necessary, and the device versions needed to get the job done.

Android Studio automatically adds each activity you create to the Android Manifest file. In the Easy Recipes app, the Android Manifest file is only aware of the initial activity named MainActivity. To see which Activities an application contains, expand the manifests folder and then double-click the AndroidManifest.xml file in the Android project view, as shown in **Figure 2-35**. Notice that Lines 19 and 20 call an activity named MainActivity. The intent in Lines 22–26 is to launch the opening screen. Lines 16 and 17 call the second activity named Recipe. The AndroidManifest.xml file must contain an entry for each activity.

Coding the Java Activity

When the user taps an application icon on their Android phone or tablet, the MainActivity.java code is read by the device processor. The entry point of the Activity class is the onCreate( ) event handler, which is called a method. A **method** is a set of Java statements that can be included inside a Java class. A method is a piece of code that performs some type of action; in our Easy Recipes app, for example, the method will open another screen on the Android phone

Figure 2-35 AndroidManifest.xml

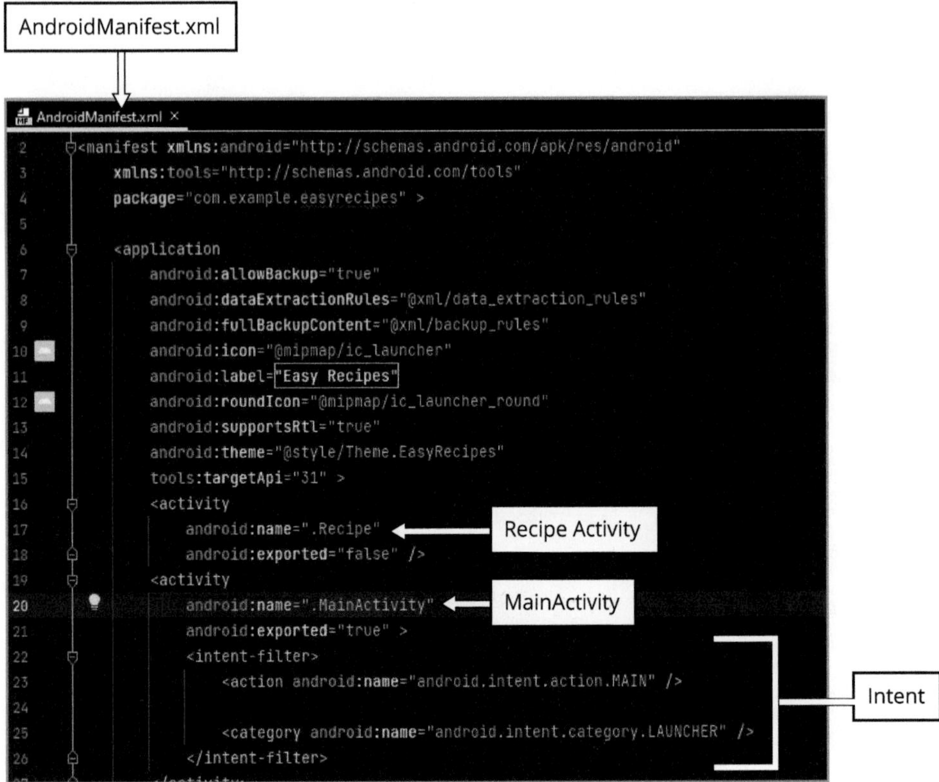

to display the recipe when you click the VIEW RECIPE button. In a large app with hundreds of recipes, the same method could execute a block of useful code that would open a particular recipe, and that method could be called repeatedly from anywhere in your program (as long as it is declared public).

The **method body** contains a collection of statements that defines what the method does. The onCreate( ) method is where you initialize the Activity. Imagine a large stack of papers on your desk; the paper on top of the stack is what you are reading right now. Android also has a stack of activities. The onCreate( ) method places the new activity on top of the stack.

2.7 Writing Code Using the onCreate( ) Method

In the chapter project, the first activity displayed in the opening screen layout designed in activity_main.xml is the currently running activity. When the user clicks the VIEW RECIPE button, the activity_main.xml screen closes and a new Activity that displays the actual recipe (activity_recipe.xml) is placed on top of the stack and becomes the running activity. The syntax for the onCreate( ) method is:

Code Syntax

```
public void onCreate(Bundle savedInstanceState) {
 super.onCreate(savedInstanceState);
}
```

The method begins with *public void*, which are special keywords that Java uses to determine the type of method. They must always be in all lowercase letters. *Void* is called the **return type** of the method. A void return type means the method does not return anything. At the end of the public void statement is an opening curly brace. The closing curly brace appears at the end of the method. Inside the braces is the onCreate( ) method, where the first user interface must be opened. Activities have no clue which user interface should be displayed on the screen. For a particular user interface to open, code must be added inside the onCreate( ) method to place that specific activity on top of the stack. The Java code necessary to display the content of a specific screen is called **setContentView**, which has the following syntax:

Code Syntax

```
setContentView(R.layout.activity_main);
```

In the code syntax, R.layout.*activity_main* represents the user interface of the activity_main.xml layout (the opening screen), which displays the opening title, sorbet image, and VIEW RECIPE button. The R represents "Resource," as the layout folder resides in the res folder.

Displaying the User Interface

The MainActivity.java file was created automatically by Android Studio; it already contains the onCreate( ) method and setContentView(R.layout.activity_main) code, as shown in Lines 10 and 12 in **Figure 2-36**. Line 10 starts the method and Line 12 displays the activity_main.xml layout when the application begins. Android Studio automatically codes the onCreate( ) method for opening the activity_recipe.xml layout when the Recipe.Java class is launched.

Figure 2-36 MainActivity.java code for onCreate( ) method

```
1  package com.example.easyrecipes;
2
3  import androidx.appcompat.app.AppCompatActivity;
4
5  import android.os.Bundle;
6
7  public class MainActivity extends AppCompatActivity {
8
9      @Override
10     protected void onCreate(Bundle savedInstanceState) {
11         super.onCreate(savedInstanceState);
12         setContentView(R.layout.activity_main);
13     }
14 }
```

2.8 Creating a Button Event Handler

Android phones and tablets have touchscreens that create endless possibilities for user interaction, allowing the user to tap, swipe, and pinch in or out to change the size of the screen. The result of an event-driven language is that users typically see an interface containing components, buttons, menus, and other graphical elements. After displaying the interface, the program waits until the user touches the device. When the user reacts, the app initiates an event that executes code in an **event handler**, a part of the program coded to respond to a specific event. In the Easy Recipes app, users have only one interaction—they can tap the Button component to start an event that displays the sorbet recipe. When the user taps the Button component, code for an event listener is necessary to begin the event that displays the activity_recipe.xml file on the Android screen. This tap event is actually known as a click event in Java code. In the Easy Recipes application, the MainActivity.java code must first contain the following sections:

- A class attribute to hold a reference to the Button object
- An OnClickListener( ) method to await the button click action's onClick( ) method to respond to the click event

The Easy Recipes application opens with a Button component on the screen. To use that button, a reference is required in the MainActivity.java file. To reference a Button component, use the following syntax to create a Button attribute:

Code Syntax

```
Button = (Button)findViewById(R.id.btRecipe);
```

The syntax for the Button attribute includes the findViewById( ) method, which is used by any Android Activity. This method finds a layout view in the XML files that you created when designing the user interface. The variable named "button" in the code contains the reference to the Button component.

After the code is entered to reference the Button component, you can press Alt+Enter to import the Button type as an Android widget. (You can press Option+Return on a Mac.) When you **import** the Button type as an Android widget, you make the classes from the Android Button package available throughout the application. An import statement is automatically placed at the top of the Java code. An **import statement** is a way of making more Java functions available to your specific program. Java can perform almost endless actions, but not every program needs to do everything. So, to limit the size of the code, Java has its classes divided into packages that can be imported at the top of your code.

After the Button attribute is referenced in MainActivity.java, an OnClickListener( ) method is necessary to detect when the user taps an on-screen button. Event listeners wait for user interaction; in the chapter project, this occurs when the user taps the button to view the recipe. When an OnClickListener is placed in the code window, Java creates an onClick auto-generated stub. A **stub** is a piece of code that serves as a placeholder to declare itself; it has just enough code to link to the rest of the program. The following syntax is needed for an OnClickListener( ) method that listens for the Button component:

Code Syntax

```
button.setOnClickListener(new OnClickListener() {
 public void onClick(View v) {
 // TODO Auto-generated method stub
 }
});
```

The last step to code is to call the startActivity( ) method, which opens the second Activity and displays the activity_recipe.xml user interface. The startActivity( ) method creates an **intent** to start another Activity, such as the recipe's Activity class. The intent needs two parts known as parameters: a context and the name of the Activity that is being opened. A context in Android coding means that any time you ask a program to launch another Activity, a context is sent to the Android system to show which initiating Activity class is making the request. The context of the chapter project is MainActivity.this, which references the MainActivity.java class. The following syntax line launches the Recipe Java class:

Code Syntax

```
startActivity(new Intent(MainActivity.this, Recipe.class));
```

2.9 Coding a Button Event Handler

When the activity_main.xml layout is initially launched by the MainActivity.java class, it is necessary to have code to control how the Button component interacts with the user. When this VIEW RECIPE button is tapped, the MainActivity.java class must contain code to launch and display the activity_recipe.xml layout, beginning the second Java class called Recipe.java. To initialize the Button component and code the Button handler to launch the second Activity class, follow these steps:

Step 1

- Click the MainActivity.java tab to open its code window.
- Click to the right of setContentView(R.layout.activity_main); in Line 12, and then press Enter.
- To initialize and reference the Button component with the id name of btRecipe, type:

  Button button = (Button) findViewById(R.id.btRecipe);

- After the code is entered to reference the Button component, point to the red Button command at the beginning of the line to view the error that occurred.

  The Button component named btRecipe is referenced in MainActivity.java. By pointing to the button command, an error message is displayed (**Figure 2-37**). Notice the red curly line under the MainActivity.java tab name, indicating an error within the code. A red light bulb may also appear on Line 13 to indicate the error as well.

Figure 2-37 Button instantiated with an error (missing Button library)

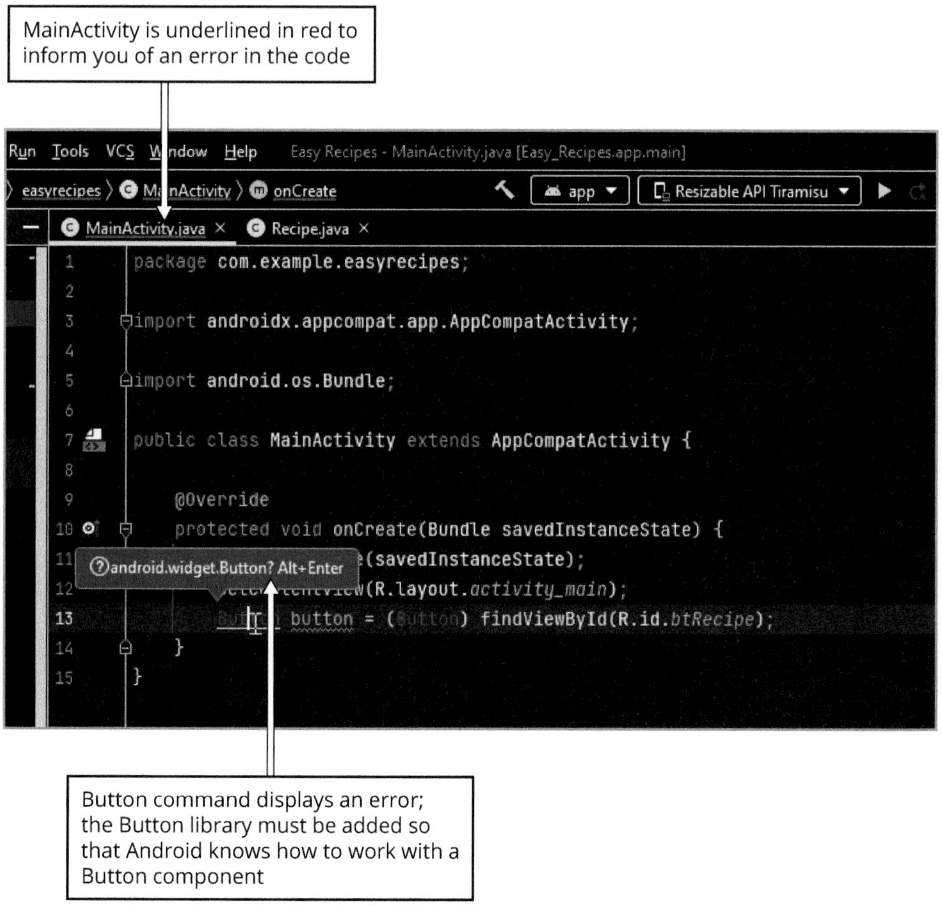

MainActivity is underlined in red to inform you of an error in the code

```
1   package com.example.easyrecipes;
2
3   import androidx.appcompat.app.AppCompatActivity;
4
5   import android.os.Bundle;
6
7   public class MainActivity extends AppCompatActivity {
8
9       @Override
10      protected void onCreate(Bundle savedInstanceState) {
11          ...(savedInstanceState);
12          ...(R.layout.activity_main);
13          Button button = (Button) findViewById(R.id.btRecipe);
14      }
15  }
```

?android.widget.Button? Alt+Enter

Button command displays an error; the Button library must be added so that Android knows how to work with a Button component

Good to Know Notice as you begin to type *find* in the preceding code that IntelliSense can help you complete the code. **IntelliSense** is a general term for automated code-editing features that are sometimes known by other names, such as code completion, content assist, and code hinting.

Step 2

- Press Alt+Enter simultaneously (or press Option+Return on a Mac) and click Button Class to resolve the syntax error and import the Button class.
- Click the expand icon (plus sign) in Line 3 to display the import statements. Notice that the Button class has been added to Line 6.
- Click the Save All button on the Standard toolbar to save your work.

The Button library is imported into this project (**Figure 2-38**).

Figure 2-38 Button instantiated with Button library added

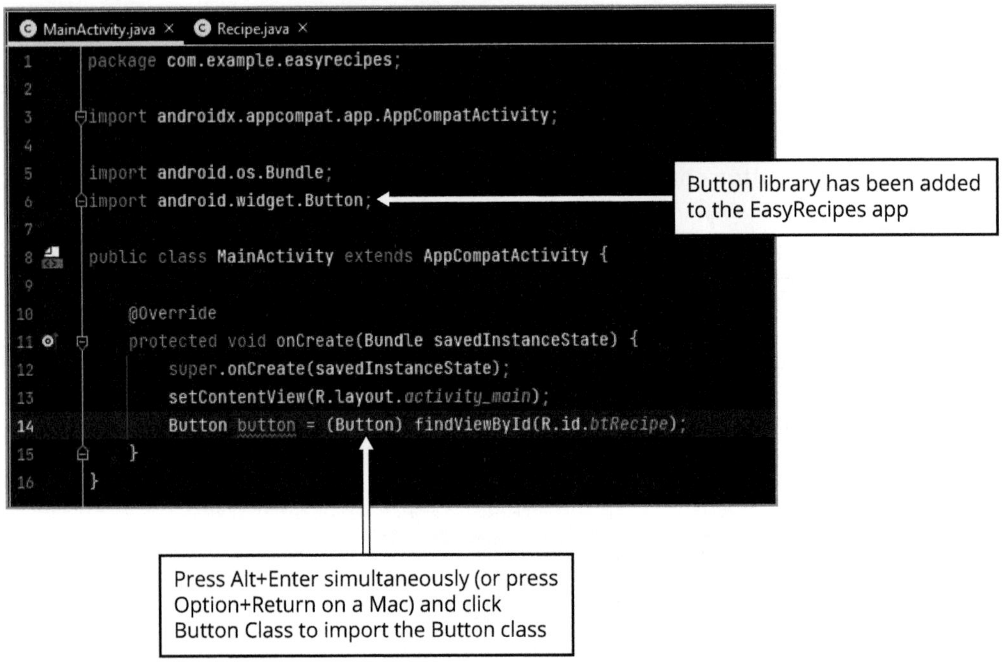

MainActivity.java × Recipe.java ×

```
1  package com.example.easyrecipes;
2
3  import androidx.appcompat.app.AppCompatActivity;
4
5  import android.os.Bundle;
6  import android.widget.Button;
7
8  public class MainActivity extends AppCompatActivity {
9
10     @Override
11     protected void onCreate(Bundle savedInstanceState) {
12         super.onCreate(savedInstanceState);
13         setContentView(R.layout.activity_main);
14         Button button = (Button) findViewById(R.id.btRecipe);
15     }
16 }
```

Button library has been added to the EasyRecipes app

Press Alt+Enter simultaneously (or press Option+Return on a Mac) and click Button Class to import the Button class

Good to Know | The lowercase "button" is the local instantiation of the Button; it is underlined because Android is reminding you that you have yet to use the button in the following code.

Step 3

- Click at the end of Line 14 and press Enter.
- To code the button listener that awaits user interaction, type **button.seton**. You see an auto-complete list of all the possible entries that are valid at that point in the code.
- Double-click the first setOnClickListener to select it from the auto-complete list.
- In the parentheses, type **new On** (you must type an uppercase *O*) to view possible auto-complete options.

The auto-complete list for the OnClickListener is displayed (**Figure 2-39**).

Step 4

- Double-click the first choice, which is OnClickListener (...) (android.view.View). Auto-generated code adds an onClick( ) method.
- Click to place the insertion point on Line 19 inside the braces for public void onClick (View view).

An OnClickListener auto-generated stub appears in the code (**Figure 2-40**).

Figure 2-39 Inserting the Button OnClickListener stub—use auto-completion to reduce typos and incorrect case of letters

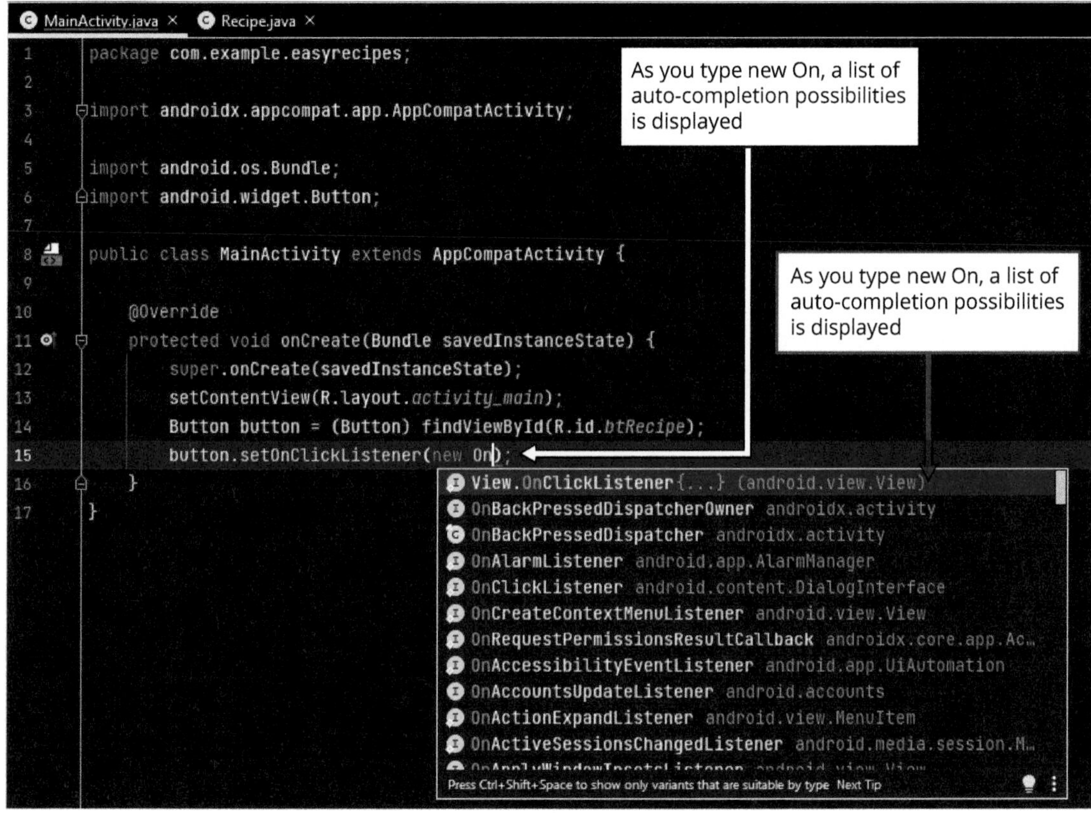

Figure 2-40 The setOnClickListener added with auto-complete feature

```java
package com.example.easyrecipes;

import androidx.appcompat.app.AppCompatActivity;

import android.os.Bundle;
import android.view.View;
import android.widget.Button;

public class MainActivity extends AppCompatActivity {

    @Override
    protected void onCreate(Bundle savedInstanceState) {
        super.onCreate(savedInstanceState);
        setContentView(R.layout.activity_main);
        Button button = (Button) findViewById(R.id.btRecipe);
        button.setOnClickListener(new View.OnClickListener() {
            @Override
            public void onClick(View view) {

            }
        });
    }
}
```

setOnClickListener added; the code typed within the brackets only executes when the user presses the app button

Step 5

- On Line 19, type **startA** and select startActivity(Intent intent) from the auto-complete list.
- In the parentheses, change the intent text by typing **new Int** and then double-click Intent (android.content) in the auto-complete list.
- In the next set of parentheses, type **MainActivity.this, Recipe.class**.
- Click the Save All button on the toolbar.

The startActivity code launches the intent to open Recipe.class (**Figure 2-41**).

Figure 2-41 Complete code for MainActivity.java—startActivity will launch the second screen's Recipe.class when the user clicks the button

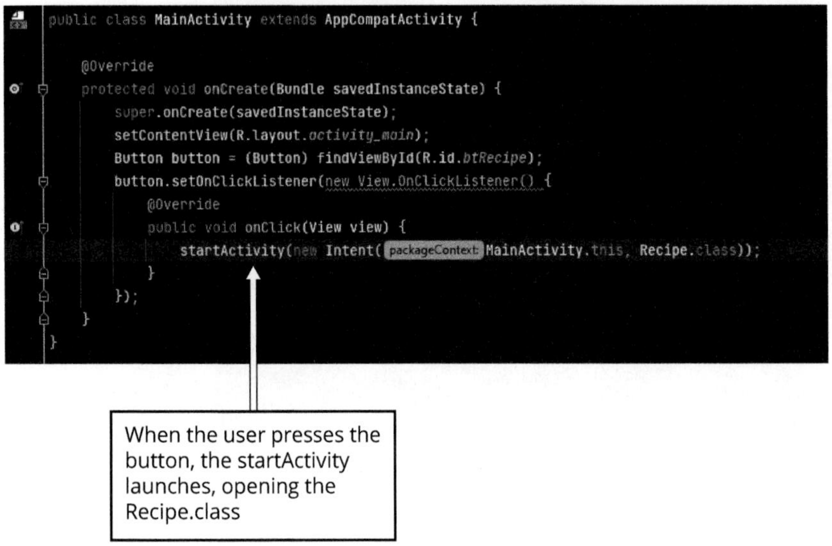

```
public class MainActivity extends AppCompatActivity {

    @Override
    protected void onCreate(Bundle savedInstanceState) {
        super.onCreate(savedInstanceState);
        setContentView(R.layout.activity_main);
        Button button = (Button) findViewById(R.id.btRecipe);
        button.setOnClickListener(new View.OnClickListener() {
            @Override
            public void onClick(View view) {
                startActivity(new Intent( packageContext: MainActivity.this, Recipe.class));
            }
        });
    }
}
```

When the user presses the button, the startActivity launches, opening the Recipe.class

On the Job

In years past, software developers would have to wait many months for their software to be published and placed in stores for sale. In today's mobile market, app stores have become the de facto app delivery channel by reducing time-to-shelf and time-to-payment and by providing developers with unprecedented reach to consumers. If your app passes the Google Play quality tests, it can be available in stores in a matter of days.

Quick Check

When the chapter's example app is run, what does the user need to do in the app to make the startActivity launch the Recipe.class?

Answer: Click the VIEW RECIPE button.

2.10 Correcting Errors in Code

Using the auto-complete feature when entering code considerably reduces the likelihood of coding errors. Nevertheless, because you could create errors when entering code, you should understand what to do when a coding error occurs. One error would be to forget the semicolon at the end of a statement; for example, see Line 16 in **Figure 2-42**. When the application is run, a dialog box states that your project contains errors and asks you to fix them before running your application. A red underline identifies the error location and a red light bulb might identify the line that contains the error. When you point to the error icon, Java suggests the possible correction to the syntax error in the code. When you run an app that contains an error, an error listing appears at the bottom of the screen with suggestions for how to fix the error. After a semicolon is placed at the end of the line, the application is run again and the program functions properly.

Figure 2-42 Syntax error

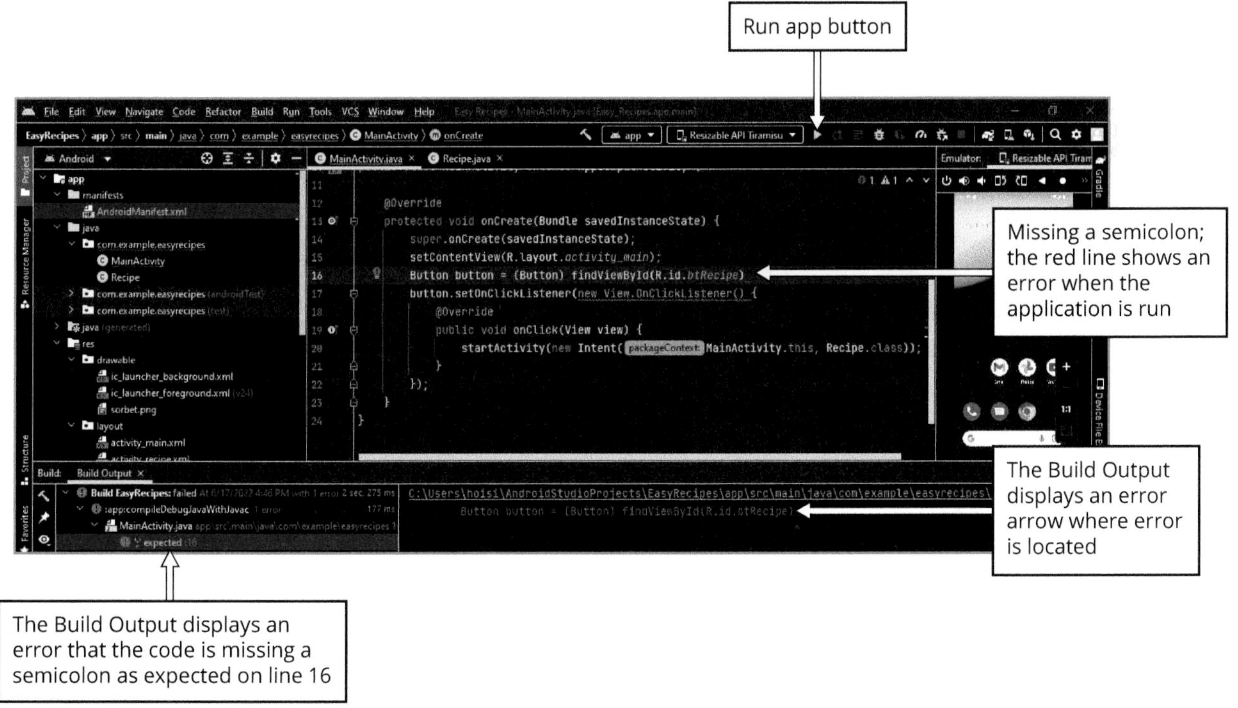
Run app button
Missing a semicolon; the red line shows an error when the application is run
The Build Output displays an error arrow where error is located
The Build Output displays an error that the code is missing a semicolon as expected on line 16

Critical Thinking

Why am I seeing black underlines on some of my code?

Android Studio may have suggestions for coding in a different way, but these suggestions may not be the best way to code your app. The suggestions can be ignored if you know better.

2.11 Saving and Running the Application

Each time an Android application is tested in the emulator, the programming design and code are automatically saved. If you start your project and need to save it before completion, click the Save All button on the toolbar. Click the Run app button on the toolbar to test the application in the emulator. A dialog box opens the first time the chapter's example application is executed and asks which emulator you want to launch. The application opens in the emulator window in **Figure 2-43**, where the sorbet recipe displays after the VIEW RECIPE button is pressed.

Figure 2-43 Execution of app in emulator

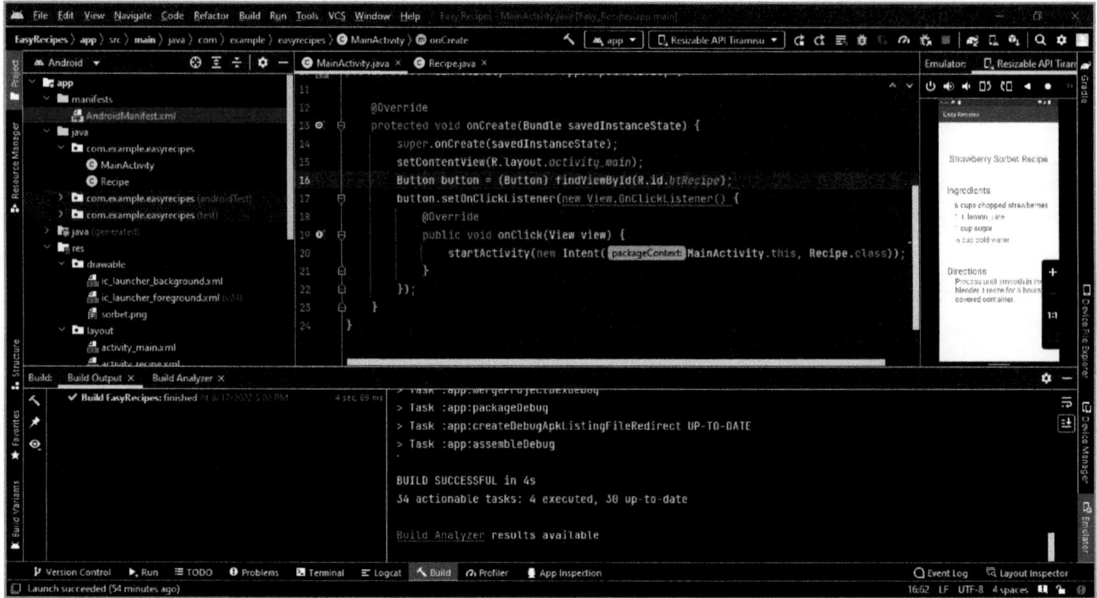

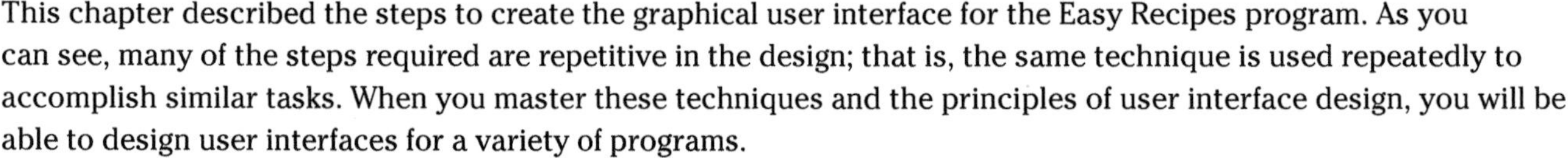

Wrap It Up—Chapter Summary

This chapter described the steps to create the graphical user interface for the Easy Recipes program. As you can see, many of the steps required are repetitive in the design; that is, the same technique is used repeatedly to accomplish similar tasks. When you master these techniques and the principles of user interface design, you will be able to design user interfaces for a variety of programs.

- Instead of adding text directly to a component's text attribute, you add it to the strings.xml file by working with the String table in the Translations Editor.
- Constraint layouts arrange screen components freely on the screen. All four sides of the component must be pulled to the edge of the screen before the component can move freely around the screen.
- Popular text properties for components include the text attribute, which specifies the string resource to use for displaying text in the component, and the textSize attribute, which specifies the size of the text.
- To display graphics such as pictures and icons in an Android app, you use an ImageView component. Before you can place an ImageView component in the emulator, you must place a graphics file in the drawable subfolder of the res folder.
- An Activity is the point at which the application makes contact with your users; it is one of the core components of the Android application. The chapter project has two Activities, one for each screen.
- Each screen represents an Activity, and each Activity must have a matching Java class file.
- Every Android application has an Android Manifest file named AndroidManifest.xml that provides essential information to the Android device, such as the name of your Java application and a listing of each Activity. Android Studio automatically adds each Activity to the file.
- A method is a set of Java statements that can be included inside a Java class. The onCreate( ) method is where you initialize an Activity. You use the setContentView command to display the content of a specific screen.
- When the user taps a Button component in an Android app, the code for an event listener, or click event, begins the event associated with the Button component. Event listeners such as the OnClickListener( ) method wait for user interaction before executing the remaining code.

- In an Android app that contains more than one Activity, or screen, you use the startActivity( ) method to create an intent to start another Activity. The intent should contain two parameters: a context and the name of the Activity being opened. A context shows which initiating Activity class is making the request.
- When you run an Android application, a dialog box opens if your project contains any errors. Look for red underlines and red light bulbs, which identify the location of the errors. Point to a red line to have Java suggest a correction to a syntax error in the code.

Key Terms

Activity
Android Manifest
backgroundTint
class
ConstraintLayout
constraints
descriptions
event handler
form factor
id attribute
ImageView component
import
import statement
instantiate
IntelliSense
intent
key
localization
method
method body
object
Pascal case
Responsive Design UI
return type
setContentView
sp
string
String table
strings.xml
stub
text attribute
textColor
textSize attribute
Translations Editor

Developer FAQs

1. What are the three components used in this chapter? (2.1)
2. If you were creating an app in many different languages, would you have to write the entire program from scratch for each language? What part of the program would stay the same? What part of the program would be different? (2.2)
3. In which subfolder in the Android project view are the XML files stored? (2.1)
4. In the chapter's example project, which kind of layout was used to lay out the components on the emulator? (2.3)
5. What is the term that describes the screen size, configuration, or physical layout of a device? (2.1)
6. What are the building blocks of an Android layout that attach or align a component to the screen either by attaching it vertically and horizontally to the edges of the screen or by aligning it with another component? (2.3)
7. Which measurement is most preferred for text size? Why? (2.3)
8. What does px stand for? (2.3)
9. What does sp stand for? (2.3)
10. What is a stub? (2.8)
11. Which picture file types are accepted for an ImageView component? (2.3)
12. Which picture file type is preferred? (2.3)

13. In which attribute can you describe an ImageView component for screen readers to improve accessibility? (2.2)
14. Which four attributes were changed in the chapter project for the Button component? (2.3)
15. What is the attribute that defines the name of an ImageView component? (2.2)
16. Write one line of code that would launch a second class named Drone from the present MainActivity class. (2.9)
17. Write one line of code that declares a Button component with a variable named button, which references a button in the XML layout with the id attribute of btBlackWidow. (2.7)
18. Write one line of code that opens the XML layout named reality. (2.9)
19. Which two keys are pressed to auto-complete a line of Java code on a PC? (2.8)
20. What character is placed at the end of most lines of Java code? (2.10)

Beyond the Book

Search the web for answers to the following questions to further your Android knowledge.

1. ConstraintLayout is not the only type of Android layout. Name three other types of layouts and write a paragraph describing each type.
2. Why are .png files the preferred type of image resource for the Android device? Write a paragraph that gives at least three reasons.
3. How much does an average Android app developer profit from an app? Research this topic and write 150–200 words on your findings.
4. Research the most expensive Android apps currently available at Google Play. Name three expensive apps, their price, and the purpose of each.

Case Programming Projects

Complete one or more of the following case programming projects. Use the same steps and techniques taught within the chapter. Successful completion of these projects requires knowledge of all chapter learning objectives. Submit the program(s) you create to your instructor. The level of difficulty is indicated for each case programming project.

Case Project 2–1: Riad Travel App (Beginner)

Requirements Document

Application title:	Riad Travel App
Purpose:	Old mansions in Morocco have been turned into reasonably priced hotels. In a Moroccan Riad Travel app, a riad is selected and its name and address are displayed.
Algorithms:	1. The opening screen displays the name of the app, an image of a riad, and a Button component (**Figure 2-44**). Research a real name of a Moroccan riad and an address to display in your own customized app. 2. When the user taps the Button component, a riad's name and address are displayed in a second screen (**Figure 2-45**).
Note:	The riad image is provided with your student files.

Figure 2-44 Riad Travel app—first screen

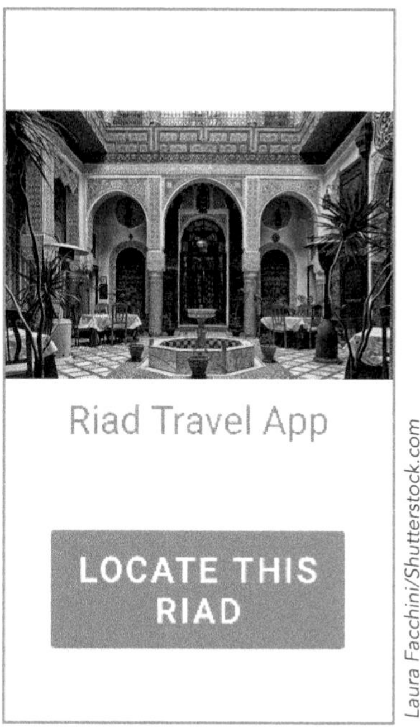

Laura Facchini/Shutterstock.com

Figure 2-45 Riad Travel app—second screen

Riad Travel App

Riad Spice Amore

23 Derb Moulay

Marrakesh, Morocco

40002

Laura Facchini/Shutterstock.com

Case Project 2–2: Electric Bike Rental App (Beginner)

Requirements Document

Application title: Electric Bike Rental App

Purpose: In an electric bike rental app, an electric bike tour is selected and a bike image is displayed with rental information.

Algorithms:

1. The opening screen displays a title line, a description, and a Button component (**Figure 2-46**).
2. When the user chooses to rent an electric bike, a second screen displays an electric bike image and a tour price (**Figure 2-47**).

Note: The bike image is provided with your student files.

Figure 2-46 Electric Bike Rental app—first screen

Join Us for an Electric Bike Ride

Ride Strong as Electric Bikes change how riders of different abilities can discover the world together on two wheels.

ELECTRIC BIKE TOUR

Figure 2-47 Electric Bike Rental app—second screen

See our beautiful city with an electric bike tour!

2 hour tour for only $25

Begalphoto/Shutterstock.com

Case Project 2–3: Your School App (Intermediate)

Requirements Document

Application title:	Your School App
Purpose:	This large app provides information about every school in your country. Create two screens for the app. You use the app to select the name of a school and then display information about the selected school.
Algorithms:	**1.** The opening screen displays the name of your school, a picture of your school, and a Button component. Create your own layout. **2.** The second screen displays the name of your school, a picture of your logo, the school address, and the phone number. Create your own layout.

Case Project 2–4: Business Card App (Intermediate)

Requirements Document

Application title:	Business Card App
Purpose:	This app provides your business card information and a picture of you. Create two screens for the business card app. You use the app to select the name of a business contact and then display detailed business card information.
Algorithms:	**1.** The opening screen displays basic information such as the name of the contact, your picture converted to a .png file, and a Button component. Create your own layout. **2.** The second screen displays a detailed business card with all of your contact information, such as your business address, email address, and phone number. Create your own layout.

Case Project 2–5: Your Contacts App—Address Book (Advanced)

Requirements Document

Application title: Your Contacts App—Address Book

Purpose: This large app provides business contact information in an address book. Create two screens for contacts for the app. You use the app to select a particular contact and then display that person's information.

Algorithms:

1. The opening screen displays two contacts who have last names starting with the letter *J*. Each contact has a separate Button component below the name. Create your own layout.
2. The second screen displays the name, address, phone number, and picture of the selected contact. Create your own layout.

Conditions: Three Java classes and three XML layouts are needed.

Case Project 2–6: Latest Music Scene App (Advanced)

Requirements Document

Application title: The Latest Music Scene

Purpose: This large app called The Latest Music Scene contains current music news. Create two screens for two music news stories. You use the app to select the title of a particular music news story and then display an image and a paragraph about the story.

Algorithms:

1. The opening screen displays the titles of two music news stories that you can create based on music stories in the news. Each news story has a separate Button component below the name and displays a small image. Create your own layout.
2. The second screen displays the name of the music story and a paragraph detailing the news. Create your own layout.

Conditions: Three Java classes and three XML layouts are needed.

Chapter 3

Engage! Android User Input, Variables, and Operations

Learning Objectives

At the completion of this chapter, you will be able to:

- **3.1** Collect user input
- **3.2** Add a Text Number component
- **3.3** Add a string array
- **3.4** Change the background attribute
- **3.5** Set the hint attribute for a Text component
- **3.6** Develop a user interface using a Spinner component
- **3.7** Add a prompt and entries to a Spinner component
- **3.8** Code the EditText class for the Text Number component
- **3.9** Code the Spinner component
- **3.10** Instantiate the Button component and variables
- **3.11** Code the getText( ) method
- **3.12** Understand arithmetic operations
- **3.13** Code the setText( ) method

3.1 Collecting User Input

In the Easy Recipes app developed earlier in this course, the user clicked a button in the user interface to trigger events, but not to enter data. In many applications, users enter data and the program uses the data in its processing. For example, you have probably opened a weather app, typed in your location, and seen the weather forecast displayed on the app. Engaging the user by requesting input customizes the user experience each time the application runs. When processing data entered by a user, a common requirement is to perform arithmetic operations on the data to generate useful output. Arithmetic operations include adding, subtracting, multiplying, and dividing numeric data.

To illustrate the use of user data input and arithmetic operations, the Android app you develop in this chapter allows the user to enter a specific number of concert tickets to purchase. The application then calculates the total cost of the concert tickets. **Figure 3-1** shows the user interface for an app named Concert Tickets with the company name, Ticket Vault, displayed at the top of the screen.

In **Figure 3-2**, the user entered 4 as the number of tickets to purchase. When the user clicked the FIND THE COST button, the program multiplied 4 tickets by the concert ticket cost ($89.99) and then displayed the total cost. To create this application, the developer must understand how to perform the following processes, among others:

1. Define all text displayed in a String table using the Translations Editor.
2. Define the text displayed in the array using XML in the strings.xml file.
3. Change the background attribute of the user interface.
4. Define a Text Number component for data entry. For this app, the quantity of tickets entered should be a number. Using a specific Text Field for positive integers prevents users from entering an incorrect value.
5. Define a Spinner component to allow users to select the musical performance group.
6. Convert data to use it for arithmetic operations.
7. Perform arithmetic operations with the data the user enters.
8. Display formatted results using the setText( ) method.

Figure 3-1 Opening screen for Concert Tickets app

AstroStar/Shutterstock.com

Figure 3-2 Four tickets purchased for a concert

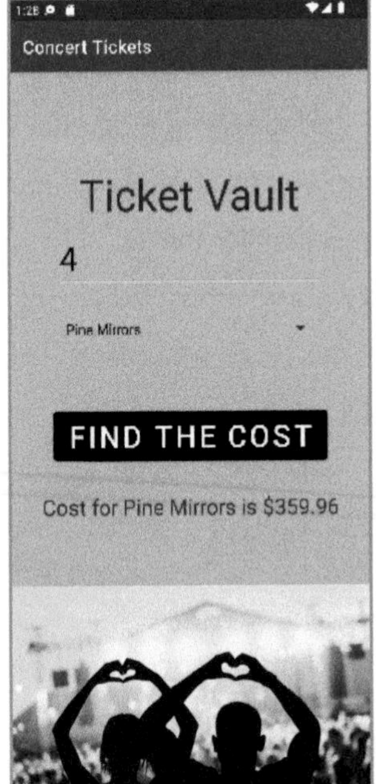

AstroStar/Shutterstock.com

Simplifying User Input

On an Android phone, users can enter text in multiple ways, including an on-screen soft keyboard, an attached flip-button hard keyboard, and even voice-to-text capabilities on most phone models. The on-screen keyboard is called a **soft keyboard**, which is positioned at the bottom of the screen over the application window. Touch input can vary from tapping the screen to using gestures. Gestures are multitouch interactions such as pressing two fingers to pan, rotate, or zoom. The primary design challenge for mobile web applications is how to simplify the user experience for an app that appears both on screens measuring a few square inches and on much larger tablets. To meet the challenge and maximize the user experience, you need to use legible fonts, simplify input, and optimize each device's capabilities. Certain Android components, such as those in the Text category, allow specific data types for user input, which simplifies data entry. For example, a numeric Text Number component only accepts numbers from the on-screen keyboard, limiting accidental user input. It is easy to tap the wrong location on a small touchscreen.

Good to Know Fifteen years ago, nearly every mobile phone offered an alphanumeric keypad as part of the device. Today, a full QWERTY touchscreen keyboard is available to allow users to enter information, engage in social networking, surf the Internet, and view multimedia.

Using Android Text Components

In the Concert Tickets application shown in Figure 3-1, users enter the quantity of tickets that they intend to purchase to attend the concert. The most common type of mobile input is text entered by touch input from an on-screen soft keyboard or the attached keyboard on a tablet. An app can request user keyboard input with the Text components in the Android Studio Palette. With Text components, input can be received on the mobile device with an on-screen keyboard or the user can use the physical keyboard on the emulator. When you click the Text Number component, a soft keyboard opens at the bottom of the Android device. Select the characters and numbers from the keyboard and tap the check mark to enter the selected values.

A mobile application's Text components can request different input types, such as plain text and numbers. Plain text includes a person's name, password, and email address. You need to select the correct Text component for the specific type of data you are requesting. Each Text component allows you to enter a specific data type from the keyboard. For example, if you select the Phone Number Text component, Android deactivates the letters on the keyboard because letters are not part of a phone number. When you are requesting a numeric value, different types of Text components are available, such as a Number for positive integer values, Number (Signed) for positive and negative numbers, and Number (Decimal) for numbers with digits to the right of the decimal point.

Good to Know The AutoComplete TextView component can suggest the completion of a word after the user begins typing the first few letters. For example, if the input component is requesting the name of a city where the user wants to book a hotel, you could suggest the completed name from a coded list of city names that match the first few letters entered by the user.

User Experience

Anytime you interact with a device, you have a user experience. This might entail navigating a mobile app or browsing a website. The term **user experience** (UX) refers to all aspects of this interaction. In the chapter project, the Concert Tickets application requests the number of concert tickets to purchase as the user interaction. This quantity is an integer value because you cannot purchase part of a ticket. When the developer selects the Text Number component, users can enter only positive integers from the keyboard. The app does not accept letters and symbols from the keyboard, which saves you time as the developer because you do not have to write lengthy data validation code. To begin designing the user experience of the Concert Tickets app and begin the application, follow these steps:

Step 1

- Open the Android Studio program.
- In the Welcome to Android Studio window, scroll down and click the New Project button in the Phone and Tablet templates to create a new Android Studio project.

- Click the Next button in the New Project window.
- Type **Concert Tickets** in the Name text box.
- If necessary, select Java in the Language text box.
- If necessary, select API 23: Android 6.0 (Marshmallow) as the Minimum SDK.

A new Java Android project named Concert Tickets is configured to save on your local computer (**Figure 3-3**).

Figure 3-3 Configuring the Concert Tickets project in the New Project window

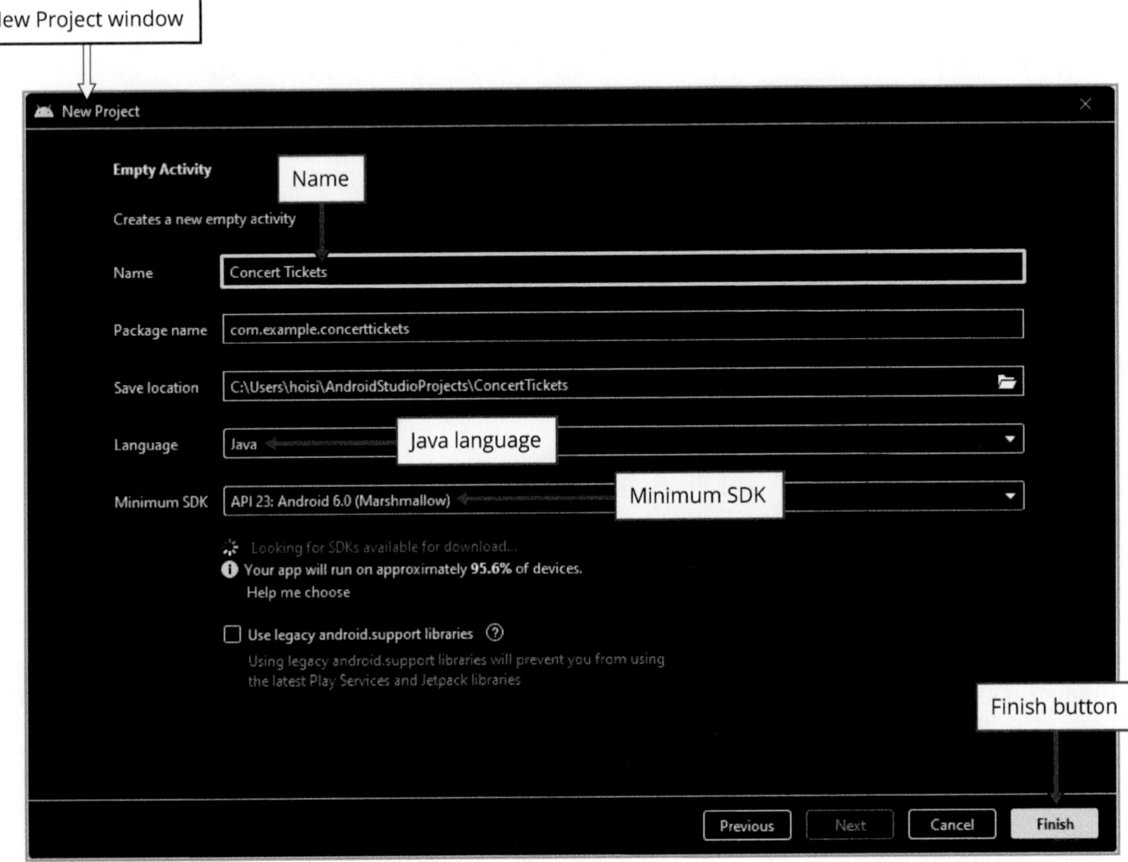

Step 2

- Click the Finish button on the New project window.
- Click the arrow (>) in front of the res folder to expand the folder.
- Click the arrow (>) in front of the layout folder to expand the folder.
- Double-click the activity_main.xml file to open the emulator design of the virtual device.
- Click the Hello world! TextView component in the emulator. This component is displayed by default.
- Press the Delete key to delete the default TextView component.
- Click the Device for Preview (D) button, also known as the emulator button, and then click Phone for the Reference Devices.

The Android Concert Tickets project files are created, the Hello world TextView components are deleted, and the Phone device for preview is selected (**Figure 3-4**).

Figure 3-4 The activity_main.xml file for the Concert Tickets project

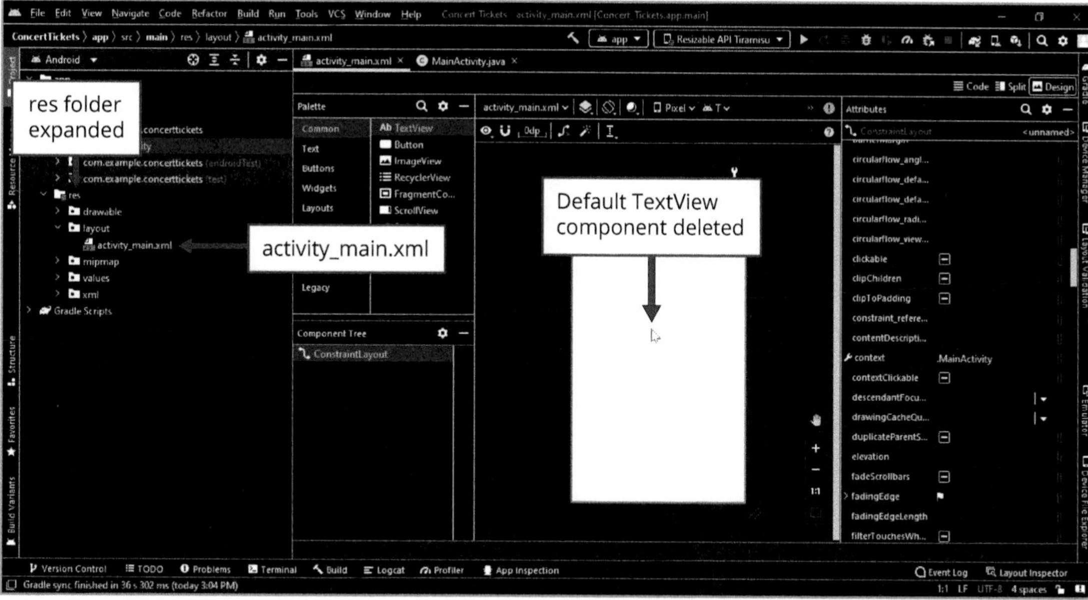

On the Job One of the top current career paths, according to Glassdoor, is that of a UX designer. UX designers determine how a product will look and feel. UX designers create working models of apps or websites and design ways for a user to enter and navigate a website.

3.2 Adding a Text Number Component

In the Concert Tickets application, a single screen opens when the application runs, and a Text Number component requests the number of concert tickets desired. One way to name a Text component is to use the id attribute in the Attributes pane and enter a name that begins with the prefix *tv*, which represents a TextView component in the code. The Java code uses the id attribute to refer to the component. A descriptive variable name such as tvTickets can turn an unreadable piece of code into one that is well documented and easy to debug.

Using the String Table

The string items displayed in the components of the chapter's example app will not be typed directly in the Attributes pane, but instead in a string array in the res/values folder. In the Concert Tickets app, the first TextView component displays the text Ticket Vault, and the Button component displays the text FIND THE COST. You also need text to prompt users to enter a selection and to display a description of the concert image shown on the screen. You add the names of musical performance groups in later steps using XML code. To add the Key and Default Value text for Text Field, Button, and ImageView components in the strings.xml file, follow these steps.

Step 1

- Expand the values folder and double-click the strings.xml file in the values subfolder to display its contents.
- Click the Open editor link.
- Click the Add Key (plus sign) button in the Translations Editor tab.
- In the Key text box, type **tvTitle** to name the string.
- In the Default Value text box, type **Ticket Vault** to define the text.

The Key and Default Value of the TextView component are entered into the strings.xml Translations Editor from the Add Key dialog box (**Figure 3-5**).

Figure 3-5 Adding strings in the Translations Editor

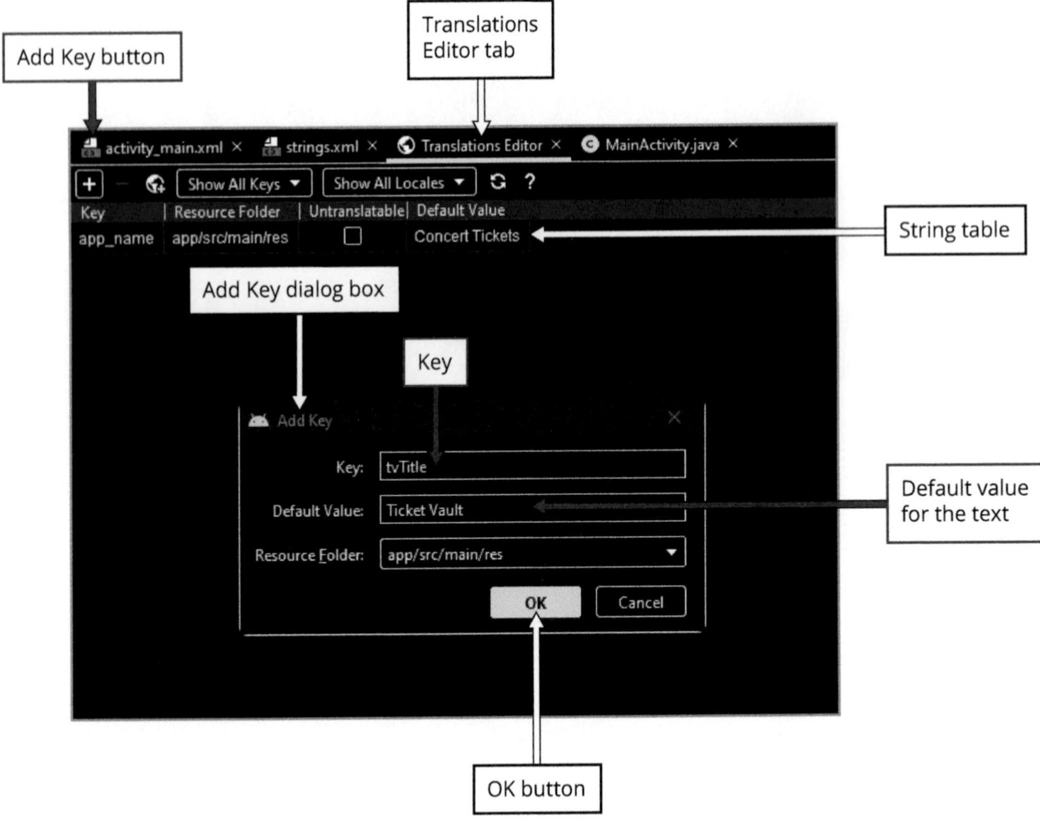

Step 2

- Click the OK button to add tvTitle to the String table.
- Click the Add Key button and then add the strings shown in **Table 3-1** to the Translations Editor using the techniques learned in earlier chapters.

The Key and Default Value of the Text Field, Button, and ImageView components are entered into the strings.xml file (**Figure 3-6**).

Table 3-1 String table text

Key	Default Value
tvTickets	Number of Tickets
Prompt	Select Group
Description	Concert Image
btCost	FIND THE COST

Figure 3-6 String table

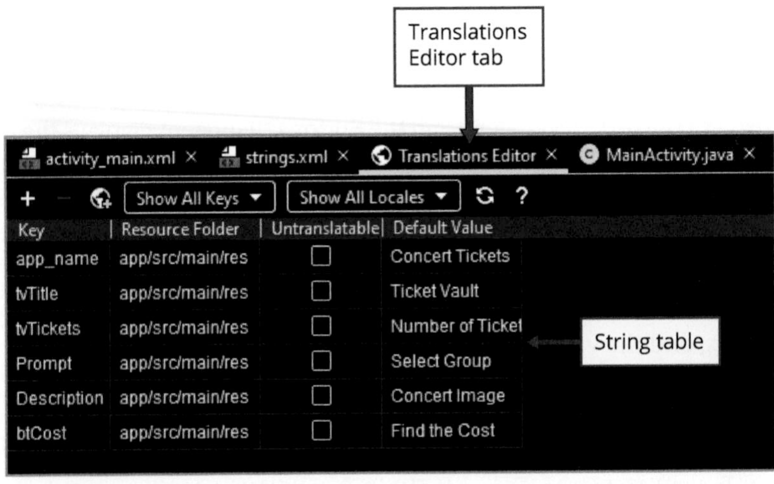

Step 3

- Close the Translations Editor tab.

Good to Know | If you accidentally make an error in the String table, you can right-click on any line of the String table and select Delete Key(s) to delete a key and add the new key again.

Quick Check

Can I type letters instead of numbers when asked for a Text Number component?

Answer: No, the soft keyboard only displays numbers.

3.3 Adding a String Array

The Text Field, Spinner, Button, and ImageView components each reference an individual string of text assigned in the strings.xml file, but if a component holds multiple text strings, it is best to use a **string array** that can be referenced from the String Resources in the application. A string array defines a string resource of related items in a central location within strings.xml. In the Concert Tickets app, the user can select one of three musical performance groups: No Filter, Fresh Haven, and Pine Mirrors. Each of the three concert groups is an **item** within the string array. An item defines an individual entry within a string array. You place the text items representing the performance groups in strings.xml as a string array resource tied together within one array name. You can populate a component such as a Spinner with a string array resource by adding XML code in strings.xml.

Android Studio has considerable built-in knowledge of XML syntax and Java programming methods that you can use to complete your code. As you type the string array XML code, the Android Studio editor offers suggestions in a panel that can complete a statement. **Figure 3-7** shows the editor suggesting possibilities for the string-array statement in the strings.xml window. By selecting the second suggestion listed in the panel in Figure 3-7 and then pressing Ctrl+period, you add the correct syntax to the statement. As you type a line of code in XML or Java, Android Studio refines the code and adds suggestions where appropriate. If a suggestion is not displayed automatically, you can press Ctrl+space to invoke code completion suggestions. All XML code begins with a less-than (<) symbol and ends with a greater-than (>) symbol. To use code completion features to add a string array to the strings.xml file to represent the three concert groups, take the following steps.

Figure 3-7 Auto-completion suggestions for XML code

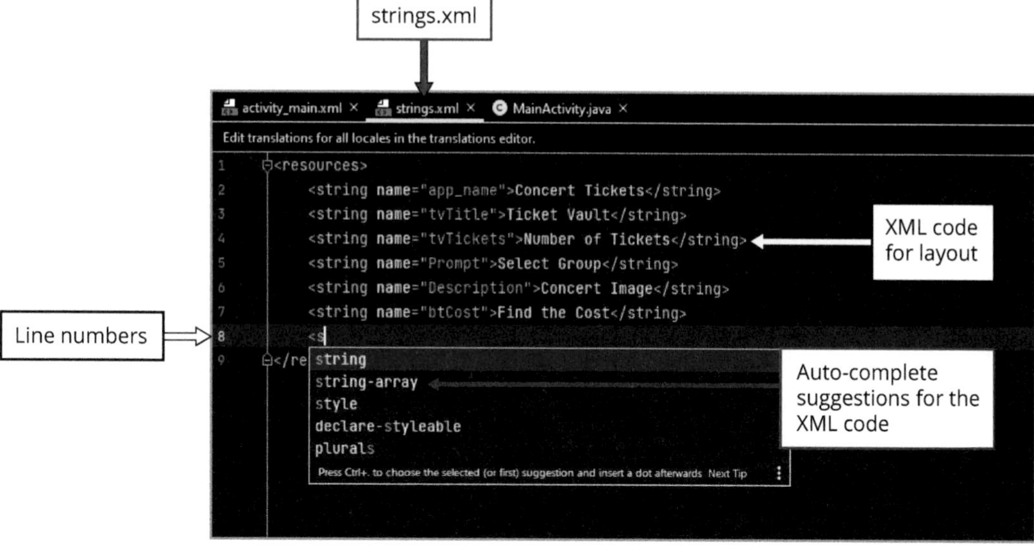

Step 1

- Click in the strings.xml window. If necessary, add line numbers by right-clicking the gray margin to the left of the code and then clicking Show Line Numbers.
- Click at the end of Line 7, press Enter, and type **<s** to view the auto-completion suggestions.

Auto-completion suggestions are displayed in the strings.xml code window (Figure 3-7).

Step 2

- Click string-array and press Ctrl+period to add the suggested XML code for a string array.
- Click between the quotation marks in Line 8 and replace the period between the quotation marks by typing **tvGroup** to name the text array that holds the three concert group names.
- Click after the closing quote, type > to end the string-array name statement, and then press Enter.

The string-array XML code named tvGroup is added. The closing statement </string-array> is added automatically by the editor in Android Studio (**Figure 3-8**).

Figure 3-8 Opening and closing XML statements of the string array

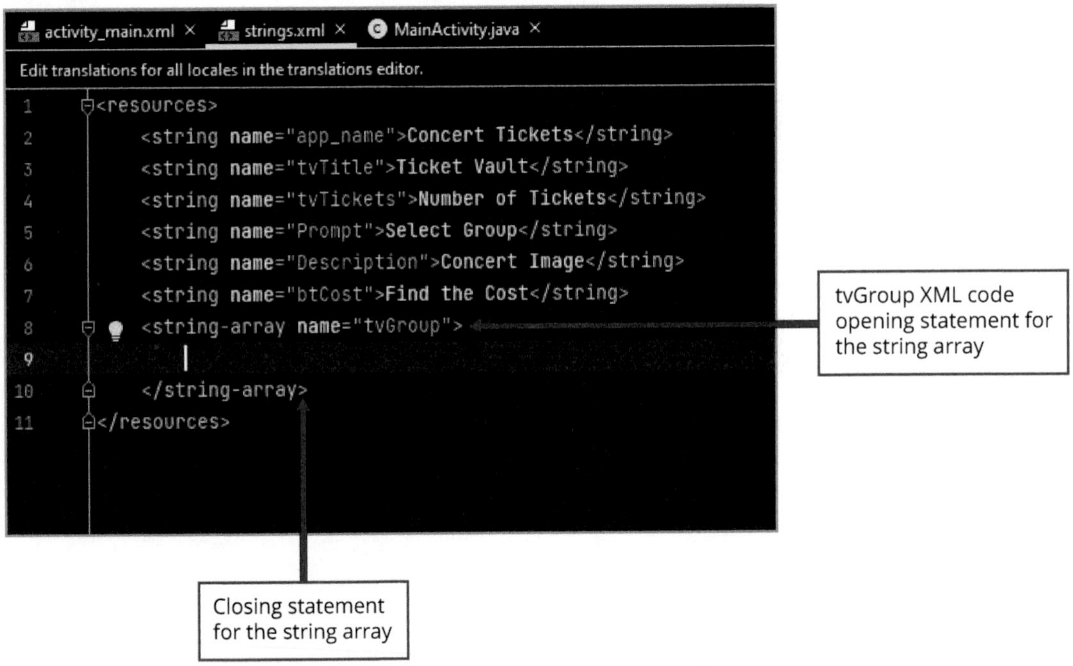

activity_main.xml × strings.xml × MainActivity.java ×

Edit translations for all locales in the translations editor.

```
1   <resources>
2       <string name="app_name">Concert Tickets</string>
3       <string name="tvTitle">Ticket Vault</string>
4       <string name="tvTickets">Number of Tickets</string>
5       <string name="Prompt">Select Group</string>
6       <string name="Description">Concert Image</string>
7       <string name="btCost">Find the Cost</string>
8       <string-array name="tvGroup">
9
10      </string-array>
11  </resources>
```

tvGroup XML code opening statement for the string array

Closing statement for the string array

Step 3

- Type **<item>** and let the editor automatically add the closing statement, </item>.
- If necessary, click between the opening and closing XML item statements and type **No Filter** as the name of the first item in the tvGroup array.
- Add a new line, type **<item>Fresh Haven**, and let the editor automatically add the closing item's XML code.
- On the next line, type **<item>Pine Mirrors** and let the editor automatically add the closing item's XML code.

Three items are added to the tvGroup string array (**Figure 3-9**).

Figure 3-9 The string array named tvGroup with three items added in XML code

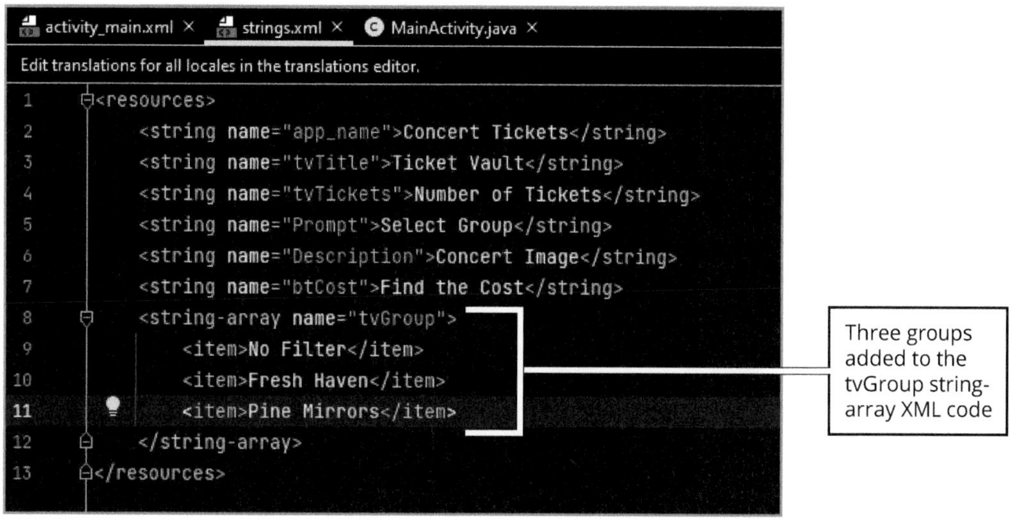

activity_main.xml × strings.xml × MainActivity.java ×

Edit translations for all locales in the translations editor.

```
<resources>
    <string name="app_name">Concert Tickets</string>
    <string name="tvTitle">Ticket Vault</string>
    <string name="tvTickets">Number of Tickets</string>
    <string name="Prompt">Select Group</string>
    <string name="Description">Concert Image</string>
    <string name="btCost">Find the Cost</string>
    <string-array name="tvGroup">
        <item>No Filter</item>
        <item>Fresh Haven</item>
        <item>Pine Mirrors</item>
    </string-array>
</resources>
```

Three groups added to the tvGroup string-array XML code

Good to Know Another use of auto-completion is statement completion. Press Shift+Ctrl+Enter (Shift+Cmd+Enter on a Mac) to automatically fill the closing code portions when possible.

3.4 Changing Background Attributes

To prevent Android apps from looking too similar, the Android background feature can help provide individual flair to each application. By default, each activity in Android has a white background. To change the background, you can set the background attribute in the Attributes pane. After the strings and string arrays are set for your app, you can add a background color and components to the emulator. To begin the design of the emulator screen with a background color and to add TextView and Text Number components, follow these steps:

Step 1

- Click the Save All button on the Standard toolbar and close the strings.xml tab.
- With activity_main.xml open and displaying the emulator screen, click the background of the emulator.
- In the Attributes pane, click the eyedropper to the right of the Background attribute.
- Click the orange color square identified as #FF9800 in hexadecimal values.

The background color of the emulator changes to an orange hue (**Figure 3-10**).

Step 2

- Drag and drop the TextView component onto the top part of the emulator.
- To center the TextView component, drag the component to the center of the screen. Drag the top Constraint handle of the TextView component to the top of the emulator screen and release the mouse.
- Drag the bottom Constraint handle of the TextView component to the bottom of the emulator screen and release the mouse. You should now have all four constraints anchored to the edge of the screen; blue curly arrows should touch the top, bottom, left, and right sides of the emulator.
- Click in the id component, name the TextView component **tvTitle**, and click the Refactor button.

Figure 3-10 Changing the background color

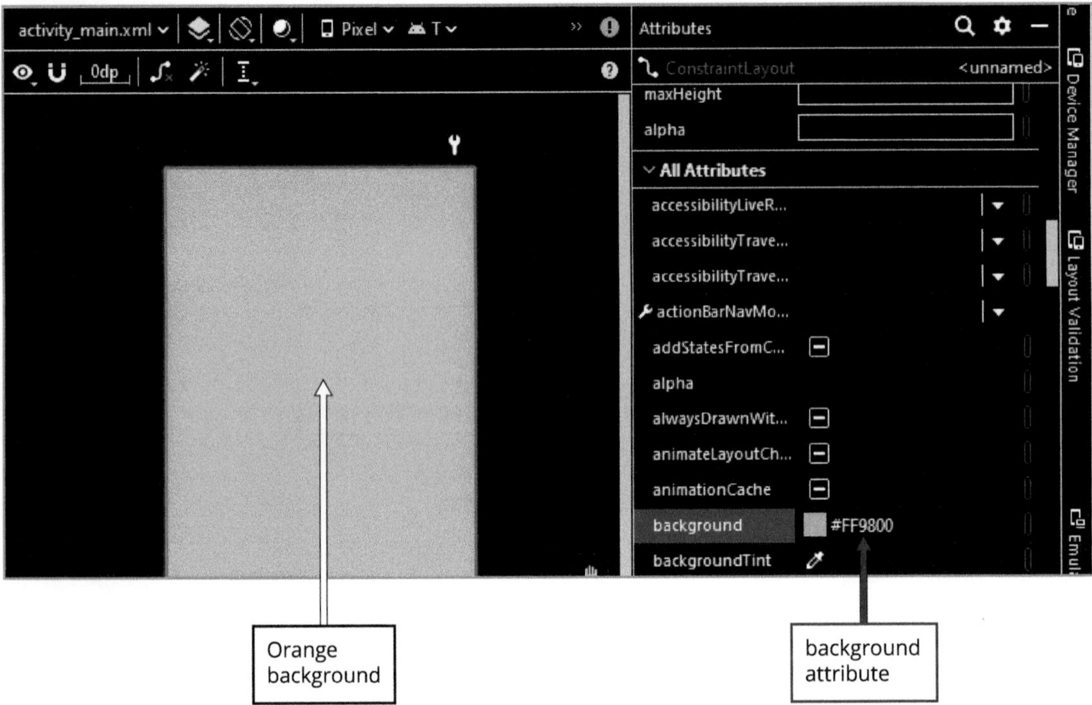

- In the Attributes pane, change the textSize attribute to **48sp** and press Enter.
- Type **@string** into the text attribute and select **@string/tvTitle** to change the text in the TextView component.

The text resource tvTitle is selected from the strings.xml file and the text Ticket Vault is displayed. The text is centered at a size of 48 scalable pixels (**Figure 3-11**).

Figure 3-11 Title added to emulator

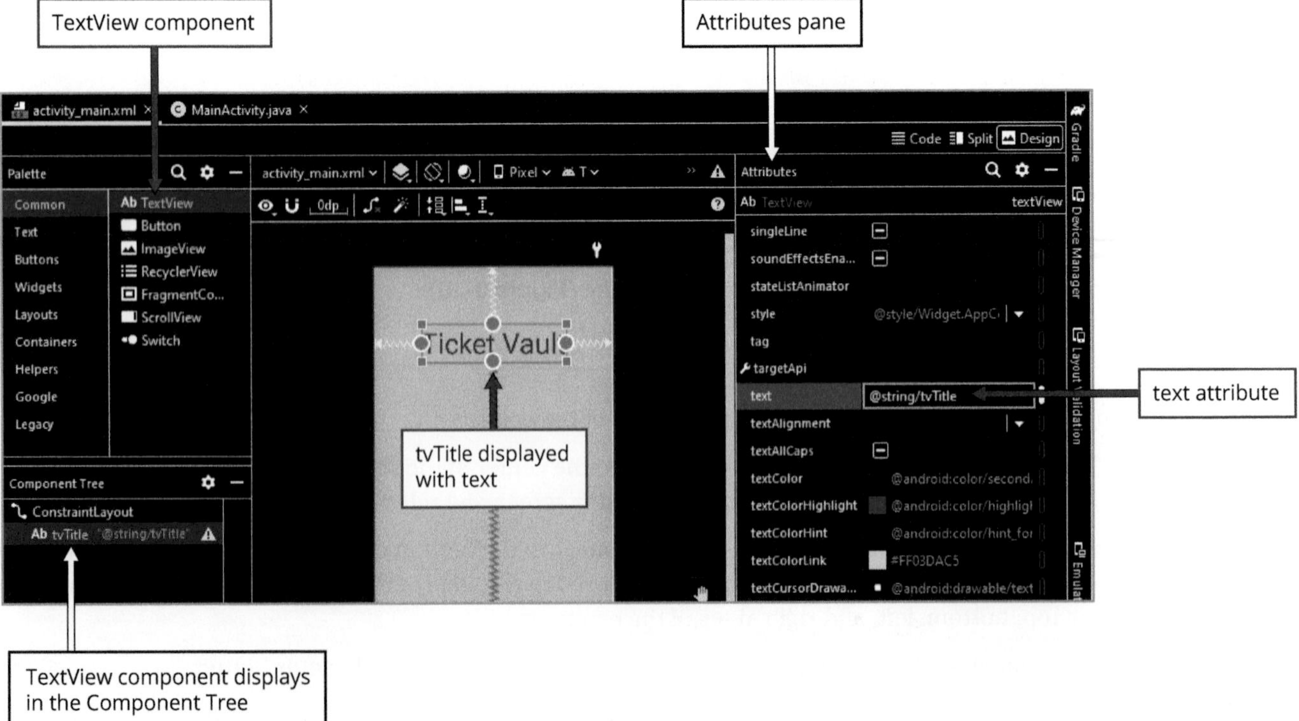

Step 3

- Click the **Text** category in the Palette.
- Drag and drop the Text Number component onto the emulator below the Ticket Vault text and center the component. Drag the Constraint handles of the Text Number component until all four constraints are anchored to the edge of the screen; blue curly arrows should touch the top, bottom, left, and right sides of the emulator.
- Type **tvTickets** in the id attribute and click the Refactor button to reference this component later in the Java code.
- Set the textSize attribute to **36sp** and press Enter to change the size of the Text Number component, as shown in **Figure 3-12**.

A Text Number component named tvTickets with the size of 36sp is added to the emulator to allow the user to enter the number of tickets (Figure 3-12).

Figure 3-12 Adding a Text Number component

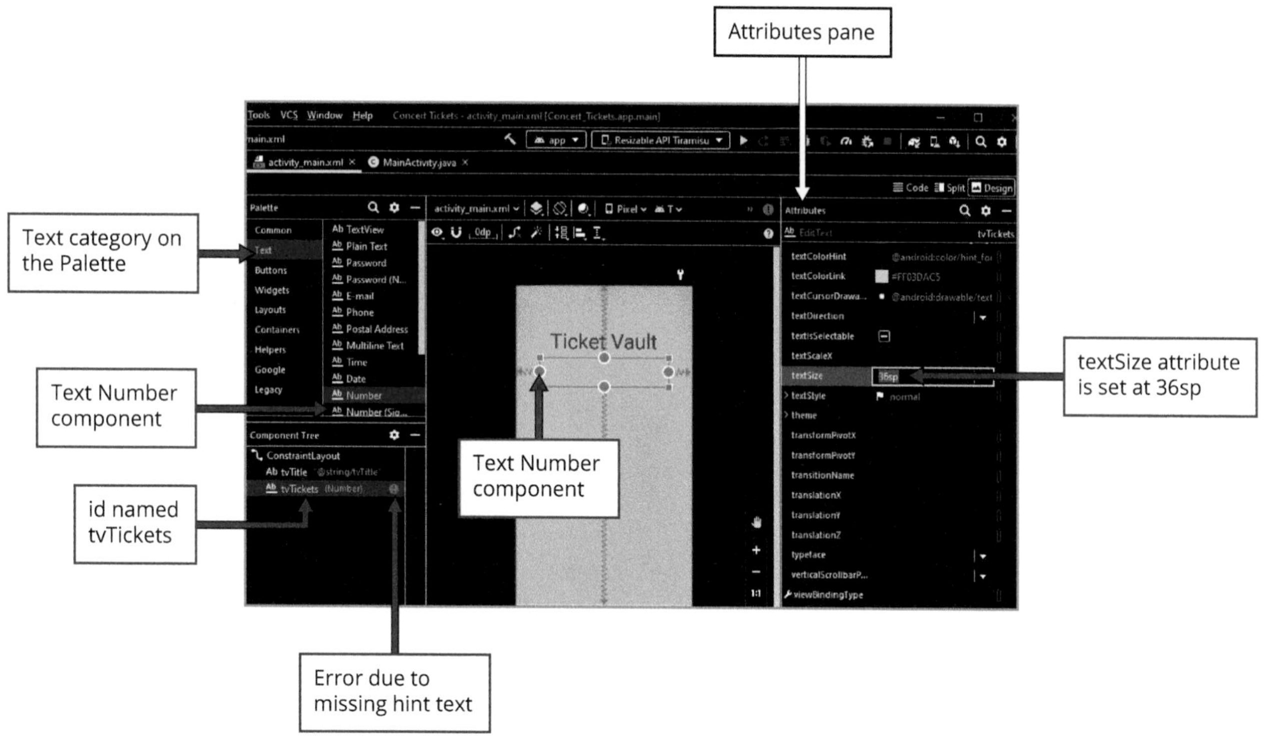

Good to Know | In addition to allowing input with an on-screen keyboard, some new Android phones come with a stylus that you can use to jot notes on the screen or to "air tap" in order to take selfie images.

3.5 Setting the Hint Attribute for a Text Component

When the Concert Tickets app runs, the user needs guidelines about the input expected in the Text Number component. These guidelines can be included in the hint attribute of the Text Number component. Notice in Figure 3-12 that an error is displayed after tvTickets in the Component Tree. The cause for the error is the missing hint text. A **hint** is a short description of a component that is visible as gray text (also called a watermark) inside a Text Number component or any Text input. Instead of typing the hint directly into the hint attribute, the preferred method is to enter the value in the String table. When the user clicks the component, the hint is removed and the user is free to type the requested input. The purpose of the hint in **Figure 3-13** is to request expected values in the Text Number component without the user having to select and delete default text. You can change the color of the hint by changing the **textColorHint** attribute. If you want to make the hint display as black text, the textColorHint attribute can be set to the #000000 hexadecimal value.

Figure 3-13 Hint attribute in Text Number component

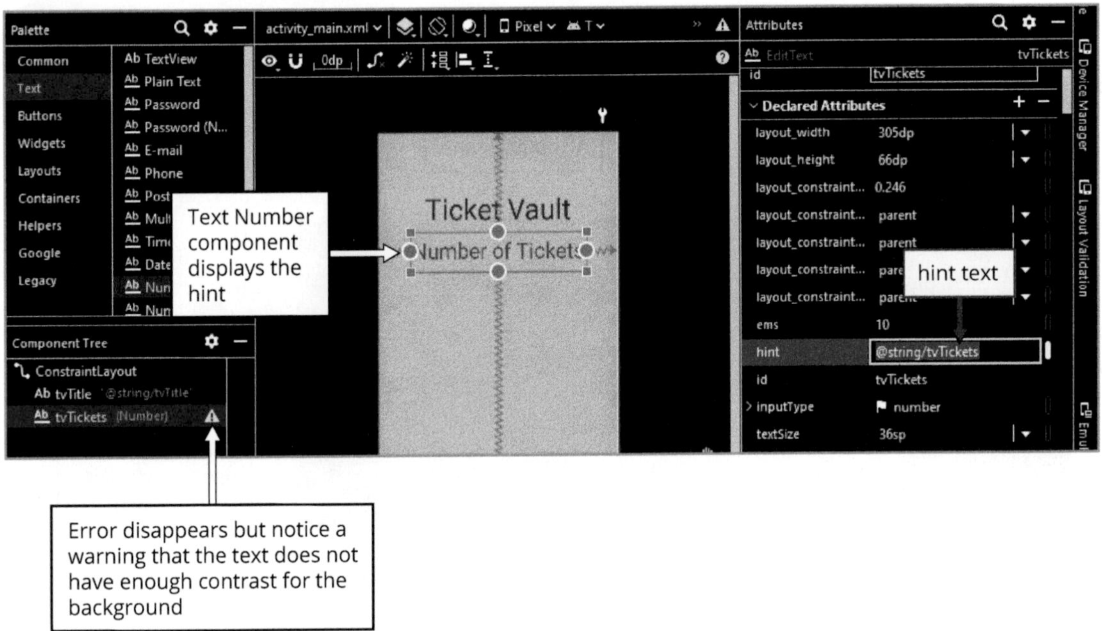

To set the hint attribute for the Text Number component, follow these steps:

Step 1

- With the tvTickets Text Number component selected on the emulator, scroll down the Attributes pane and then click to the right of the hint attribute.
- Type **@string/tvTickets** in the hint attribute and press Enter to display the text characters from the String table for the hint.

The tvTickets hint text ("Number of Tickets") is displayed in the Text Number component (Figure 3-13).

Step 2

- Click the Pick a Resource button (the thin rectangle symbol) to the right of the textColorHint attribute to display the Pick a Resource dialog box.

The Pick a Resource dialog box opens so you can select a color for the textColorHint attribute (**Figure 3-14**).

Figure 3-14 Pick a Resource dialog box for selecting colors

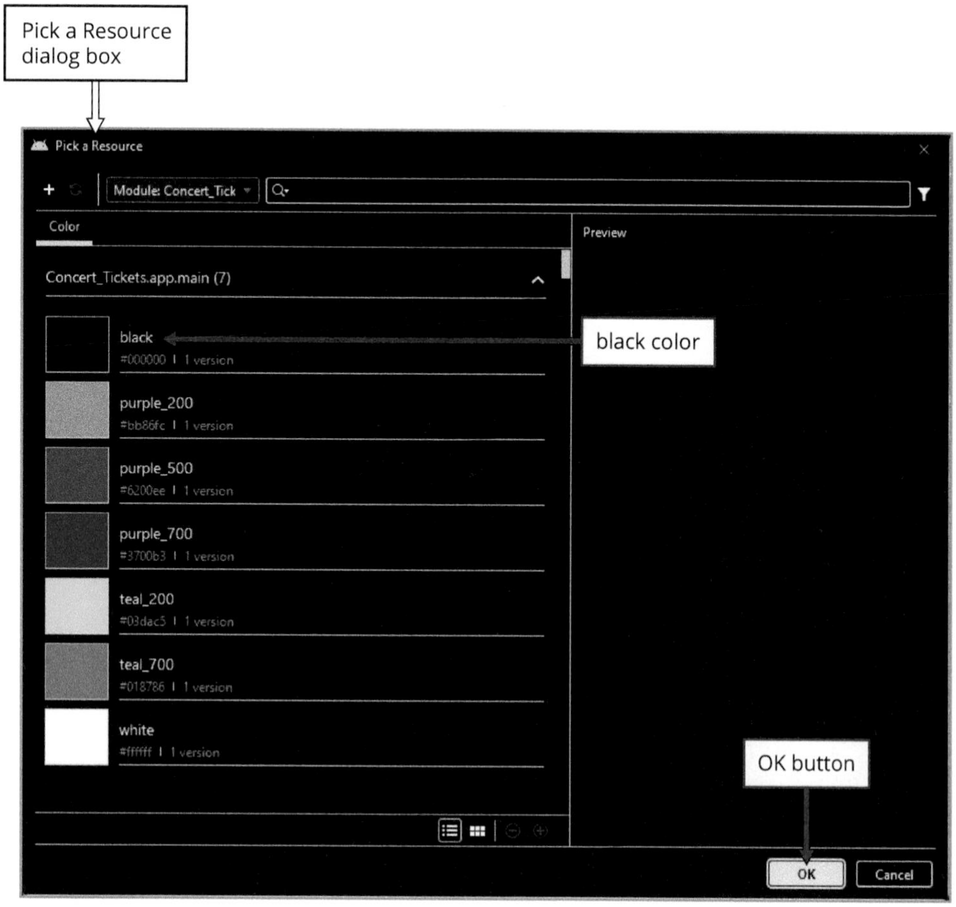

Step 3

- Click black (#000000) to change the textColorHint attribute to black.
- Click the OK button.

Step 4

- Click the yellow warning symbol for the tvTickets component in the Component Tree. This warning will not stop your app from running. The suggestion about AutoFill can be a paid service that you add to your app to automatically complete what the user enters. This service is beyond the scope of our text; note that the next step can fix the warning if you prefer.
- Scroll down the warning window and click the Fix button (Set autoFillHints).

The warning symbol is removed from the tvTickets component (**Figure 3-15**).

Good to Know

If the emulator in activity_main.xml fails to update, try saving your project to update the emulator. You can also refresh your Android Studio project by clicking Build on the menu bar and then clicking Clean Project.

Figure 3-15 Warning symbol removed from Text Number component

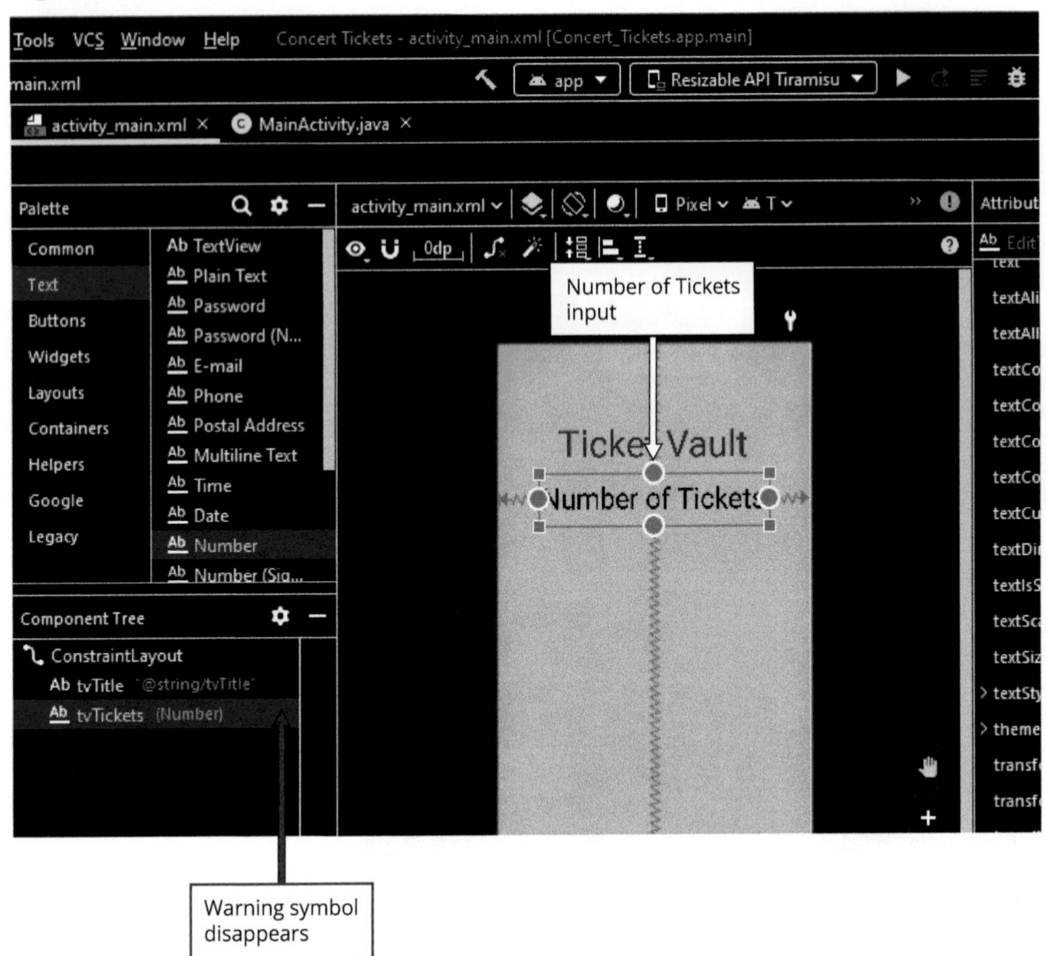

Quick Check

How does the hint in Android Studio assist you?

Answer: Hint text is text displayed in an EditText component to indicate what the user should enter. Examples of hint text include "Type your choice here," "Enter your name," or "Enter phone number."

3.6 Developing a User Interface Using a Spinner Component

After the user enters the number of tickets, the next step is to select which concert to attend. Three musical groups are performing next month: No Filter, Fresh Haven, and Pine Mirrors. User error is a distinct possibility when typing on a small on-screen keyboard; it is much easier to use a Spinner component instead of actually typing a group name. A **Spinner component** is a component similar to a drop-down list; it allows users to select a single item on a touchscreen from a fixed list, as shown in **Figure 3-16**. The Spinner component displays a prompt with a list of strings called items that are assigned in strings.xml. The items are shown in a pop-up window without taking up multiple lines on the initial display.

Figure 3-16 Spinner dialog box displaying the three concert groups

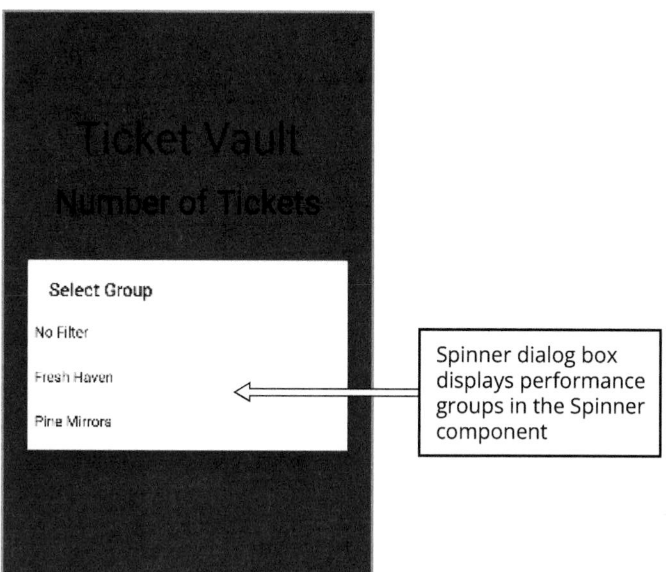

In the Concert Tickets app, a string array for a Spinner component named tvGroup is necessary to hold the three musical group names as individual string resources in strings.xml. The strings.xml file provides an easy way to update commonly used strings throughout your project, instead of searching through code and properties to alter a string array within the application. For example, each month the concert planners can simply change the text in the strings .xml file to reflect the new concert events.

3.7 Adding a Prompt and Entries to a Spinner Component

As an app designer, you always need to keep in mind the users' journey as they run your app. When users view the Spinner component, they most likely will not know what to do, so assisting them should be the focus of your design efforts. A **prompt**, which can be used to display instructions at the top of the Spinner component using the prompt attribute, is stored in strings.xml and is named prompt. This prompt explains to users what to do next.

Using Entries

Three different groups are available in the chapter's example app. The Spinner component uses an attribute called **entries** that connect the string array in strings.xml to the Spinner component so the entries can be displayed in the application. The Spinner component is located in the Containers category of the Palette. As you define the Spinner component, the **spinnerMode** attribute sets the Spinner component to either the dialog mode or drop-down mode. The dialog mode uses a pop-up dialog box to display the Spinner items. The drop-down mode displays the items in a list box. The Spinner component also has attributes associated with the width and height of the component named **layout_width** and **layout_height**. The following steps add the Spinner component to the Android application using the dialog mode:

Step 1

- With the activity_main.xml tab open, click the Containers category in the Palette.
- Drag and drop the Spinner component below the Text Number component and center it horizontally. Drag the Constraint handles of the Spinner component until all four constraints are anchored to the edge of the screen; blue curly arrows should touch the top, bottom, left, and right sides of the emulator.

- Click the id attribute and type **spGroup** in the id text box. If necessary, click the Refactor button.
- Click the spinnerMode attribute arrow.

The spinnerMode attribute displays the options for the Spinner component named spGroup (**Figure 3-17**).

Figure 3-17 Spinner component with spinnerMode attribute

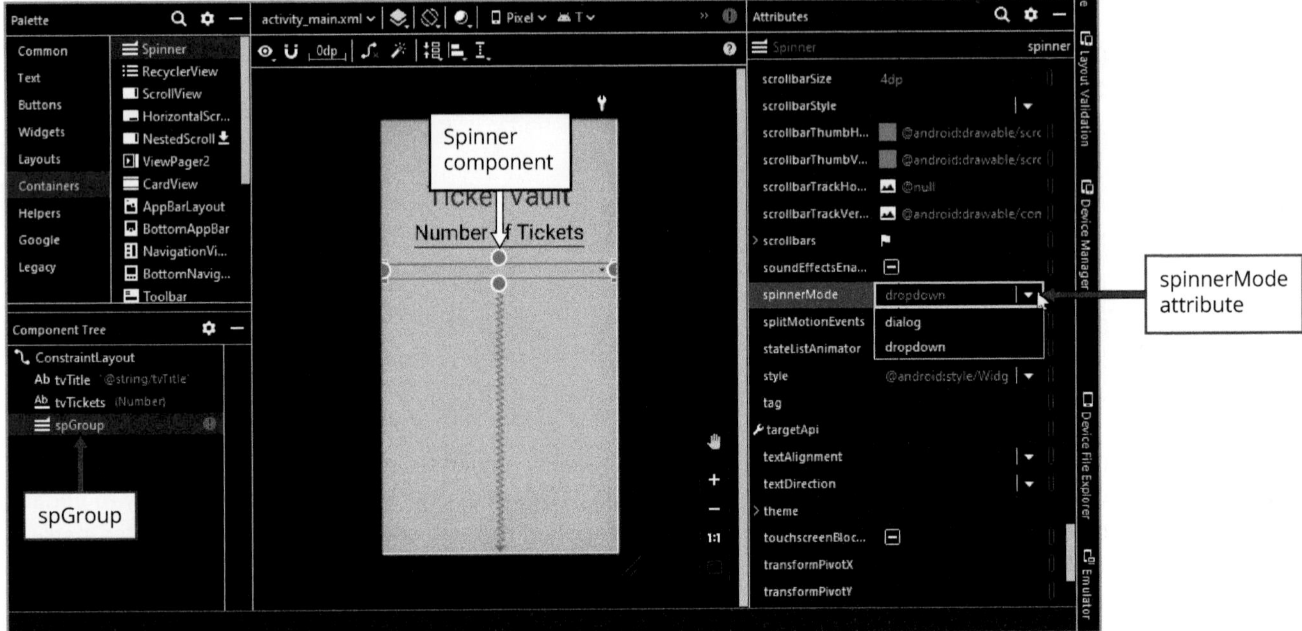

Step 2

- Click **dialog** for the spinnerMode attribute.
- In the Attributes pane, click to the right of the prompt attribute.
- Click the Pick a Resource button (the thin rectangle symbol) to display the Pick a Resource dialog box.
- Scroll down and click Prompt to display instructions when the user touches the Spinner component.
- Click the OK button.
- In the Attributes pane, click to the right of the entries attribute.
- Click the Pick a Resource button (the thin rectangle symbol) to display the Pick a Resource dialog box.
- Click **tvGroup** to reference the three items added to the strings.xml file. These items will be displayed in the string array of the Spinner component when the app runs.

The prompt attribute connects to the resource named @string/prompt. The entries attribute connects to the resources of the string array @array/tvGroup (**Figure 3-18**).

Step 3

- Click the OK button in the Pick a Resource dialog box.
- Scroll up the Attributes pane, change the layout_width attribute to **300dp**, and change the layout_height attribute to **60dp**.

The actual group names are displayed in the Spinner component when the app is executed in the emulator. The Spinner component has a width of 300dp and a height of 60dp to make it large enough to touch (**Figure 3-19**).

Figure 3-18 Pick a Resource dialog box with tvGroup string array selected

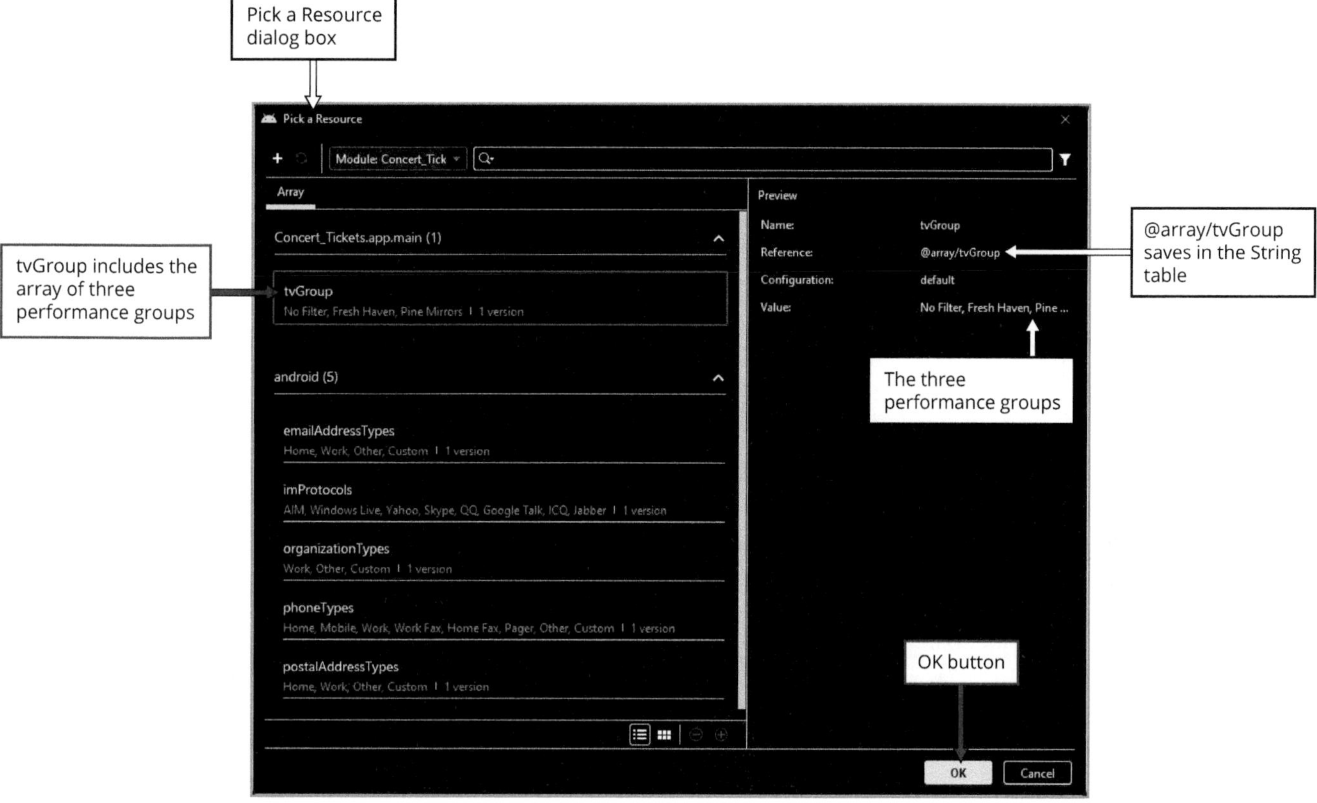

Figure 3-19 The layout_width and layout_height attributes

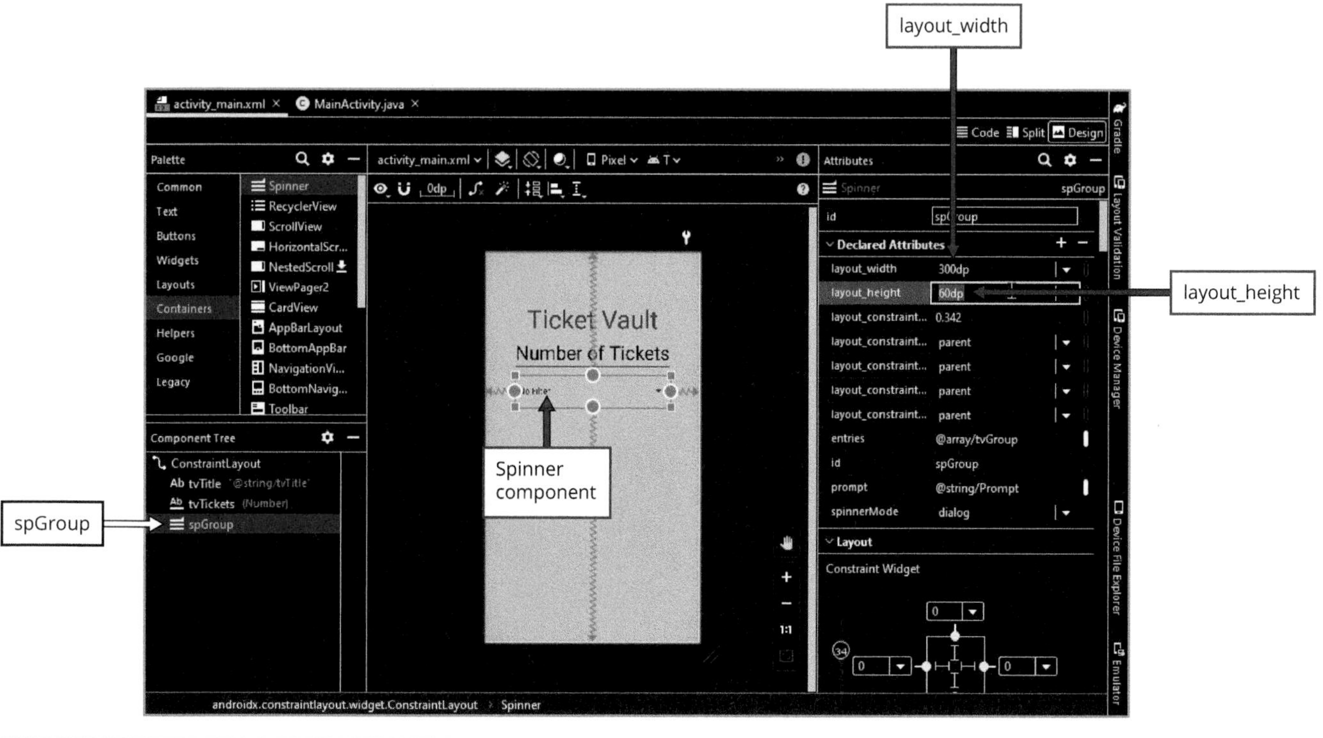

Quick Check

What are the two ways that you can connect the String table text with the text attribute?

Answer: Either type @string/*variable name* or click the Pick a Resource button (the thin rectangle symbol) to display the Pick a Resource dialog box.

Adding the Button, TextView, and ImageView Controls

After the user enters the number of tickets and the concert group name, the user clicks the FIND THE COST button to calculate the cost. The app calculates the total cost by multiplying the number of tickets by the cost of each ticket ($89.99), and then displays the name of the group and total cost of the tickets in a TextView component.

An ImageView component displayed on an Android device should be accessible to everyone. Accessibility issues should be addressed for those who are blind, users with limited vision, and users who might need a built-in screen reader to assist them in using an app. An ImageView component should have a content description for those who cannot see the image. For example, the Concert Tickets app displays a picture of a concert. By setting the contentDescription attribute for the ImageView component to the String text "Concert Image," the viewer can imagine what the image looks like based on your description.

An image file named concert.png, provided with your student files, is displayed in an ImageView component for the Concert Tickets app. You should already have the student files for this textbook; if not, ask your instructor for the files or download them from the book's webpage (www.cengage.com). To add the Button, TextView, and ImageView components to the emulator, follow these steps:

Step 1

- In the activity_main.xml tab, drag the Button component from the Common category in the Palette to the emulator and center it below the Spinner component. Release the mouse button.
- Drag the top and bottom Constraint handles of the Button component to the top and bottom of the emulator screen and release the mouse.
- Click in the id component and type **btCost** in the id text box within the Attributes pane. Click the Refactor button.
- Click to the right of the text attribute. Click the Pick a Resource button (the thin rectangle symbol) to display the Pick a Resource dialog box.
- Click **btCost** to reference the text added to the strings.xml file. Click the OK button to close the Pick a Resource dialog box.
- Change the textSize attribute to **34sp**.
- Change the backgroundTint attribute to the color **black**. Save your work.

The Button component named btCost displays the text FIND THE COST from the btCost String, the backgroundTint is changed to black, and the size is changed to 34sp (**Figure 3-20**).

Step 2

- From the Common category in the Palette, drag the TextView component to the emulator and center it below the Button component. Drag the top and bottom Constraint handles of the TextView component to the top and bottom of the emulator screen and release the mouse.

Figure 3-20 Adding a Button component

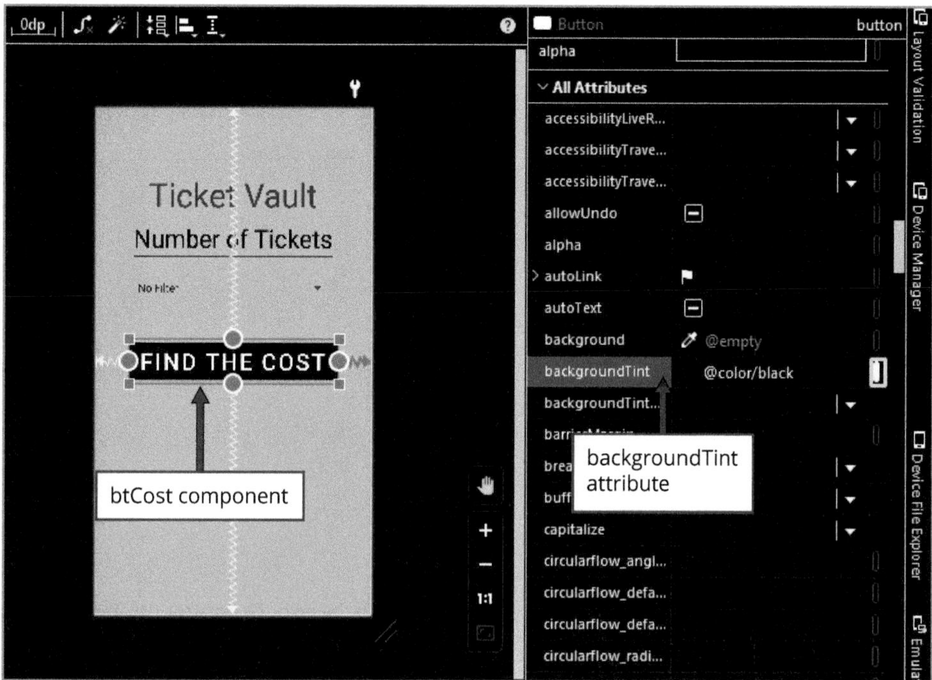

- Click the id attribute, type **tvResult** to the right of the id attribute, and click the Refactor button.
- Delete the text New Text shown in the text attribute.
- In the Attributes pane, click to the right of the textSize attribute, type **24sp**, and then press Enter.

The tvResult TextView component is added to the emulator. The text attribute will be filled in when the code is run and the calculation is computed (**Figure 3-21**).

Figure 3-21 Adding a TextView component

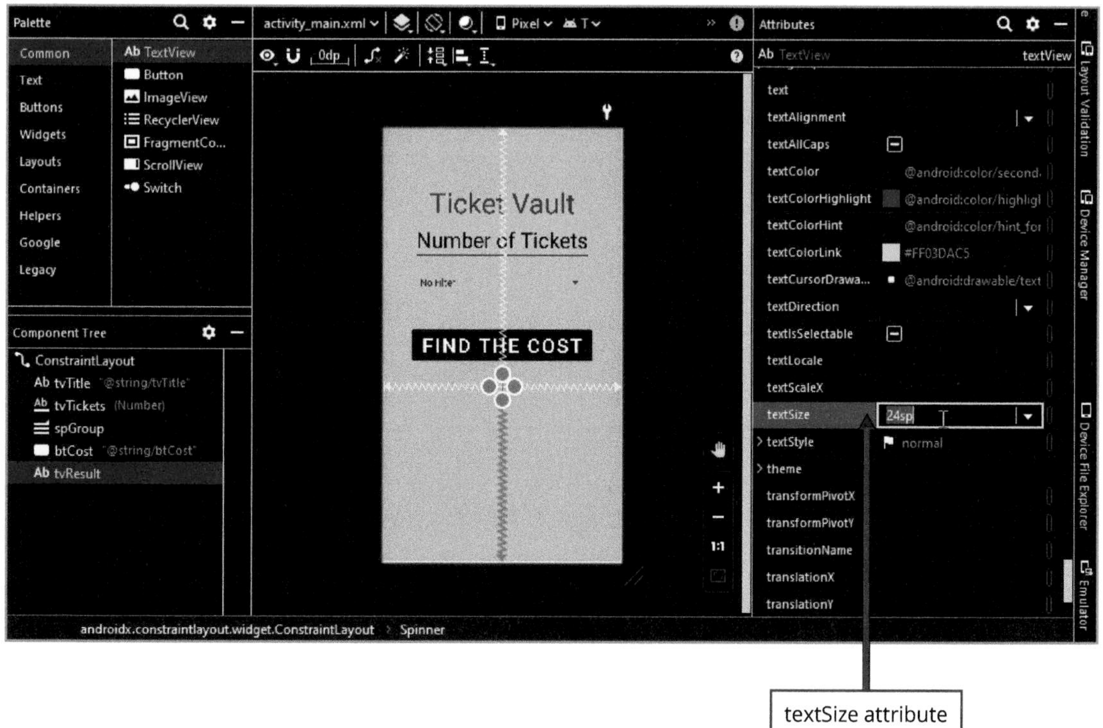

Critical Thinking

The Text component is difficult to locate because it does not have text in the text attribute. Is there an easier way to locate it?

Yes. Click the tvResult object in the Component Tree.

Step 3

- To add the ImageView component, first download the student files to your computer (if necessary).
- Open the folder containing the student files.
- Drag the concert.png file from the folder to the drawable folder in the Android project view pane. Release the mouse to place the file in the drawable folder.
- Click the OK button in the Copy dialog box. Click the Refactor button.
- In the activity_main.xml tab, drag the ImageView component from the Common category in the Palette to the emulator. Center the component below the TextView component at the bottom of the emulator.
- When the Pick a Resource dialog box opens, click **concert** and then click the OK button.
- Drag the top and bottom Constraint handles of the ImageView component to the top and bottom of the emulator screen and then release the mouse. Make sure you place the component below the tvResult TextView component that will display the cost of the tickets.
- In the id attribute of the Attributes pane, type **ivConcert** to name the ImageView component.
- Click to the right of the contentDescription attribute. Click the Pick a Resource button (the thin rectangle symbol) to display the Pick a Resource dialog box.
- Click **Description** to reference the accessibility text added to the strings.xml file. Click the OK button to close the Pick a Resource dialog box.

The concert image is displayed at the bottom of the emulator with a content description for accessibility purposes (**Figure 3-22**).

Figure 3-22 Adding an ImageView component with a contentDescription attribute

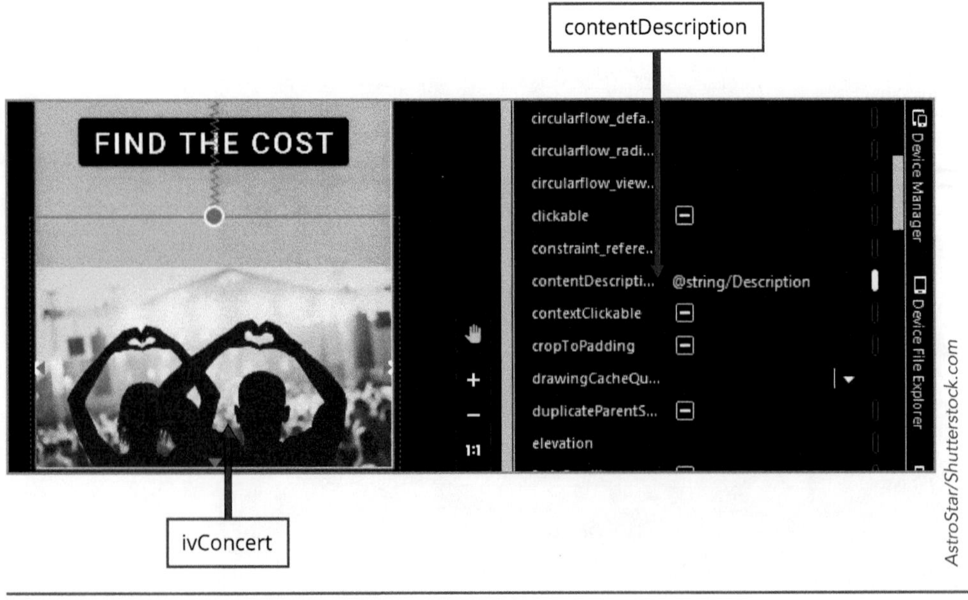

AstroStar/Shutterstock.com

3.8 Coding the EditText Class for the Text Number Component

To handle the input that users enter into the numeric Text Number component in the chapter project, you use the EditText class, which extracts the text and converts it for use in the Java code. The code must assign the extracted text to a variable. A Java program uses a **variable** to contain data that changes during the execution of the program. In the chapter project, a variable named tickets holds the text entered in the Text Number component for the amount of tickets desired. The following code syntax declares (or initializes) the tickets variable, which contains the extracted EditText class text from the user's input. Notice the code syntax begins with the word **final**, indicating that tickets is a final variable. A final variable can be initialized only once; any attempt to reassign the value results in a compile error when the application runs.

Code Syntax

```
final EditText tickets = (EditText)findViewById(R.id.tvTickets);
```

Good to Know | You can include spaces before and after the equal sign or you can omit them. Java considers either format correct.

Recall that if you want to refer to a component in the Java code, you can use the id attribute to name the component when you add it to the interface. For example, the Text Number component has the id tvTickets. You can access the component in the code using the findViewById( ) method. In the parentheses of the previous code syntax statement, the R refers to resources available to the app, such as a layout component, the id indicates that the resource is identified by the id attribute, and tvTickets is the assigned id.

Next, you assign the tvTickets Text Number component to the variable named tickets. To collect the ticket input from the user, code the EditText class for the Text Number component by following this step:

Step 1

- In the Android project view, expand the java folder and the first instance of com.example.concerttickets, and then double-click MainActivity to open the code window.
- Click to the right of the line setContentView(R.layout.*activity_main*);.
- Press Enter to insert a blank line.
- To initialize and reference the EditText class with the id name of tvTickets, type **final EditText tickets = (EditText)findViewById(R.id.tvTickets);**.
- Click the first instance of EditText displayed in red text, and then press Alt+Enter to import the Java library for the EditText component.

The EditText class extracts the value for the number of tickets from the user's input and assigns the value to the variable named tickets. Variables that the program has not used appear with a curly underline. This underline is removed when a value is assigned later in the program (**Figure 3-23**).

Figure 3-23 EditText code for Text Number component

MainActivity.java

activity_main.xml × concert.png × MainActivity.java ×

```
package com.example.concerttickets;

import ...

public class MainActivity extends AppCompatActivity {

    @Override
    protected void onCreate(Bundle savedInstanceState) {
        super.onCreate(savedInstanceState);
        setContentView(R.layout.activity_main);
        final EditText tickets = (EditText)findViewById(R.id.tvTickets);
    }
}
```

EditText code

3.9 Coding the Spinner Control

The user's selection of the concert group must also be assigned to a text variable and stored in the computer's memory. For this application, assign the selection made from the Spinner component (spGroup) to a variable named group using the following code:

Code Syntax

```
final Spinner group = (Spinner)findViewById(R.id.spGroup);
```

To collect the input from the user's group selection, code the Spinner component by following this step:

Step 1

- After the EditText line of code, press Enter to create a new line.
- To initialize and reference the Spinner component with the id name of spGroup, type **final Spinner group = (Spinner)findViewById(R.id.spGroup);**.
- Click the first instance of Spinner displayed in red text, and then press Alt+Enter to import the Spinner component.

The Spinner component assigns the value from the user's input to the variable named group (**Figure 3-24**).

Figure 3-24 Spinner component code

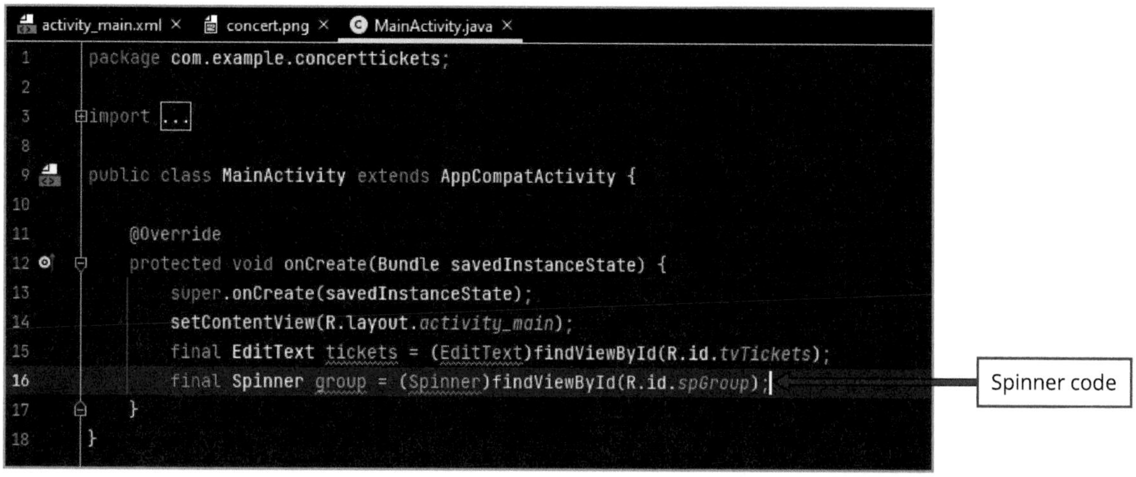

```
activity_main.xml ×   concert.png ×   MainActivity.java ×

package com.example.concerttickets;

import ...

public class MainActivity extends AppCompatActivity {

    @Override
    protected void onCreate(Bundle savedInstanceState) {
        super.onCreate(savedInstanceState);
        setContentView(R.layout.activity_main);
        final EditText tickets = (EditText)findViewById(R.id.tvTickets);
        final Spinner group = (Spinner)findViewById(R.id.spGroup);
    }
}
```

Spinner code

3.10 Instantiating the Button Component and Variables

After the user inputs the number of tickets and the concert group name, the onClickListener waits patiently in the background and listens for the user to click the FIND THE COST button to calculate the cost in a Button event. The Button event OnClick handler executes the portion of code that calculates the cost of the tickets when the button is touched. After the app calculates the total cost by multiplying the number of tickets by the cost of each ticket ($89.99), the name of the group and total cost of the tickets are displayed in a TextView component. The TextView component is instantiated to the variable named result using the following code:

Code Syntax

```
final TextView result = ((TextView)findViewById(R.id.tvResult));
```

To instantiate the Button component, set up the Button listener and initiate the TextView component. To display the results, follow these steps:

Step 1

- If necessary, click to the right of the code line that assigned the Spinner component to the variable named group, and then press Enter.
- To initialize the Button component with the id of btCost, type **Button cost = (Button)findViewById(R.id.btCost);**.
- Click the first instance of Button displayed in red text, press Alt+Enter, and then select Import Class to import the Button component as an Android component.

The Button component is initialized and the Button type is imported (**Figure 3-25**).

Step 2

- Press Enter at the end of the Button statement.
- To code the button listener that awaits user interaction, type **cost.seton** to display a list of auto-complete suggestions with all the possible entries that are valid at that point in the code.
- Double-click the first setOnClickListener to select it from the auto-complete list.
- In the parentheses, type **new On** (with an uppercase *O*) to view possible auto-complete options, and then double-click the OnClickListener option.

Figure 3-25 Instantiated Button class

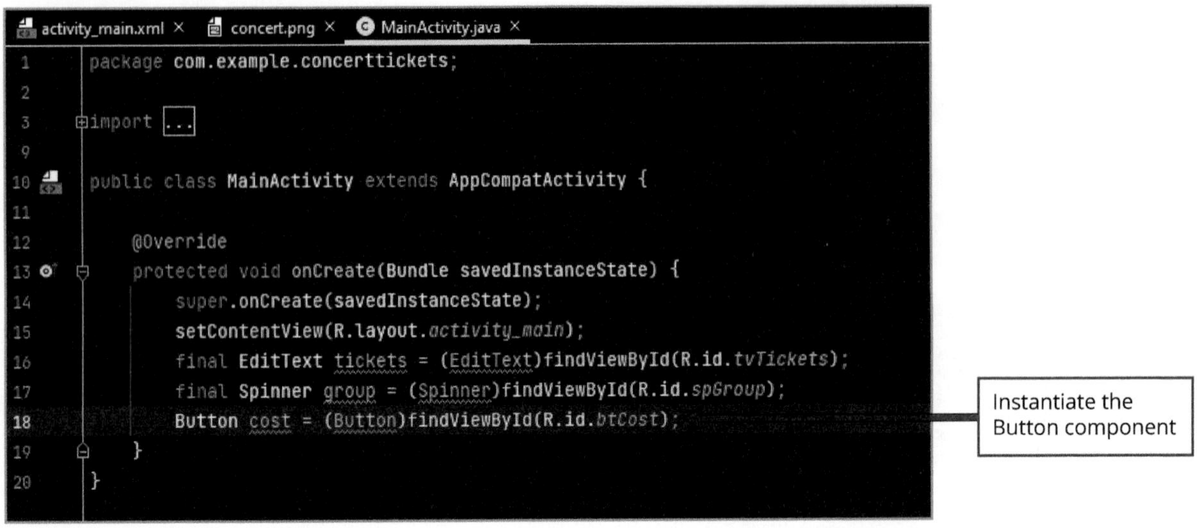

activity_main.xml × concert.png × MainActivity.java ×

```
package com.example.concerttickets;

import ...

public class MainActivity extends AppCompatActivity {

    @Override
    protected void onCreate(Bundle savedInstanceState) {
        super.onCreate(savedInstanceState);
        setContentView(R.layout.activity_main);
        final EditText tickets = (EditText)findViewById(R.id.tvTickets);
        final Spinner group = (Spinner)findViewById(R.id.spGroup);
        Button cost = (Button)findViewById(R.id.btCost);
    }
}
```

Instantiate the Button component

The Button component is initialized and an OnClickListener auto-generated stub appears in the code window (**Figure 3-26**).

Figure 3-26 Initializing the OnClickListener

activity_main.xml × concert.png × MainActivity.java ×

```
1  package com.example.concerttickets;
2
3  import ...
10
11 public class MainActivity extends AppCompatActivity {
12
13     @Override
14     protected void onCreate(Bundle savedInstanceState) {
15         super.onCreate(savedInstanceState);
16         setContentView(R.layout.activity_main);
17         final EditText tickets = (EditText)findViewById(R.id.tvTickets);
18         final Spinner group = (Spinner)findViewById(R.id.spGroup);
19         Button cost = (Button)findViewById(R.id.btCost);
20         cost.setOnClickListener(new View.OnClickListener() {
21             @Override
22             public void onClick(View view) {
23
24             }
25         });
26     }
27 }
```

OnClickListener auto-generated stub

Step 3

- After the line of code beginning with cost.setOnClickListener in Line 20, press Enter, and then type **final TextView result = ((TextView)findViewById(R.id.tvResult));**.
- Click the first instance of TextView displayed in red text and then press Alt+Enter to import the TextView component.

The TextView component tvResult is assigned to the variable named result (**Figure 3-27**).

Figure 3-27 TextView component code for the result

activity_main.xml × concert.png × MainActivity.java ×

```
package com.example.concerttickets;

import ...

public class MainActivity extends AppCompatActivity {

    @Override
    protected void onCreate(Bundle savedInstanceState) {
        super.onCreate(savedInstanceState);
        setContentView(R.layout.activity_main);
        final EditText tickets = (EditText)findViewById(R.id.tvTickets);
        final Spinner group = (Spinner)findViewById(R.id.spGroup);
        Button cost = (Button)findViewById(R.id.btCost);
        cost.setOnClickListener(new View.OnClickListener() {
            final TextView result = ((TextView)findViewById(R.id.tvResult));
            @Override
            public void onClick(View view) {

            }
        });
    }
}
```

tvResult is assigned to variable named result

Critical Thinking

How can I combine the Button component with the ImageView component to create a button with an image overlay?

The ImageButton component displays a button with an image instead of text that the user can click. Place the image in the drawable folder and then reference the picture as the source of your ImageButton.

Good to Know

Variable names are case sensitive and should be mixed case (camel case) when they include more than one word, as in costPerItem. Java variable names cannot start with a number or special symbol. Subsequent characters in the variable name may be letters, digits, dollar signs, or underscore characters.

Declaring Variables

As you have seen, the user can enter data in the chapter's example program using a Text Number component. In the Concert Tickets app, a mathematical equation multiplies the number of tickets by the cost of the tickets to calculate the total cost. When writing programs, it is convenient to use variables instead of the actual data, such as the cost of a ticket ($89.99). As you learned in the previous section, two steps are necessary in order to use a variable:

1. Declare the variable.
2. Assign a value to the variable.

The declared type of a value determines which operations are allowed. At the core of Java code are eight built-in primitive (simple) types of data.

Primitive Data Types

Java requires all variables to have a data type. **Table 3-2** lists the primitive data types that all computer platforms support, including the Android SDK.

Table 3-2 Primitive data types in Java

Type	Meaning	Range	Default Value
byte	Often used with arrays	−128 to 127	0
short	Often used with arrays	−32,768 to 32,767	0
int	Most commonly used number value	−2,147,483,648 to 2,147,483,647	0
long	Used for numbers that exceed int	−9,223,372,036,854,775,808 to 9,223,372,036,854,775,807	0
float	A 32-bit floating-point number	+/−3.40282347 ^38	0
double	Most common for decimal values	+/−1.79769313486231570 ^308	0
char	Used for single characters	Characters	0
boolean	Used for conditional statements	True or false	False

Quick Check

Which data type would be best to represent the population of the world?

Answer: The best integer to use would be long.

In the Concert Tickets program, the tickets cost $89.99 each. To declare this cost, use a double data type, which is appropriate for decimal values. A statement should both declare the variable and assign a value for costPerTicket, as shown in the following code syntax. The requested quantity of tickets is assigned to a variable named numberOfTickets, which represents an integer. For example, if you want to purchase four concert tickets at $89.99 each, the cost would be $359.96. To multiply two values, the values must be stored in one of the numeric data types. When the program computes the total cost of the tickets, it assigns the value to a variable named totalCost, also a double data type, as shown in the following code:

Code Syntax

```
double costPerTicket = 89.99;
int numberOfTickets;
double totalCost;
String groupChoice;
```

The String Data Type

In addition to the primitive data types, Java has another data type for working with text. The String type is a class and not a primitive data type. Most strings that you use in the Java language are an object of type String. A string can be a character, word, or phrase. If you assign a phrase to a String variable, place the phrase between double quotation marks. In the Concert Tickets app, after the user selects a musical group from the Spinner component, the program assigns that group to a String type variable named groupChoice, as shown in the following code:

Code Syntax

```
String groupChoice;
```

Good to Know

When defining variables, good programming practice dictates that the variable names you use should reflect the actual values to place in the variable. That way, anyone reading the program code can easily understand the use of the variable from its descriptive names.

Critical Thinking

Should I assign a postal code to a number variable or a String variable?

Assign a postal code to a String variable. Assign numbers to a String variable when you do not plan to use the values mathematically.

Declaring the Variables in the Project

You typically declare variables in an Android application at the beginning of an activity. The code must declare a variable before it can be used in the application. To initialize, or declare, the variables in the chapter's example project, follow this step:

Step 1

- In MainActivity.java, on Line 12 within the class, press the Tab key to indent the text, and then insert the following four lines of code to initialize the variables in this activity:

  double costPerTicket = 89.99;

  int numberOfTickets;

  double totalCost;

  String groupChoice;

The variables are declared at the beginning of the activity (**Figure 3-28**).

Figure 3-28 Declaring variables for the activity

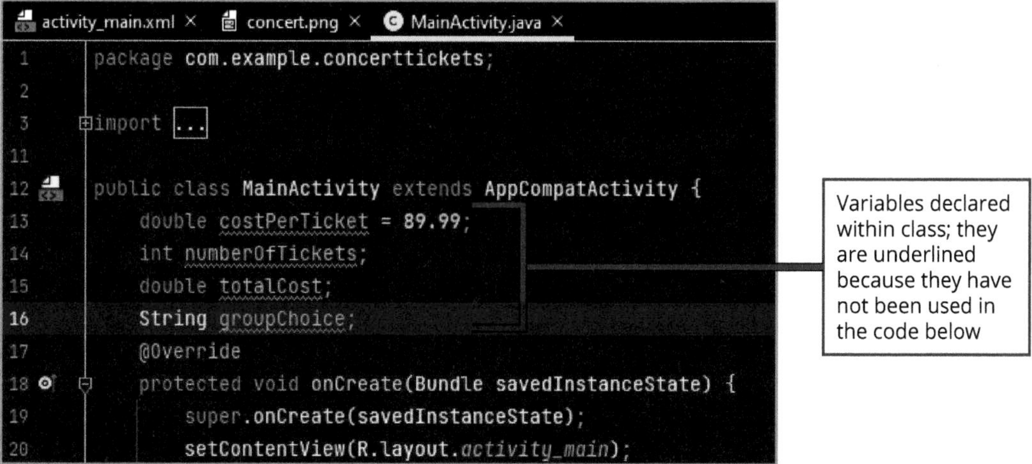

3.11 Coding the getText( ) Method

At this point in the application's development, all the components have been assigned variables to hold their values. The next step is to convert the values in the assigned variables to the correct data type for calculation purposes. After the user enters the number of tickets and the concert group name, the user clicks the FIND THE COST button. Inside the OnClickListener code for the button component, the text stored in the tickets EditText component can be read with the **getText( )** method. By default, Java reads the text in the EditText component as a String type. However, you cannot use a String type in a mathematical function because it is not a numeric value. To convert a string into a numerical data type, you use a **Parse** class. **Table 3-3** displays the Parse types that convert a string to a common numerical data type.

Table 3-3 Parse type conversions

Numerical Data Type	Parse Types
Integer	Integer.parseInt( )
Float	Float.parseFloat( )
Double	Double.parseDouble( )
Long	Long.parseLong( )

To extract the string of text entered in the EditText component and convert it to an integer data type for the number of tickets, the following syntax is necessary:

Code Syntax

```
numberOfTickets = Integer.parseInt(tickets.getText( ).toString( ));
```

To code the getText() method, convert the value in the tickets variable into an integer data type, assign it to a variable named numberOfTickets, and follow this step:

Step 1

- In MainActivity.java, inside the OnClickListener onClick( ) method stub on Line 28, press the Tab key and then type **numberOfTickets = Integer.parseInt(tickets.getText( ).toString( ));**.

The getText( ) method extracts the text from tickets, converts the string to an integer, and assigns the value to numberOfTickets (**Figure 3-29**).

Working with Mathematical Operations

The ability to perform arithmetic operations on numeric data is fundamental to many applications. Many programs require arithmetic operations to add, subtract, multiply, and divide numeric data. For example, the Concert Tickets app must multiply the cost of each ticket by the number of tickets purchased in order to calculate the total cost of the concert tickets.

Figure 3-29 Converting the string input to an integer with parseInt

```
package com.example.concerttickets;

import ...

public class MainActivity extends AppCompatActivity {
    double costPerTicket = 89.99;
    int numberOfTickets;
    double totalCost;
    String groupChoice;
    @Override
    protected void onCreate(Bundle savedInstanceState) {
        super.onCreate(savedInstanceState);
        setContentView(R.layout.activity_main);
        final EditText tickets = (EditText)findViewById(R.id.tvTickets);
        final Spinner group = (Spinner)findViewById(R.id.spGroup);
        Button cost = (Button)findViewById(R.id.btCost);
        cost.setOnClickListener(new View.OnClickListener() {
            final TextView result = ((TextView)findViewById(R.id.tvResult));
            @Override
            public void onClick(View view) {
                numberOfTickets = Integer.parseInt(tickets.getText( ).toString( ));
            }
        });
    }
}
```

getText( ) method extracts the text from tickets

Quick Check

When requesting input from the user, what is the programming method that accepts the input?

Answer: The getText( ) method.

3.12 Understanding Arithmetic Operators

Table 3-4 shows a list of the Java arithmetic operators, along with their uses and examples of arithmetic expressions showing their use.

Table 3-4 Java arithmetic operators

Arithmetic Operator	Use	Assignment Statement
+	Addition	value = itemPrice + itemTax;
−	Subtraction	score = previousScore − 2;
*	Multiplication	totalCost = costPerTicket * numberOfTickets;
/	Division	average = totalGrade / 5.0;
%	Remainder	leftover = widgetAmount % 3; (If widgetAmount = 11, the remainder = 2)
++	Increment (adds 1)	golfScore ++
− −	Decrement (subtracts 1)	points − −

When multiple operations are included in a single assignment statement, the sequence for performing the calculations is determined by the rules shown in **Table 3-5**. These rules are called the order of operations. The order of evaluation of equal-precedence operators is usually from left to right.

Table 3-5 Order of operations

Highest to Lowest Precedence	Description of Order of Operations
()	Operations in parentheses are performed first
++ --	Left to right
* / %	Left to right
+ -	Left to right

For example, the result of 2 + 3 * 4 is 14 because the multiplication is of higher precedence than the addition operation.

Formatting Numbers

After computing the total ticket cost, the program should display the result in currency format, which includes a dollar sign, inserts commas if needed for larger values, and rounds off the result to two places past the decimal point. Java includes a class called **DecimalFormat** that provides patterns for formatting numbers for output on the Android device. Using the DecimalFormat class in Java enables you to round numbers off to your preferred number of decimal places. For example, the pattern "$###,###.##" establishes that a number begins with a dollar sign character, displays a comma if the number has more than three digits, and rounds off the result to the nearest penny. If the pattern "###.#%" is used, the number is multiplied by 100 and rounded to the first digit past the decimal point. To establish a currency decimal format for the result of the ticket cost, use the following code syntax. The code assigns the decimal format to a variable named currency and later applies it to the totalCost variable to display a currency value:

Code Syntax

```
DecimalFormat currency = new DecimalFormat("###,###.##");
```

To code the calculation that computes the cost of the tickets and to create a currency decimal format, follow this step:

Step 1

- In MainActivity.java, after the last line entered, insert a new line, type **totalCost = costPerTicket * numberOfTickets;**, and then press Enter.
- To establish a currency format, type **DecimalFormat currency = new DecimalFormat("$###,###.##");**.
- Import the DecimalFormat class, if necessary. Notice that Android Studio places the hint for Pattern.

The equation computes the total cost of the tickets and DecimalFormat creates a currency format to use when the total cost is displayed (**Figure 3-30**).

Figure 3-30 Calculating and formatting the ticket cost

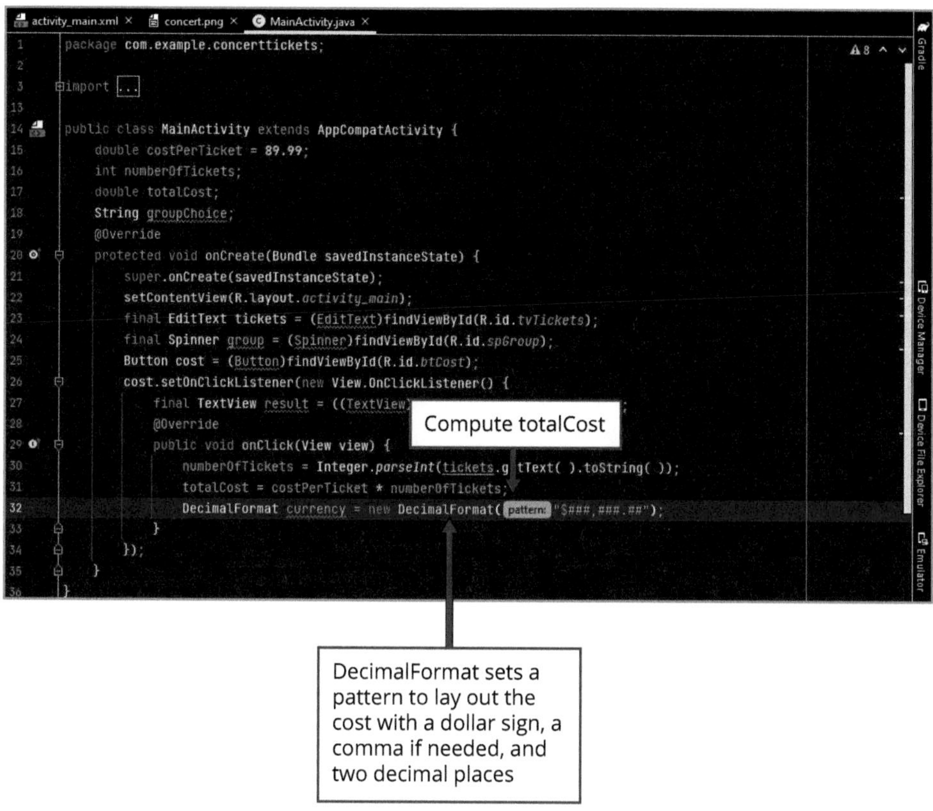
Compute totalCost
DecimalFormat sets a pattern to lay out the cost with a dollar sign, a comma if needed, and two decimal places

Quick Check

How would you display a three-digit number with a decimal value rounded to three places past the decimal?

Answer: DecimalFormat currency = new DecimalFormat("###.###");.

Displaying Android Output

In Java, computing the results does not mean displaying the results. To display the results of the chapter's example project, including the name of the group and the final cost of the tickets, first assign the name of the group to a String variable.

Using the getSelectedItem( ) Method

To obtain the text name of the musical group that the user selected in the Spinner component, you use a method named getSelectedItem( ). The **getSelectedItem( )** method returns the text label of the currently selected Spinner item. For example, if the user selected Fresh Haven, the getSelectedItem() method assigns this group to a String variable named groupChoice that was declared at the beginning of the activity, as shown in the following code:

Code Syntax

```
groupChoice = group.getSelectedItem( ).toString( );
```

Good to Know

A method named getSelectedIndex( ) can be used with a Spinner component to determine if the user selected the first, second, or subsequent choice. For example, if getSelectedIndex( ) is equal to the integer 0, the user selected the first choice.

3.13 Coding the setText( ) Method

Earlier in the chapter's example Android project, the getText( ) method extracted the text from the Text Field component. The setText( ) method displays text in a TextView component. setText( ) accepts a string of data for display. To join variable names and text, you can concatenate the text with a plus sign (+). In the following example, the variable completeSentence is assigned *Android is the best phone platform.* This sentence is displayed in a TextView object named result.

For example:

String mobile = "Android";

String completeSentence = mobile + " is the best phone platform";

result.setText(completeSentence);

The syntax for the setText( ) method is shown in the following code. In this example, the result is displayed in the TextView component named result and includes the string that uses the concatenation operator—the plus sign connecting variables to the string text.

Code Syntax

```
result.setText("Cost for " + groupChoice + " is " + currency.format(totalCost));
```

The currency.format portion of the code displays the variable totalCost with a dollar sign and rounds off the total to the nearest penny. The output for the result was displayed earlier in Figure 3-2: Cost for Pine Mirrors is $359.96. To complete the app by coding the getSelectedItem( ) method and the setText( ) method, follow these steps:

Step 1

- In MainActivity.java after the last line of code entered, insert a new line and type **groupChoice = group.getSelectedItem().toString();** to assign the concert group to the String variable groupChoice.
- Insert a new line, and then type **result.setText("Cost for " + groupChoice + " is " + currency.format(totalCost));** to display the output.

The getSelectedItem( ) method identifies the selected group and setText( ) displays the selected group with the total cost of the tickets (**Figure 3-31**).

Step 2

- Click the Run app button on the Standard toolbar to test the application in the emulator.
- When the application opens in the emulator, enter the number of tickets using the on-screen keyboard (**Figure 3-32**) and select a group from the Spinner component. To view the results, click the FIND THE COST button.

Figure 3-31 Identifying and displaying the selected group

```
public class MainActivity extends AppCompatActivity {
    double costPerTicket = 89.99;
    int numberOfTickets;
    double totalCost;
    String groupChoice;
    @Override
    protected void onCreate(Bundle savedInstanceState) {
        super.onCreate(savedInstanceState);
        setContentView(R.layout.activity_main);
        final EditText tickets = (EditText)findViewById(R.id.tvTickets);
        final Spinner group = (Spinner)findViewById(R.id.spGroup);
        Button cost = (Button)findViewById(R.id.btCost);
        cost.setOnClickListener(new View.OnClickListener() {
            final TextView result = ((TextView)findViewById(R.id.tvResult));
            @Override
            public void onClick(View view) {
                numberOfTickets = Integer.parseInt(tickets.getText( ).toString( ));
                totalCost = costPerTicket * numberOfTickets;
                DecimalFormat currency = new DecimalFormat( pattern: "$###,###.##");
                groupChoice = group.getSelectedItem( ).toString( );
                result.setText("Cost for " + groupChoice + " is " + currency.format(totalCost));
            }
        });
    }
}
```

Print out the result using setText( )

The Concert Tickets Android app is executed. Figures 3-1 and 3-2, shown earlier in the chapter, illustrate how the app should look.

Figure 3-32 Completed Concert Tickets app

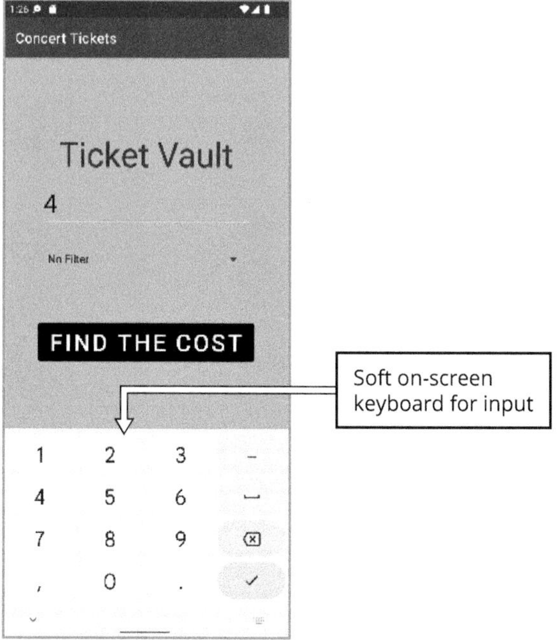

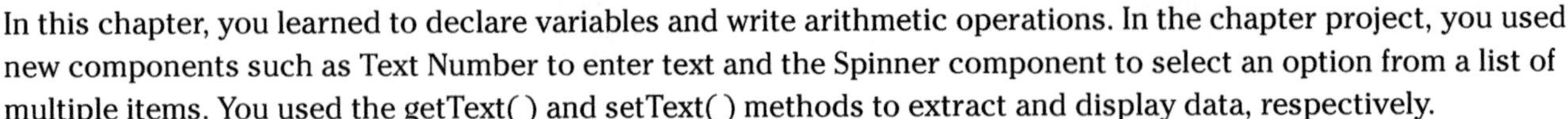

Wrap It Up—Chapter Summary

In this chapter, you learned to declare variables and write arithmetic operations. In the chapter project, you used new components such as Text Number to enter text and the Spinner component to select an option from a list of multiple items. You used the getText( ) and setText( ) methods to extract and display data, respectively.

- Use a Text Number component or other text fields to request input from users, who can enter characters using an on-screen keyboard or a physical keyboard. You need to select the correct type of Text component for the type of data you are requesting.
- The strings.xml file is part of every Android application by default and contains strings used in the application, such as text displayed in a TextView, Spinner, or Button component. You can edit a string in strings.xml to update the text wherever it is used in the application. In strings.xml, you can also include prompt text that provides instructions in a Spinner component. In the Java code, use the getSelectedItem( ) method to return the text of the selected Spinner item.
- To provide guidelines so users enter the correct data in a Text Number component, use the component's hint attribute to display light-colored text, also called a watermark, that describes what to enter. The user clicks the component to remove the hint and type the requested input.
- To handle the input that users enter into a Text Number component, you use the EditText class, which extracts the text and converts it for use in the Java code. The extracted text must be assigned to a variable, which holds data that changes during the execution of the program. To extract the string of text entered in an EditText component, use the getText( ) method. To display the extracted text in a TextView component, use the setText( ) method.
- To use a variable, you must first declare the variable and then assign a value to it. The declared type of a value determines which mathematical operations are allowed. Variables in an Android application are typically declared at the beginning of an activity.
- After assigning variables to hold the values entered in components, you often need to convert the values in the assigned variables to the correct data type so the values can be used in calculations. To use string data in a mathematical function, you use the Parse class to convert the string into a numerical data type.

Key Terms

DecimalFormat
entries
final
getSelectedItem( )
getText( )
hint
item
layout_height
layout_width
Parse
prompt
soft keyboard
Spinner component
spinnerMode
string array
textColorHint
user experience
variable

Developer FAQs

1. Where do you type numbers on the screen on an Android phone? (3.1)
2. Where is the soft keyboard? Be sure to include its location in your answer. (3.1)
3. What does UX stand for? (3.1)

4. Which five components were used in the chapter project? (All)
5. Which Text component is best for entering a value such as Pi? (3.1)
6. Which Text component is best for entering an amount for an overdrawn checking account? (3.1)
7. Which attribute of the Spinner component adds text at the top of the component, such as instructions? (3.7)
8. What is the name of the file that holds commonly used phrases (arrays) of text in an application? (3.3)
9. What is a single string of information called in a string array? (3.3)
10. Which attribute do you assign to the string array that you create for a Spinner? (3.3 and 3.7)
11. Write the following variable in camel case: NUMBEROFDELAYS. (3.10)
12. Write a declaration statement for each of the following variables using the variable type and variable name that would be best for each value. Assign values if directed. (3.10)
    a. The smallest data type you can use for your age
    b. The population of the state of Maine
    c. Your weekly pay using the most common type for this type of number
    d. The first initial of your first name
    e. The present minimum wage using the most common type for this type of number
    f. The name of the city in which you live
    g. The answer to a true/false question for whether your age is over 16
13. Name two numeric data types that can contain a decimal point. (3.10)
14. What is the solution to each of the following arithmetic expressions? (3.12)
    a. 3 + 4 * 2 + 9
    b. 16 / 2 * 4 + 4
    c. 40 – (6 + 2) / 8
    d. 3 + 68 % 9
15. Write a getText( ) statement that converts a variable named deficit to a double data type and assigns the value to the variable named financeDeficit. (3.11)
16. Assign the text of the user's choice of a Spinner component named careerName to the variable named topCareers. (3.7)
17. If a variable named amount is assigned the value 57,199.266, what would the following statements display in the variable called price? (3.12)

    DecimalFormat money = new DecimalFormat("$###,###.##"); price.setText("Salary = " + money.format(amount));
18. Write a line of Java code that assigns the variable jellyBeans to a decimal format with six digits and a comma if needed, but no dollar sign or decimal places. (3.12)
19. Write a line of Java code to use concatenation to join the phrase "Welcome to the ", versionNumber (an int variable), and the phrase "th version" to the variable combinedStatement. (3.13)
20. Write a line of Java code that assigns a number to the variable numberChoice, which indicates the user's selection. If the user selects the first group, the number 0 is assigned; if the user selects the second group, the number 1 is assigned; and if the user selects the third group, the number 2 is assigned with the same variables used in the chapter project. (3.12)

Beyond the Book

Search the web for answers to the following questions to further your Android knowledge.

1. Research a smartphone that allows you to input data with a stylus. Show a screenshot of the phone displaying the features and price.
2. Search for three Android apps that sell any types of tickets. Name five features of each of the three apps.
3. A good Android developer always keeps up with the current market. Open the webpage *https://play.google.com*. Find this week's featured tablet apps and write about the top five. Write a paragraph on the purpose and cost of each app, for a total of five paragraphs.
4. Open the search engine Bing.com and then click the News tab. Search for an article about Android devices using this week's date. Insert the URL link at the top of a new document. Write a summary of the article in 150 to 200 of your own words.

Case Programming Projects

Complete one or more of the following case programming projects. Use the same steps and techniques taught within the chapter. Successful completion of these projects requires knowledge of all chapter learning objectives. Submit the program(s) you create to your instructor. The level of difficulty is indicated for each case programming project.

Case Project 3–1: Night Sky Tours App (Beginner)

Requirements Document

Application title:	Night Sky Tours App
Purpose:	A city planetarium is offering Night Sky Tours to view the celestial stars. Create a simple app that determines how many tour tickets the user needs and whether the ticket is for weekday or weekend tours. The app displays the total price for the tour tickets.
Algorithms:	1. The app displays a title, an image, and Text Number, Spinner, and Button components (**Figure 3-33**). The two options in the Spinner component include Weekday and Weekend. Each nightly tour is $7.50 per person. The background color is #4DFFEB3B. 2. When the user clicks the Button component, the number of tickets purchased and the total cost of the tour is displayed (**Figure 3-34**).
Conditions:	Use an image (stars.png), Spinner prompt, string array, and hint attribute.

Figure 3-33 Night Sky Tours app—opening screen

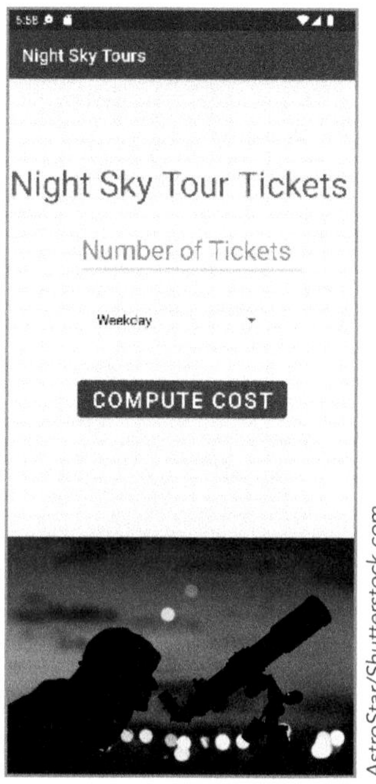

Figure 3-34 Night Sky Tours app results

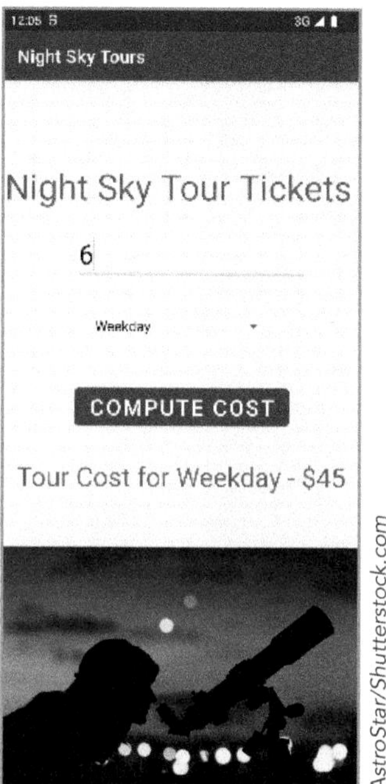

Case Project 3–2: Hiking Registration App (Beginner)

Requirements Document

Application title:	Hiking Registration App
Purpose:	A hiking registration app allows hikers to register for one of three Virginia guided hikes to qualify for the Great Outdoors badge.
Algorithms:	**1.** The hiking registration app has two text fields: One requests the number of hikers who want a guided tour ($16.99 each) and the other requests the location. A Spinner component allows the hiker to select one of the three possible locations: Peaks of Otter, New River Trail, and Crabtree Falls. The app also displays a title, an image, and a Button component (**Figure 3-35**). **2.** After the user clicks the Button component (color #7E977E), the selected location and the total cost are displayed in a TextView component (**Figure 3-36**). The background color is #7E977E.
Conditions:	Use a title, an image (hike.png), a Spinner prompt, a string array, and a hint attribute.

Figure 3-35 Hiking Registration app—opening screen

Jacob Lund/Shutterstock.com

Figure 3-36 Hiking Registration app results

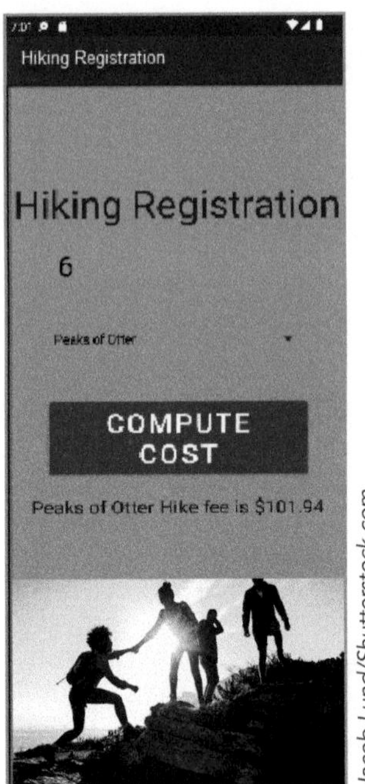

Jacob Lund/Shutterstock.com

Case Project 3–3: Paint Calculator App (Intermediate)

Requirements Document

Application title:	Paint Calculator App
Purpose:	The paint section of a large home store wants to provide a paint calculator app to determine the number of gallons needed to paint a room. The amount of paint in gallons is displayed.
Algorithms:	**1.** The app displays a title, an image, two text fields, and Spinner, Button, and TextView components. The Spinner component shows five colors of paint for selection. The user enters measurements to determine the area of the room. **2.** The color and the exact number of gallons needed are displayed in decimal form.
Conditions:	A gallon is needed for every 250 square feet to create a single coat of paint. Display the result rounded to two decimal places. Select five names of paint colors for the Spinner component. Use an image (paint.png), Spinner prompt, string array, and hint attribute.

Case Project 3–4: Chicago Cab Fare App (Intermediate)

Requirements Document

Application title: Chicago Cab Fare App

Purpose: Create an app that estimates the cost of cab fare in Chicago. The app calculates the cost of the trip and requests a reservation for a smart car, traditional sedan, or minivan.

Algorithms:

1. The app requests the distance in miles for the cab ride and your preference for the requested cab: a smart car, traditional sedan, or minivan. The cab fare has an initial fee of $3.00. A rate of $3.25 per mile is also charged.
2. The app displays the name of a cab company, a logo, and the results of the requested type of cab with the cost of the fare. Create your own layout.

Conditions: Use an image, Spinner prompt, string array, and hint attribute. Decimal mileage is possible.

Case Project 3–5: Split the Bill App (Advanced)

Requirements Document

Application title: Split the Bill App

Purpose: You are out with friends at a nice restaurant. This app splits the bill, including the tip, among the members of your party.

Algorithms:

1. A welcome screen displays the title, an image, and a button that displays a second screen. The input/output screen requests the amount of the restaurant bill and the number of people in your group. The Spinner component asks about the quality of service: Excellent, Average, or Poor.
2. Calculate an 18 percent tip and divide the restaurant bill with the tip included among the members of your party. Display the tip amount and the individual share of the bill.

Conditions: Use an image, Spinner prompt, string array, and hint attribute.

Case Project 3–6: Piggy Bank Children's App (Advanced)

Requirements Document

Application title:	Piggy Bank Children's App
Purpose:	A piggy bank app allows children to enter the number of quarters, dimes, nickels, and pennies that they have. The child can select whether to save the money or spend it. Calculate the amount of money the child has and display the amount that the child is saving or spending. Create two screens: a welcome screen and an input/output screen.
Algorithms:	**1.** A welcome screen displays a title, an image, and a button that takes the user to a second screen. The input/output screen requests the number of quarters, dimes, nickels, and pennies the child has. A Spinner component should indicate whether the child is saving or spending the coins. Create your own layout. **2.** The results display how much the child is saving or spending.
Conditions:	Use an image, Spinner prompt, string array, and hint attribute.

Chapter 4

Explore! Icons and Decision-Making Components

Learning Objectives

At the completion of this chapter, you will be able to:

- **4.1** Create an Android project with a custom icon
- **4.2** Display the Action bar icon using code
- **4.3** Place a RadioGroup and RadioButtons in Android applications
- **4.4** Determine layouts with the layout:margin attributes
- **4.5** Align components using the foregroundGravity attributes
- **4.6** Add a RadioButton Group
- **4.7** Write code for a RadioButton component
- **4.8** Make decisions with conditional statements
- **4.9** Make decisions using an If statement
- **4.10** Make decisions using an If Else statement
- **4.11** Make decisions using logical operators
- **4.12** Display an Android toast notification
- **4.13** Use the isChecked( ) method with RadioButtons
- **4.14** Make decisions using nested If statements

Developers can code Android applications to make decisions based on the input of users or other conditions that occur. Decision making is one of the fundamental activities of a computer application. In this chapter, you learn to write decision-making statements in Java, which allows you to test conditions and perform different operations depending on the results of that test. You can test for a condition being true or false and change the flow of what happens in a program based on the user's input.

4.1 Creating an Android Project with a Custom Icon

An app icon is an important way to distinguish your app. It appears in a number of places in the app, including the Home screen, the All Apps screen, and the Settings app on your smartphone or tablet. The sample program in this chapter is designed to run on an Android phone or a tablet device at a hospital. The Medical Calculator application provides healthcare workers with a mobile way to convert the weight of a patient from pounds to kilograms and from kilograms to pounds. The app is useful because most medication amounts are prescribed based on the weight of the patient. Most hospital scales display weight in pounds, but the prescribed medication is often based on the weight of a patient in kilograms. For safety reasons, the exact weight of the patient must be correctly converted between pounds and kilograms.

In the Medical Calculator app, the doctor or nurse enters the weight of the patient and selects a radio button, as shown in **Figure 4-1**, to determine whether pounds are being converted to kilograms or kilograms are being converted to pounds. The mobile application then computes the converted weight based on two conversion formulas: kilograms = pounds * 2.2 and pounds = kilograms / 2.2. The app also validates that correct weights are entered; if the weight value entered is greater than 500 for the conversion from pounds to kilograms or greater than 225 for the conversion from kilograms to pounds, the user is asked for a valid entry. If the user enters a number outside of the acceptable range, a warning called a toast message appears on the screen.

When the app is running, a nurse might enter 260 as the weight of the patient and select the Convert Pounds to Kilograms radio button shown in Figure 4-1. After the nurse taps the CONVERT WEIGHT button, the application displays 118.2 kilograms (rounded to the nearest tenth place) in a red font, as shown in **Figure 4-2**. By using a mobile device, the nurse can capture patient information directly at the point of care, anywhere and anytime. Healthcare workers can also reduce errors made by delaying data entry on a traditional computer in another location.

Figure 4-1 Opening screen of the Medical Calculator

Figure 4-2 Results screen of the Medical Calculator

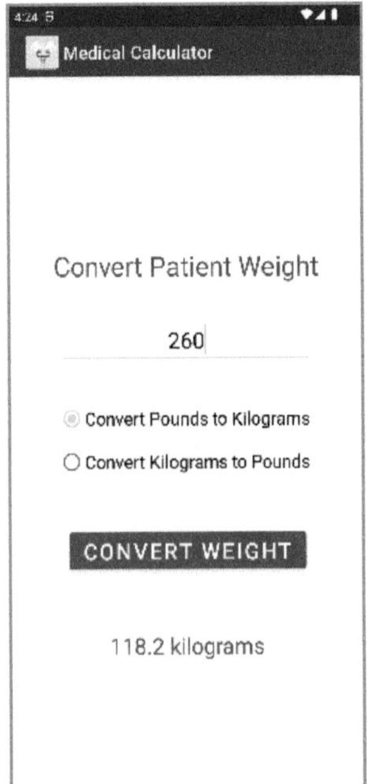

To create this application, the developer must understand how to perform the following processes:

1. Create a customized launcher icon.
2. Use code to add the icon for display in the Action bar.
3. Define a TextField for the user to enter the weight of the patient.

4. Define a RadioGroup to select a conversion of pounds to kilograms or kilograms to pounds.
5. Display a toast message for data validation.
6. Convert data so it can be used for arithmetic operations.
7. Perform arithmetic operations on data the user enters.
8. Display formatted results.

On the Job | Medical device apps are changing the entire patient point-of-care system. Apps now used in hospitals facilitate the mobile use of patient records, drug prescriptions, medical journals, surgical checklists, dosage calculators, radiology imagery, and disease pathology.

Using the Launcher Icon

By default, Android places a standard Android icon as the graphic that represents your application on the device's home screen and in the Launcher window. To view the opening icon, called the **launcher icon**, on the home screen, click the application icon at the bottom of the emulator when an application begins to execute. Instead of a default icon that displays an Android logo, each app published to Google Play should have a custom graphic (**Figure 4-3**) representing the contents of your application. Launcher icons form the first impression of your app to prospective users in Google Play. With so many apps available, a high-quality launcher icon can influence users to purchase your Android app.

Good to Know | You can resize a .png image file in Microsoft Paint or another graphics program to be 48 pixels high by 48 pixels wide.

An icon is a graphic that takes up a small portion of screen space and provides a quick, intuitive representation of an app. As you design a launcher icon, consider that an icon can establish brand identity. A unique image logo and program name can communicate your brand to potential customers. In the Medical Calculator app, the icon shown in Figure 4-3 clearly communicates that the app examines a patient's medical status. A simple image with a clear visual cue like the medical fiducia symbol has a memorable impact. It also helps users find the app on the Google Play site. Google Play suggests that icons should be simple and bold in design. For example, for a paint graphics program, an icon shaped like a thin art paintbrush may be hard to distinguish from a pencil image, but a large cartoon-like paintbrush can convey its purpose easily.

Figure 4-3 Launcher icon for the Medical Calculator app

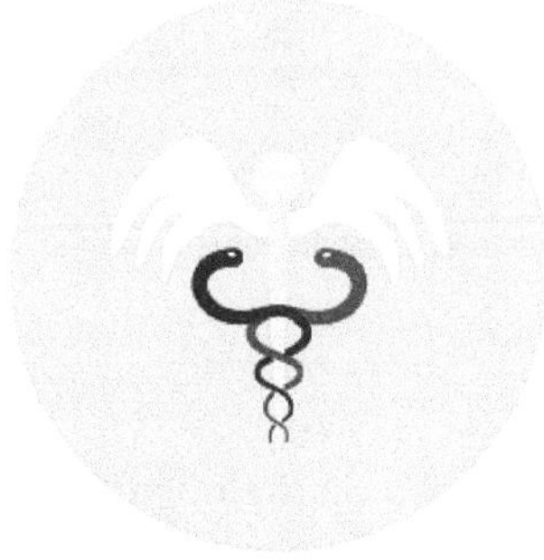

Google Play also specifies the size and format of all launcher icons for uniformity. Launcher icons should be saved with the .png file format or file extension. Based on your target device, **Table 4-1** specifies the size of a finished launcher icon. You can use programs such as Microsoft Paint, Mac Paintbrush, and Adobe Photoshop to resize the icon to the correct number of pixels. In the chapter project, the icon dimensions are 48 × 48 pixels for the high-density screen used by the application, but the Asset Studio within Android Studio can automatically resize icons to the appropriate size necessary for different device platforms.

Table 4-1 Launcher icon sizes

Resolution	Dots Per Inch (dpi)	Size (px)
ldpi (low-density screen)	120	36 × 36
mdpi (medium-density screen)	160	48 × 48
hdpi (high-density screen)	240	72 × 72
xhdpi (extra high-density screen)*	320	96 × 96
xxhdpi (extra extra high-density screen)*	480	144 × 144
xxxhdpi (extra extra extra high-density screen)*	640	192 × 192

*Used by some tablets

Good to Know

When you publish an app to Google Play, you must provide a 512 × 512–pixel, high-resolution application icon in the developer console as you upload your program. This icon is displayed on the Google Play site to provide a description of the app and does not replace your launcher icon. When you use the Image Asset Studio (part of Android Studio), the 512 × 512–pixel image will be created for you.

Google Play recommends a naming convention for launcher icons. Typically, the prefix ic_launcher is used to name launcher icons for Android apps. In the Medical Calculator app, the launcher icon is named medical.png. After a custom icon is placed within the project, Android renames the icon as ic_launcher.png.

Good to Know

Vector-based graphics are best to use for icon design because the images can be scaled without loss of detail and are easily resized.

Quick Check

What is the preferred file extension for a launcher icon?

Answer: .png.

Customizing a Launcher Icon

Instead of using the built-in, generic Android logo icon, you can display a custom launcher icon on the home screen. Android Studio includes a tool called **Image Asset Studio** that helps you generate your own app icons from images. It generates a set of icons at the appropriate resolution for each pixel density that your app supports. The custom icon image can be automatically placed in the res/mipmap folder by adding an image asset using the built-in Image

Asset Studio wizard in Android Studio. The Image Asset Studio creates multiple icons for different screen resolutions and provides a live preview of the resized icons. The Image Asset wizard uploads and replaces the current launcher icon named ic_launcher.png with a custom icon of your choice. To perform the following steps, you need an image file named medical.png, which is provided with your student files, to use as the custom launcher icon for the Medical Calculator app. You should already have the student files for this text, either from your instructor or a download from this book's webpage (*www.cengage.com*). To begin the chapter project, add a customized launcher icon using the Image Asset Studio by following these steps:

Step 1

- Open the Android Studio program.
- In the Welcome to Android Studio window, scroll down and click the New Project button in the Phone and Tablet templates to create a new Android Studio project.
- Click the Next button in the New Project window.
- Type **Medical Calculator** in the Name text box.
- If necessary, select Java in the Language text box.
- If necessary, select API 23: Android 6.0 (Marshmallow) in the Minimum SDK text box.

A new Java Android project named Medical Calculator is configured to save on your local computer (**Figure 4-4**).

Figure 4-4 New Android application named Medical Calculator

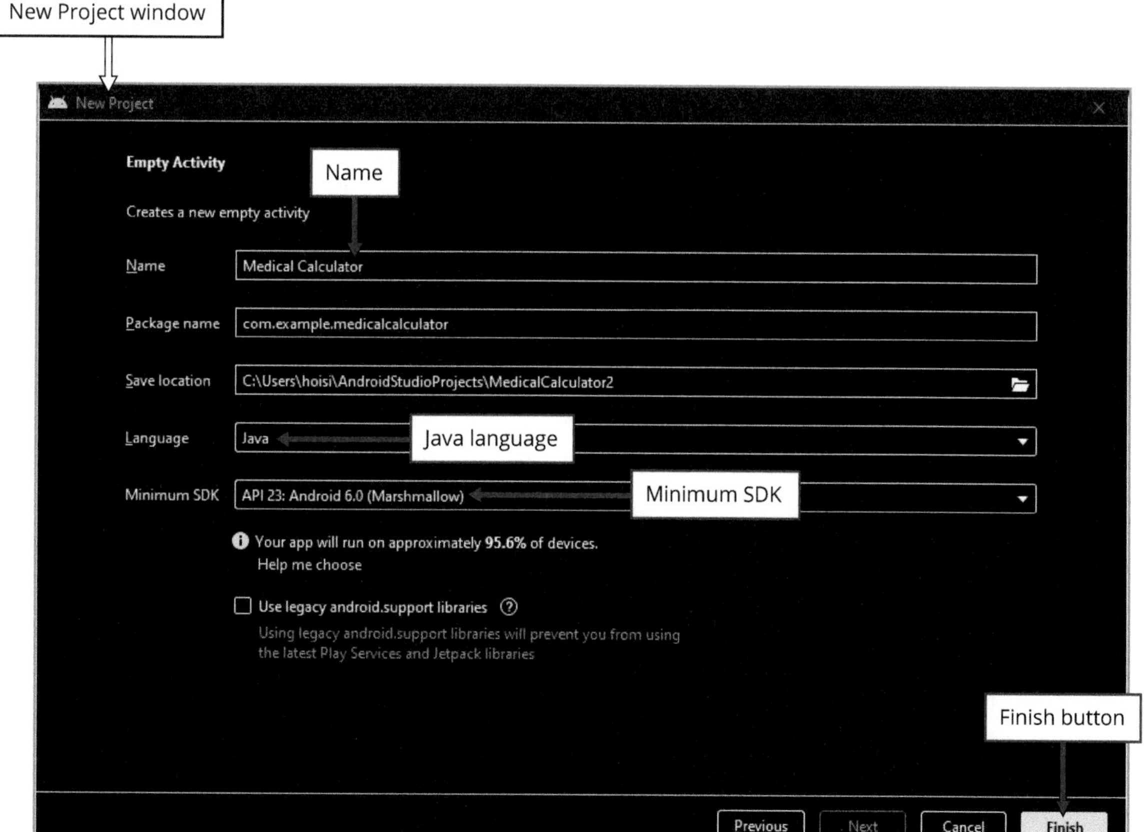

Step 2

- Click the Finish button in the New Project window.
- In the Android Project view, click the activity_main.xml file.
- Click the Hello world! TextView widget displayed by default in the emulator and press the Delete key.
- Click File on the menu bar and then click New.

The New menu opens in Android Studio (**Figure 4-5**).

Figure 4-5 New menu

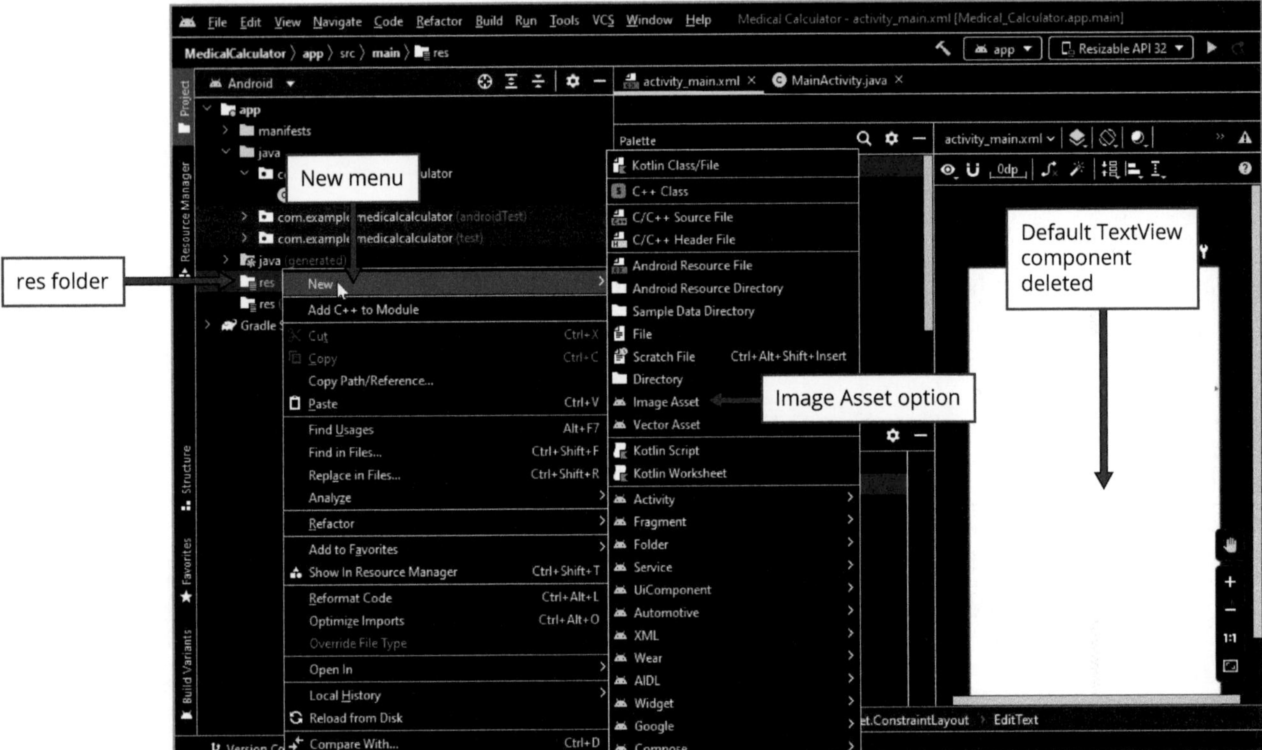

Step 3

- Click Image Asset on the New menu.

The Asset Studio dialog box opens to display the default launcher icons for the resolutions of various devices (**Figure 4-6**).

Step 4

- Click the folder symbol in the Path box to open the Select Path dialog box.
- To add the custom launcher icon, copy the student files to your computer (if necessary). Open the folder that contains the student files, then locate and select the file medical.png.
- In the Select Path dialog box, navigate to the location of the medical.png file, and then select the file.
- Click the OK button to add the custom launcher icon.

The custom launcher icon of a medical symbol is displayed in different sizes in the Asset Studio dialog box. The icon's background is removed (**Figure 4-7**). The Asset Studio replaces the current ic_launcher icon with the updated scale icon automatically.

Figure 4-6 Default launcher icons in the Asset Studio

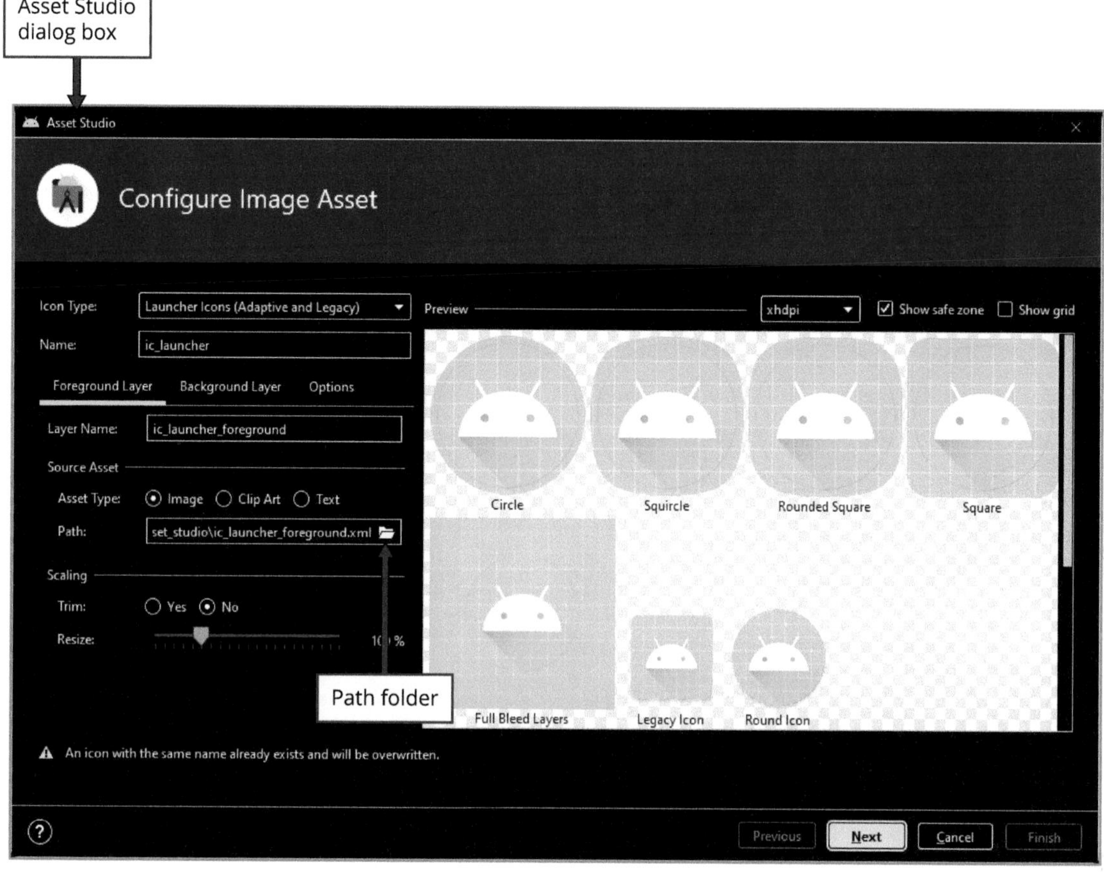

Figure 4-7 Custom launcher icons

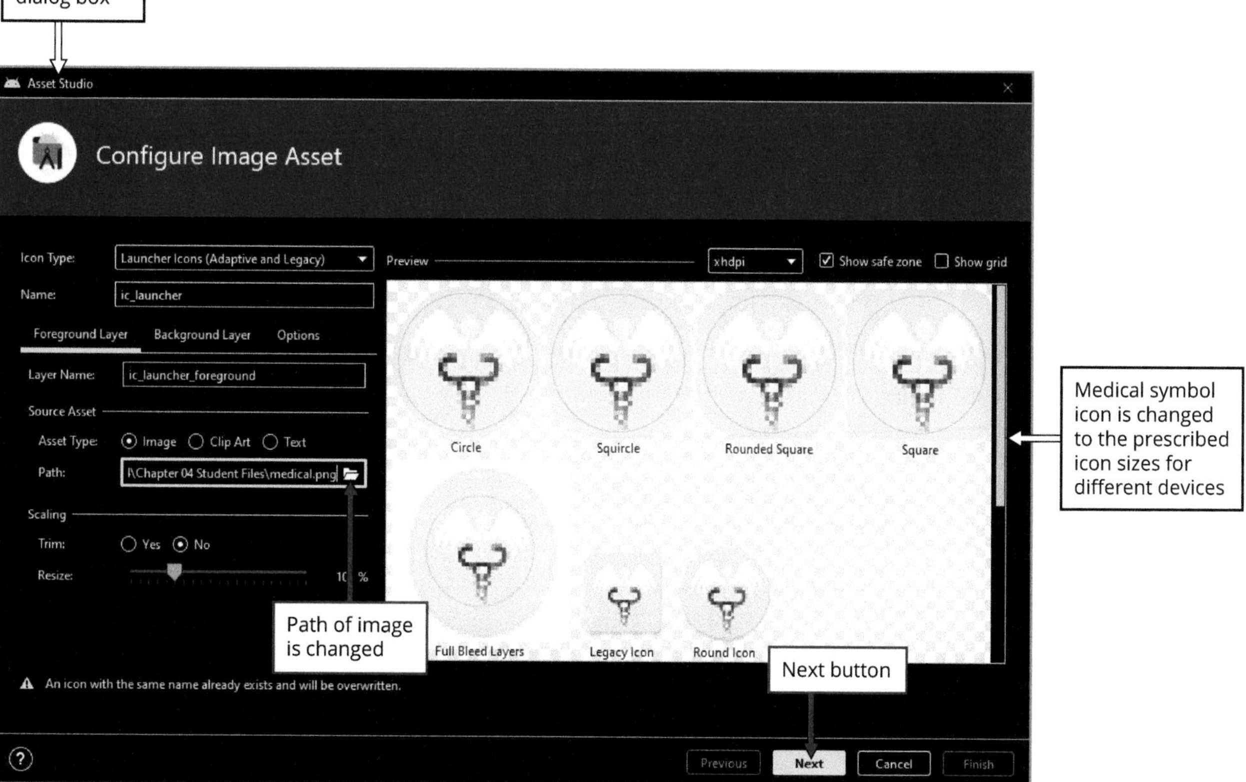

Step 5

- Click the Next button.

The launcher icon is also resized to 512 × 512 pixels for the Google Play Store. The resized launcher icons will replace the standard Android icon in the appropriate mipmap folders based on their size and resolution (**Figure 4-8**).

Figure 4-8 Confirmed icon path in Asset Studio displayed in res/mipmap folders

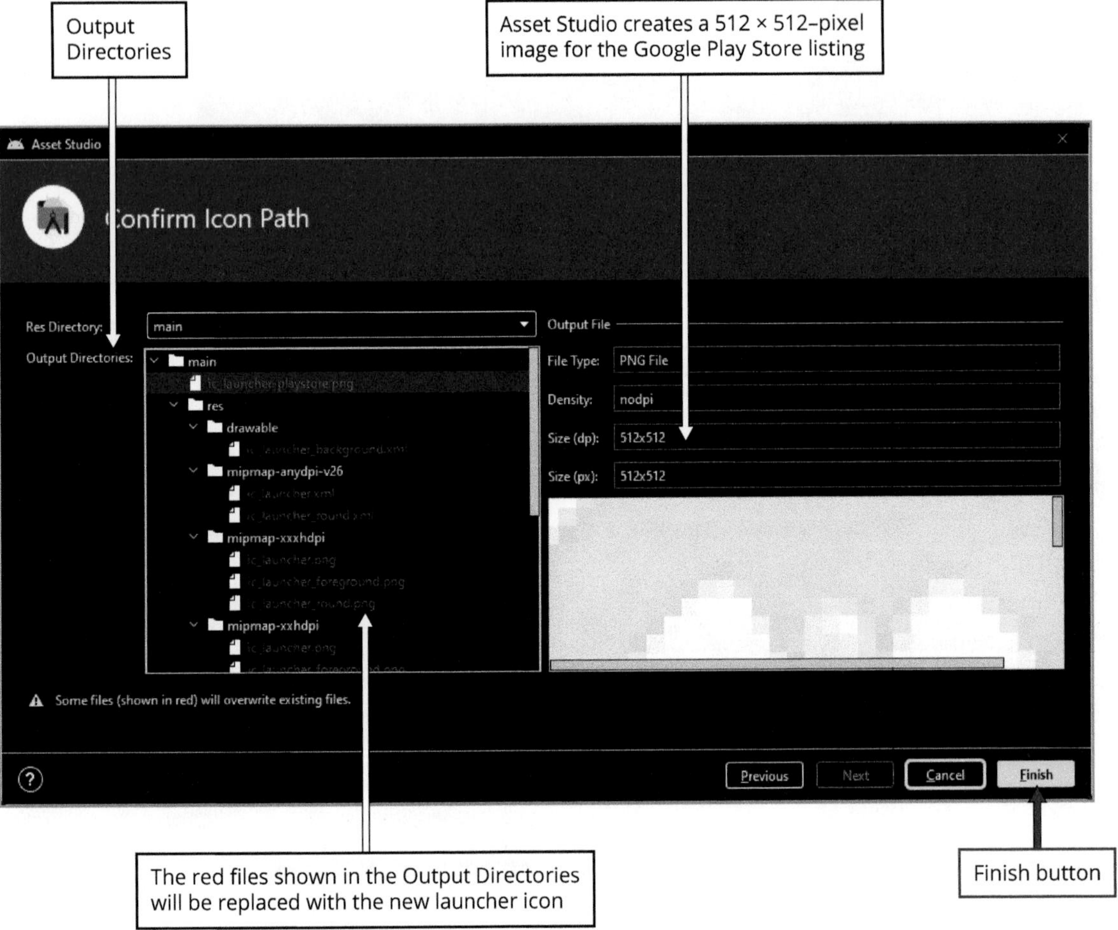

Step 6

- Click the Finish button.
- Expand the res folder.
- Expand the mipmap folder.
- Expand the ic_launcher (5) folder.
- Double-click ic_launcher.png (xxxhdpi).

Android Studio displays the new ic_launcher app image (**Figure 4-9**). If you execute the app at this point, the new ic_launcher icon does not appear in the Action bar.

Figure 4-9 Resized custom icons and their pathways in the mipmap folder

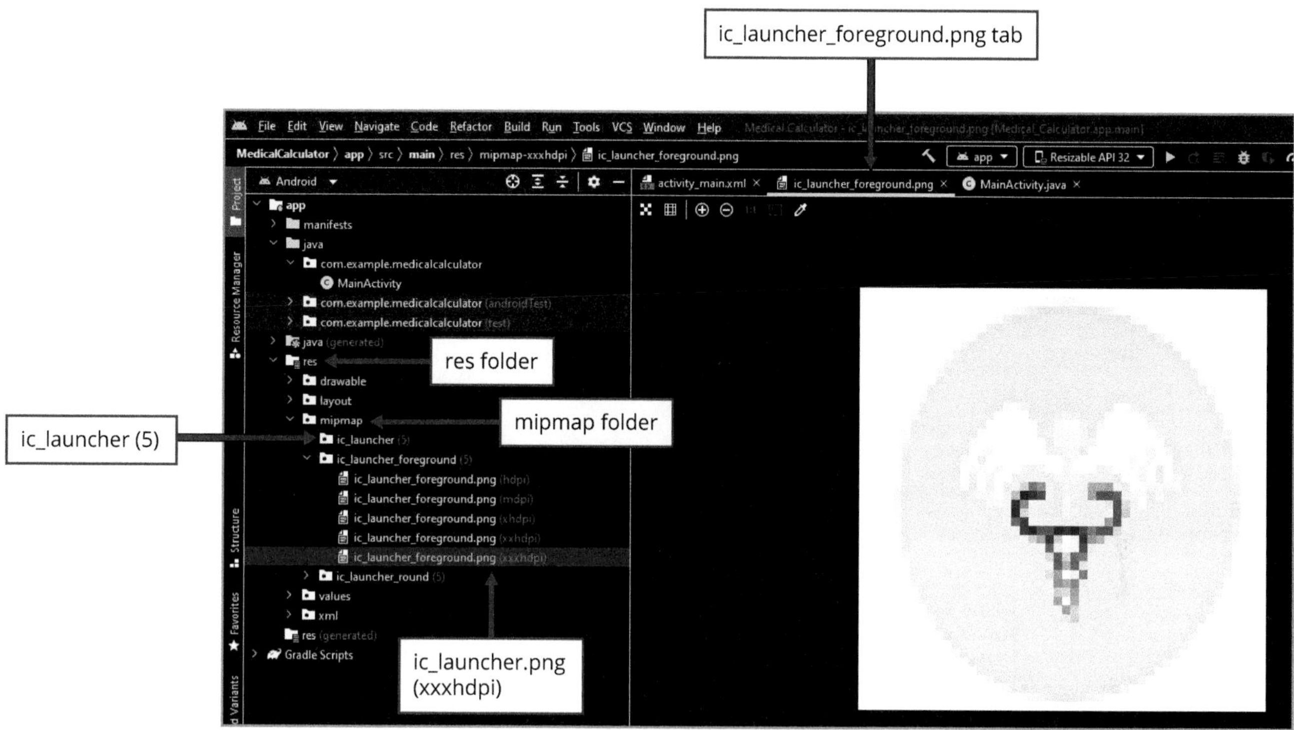

Step 7

- Close the ic_launcher.png tab and click the Save All button.

4.2 Displaying the Action Bar Icon Using Code

The Medical Calculator app has replaced the ic_launcher icon with the medical image, but without supporting code, the image will not appear in the Action bar when you run the completed app. An **Action bar icon** is considered a **logo** that represents the program's function; for example, the medical symbol conveys the purpose and identity of the app. To display the Action bar logo in the completed app, follow these steps:

Step 1

- In the Android project view, if necessary, expand the java folder and the first com.example.medicalcalculator folder and then double-click MainActivity to open the code window.
- Click at the end of Line 12 (setContentView), press Enter, and type the following three statements to display the logo in the Action bar:

  getSupportActionBar().setDisplayShowHomeEnabled(true);

  getSupportActionBar().setLogo(R.mipmap.ic_launcher);

  getSupportActionBar().setDisplayUseLogoEnabled(true);

MainActivity.java has three new statements to display the logo named ic_launcher that was placed in the mipmap folder (**Figure 4-10**). Line 14 displays a miniature logo image near the line number.

Figure 4-10 Action bar displays icon launcher in activity_main.xml

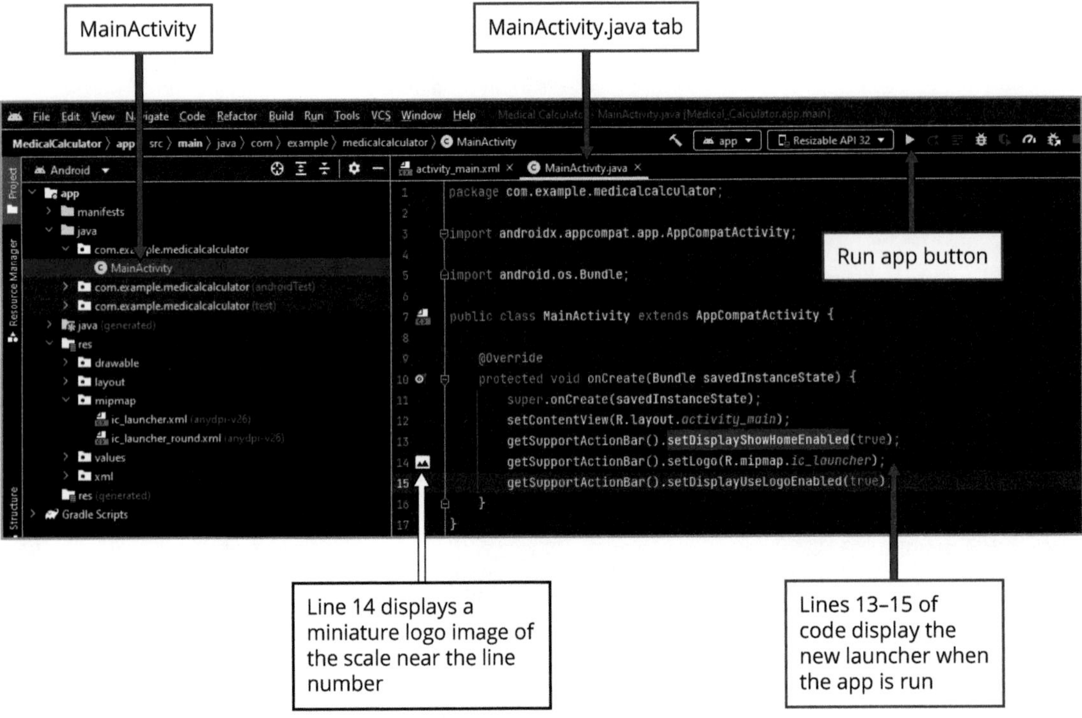
MainActivity
MainActivity.java tab
Run app button
Line 14 displays a miniature logo image of the scale near the line number
Lines 13–15 of code display the new launcher when the app is run

Step 2

- To view the new launcher icon, click Run app on the Standard toolbar and then allow the emulator to load.

The emulator displays the Action bar at the top of the app. The new launcher icon of the medical symbol is placed before the app name (**Figure 4-11**).

Figure 4-11 Icon displayed in running app in the emulator

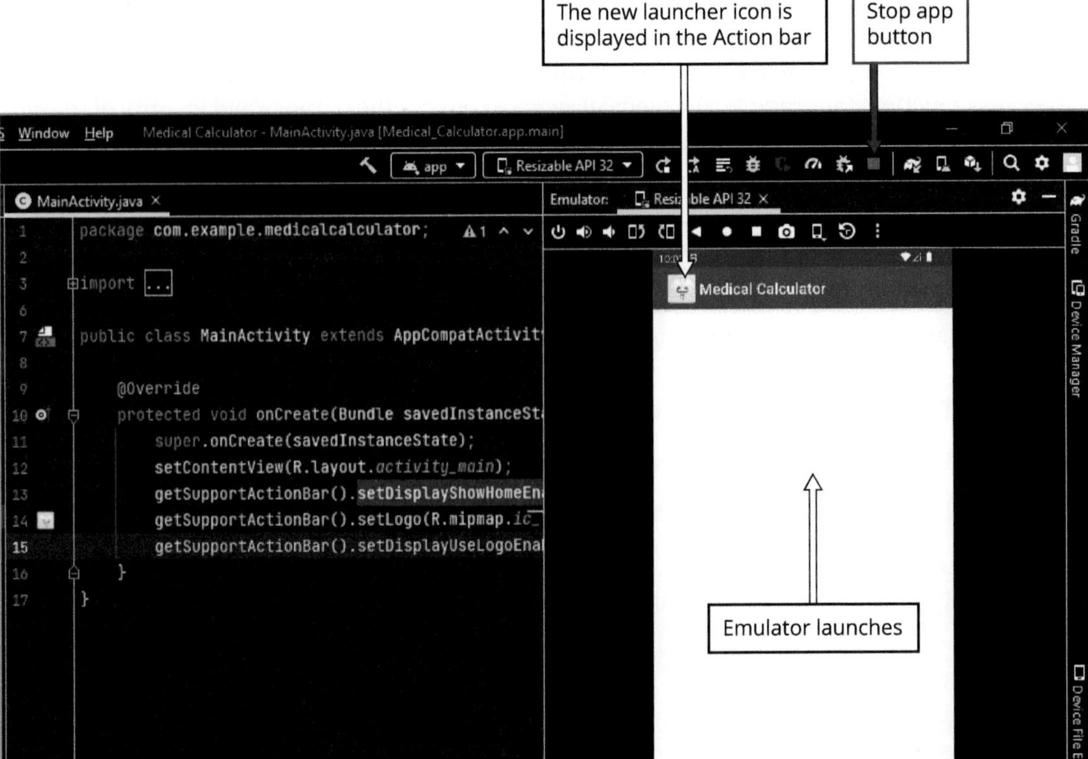
The new launcher icon is displayed in the Action bar
Stop app button
Medical Calculator
Emulator launches

Step 3

- Click the Stop app button and minimize the emulator that launched.

The app stops running and the emulator is closed.

Good to Know Google provides an Android Asset Studio that allows you to generate your own custom launcher icons for apps using Creative Commons images. The images are available at *http://romannurik.github.io/AndroidAssetStudio*.

String Table

In the Medical Calculator app, the String resources are stored within the /res/values/strings.xml file of the resource hierarchy. These resources are for the text displayed in the TextView, RadioButton, EditText, and Button components. Any strings you add to the strings.xml file are accessible within your application. In the following steps, you insert the string names and values shown in **Table 4-2**.

Table 4-2 String names and values to add

String Name	String Value
hint	Weight of Patient
rbLbToKilo	Convert Pounds to Kilograms
rbKiloToLb	Convert Kilograms to Pounds
btConvert	CONVERT WEIGHT

To begin the design of the Android user interface and create the String table, follow this step:

Step 1

- In the Android project view, open the strings.xml file in the res/values folder.
- Click the Open editor link.
- Click the Add Key (plus sign) button in the Translations Editor.
- In the Key text box, type **tvTitle** to name the string for the TextView component.
- In the Default Value text box, type **Convert Patient Weight** to define the text to display and then click the OK button.
- Click the Add Key button again and repeat the same process to add the remaining items listed in Table 4-2.
- Click the Reload string resources button to reload the list of strings.

The strings.xml file is populated with the text used in the app (**Figure 4-12**).

Figure 4-12 Translations Editor with new strings in the String table

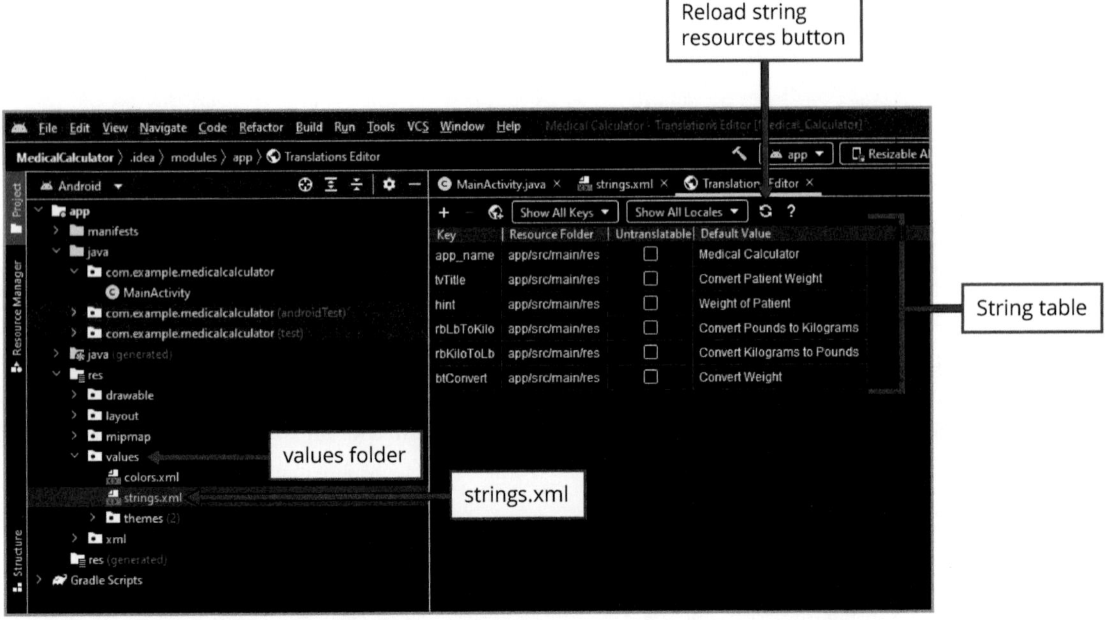

4.3 Placing a RadioGroup and RadioButtons in Android Applications

RadioButton components are used to select or deselect an option. In the chapter project, radio buttons are used to select which mathematical conversion is needed—pounds to kilograms or vice versa. When RadioButtons are placed on the emulator, each component is arranged vertically by default. If you prefer the RadioButton components to be listed horizontally, you can set the orientation attribute to horizontal. Each RadioButton component has a label defined by the Text attribute and a Checked attribute set to either true or false. RadioButton components are typically used together in a **RadioGroup** container. Checking one radio button unchecks the other radio buttons within the group. In other words, within a RadioGroup component, only one RadioButton component can be selected at a time.

When the RadioGroup container component is placed in the emulator window from the Buttons category in the Palette, three RadioButton components are included in the group by default. If you need additional RadioButton components, drag them from the Palette in the Buttons category into the group. In the case of the Medical Calculator app, two radio buttons are needed for converting from pounds to kilograms or from kilograms to pounds. To make the user's input as simple as possible, offer a default selection. For example, nurses more often convert weight from pounds to kilograms, so that RadioButton option should be checked initially. The Checked attribute of this RadioButton component is set to true to provide a default selection. You do not have to provide a default selection, but if one of the options is more common, it saves the user a step of having to select a RadioButton component.

Good to Know

Like RadioButton components, a CheckBox component allows a user to check or uncheck a listing. A user may select any number of check boxes, including zero or one. In other words, each check box is independent of all other check boxes in the list, so checking one box does not uncheck the others. The shape of a radio button is circular and a check box is square.

Changing the Text Color of RadioButton and CheckBox Components

Thus far, each application in this text has changed some of the text colors of the app's Android components. The Android platform uses a color system called hexadecimal color codes to display different colors. A **hexadecimal color code** is a triplet of three colors. Colors are specified by a pound sign followed by the amount of red, green, and blue contained in the final color. Each of the three colors in the code is represented by two characters on the hexadecimal scale of 00 to FF. For example, the hexadecimal color of #FF0000 is a true red. The TextView and Button components displayed in the chapter project are red, which you designate by typing #FF0000 as the textColor or backgroundTint attribute. To look up these color codes, search for hexadecimal color codes in a search engine or refer to *http://html-color-codes.com*. On the Color tab, you can select any color within the circle, enter RGB (Red, Green, Blue) values, or enter hexadecimal color values.

Critical Thinking

I noticed that the Color Resource dialog box has RBG text boxes. How do I locate a color using RGB coding?

A site such as https://rgbcolorcode.com/ can provide a list of all the possible color codes using RGB coding.

4.4 Determining Layouts with the layout:margin Attributes

After placing a component on the user interface, you can change the alignment by adjusting the component's **Gravity** settings. For more flexibility in deciding your layout, use the **layout:margin** attribute to set the spacing around each object by changing all the margins equally or changing the left, top, right, and bottom margins individually. Each component in the Medical Calculator app has adjustable margins you can use to add a certain amount of blank space on each of its four sides. This spacing is measured in density-independent pixels (dp); density refers to the physical density of the screen. Instead of "eyeballing" components on the user interface for alignment, you can use the layout:margin attribute to create equal spacing around components. Using the layout:margin attribute helps organize your user interface and ultimately makes it easier to use. For example, in Figure 4-14, a margin spacing of 15dp (pixels) for the layout_marginTop attribute specifies 15 extra pixels on the top side of the selected TextView component that displays the title. These dp units are relative to a 160-dpi screen, so one dp is one pixel on a 160-dpi screen. As you design the user interface, specify the same margins around each component to provide a symmetrical layout.

4.5 Aligning Components Using the foregroundGravity Attributes

The Medical Calculator app displays components from the Palette with a ConstraintLayout. At times, you may find that the emulator displays a component in a different location than where you placed it on the screen. The layout can be set for each component using an attribute named foregroundGravity to center the component horizontally as well as position it at other locations on the screen. After each component is placed on the emulator, a toolbar appears above the emulator screen. The gravity can be changed using the Attributes pane or with a shortcut on the toolbar [0dp]. The foregroundGravity tool shown in **Figure 4-13** changes the linear alignment to center the hint in the Text Number component. Layout gravity is similar to the alignment feature in Microsoft Office that allows a component to snap to the left, center, right, top, or bottom. The foregroundGravity attribute in the Attributes pane provides additional options, such as fill_horizontal, top, left, bottom, center_vertical, fill_vertical, clip_vertical, clip_horizontal, and fill.

Figure 4-13 The foregroundGravity attribute to center hint text with the center_horizontal option

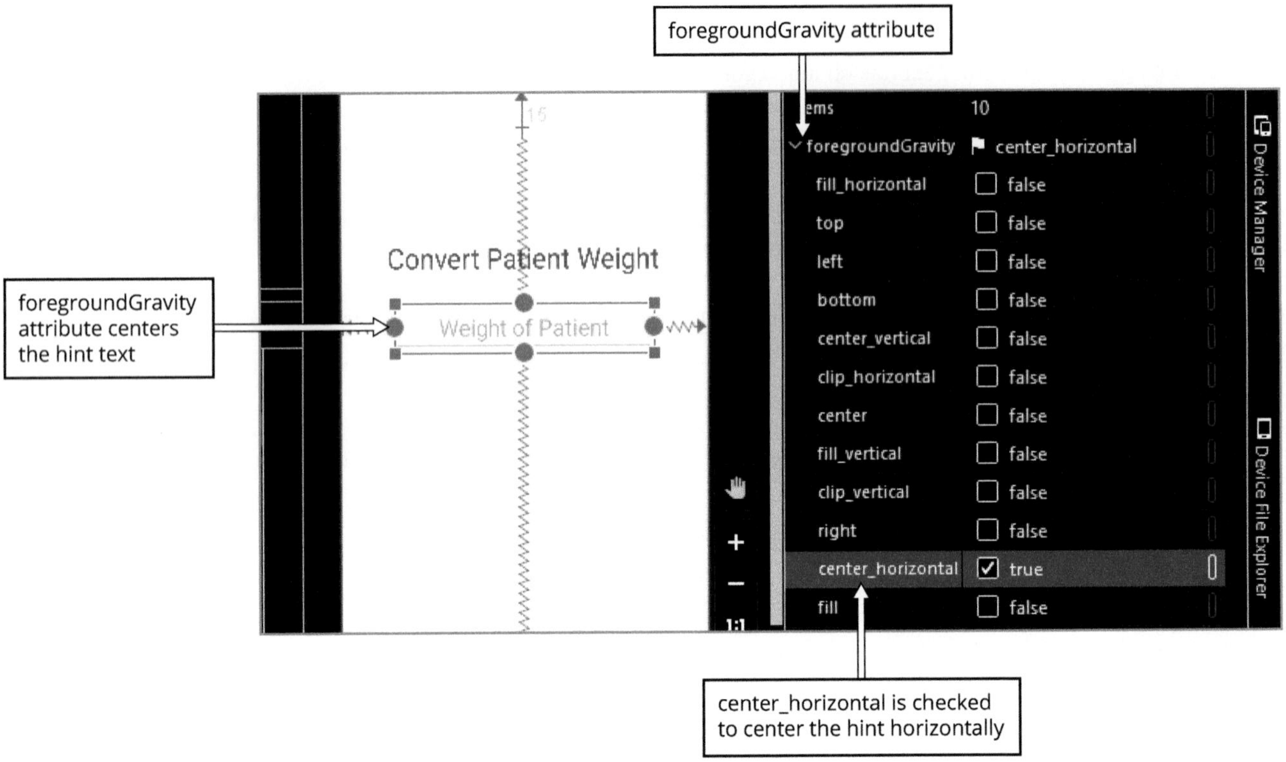

4.6 Adding the RadioButton Group and Other Components

Earlier, you created a strings.xml file to hold the text used within the app. The app uses the text in the String table to assign the TextView title, the hint attribute of the EditText component, the text on both RadioButton components, and the Button component text. After creating the strings.xml file, you can add components to the user interface. The Medical Calculator app displays a TextView component, Text Number field, and RadioGroup component, all centered horizontally. The TextView and RadioGroup components use the text color of gray. To name a RadioButton component, use the id attribute in the Attributes pane; enter a name that begins with the prefix *rb*, which represents a radio button in the code. To name a RadioGroup component, again use the id attribute in the Attributes pane; enter a name that begins with the prefix *rg*, which represents a radio group in the code. The hint text color within the Text Number Component can be changed using the textColorHint attribute. To add TextView, Text Number, and RadioGroup components to the Medical Calculator app, follow these steps:

Step 1

- Click the Save All button on the toolbar.
- Close the Translations Editor tab and the strings.xml tab.
- With activity_main.xml open and displaying the emulator screen, drag and drop the TextView component onto the top part of the emulator.
- Drag the top Constraint handle of the TextView component to the top of the emulator screen and release the mouse.
- Drag the bottom Constraint handle of the TextView component to the bottom of the emulator screen and release the mouse. You should now have all four constraints anchored to the edge of the screen; blue curly arrows should touch the top, bottom, left, and right sides of the emulator.
- Click in the id component, name the TextView component **tvTitle**, and click the Refactor button.

- Click the Pick a Resource rectangle in the text attribute, click tvTitle in the Pick a Resource dialog box to select the assigned string, and then click the OK button.
- Change the textSize attribute to **30sp**.
- Click the textColor attribute, type **#FF0000** in the Hex box, and then press Enter to change the text color to red. Click on the back of the emulator to see the app title change to red.
- Expand the layout:margin attribute by clicking the arrow preceding the attribute.
- In the layout_marginTop attribute, enter **15dp** and press the Enter key to place 15 pixels of space above the component.

The layout_marginTop attribute is displayed with 15dp entered. The TextView component is added to the form with the text, size, text color, and margin changed (**Figure 4-14**).

Figure 4-14 Title TextView component and layout_marginTop attribute

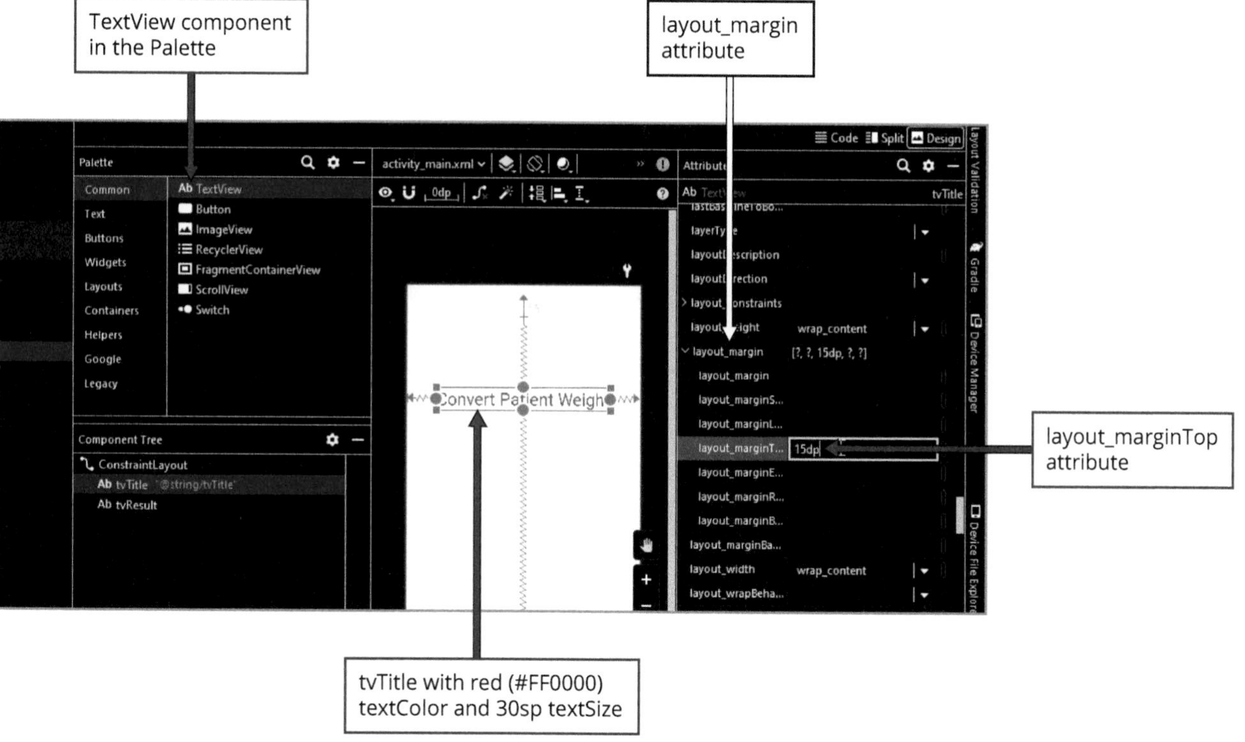

Step 2

- To add the Text Number component, click the Text category in the Palette.
- Drag and drop the Text Number component into the center of the emulator below the TextView component.
- Drag the top Constraint handle of the Text Number component to the top of the emulator screen and release the mouse.
- Drag the bottom Constraint handle of the Text Number component to the bottom of the emulator screen and release the mouse. You should now have all four constraints anchored to the edge of the screen; blue curly arrows should touch the top, bottom, left, and right sides of the emulator.
- Change the id attribute to the name **tvWeight** and click the Refactor button.
- Click the Pick a Resource rectangle button in the hint attribute of the Attributes pane.
- Click "hint" in the Pick a Resource dialog box to select the assigned string and then click the OK button to display the hint.

- Change the textSize attribute to **25sp**.
- Change the textColorHint attribute to #78909C in the Attributes pane of the Text number component.
- To fix the Autofill warning, click the warning badge in the Component Tree next to tvWeight and click the Fix button for Set autoFillHints.
- Expand the foregroundGravity attribute and then select center_horizontal to center the hint within the component.
- In the layout:margin attribute, click to the right of the layout_marginTop attribute, enter **15dp**, and press Enter to place 15 pixels of space between the tvTitle TextView component and the Text Number component.

A Text Number component is placed on the emulator with the id, text size, text hint, gravity, and margins changed (**Figure 4-15**).

Figure 4-15 Text Number component and foregroundGravity attribute to center hint text

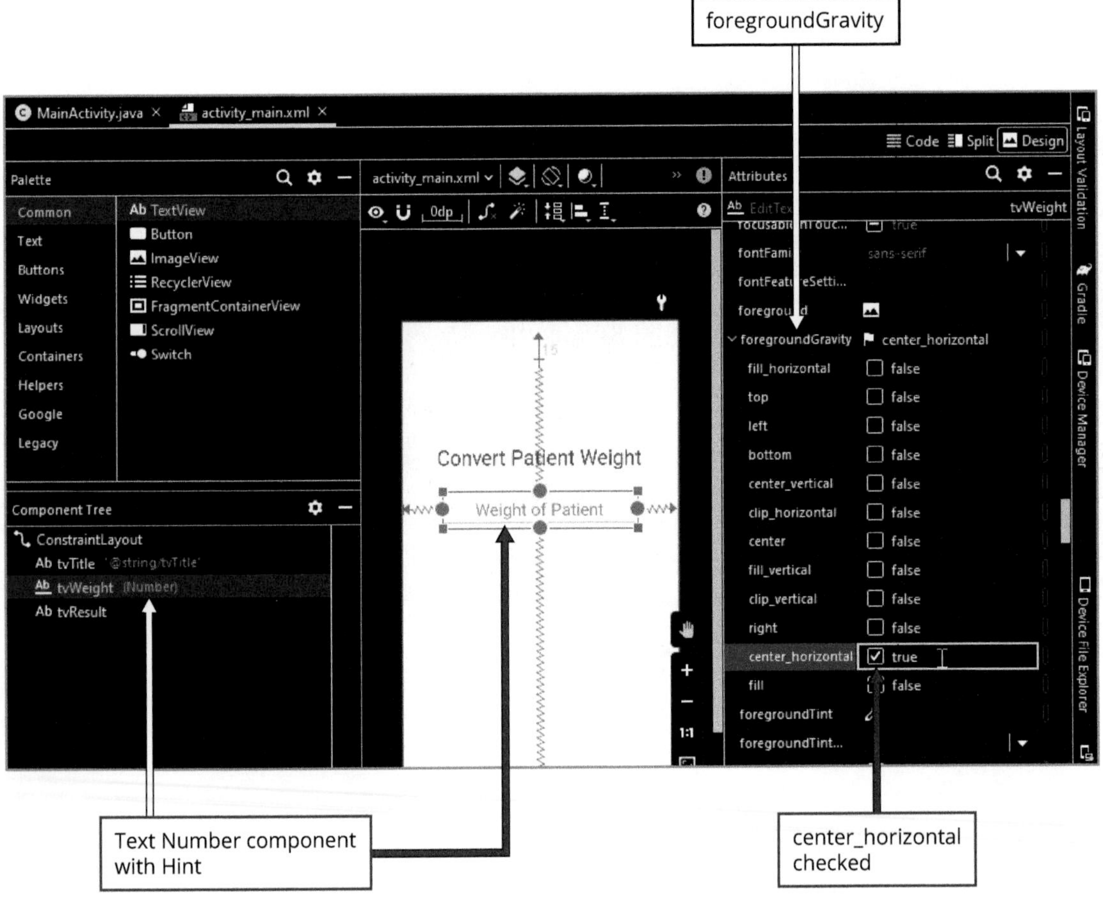

Critical Thinking

Why did I originally get a warning before I changed the textColorHint attribute?

The textColorHint attribute in the Text Number component's Attributes pane allows you to change the hint color. It must have enough contrast with your current background.

Step 3

- In the Palette, click the Buttons category, select the Button named RadioGroup, and then drag and drop the RadioGroup component onto the user interface below the Text Number component.

- Drag the top Constraint handle of the RadioGroup component to the top of the emulator screen and release the mouse.
- Drag the bottom Constraint handle of the RadioGroup component to the bottom of the emulator screen and release the mouse. You should now have all four constraints anchored to the edge of the screen; blue curly arrows should touch the top, bottom, left, and right sides of the emulator.
- Change the layout_width attribute to 300dp to resize the RadioGroup component to 300 pixels wide.
- Change the layout_height attribute to 100dp to resize the RadioGroup component to 100 pixels tall.
- Change the id attribute of the RadioGroup component to **rgWeight**.

The RadioGroup component is placed on the emulator with an id (**Figure 4-16**).

Figure 4-16 RadioGroup component

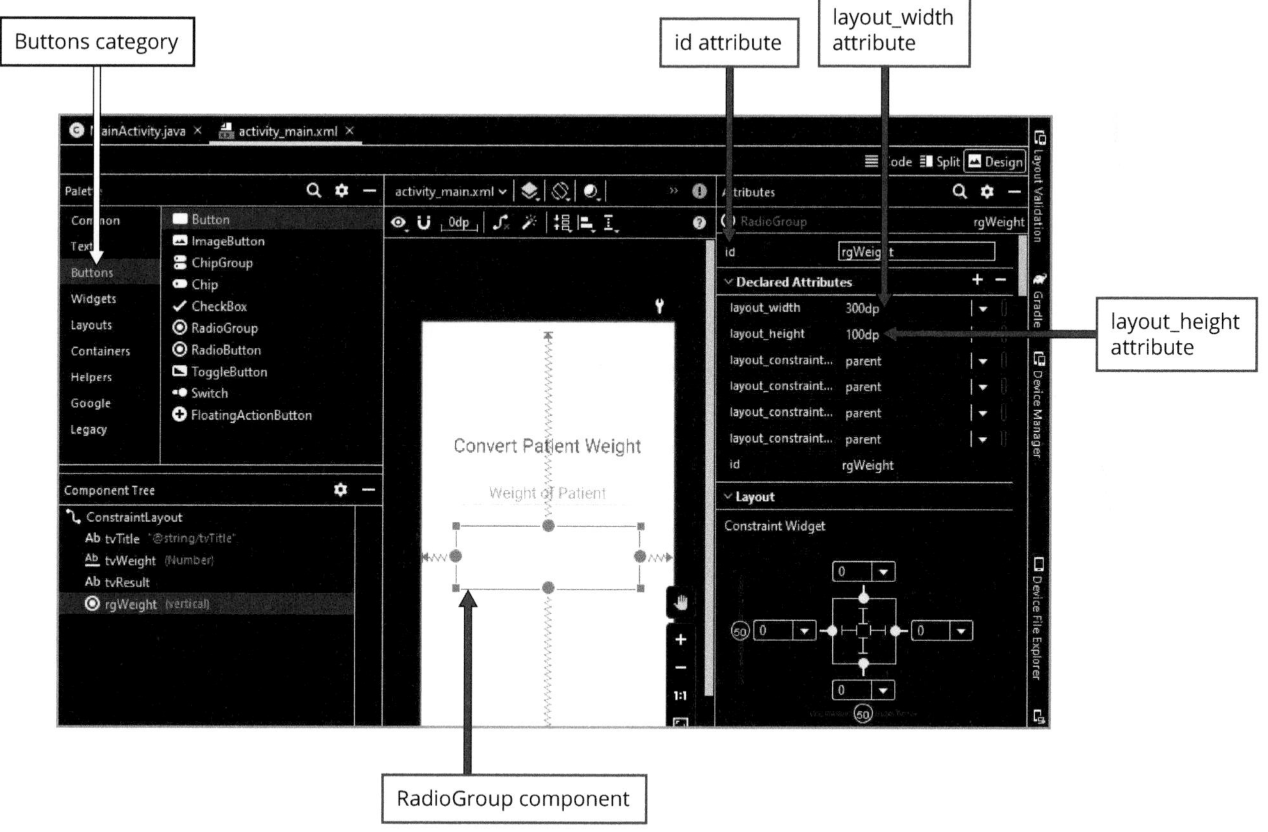

Step 4

- Two radio buttons are needed for this app, so click the RadioButton component in the Buttons category and then drag and drop two radio buttons inside the RadioGroup component.
- Change the id attribute of the first RadioButton component to **rbLbToKilo** and click the Refactor button.
- Click the Pick a Resource rectangle button in the text attribute, click rbLbToKilo in the Pick a Resource dialog box to select the assigned string, and then click the OK button.
- Change the textSize attribute to **20sp**.
- Click the checked attribute to True to indicate that the first radio button is the default selection.

Two RadioButton components are placed on the emulator; the first RadioButton has an id, text, and textSize. The checked attribute of the first RadioButton is set to True as the default selection (**Figure 4-17**).

Figure 4-17 Two RadioButton components with first RadioButton checked

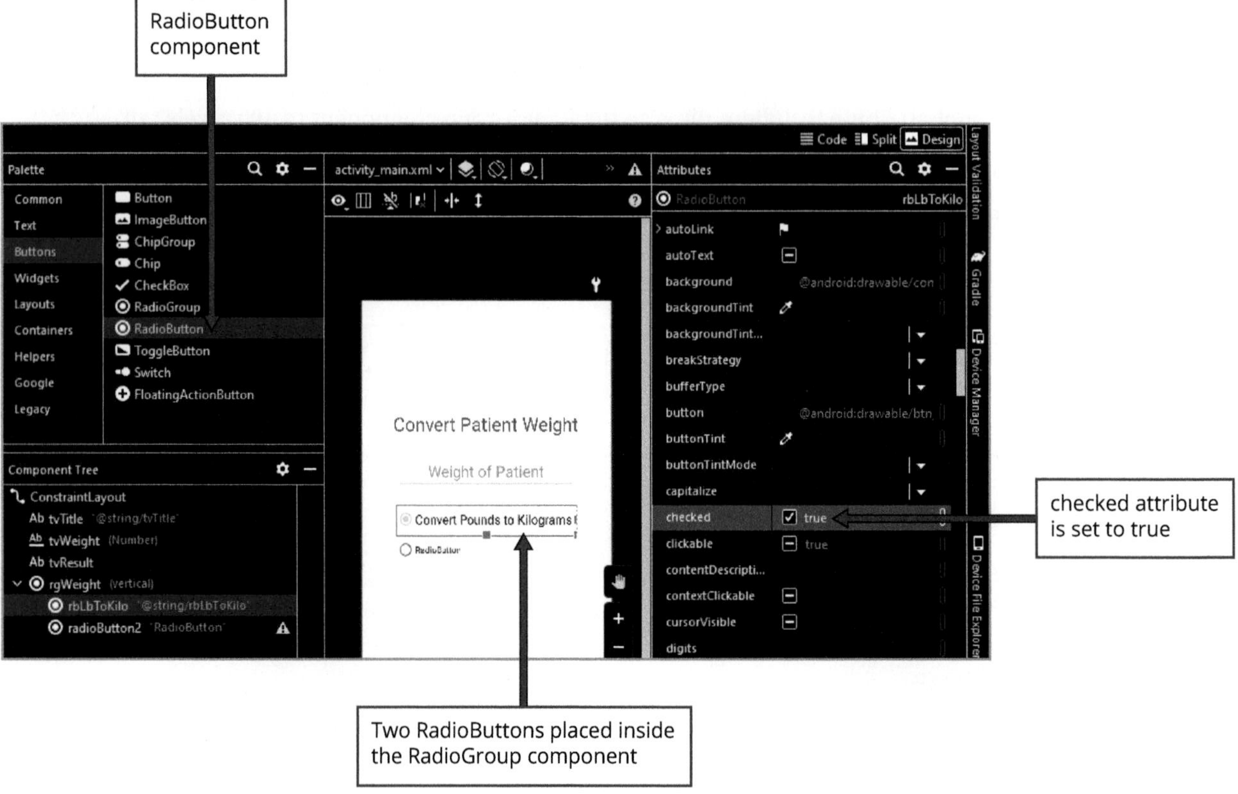

Step 5

- Click the second RadioButton component, change the id attribute to **rbKiloToLb**, and click the Refactor button.
- Click the Pick a Resource rectangle button in the text attribute, click rbKiloToLb in the Pick a Resource dialog box to select the assigned string, and then click the OK button.
- Change the textSize attribute to **20sp**.

The second RadioButton component has id, text, and textSize attributes (**Figure 4-18**).

Completing the User Interface

As you design the Android interface, it is important to have a clean layout and use the entire screen effectively. To complete the user interface by adding Button and TextView components and then coding them, follow these steps:

Step 1

- In the activity_main.xml tab, drag the Button component in the Buttons category from the Palette to the emulator below the RadioGroup component.
- Drag the top Constraint handle of the Button component to the top of the emulator screen and release the mouse.
- Drag the bottom Constraint handle of the Button component to the bottom of the emulator screen and release the mouse. You should now have all four constraints anchored to the edge of the screen; blue curly arrows should touch the top, bottom, left, and right sides of the emulator.
- Change the id attribute of the Button component to **btConvert** and click the Refactor button.
- Click the Pick a Resource rectangle button in the text attribute of the Attributes pane.

Figure 4-18 Second RadioButton component

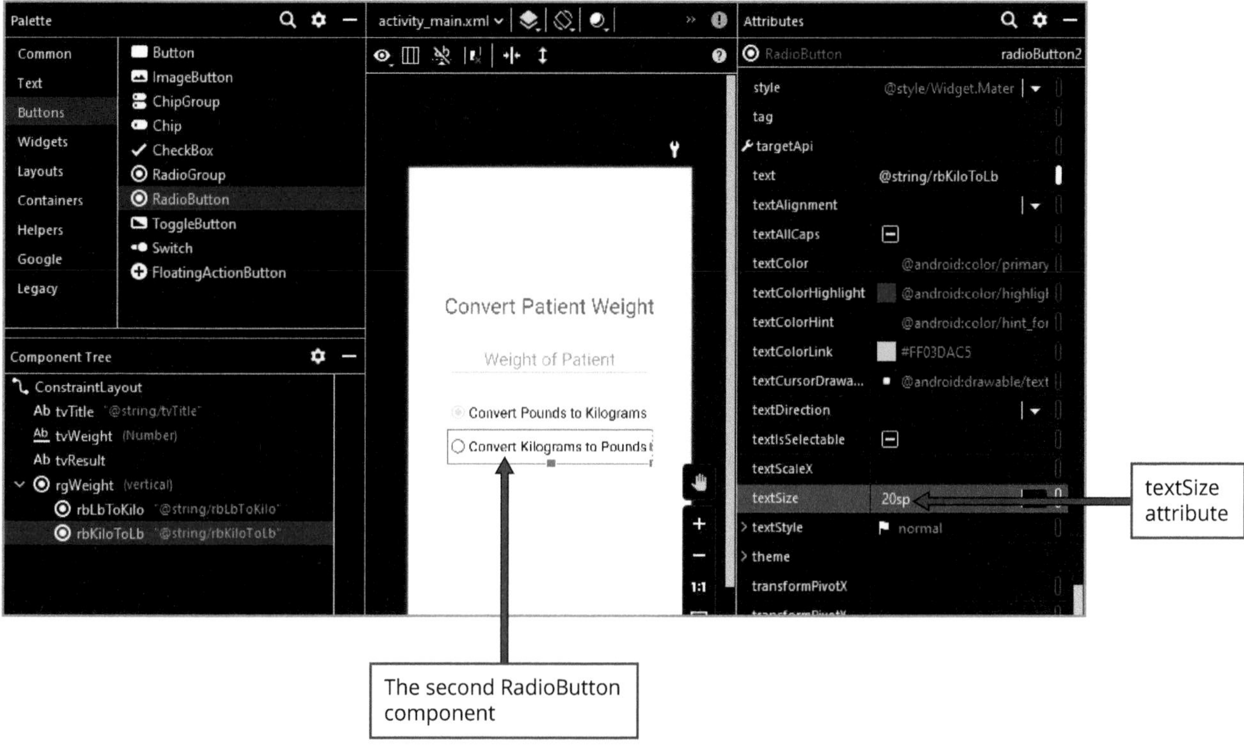

- Click btConvert in the Pick a Resource dialog box to select the assigned string and then click the OK button to display the text.
- Change the textSize attribute to **25sp**.
- Change the backgroundTint attribute to the hexadecimal value of **#FF0000** (red).
- In the gravity attribute, click **center_horizontal** to center the component.
- In the layout_marginTop attribute, type **15dp** to place 15 pixels of space above the component.

The Button component named btConvert displays the text CONVERT WEIGHT and its id, text size, gravity, and margins are changed (**Figure 4-19**).

Figure 4-19 Button component

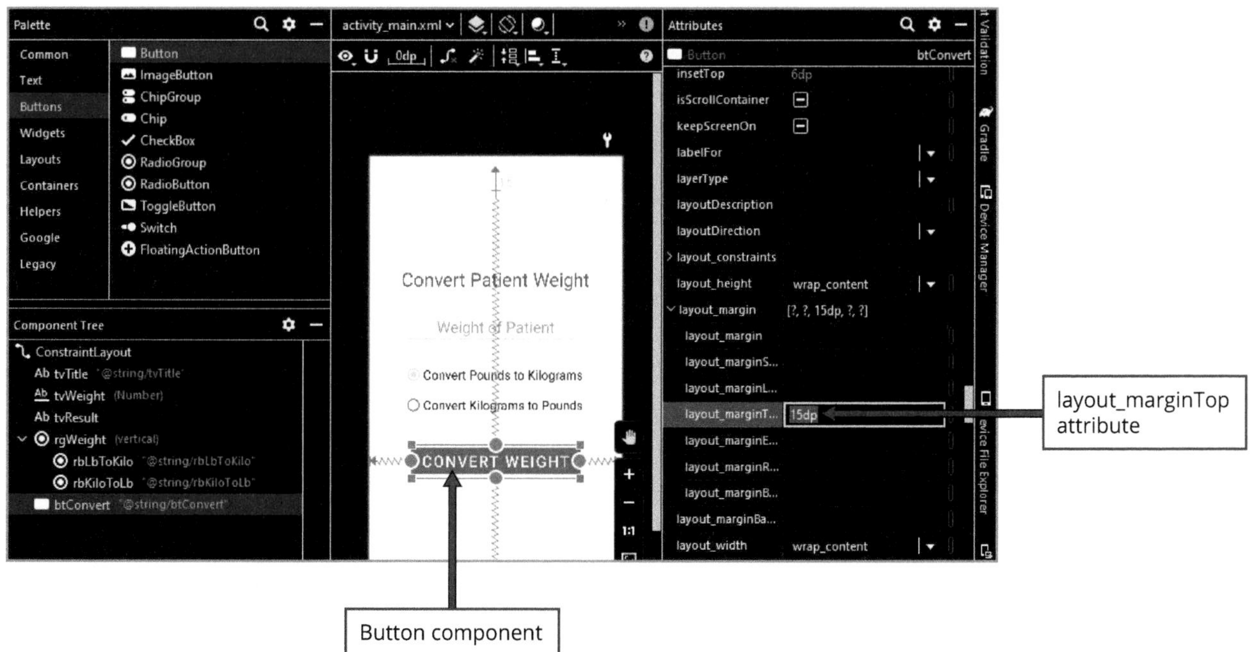

Step 2

- Drag another TextView component from the Text category of the Palette to the emulator below the Button.
- Change the id attribute of the TextView component to **tvResult** and click the Refactor button.
- Drag the top Constraint handle of the TextView component to the top of the emulator screen and release the mouse.
- Drag the bottom Constraint handle of the TextView component to the bottom of the emulator screen and release the mouse. You should now have all four constraints anchored to the edge of the screen; blue curly arrows should touch the top, bottom, left, and right sides of the emulator.
- Delete the text in the text attribute.
- Change the textSize attribute to **25sp**.
- For the textColor attribute, enter **#FF0000** (red).
- In the layout_marginTop attribute, enter **25dp** to place 25 pixels of space above the component.
- Click the Save All button on the Standard toolbar.

The TextView component is placed on the emulator with an empty text attribute (**Figure 4-20**).

Figure 4-20 TextView component to display results

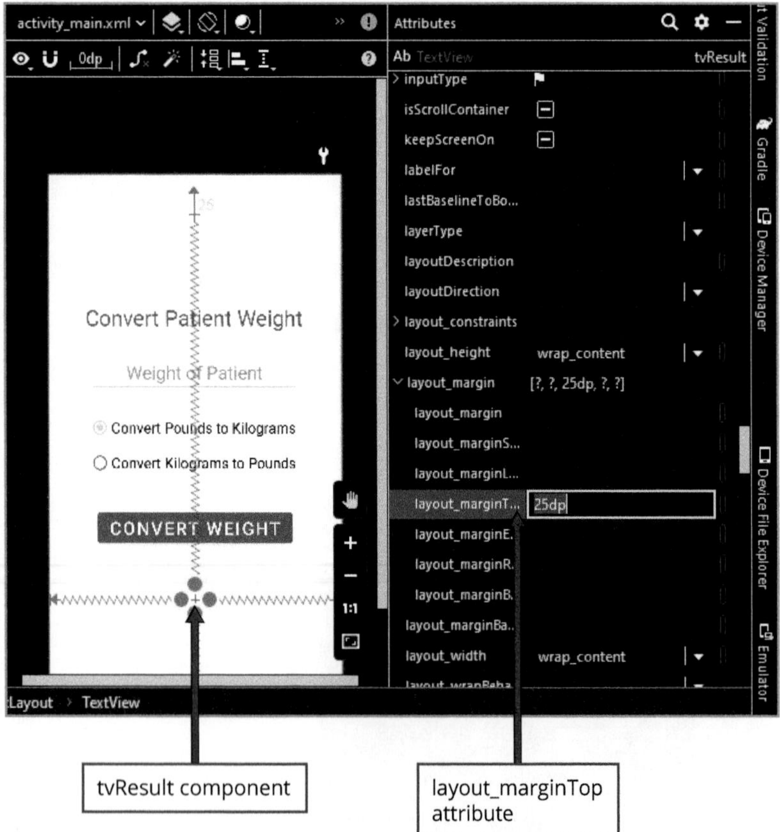

4.7 Coding a RadioButton Component

Each of the RadioButton components placed on the emulator needs to be referenced by using the findViewById Java command. In the following code syntax, lbToKilo and kiloToLb reference the two RadioButton components in the Medical Calculator application:

Code Syntax

```
final RadioButton lbToKilo = (RadioButton) findViewById(R.id.rbLbToKilo);
final RadioButton kiloToLb = (RadioButton) findViewById(R.id.rbKiloToLb);
```

The keyword *final* means that the variable can be assigned only once. This variable can only be referenced within this class. After the RadioButton components have been referenced, the next priority is to determine which of the two radio buttons the user selected. If the user selected the Convert Pounds to Kilograms radio button, the weight entered is divided by 2.2, but if the user selected the Convert Kilograms to Pounds radio button, the weight is multiplied by 2.2. A variable named conversionRate is assigned the decimal value 2.2. The variables weightEntered and convertedWeight contain the patient weight and converted weight result, respectively.

To create the Java code that declares the variables used in the application and to assign variables to reference the components, follow these steps:

Step 1

- Display the MainActivity.java tab.
- Click in the blank line (Line 8) inside the MainActivity class, and then press Tab to indent the line.
- To initialize the conversion rate value of 2.2, type **double conversionRate = 2.2;** and press the Enter key.
- To initialize the weightEntered variable, type **double weightEntered;** and press the Enter key.
- To initialize the variable that will hold the converted weight, type **double convertedWeight;** and press the Enter key.

Three variables are declared in the Java code (**Figure 4-21**).

Figure 4-21 Variables declared

MainActivity.java

MainActivity.java × activity_main.xml ×

```
1   package com.example.medicalcalculator;
2
3   import ...
6
7   public class MainActivity extends AppCompatActivity {
8       double conversionRate = 2.2;
9       double weightEntered;
10      double convertedWeight;
11
12      @Override
13      protected void onCreate(Bundle savedInstanceState) {
14          super.onCreate(savedInstanceState);
15          setContentView(R.layout.activity_main);
16          getSupportActionBar().setDisplayShowHomeEnabled(true);
17          getSupportActionBar().setLogo(R.mipmap.ic_launcher);
18          getSupportActionBar().setDisplayUseLogoEnabled(true);
19      }
20  }
```

Three variables are declared

Step 2

- Click at the end of Line 18, which is getSupportActionBar().setDisplayUseLogoEnabled(true);. Press the Enter key.
- To instantiate and reference the EditText class with the id name of tvWeight, type **final EditText weight = (EditText) findViewById(R.id.tvWeight);**.
- Click EditText (displayed in red), press Alt+Enter, and then import the EditText class. After the closing semicolon, press the Enter key.
- To instantiate and reference the RadioButton class with the id name of rbLbToKilo, type **final RadioButton lbToKilo = (RadioButton) findViewById(R.id.rbLbToKilo);**.
- If necessary, click the RadioButton text in red and press Alt+Enter to import the RadioButton class. After the closing semicolon, press the Enter key.
- To instantiate and reference the RadioButton class for the second radio button with the id name of rbKiloToLb, type **final RadioButton kiloToLb = (RadioButton) findViewById(R.id.rbKiloToLb);**.
- Save your work.

The EditText class extracts the value from the user's input for the patient weight and the RadioButton class extracts the checked value from the radio buttons (**Figure 4-22**).

Figure 4-22 EditText and RadioButtons referenced

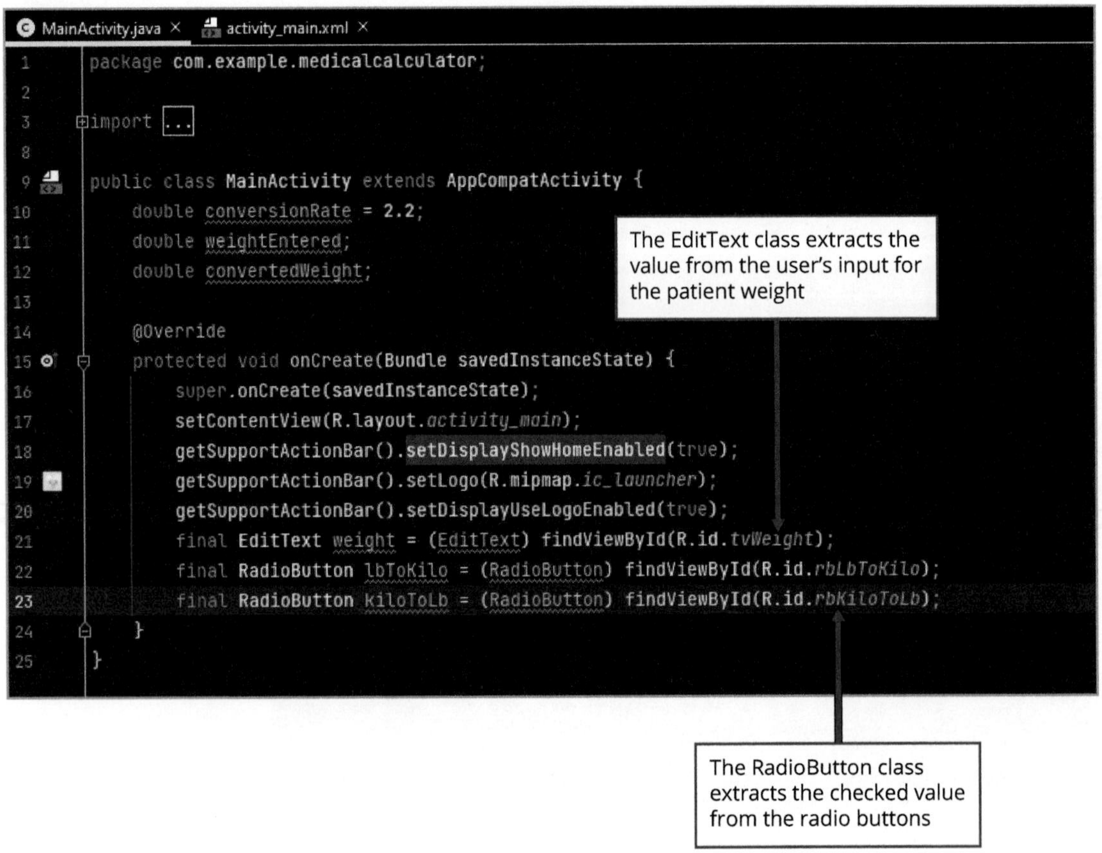
MainActivity.java ×
activity_main.xml ×
1 package com.example.medicalcalculator;
2
3 import ...
8
9 public class MainActivity extends AppCompatActivity {
10 double conversionRate = 2.2;
11 double weightEntered;
12 double convertedWeight;
13
14 @Override
15 protected void onCreate(Bundle savedInstanceState) {
16 super.onCreate(savedInstanceState);
17 setContentView(R.layout.activity_main);
18 getSupportActionBar().setDisplayShowHomeEnabled(true);
19 getSupportActionBar().setLogo(R.mipmap.ic_launcher);
20 getSupportActionBar().setDisplayUseLogoEnabled(true);
21 final EditText weight = (EditText) findViewById(R.id.tvWeight);
22 final RadioButton lbToKilo = (RadioButton) findViewById(R.id.rbLbToKilo);
23 final RadioButton kiloToLb = (RadioButton) findViewById(R.id.rbKiloToLb);
24 }
25 }
The EditText class extracts the value from the user's input for the patient weight
The RadioButton class extracts the checked value from the radio buttons

Coding the Button Component

The Button component detects user interaction using an event listener. The following steps instantiate the second TextView component, the Button component, and the OnClickListener.

Step 1

- After the two lines of code referring to the RadioButton components, type a new line with the code **final TextView result = (TextView) findViewById(R.id.tvResult);**.
- Import the TextView class.

The TextView component is instantiated to the variable tvResult (**Figure 4-23**).

Figure 4-23 TextView component referenced

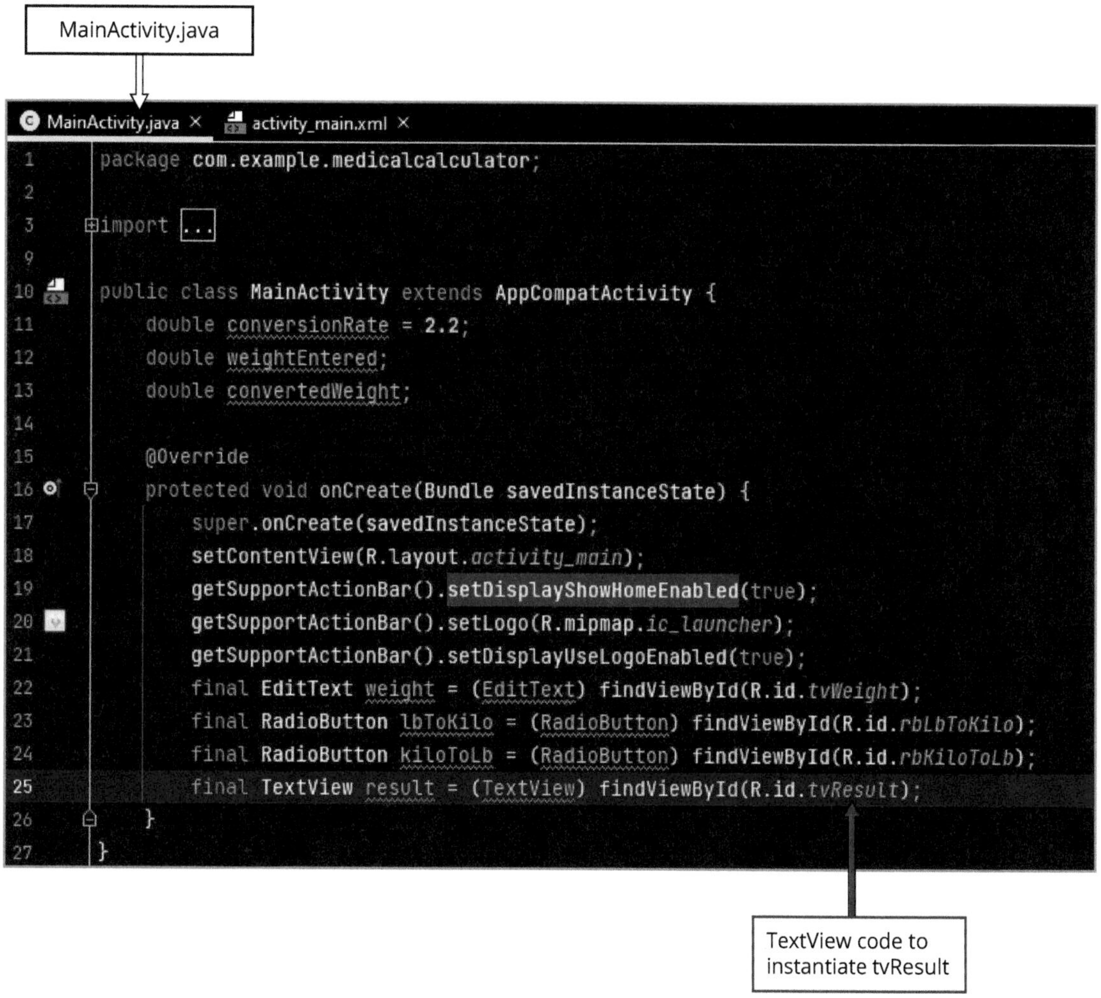

MainActivity.java

MainActivity.java × activity_main.xml ×

```
package com.example.medicalcalculator;

import ...

public class MainActivity extends AppCompatActivity {
    double conversionRate = 2.2;
    double weightEntered;
    double convertedWeight;

    @Override
    protected void onCreate(Bundle savedInstanceState) {
        super.onCreate(savedInstanceState);
        setContentView(R.layout.activity_main);
        getSupportActionBar().setDisplayShowHomeEnabled(true);
        getSupportActionBar().setLogo(R.mipmap.ic_launcher);
        getSupportActionBar().setDisplayUseLogoEnabled(true);
        final EditText weight = (EditText) findViewById(R.id.tvWeight);
        final RadioButton lbToKilo = (RadioButton) findViewById(R.id.rbLbToKilo);
        final RadioButton kiloToLb = (RadioButton) findViewById(R.id.rbKiloToLb);
        final TextView result = (TextView) findViewById(R.id.tvResult);
    }
}
```

TextView code to instantiate tvResult

Step 2

- After the closing semicolon, press the Enter key.
- To code the button, type **Button convert = (Button) findViewById(R.id.btConvert);**.
- Click the Button code and import the Button class.
- After the closing semicolon, press the Enter key two times to separate the variables from the rest of the code.
- To code the Button listener, type **convert.setOn**. Then, if necessary, press Ctrl+spacebar to display an auto-complete code list.

- Double-click the setOnClickListener displayed in the auto-complete list.
- Inside the parentheses, type **new On** and double-click the first choice, which lists an OnClickListener with an Anonymous Inner Type event handler.

The btConvert Button component and OnClickListener are coded (**Figure 4-24**).

Figure 4-24 OnClickListener for the Button component

```
public class MainActivity extends AppCompatActivity {
    double conversionRate = 2.2;
    double weightEntered;
    double convertedWeight;

    @Override
    protected void onCreate(Bundle savedInstanceState) {
        super.onCreate(savedInstanceState);
        setContentView(R.layout.activity_main);
        getSupportActionBar().setDisplayShowHomeEnabled(true);
        getSupportActionBar().setLogo(R.mipmap.ic_launcher);
        getSupportActionBar().setDisplayUseLogoEnabled(true);
        final EditText weight = (EditText) findViewById(R.id.tvWeight);
        final RadioButton lbToKilo = (RadioButton) findViewById(R.id.rbLbToKilo);
        final RadioButton kiloToLb = (RadioButton) findViewById(R.id.rbKiloToLb);
        final TextView result = (TextView) findViewById(R.id.tvResult);
        Button convert = (Button) findViewById(R.id.btConvert);
        convert.setOnClickListener(new View.OnClickListener() {
            @Override
            public void onClick(View v) {

            }
        });
    }
}
```

Button instantiated

convert.setOnClickListener and onClick method stub

4.8 Making Decisions with Conditional Statements

In the Medical Calculator chapter project, which converts an entered weight to pounds or kilograms, the user selects one of two radio buttons. Then, based on the choice, the application either divides by 2.2 or multiplies by 2.2.

Java uses decision structures to deal with the different conditions that occur based on the values entered into an application. A **decision structure** is a fundamental component structure used in computer programming. A statement that tests the radio button is called a conditional statement, and the condition checked is whether the first or second radio button is selected. If the first radio button is selected, the weight is divided by 2.2. When a condition is tested in a Java program, it is either true or false. Conditional statements allow the user to make a decision and to follow a path after the decision is made. To execute a conditional statement and the statements that are executed when a condition is true, Java uses the If statement and its variety of formats.

In coding, when we compare two values—for example, is the number five less than seven?—the result will either be true or false. In this case, five is less than seven, so the result is true. Another name in Java for true-or-false results is **Boolean operators**. Boolean operators have two values, which are either true (designated as a 1) or false (designated as a 0). When you compare two values, Java simply returns a Boolean value of true or false.

4.9 Making Decisions Using an If Statement

In the chapter program, an **If statement** is used to determine which RadioButton component is selected. The simplest form of the If statement is shown in the following code:

Code Syntax

```
if (condition) {
        //Statements completed if true
}
```

The statement(s) between the opening and closing braces are executed if the condition is true. If the condition is not true, no statements between the braces are executed, and program execution continues with the statement(s) after the closing brace.

Another example of using an If decision structure is determining if a child is old enough to begin elementary school when the age requirement is that the child be more than four years old:

Code Syntax

```
if (age>4) {
   // If the age is less than four then the Boolean value is true
   // then this block of code between the braces is executed
 result.setText("Your child can be enrolled in school");
}
```

4.10 Making Decisions Using an If Else Statement

In many applications, the logic requires one set of instructions to be executed if a condition is true and another set of instructions to be executed if a condition is false. Making decisions in Java assists programmers in writing decision-driven statements and determining whether to execute a block of statements in braces. For example, a program requirement may specify that if a student's test score is 60 or greater, a message stating "You passed the examination" is displayed, but if the test score is less than 60, a message stating "You failed the examination" is displayed.

```
if (score>=60) {
  result.setText("You passed the examination");
} else {
  result.setText("You failed the examination");
}
```

To execute one set of instructions if a condition is true and another set of instructions if the condition is false, you can use the **If Else statement**, as shown in the following code:

Code Syntax

```
if (condition) {
 //Statements completed if condition is true
} else {
 //Statements completed if condition is false
}
```

Another example of using an If Else decision structure is determining if a child is old enough to begin elementary school when the age requirement is that the child be more than four years old. The If Else structure could be written to state that the child either can be enrolled or not enrolled:

Code Syntax

```
if (age>4) {
    result.setText("Your child can be enrolled in school");
} else {
    result.setText("Your child cannot be enrolled in school");
}
```

Good to Know Java automatically indents statements to be executed when a condition is true or not true to indicate that the lines of code are within the conditional If structure.

Relational Operators

In the syntax of the condition portion of the If statement, a condition is tested to determine if it is true or false. The conditions that can be tested are:

- Is one value equal to another value?
- Is one value not equal to another value?
- Is one value greater than another value?
- Is one value less than another value?
- Is one value greater than or equal to another value?
- Is one value less than or equal to another value?

To test these conditions, Java provides relational operators that are used within the conditional statement to express the relationship between the numbers being tested. **Table 4-3** shows these relational operators.

Table 4-3 Relational operators

Relational Operator	Meaning	Example	Resulting Condition
= =	Equal to	6 = = 6	True
! =	Not equal to	4! = 7	False
>	Greater than	3 > 2	True
<	Less than	8 < 1	False
>=	Greater than or equal to	5 >= 5	True
<=	Less than or equal to	9 <= 6	False

In the chapter project, an If Else statement determines if the entered weight is valid. If a nurse is converting pounds to kilograms, the weight entered must be less than or equal to 500 to fall within the valid range of acceptable entries. If the entered weight is valid, the weight is converted by dividing it by the conversion rate of 2.2, as shown in the following code:

Code Syntax

```
if (weightEntered <= 500) {
      convertedWeight = weightEntered / conversionRate;
} else {
      //Statements completed if condition is false
}
```

Good to Know | The most common mistake made with an If statement is the use of a single equal sign to compare equality. A single equal sign (=) is used for assigning a value to a variable, not for comparison.

In addition to numbers, strings can be compared in a conditional statement. A string value comparison is used to compare each character in two strings, starting with the first character in each string. All characters found in strings, including letters, numbers, and special characters, are ranked in sequence from lowest to highest based on how the characters are coded internally in the computer. The relational operators in Table 4-3 cannot be used with string comparisons. If you are comparing equality, string characters cannot be compared with the = = operator. Java strings are compared with the **equals( ) method** of the String class.

If you are comparing whether a string comes alphabetically before another string, use the compareTo( ) method to determine the order of strings. Do not use the less-than or greater-than symbols shown in Table 4-3 to compare string data types. The compareTo( ) method returns a negative integer if the first string precedes the second string. It returns zero if the two strings being compared are equal. It returns a positive integer if the first string follows the second string. Examples of the equals( ) and compareTo( ) methods are shown in **Table 4-4** using the following initialized variables:

```
String name1 = "Sara";
String name2 = "Shawna";
String name3 = "Ryan";
```

Table 4-4 Examples of the equals( ) and compareTo( ) methods

If Statement	Comparison	Resulting Condition
if (name1.equals(name2))	Strings are not equal	False
if (name1.compareTo(name1) = = 0)	Strings are equal	True
if (name1.compareTo(name3) = = 0)	Strings are not equal	False
if (name1.compareTo(name2) > 0)	The first string precedes the second string; returns a negative number	False
if (name1.compareTo(name3) < 0)	The first string follows the third string; returns a negative number	True
if (name3.compareTo(name2) > 0)	The third string follows the second string; returns a positive number	True

Quick Check

Write a code statement with empty braces to determine if your shoe size is a 9.

Answer:
```
if (shoeSize = = 9) {
}
```

4.11 Making Decisions Using Logical Operators

An If statement can test more than one condition within a single statement. In many cases, more than one condition must be true or one of several conditions must be true in order for the statements within the braces to be executed. When more than one condition is included in an If statement, the conditions are called a **compound condition**. Logical operators are needed to control the flow of execution. For example, consider the following business travel rule for a company: "If the flight costs less than $500 and the hotel is less than $150 per night, the business trip is approved." In this case, both conditions (flight less than $500 and hotel less than $150 per night) must be true for the trip to be approved. If either condition is not true, then the business trip is not approved.

Code Syntax

```
if (flightCost < 500 && hotelCost < 150) {
    result.setText("Your business trip is approved");
} else {
    result.setText("Your business trip is not approved");
}
```

To create an If statement that processes the business travel rule, you must use a logical operator. The most common set of logical operators is listed in **Table 4-5**.

Table 4-5 Common logical operators

Logical Operator	Meaning	Example
&&	And—all Boolean conditions must be true	if (flightCost < 500 && hotelCost < 150)
||	Or—at least one Boolean condition must be true	if (stamp < 0.49 || rate = = 2)
!	Not—reverses the meaning of a Boolean condition	if (! (grade > 70))

Quick Check

Write a code statement with empty braces to determine if your zip code is 40345 or your rental cost is under 700.

Answer:
```
if (zipCode = = 40345 | | rentalCost<700) {
}
```

Data Validation

Data validation is the practice of checking the integrity, accuracy, and structure of a program before it is used for a business operation. It may seem as though data validation is a step that slows down your pace of work, but it is essential because it helps you create the best results possible. In the chapter project, it is important to confirm that the number entered by the user is not a typo or another type of mistake. If a value greater than 500 is entered for the conversion from pounds to kilograms or a value greater than 225 is entered for the conversion from kilograms to pounds, the user should be notified and asked for a valid entry. To alert the user that an incorrect value was entered, a message called a toast notification (or toast message) can appear on the screen temporarily. It does not require extensive effort to validate that a user is entering correct and expected values. Testing is necessary to ensure that data entered into a smartphone is correct and meets the desired quality standards for security.

4.12 Displaying an Android Toast Notification

A **toast notification** communicates messages to the user as an unobtrusive element that appears on the screen when an event occurs. It is used to provide feedback or show a message to the user. These messages pop up as an overlay on the user's current screen, often displaying a validation warning message. For example, a weather application may display a toast notification if a town is under a tornado warning, or an instant messaging app might display a toast notification that a text message has been sent. In the chapter project, a toast notification displays a message warning the user that an invalid number was entered. A toast message only fills the amount of space required for the message to be displayed while the user's current activity remains visible and interactive. Toasts can be dismissed by tapping on them or by swiping them off the screen. If you do not dismiss a toast, the notification automatically fades in and out on the screen after a few seconds.

The toast notification code uses a Toast object and the makeText( ) method with three parameters: the context (which displays the activity name), the text message, and the duration of the interval that the toast is displayed (LENGTH_SHORT or LENGTH_LONG). To display the toast notification, a show( ) method displays the Toast object.

Code Syntax

```
Toast toast = Toast.makeText(context, text, duration).show( );
```

The toast message is best used for short messages. If the user enters an invalid number into the Medical Calculator, a warning toast notification appears. Notice in the following syntax that the text notification message displays *Pounds must be less than 500.*

Code Syntax

```
Toast.makeText(MainActivity.this, "Pounds must be less than 500",
Toast.LENGTH_LONG).show( );
```

Good to Know | A Google employee is credited with coining the term *toast*, which is a small notification window that slides upward into view, like toast popping out of a toaster.

Quick Check

What do you call the message that appears temporarily on the app screen to provide a warning or other important message?

Answer: A toast notification.

4.13 Using the isChecked( ) Method with RadioButton Components

You will recall that the RadioButton components in the Medical Calculator application allow the user to select a conversion option. When the user selects the second radio button, a small, shaded circle is displayed in that radio button. When the RadioButton is selected, the Checked attribute of the second RadioButton component changes from False (unselected) to True (selected). The Java code must check each RadioButton to determine if it has been selected by the user. This checked attribute can be tested in an If statement using the **isChecked( ) method** to determine if the RadioButton object has been selected.

Code Syntax

```
if (lbToKilo.isChecked) {
    //Statements completed if condition is true (Boolean value)
} else {
    //Statements completed if condition is false (Boolean value)
}
```

If the user selects the lbToKilo RadioButton component, the statements between the braces within the If portion are completed. If the user selects the kiloToLb RadioButton component, the statements within the Else portion are completed.

4.14 Using Nested If Statements

At times, more than one decision must be made to determine what processing must occur. For example, if one condition is true, a second condition might need to be tested before the correct code is executed. To test a second condition only after determining that a first condition is true (or false), you must place an If statement within another If statement. When you do this, the inner If statement is said to be **nested** within the outer If statement. In the chapter Android app, if the user checks the first radio button to convert pounds to kilograms and if the entered weight is equal to 500 pounds or less, then the weight can be converted. If the weight is above 500 pounds, a toast notification appears with a warning. A second nested If statement evaluates whether the second radio button is checked and if the user entered 225 kilograms or less.

Code Syntax

```
if (lbToKilo.isChecked( )) {
   if (weightEntered <= 500) {
```

```
        convertedWeight = weightEntered / conversionRate;
    } else {
    Toast.makeText(MainActivity.this, "Pounds must be less than
        500", Toast.LENGTH_LONG).show( );
    }
}
```

Coding the Button Event

After the user enters the weight and selects the desired RadioButton in the chapter example app, the user taps or clicks the Button component. The OnClickListener event is triggered and the entered weight is converted. Within the onClick( ) method, the weight entered must be converted to the Double data type. The syntax Double.parseDouble converts input to a Double, and Integer.parseInt converts input to an Integer data type. A DecimalFormat layout is necessary to format the result to one place past the decimal point ("#.#"). If you want to display a result two places past the decimal point, use the format ("#.##"). To convert the weight to a Double data type and establish the format for the output, follow these steps:

Step 1

- On Line 32, inside the OnClick method stub of the MainActivity.java code, type **weightEntered=Double.parseDouble(weight.getText( ).toString());** to convert the weight entered to a Double data type.

The weight entered by the user is converted to a Double data type (**Figure 4-25**).

Figure 4-25 Weight converted to a Double data type

```
11
12  public class MainActivity extends AppCompatActivity {
13      double conversionRate = 2.2;
14      double weightEntered;
15      double convertedWeight;
16
17      @Override
18      protected void onCreate(Bundle savedInstanceState) {
19          super.onCreate(savedInstanceState);
20          setContentView(R.layout.activity_main);
21          getSupportActionBar().setDisplayShowHomeEnabled(true);
22          getSupportActionBar().setLogo(R.mipmap.ic_launcher);
23          getSupportActionBar().setDisplayUseLogoEnabled(true);
24          final EditText weight = (EditText) findViewById(R.id.tvWeight);
25          final RadioButton lbToKilo = (RadioButton) findViewById(R.id.rbLbToKilo);
26          final RadioButton kiloToLb = (RadioButton) findViewById(R.id.rbKiloToLb);
27          final TextView result = (TextView) findViewById(R.id.tvResult);
28          Button convert = (Button) findViewById(R.id.btConvert);
29          convert.setOnClickListener(new View.OnClickListener() {
30              @Override
31              public void onClick(View v) {
32                  weightEntered=Double.parseDouble(weight.getText( ).toString( ));
33              }
34          });
35      }
36  }
```

Logcat Build Profiler App Inspection

weight is converted from a String to a Double data type

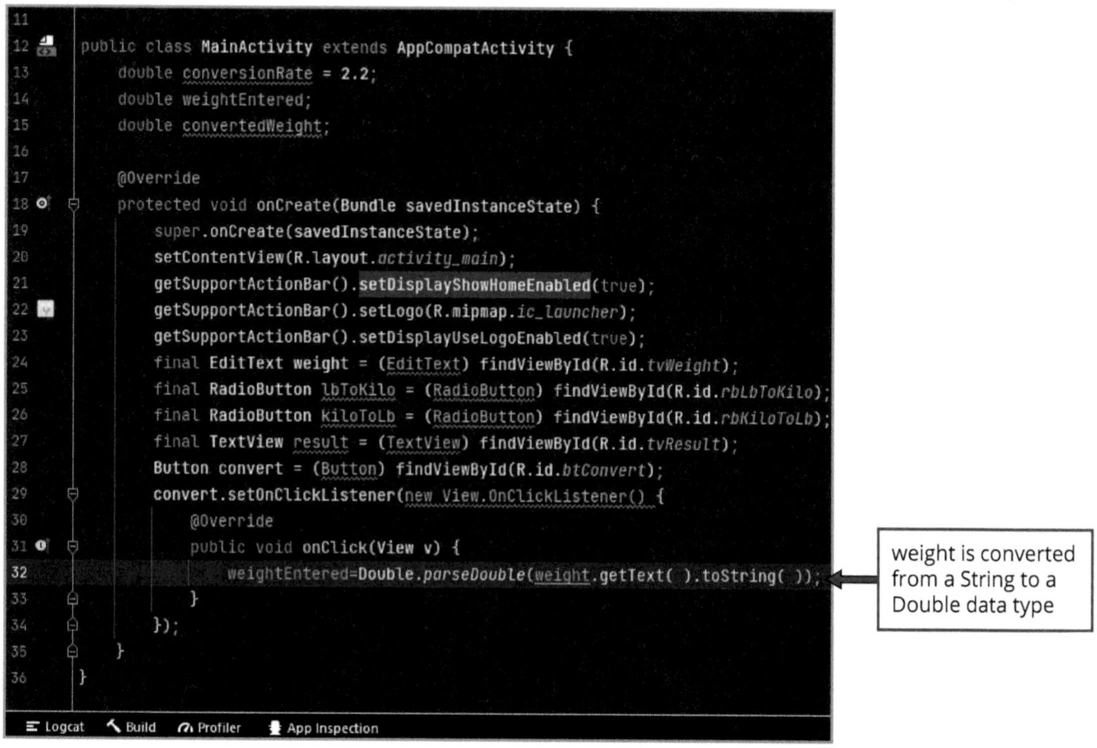

Step 2

- After the closing semicolon, press the Enter key.
- To create a decimal layout that changes the weight to a decimal value rounded to the nearest tenth for use in the result later, type **DecimalFormat tenth = new DecimalFormat("#.#");**.
- Click DecimalFormat, press Alt+Enter, and then import the DecimalFormat class.

The DecimalFormat code rounds off to the nearest tenth (**Figure 4-26**).

Figure 4-26 DecimalFormat code used to round to the nearest tenth

```
public class MainActivity extends AppCompatActivity {
    double conversionRate = 2.2;
    double weightEntered;
    double convertedWeight;

    @Override
    protected void onCreate(Bundle savedInstanceState) {
        super.onCreate(savedInstanceState);
        setContentView(R.layout.activity_main);
        getSupportActionBar().setDisplayShowHomeEnabled(true);
        getSupportActionBar().setLogo(R.mipmap.ic_launcher);
        getSupportActionBar().setDisplayUseLogoEnabled(true);
        final EditText weight = (EditText) findViewById(R.id.tvWeight);
        final RadioButton lbToKilo = (RadioButton) findViewById(R.id.rbLbToKilo);
        final RadioButton kiloToLb = (RadioButton) findViewById(R.id.rbKiloToLb);
        final TextView result = (TextView) findViewById(R.id.tvResult);
        Button convert = (Button) findViewById(R.id.btConvert);
        convert.setOnClickListener(new View.OnClickListener() {
            @Override
            public void onClick(View v) {
                weightEntered=Double.parseDouble(weight.getText( ).toString( ));
                DecimalFormat tenth = new DecimalFormat( pattern: "#.#");
            }
        });
    }
}
```

DecimalFormat code used to round off to the nearest tenth

Coding the Nested If Statements

After the weight entered is converted to Double data and a format is set, the next set of code determines which RadioButton was selected by using the isChecked attribute. Within each RadioButton If statement, the weight entered is converted to the appropriate weight unit and displayed, but only if the weight is within the valid range limits (500 pounds or 225 kilograms). If the weight is not within the valid range, a toast notification warns the user to enter a value within the acceptable range. To code a nested If statement that displays the result, follow these steps:

Step 1

- To determine if the first RadioButton component is selected, insert a new line after the DecimalFormat line of code, type **if(lbToKilo.isChecked())** {, and press Enter. Java automatically adds the closing brace.

An If statement determines if the lbToKilo RadioButton component is checked (**Figure 4-27**).

Figure 4-27 If statement to test whether the first radio button is checked

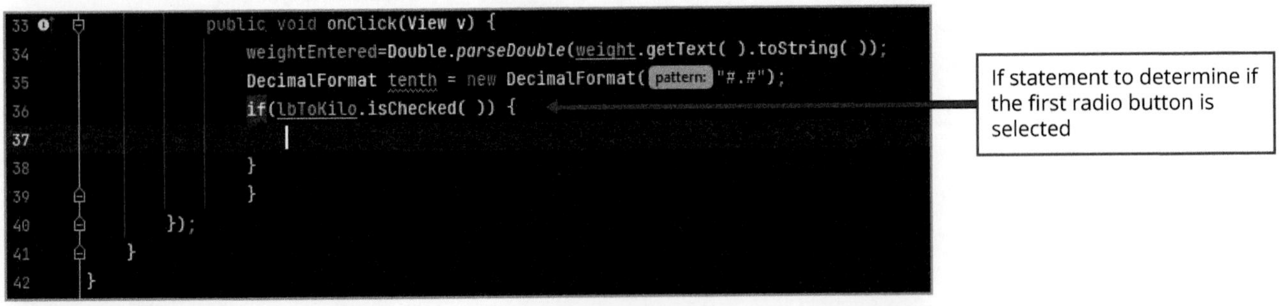

```
            public void onClick(View v) {
                weightEntered=Double.parseDouble(weight.getText( ).toString( ));
                DecimalFormat tenth = new DecimalFormat( pattern: "#.#");
                if(lbToKilo.isChecked( )) {
                    |
                }
            }
        });
    }
}
```

If statement to determine if the first radio button is selected

Step 2

- Within the first If statement, braces create a nested If Else statement that determines if the weight entered for pounds is less than or equal to 500. Type **if (weightEntered <= 500) {** and press Enter. Java automatically adds the closing brace.
- On Line 39, after the closing brace, type **else** { and press Enter. Java automatically adds the closing brace.

A nested If Else statement determines whether the number of pounds entered is valid—in other words, under 500 pounds (**Figure 4-28**).

Figure 4-28 Nested If Else statement

```
33      public void onClick(View v) {
34          weightEntered=Double.parseDouble(weight.getText( ).toString( ));
35          DecimalFormat tenth = new DecimalFormat( pattern: "#.#");
36          if(lbToKilo.isChecked( )) {
37              if (weightEntered <=500) {
38
39              } else {
40
41              }
42              }
43          }
44      });
45  }
46 }
```

If statement confirms if the weightEntered is under 500 lbs

Else statement

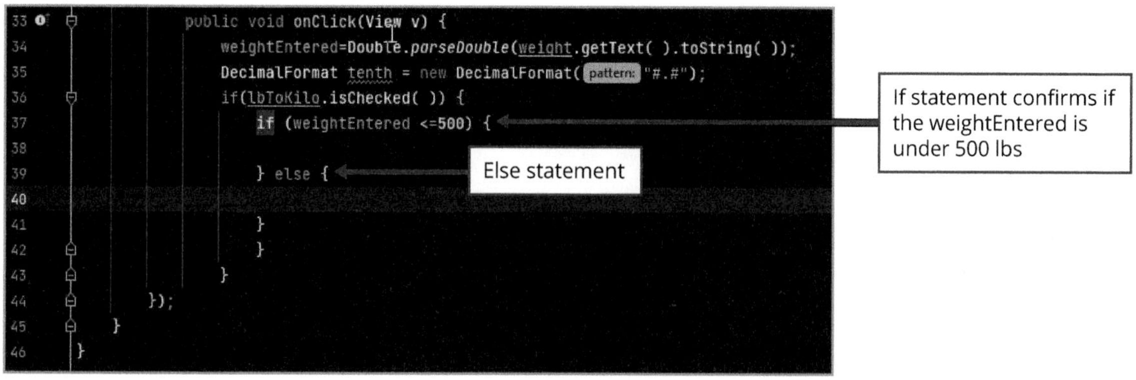

Step 3

- After the pounds variable is validated, the weight must be converted, so you divide the weight by the conversion rate of 2.2. Inside the nested If statement (Line 38), after the weightEntered <= 500) { line, type **convertedWeight = weightEntered / conversionRate;** and press the Enter key.
- To display the result of the equation rounded to one place past the decimal point, type **result.setText(tenth.format(convertedWeight) + " kilograms");**.

The number of pounds is converted to kilograms and displayed in the result TextView component if the value entered is under 500 pounds (**Figure 4-29**).

Figure 4-29 Equation for weight conversion and displayed results

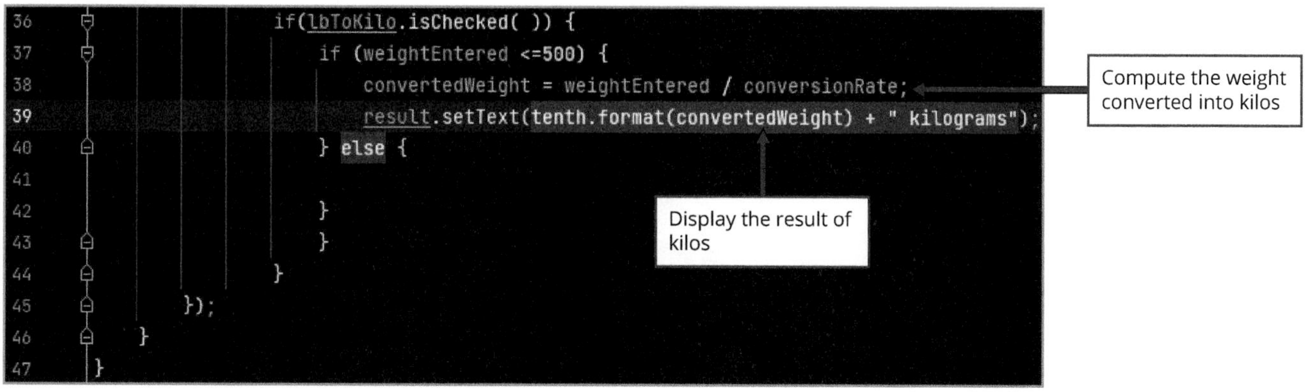

```
36          if(lbToKilo.isChecked( )) {
37              if (weightEntered <=500) {
38                  convertedWeight = weightEntered / conversionRate;
39                  result.setText(tenth.format(convertedWeight) + " kilograms");
40              } else {
41
42              }
43              }
44          }
45      });
46  }
47 }
```

Compute the weight converted into kilos

Display the result of kilos

Step 4

- If the weight is not within the valid range, a toast message requests that the user enter a valid weight. Click the line after the Else statement and type **Toast.makeText(MainActivity.this,"Pounds must be less than 500", Toast.LENGTH_LONG).show( );**.
- Click Toast and import the Toast class.

A toast message displays a reminder to enter a valid weight (**Figure 4-30**).

Figure 4-30 Toast message

```
File Edit View Navigate Code Refactor Build Run Tools VCS Window Help   Medical Calculator - MainActivity.java [Medical_Calculator.app.main]
in 〉 java 〉 com 〉 example 〉 medicalcalculator 〉 MainActivity 〉 onCreate 〉 anonymous OnClickListener 〉 onClick   app ▾   Resizable API 32 ▾
MainActivity.java ×   activity_main.xml ×
27            final EditText weight = (EditText) findViewById(R.id.tvWeight);
28            final RadioButton lbToKilo = (RadioButton) findViewById(R.id.rbLbToKilo);
29            final RadioButton kiloToLb = (RadioButton) findViewById(R.id.rbKiloToLb);
30            final TextView result = (TextView) findViewById(R.id.tvResult);
31            Button convert = (Button) findViewById(R.id.btConvert);
32            convert.setOnClickListener(new View.OnClickListener() {
33                @Override
34                public void onClick(View v) {
35                    weightEntered=Double.parseDouble(weight.getText( ).toString( ));
36                    DecimalFormat tenth = new DecimalFormat( pattern: "#.#");
37                    if(lbToKilo.isChecked( )) {
38                        if (weightEntered <=500) {
39                            convertedWeight = weightEntered / conversionRate;
40                            result.setText(tenth.format(convertedWeight) + " kilograms");
41                        } else {
42                            Toast.makeText( context: MainActivity.this, text: "Pounds must be less than 500", Toast.LENGTH_LONG).show( );
43                        }
44                    }
45                }
46            });
47        }
48    }
```

Toast message is displayed if user enters 500 or more

Step 5

- For cases when the user selects the Convert Kilograms to Pounds RadioButton component, type the following lines of code starting after the closing brace in Line 43 and press Enter after each line, as shown in **Figure 4-31**:

```
if(kiloToLb.isChecked( )) {
   if (weightEntered <= 225) {
      convertedWeight = weightEntered * conversionRate;
      result.setText(tenth.format(convertedWeight) + " pounds");
   } else {
Toast.makeText(MainActivity.this, "Kilos must be less than 225",
     Toast.LENGTH_LONG).show( );
```

The nested If statement is executed if the second RadioButton component is selected (Figure 4-31).

Figure 4-31 Completed code for If Else statements

```
34                public void onClick(View v) {
35                    weightEntered=Double.parseDouble(weight.getText( ).toString( ));
36                    DecimalFormat tenth = new DecimalFormat( pattern: "#.#");
37                    if(lbToKilo.isChecked( )) {
38                        if (weightEntered <=500) {
39                            convertedWeight = weightEntered / conversionRate;
40                            result.setText(tenth.format(convertedWeight) + " kilograms");
41                        } else {
42                            Toast.makeText( context: MainActivity.this, text: "Pounds must be less than 500", Toast.LENGTH_LONG).show( );
43                        }
44                        if(kiloToLb.isChecked( )) {
45                            if (weightEntered <= 225) {
46                                convertedWeight = weightEntered * conversionRate;
47                                result.setText(tenth.format(convertedWeight) + " pounds");
48                            } else {
49                                Toast.makeText( context: MainActivity.this, text: "Kilos must be less than 225", Toast.LENGTH_LONG).show( );
50                            }
51                        }
52                    }
53                }
54            });
55        }
56    }
```

Second nested If Else statement

Good to Know | The Else statement only has one line, so technically it does not need braces, but if more lines are added later, the braces are useful to have in place.

Running and Testing the App

An app can be run and tested on an actual Android device or the emulator. It is best to leave the emulator running and run the app to test your code each time you make a change. To run your app, follow this step.

Step 1

- To view the finished application, click Run app on the Standard toolbar, and then select an emulator to open it. Unlock the emulator. Run the app again to send the code to the emulator and test the application in it.
- The application opens in the emulator, where you enter a weight and select a radio button.
- To view the results, click the CONVERT WEIGHT button.

The Medical Calculator Android app is executed, as shown in **Figure 4-32** as well as in Figures 4-1 and 4-2 earlier in the chapter. Notice that in Figure 4-32, the Toast notification is displayed at the bottom when the weight exceeds the If statement limit for pounds.

Figure 4-32 Running app and toast notification

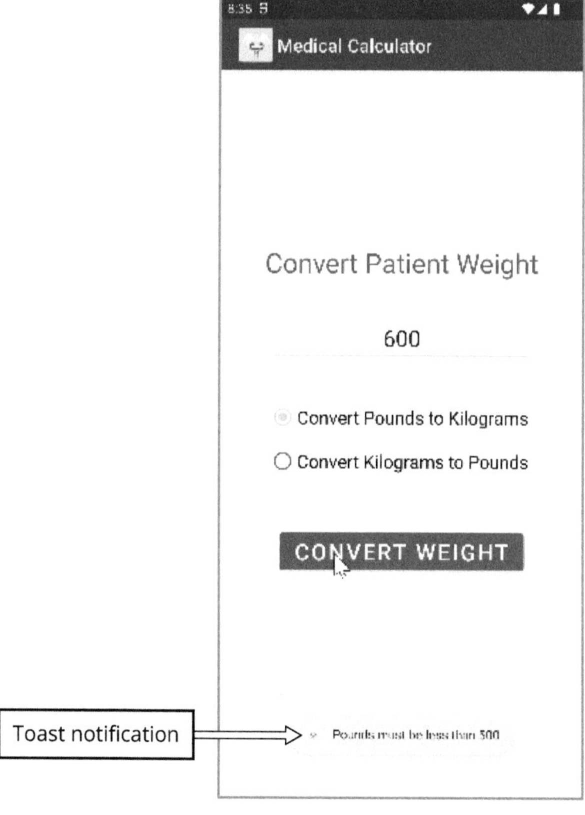

Wrap It Up—Chapter Summary

Beginning with selecting a customized icon, this chapter has completed the steps to create a graphical user interface that included a RadioGroup component for the Medical Calculator program. The decision structure included a nested If Else statement to determine different outcomes based on user input. If necessary, a toast message reminded the user of the expected input. You learned to customize feedback and make decisions based on any user's input.

- To display a custom launcher icon instead of the default icon on the home screen of an Android device, click Image Asset on the New menu to open the Asset Studio dialog box.
- Include RadioButton components to allow users to select or deselect an option. Each RadioButton component has a label defined by the Text attribute and a Checked attribute set to either true or false. In a RadioGroup component, only one RadioButton component can be selected at a time.
- Android apps can use hexadecimal color codes to set the colors displayed in components.
- For more flexibility in controlling your layout, use the layout:margin attributes to change the spacing between objects. Use the Gravity attributes to position a component precisely on the screen. You can change this attribute using the Attributes pane or the Gravity tool on the toolbar.
- A decision structure includes a conditional statement that checks whether the condition is true or false. To execute a conditional statement and the statements that are executed when a condition is true, Java uses the If statement and its variety of formats, including the If Else statement. An If statement executes one set of instructions if a specified condition is true and takes no action if the condition is not true. An If Else statement executes one set of instructions if a specified condition is true and another set of instructions if the condition is false.
- To test the conditions in a conditional statement such as an If statement, Java provides relational operators that are used within the statement to express the relationship between the numbers being tested. For example, you can use a relational operator to test whether one value is greater than another.
- If more than one condition is tested in a conditional statement, the conditions are called a compound condition. To create an If statement that processes a compound condition, you must use a logical operator such as && (And).
- After including code that validates data, you can code a toast notification (also called a toast message) to display a brief message indicating that an incorrect value was entered.
- To test a second condition only after determining that a first condition is true or false, you nest one If statement within another If statement.

Key Terms

Action bar icon
Boolean operators
compound condition
data validation
decision structure
equals( ) method
Gravity
hexadecimal color code
If statement
If Else statement
Image Asset Studio
isChecked( ) method
launcher icon
layout:margin
logo
nested
RadioGroup
toast notification

Developer FAQs

1. Who specifies the size and format of all launcher icons for uniformity on their platform? (4.1)
2. What is the name of the icon that appears on the upper-left side of the opening bar across the opening screen of the app? (4.1)
3. What is the preferred prefix for a filename and the file extension of the icon described in question 1? (4.1)
4. To display a custom icon, what wizard can you use in Android Studio? (4.1)
5. After adding an image as a launcher icon to the Image Asset Studio, is the launcher icon displayed when you run the app? (4.2)
6. Which primary color is represented by the hexadecimal code of #00FF00? (4.3)
7. What is the name of the attribute used to horizontally center the hint attribute of a Text Number component? (4.5)
8. Using the layout_marginTop attribute, in which text box would you type 18dp to move a component 18 density pixels down from the upper edge of the emulator? (4.4)
9. When a RadioGroup component is placed on the emulator, the first RadioButton component is selected by default. Which attribute is set as true by default? (4.3)
10. Write an If statement with empty braces that tests if the value in the variable *age* is between 18 and 21 years inclusive. (4.11)
11. Write an If statement with empty braces that tests if the radio button named *gender* is selected. (4.14)
12. Rewrite the following line of code without a Not logical operator but keeping the same logical processing: if (! (height <= 60) {. (4.11)
13. Write an If statement with empty braces to compare if a string variable named *company* is equal to *AT&T*. (4.10)
14. Fix this statement: if (hours < 2 || > 8) {. (4.11)
15. How many radio buttons can be selected at one time in a RadioGroup component? (4.3)
16. Write an If statement with empty braces that compares if *wage* is equal to 7.25. (4.10)
17. If you compare two strings and the result is a positive number, what is the order of the two strings? (4.10)
18. Using a relational operator with empty braces, write an If statement that evaluates if a variable named *tipPercent* is not equal to .15. (4.10)
19. Write a warning message that would display the comment "The maximum credits allowed is 18" with a long interval. (4.12)
20. Write a quick reminder message that would display the comment "File saved" with a short interval. (4.12)

Beyond the Book

Search the web for answers to the following questions to further your Android knowledge.

1. You have developed an application for music downloads. Search using Google Images to locate an appropriate icon and resize it using a program like Microsoft Paint for use as a tablet app launcher icon (xxhdpi).
2. Search the Google Play site for a popular app that has a Sudoku puzzle. Take a screenshot of one Sudoku puzzle's launcher icon and another screenshot of the larger graphic used for the description of the app.

3. An Android toast message can be coded to appear at an exact location on the screen. Explain how this works and give an example of the code that would do this.
4. Research the average price of an individual paid app. Write 75 to 100 words on the average selling prices of Android and iPhone apps.

Case Programming Projects

Complete one or more of the following case programming projects. Use the same steps and techniques taught within the chapter. Successful completion of these projects requires knowledge of all chapter learning objectives. Submit the program(s) you create to your instructor. The level of difficulty is indicated for each case programming project.

Case Project 4–1: Phone Photo Prints App (Beginner)

Requirements Document

Application title:	Phone Photo Prints App
Purpose:	This phone app determines the cost of printing photos. The pictures are delivered directly to your home.
Algorithms:	1. The opening screen requests the number of photos the user wants to have printed (**Figure 4-33**). 2. The user selects one of three radio buttons labeled 4 × 6 (19 cents), 5 × 7 (49 cents), or 8 × 10 (79 cents) and then selects the ORDER PRINTS button. 3. The cost is displayed for the number of prints (**Figure 4-34**).
Conditions:	1. Use a customized launcher icon named photo.png from the student files and display the icon in the Action bar.

Figure 4-33 Phone Photo Prints opening screen

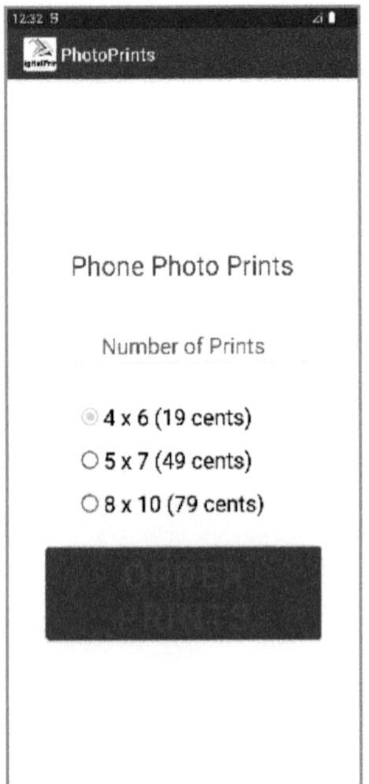

Figure 4-34 Number of prints and cost

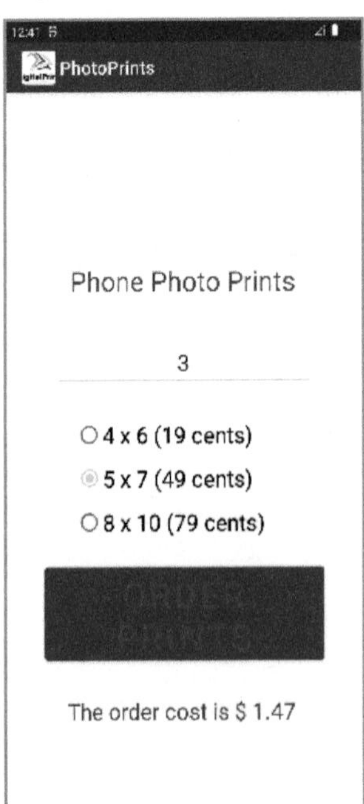

Case Project 4–2: Car Wash App (Beginner)

Requirements Document

Application title: Car Wash App

Purpose: Large cities provide car wash apps where you can purchase cleaning packages for your vehicle.

Algorithms:

1. The opening screen requests the number of car washes and the type of car wash package you want to purchase (**Figure 4-35**).
2. The user selects a type of car wash: exterior only or exterior with interior vacuum services. For a package of 12 or more car washes, the Car Wash app charges $8 for an exterior wash and $10 for an exterior wash with an interior vacuum. If you select fewer than 12 washes, the charge is $13 for an exterior wash or $15 for an exterior wash and interior vacuum.
3. When the CALCULATE PACKAGE button is selected, the total price is displayed for the number of car washes purchased (**Figure 4-36**).

Conditions:

1. Find a custom launcher icon online, add it to the Action Bar, and name the icon file carwashicon.png.
2. Add an image named carwash.png to the bottom of the app screen. The image is available in the student files.
3. Display the result with a dollar sign and no decimal places.

Figure 4-35 Car Wash Packages opening screen

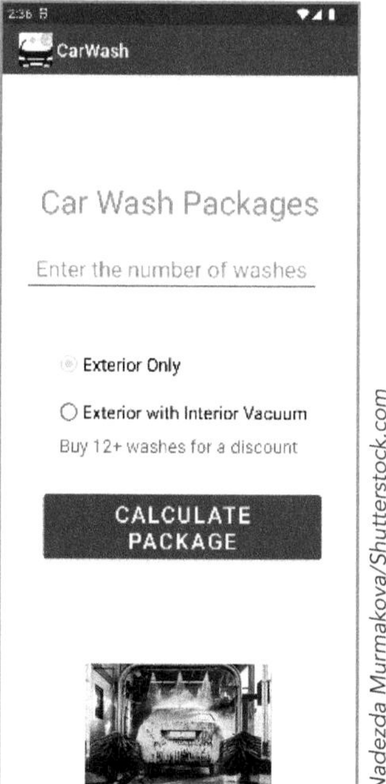

Nadezda Murmakova/Shutterstock.com

Figure 4-36 Number of washes and cost

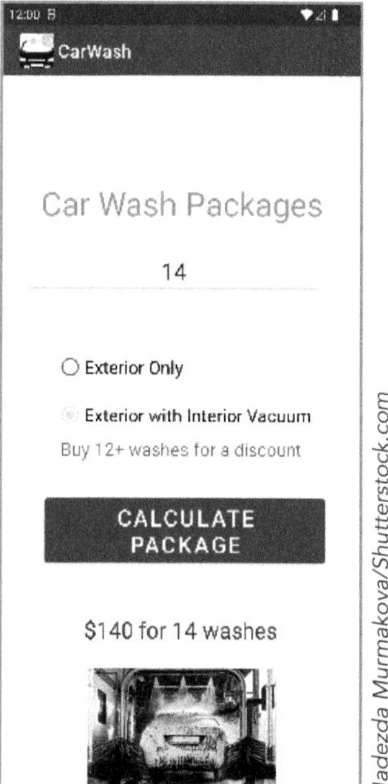

Nadezda Murmakova/Shutterstock.com

Case Project 4–3: Power Tool Rental App (Intermediate)

Requirements Document

Application title:	Power Tool Rental App
Purpose:	The app determines the cost of a power washer or tiller.
Algorithms:	1. The opening screen requests the number of days that the power tool will be rented. 2. The user selects a radio button labeled Power Washer or Tiller and then selects the Compute Cost button. 3. The final cost is displayed for the number of days rented.
Conditions:	1. The result is rounded off to the nearest penny. 2. The power washer costs $55.99 a day and the tiller $68.99 a day. 3. Do not enter more than seven days. 4. Locate an image online and resize it for use as a custom launcher icon and Action bar icon.

Case Project 4–4: Floor Tiling App (Intermediate)

Requirements Document

Application title:	Floor Tiling App
Purpose:	The tiling app allows you to calculate how many tiles you need to cover a rectangular area.
Algorithms:	1. The opening screen requests the length and the width of a room in feet. Use whole numbers only. 2. The user selects whether the tiles are 12 inches by 12 inches or 18 inches by 18 inches. 3. The app displays the number of tiles needed to cover the area in square feet.

Case Project 4–5: Currency Conversion App (Advanced)

Requirements Document

Application title:	Currency Conversion App
Purpose:	The Currency Conversion app converts U.S. dollars into euros, Mexican pesos, or Canadian dollars.
Algorithms:	1. The opening screen requests the amount of U.S. dollars to be converted. 2. The user selects euros, Mexican pesos, or Canadian dollars. The conversion of U.S. dollars to the selected currency is displayed.
Conditions:	1. Use *http://xe.com* to locate current conversion rates. 2. The program only converts values below $100,000 U.S. dollars. 3. Use a customized launcher icon.

Case Project 4–6: Average Income Tax by Country App (Advanced)

Requirements Document

Application title: Average Income Tax by Country App

Purpose: The Average Income Tax by Country app allows the user to enter the amount of taxable income earned in the past year. The user selects a country of residence and the yearly income tax is displayed.

Algorithms:

1. The opening screen requests two integer values.
2. The user can select addition, subtraction, or multiplication.
3. The entire math problem is displayed with the result.

Conditions: The following table displays the annual income tax percentages.

Country	Average Income Tax
China	25%
Germany	32%
Sweden	52%
USA	18%

Chapter 5

Investigate! Android Lists, Arrays, Switch Statements, and Web Browsers

Learning Objectives

At the completion of this chapter, you will be able to:

5.1 Create an Android project using a list

5.2 Add a ListView layout with XML code

5.3 Create an array

5.4 Initialize a ListView layout component

5.5 Display an array in the ListView with an ArrayAdapter

5.6 Call the setOnItemClick( ) method

5.7 Create a decision structure using a Switch statement

5.8 Describe the purpose of intents in Android

5.9 Launch a browser from an Android device

5.10 Test an application with multiple decisions

5.1 Creating an Android Project Using a List

Displaying a list is one of the most common design patterns used in mobile applications. This morning, you likely read the news or your favorite social media postings from a list on a phone or tablet. You scrolled down the list of articles or posts and then selected one by tapping the screen to display a full story with text, images, and hyperlinks. As you walked to class today, you probably scrolled a list of songs on a mobile device and listened to your favorite tunes.

From a list, you can open an article, play a song, open a website, or even launch a video. A list created with a ListView component may be one of the most important Android design elements because it is used so frequently. When using list items, a design structure is necessary to route your request to the intended content. In Chapter 4, you learned about the decision structure called an If statement, one of the major component structures used in computer programming. In this chapter, you learn about another decision structure called the Switch statement.

To demonstrate the process of using a list to navigate to different content, you design a travel guide for Chicago that highlights the best attractions the city has to offer. The City Guide application shown in **Figure 5-1** provides a list of city attractions. A guide for a large city can provide easy access to all its sights, activities, and restaurants in one handy place on your phone.

Figure 5-1 The City Guide Android app

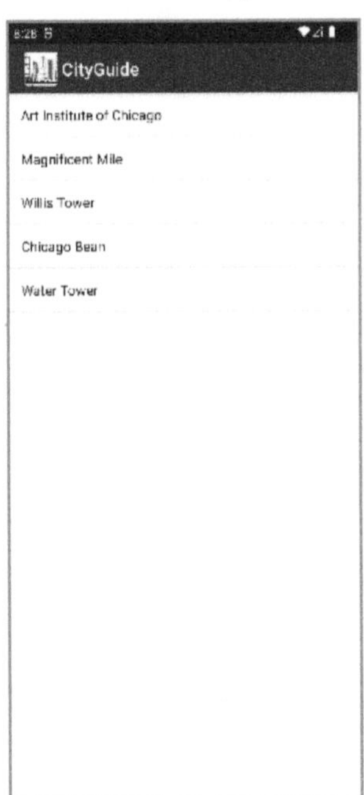

The Android app in Figure 5-1 could be part of a larger app that displays city maps, detailed site information, and restaurant recommendations. This mobile app provides information about popular places that tourists visit in Chicago. The City Guide app displays five Chicago attractions. When the user taps one of the attractions, a second window opens to display either an image or a website that provides more information. The first two items on the list link to websites, as shown in **Figure 5-2**. A browser opens to display a website for the Art Institute of Chicago or the Magnificent Mile. If the user selects Willis Tower, Chicago Bean, or Water Tower, an image appears on a second screen, as shown in **Figure 5-3**. By clicking the left-arrow button on the emulator, you can return to the list of attractions and select another one.

Figure 5-2 Art Institute of Chicago and Magnificent Mile websites

Source: Artic.edu, Source: www.themagnificentmile.com

Figure 5-3 Chicago attractions

Songquan Deng/Shutterstock.com, Photo.ua/Shutterstock.com, AevanStock/Shutterstock.com

On the Job | To see a professional city guide app in action, download a free app created by Trip Advisor or Triposo.

To create this application, the developer must understand how to perform the following processes, among others:

1. Create a list using a ListView component.
2. Define an array to establish the items in the list.
3. Add the images used in the project.
4. Define an XML file to design a list.
5. Code a Switch decision structure to handle the selection of items.
6. Open an Android web browser to display a specified Uniform Resource Identifier.
7. Create multiple classes and XML layout files to display pictures of attractions.

Beginning the City Guide App

The Chicago City Guide app begins with a vertical list of attractions on the opening screen, as shown in Figure 5-1. The Java View class creates the list and makes it scrollable if it exceeds the length of the screen. Lists can be used to display to-do items, your personal contacts, recipe names, shopping items, weekly weather, Twitter messages, and Facebook postings, for example. You use a ListView component to contain the list items. Android also has a TableLayout view that looks similar to a ListView, but a ListView allows you to select each row in the list for further action.

Selecting a list item in the City Guide app opens a web browser to a related webpage or displays an image of an attraction. You could create the list using the ListView component in the Composite category of the Palette within the emulator layout, just as you can with any other user interface component, but coding the list in XML code is the preferred method and is used in the chapter project.

The ListView component can display a vertical scroll bar if you have more items than the screen space can display. In our case, with only five attractions, the ListView will not display a vertical scroll bar because it is not needed. To begin the City Guide app by adding a custom icon launcher, follow these steps:

Step 1

- Open the Android Studio program.
- In the Welcome to Android Studio window, scroll down and click the New Project button in the Phone and Tablet templates to create a new Android Studio project.
- Click the Next button in the New Project window.
- Type **City Guide** in the Name text box.
- If necessary, select Java in the Language text box.
- If necessary, select API 23: Android 6.0 (Marshmallow) as the Minimum SDK.

A new Java Android project named City Guide is configured to save on your local computer (**Figure 5-4**).

Step 2

- Click the Finish button in the New Project window.
- Click the Hello world! TextView widget displayed by default in the emulator and press the Delete key.
- Click File on the menu bar and then click New to open the New menu.
- Click Image Asset on the New menu.
- Click the folder symbol in the Path box to open the Asset Studio dialog box.
- To add the custom launcher icon, copy the student files to your computer, if necessary. Open the folder that contains the student files and then select the file city.png.
- In the Asset Studio dialog box, navigate to the location of the city.png file and then select the file.
- Click the OK button to add the custom launcher icon.

The custom launcher icon of the Chicago skyline is displayed in different shapes and sizes (**Figure 5-5**).

Figure 5-4 Application information for the new Android project

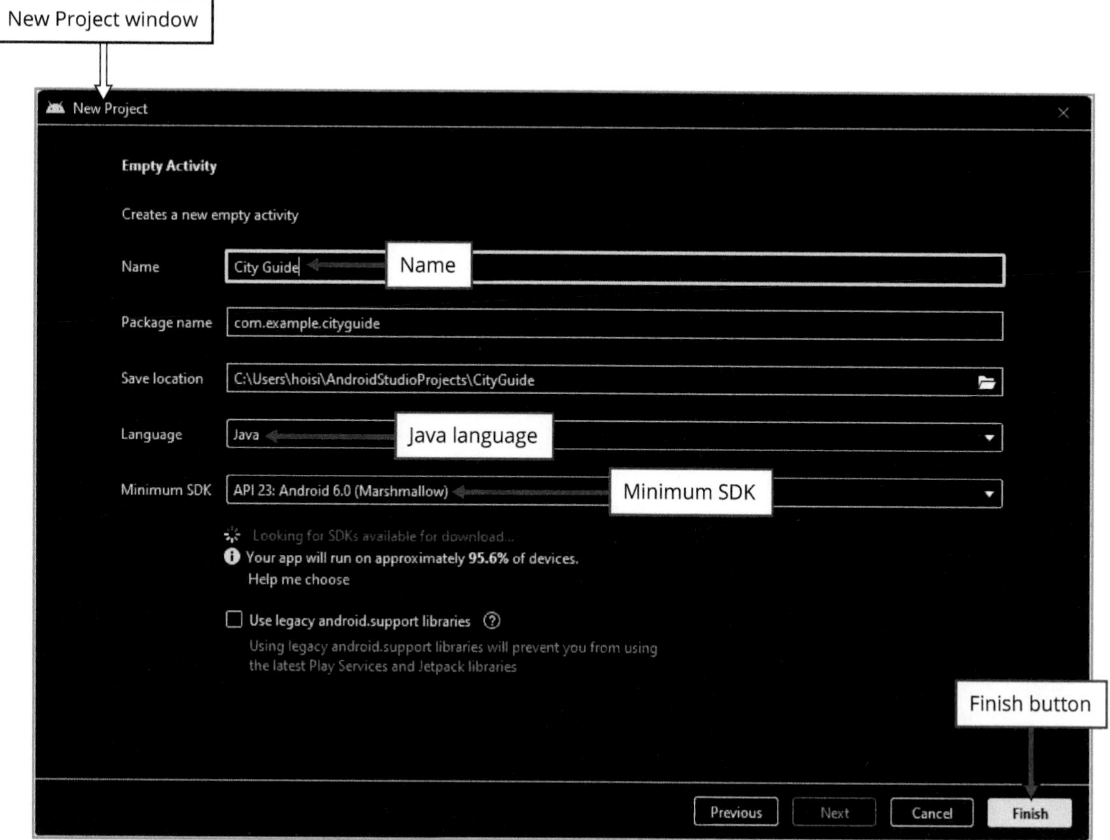

Figure 5-5 Asset Studio dialog box

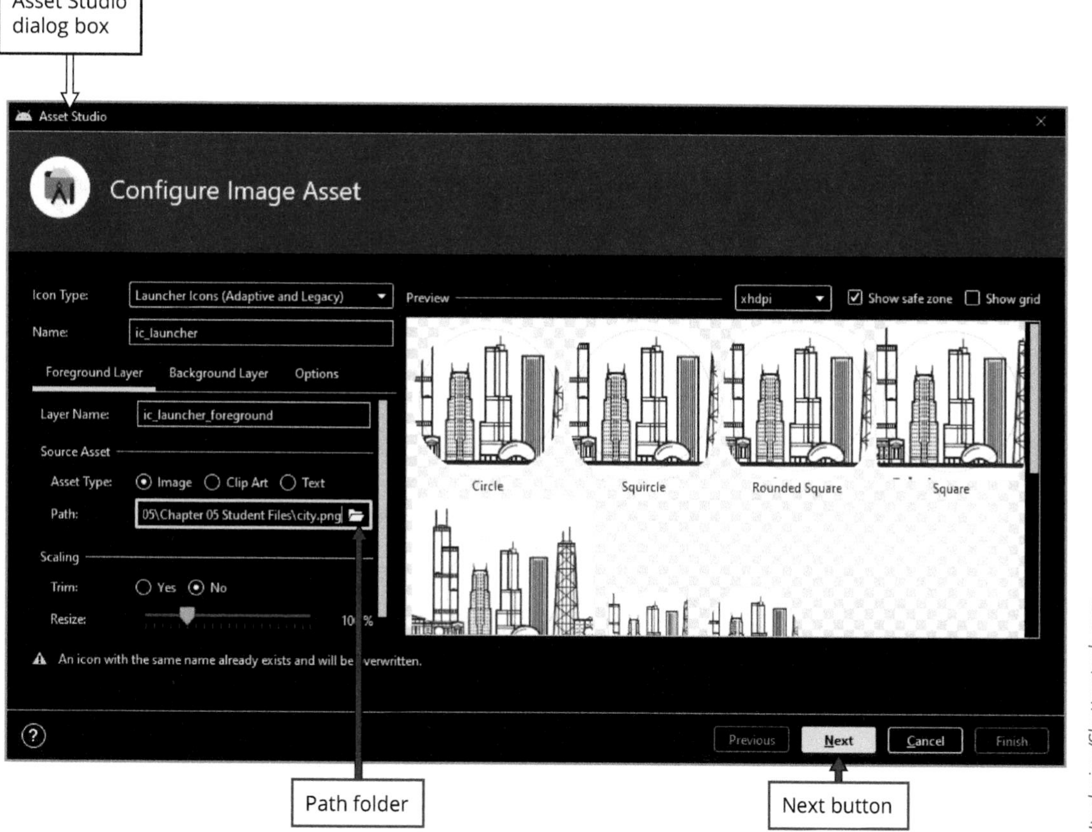

Its design/Shutterstock.com

Step 3

- Click the Next button to view the output directories and then click the Finish button to update the launcher icon.
- Open the MainActivity.java tab.
- Click at the end of Line 12 (setContentView), press Enter, and type the following three statements to display the logo in the Action bar:

  getSupportActionBar().setDisplayShowHomeEnabled(true);

  getSupportActionBar().setLogo(R.mipmap.ic_launcher);

  getSupportActionBar().setDisplayUseLogoEnabled(true);

MainActivity.java has three new statements to display the logo named city.png that was placed in the mipmap folder (**Figure 5-6**). Line 13 displays a miniature logo image near the line number.

Figure 5-6 Code to display launcher icon

MainActivity.java tab open

MainActivity.java × activity_main.xml ×

```
1   package com.example.cityguide;
2
3   import ...
5
6   public class MainActivity extends AppCompatActivity {
7
8       @Override
9       protected void onCreate(Bundle savedInstanceState) {
10          super.onCreate(savedInstanceState);
11          setContentView(R.layout.activity_main);
12          getSupportActionBar().setDisplayShowHomeEnabled(true);
13          getSupportActionBar().setLogo(R.mipmap.ic_launcher);
14          getSupportActionBar().setDisplayUseLogoEnabled(true);
15      }
16  }
```

Code added to display launcher icon

On the Job

Another type of ListView component is the ExpandableListView, which provides a two-level list. For example, if you were renting a car, a list of all the compact cars might be displayed in one category on the top half of your phone and the economy cars might be listed in a separate category at the bottom. The ExpandableListView provides two separate listings.

5.2 Adding a ListView Layout with XML Code

The Layout Editor is one of the companion windows in Android Studio that allows you to customize every step of app design. For a beginner, this is one of the places to start building apps. In the Layout Editor, you can design screens and add components that you will use later in the code. You can design a layout by using the emulator window and then drag and drop components from the Palette, or you can code the activity_main.xml file using XML code in the Layout Editor. The XML code uses an auto-complete feature that assists you as you type XML code. As soon as you start typing an XML command or phrase, the XML code editor shows a list of words or phrases that you can enter without having to type the command completely. This feature makes the application easier to use and improves the user experience.

It is often easier to use the Palette for a simple layout, but understanding how to manipulate XML code can assist you greatly in app design. Android Studio provides a live layout editing mode that lets you preview XML code changes in an emulator directly to the right of the XML code window. The opening screen for the City Guide chapter project (Figure 5-1) requires a custom layout that includes a ListView component to hold a list of Chicago attractions. In the XML code, you must add a ListView component with an id name and determine where the component should appear on the emulator screen. If you type XML code to add a component, the component shows up in the Component Tree of the Layout Editor. To create an XML layout for activity_main.xml, follow these steps:

Step 1

- Click the activity_main.xml tab.
- Click Code in the upper-right portion of the window to display the XML code and show line numbers. By default, a ConstraintLayout is already set.
- Click Line 7 and then press Enter.
- Type **<ListView** and press Enter.

The ListView component is added by entering XML code instead of dragging the ListView component to the emulator from the Palette (**Figure 5-7**).

Figure 5-7 ListView component coded in XML

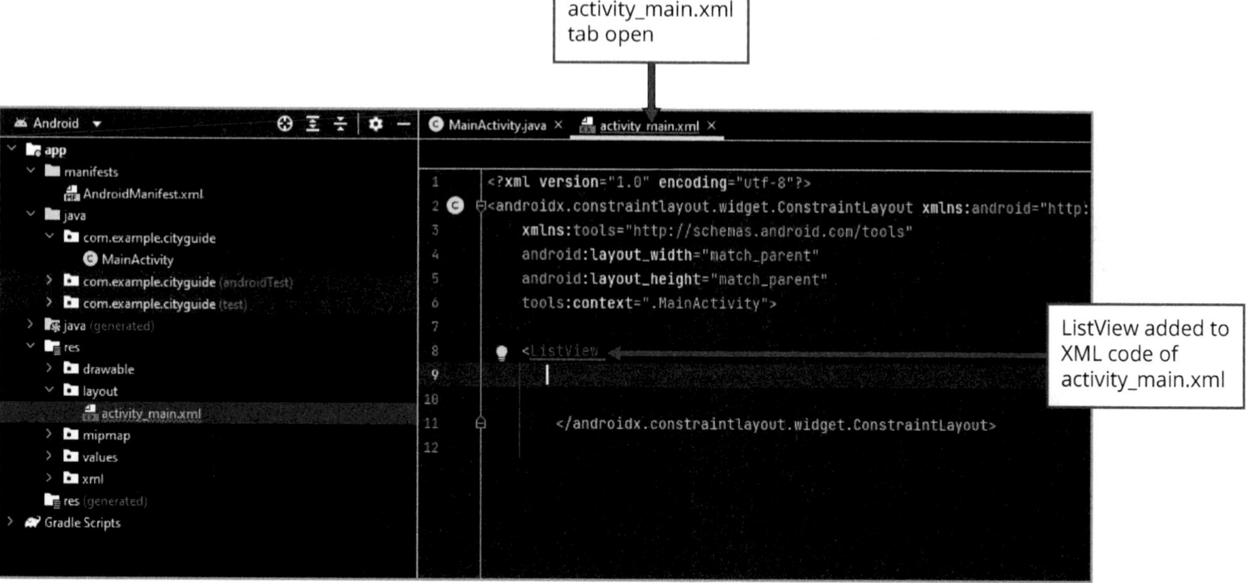

Step 2

- Type the following code using auto-completion as much as possible:

  android:id="@+id/listView"

  android:layout_width="match_parent"

  android:layout_height="fill_parent"

  tools:ignore="MissingConstraints" />

- Press Enter after the closing angle bracket and save your work.

The ListView layout is added in XML code in the activity_main.xml file to display the list of attractions (**Figure 5-8**). The id code represents the name of the ListView component. The next two lines, layout_width and layout_height, are used to define the basic width and height of the element in your layout. The width and height can be specified in any valid dimensional measure (dp, in, mm, pt, sp, px) or you can use a special constant for the width: match_parent and wrap_content. The last line of the preceding code means to ignore the fact that constraint handles have not been pulled to the edges of the emulator. Code is still needed to initialize the ListView component in the MainActivity.java file.

Figure 5-8 ListView layout

MainActivity.java × activity_main.xml ×

```
<?xml version="1.0" encoding="utf-8"?>
<androidx.constraintlayout.widget.ConstraintLayout xmlns:android="http:/
    xmlns:tools="http://schemas.android.com/tools"
    android:layout_width="match_parent"
    android:layout_height="match_parent"
    tools:context=".MainActivity">

    <ListView
        android:id="@+id/listView"
        android:layout_width="match_parent"
        android:layout_height="fill_parent"
        tools:ignore="MissingConstraints" />

</androidx.constraintlayout.widget.ConstraintLayout>
```

ListView layout component and attributes coded in XML

Critical Thinking

What does the Split button in activity_main.xml do?

The Split button provides a powerful option by displaying the code directly to the left of the emulator so you can change attributes in the code or directly in the Attributes pane.

Quick Check

Instead of designing an app with the components in the Palette, what is your other option?

Answer: Code the components with XML code.

5.3 Creating an Array

Before the list of attractions can be displayed in the ListView Layout component, the string of Chicago attraction names must be declared in an array. An **array** is a container object that holds a fixed number of values of a single type. By using an **array variable**, which can store more than one value, you can avoid assigning a separate variable for each item in the list. Each individual item in an array that contains a value is called an **element**.

Every application developed thus far in this book has involved a limited number of variables, but professional programming applications commonly require much larger sets of data using multiple variables. You have learned that data type variables can store only one value at a time; therefore, if you change a variable's value, the previous value is deleted.

Arrays provide access to data by using a numeric index, or subscript, to identify each element in the array. Using an array, you can store a collection of values of similar data types. For example, you can store five string values without having to declare five different variables. Instead, each value is stored in an individual element of the array, and you refer to each element by its index within the array. The index used to reference a value in the first element within an array is zero. Each subsequent element is referenced by an increasing index value, as shown in **Table 5-1**.

Table 5-1 The attraction array with index values

Element	Value
attraction[0]	Art Institute of Chicago
attraction[1]	Magnificent Mile
attraction[2]	Willis Tower
attraction[3]	Chicago Bean
attraction[4]	Water Tower

In Table 5-1, an array named attraction holds five attractions. Each attraction is stored in an array element, and each element is assigned a unique index. The first string is stored in the element with the index of 0. The element is identified by the term attraction[0], pronounced "attraction sub zero."

Declaring an Array

Like declarations for variables of other types, an array declaration has two components: the array's data type and its name. As mentioned, an array is a container object that holds a fixed number of values of a single type. You can declare an array containing numeric values, as in the following coding examples:

```
int[] age={18,21,38,88};
double[] weather={72.3, 65.0, 25.7, 99.5};
char[] initials={'P','N','D'};
```

To declare a String array containing the text values used in the chapter project, use the following code:

Code Syntax

```
String[] attraction = new String[]{"Art Institute of Chicago", "Magnificent
Mile", "Willis Tower", "Chicago Bean", "Water Tower"};
```

The attraction list initialized in the array can easily be expanded to include more items at any time. To assign the list of attractions to the String data type in an array named attraction, follow these steps:

Step 1

- Open the MainActivity.java tab.
- After Line 15 in MainActivity.java, insert a new line.
- Type **String[ ] attraction = new String[]{"Art Institute of Chicago", "Magnificent Mile", "Willis Tower", "Chicago Bean", "Water Tower"};**.

The String array named attraction is assigned the five attractions (**Figure 5-9**).

Figure 5-9 Array of attractions assigned

```
1   package com.example.cityguide;
2
3   import ...
5
6   public class MainActivity extends AppCompatActivity {
7
8       @Override
9       protected void onCreate(Bundle savedInstanceState) {
10          super.onCreate(savedInstanceState);
11          setContentView(R.layout.activity_main);
12          getSupportActionBar().setDisplayShowHomeEnabled(true);
13          getSupportActionBar().setLogo(R.mipmap.ic_launcher);
14          getSupportActionBar().setDisplayUseLogoEnabled(true);
15          String[] attraction = new String[]{"Art Institute of Chicago", "Magnificent Mile", "Willis Tower", "Chicago Be
16      }
```

Five Chicago attractions assigned to a String array named attraction

Step 2

- Save your work.

Good to Know

To declare an array without assigning actual values, allocate the size of the array in the brackets to reserve the room needed in memory, as in int[ ] ages = new int[100];. The first number assigned to the ages array is placed in ages [0]. This array holds 101 elements, one more than the maximum index. The actual values can be assigned later as input values.

Quick Check

Use Java code to create a string array called months for the first three months of the year.

Answer: Type **String[ ] month={"January", "February", "March"};**.

5.4 Initializing a ListView Layout Component

After declaring the array of attractions, use the Android ListView layout to display the attraction in a vertical scrollable list. The list items in the array are automatically inserted in the ListView component using a Java Adapter that pulls content from a source such as an array or database. To initialize the ListView component, follow these steps:

Step 1

- In Line 7, type **ListView listView;** to declare the ListView component.
- Click the red ListView text and import the ListView class by pressing Alt+Enter.

The ListView component is initialized (**Figure 5-10**).

Figure 5-10 ListView component initialized

MainActivity.java × activity_main.xml ×

```
1   package com.example.cityguide;
2
3   import ...
7
8   public class MainActivity extends AppCompatActivity {
9       ListView listView;
10      @Override
11      protected void onCreate(Bundle savedInstanceState) {
12          super.onCreate(savedInstanceState);
13          setContentView(R.layout.activity_main);
14          getSupportActionBar().setDisplayShowHomeEnabled(true);
15          getSupportActionBar().setLogo(R.mipmap.ic_launcher);
16          getSupportActionBar().setDisplayUseLogoEnabled(true);
17          String[] attraction = new String[]{"Art Institute of Chicago", "Magnificent Mile", "Willis Tower", "Chicago Bean", "Water Tower"};
18      }
19  }
```

ListView component initialized

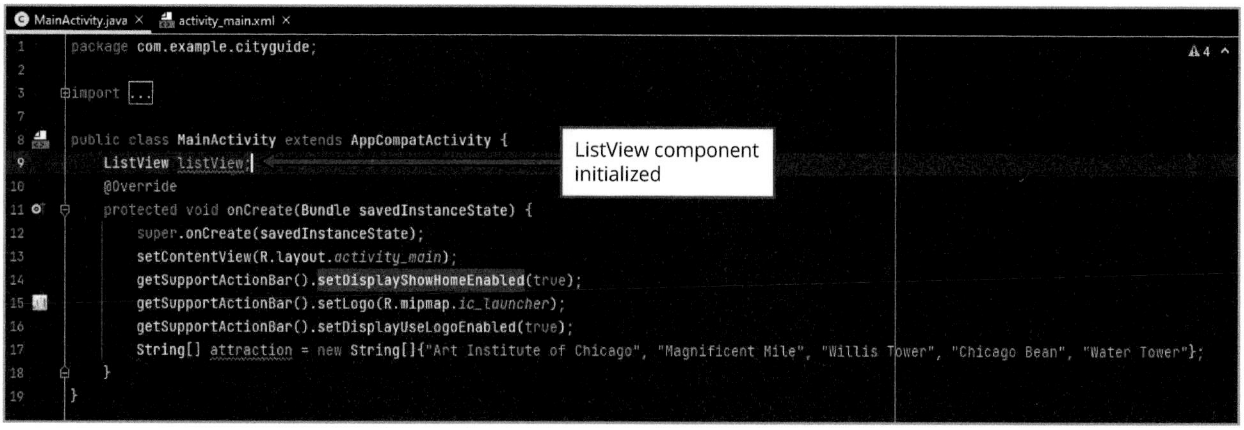

Step 2

- On Line 18, type **listView = findViewById(R.id.listView);** to assign the listView variable.

The ListView component is defined in code (**Figure 5-11**).

Figure 5-11 ListView layout defined

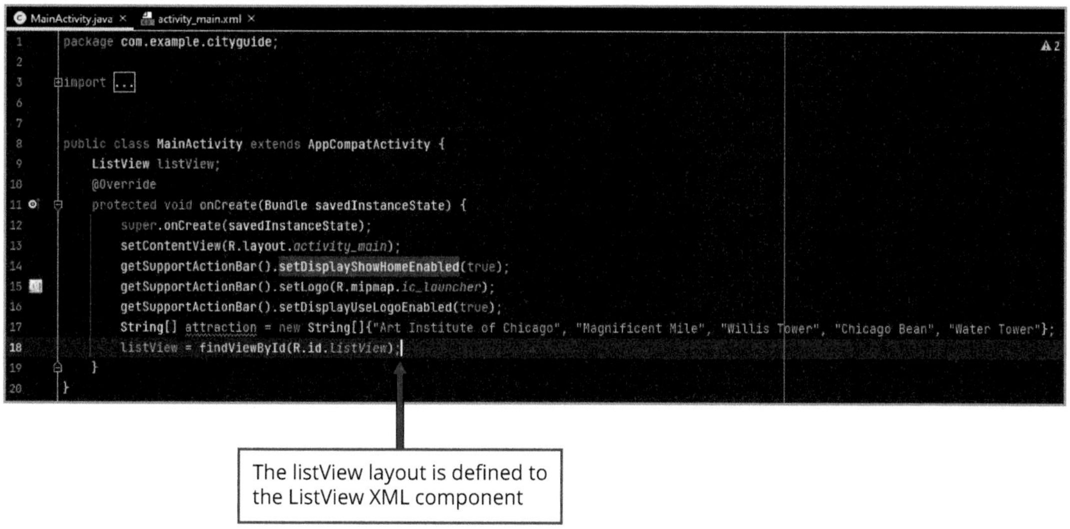

MainActivity.java × activity_main.xml ×

```
1   package com.example.cityguide;
2
3   import ...
6
7
8   public class MainActivity extends AppCompatActivity {
9       ListView listView;
10      @Override
11      protected void onCreate(Bundle savedInstanceState) {
12          super.onCreate(savedInstanceState);
13          setContentView(R.layout.activity_main);
14          getSupportActionBar().setDisplayShowHomeEnabled(true);
15          getSupportActionBar().setLogo(R.mipmap.ic_launcher);
16          getSupportActionBar().setDisplayUseLogoEnabled(true);
17          String[] attraction = new String[]{"Art Institute of Chicago", "Magnificent Mile", "Willis Tower", "Chicago Bean", "Water Tower"};
18          listView = findViewById(R.id.listView);
19      }
20  }
```

The listView layout is defined to the ListView XML component

5.5 Displaying an Array in the ListView with an ArrayAdapter

In the City Guide application, after the array is assigned and the ListView component is initialized, you can display an array listing using adapters. An **adapter** provides a data model for the layout of the list and for converting the array data into list items. The ListView and ArrayAdapter work together to display a list. You can use an ArrayAdapter when your data source is an array. For example, if you want to share an iPad screen with a group, you need an adapter to connect to a projector and display the image on a large screen. Similarly, an ArrayAdapter is the most commonly used adapter in Android. When you have a list of single-type items that are stored in an array, you can use an ArrayAdapter.

The **ArrayAdapter<String>** supplies the String array data to the ListView. The three parameters that follow ArrayAdapter refer to the *this* class, a generic layout called simple_list_item_l, and the array named attraction. The following code syntax shows the complete statement:

Code Syntax

```
ArrayAdapter<String> adapter = new ArrayAdapter<>(this, android.R.layout.simple_
list_item_1, android.R.id.text1, attraction);
```

Follow these steps to add the ArrayAdapter that displays the array as a list:

Step 1

- After the line of code that includes findViewbyId, press Enter.
- Type **ArrayAdapter<String> adapter = new ArrayAdapter<>(this, android.R.layout.simple_list_item_1, android.R.id.text1, attraction);** and press Enter.
- Click the red ArrayAdapter text and import ArrayAdapter by pressing Alt+Enter.

The ArrayAdapter displays the attraction array as text in a generic ListView layout (**Figure 5-12**).

Figure 5-12 ArrayAdapter code

Step 2

- On the next line, type **listView.setAdapter(adapter);**.
- To display the attraction list in the generic ListView layout, click Run app on the toolbar.

The application opens in the emulator window and displays the ListView component with the five Chicago attractions (**Figure 5-13**). At this point, the list items do not respond when you click them because you have not created that portion of the app.

Figure 5-13 Line of setAdapter code

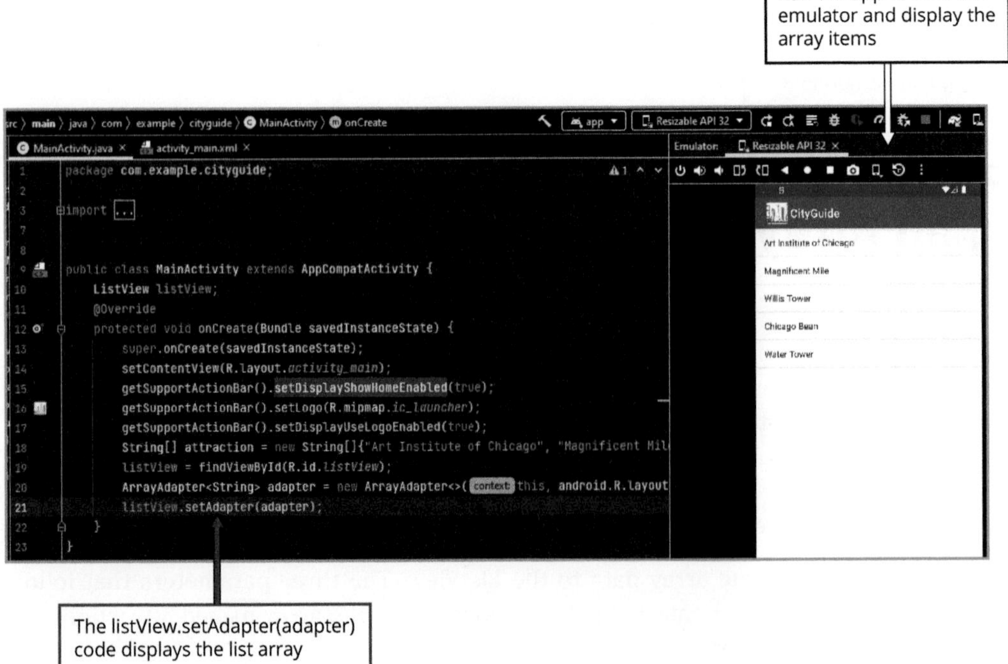

Step 3

- Close the emulated application window.

Good to Know Other generic layouts of the ListView object include simple_list_item_2, simple_list_item_checked (which displays check boxes), and simple_list_item_multiple_choice, which simply displays different layouts. Feel free to try these layouts.

Adding the Images to the Resources Folder

The City Guide application uses several images throughout the app. Images of the Willis Tower, the Chicago Bean, and the Water Tower appear when the user selects those items from the opening list. To place a copy of the images from your computer into the res/drawable folder, follow these steps:

Step 1

- To add the three image files to the drawable resource folder, select willis.png, bean.png, and water.png, then press Ctrl+C.
- To paste the image files to the drawable folder, press and hold or right-click the drawable folder in the Android project view pane.
- Release the mouse button. Click the OK button in the Copy dialog box and then click the OK button. Expand the drawable folder, if necessary.

Copies of the three files appear in the drawable folder (**Figure 5-14**).

Figure 5-14 Images copied

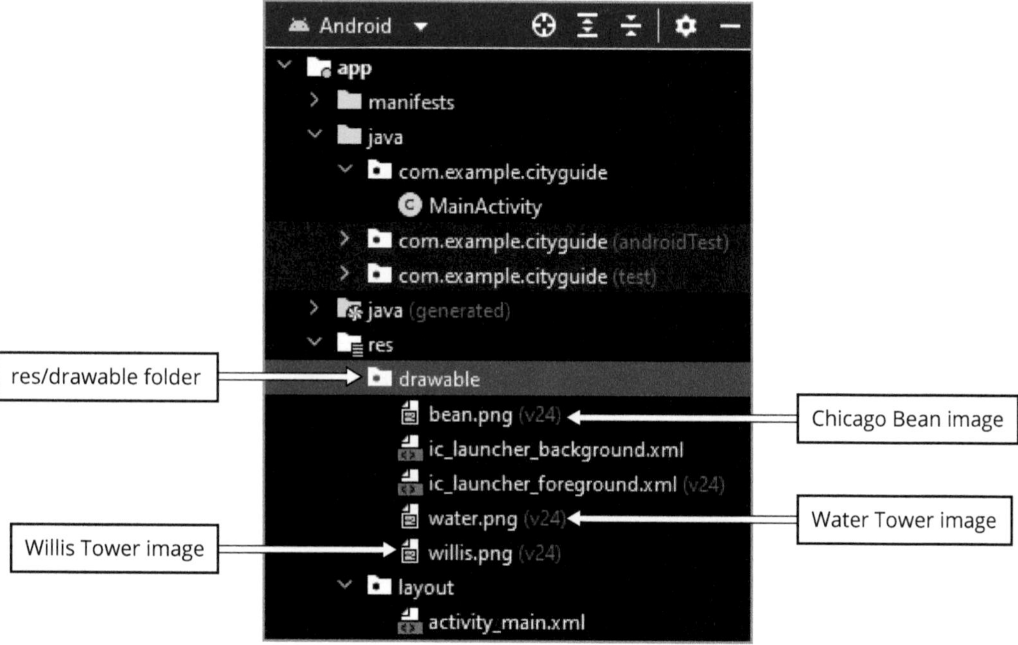

Step 2

- Close the image tabs and click the Save All button on the Standard toolbar to save your work.

On the Job

When publishing Android apps, you must follow copyright laws that apply to any copyrighted images you use. Copyright is the legal protection extended to the authors or owners of original artistic and intellectual works; you must seek copyright permissions to use such work. A copyright holder can seek monetary or statutory damages for a violation of the copyright. However, if an image is accompanied by the statement "This work is dedicated to the public domain," the image is available for fair use in your app. When you use the Google search engine to find an image, you can click Tools, Usage Rights, and then Creative Common licenses to find public-domain images.

Adding the String Table

To add three strings for the three ImageView component descriptions, follow these steps:

Step 1

- In the res\values folder, double-click the strings.xml file.
- Click the Open editor link in strings.xml.
- Click the Add Key button (plus sign), type **willis** in the Key text box, and then type **Willis Tower Image** in the Default Value text box. Click the OK button.
- Click the Add Key button again, type **bean** in the Key text box, and then type **Chicago Bean Image** in the Default Value text box. Click the OK button.
- Click the Add Key button again, type **water** in the Key text box, and then type **Water Tower Image** in the Default Value text box. Click the OK button.
- Click the Reload string resources button.

The image description keys are entered in the Translations Editor (**Figure 5-15**).

Figure 5-15 String table

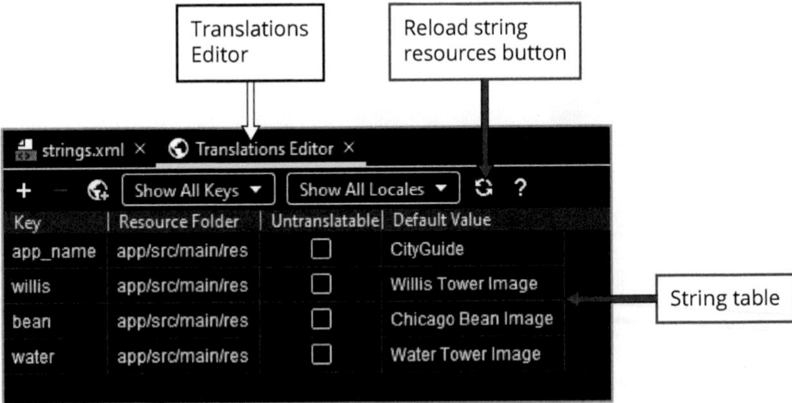

Step 2

- Save your work and close the Translations Editor and strings.xml tabs.

5.6 Calling the setOnItemClick( ) Method

The City Guide opening screen has a list shown in Figure 5-1. Each of the attractions displayed in the list can be selected by tapping the attraction name on a mobile device. The method **setOnItemClick( )** is called when an item in the list is selected. The setOnListItemClick( ) method is similar to the Button OnClickListener, which awaits user interaction. When an attraction in the list is selected, the **position** of the item is passed from setOnItemClick( ) and evaluated with a decision structure, as shown in the following code syntax. If the user selects the first attraction (Art Institute of Chicago), the position parameter is assigned an integer value of 0. The second item is assigned the position of 1, and so forth. The first position or index of an array is always zero.

Code Syntax

```
listView.setOnItemClickListener(new AdapterView.OnItemClickListener()
```

When you type in the preceding line of code, Android Studio automatically creates the following method stub:

```
public void onItemClick(AdapterView<?> parent, View view, int position,
long id) {
}
```

In the preceding code, the int position argument represents the position number of the selected attraction. To code the onItemClick( ) method to respond to the event of the user's selection, follow these steps:

Step 1

- In MainActivity.java, click after Line 24 to add a new line.
- To respond to the user's selection from the attraction list, type **listView.setOnItemClickListener(new AdapterView.OnItemClickListener()**. This code creates a setOnItemClick( ) method to await the user's selection from the ListView items.
- Type an opening brace { after the statement and press Enter. A closing brace is automatically placed in the code.
- After the code is entered to reference the ListView, click the red AdapterView text, press Alt+Enter, and select Import Class, if necessary.

The onListItemClick( ) method detects the selection's position and adds the onItemClick( ) method stub (**Figure 5-16**).

Figure 5-16 Adding the onItemClick( ) method stub

```
MainActivity.java ×   activity_main.xml ×
11  public class MainActivity extends AppCompatActivity {
12      ListView listView;
13
14      @Override
15      protected void onCreate(Bundle savedInstanceState) {
16          super.onCreate(savedInstanceState);
17          setContentView(R.layout.activity_main);
18          getSupportActionBar().setDisplayShowHomeEnabled(true);
19          getSupportActionBar().setLogo(R.mipmap.ic_launcher);
20          getSupportActionBar().setDisplayUseLogoEnabled(true);
21          String[] attraction = new String[]{"Art Institute of Chicago", "Magnificent Mile", "Willis Tower", "Chicago Bean", "Water Tower"};
22          listView = findViewById(R.id.listView);
23          ArrayAdapter<String> adapter = new ArrayAdapter<>( context: this, android.R.layout.simple_list_item_1, android.R.id.text1, attraction);
24          listView.setAdapter(adapter);
25          listView.setOnItemClickListener(new AdapterView.OnItemClickListener() {
26              @Override
27              public void onItemClick(AdapterView<?> parent, View view, int position, long id) {
28
29              }
30          });
31      }
32  }
33
```

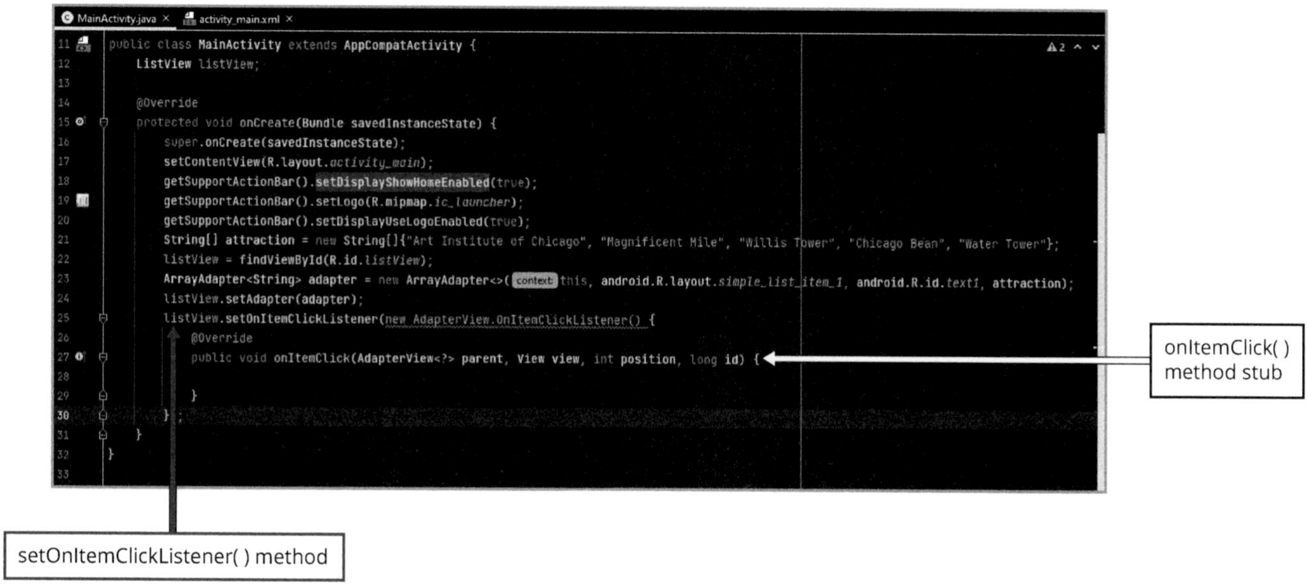

Step 2

- Save your work.

5.7 Creating a Decision Structure with a Switch Statement

Each item in a list produces a different result when selected, such as opening a web browser or displaying a picture on a second screen. In Chapter 4, If statements evaluated the user's selection and the decision structure determined the results. You can use another decision structure called a Switch statement with a list or menu. The **Switch** statement allows you to choose from many statements based on an integer or single character (char) input. The switch keyword is followed by an integer expression in parentheses, which is followed by its cases, all enclosed in braces, as shown in the following code syntax:

Code Syntax

```
switch(position){
case 0:
   //statements that are executed if position == 0
break;
case 1:
   //statements that are executed if position == 1
break;
default:
   //statements that are executed if position != any of the cases
}
```

The integer named *position* is evaluated in the Switch statement and executes the corresponding case. The **case** keyword is followed by a value and a colon. Typically, the statement within a case ends with a **break** statement, which exits the Switch decision structure and continues with the next statement. Be careful not to omit the break statement or the subsequent case statement will be executed as well. If there is no matching case value, the default option is executed. A default statement is optional. In the chapter project, a default statement is not necessary because the user must select one of the items in the list for an action to occur.

Critical Thinking

When should I use an If statement instead of a Switch statement decision structure?

Technically, these statements are interchangeable, but a Switch statement is better when you would otherwise be using a list of If statements that all compare the value of the same variable.

In the City Guide app, five attractions make up the list, so the following positions are possible for the Switch statement: case 0, case 1, case 2, case 3, and case 4. To code the Switch decision structure, follow these steps:

Step 1

- On Line 28, within the braces of the onItemClick( ) method, type **switch(position){** and press Enter for the closing brace to appear.

The Switch decision structure is coded within the onListItemClick( ) method to determine which attraction is selected (**Figure 5-17**).

Figure 5-17 Switch statement

```
@Override
public void onItemClick(AdapterView<?> parent, View view, int position, long id) {
    switch(position){

    }
}
});
}
}
```

Step 2

- Within the braces of the Switch statement, add the case integer options. Type the following code, inserting a blank line after each case statement:

```
case 0:
    break;
case 1:
    break;
case 2:
    break;
case 3:
    break;
case 4:
    break;
```

The case statements for the five selections in the attractions list are coded (**Figure 5-18**).

Figure 5-18 Case statements

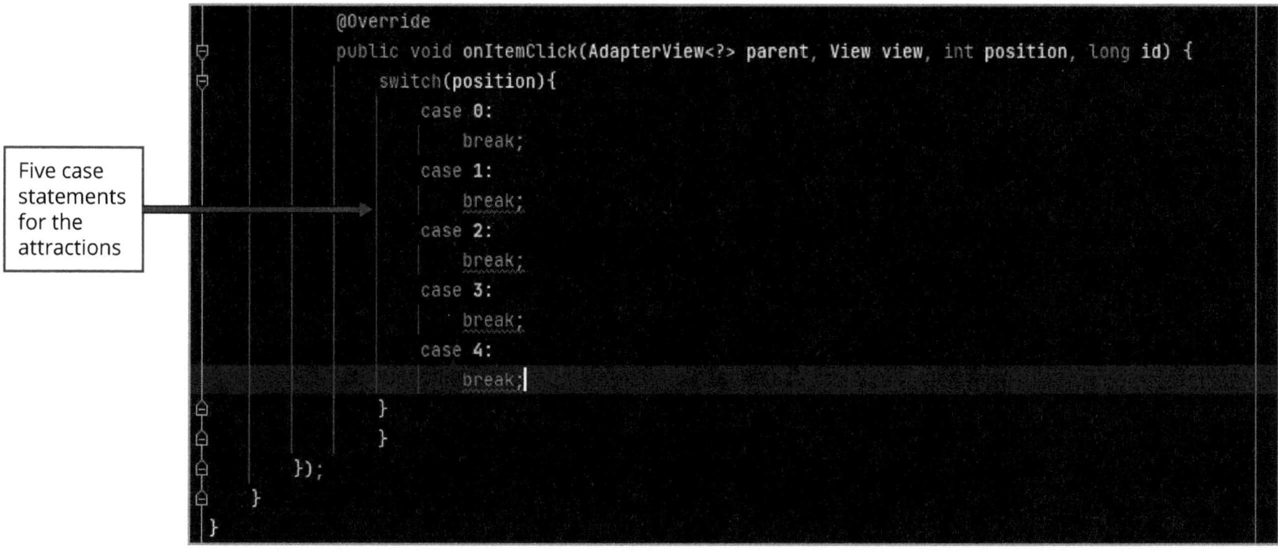

Critical Thinking

Is the last break statement necessary after case 4, considering the Switch statement ends after case 4?

Technically, the last break is not required, but it is recommended so that modifying the code is less error prone. For example, if another attraction is added to the City Guide app, case 5 would be placed after the last break statement.

Good to Know

Switch statements do not allow ranges such as 10–50 (as in 10 to 50). Use If statements when evaluating a range of numbers or specific strings.

Quick Check

Write a Switch statement named month for determining the first three months of the year, and display a comment with the month name.

Answer:

```
switch (month) {
case 0:
//January
    break;
case 1:
//February
    break;
case 2:
//March
    break;
}
```

5.8 Understanding Android Intents

When the user selects one of the first two list items in the chapter project, Art Institute of Chicago or Magnificent Mile, a built-in Android browser launches a website about the attraction. A browser is launched with Android code using an intent. Android intents send and receive activities and services that include opening a webpage in a browser, calling a phone number, locating a GPS position on a map, posting your notes to a note-taking program such as Evernote, opening your contacts list, sending a photo, or even posting to your social network. Additional Android intents are explored throughout the rest of this book. Android intents are powerful features that allow apps to talk to each other in a very simple way.

To better understand an intent, imagine a student sitting in a classroom. To ask a question or make a request, the student raises a hand. The teacher is alerted and responds to the student. An intent works the same way. Your app "raises its hand" and the other apps state that they are ready to handle the request. When the chapter project sends an intent, the browser app handles the request and opens the website.

On the Job

Android platform devices have many options for supported browsers. As a developer, you can test an app on your actual Android phone using popular browsers that include Chrome, Microsoft Edge, Opera, Mozilla Firefox Mobile, and Samsung Internet.

5.9 Launching a Browser from an Android Device

Android phones have a built-in browser with an intent filter that accepts intent requests from other apps. The intent sends the browser a **URI** (Uniform Resource Identifier), a string that identifies web resources. You might already be familiar with the term **URL** (Uniform Resource Locator), which means a website address. A URI is a URL with additional information necessary for gaining access to the resources required for posting a webpage.

Depending on the browsers installed on an Android device, Android selects a suitable browser (usually a user-set preferred browser), which accepts an action called ACTION_VIEW (it must be in caps) and displays the site. **ACTION_VIEW** is the most common action performed on data. It is a generic action you can use to send any request to get the most reasonable action to occur. As shown in the following code syntax for the chapter project, a startActivity statement informs the current Activity that a new Activity is being started and the browser opens the website—in this case, the Art Institute of Chicago site:

Code Syntax

```
startActivity(new Intent(Intent.ACTION_VIEW, Uri.parse("http://artic.edu")));
```

When the user selects the Art Institute of Chicago item from the attractions list, the Switch statement sends an integer value of zero to the case statements. The case 0: statement is true, so the program executes the startActivity statement, which sends the browser a parsed string containing the URI web address. The browser application then launches the Art Institute of Chicago website. When you click the Back button in some browser windows or the left arrow to the right of the menu button on the right side of the emulator, the previous Activity opens. In the chapter project, the attractions list is displayed again.

To code the startActivity that launches a website in an Android browser, follow these steps:

Step 1

- In MainActivity.java, add a blank line after the line containing case 0: inside the Switch decision structure.
- Type **startActivity(new Intent(Intent.ACTION_VIEW, Uri.parse ("*http://artic.edu*")));**.
- Click Intent and press Alt+Enter, if necessary.
- Click Uri and then press Alt+Enter.

The startActivity code launches the Art Institute of Chicago website when the user selects the first list item (**Figure 5-19**). Some websites, such as this one, are especially designed for mobile devices.

Figure 5-19 Code for launching the Art Institute of Chicago website

startActivity code launches the Art Institute website

```
switch(position){
    case 0:
        startActivity(new Intent(Intent.ACTION_VIEW, Uri.parse ("http://artic.edu ")));
        break;
    case 1:
        break;
```

Step 2

- In MainActivity.java, click the blank line after the line containing case 1:.
- Type **startActivity(new Intent(Intent.ACTION_VIEW, Uri.parse ("*http://themagnificentmile.com*")));**.

The startActivity code launches the Magnificent Mile website when the user selects the second list item (**Figure 5-20**).

Figure 5-20 Code for launching the Magnificent Mile website

```
case 0:
    startActivity(new Intent(Intent.ACTION_VIEW, Uri.parse ("http://artic.edu ")));
    break;
case 1:
    startActivity(new Intent(Intent.ACTION_VIEW, Uri.parse ("http://themagnificentmile.com" )));
    break;
```

Launches the Magnificent Mile website

Step 3

- To display the Magnificent Mile website in the browser, click Run on the menu bar and then select Run.
- If necessary, select Android Application and click the OK button.
- Save all the files in the next dialog box, if necessary, and unlock the emulator.
- Select the Magnificent Mile list item.

The item is selected from the list in the emulator and the Android browser displays the Magnificent Mile website. The site loads slowly in the emulator (**Figure 5-21**).

Figure 5-21 Browser opens in the emulator to display *www.themagnificentmile.com*

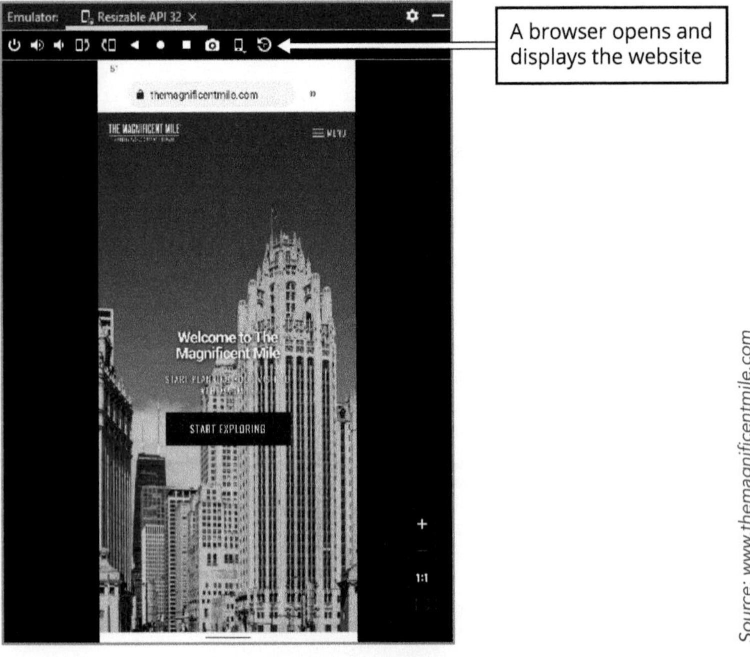

Source: www.themagnificentmile.com

Step 4

- Close the emulated application window.

On the Job | Be sure to test any links within your Android apps often. If you have hundreds of web links, verifying the links can be simple in concept but very time-consuming in practice. A good place to start is with the World Wide Web Consortium's free Web Site Validation Service (*http://validator.w3.org*).

Quick Check

What does URI stand for?

Answer: Uniform Resource Identifier.

Adding Multiple Class Files

Multiple classes are needed to display images on the screen when the user selects Willis Tower, Chicago Bean, or Water Tower on the opening ListView component. An onCreate( ) method requests that the user interface opens to display an image of the attraction. Remember, each time you add a class to an application, the class must begin with a capital letter; a coordinating XML layout file with the same name but a lowercase beginning letter is automatically created. To create three class files and the coordinating XML layout files, follow these steps:

Step 1

- In the Android project view, create a second class: Expand the java folder, right-click the first com.example.cityguide folder, point to New on the shortcut menu, and then click Activity. Next, click Empty Activity.
- Type **Willis** in the Activity Name text box to create a second class that will define the Willis Activity and a layout named activity_willis associated with the class.

A new class named Willis that creates activity_willis.xml appears in the New Android Activity dialog box with the title Willis Tower (**Figure 5-22**).

Figure 5-22 Creating the Willis.java class file

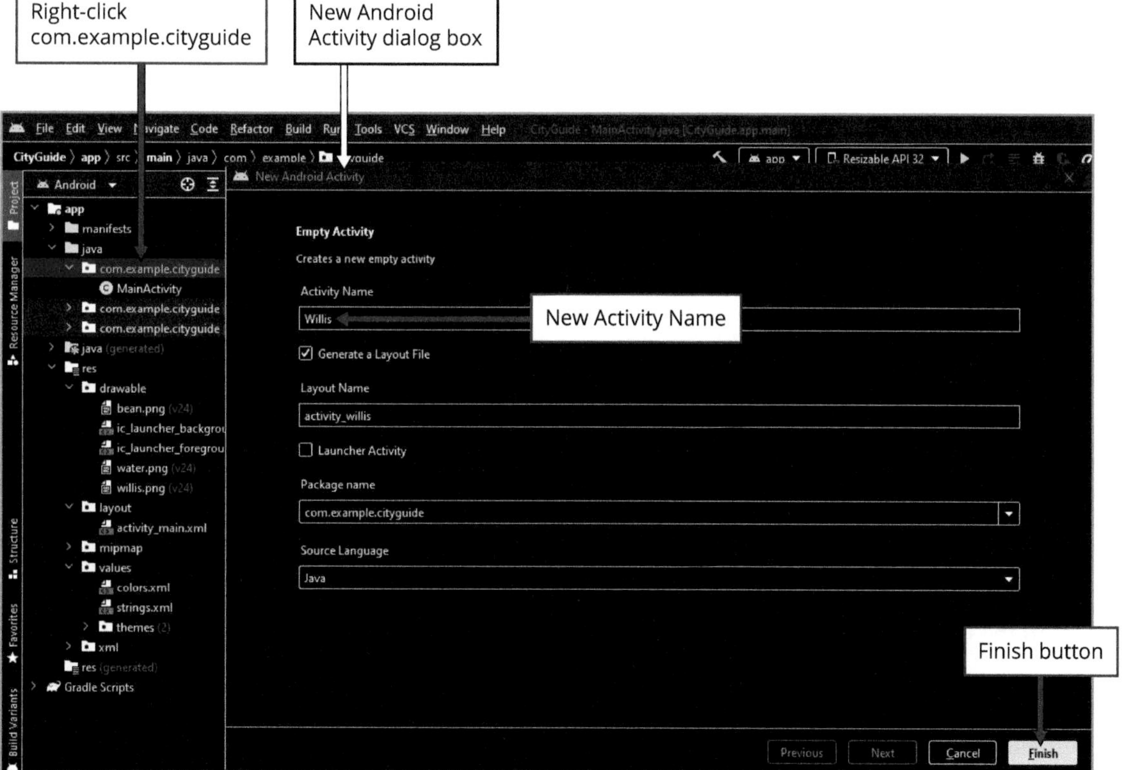

Step 2

- Click the Finish button. Notice the Activity includes an onCreate( ) method to launch activity_willis.
- Close the Willis.java file tab.
- To create a third class, right-click the first com.example.cityguide folder, point to New on the shortcut menu, and then click Activity. Next, click Empty Activity.
- Type **Bean** in the Activity Name text box to create a third class that will define the Bean Activity.
- Click the Finish button.
- Close the Bean.java file tab.
- To create a fourth class, right-click the com.example.cityguide folder, point to New on the shortcut menu, and click Activity. Next, click Empty Activity.
- Type **Water** in the Activity Name text box to create a fourth class that will define the Water Activity.
- Click the Finish button and save your work.
- Close the Water.java tab.

Three new Activity java files are created with three XML layout files in Android project view (**Figure 5-23**).

Figure 5-23 Four Java Activity classes and four XML layout files

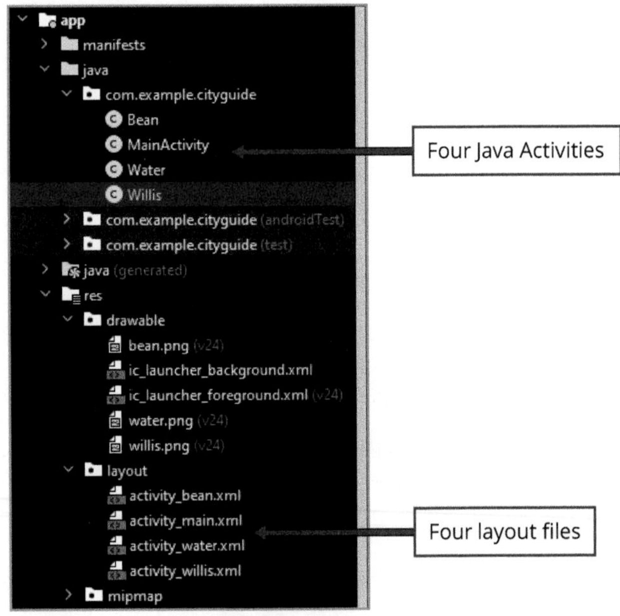

Designing XML Layout Files

The last three case statements are used to open a second screen that displays a picture of the selected attraction. Three XML layout files must be designed to display an ImageView component with an image source file. To add an ImageView component in the three XML layout files, follow these steps:

Step 1

- Open the activity_willis.xml tab and click the Design button, if necessary.
- In the Palette, drag the ImageView component to the top of the emulator.

- Drag all four constraint handles to the edges of the emulator.
- Type **imgWillis** in the id attribute to name the ImageView component and click the Refactor button.
- Click the Pick a Resource rectangle to the right of the contentDescription attribute and click willis in the Pick a Resource dialog box. Click the OK button.

The willis XML file is designed with an image of the Willis Tower and with the accessibility text set in the contentDescription property (**Figure 5-24**).

Figure 5-24 The activity_willis.xml layout file

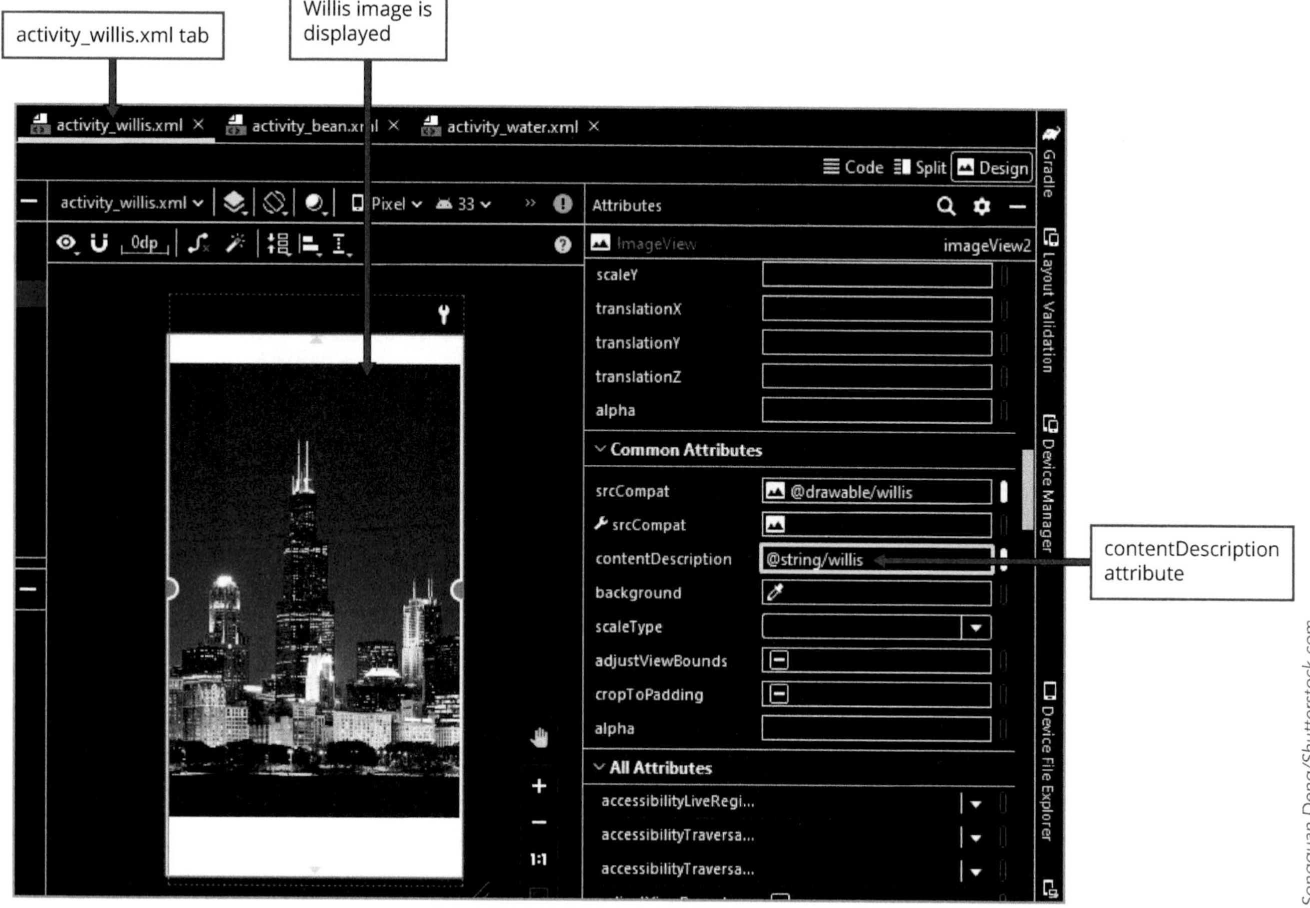

Step 2

- Close the activity_willis.xml file tab and save your work.
- Click the activity_bean.xml tab. If necessary, click the Design button to open the emulator window.
- In the Palette, drag the ImageView component to the top of the emulator.
- Type **imgBean** in the id attribute to name the ImageView component and click the Refactor button.
- Drag all four constraint handles to the edges of the emulator.
- Click the Pick a Resource rectangle to the right of the contentDescription attribute and click bean in the Pick a Resource dialog box. Click the OK button.

The activity_bean XML file is designed with an image of the Chicago Bean (**Figure 5-25**).

Figure 5-25 The activity_bean.xml file

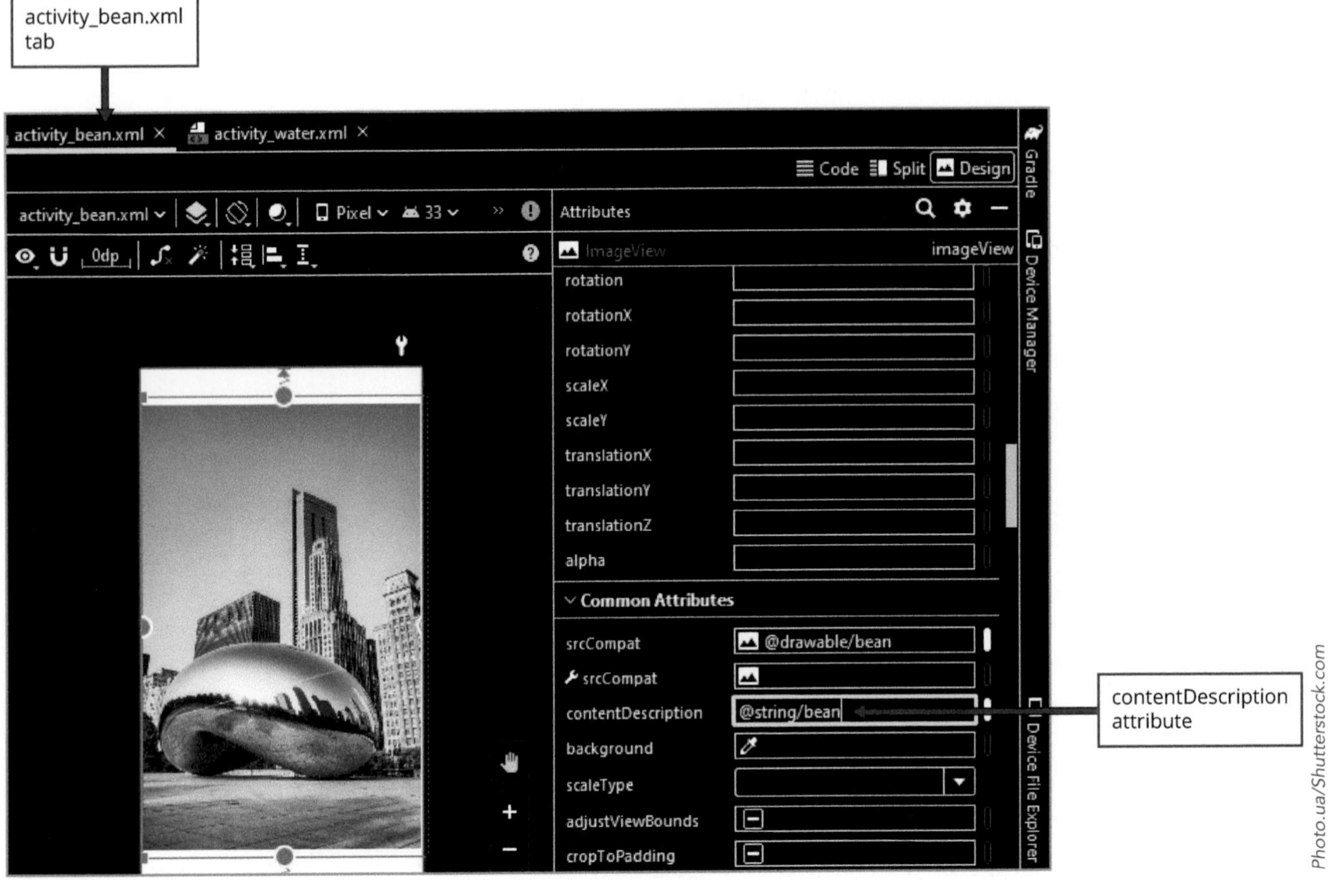

Photo.ua/Shutterstock.com

Step 3

- Close the activity_bean.xml file tab and save your work.
- Click the activity_water.xml tab. If necessary, click the Design button to open the emulator window.
- In the Palette, drag the ImageView component to the top of the emulator.
- Type **imgWater** in the id attribute to name the ImageView component and click the Refactor button.
- Drag all four constraint handles to the edges of the emulator.
- Click the Pick a Resource rectangle to the right of the contentDescription attribute and click water in the Pick a Resource dialog box. Click the OK button.

The water XML file is designed with an image of the Chicago Water Tower (**Figure 5-26**).

Figure 5-26 The activity_water.xml file

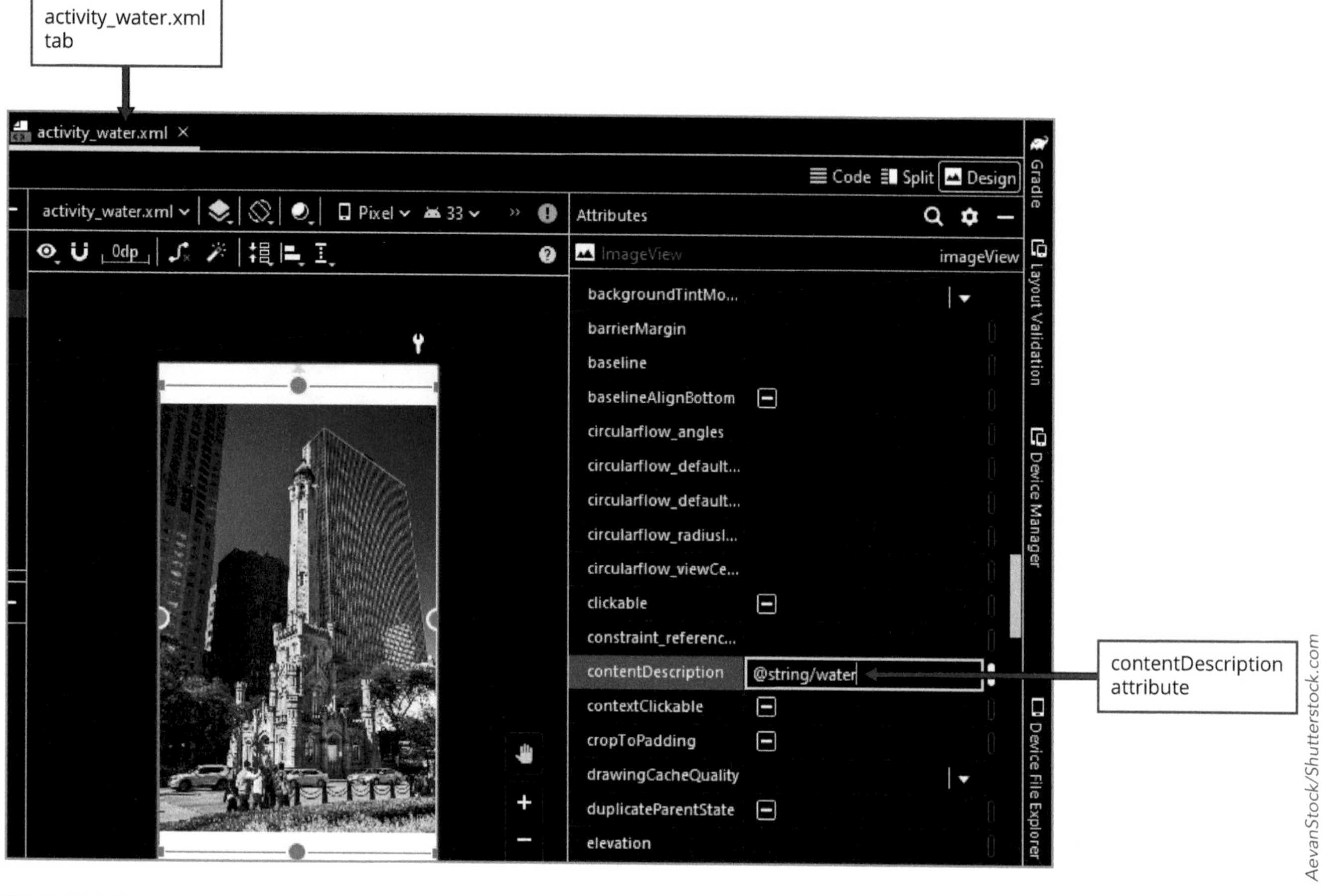

Coding the Multiple Class Files

The last step in the development of the Chicago City Guide app is to launch the class files when the user selects Willis Tower (case 2), Chicago Bean (case 3), or Water Tower (case 4) from the ListView component. A startActivity( ) method opens the next Activity, which in turn launches the appropriate XML layout that displays an image of the attraction. To code the remaining case statements within the Switch decision structure that start each of the Activities, follow these steps:

Step 1

- Close the activity_water.xml tab.
- In MainActivity.java, add a blank line below the statement containing case 2: and type **startActivity(new Intent(MainActivity.this, Willis.class));**.
- Add a blank line below the one containing case 3: and type **startActivity(new Intent(MainActivity.this, Bean.class));**.
- Add a blank line below the one containing case 4: and type **startActivity(new Intent(MainActivity.this, Water.class));**.

The case statements 2 through 4 are coded with a startActivity that executes the appropriate class (**Figure 5-27**).

Figure 5-27 Complete code for MainActivity.java class

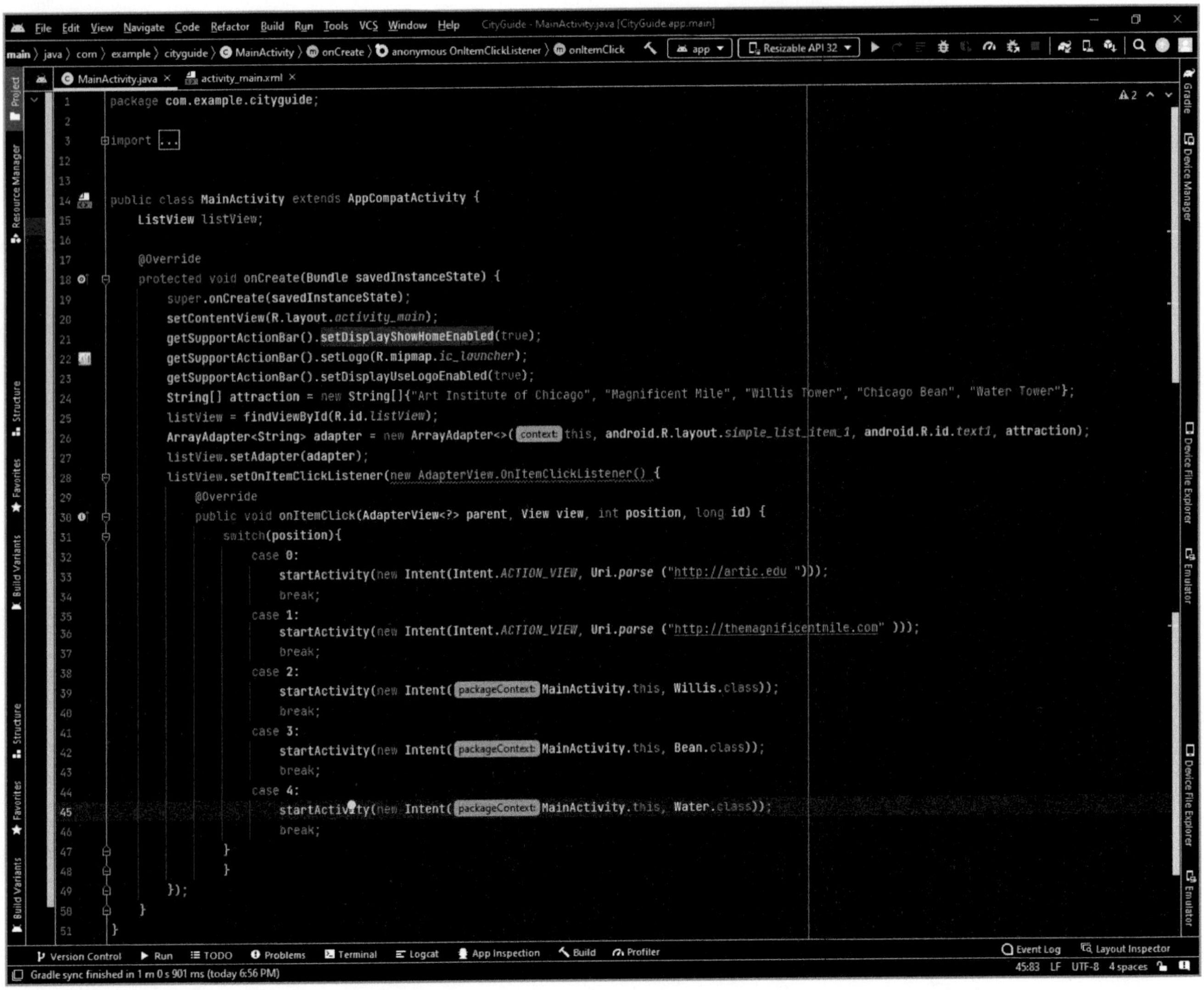

```
package com.example.cityguide;

import ...


public class MainActivity extends AppCompatActivity {
    ListView listView;

    @Override
    protected void onCreate(Bundle savedInstanceState) {
        super.onCreate(savedInstanceState);
        setContentView(R.layout.activity_main);
        getSupportActionBar().setDisplayShowHomeEnabled(true);
        getSupportActionBar().setLogo(R.mipmap.ic_launcher);
        getSupportActionBar().setDisplayUseLogoEnabled(true);
        String[] attraction = new String[]{"Art Institute of Chicago", "Magnificent Mile", "Willis Tower", "Chicago Bean", "Water Tower"};
        listView = findViewById(R.id.listView);
        ArrayAdapter<String> adapter = new ArrayAdapter<>( context: this, android.R.layout.simple_list_item_1, android.R.id.text1, attraction);
        listView.setAdapter(adapter);
        listView.setOnItemClickListener(new AdapterView.OnItemClickListener() {
            @Override
            public void onItemClick(AdapterView<?> parent, View view, int position, long id) {
                switch(position){
                    case 0:
                        startActivity(new Intent(Intent.ACTION_VIEW, Uri.parse ("http://artic.edu ")));
                        break;
                    case 1:
                        startActivity(new Intent(Intent.ACTION_VIEW, Uri.parse ("http://themagnificentmile.com" )));
                        break;
                    case 2:
                        startActivity(new Intent( packageContext: MainActivity.this, Willis.class));
                        break;
                    case 3:
                        startActivity(new Intent( packageContext: MainActivity.this, Bean.class));
                        break;
                    case 4:
                        startActivity(new Intent( packageContext: MainActivity.this, Water.class));
                        break;
                }
            }
        });
    }
}
```

Step 2

- Compare your code to Figure 5-27, make changes as necessary to match the code in the figure, and then save your work.

5.10 Testing an Application with Multiple Decisions

As you save and run the Chicago City Guide application, be sure to test every option. Before publishing any Android app to Google Play, it is critical to make sure all the fields can gracefully handle any click or any value entered. Click Run on the menu bar and then select Run to save and test the application in the emulator. The first time the application is executed, a dialog box asks how you would like to run the application. Select Android Application and click the OK button. Save all the files in the next dialog box, if necessary, and unlock the emulator. The application opens in the emulator window where you can test each list item in the Chicago City Guide app, as shown in Figures 5-1, 5-2, and 5-3.

On the Job

Testing an Android app is called usability testing. In addition to the traditional tests of navigation and ease of use, Section 508 compliance is a third component to be tested. The 1998 Amendment to Section 508 of the Rehabilitation Act spells out accessibility requirements for people with certain disabilities. For more details, refer to *www.section508.gov.*

Wrap It Up—Chapter Summary

This chapter described the steps to create a list with items that users select to launch websites and XML layouts through the use of a Switch decision structure. The introduction of intents to outside services such as a web browser begins our adventure of many other intent options used throughout the rest of this book.

- The Java View class creates a list and makes it scrollable if it exceeds the length of the screen. To contain the list items, use a ListView component, which allows you to select each row in the list for further action, such as displaying an image or webpage.
- When you want to display a ListView component, you can drag and drop a ListView component from the Palette or create the component in XML code.
- Before you can specify the items in a list, you must declare the item names using an array variable, which can store more than one value of similar data types. For example, you can store five string values in an array without having to declare five variables.
- Arrays provide access to data by using a numeric index to identify each element in the array. Each value is stored in an element of the array, which you refer to by its index. The index for the first element in an array is zero. For example, attraction[0] is the first element in the attraction array.
- To declare an array, specify the array's data type and name followed by the values in braces, as in: String[ ] attraction = newString[]{"Art Institute of Chicago", "Magnificent Mile", "Willis Tower", "Chicago Bean", "Water Tower"};.
- You can display the values in an array using an adapter, which provides a data model for the layout of the list and for converting the array data into list items. A ListView component is the container for the list items, and an adapter connects the array data to the ListView component so the items are displayed on the device screen. In other words, calling a setAdapter in the Java code binds the elements of an array to a ListView layout.
- To have an app take action when a user selects an item in a list, you code the onItemClick( ) method to respond to the event of the user's selection.
- You can use the Switch decision structure with a list or menu. In a Switch statement, an integer or character variable is evaluated and the corresponding case is executed. Each case is specified using the *case* keyword followed by a value and a colon. For example, if a list contains five items, the Switch statement will have five cases, such as case 0, case 1, case 2, case 3, and case 4. End each case with a break statement to exit the Switch decision structure and continue with the next statement.
- Android intents send and receive activities and services, including opening a webpage in a browser. An intent can use the ACTION_VIEW action to send a URI to a built-in Android browser and display the specified website.
- As you develop an application, you must test every option and possible user action, including incorrect values and selections. Thoroughly test an Android app before publishing it to Google Play.

Key Terms

ACTION_VIEW
adapter
array
array variable
ArrayAdapter<String>
break
case
element
position
setOnItemClick( )
Switch
URI
URL

Developer FAQs

1. In the chapter example project, which Android component is used to display a vertical list of attractions? (5.1)
2. After you display the second page in the City Guide app, which button do you click to return to the first page of the app? (5.1)
3. When does a vertical scroll bar appear in a list? (5.1)
4. Initialize an array named temps with the integers 21, 56, 38, 30, and 57. (5.3)
5. Answer the following questions about the following initialized array: (5.3)

   ```
   String[]pizzaToppings = new String[10];
   ```

   a. What is the statement to assign mushrooms to the first array location?
   b. What is the statement to assign green peppers to the fourth location in the array?
   c. How many toppings can this array hold?
   d. Rewrite the statement to initially be assigned the following four toppings only: extra cheese, black olives, mushrooms, and bacon.
6. Write a line of code that assigns the values Samsung, HTC, Sony, Huawei, and Pixel to the elements in the array phoneBrands. (5.3)
7. Fix this array statement: (5.3)

   ```
   doubles { } driveSize = ["32.0", "64.0", "128.0"]
   ```

8. Write two lines of code that assign an array named coding with the items Java, C#, Python, Visual Basic, and Ruby and then display the array as a generic list. (5.3)
9. Which type of pictures are permissible for free fair use without copyright? (5.5)
10. What does URI stand for? (5.9)
11. Write a statement that opens the Android Help website *http://developer.android.com*. (5.9)
12. Write a single line of XML code that ignores the constraint layout of a component. (5.2)
13. Write two lines of XML code that display the id "Winners" in a ListView component. (5.2)
14. Write a Switch decision structure that tests the user's age in an integer variable named teenAge and assigns the variable schoolYear, as shown in **Table 5-2**. (5.7)

Table 5-2 Data for Switch decision structure

Age	High School Year
14	Freshman
15	Sophomore
16	Junior
17	Senior
Any other age	Not in high school

15. Change the following If decision structure to a Switch decision structure. (5.7)

```
if (count == 3) {
   result = "Password incorrect";
} else {
   result = "Request password";
}
```

16. What is the purpose of a default statement in a decision structure? (5.7)
17. Name two decision structures. (5.7)
18. What happens when a webpage opens in the emulator and the Back button is clicked in the chapter project? (5.9)
19. The first element in each array has what number subscript? (5.3)
20. Write a startActivity statement that launches a class named Studio. (5.9)

Beyond the Book

Search the web for answers to the following questions to further your Android knowledge.

1. Create a five-item list array program of your favorite hobby and test three types of built-in Android list formats. Take a screenshot comparing the three layouts identified by the layout format.
2. Compare four different Android browsers. Write a paragraph about each browser.
3. Research the 508 standards for Android app design. Create a list of 10 standards that should be met while designing Android applications.
4. Besides the 508 standards, research the topic of Android usability testing. Write one page on testing guidelines that assist in the design and testing process.

Case Programming Projects

Complete one or more of the following case programming projects. Use the same steps and techniques taught within the chapter. Successful completion of these projects requires knowledge of all chapter learning objectives. Submit the program(s) you create to your instructor. The level of difficulty is indicated for each case programming project.

Case Project 5–1: Watersports Rental App (Beginner)

Requirements Document

Application title:	Watersports Rental App
Purpose:	A watersports rental shop would like an app that displays information about their glass kayak and paddleboard rental services. As each watersport is selected, an image of that sport is displayed.
Algorithms:	1. The opening screen displays a list that includes a glass kayak, a paddleboard, and the shop's full website (**Figure 5-28**). 2. When the user selects an item from the list, a full-screen image of the item is displayed for one of the first two rentals (**Figure 5-29**). The third option opens the website *http://jopaddle.com*.
Conditions:	1. Pictures of the two types of watersports are provided with your student files (kayak.png and paddleboard.png). 2. Use the Switch decision structure. 3. Use a String table for image descriptions.

Figure 5-28 Watersports Rental app opening screen

Figure 5-29 Glass Kayak option selected

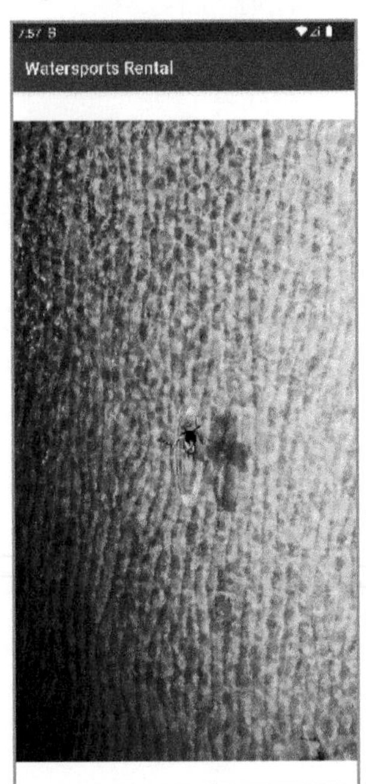

HishamHaroon/Shutterstock.com

Case Project 5–2: Paris Cafe App (Beginner)

Requirements Document

Application title: Paris Cafe App

Purpose: The Paris Cafe specializes in desserts and would like an app that lists the specials of the day. As each dessert special is selected, an image is displayed.

Algorithms:

1. The opening screen lists the three dessert specials of the day and an item for accessing the cafe's full website (**Figure 5-30**).
2. When the user selects one of the three specials (macaron, cupcakes, or donuts), an image of the special is displayed. In **Figure 5-31**, the user has selected the Macaron option. If the full website is requested, *http://pariscafenyc.com* opens.

Conditions:

1. The three images for the specials are named macaron.png, cupcakes.png, and donuts.png.
2. Use the Switch decision structure.
3. Use a String table.

Figure 5-30 Paris Cafe app

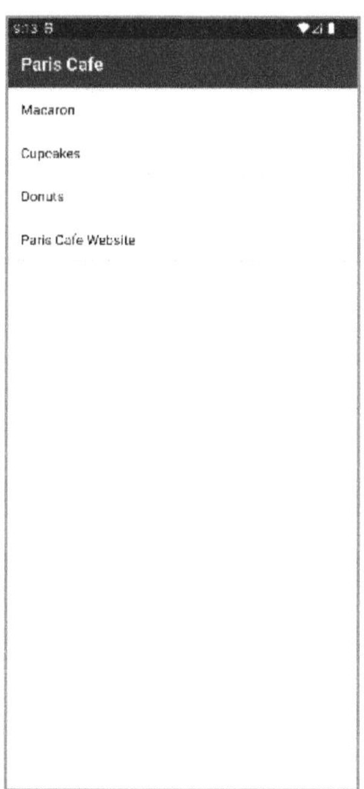

Figure 5-31 Macaron option selected

Melica/Shutterstock.com

Case Project 5–3: Rent a Car App (Intermediate)

Requirements Document

Application title:	Rent a Car App
Purpose:	A rental car app provides a list of six nationally known car rental companies. By selecting a company, a car rental site opens.
Algorithms:	**1.** An opening screen displays an image of a car and a button. **2.** The second screen displays a list of six car rental companies. This screen also contains a custom icon and layout. **3.** Each car rental agency can be selected to view a website of the corresponding company.
Conditions:	**1.** Select your own images. **2.** Create a custom icon launcher.

Case Project 5–4: Coffee Finder App (Intermediate)

Requirements Document

Application title:	Coffee Finder App
Purpose:	The Coffee Finder app locates four places in your town or city to get a great cup of joe.
Algorithms:	**1.** The opening screen displays the names of four coffee shops. **2.** When the user selects a coffee shop, a second screen displays the name and address of the selected coffee shop with an appropriate picture or logo.
Conditions:	**1.** Select your own images. **2.** Create a custom launcher icon.

Case Project 5–5: Tech Gadgets App (Advanced)

Requirements Document

Application title:	Tech Gadgets App
Purpose:	The Tech Gadgets app shows the top five technology gifts on your wish list.
Algorithms:	**1.** The opening screen displays names of five technology gadgets of your choosing. **2.** If the user selects any of the gadgets, a second screen opens to display an image and a button. If the user clicks the button, a webpage opens and displays more information about the tech gadget.
Conditions:	**1.** Select your own images. **2.** Create a custom launcher icon.

Case Project 5–6: Create Your Own App (Advanced)

Requirements Document

Application title:	Create Your Own App
Purpose:	Get creative! Create an app with five to eight list items. Use a custom layout and a custom icon that links to webpages and other XML layout screens.
Algorithms:	**1.** Create an app on a topic of your choice. Create a list. **2.** Display XML layout pages as well as webpages on different list items.
Conditions:	**1.** Select your own images. **2.** Use a custom launcher icon.

Chapter 6

Jam! Implementing Audio in Android Apps

Learning Objectives

At the completion of this chapter, you will be able to:

6.1 Create an Android project using a splash screen

6.2 Launch the splash screen before the MainActivity

6.3 Design a TextView component with a background image

6.4 Create a timer

6.5 Describe the life and death of an Activity

6.6 Assign class variables

6.7 Play music

6.8 Create a raw folder for music files

6.9 Play music with a MediaPlayer method

6.10 Start and resume music playback

6.11 Change the text attribute of a component

6.12 Change the visibility of a component

Playing music on a smartphone is one of the primary uses of a mobile device, especially as MP3 players are losing popularity. The most common phone activities include texting, talking, gaming, and playing music. Talking and texting continue to be mainstream communication channels, but a growing proportion of users take advantage of apps, games, and multimedia on their phones. The principal specification to consider when purchasing a smartphone is typically the amount of memory it has. Consumers often purchase a phone with more memory so they can store music.

6.1 Creating an Android Project Using a Splash Screen

To demonstrate how to play music through an Android built-in media player, the Chapter 6 project is named Aloha Music and opens with an image and the text "Sounds of Hawaii." The opening screen (**Figure 6-1**), also called a splash screen, is displayed for approximately five seconds, and then the program automatically opens the second window. The Aloha Music application (**Figure 6-2**) plays two songs that feature different instruments: a ukulele, a small guitar that originated in Hawaii, and drums. If the user selects the first button, the Ukulele song plays until the user selects the first button again to pause the song. If the user selects the second button, the Drums song plays until the user selects the second button again. The emulator plays the music through your computer's speakers.

Figure 6-1 Aloha Music Android app

Natalya Timofeeva/Shutterstock.com

Figure 6-2 Music played in the Android app

Anut21ng Stock/Shutterstock.com, Uwe Kreth/Shutterstock.com

Good to Know Android music apps can play music on the memory card (a flash drive often used in mobile devices), download music available for purchase or for free from music-sharing sites, tune into Internet-based streaming radio stations, or connect to music saved in a cloud service.

To create this application, the developer must understand how to perform the following processes, among others:

1. Create a splash screen with a timer.
2. Design a TextView component with a background image.
3. Initialize a TimerTask and a timer.
4. Launch a second Activity.
5. Design a second XML layout.
6. Add music files to the raw folder.
7. Initialize the MediaPlayer class.
8. Play and pause music with a Button component.

Beginning the Aloha Music App

The Aloha Music app opens with a window that is displayed for approximately five seconds before the next window is automatically launched. Unlike the project in Chapter 2 (Easy Recipes), which required a button to be tapped to begin a click event that opened a second screen, the music app does not require user interaction to open the second

Activity class. Many Android applications on the market show splash screens that often include the name of the program, display a brand logo for the application, or identify the author. A splash screen opens as you launch your app, providing time for Android to initialize its resources. Extending the length of time that your splash screen is displayed enables your app to load necessary files.

Critical Thinking

What kind of Android resources are loaded while a splash screen is displayed?

Background processes can consume multiple seconds when an app is initiated. Such processes include loading a mobile database to view a list of inventory or making a call over a network.

The Aloha Music app, instead of using Main as the name of the initial Activity, has an opening Activity (Figure 6-4) named SplashActivity. A second .java Activity is needed to launch at the beginning of the app to quickly display its name with an appropriate image. Next, the MainActivity class loads; it is responsible for playing the two songs. To start the Aloha Music application with a splash screen as a second Activity, complete the following steps.

Step 1

- In the Welcome to Android Studio window, scroll down and click the New Project button in the Phone and Tablet templates to create a new Android Studio project.
- Click the Next button in the New Project window.
- Type **Aloha Music** in the Name text box.
- If necessary, select Java in the Language text box.
- If necessary, select API 23: Android 6.0 (Marshmallow) as the Minimum SDK.

A new Java Android project named Aloha Music is configured to save on your local computer (**Figure 6-3**).

Figure 6-3 Setting up the Aloha Music project in the New Project window

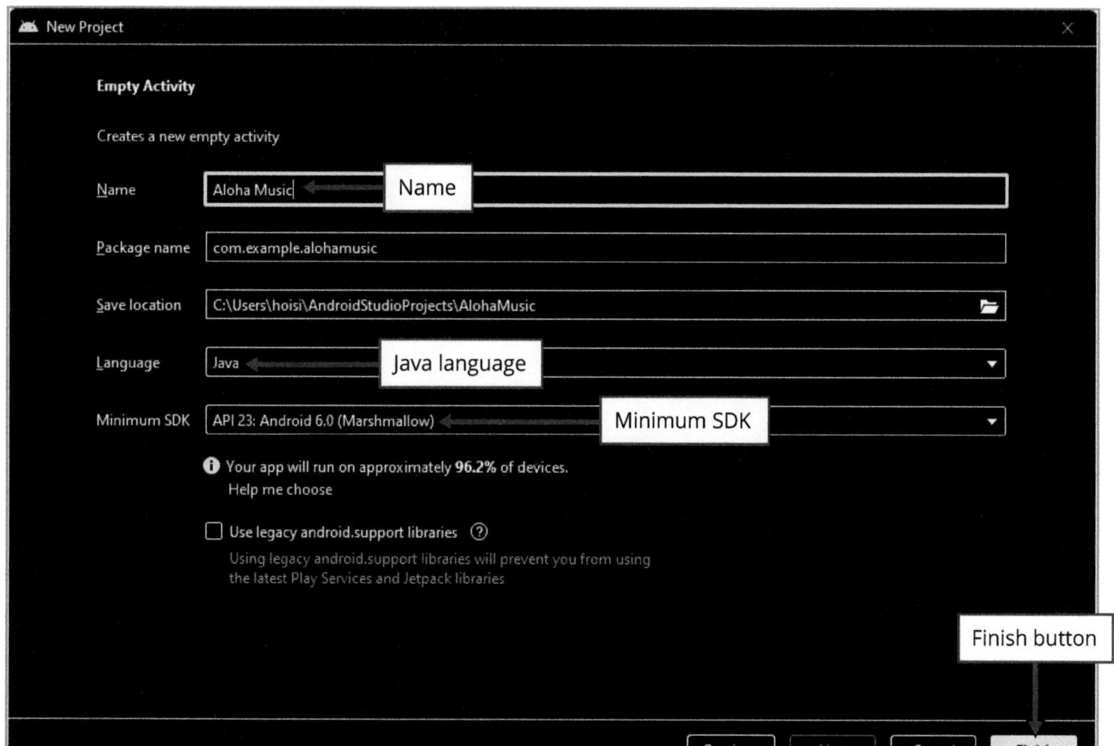

Step 2

- Click the Next button on the Configure your new project page of the Create New Project dialog box.
- Click the Finish button in the New Project window.
- Click the arrow (>) in front of the res folder to expand the folder.
- Click the arrow (>) in front of the layout folder to expand the folder.
- Double-click the activity_main.xml file to open the emulator design of the virtual device.
- Click the Hello world! TextView component in the emulator. This component is displayed by default.
- Press the Delete key to delete the default TextView component.
- Add a second Empty Activity by clicking **File** and then **New** to display the menu listing.
- Click **Activity** and then **Empty Activity** to display the New Android Activity dialog box.
- Type **SplashActivity** in the Activity Name text box.

The new Aloha Music project has a second activity named SplashActivity added (**Figure 6-4**).

Figure 6-4 Adding the Splash Activity (splash screen)

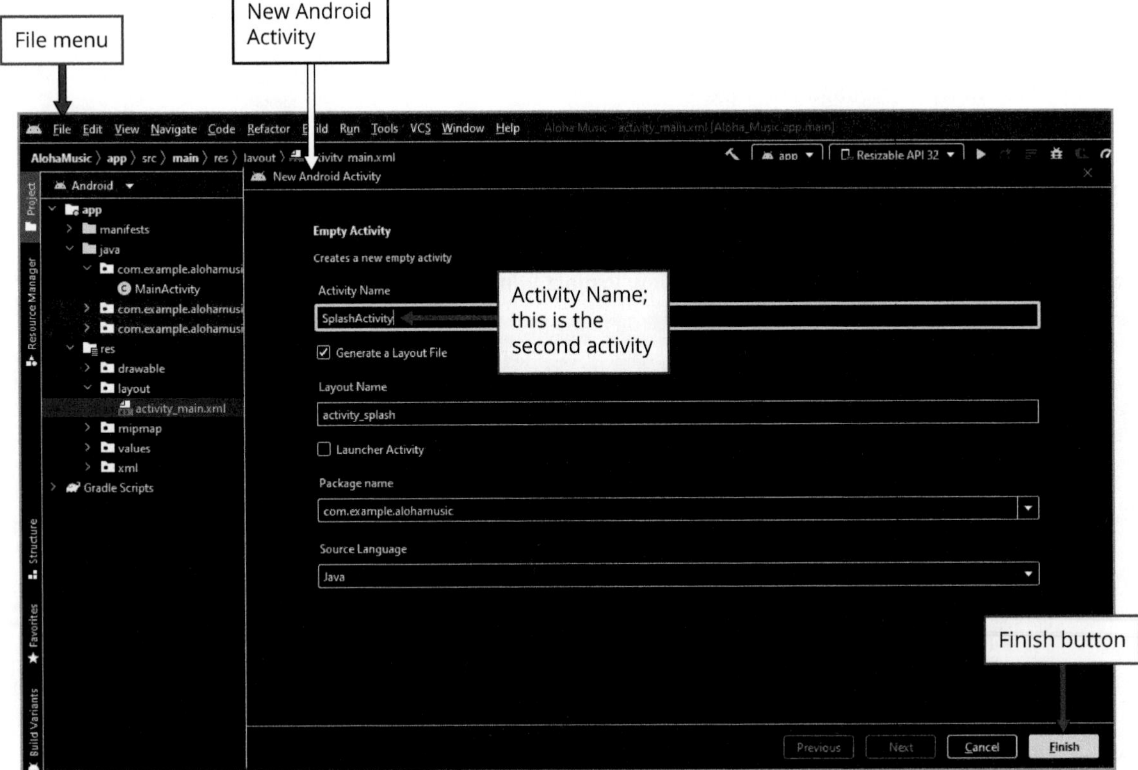

Step 3

- Click the Finish button to display the Android project view of the Aloha Music app.

6.2 Launching the Splash Screen before the MainActivity

A splash screen will be the first screen visible to the user when the Aloha Music application is launched. The splash screen is one of the most vital screens in an application because it is the user's first experience with the application. By default, the first Activity that launches is the MainActivity, but when a splash screen is added, the SplashActivity needs to launch first. In Chapter 2, the AndroidManifest.xml file was introduced; this file includes the package name and activity names. In addition, the AndroidManifest file includes Android version support, hardware features support, and permissions. The Android Manifest file needs code that declares a Java class named SplashActivity is the launcher activity for your Android application. To launch the splash screen first when the app begins, complete the following steps.

Step 1

- Expand the manifests folder to display the AndroidManifest.xml file.
- Double-click the AndroidManifest.xml file to display the AndroidManifest.xml tab.
- Select Lines 22 through 26 to highlight the MainActivity intent lines, which code the launch of the first activity.

The intent lines that launch the MainActivity class are highlighted (**Figure 6-5**).

Figure 6-5 Updating the Android Manifest file

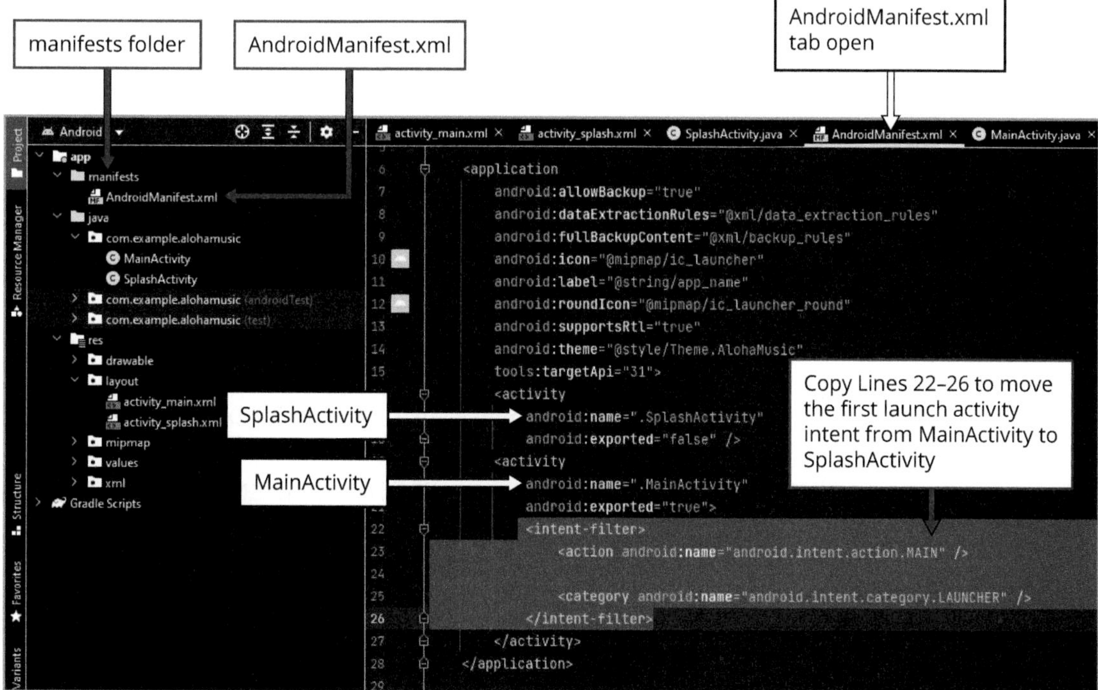

Step 2

- Right-click the mouse and click Cut.
- Click at the end of Line 18 and press Enter.
- Right-click the mouse and click Paste.
- On Line 18, delete the code for false and change it to true. Delete the closing brace backslash. Line 18 should now be android:exported="true" >.
- Add a line after Line 23 and type **</activity>** to close the activity.

The intent lines are moved after the SplashActivity class to launch this class first (**Figure 6-6**).

Figure 6-6 Launching the Splash Activity first in the Android Manifest file

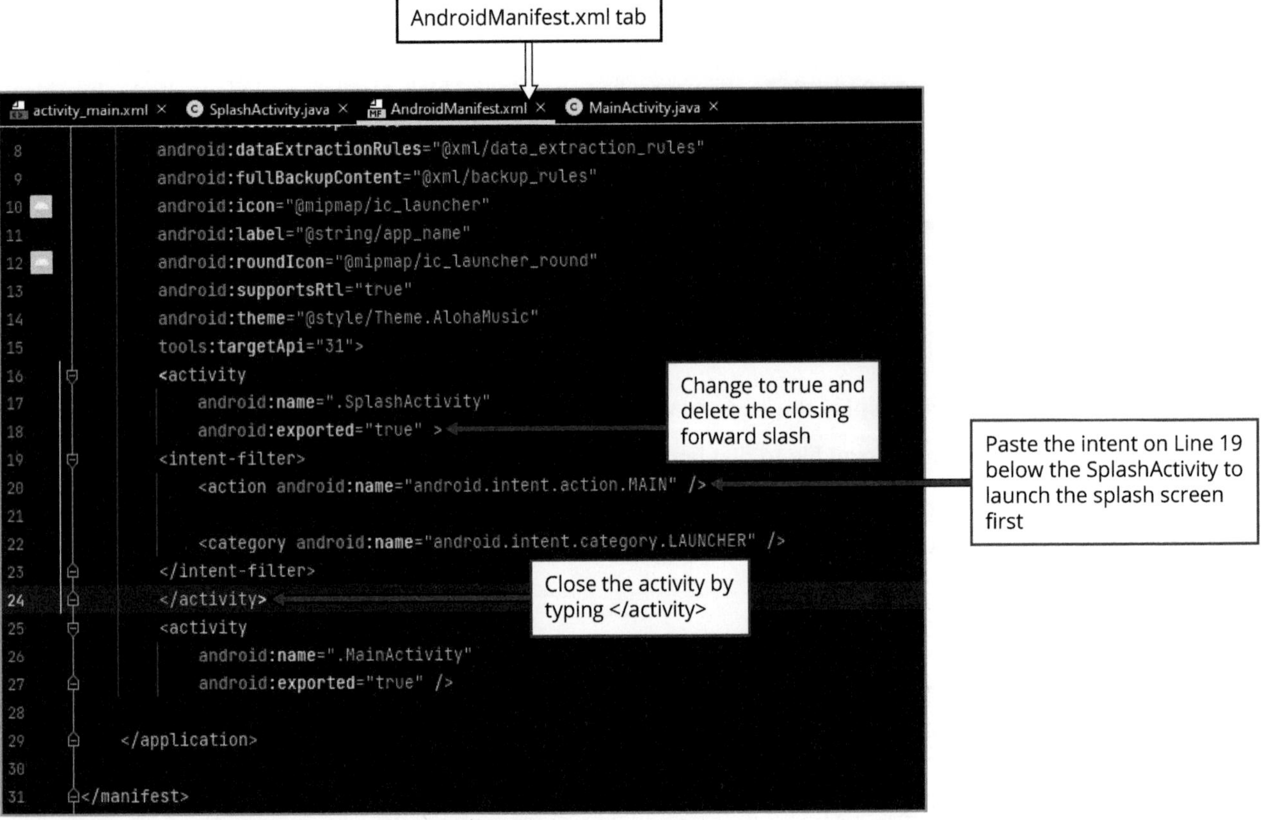

6.3 Designing a TextView Component with a Background Image

On the splash screen in Figure 6-1, an image with the text "Sounds of Hawaii" is displayed. The text for the TextView image as well as the image descriptions for the two ImageView components and button text are stored in the strings.xml file. The opening image is not an ImageView component, but a TextView component with a background image. You use a TextView attribute named background to specify the image. The image is first placed in the drawable folder and then referenced in the TextView background. The TextView background can display an image or a solid-color fill such as the hexadecimal color #F4511E for brown. The margins and gravity properties are used to place text in the location of your choice. To add the images for this project and an activity_splash.xml file with a TextView widget that contains a background image, follow these steps.

Step 1

- Close the AndroidManifest.xml tab.
- Open the folder that contains the student files.
- To add the three project image files to the drawable resource folder, click hawaii.png, ukulele.png, and drums.png, then press Ctrl+C.
- To paste the image files to the drawable folder, right-click the drawable folder in the Android project view pane.

- Click Paste on the shortcut menu.
- Click the OK button in the Copy dialog box.

Copies of the three image files appear in the drawable folder (**Figure 6-7**).

Figure 6-7 Image files in the drawable folder

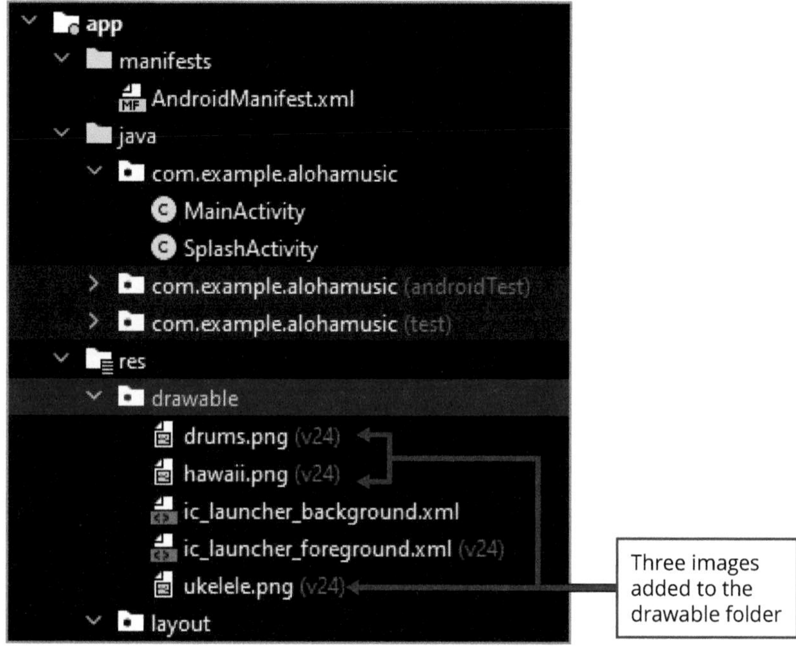

Step 2

- Expand the res\values folder and then double-click the strings.xml file.
- Click the Open editor link.
- Click the Add Key (plus sign) button in the Translations Editor.
- In the Key text box, type **tvSplash** to name the string for the TextView component.
- In the Default Value text box, type **Sounds of Hawaii** to define the text to display.
- Using the same technique explained earlier in this step, add the strings in **Table 6-1** to the String table in the Translations Editor.

Table 6-1 Strings for the Aloha Music app

Key	Default Value
ukulele	Ukulele Image
drums	Drums Image
btUkulele	PLAY UKULELE SONG
btDrums	PLAY DRUMS SONG

The Translations Editor contains the String values necessary in this app (**Figure 6-8**).

Figure 6-8 Translations Editor

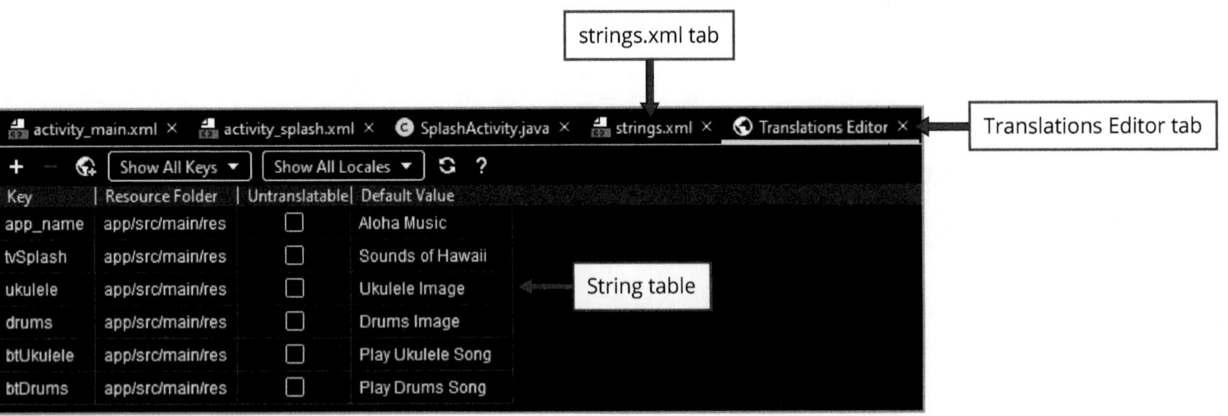

Step 3

- Save your work and close the Translations Editor and strings.xml tabs.
- Open the activity_splash.xml layout file.
- In the Palette, drag the TextView component to the upper-left part of the emulator.
- Drag all four constraint handles to the edges of the emulator. You should have all four constraints anchored to the edges of the screen; blue curly arrows should touch the top, bottom, left, and right sides of the emulator.
- Type **tvTitle** in the id attribute and click the Refactor button to change the id name.
- Click the rectangle to the right of the text attribute, click **tvSplash** in the Pick a Resource dialog box, and then click the OK button.
- Type **#F4511E** for the textColor attribute to create a brown font color.
- Set the textSize attribute to **34sp**.
- Expand the textStyle attribute and then click the bold check box.
- Expand the gravity attribute, then select the top check box and the center check box to place the text in the top center of the screen.
- In the background attribute, click the rectangle to open the Pick a Resource dialog box.
- In the Pick a Resource dialog box, click hawaii to select the background image and then click the OK button.

A TextView component with an image background is displayed in the activity_splash.xml file (**Figure 6-9**).

Step 4

- Close the activity_splash.xml tab and save your work.

Figure 6-9 The activity_splash.xml file displays a TextView component with a background image

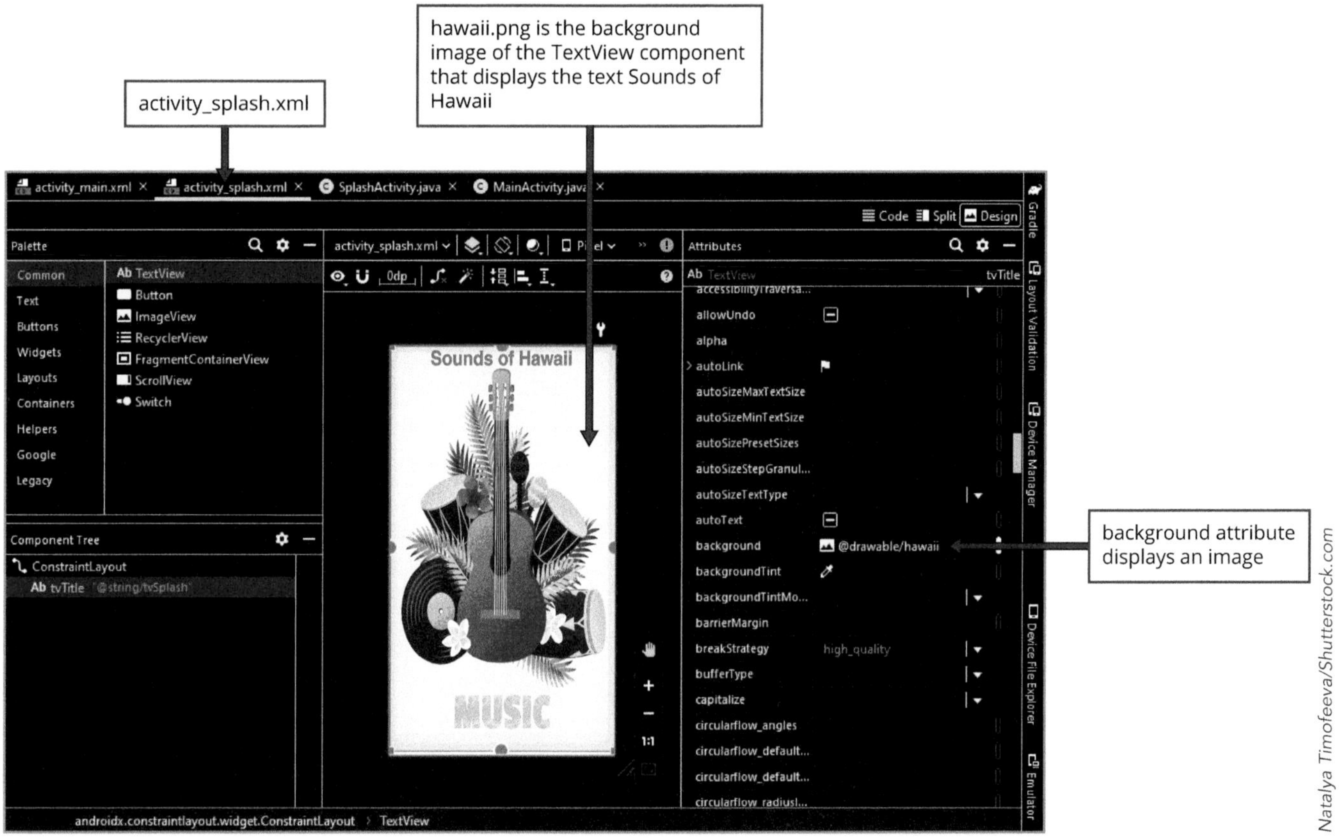

activity_splash.xml

hawaii.png is the background image of the TextView component that displays the text Sounds of Hawaii

background attribute displays an image

Natalya Timofeeva/Shutterstock.com

Quick Check

Which attribute sets the background image for a TextView component?

Answer: The background attribute.

6.4 Creating a Timer

When most Android apps open, a splash screen is displayed for a few seconds. Large-scale applications often preload database files and information behind the scenes. In the Aloha Music app, a timer is necessary to display the splash.xml file for approximately five seconds before the Main Activity intent is called. A **timer** in Java executes a one-time task such as displaying an opening splash screen, or it performs a continuous process, such as a morning wake-up call set to run at regular intervals.

Timers can be used to pause an action temporarily or for time-dependent or repeated activities, such as animation in a cartoon application. The timer object uses milliseconds as the unit of time. On an average Android device, 1,000 milliseconds is equivalent to about one second. This fixed period of time is supported by two Java classes called **TimerTask** and **Timer**. The first step in creating a timer is to create a TimerTask object, as shown in the following syntax.

Code Syntax

```
TimerTask task = new TimerTask( ) {
}
```

Good to Know

Each time a timer runs its tasks, it executes within a single thread. A **thread** is a single sequential flow of components within a program. Java allows an application to have multiple threads of execution running concurrently. You can assign multiple threads so they occur simultaneously, completing several tasks practically at the same time. For example, a program could display a splash screen, download files needed for the application, and even play an opening sound at the same time.

A TimerTask invokes a scheduled timer. A timer may remind you of the childhood game Hide-and-Seek. Do you remember covering your eyes and counting to 50 while your friends found a hiding spot before you began searching for everyone? A timer might only count to five seconds (5,000 milliseconds), but in a similar fashion, the application pauses while the timer counts to the established time limit. After the timed interval is completed, the program resumes and continues with the next task.

After entering the TimerTask code, click the red error line under TimerTask( ) to add the run( ) method, an auto-generated method stub, as shown in the following code syntax. Any statements within the braces of the run( ) method are executed after the TimerTask class is invoked.

Code Syntax

```
TimerTask task = new TimerTask( ) {
     @Override
     public void run() {
     // TODO Auto-generated method stub
}
```

The TimerTask must implement a run( ) method that is called by the timer when the task is scheduled for execution. To add a TimerTask class to the SplashActivity, follow these steps.

Step 1

- In the Android project view, expand the java folder, expand the first com.example.alohamusic folder, and then double-click SplashActivity.java to open the code window.
- After the setContentView(R.layout.activity_splash); statement, press the Enter key to insert a new line, type **TimerTask task = new TimerTask() {** to add the TimerTask, and then press the Enter key.
- Click the red text, TimerTask( ), and press Alt+Enter to import the TimerTask.

The TimerTask class is initialized and a red curly line appears below TimerTask (**Figure 6-10**).

Step 2

- Click the red curly line below TimerTask( ) and press Alt+Enter to view the quick-fix suggestion.
- Click Implement Method and click the OK button in the Select Methods to implement dialog box to add the auto-generated method stub for the run( ) method.
- To complete the stub, click to the right of } in Line 21 at the end of the stub and then type a semicolon to close the class.

The auto-generated stub for the run( ) method is created automatically for the TimerTask (**Figure 6-11**).

Figure 6-10 TimerTask statement

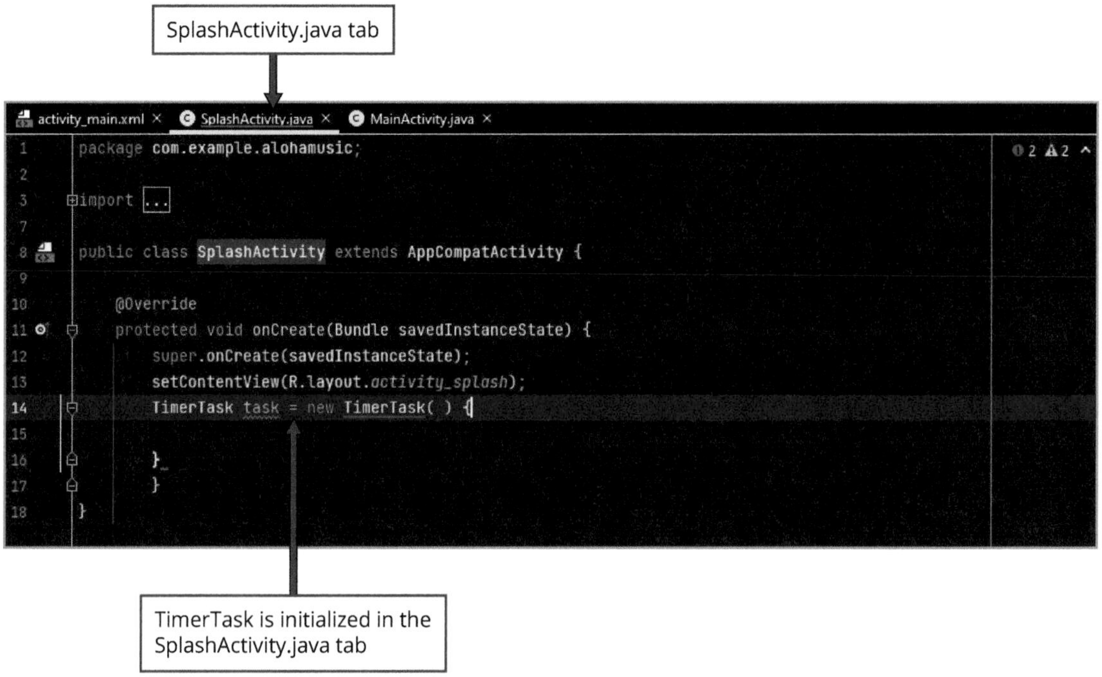

SplashActivity.java tab

activity_main.xml × SplashActivity.java × MainActivity.java ×

```
package com.example.alohamusic;

import ...

public class SplashActivity extends AppCompatActivity {

    @Override
    protected void onCreate(Bundle savedInstanceState) {
        super.onCreate(savedInstanceState);
        setContentView(R.layout.activity_splash);
        TimerTask task = new TimerTask( ) {

        }
        }
}
```

TimerTask is initialized in the SplashActivity.java tab

Figure 6-11 The run( ) method

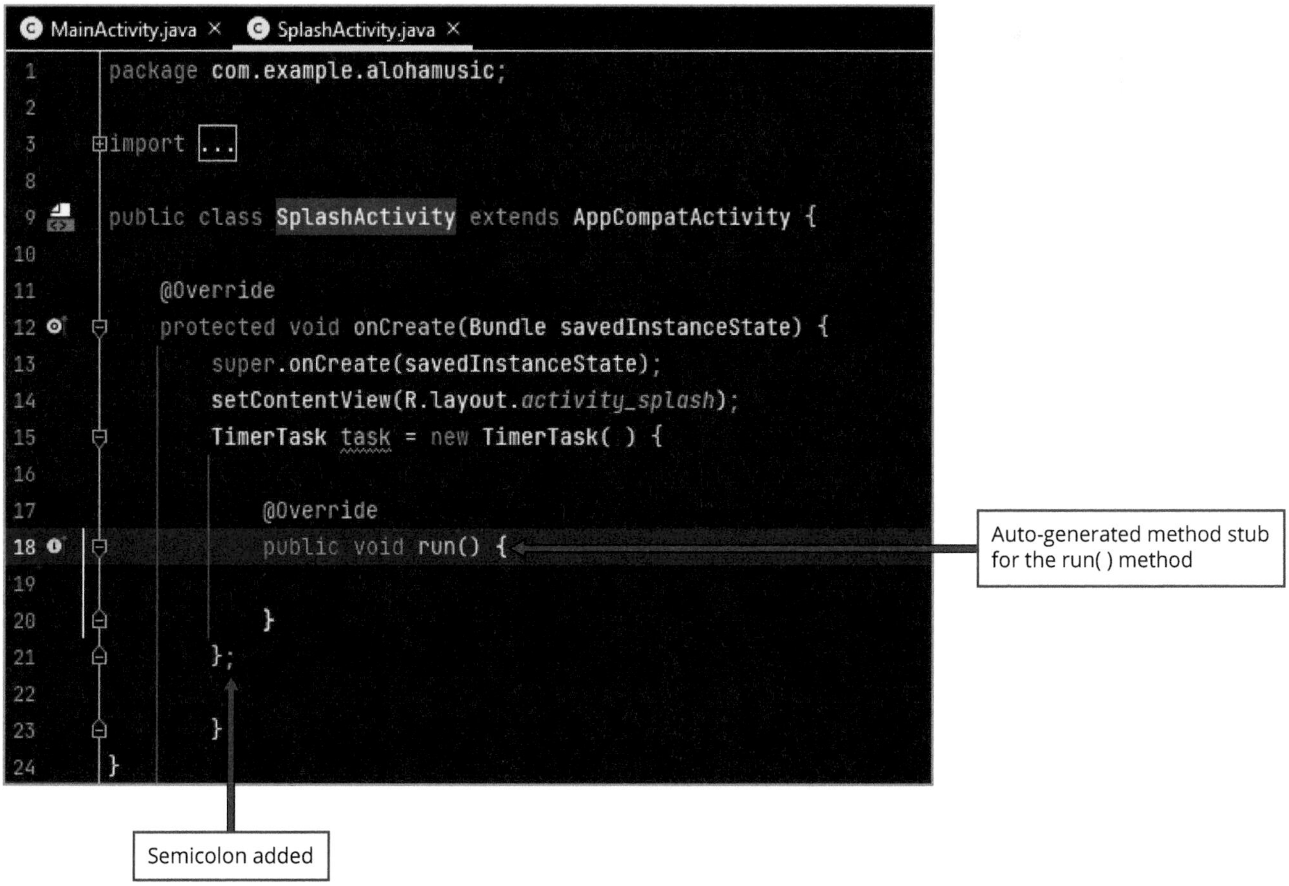

MainActivity.java × SplashActivity.java ×

```
package com.example.alohamusic;

import ...

public class SplashActivity extends AppCompatActivity {

    @Override
    protected void onCreate(Bundle savedInstanceState) {
        super.onCreate(savedInstanceState);
        setContentView(R.layout.activity_splash);
        TimerTask task = new TimerTask( ) {

            @Override
            public void run() {

            }
        };

    }
}
```

Auto-generated method stub for the run( ) method

Semicolon added

Good to Know | Timers can also be used to monitor what a user is doing, execute other routines while an Activity is running, or display updates of how long an installation is taking by displaying a countdown.

Scheduling a Timer

After a reference is included to the TimerTask class, a timer must be scheduled for the amount of time that the splash screen is displayed. The Timer class shown in the following code syntax creates a timed event when the schedule( ) method is called. A delay timer is scheduled in milliseconds using the Timer class. Delay schedules simply prompt an event to occur once at a specified time.

Code Syntax

```
Timer opening = new Timer();
opening.schedule(task,5000);
```

In the first line of the code syntax, the object named opening initializes a new instance of the Timer class. When the schedule( ) method of the Timer class is called in the second line, two arguments are required. The first parameter (task) is the name of the variable that was initialized for the Timer class. The second parameter represents the number of milliseconds (5,000 milliseconds = about 5 seconds). Follow these steps to add the scheduled timer.

Step 1

- In the code on the SplashActivity.java tab, after the closing braces for the TimerTask class and the semicolon (Line 20), insert a new line.
- Type **Timer opening = new Timer();**.
- Click Timer and press Alt+Enter. Click Import Class.

An instance of the Timer class is created (**Figure 6-12**).

Figure 6-12 Timer class

```
12    protected void onCreate(Bundle savedInstanceState) {
13        super.onCreate(savedInstanceState);
14        setContentView(R.layout.activity_splash);
15        TimerTask task = new TimerTask( ) {
16
17            @Override
18            public void run() {
19
20            }
21        };
22        Timer opening = new Timer( );
23        }
24 }
```

Instance of the Timer class added

Step 2

- To schedule a timer to pause for five seconds using the schedule( ) method from the Timer class, press the Enter key at the end of the line.
- Type **opening.schedule(task,5000);**.

The timer named opening, which lasts five seconds, is scheduled (**Figure 6-13**).

Figure 6-13 Timer scheduled for 5 seconds

```
12      protected void onCreate(Bundle savedInstanceState) {
13          super.onCreate(savedInstanceState);
14          setContentView(R.layout.activity_splash);
15          TimerTask task = new TimerTask( ) {
16
17              @Override
18              public void run() {
19
20              }
21          };
22          Timer opening = new Timer( );
23          opening.schedule(task, delay: 5000);
24      }
25  }
```

Five-second timer to display the splash screen

On the Job | Be careful not to code excessively long timers that waste the time of the user. A user-friendly program runs smoothly without long delays.

Quick Check

For how many seconds, approximately, would a timer that counts to 12,000 hold the screen?

Answer: 12 seconds.

6.5 Understanding the Life and Death of an Activity

In Line 12 of the Aloha Music app, as shown in Figure 6-13, the SplashActivity begins its life in the Activity life cycle with the onCreate( ) method. Each Activity has a **life cycle**, which is the series of actions from the beginning of an Activity to its end. Actions that occur during the life cycle provide ways to manage how users interact with your app. Each Activity in this book begins with the onCreate( ) method, which initializes the user interface with an XML layout; the life of the Activity is started. As in any life cycle, the opposite of birth is death. In this case, the **onDestroy( ) method** is the end of the Activity. The onCreate( ) method sets up all the resources required to perform the Activity, and onDestroy( ) releases those same resources to free up memory on your mobile device. The life cycle of the SplashActivity begins with onCreate( ) and ends with onDestroy( ).

Other actions can take place during the life of the Activity. For example, when the scheduled timer starts (Line 23 in Figure 6-13), the SplashActivity is paused. If you open multiple apps on a smartphone and receive a phone call, you must either pause or terminate the other apps to secure enough available memory to respond to the incoming call. To handle the life cycle actions between onCreate( ) and onDestroy( ), you use methods such as onRestart( ), onStart( ), onResume( ), onPause( ), and onStop( ). Each of these methods changes the state of the Activity. The four **states** of an Activity determine whether it is active, paused, stopped, or dead. The life cycle of an application affects how an app works and how the different parts are being orchestrated. **Table 6-2** shows the development of an Activity throughout its life cycle.

Table 6-2 Methods used in the life cycle of an Activity

Method	Description
onCreate( )	The onCreate( ) method begins each Activity. This method also provides a Bundle containing the Activity's previously frozen state, if it had one.
onRestart( )	If the Activity is stopped, onRestart( ) begins the Activity again. If this method is called, it indicates your Activity is being redisplayed to the user from a stopped state. The onRestart( ) method is always followed by onStart( ).
onStart( )	If the Activity is hidden, onStart( ) makes the Activity visible.
onResume( )	The onResume( ) method is called when the user begins interacting with the Activity. The onResume( ) method always follows onPause( ).
onPause( )	This method is called when an Activity is about to resume.
onStop( )	This method hides the Activity.
onDestroy( )	This method destroys the Activity. Typically, the finish( ) method (part of the onDestroy( ) method) is used to declare that the Activity is finished; when the next Activity is called, the method releases all the resources from the first Activity.

When an Activity is launched using onCreate( ), the app performs the actions in the Activity. In other words, the Activity becomes the top sheet of paper on a stack of papers. When the methods shown in Table 6-2 are used between the onCreate( ) and onDestroy( ) methods, they shuffle the order of the papers in that stack. When onDestroy( ) is called, imagine that the pile of papers is thrown away. The finish( ) method is part of the onDestroy( ) method and is called when the Activity is completed and should be closed. Typically, the finish( ) method occurs directly before another Activity is launched. As an Android developer, you should be well acquainted with the life cycle of Activities because an app that you publish in the Android market must "play" well with all the other apps on a mobile device. For example, your Android app must pause when a text message, phone call, or other event occurs.

The diagram in **Figure 6-14** shows the life cycle of an Activity. The rectangles represent the methods you can implement to perform operations when the Activity moves between states. The colored ovals are the possible major states of the Activity.

As an example of how an app transitions through each stage of the Activity life cycle, consider the native Android application designed for taking a picture using the built-in camera. When the user launches the camera app, the camera Activity executes the onCreate( ) method to display the opening screen and the image captured through the camera lens. The user taps a Button component to take a picture. The onStop( ) method is called to hide the live image displayed after the picture is taken. The onRestart( ) method is called after the picture is taken to restart the rest of the app. The onStart( ) method is called to display the picture that was just taken. If the user taps the screen to upload the image to Facebook, the onPause( ) method is called to pause operations of the camera app while the image is uploaded. The onResume( ) method is launched after the picture is uploaded to reactivate the camera. The user can choose to take another image, which repeats the process, or to exit the camera app. If the user selects the exit option, onDestroy( ) or finish( ) frees the saved resources from the temporary memory of the device and closes the camera application.

Figure 6-14 Android life cycle

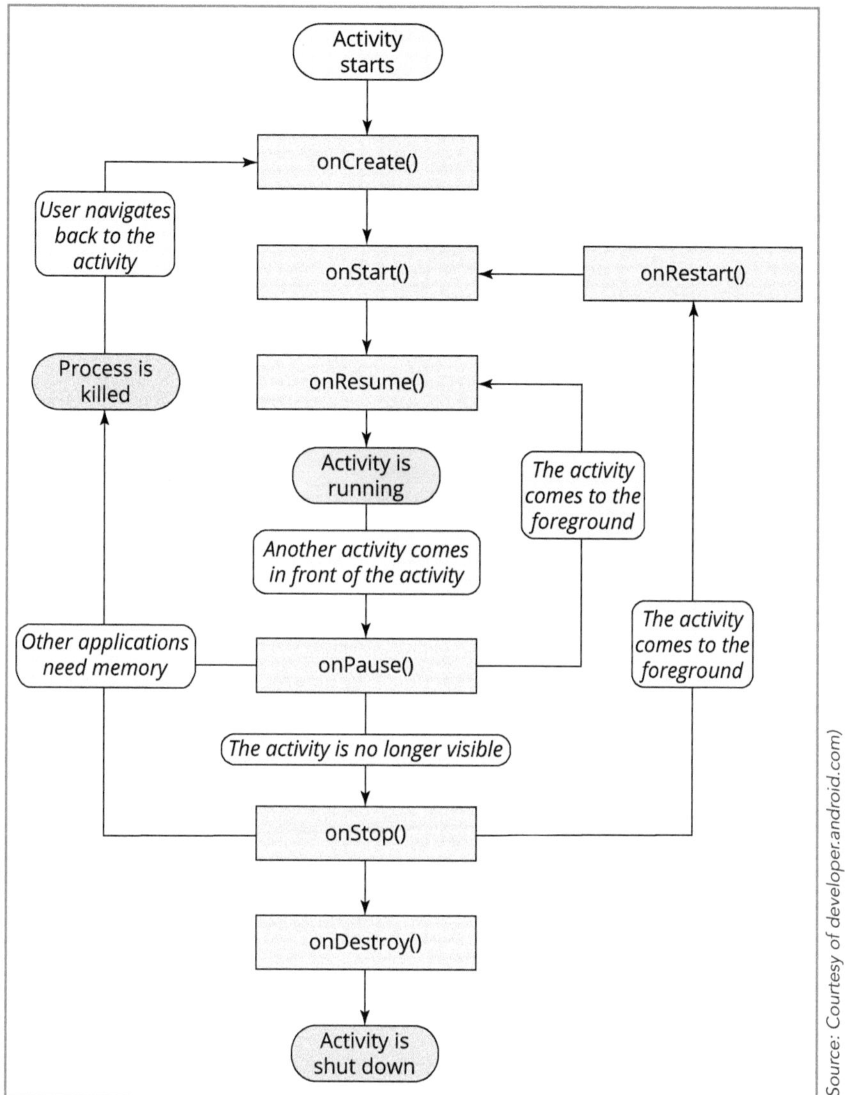

(Source: Courtesy of developer.android.com)

In the Aloha Music application, after the timer pauses the program temporarily, the SplashActivity should be destroyed with onDestroy( ) before launching the second Activity. The app should call the onDestroy( ) method from within the run( ) method of the timer task that was invoked by TimerTask. Doing so guarantees that the ongoing task execution is the last task this timer performs. To close the SplashActivity, follow these steps.

Step 1

- In SplashActivity.java, click inside the run( ) auto-generated method stub in Line 19.
- Type **finish();**.

The finish() statement releases the resources that were created for the SplashActivity and closes the Activity (**Figure 6-15**).

Step 2

- Save your work.

Figure 6-15 After the finish( ) method is called

```
public class SplashActivity extends AppCompatActivity {

    @Override
    protected void onCreate(Bundle savedInstanceState) {
        super.onCreate(savedInstanceState);
        setContentView(R.layout.activity_splash);
        TimerTask task = new TimerTask( ) {

            @Override
            public void run() {
                finish();
            }
        };
        Timer opening = new Timer( );
        opening.schedule(task, delay: 5000);
        }
}
```

End the life cycle of the SplashActivity by closing the activity

Launching the Next Activity

After the Activity for the splash screen is destroyed, an intent must request that the next Activity is launched. An XML layout named main.xml already exists as the default layout. The initial class named MainActivity is responsible in this app for playing music. To launch the MainActivity as the second class opened, follow this step.

Step 1

- To launch the MainActivity class from the splash screen, insert a new line in the run( ) auto-generated method stub after the finish( ); statement.
- Type **startActivity(new Intent(SplashActivity.this, MainActivity.class));** to launch the second Activity.
- Click the red text, Intent, and press Alt+Enter to import the intent statement. Save your work.

The second Activity named MainActivity is launched with an intent statement (**Figure 6-16**).

Figure 6-16 The second Activity, which is called MainActivity

```
public class SplashActivity extends AppCompatActivity {

    @Override
    protected void onCreate(Bundle savedInstanceState) {
        super.onCreate(savedInstanceState);
        setContentView(R.layout.activity_splash);
        TimerTask task = new TimerTask( ) {

            @Override
            public void run() {
                finish();
                startActivity(new Intent( packageContext: SplashActivity.this, MainActivity.class));
            }
        };
        Timer opening = new Timer( );
        opening.schedule(task, delay: 5000);
        }
}
```

Launch MainActivity after the splash screen is finished displaying

Designing the activity_main.xml File

After the first Activity finishes displaying the splash screen in the Aloha Music app and the second Activity named MainActivity is launched, a second XML layout file is displayed when the onCreate( ) method is called within the MainActivity.java file. The MainActivity.java file uses the default Relative layout with two ImageView and Button components. To create and design the XML layout for activity_main.xml, follow these steps.

Step 1

- Close the SplashActivity.java tab.
- Open the activity_main.xml tab.
- Drag an ImageView component from the Palette to the emulator window and center the placeholder in the upper third of the emulator.
- Click **ukulele** when the Pick a Resource dialog box opens and then click the OK button to display the ukulele image.
- Drag all constraint handles as necessary and place the image in the upper third of the emulator.
- Type **ivUkulele** in the id text box to name the ImageView component and then click the Refactor button.
- Click the rectangle to the right of the contentDescription attribute in the Attributes pane, click **ukulele** in the Pick a Resource dialog box, and then click the OK button.
- Change the layout_height attribute to **250dp** and the layout_width to **400dp**.
- Expand the layout_margin attribute and type **15dp** in the layout_marginTop text box.

The Ukulele image for the first song is placed in activity_main.xml (**Figure 6-17**).

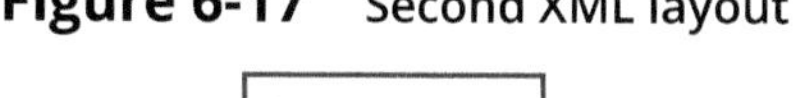

Figure 6-17 Second XML layout

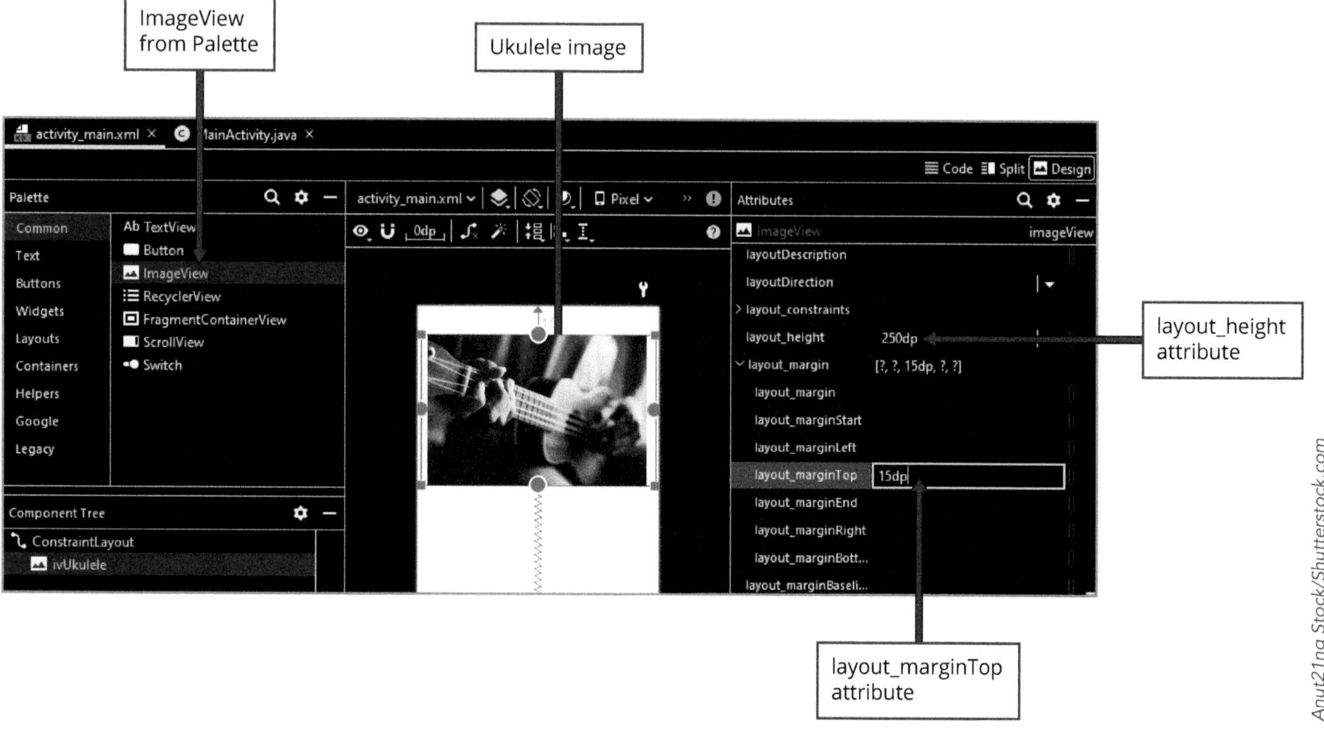

Step 2

- Drag a Button from the Palette and center it below the image after dragging the four constraint handles.
- Type **btUkulele** to the right of the id attribute and click the Refactor button.
- Click the rectangle to the right of the text attribute, click **btUkulele** in the Pick a Resource dialog box, and then click the OK button.
- Set the textSize attribute to **22sp**.
- Set the backgroundTint attribute to **#F4511E**.
- Expand the layout_margin attribute and type **10dp** in the layout_marginTop and layout_marginBottom text boxes.

The Ukulele button to select the first song is placed on the emulator (**Figure 6-18**).

Figure 6-18 Second XML layout complete

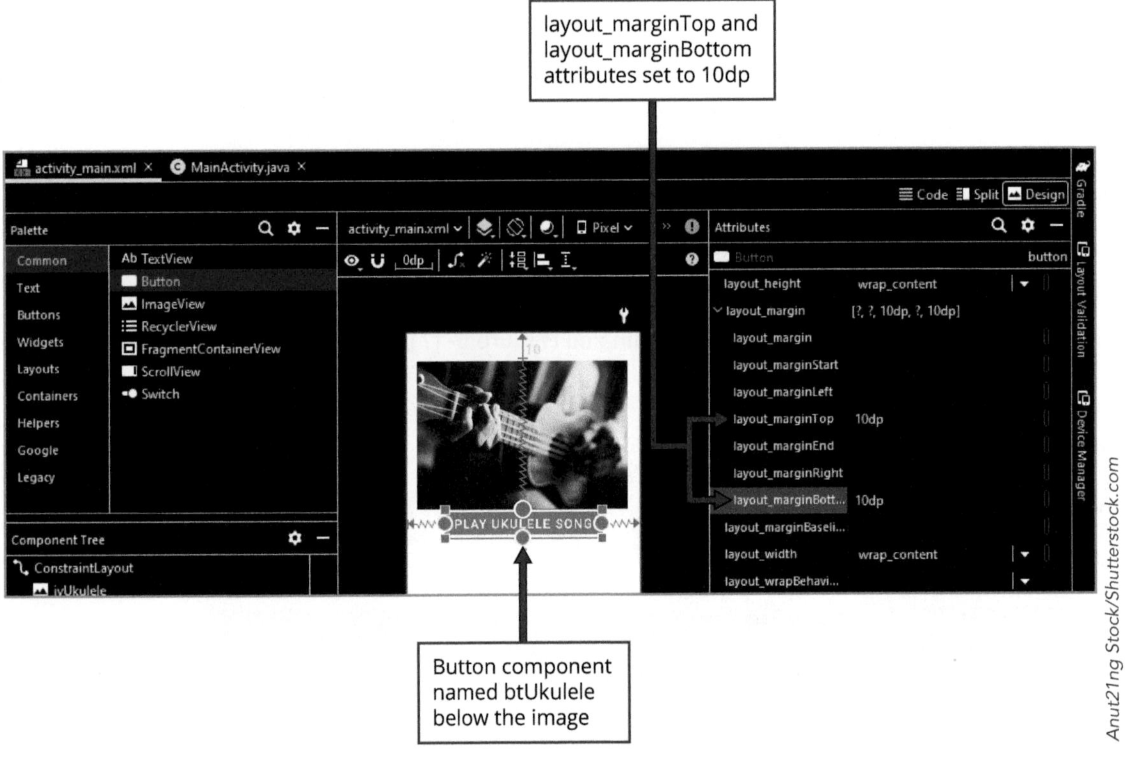

Anut21ng Stock/Shutterstock.com

Step 3

- Drag another ImageView component to the emulator and center it below the Button component.
- Click **drums** when the Pick a Resource dialog box opens and then click the OK button to display the drums image.
- Drag all constraint handles as necessary.
- Type **ivDrums** in the id text box to name the ImageView component, and then click the Refactor button.
- Click the rectangle to the right of the contentDescription attribute in the Attributes pane, click **drums** in the Pick a Resource dialog box, and then click the OK button.
- Change the layout_height attribute to **250dp** and the layout_width to **400dp**.
- Expand the layout_margin attribute and type **10dp** in the layout_marginTop text box.
- Drag another Button to the emulator, center it below the drums image, type **btDrums** to the right of the id attribute, and click the Refactor button.
- Click the rectangle to the right of the text attribute, click **btDrums** in the Pick a Resource dialog box, and then click the OK button.

- Set the textSize attribute to **22sp**.
- Set the backgroundTint attribute to **#F4511E**.
- Expand the layout_margin attribute and type **10dp** in the layout_marginTop and layout_marginBottom text boxes.

The Drum image and button to select the second song are designed in activity_main.xml (**Figure 6-19**).

Figure 6-19 The activity_main.xml layout is complete

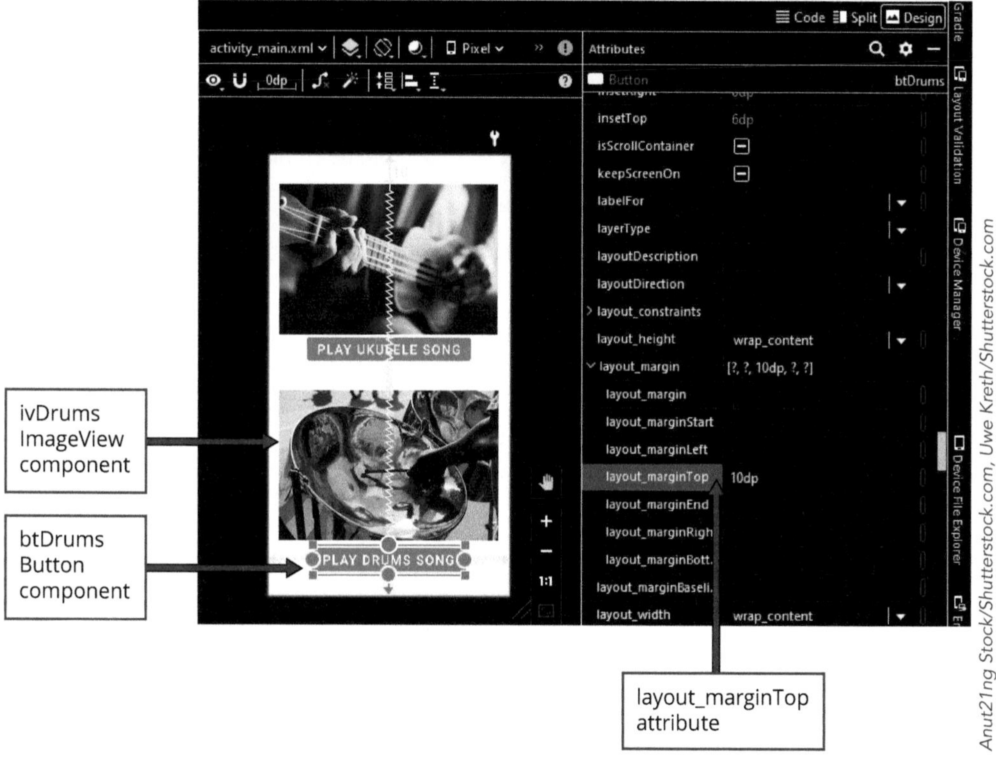

6.6 Assigning Class Variables

In the coding examples used thus far in this book, variables have been local variables. **Local variables** are declared by variable declaration statements within a method, such as a primitive integer variable within an onCreate( ) method. The local variable effectively ceases to exist when the execution of the method is complete. The **scope** of a variable refers to the variable's visibility within a class. Variables that are accessible only to a restricted portion of a program, such as a single method, are said to have local scope. A local variable declared inside a block or method is not visible to outside classes, so a local variable declared inside the MainActivity cannot be accessed outside the MainActivity class.

Variables that are accessible from anywhere in a class, however, are said to have **global scope**. If a variable is needed in multiple methods within a class, the global variable is assigned at the beginning of a class, not within a method. This global scope variable is called a **class variable** in Java and can be accessed by multiple methods throughout the program. In the chapter project, a Button, a MediaPlayer (necessary for playing sound), and an integer variable named playing are needed in the onCreate() method and within both onClick() methods for each Button component. To keep the value of these variables throughout multiple classes, the variables are defined as class variables that cease to exist when their class or activity is unloaded.

After class variables are defined in MainActivity.java, the onCreate( ) method opens the activity_main.xml layout and defines the two Button components. The Activity waits for the user to select one of the two buttons, each of which plays a song. If a button is clicked twice, the music pauses. Each button must have a setOnClickListener that awaits the user's click. After the user taps a button, the setOnClickListener( ) method implements the Button.OnClickListener, creating an instance of the OnClickListener and calling the onClick( ) method. The onClick( ) method responds to the user's action. For example, in the chapter project, the response is to play a song. The onClick( ) method is where you place the code to handle playing the song. To code the class variables, display the activity_main.xml layout, reference the two Button components, and set an OnClickListener, follow these steps.

Step 1

- Close the activity_main.xml window and save your work.
- Open the MainActivity.java tab.
- After the public class MainActivity extends AppCompatActivity statement, type **Button button1, button2;** on the next line to create a class variable that refers to the two Button components. When you finish, press Enter.
- Click the red text, Button, and press Alt+Enter to import the Button class.
- On the next line, type **MediaPlayer mpUkulele, mpDrums;** to create a class variable reference for the media player.
- Click MediaPlayer and press Alt+Enter to import the MediaPlayer class.
- Insert a new line and then type **int playing;** to create a primitive class variable named playing, which keeps track of whether a song is playing. When you finish, press the Enter key.

Class variables that can be accessed by the rest of the program are initialized (**Figure 6-20**).

Figure 6-20 Class variables

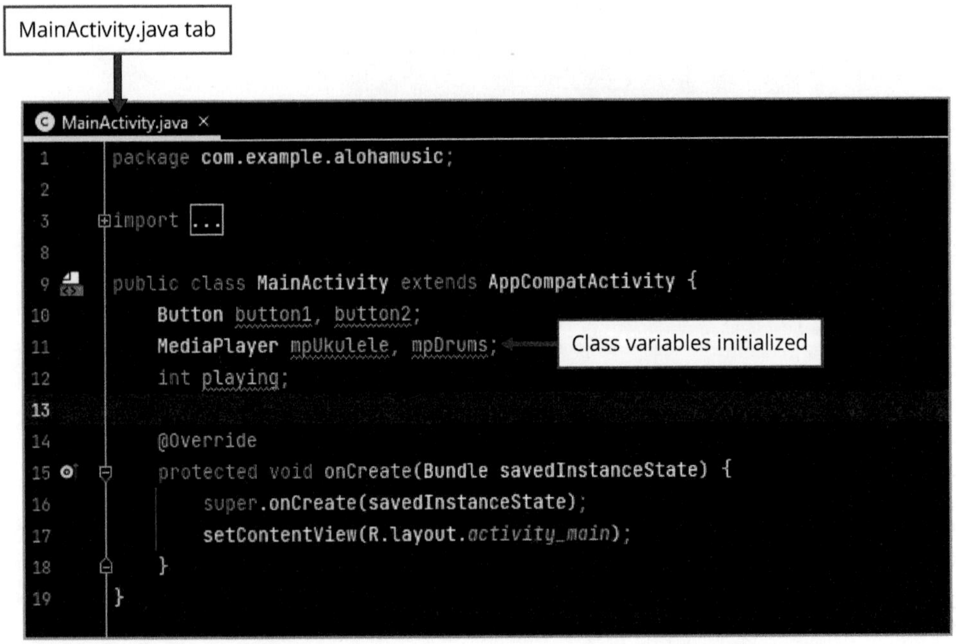

MainActivity.java tab

MainActivity.java ×

```
1   package com.example.alohamusic;
2
3   import ...
8
9   public class MainActivity extends AppCompatActivity {
10      Button button1, button2;
11      MediaPlayer mpUkulele, mpDrums;
12      int playing;
13
14      @Override
15      protected void onCreate(Bundle savedInstanceState) {
16          super.onCreate(savedInstanceState);
17          setContentView(R.layout.activity_main);
18      }
19  }
```

Class variables initialized

Step 2

- To create an instance of each Button component referenced as class variables, press the Enter key after Line 17 (the setContentView statement) and type **button1 = (Button)findViewById(R.id.btUkulele);**.
- Press the Enter key and then type **button2 = (Button)findViewById(R.id.btDrums);**.

The Button components named button1 and button2 are referenced in MainActivity.java (**Figure 6-21**).

Step 3

- To create a setOnClickListener( ) method so the first Button (button1) waits for the user's tap, press the Enter key and type **button1.setOnClickListener(Ukulele);**.
- To create an instance of the Button OnClickListener, click between the two ending braces (Line 22), type **Button.OnClickListener Ukulele = new Button.OnClickListener(){**, and then press the Enter key.

Figure 6-21 Adding Button components

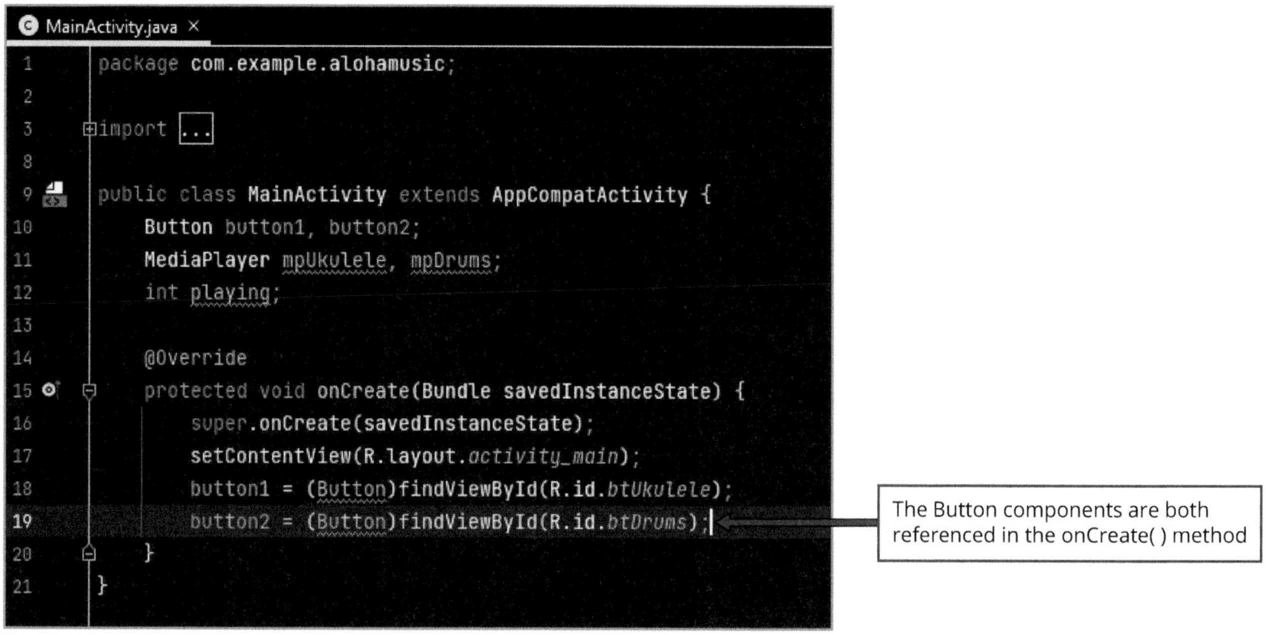

MainActivity.java ×

```
1   package com.example.alohamusic;
2
3   import ...
8
9   public class MainActivity extends AppCompatActivity {
10      Button button1, button2;
11      MediaPlayer mpUkulele, mpDrums;
12      int playing;
13
14      @Override
15      protected void onCreate(Bundle savedInstanceState) {
16          super.onCreate(savedInstanceState);
17          setContentView(R.layout.activity_main);
18          button1 = (Button)findViewById(R.id.btUkulele);
19          button2 = (Button)findViewById(R.id.btDrums);
20      }
21  }
```

The Button components are both referenced in the onCreate( ) method

- Place a semicolon after the new closing brace on Line 24.
- This OnClickListener is designed for a class variable for a Button. Click the red curly error line below Button. OnClickListener, press Alt+Enter, select Implement Method to add the quick fix, and then click the OK button.

An OnClickListener auto-generated stub appears in the code for the first button (**Figure 6-22**).

Figure 6-22 Inserting the first Button OnClickListener stub

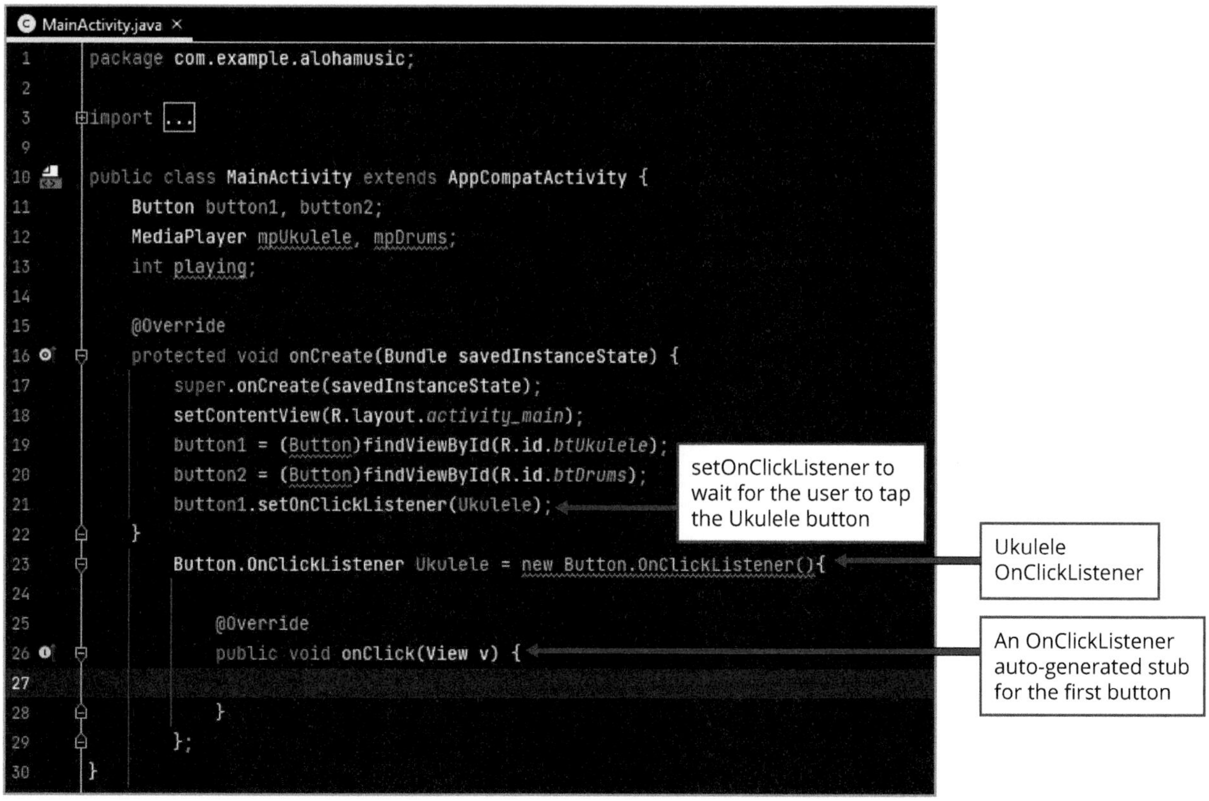

MainActivity.java ×

```
1   package com.example.alohamusic;
2
3   import ...
9
10  public class MainActivity extends AppCompatActivity {
11      Button button1, button2;
12      MediaPlayer mpUkulele, mpDrums;
13      int playing;
14
15      @Override
16      protected void onCreate(Bundle savedInstanceState) {
17          super.onCreate(savedInstanceState);
18          setContentView(R.layout.activity_main);
19          button1 = (Button)findViewById(R.id.btUkulele);
20          button2 = (Button)findViewById(R.id.btDrums);
21          button1.setOnClickListener(Ukulele);
22      }
23          Button.OnClickListener Ukulele = new Button.OnClickListener(){
24
25              @Override
26              public void onClick(View v) {
27
28              }
29          };
30  }
```

setOnClickListener to wait for the user to tap the Ukulele button

Ukulele OnClickListener

An OnClickListener auto-generated stub for the first button

Step 4

- To create a setOnClickListener( ) method so the second Button (button2) for the Drums song waits for the user's click, click after the button1.setOnClickListener(Ukulele); statement and then press the Enter key.
- Type **button2.setOnClickListener(Drums);**.
- To create an instance of the button2 OnClickListener, click after the brace with the semicolon at the end of the code in Line 30 and then press the Enter key.
- Type **Button.OnClickListener Drums = new Button.OnClickListener()** { and then press the Enter key to create the closing brace.
- Place a semicolon after the new closing brace.
- Click the red error line below Button.OnClickListener, press Alt+Enter, select Implement Method to add the quick fix, and then click the OK button. Save your work.

An OnClickListener auto-generated stub appears in the code for the second button (**Figure 6-23**).

Figure 6-23 Inserting the second Button OnClickListener stub

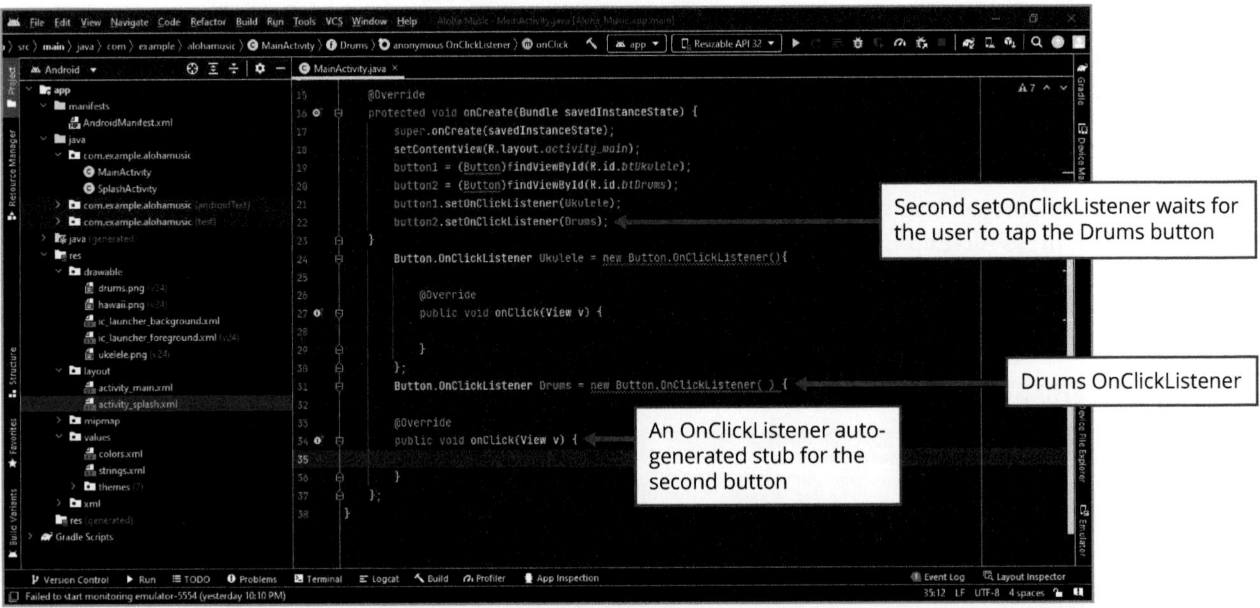

Quick Check

Which variable type has global scope?

Answer: A class variable.

6.7 Playing Music

Every Android phone and tablet includes a built-in music player where you can store your favorite music. You can also write your own applications that offer music playback capabilities. To enable the Aloha Music chapter project to play two songs, Android includes a MediaPlayer class that can play both audio and music files. Android lets you play audio and video from several types of data sources. You can play audio or video from media files stored in the application's resources (a folder named raw), from stand-alone files in the Android file system of the device, from an SD (Secure Digital) memory card in the phone itself, or from a data stream provided through an Internet connection with services such as Amazon Music and Pandora. The most common file type supported for audio playback with the MediaPlayer class is .mp3, but other audio file types such as .wav, .ogg, and .midi are typically supported by most Android hardware. The Android device platform supports a wide variety of media types based on the codecs included in the device by the manufacturer. A **codec** is a computer technology used to compress and decompress audio and video files.

On the Job

The Android platform provides a class to record audio and video if it is supported by the mobile device hardware. To record audio or video, use the MediaRecorder class. The emulator does not provide the capability to capture audio or video, but an actual mobile device can record media input through the MediaRecorder class.

Critical Thinking

What types of video file formats can be played on an Android device?

Android currently supports the following video formats: MPEG-4, H.263, H.264, H.265, VP8, VP9, and the newest AV1.

6.8 Creating a Raw Folder for Music Files

In an Android project, music files are typically stored in a new resource directory called raw, which is a subfolder created in the res folder. The raw resource directory must be created before music files can be placed in the folder. The two .mp3 files played in the Aloha Music app are named ukulele.mp3 and drums.mp3, and they should be placed in the raw folder. To create a raw folder that contains music files, follow these steps.

Step 1

- In the Android project view, right-click the res folder.
- Click **New** on the shortcut menu and then click **Android resource directory**. The New Resource Directory dialog box opens.
- Click the arrow to the right of the Resource type text box and select raw from the drop-down entries.

A resource directory named raw is created using the New Resource Directory dialog box (**Figure 6-24**).

Figure 6-24 The raw folder added for sound files

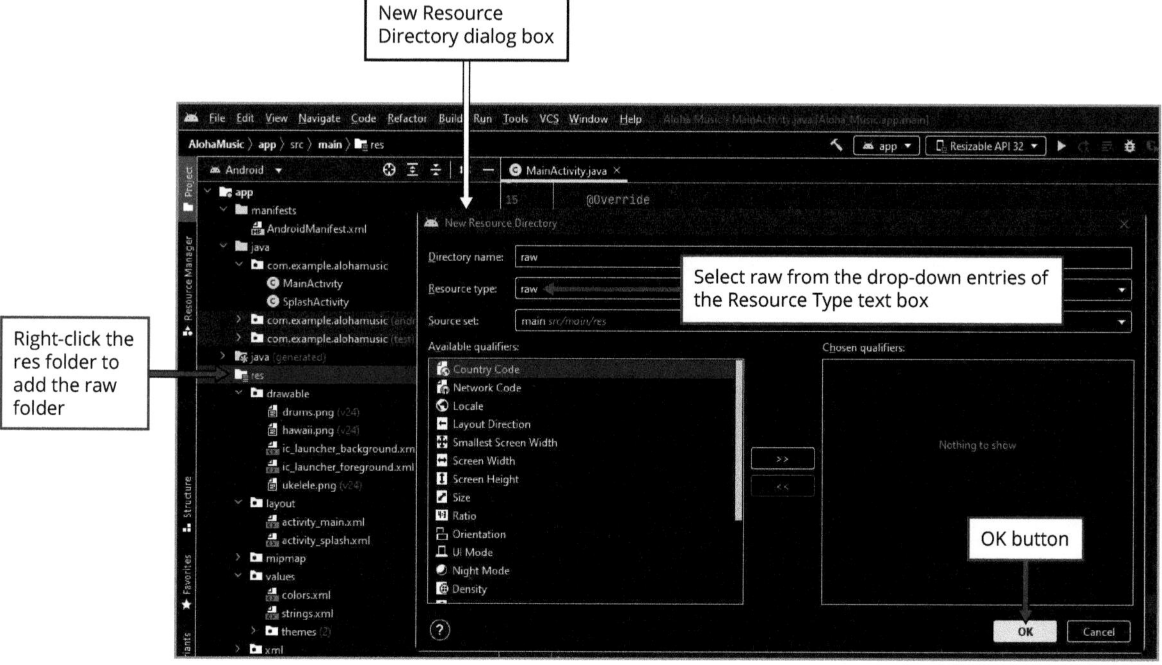

Step 2

- Click the OK button.
- To add the project music files to the raw folder, open the folder that contains your student files.
- To add the two music files to the raw resource folder, copy ukulele.mp3 and drums.mp3 by pressing Ctrl+C, right-click the raw folder, and click Paste.
- Click the Reformat button in the dialog box.

Copies of the music files appear in the raw folder (**Figure 6-25**).

Figure 6-25 MP3 files added to the raw folder

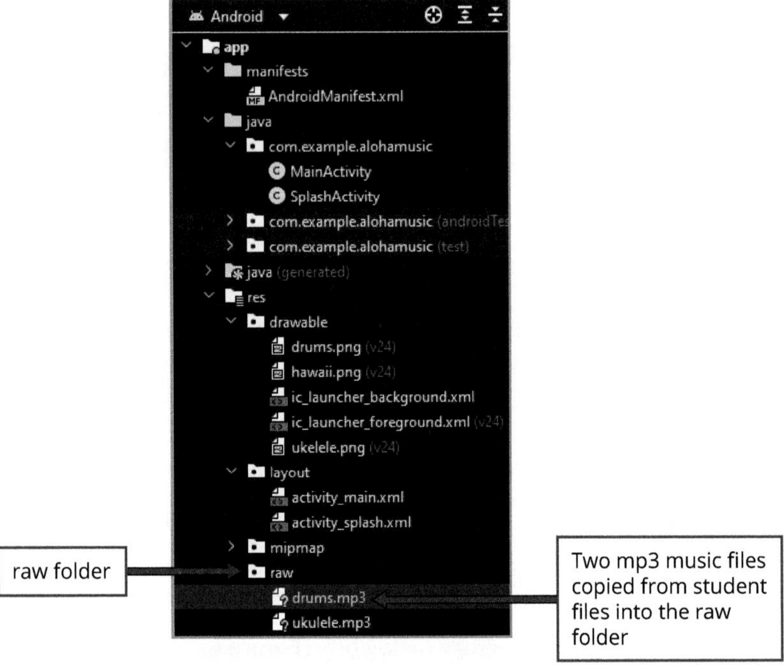

Quick Check

Music .mp3 files should be stored in which subfolder?

Answer: The raw folder.

6.9 Playing Music with a MediaPlayer Method

The **MediaPlayer class** provides the methods for component audio playback on an Android device. The Android MediaPlayer class provides access to built-in MediaPlayer services for playing audio and video files. At the beginning of the MainActivity.java code, two MediaPlayer class variables are declared. After the variables are declared, an instance of the MediaPlayer class is assigned to each variable. In the following code syntax, mpUkulele is assigned to an instance of the MediaPlayer class that accesses the ukulele music file in the raw folder.

Code Syntax

```
mpUkulele = MediaPlayer.create(this, R.raw.ukulele);
```

The class variables mpUkulele and mpDrums are assigned the music files from the raw folder. To declare an instance of the MediaPlayer class, follow this step.

Step 1

- In MainActivity.java, press the Enter key after the button2.setOnClickListener(Drums); statement (Line 22) to create a new line.
- Type **mpUkulele = new MediaPlayer();** to create a new instance of MediaPlayer.
- Insert a new line and type **mpUkulele = MediaPlayer.create(this, R.raw.ukulele);** to assign the first song to mpUkulele in order to play the Ukulele song. Press the Enter key after the closing semicolon.
- Type **mpDrums = new MediaPlayer();** to add an instance for the second MediaPlayer variable.
- Insert a new line and type **mpDrums = MediaPlayer.create(this, R.raw.drums);** to assign the second song to mpDrums.

The two class variables are assigned an instance of the MediaPlayer class (**Figure 6-26**).

Figure 6-26 MediaPlayer instance statements

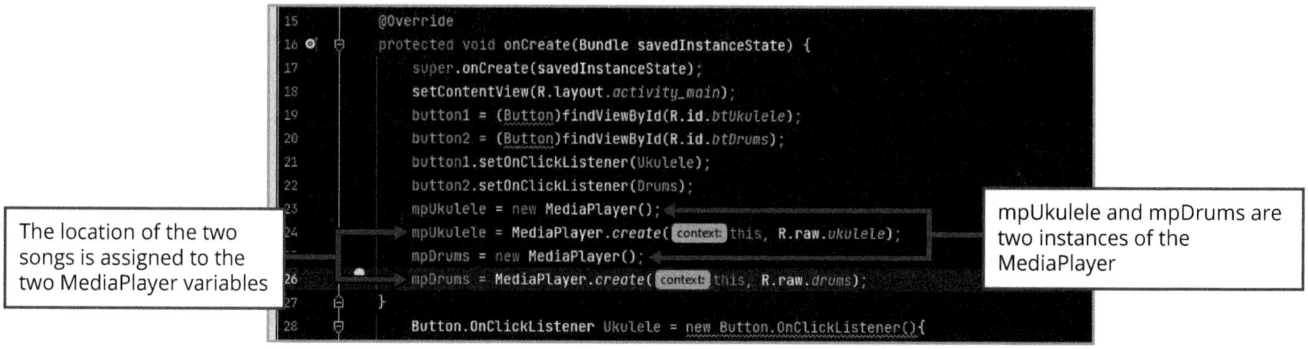

```
15      @Override
16      protected void onCreate(Bundle savedInstanceState) {
17          super.onCreate(savedInstanceState);
18          setContentView(R.layout.activity_main);
19          button1 = (Button)findViewById(R.id.btUkulele);
20          button2 = (Button)findViewById(R.id.btDrums);
21          button1.setOnClickListener(Ukulele);
22          button2.setOnClickListener(Drums);
23          mpUkulele = new MediaPlayer();
24          mpUkulele = MediaPlayer.create( context: this, R.raw.ukulele);
25          mpDrums = new MediaPlayer();
26          mpDrums = MediaPlayer.create( context: this, R.raw.drums);
27      }
28          Button.OnClickListener Ukulele = new Button.OnClickListener(){
```

The location of the two songs is assigned to the two MediaPlayer variables

mpUkulele and mpDrums are two instances of the MediaPlayer

> **Good to Know** Music can be used in many ways throughout Android apps. Music can provide sound effects to inform the user of a recent email or to praise you when you reach the winning level on your favorite game. Background music is often used as a soundtrack to create a theme in an adventure game.

6.10 Starting and Resuming Music Playback

Android uses the MediaPlayer class to control the playing of an audio file. The audio file can be saved locally on the phone device, within the app, or even from a URL via HTTP streaming. The **playback state** of the MediaPlayer determines whether an audio file is playing. By informing the Android app that a file is playing, control of the playback state can be delegated to the app. The three common playback states of an audio file are when the music starts, when the music pauses, and when the music stops, as shown in **Table 6-3**.

Table 6-3 Common MediaPlayer playback states

Method	Purpose
start( )	Starts media playback
pause( )	Pauses media playback
stop( )	Stops media playback

In the Aloha Music project, the user first taps a button to start playing the music. The start( ) method is used to begin the playback of the selected music file. When the user taps the same button again, the app temporarily pauses the music file by calling the pause( ) method. To restart the song, the start( ) method must be called again. To determine the state of the MediaPlayer, the code must assess whether this is the first time the user is tapping the button to start the song or if the user is tapping the same button twice to pause the song. The user can tap the button a third time to start the song again. This cycle continues until the user exits the project. In the chapter project, an integer variable named playing is initially set to zero. Each time the user taps the button, the playing variable changes value. The first time the user taps the button, the variable is changed to the value of 1 to assist the program in determining the state of the MediaPlayer. If the user taps the same button again to pause the song, the variable changes to the value of 0. Android does not have a method for determining the current state of the MediaPlayer, but by using this simple primitive variable, you can keep track of the state of the music. A Switch decision structure uses the variable named playing to change the state of the music. The onClick( ) method is called every time the user selects a button. To initiate the variable used to determine the state of the MediaPlayer and to code a Switch decision structure to determine the state, follow these steps.

Step 1

- In MainActivity.java, press the Enter key after the mpDrums = MediaPlayer.create(this, R.raw.drums); statement (Line 26) to create a new line.
- Type **playing = 0;** to initialize the variable named playing as the value 0. When the user clicks a button, the Switch statement follows the path of case 0, which begins the audio playback of one of the songs.

The variable named playing is initialized as the value 0 to identify that the music is not playing (**Figure 6-27**).

Figure 6-27 Variable named playing is set to 0

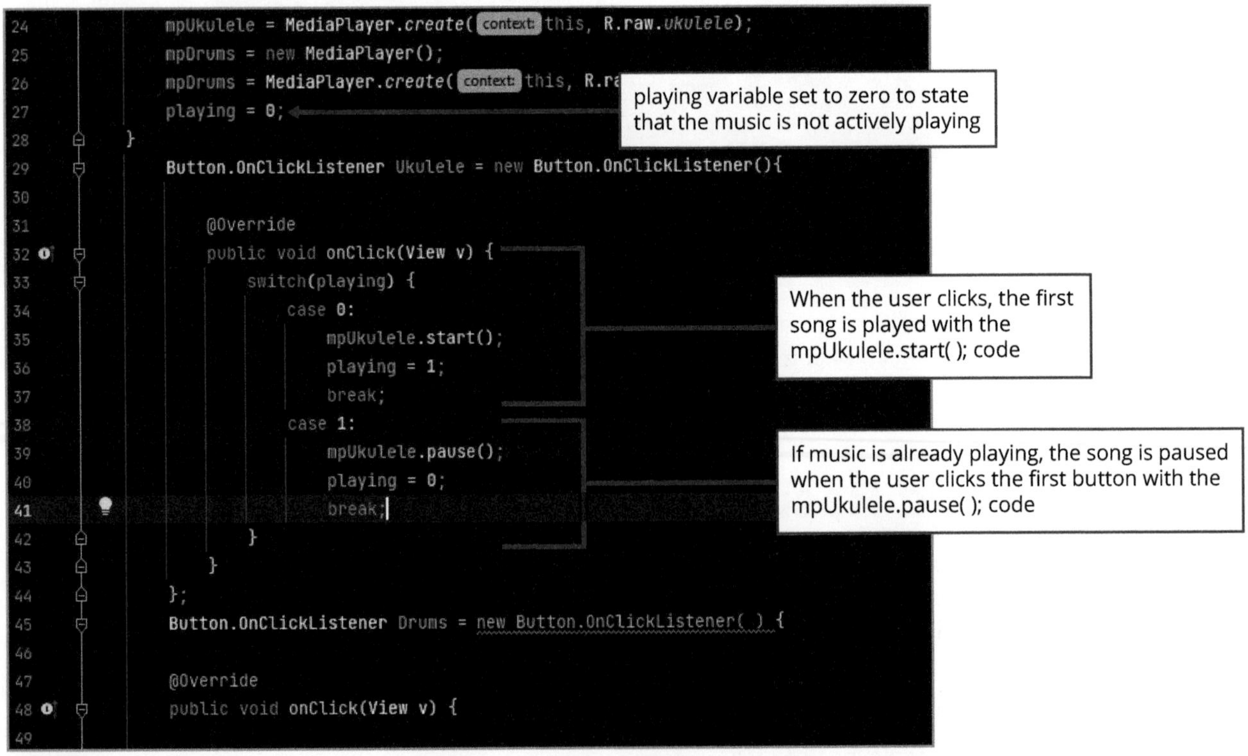

```
24        mpUkulele = MediaPlayer.create( context: this, R.raw.ukulele);
25        mpDrums = new MediaPlayer();
26        mpDrums = MediaPlayer.create( context: this, R.ra
27        playing = 0;
28    }
29    Button.OnClickListener Ukulele = new Button.OnClickListener(){
30
31        @Override
32        public void onClick(View v) {
33            switch(playing) {
34                case 0:
35                    mpUkulele.start();
36                    playing = 1;
37                    break;
38                case 1:
39                    mpUkulele.pause();
40                    playing = 0;
41                    break;
42            }
43        }
44    };
45    Button.OnClickListener Drums = new Button.OnClickListener( ) {
46
47        @Override
48        public void onClick(View v) {
49
```

playing variable set to zero to state that the music is not actively playing

When the user clicks, the first song is played with the mpUkulele.start( ); code

If music is already playing, the song is paused when the user clicks the first button with the mpUkulele.pause( ); code

Step 2

- Inside the braces of the first onClick( ) method, click the blank Line 33 and then type the following Switch decision structure, which is used to determine the state of the music:

```
switch(playing) {
    case 0:
        mpUkulele.start();
        playing = 1;
        break;
    case 1:
        mpUkulele.pause();
        playing = 0;
        break;
}
```

The Switch decision structure that determines the state of the music is coded for the first onClick( ) method (Figure 6-27). When the user taps the first button to play the ukulele song, the variable playing is set to the value of 1 so the app knows the music is playing.

Good to Know | Music playback may fail due to various reasons, such as an unsupported audio/video format, poorly interleaved audio/video, a file size that overwhelms memory capabilities, or a streaming timeout on the Internet.

6.11 Changing the Text Attribute of a Component

To play the first song in the chapter project, the user taps the Button component with the text "PLAY UKULELE SONG." To pause the song, the user must tap the same button, but the text should be changed to a more fitting action, such as "PAUSE UKULELE SONG." An attribute can initially be entered in the XML layout or coded in Java. In Chapter 4, the setText() method displays text in the TextView component. To change the text attribute for a Button component using Java code, the component name and the setText( ) method are separated by a period and followed by a string of text within parentheses, as shown in the following code syntax.

Code Syntax

```
button1.setText("Pause Ukulele Song");
```

The code enables the btUkulele Button component to display the text "PAUSE UKULELE SONG." If the user wants to restart the song, a second setText() method changes the text back to "PLAY UKULELE SONG." Thus, the buttons in this app serve as a way to communicate that you are currently playing a song or pausing a song. To change the text on the first Button component, follow these steps.

Step 1

- In MainActivity.java, in the first onClick( ) method, press the Enter key after the statement playing = 1; in case 0 (Line 36).
- Type **button1.setText("Pause Ukulele Song");** to change the text displayed on the Button component.
- To change the text back to the original text if the user restarts the music, go to case 1 of the Switch decision structure and press the Enter key after the statement playing = 0; (Line 41).
- Type **button1.setText("Play Ukulele Song");** to change the text displayed on the Button component.

The first button changes text while the music is paused or restarted (**Figure 6-28**).

Figure 6-28 The setText( ) method changes the button text in both case statements

```
            playing = 0;
        }
        Button.OnClickListener Ukulele = new Button.OnClickListener(){

            @Override
            public void onClick(View v) {
                switch(playing) {
                    case 0:
                        mpUkulele.start();
                        playing = 1;
                        button1.setText("Pause Ukulele Song");
                        break;
                    case 1:
                        mpUkulele.pause();
                        playing = 0;
                        button1.setText("Play Ukulele Song");
                        break;
                }
            }
        };
        Button.OnClickListener Drums = new Button.OnClickListener( ) {
```

Text changes on the button when the music is playing

Text changes on the button when the music is paused

Step 2

- To test the music and text on the first Button component, save and run the program. The second Button component has not been coded yet.

The app loads with a five-second splash screen and then launches the MainActivity class. When you tap the first Button component, the Ukulele song plays and the Button text is changed. You can restart or pause the music by pressing the button again (**Figure 6-29**).

Figure 6-29 Coding the button

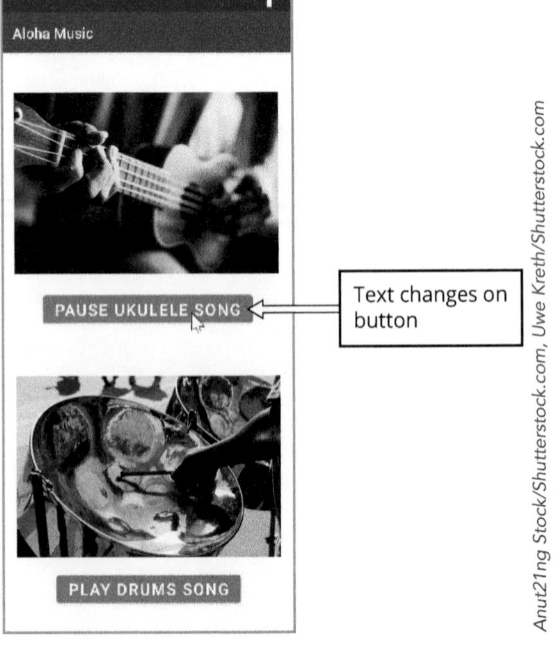

Anut21ng Stock/Shutterstock.com, Uwe Kreth/Shutterstock.com

6.12 Changing the Visibility of a Component

When the program is complete, the user can select the button that plays the Ukulele song or the Drums song. One problem is that a user can tap the Ukulele button and then tap the Drums button, playing both songs at once. To resolve this problem when the user has already selected one of the songs, the button to the other song can be coded to disappear until the user has paused the current song from playing. The Java attribute that determines whether a component is displayed on the emulator is the **visibility attribute**. By default, the visibility attribute is set to display any component you place on the emulator when the program runs. To cause the component not to appear, you must code the setVisibility attribute to change the view to invisible. To change the visibility of the button to reappear, set the setVisibility attribute to visible, as shown in the following code syntax:

Code Syntax

To hide the component:

```
button2.setVisibility(View.INVISIBLE);
```

To display the component:

```
button2.setVisibility(View.VISIBLE);
```

To set the setVisibility attribute for the Ukulele button component and to copy and paste the first onClick() method code to create a Switch decision structure for the second button, you can complete the following steps.

Step 1

- In MainActivity.java, within the first onClick( ) method in the case 0 option, press the Enter key after the statement button1.setText("Pause Ukulele Song");.
- Type **button2.setVisibility(View.INVISIBLE);** to hide the Drums button when the Ukulele song is playing. When the music is paused, the Drums button should be visible again.
- In the case 1 option, press the Enter key after the statement button1.setText("Play Ukulele Song");.
- Type **button2.setVisibility(View.VISIBLE);** to change the visibility of the Drums button.

The Drums button is hidden when the ukulele music plays and displayed when the music stops (**Figure 6-30**).

Figure 6-30 The setVisibility( ) method changes the visibility of the Button component

Step 2

- To code the second onClick( ) method for the Drums button, select and copy Lines 33–46 in Figure 6-30 by clicking Edit on the menu bar and then clicking Copy. Click Line 53 inside the second onClick() method, click Edit on the menu bar, and then click Paste. Change every reference of mpUkulele to **mpDrums**. Change every reference of button1 to **button2** or vice versa.
- Change the setText( ) messages to **Pause Drums Song** and **Play Drums Song**. You might need to add **};** as the second-to-last line of code. Compare your code with the complete code for the app, making changes as necessary.

The second onClick( ) method is coded using a Switch decision structure (**Figure 6-31**). The code for MainActivity.java is complete.

Figure 6-31 Completed code for MainActivity.java

```
48          };
49          Button.OnClickListener Drums = new Button.OnClickListener( ) {
50
51              @Override
52              public void onClick(View v) {
53                  switch(playing) {
54                      case 0:
55                          mpDrums.start();
56                          playing = 1;
57                          button2.setText("Pause Drums Song");
58                          button1.setVisibility(View.INVISIBLE);
59                          break;
60                      case 1:
61                          mpDrums.pause();
62                          playing = 0;
63                          button2.setText("Play Drums Song");
64                          button1.setVisibility(View.VISIBLE);
65                          break;
66                  }
67              }
68          };
69      }
```

Lines 33–46 from Figure 6-30 are copied, pasted, and revised

Critical Thinking

What would have happened if the second button was visible while the first song was playing and both buttons were pressed?

Both songs would play at the same time.

Running and Testing the Application

Your first experience with media in an Android application is complete. Click Run on the menu bar and then select Run to save and test the application in the emulator. If necessary, select Android Application and click the OK button. Save all the files in the next dialog box, if necessary, and unlock the emulator. The application opens in the emulator window, as shown in Figures 6-1 and 6-2. The splash screen opens for five seconds. The activity_main layout screen opens next, requesting your button selection to play one of the songs. Test both buttons and make sure your speakers are on so you can hear the music play.

Wrap It Up—Chapter Summary

In this chapter, the Android platform created a memorable multimedia experience with the sounds of Hawaiian music. A splash screen provided time to load extra files if needed and displayed an initial logo for brand recognition. Methods such as setText( ) and setVisibility( ) helped to create an easy-to-use Android application that was clear to the user. The app used the start( ) and pause( ) methods of the MediaPlayer to fill your classroom or home with music.

- An Android application can show a splash screen that displays the name of the program, a brand logo for the application, or the name of the author. The splash screen opens as you launch your app, providing time for Android to initialize its resources.
- A TextView widget can display a background color or image stored in one of the project's drawable folders.
- A timer in Java executes a one-time task such as displaying an opening splash screen, or it performs a continuous process, such as a wake-up call that rings each morning at the same time. Timers can be used to pause an action temporarily or for time-dependent or repeated activities. The timer object uses milliseconds as the unit of time.
- After including a reference to the TimerTask class in your code, schedule a timer for the amount of time that an event occurs, such as a splash screen being displayed.
- Each Activity has a life cycle, which is the series of actions from the beginning of an Activity to its end. An Activity usually starts with the onCreate( ) method, which sets up all the resources required to perform the Activity. An Activity usually ends with the onDestroy( ) method, which releases those same resources to free up memory on the mobile device. Other actions can take place during the life of the Activity, including onRestart( ), onStart( ), onResume( ), onPause( ), and onStop( ).
- Local variables are declared by variable declaration statements within a method. The local variable effectively ceases to exist when the execution of the method is complete.
- The scope of a variable refers to the variable's visibility within a class. Variables that are accessible only to a restricted portion of a program, such as a single method, have local scope. Variables that are accessible from anywhere in a class, however, have global scope. If a variable is needed in multiple methods within a class, the global variable is assigned at the beginning of a class, not within a method. This global scope variable is called a class variable in Java and can be accessed by multiple methods throughout the program.
- Every Android phone and tablet includes a built-in music player where you can store music. You can also write applications that offer music playback capabilities. The media types an Android device platform supports are determined by the codecs the manufacturer included in the device. A codec is a computer technology used to compress and decompress audio and video files.
- In an Android project, music files are typically stored in the res\raw subfolder. In newer versions of Android, you must create the raw subfolder before storing music files.
- The MediaPlayer class provides the methods for component audio playback on an Android device. First, declare the MediaPlayer class variables and then assign an instance of the MediaPlayer class to each variable. The playback state of the MediaPlayer determines whether the music file is playing. The three common states of an audio file are when the music starts, when it pauses, and when it stops.
- The Java attribute that determines whether a component is displayed on the emulator is the visibility attribute. By default, the visibility attribute is set to display any component you place on the emulator when the program runs. To cause the component not to appear, you must code the setVisibility attribute in Java to change the view to invisible. To change the visibility of the component to reappear, change the setVisibility attribute to visible.

Key Terms

class variable
codec
global scope
life cycle
local variable
MediaPlayer class
onDestroy( ) method
playback state
scope
state
thread
Timer
timer
TimerTask
visibility attribute

Developer FAQs

1. What is the name of the initial window in an app that typically displays a company logo for a few seconds? (6.1)
2. Which attribute of TextView displays a solid color behind the text? (6.2)
3. Which attribute of TextView displays an image as a backdrop behind the text? (6.2)
4. Write a line of code that creates an instance of the TimerTask class with an object named welcome. (6.4)
5. Write a line of code that creates an instance of the Timer class with an object named stopwatch. (6.4)
6. Write a line of code that would hold the initial opening screen for four seconds. The Timer object is named stopwatch and the TimerTask object is named welcome. (6.4)
7. How long does the following statement schedule a pause in the execution? Identify the unit of measurement. (6.4)

```
logo.schedule(task, 8000);
```

8. Write a line of code that closes the resources of the existing Activity. (6.5)
9. Typically, which method begins an Activity? (6.5)
10. Typically, which method releases the resources used within an Activity and ends the Activity? (6.5)
11. What are the four states of an Activity? (6.5)
12. Which method follows an onPause( ) method? (6.5)
13. Write two statements that initialize the MediaPlayer to create an instance of a file named blues stored in your raw folder. Name the variable mpJazz. (6.8)
14. Write a statement that is needed to begin playing the song from Question 13. (6.9)
15. Write a statement that pauses the song from Question 14. (6.9)
16. Write a statement that changes the text on a button named btJazz to "Pause Unforgettable." (6.10)
17. Write a statement that hides the button in Question 16. (6.11)
18. What is the name of the folder that typically holds media files in an Android project? (6.7)
19. Why are class variables sometimes used instead of local variables? (6.6)
20. What is the most common extension for a song played on an Android device? (6.7)

Beyond the Book

Search the web for answers to the following questions to further your Android knowledge.

1. Research the four most common music file types played on an Android device. Write a paragraph about each music file type. Compare the file size, music quality, and usage of each file type.
2. Using a typical weather app as an example, describe the Android life cycle using each of the methods and a process that happens within the weather app. (*Hint:* See the example using the camera app in this chapter.)
3. In Google Play, research five music apps. Write a paragraph that includes the name, features, and purpose of each app.
4. The MediaPlayer class has a method named seekTo( ). Research the purpose of this method.

Case Programming Projects

Complete one or more of the following case programming projects. Use the same steps and techniques taught within the chapter. Successful completion of these projects requires knowledge of all chapter learning objectives. Submit the program(s) you create to your instructor. The level of difficulty is indicated for each case programming project.

Case Project 6–1: Celtic Songs App (Beginner)

Requirements Document

Application title:	Celtic Songs App
Purpose:	A music app compares the different types of Celtic music.
Algorithms:	1. A splash screen opens and displays the opening.png image with the title “Celtic Songs” for four seconds (**Figure 6-32**). 2. Two types of Celtic music are available in this app. An Irish jig, jig.mp3, can be played while displaying an image of Irish dancers (jig.png). A selection of bagpipe music plays from bagpipes.mp3 while the app displays an image of a person playing bagpipes (**Figure 6-33**).
Conditions:	1. The picture from the opening file and the two music files are provided with your student files. 2. The music should be played and paused by a button component. 3. When a song is playing, the other button should not be displayed.

Figure 6-32 Celtic Songs splash screen

Figure 6-33 Two types of Celtic songs

Case Project 6–2: Animal Sounds Children's App (Beginner)

Requirements Document

Application title:	Animal Sounds Children's App
Purpose:	The Animal Sounds app plays sounds of sheep and pigs in the barnyard.
Algorithms:	**1.** The opening screen displays an image of farm animals and the title "Animal Sounds" for six seconds (**Figure 6-34**). **2.** The second screen displays two buttons with two images that allow the user to select sheep sounds or pig sounds (**Figure 6-35**).
Conditions:	**1.** The sheep.jpg, pig.jpg, and farm.png images are available in the student files; the sound effects are named sheep.mp3 and pig.mp3. **2.** When a sound effect is playing, the other button should not be displayed. Each sound effect can play and pause on the user's selection.

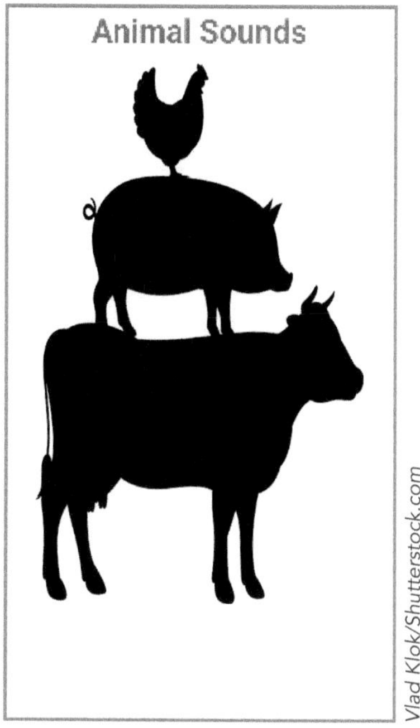

Figure 6-34 Animal Sounds splash screen

Vlad Klok/Shutterstock.com

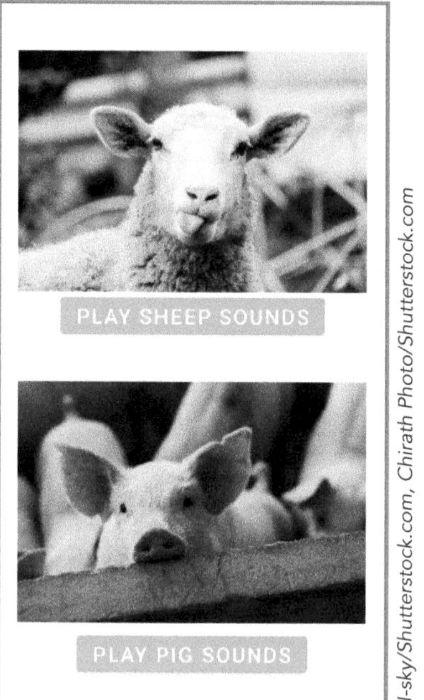

Figure 6-35 Two types of animal sounds

N-sky/Shutterstock.com, Chirath Photo/Shutterstock.com

Case Project 6–3: Serenity Sounds App (Intermediate)

Requirements Document

Application title: Serenity Sounds App

Purpose: A relaxation app provides songs to allow you to breathe deeply and meditate.

Algorithms:

1. An opening screen displays an image of a relaxing location.
2. The second screen displays two song names with a description of each song. A button is available to play or pause each song.

Conditions:

1. Choose your own image for the splash screen from images available on the web.
2. Choose your own songs from songs available at free sites online. Listen to each song and create your own description of each song.
3. When a song is playing, the other button should not be displayed. Each song can play and pause on the user's selection.

Case Project 6–4: Guitar Solo App (Intermediate)

Requirements Document

Application title:	Guitar Solo App
Purpose:	A new guitar performance artist needs an Android app to demonstrate her talent.
Algorithms:	**1.** The opening screen displays the text "Solo Guitar Demo" and an image of a guitar. **2.** A second screen displays the guitar image and a button. When the user selects the Play Guitar Solo button, a guitar solo plays.
Conditions:	**1.** The opening screen is displayed for three seconds. **2.** The song can be paused by the user and restarted. **3.** Locate images and music files on free sites online.

Case Project 6–5: Ring Tones App (Advanced)

Requirements Document

Application title:	Ring Tones App
Purpose:	The Ring Tones app allows you to listen to three different ring tones using RadioButton components for making a selection.
Algorithms:	**1.** Create an app that opens with a picture of a mobile phone and a title for three seconds. **2.** The second screen shows three RadioButton components that display different ring tone titles and a description of each ring tone.
Conditions:	**1.** Select your own images and free ring tones available by searching the web. **2.** When a ring tone is playing, the other buttons should not be displayed. Each ring tone can play and pause on the user's selection.

Case Project 6–6: Your Personal Playlist App (Advanced)

Requirements Document

Application title:	Your Personal Playlist App
Purpose:	Get creative! Play your favorite three songs on your own personal playlist app.
Algorithms:	**1.** Create an app that opens with your own picture and a title for six seconds. **2.** The second screen shows three buttons that display different song titles and an image of the artist or group.
Conditions:	**1.** Select your own images and music files. **2.** When a song is playing, the other buttons should not be displayed. Each song can play and pause on the user's selection.

Chapter 7

Reveal! Displaying Pictures in a GridView

Learning Objectives

At the completion of this chapter, you will be able to:

- **7.1** Create an Android project using a GridView component
- **7.2** Add a GridView to display a two-dimensional grid of images
- **7.3** Add the ImageView component in XML code
- **7.4** Create an array for images
- **7.5** Instantiate the GridView and ImageView components
- **7.6** Use a setAdapter with an ImageAdapter
- **7.7** Code the OnItemClickListener
- **7.8** Code a custom toast notification
- **7.9** Display the setImageResource image
- **7.10** Define a Context resource
- **7.11** Determine the length of an array
- **7.12** Code the getView( ) method

7.1 Creating an Android Project Using a GridView Component

Using multimedia in an Android program brings personality and imagery to your app. Images are a powerful marketing tool that add visual appeal to any Android application, but it is essential to create a clean, professional effect with those images. To meet this goal, Android provides a layout tool called GridView, which shows items in a two-dimensional scrolling grid.

To demonstrate the visual appeal of a GridView component, you will design a grid that displays animals on the endangered species list. The Endangered Species application shown in **Figure 7-1** allows users to select an animal they want to symbolically adopt and to contribute funds for support groups that work to protect these iconic animals from extinction. Users can scroll the image grid by flicking their fingers across a horizontal list of thumbnail-sized pictures. To view a larger image of one of the endangered animals, users can tap a thumbnail.

Figure 7-1 Endangered Species app

Bundit Jonwises/Shutterstock.com, Pfotenpaparazzi/Shutterstock.com, Jiri Fejkl/Shutterstock.com, Hung Chung Chih/Shutterstock.com, Sergey Uryadnikov/Shutterstock.com, Roger de la Harpe/Shutterstock.com

Figure 7-2 Panda image selected in the grid

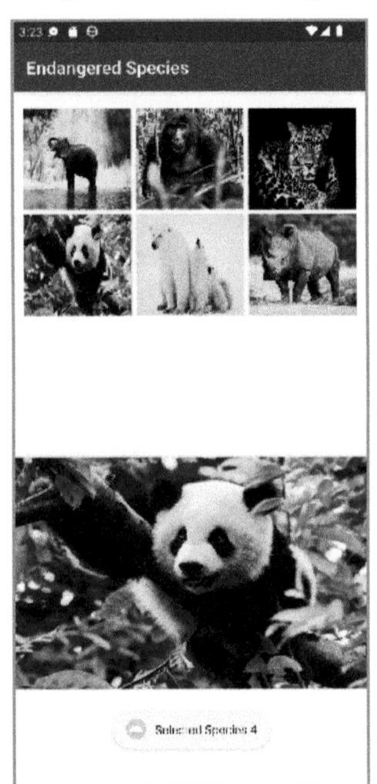

Bundit Jonwises/Shutterstock.com, Pfotenpaparazzi/Shutterstock.com, Jiri Fejkl/Shutterstock.com, Hung Chung Chih/Shutterstock.com, Sergey Uryadnikov/Shutterstock.com, Roger de la Harpe/Shutterstock.com, Hung Chung Chih/Shutterstock.com

The Android app in Figure 7-1 is more visually appealing than one that simply displays images of the six endangered species in a tiled layout or grid view. The app also provides an easy way for a donor to select an animal to symbolically adopt. The app displays six animals on the endangered species list, including an Asian elephant, mountain gorilla, leopard, giant panda, polar bear, and rhinoceros. When a user selects the panda bear in the GridView component, for example, a larger image is displayed with the toast message "Selected Species 4," as shown in **Figure 7-2**. A different image is displayed each time the user selects another thumbnail in the grid.

> **Good to Know**
>
> A GridView component of images is typically used to select a wallpaper image for the background of an Android device.

To create the Endangered Species application, the developer must understand how to perform the following processes, among others:

1. Add a GridView component and an ImageView component to the emulator.
2. Update the XML code for an ImageView component not linked to a particular image.
3. Place six images in a drawable folder.
4. Define an array to hold the image files.
5. Instantiate the GridView and ImageView components.
6. Create an ImageAdapter class.
7. Display a custom toast message.
8. Display the selected image.
9. Customize the ImageAdapter class.
10. Define the layout using the getView( ) method.

7.2 Adding a GridView to Display a Two-Dimensional Grid of Images

The Endangered Species app opens with a horizontal scrolling list of animal pictures in a View container called a GridView, as shown in Figure 7-1. A **View** container is a rectangular area of the screen that displays an image or text object. A View container can include layouts such as GridView, RadioGroup, ScrollView, TabHost, and ListView.

In Chapter 5, you used the ListView layout to create a vertical list of Chicago attractions. In the Endangered Species project, the **GridView** container displays a horizontal list of objects. A GridView is mainly useful when you want to show data in a grid layout to display images or icons, for example. This layout can be used to build applications such as image viewers and audio or video players to show elements in a table or grid. If you have more images than can be displayed on the screen, you can move through the grid by scrolling the page. The photos in a grid can be sized as small as thumbnail images or as large as full-screen images. The photos can be stored in the Android drawable folders, in your phone's storage (SD card), or even on a website such as Picasa.

The GridView prefix in XML code is *gv*. Each GridView component can be customized with the attributes shown in **Table 7-1**. The GridView attributes can be changed within the XML code.

Table 7-1 GridView component attributes

GridView Attribute Name	Description
android:columnWidth	Specifies the fixed width for each column of the grid
android:numColumns	Defines the number of columns in the grid
android:horizontalSpacing	Defines the default horizontal spacing between columns in the grid
android:verticalSpacing	Defines the default vertical spacing between rows in the grid

To begin the app by adding a GridView component to activity_main.xml, follow these steps.

Step 1

- Open the Android Studio program.
- In the Welcome to Android Studio window, scroll down and click the New Project button in the Phone and Tablet templates to create a new Android Studio project.
- Click the Next button in the New Project window.
- Type **Endangered Species** in the Name text box.
- If necessary, select Java in the Language text box.
- If necessary, select API 23: Android 6.0 (Marshmallow) as the Minimum SDK.

A new Java Android project named Endangered Species is configured to save on your local computer (**Figure 7-3**).

Step 2

- Click the Finish button in the New Project window.
- Click the Hello world! TextView widget displayed by default in the emulator and press the Delete key.
- Click the Next button on the Configure your new project page of the Create New Project dialog box.
- In the Search tool of the Palette, type **GridView** and drag the GridView component to the upper-center part of the emulator on the activity_main.xml tab.
- Drag all four constraint handles of the GridView component to the edges of the emulator and resize the component to fill the top half of the emulator.

The activity_main.xml file is displayed in the emulator with the GridView component (**Figure 7-4**).

Step 3

- Click the Code tab at the upper-right side of the activity_main.xml view to display the XML code.
- To name the GridView component using XML code, click after Line 9 and press Enter. On Line 10, type **android:id="@+id/gvAnimals"** to name the GridView component and press Enter.

Figure 7-3 Application information for the Endangered Species project

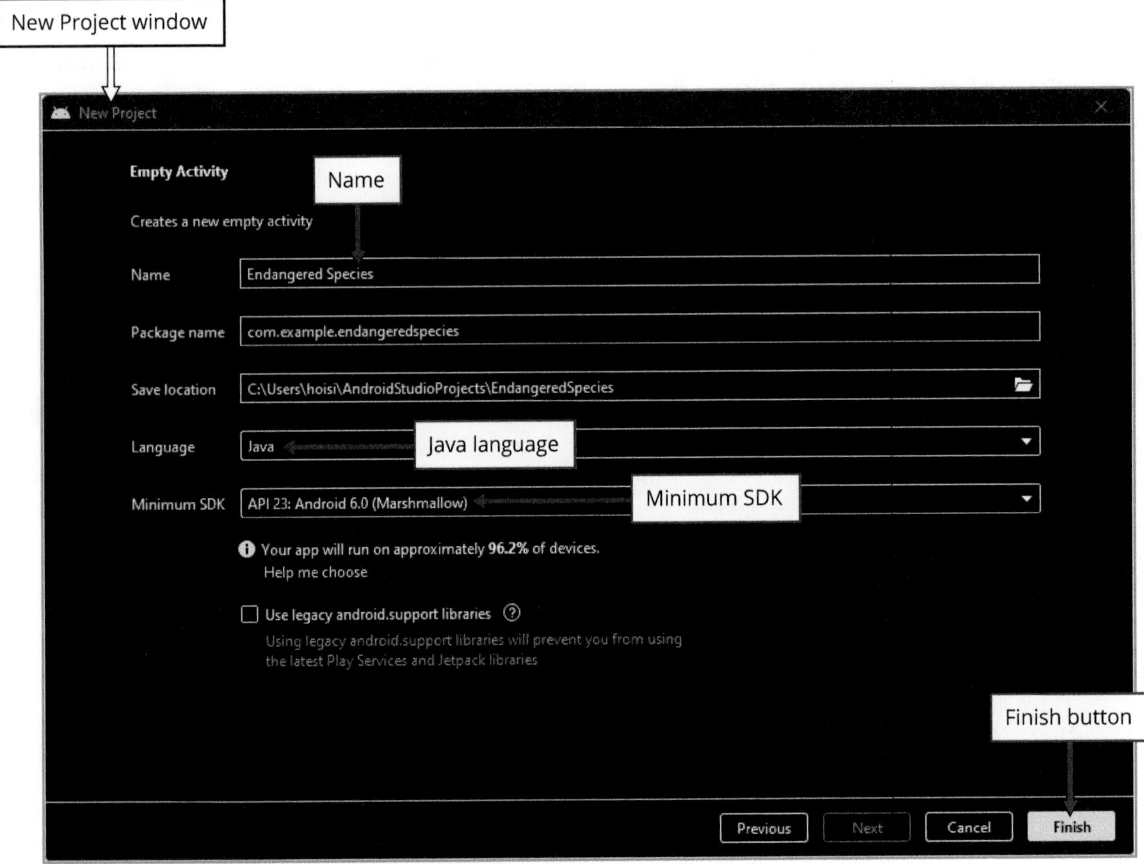

- To customize the layout, change the size of the GridView component. On Lines 11 and 12 of the XML code, change the size to the following values:

  android:layout_width="380dp"

  android:layout_height="320dp"

The activity_main.xml file is displayed in the emulator with the GridView component (**Figure 7-5**). The GridView component's id and size are changed within the XML code.

Step 4

- Press Enter after Line 12.
- Beginning on Line 13, type the following XML code to add the desired number of columns and spacing to the GridView component:

  android:numColumns="3"

  android:columnWidth="160dp"

  android:horizontalSpacing="5dp"

  android:verticalSpacing="5dp"

The GridView component is customized with three columns, each 160dp wide, with the horizontal and vertical spacing set to 5dp between the individual grid items (**Figure 7-6**).

Figure 7-4 GridView component in the emulator for the Endangered Species project

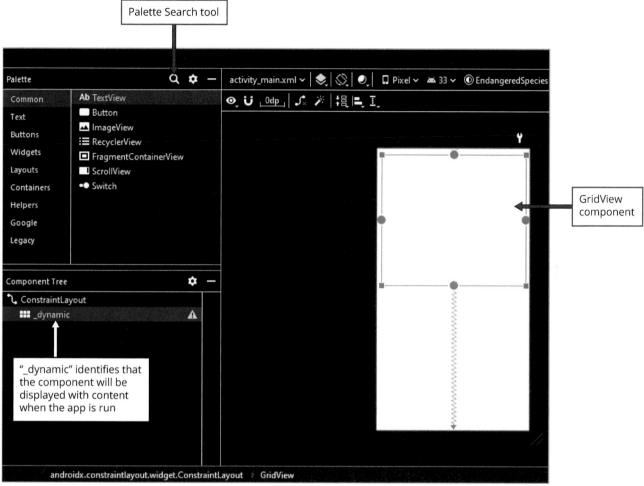

Figure 7-5 Displaying the activity_main XML code

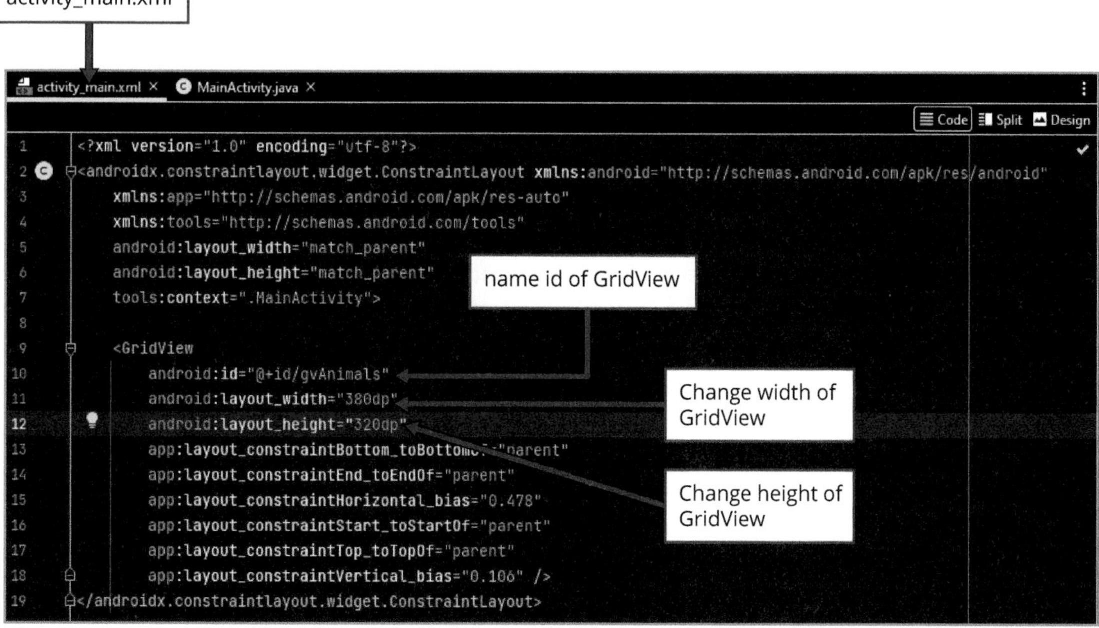

Figure 7-6 Customized GridView XML code

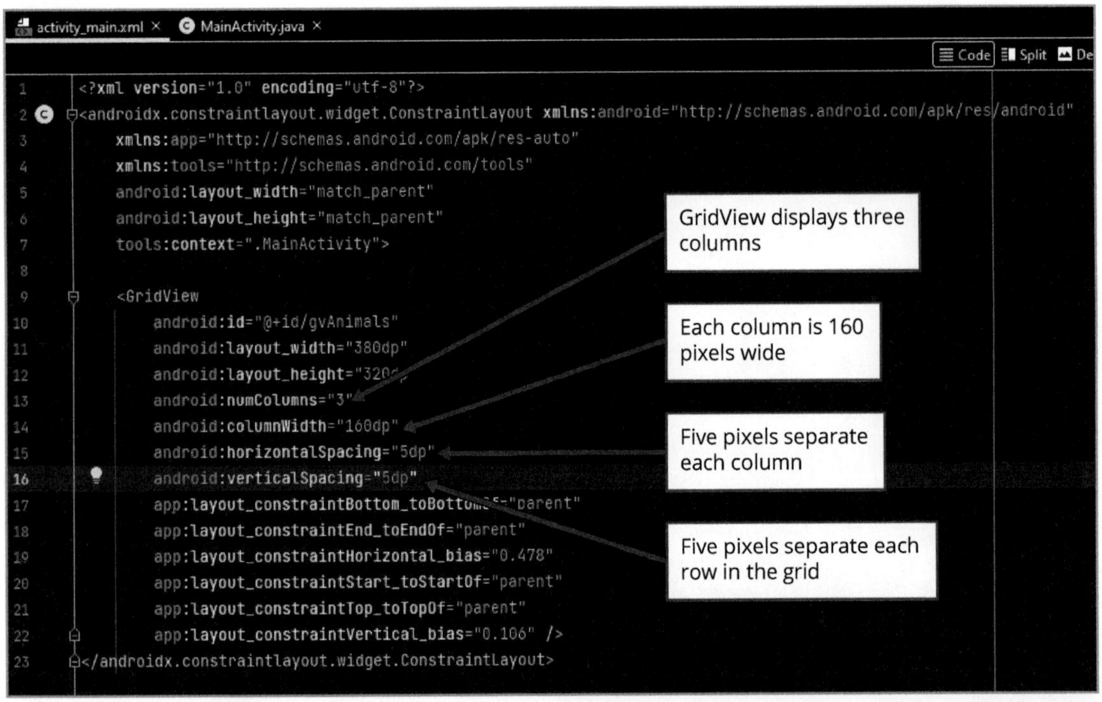

activity_main.xml × MainActivity.java ×

Code Split De

```
1  <?xml version="1.0" encoding="utf-8"?>
2  <androidx.constraintlayout.widget.ConstraintLayout xmlns:android="http://schemas.android.com/apk/res/android"
3      xmlns:app="http://schemas.android.com/apk/res-auto"
4      xmlns:tools="http://schemas.android.com/tools"
5      android:layout_width="match_parent"
6      android:layout_height="match_parent"
7      tools:context=".MainActivity">
8
9      <GridView
10         android:id="@+id/gvAnimals"
11         android:layout_width="380dp"
12         android:layout_height="320dp"
13         android:numColumns="3"
14         android:columnWidth="160dp"
15         android:horizontalSpacing="5dp"
16         android:verticalSpacing="5dp"
17         app:layout_constraintBottom_toBottomOf="parent"
18         app:layout_constraintEnd_toEndOf="parent"
19         app:layout_constraintHorizontal_bias="0.478"
20         app:layout_constraintStart_toStartOf="parent"
21         app:layout_constraintTop_toTopOf="parent"
22         app:layout_constraintVertical_bias="0.106" />
23 </androidx.constraintlayout.widget.ConstraintLayout>
```

GridView displays three columns

Each column is 160 pixels wide

Five pixels separate each column

Five pixels separate each row in the grid

Quick Check

If you wanted this GridView to display four columns, what XML code would you type?

Answer: android:numColumns="4"

7.3 Adding the ImageView Component in XML Code

In the Endangered Species chapter project, the GridView component displays a grid containing two rows with three columns of six thumbnail-sized animal photos stored in the drawable folder. When the user taps one of these images, a full-size image appears in an ImageView component below the GridView component, as shown in Figure 7-2. Typically, you add an ImageView component by dragging the component onto the emulator. A dialog box automatically opens and asks which image file in the drawable folder should be displayed. In the case of the chapter project, an image appears in the ImageView only if the user taps the thumbnail image in the grid. Otherwise, no image should appear in the ImageView component. To prevent an image from being assigned to (and displayed in) the ImageView component, you must enter the XML code for the ImageView component in the activity_main.xml file. The ImageView source will be displayed in the component when the user selects a particular animal. The source display will be coded in the MainActivity.java file. To add the XML code to create the ImageView component named ivLarge, add the String table, and add the six image files to the drawable folder, follow these steps.

Step 1

- On Line 22 of the GridView XML code, press the Enter key twice to insert two blank lines, and then type the following custom ImageView XML code on Line 24 using auto-completion as much as possible:

```
<ImageView
    android:id="@+id/ivLarge"
```

```
android:layout_marginTop="10dp"
android:layout_width="270dp"
android:layout_height="300dp"
android:layout_gravity="center_horizontal"
android:contentDescription="@string/ivLarge" />
```

The ImageView component named ivLarge is coded in the activity_main.xml file (**Figure 7-7**). The ImageView component includes a top margin of 10dp, has a size of 270 by 300 pixels, and is centered below the GridView layout. The contentDescription appears in red text because the description has not yet been added to the Translations Editor.

Figure 7-7 ImageView XML code

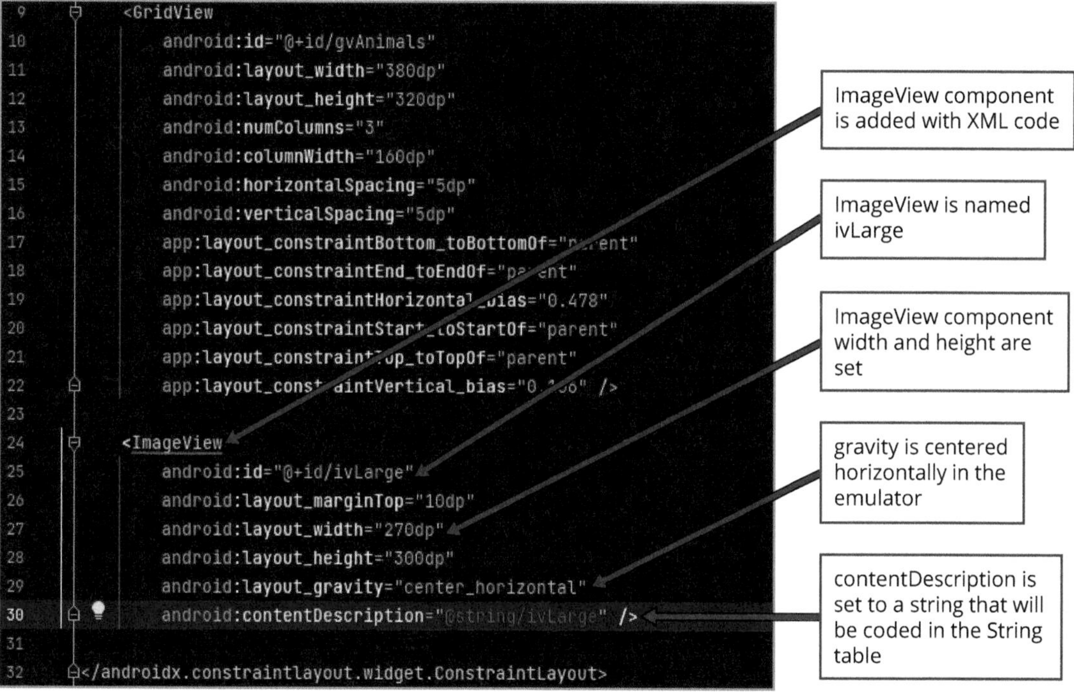

Step 2

- Close and save the activity_main.xml tab.
- To add the content description to the String table, open the values folder in the Android project view and then open strings.xml.
- Click the Open editor link.
- Click the Add Key button in the Translations Editor. Type **ivLarge** in the Key text box and type **Endangered Species Image** in the Default Value text box.

The strings.xml file contains the needed String value for the contentDescription attribute of the ImageView component (**Figure 7-8**).

Step 3

- Click the OK button and then close the Translations Editor and strings.xml tabs.
- To add the six image files to the drawable subfolder, download the images from the student files, if necessary.

Figure 7-8 Adding a String value

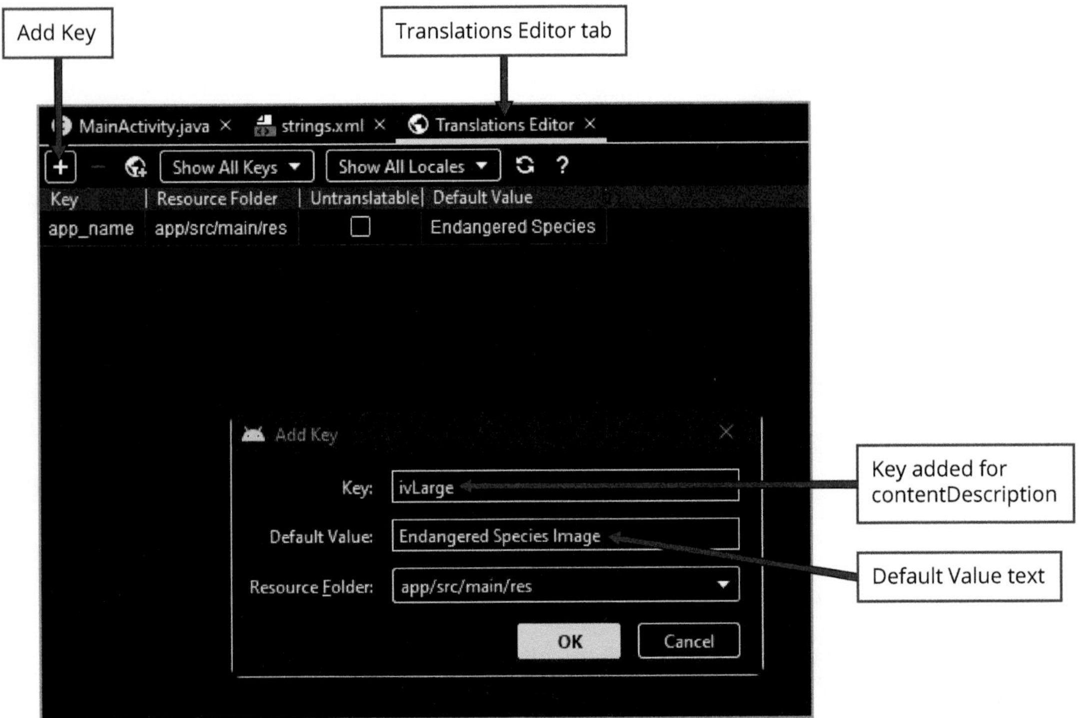

- Select the files and press Ctrl+C to copy the images.
- To add the six image files to the drawable resource folder, right-click the drawable folder and then click Paste.
- Click the OK button in the Copy dialog box.

Copies of the six image files appear in the drawable subfolder (**Figure 7-9**).

Figure 7-9 Images copied

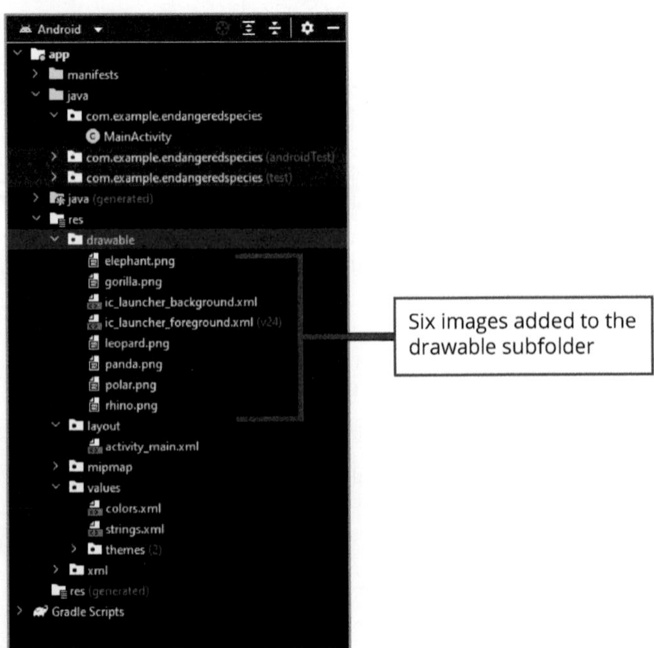

Good to Know The ImageView component could have been added by dragging the component from the Palette and placing it on the emulator, but understanding XML code will make you a more competent Android developer.

7.4 Creating an Array for Images

Before the images can be displayed in the GridView component, the images in the drawable folder must be referenced in the code and assigned to an array. By using an array variable, which can store more than one value, you can avoid assigning a separate variable for each image in the folder. You could add dozens of images to be displayed in the GridView component based on the needs of your app. For example, an app can display three rows of four images each in a grid to represent the 12 top-selling Android phones on the market, and then users can scroll over the grid to select an image of their favorite phone. If more phone images are added to the grid, the GridView component automatically becomes scrollable, allowing users to view every image in the grid. The GridView component is a view group that displays items in a two-dimensional scrolling grid with rows and columns, in the same fashion as a table in a word-processing document.

Arrays provide access to data by using a numeric index, or subscript, to identify each element in the array. In the chapter project, the images are assigned to an integer array named Animals and each image is associated with an integer value. For example, the first image of the elephant is assigned a subscript of 0, as shown in **Table 7-2**; there are six elements in the array. Typically, an array is used to assign values to a GridView component that has multiple items.

Table 7-2 Animals array

Element of Array	Image File
Animals[0]	elephant.png
Animals[1]	gorilla.png
Animals[2]	leopard.png
Animals[3]	panda.png
Animals[4]	polar.png
Animals[5]	rhino.png

In MainActivity.java, the Animals array and ImageView component are declared as class-level variables because they are referenced in multiple methods throughout the application. Recall that class-level variables are accessible from anywhere within a Java class. The array is available throughout the entire Activity. To declare the Animals array and ImageView component in MainActivity.java, follow these steps.

Step 1

- If necessary, open the MainActivity.java tab to open its code window.
- Click at the end of the public class MainActivity extends AppCompatActivity { line, press the Enter key, and then use auto-completion as much as possible to type the following code as a class variable and create the Animals array, which can be used by multiple methods. Press Enter after typing **R.drawable.gorilla** to have your code match the figures in this chapter.

  Integer[] Animals = {R.drawable.elephant, R.drawable.gorilla, R.drawable.leopard, R.drawable.panda, R.drawable.polar, R.drawable.rhino};

The Animals array references the images stored in the drawable folder (**Figure 7-10**).

Figure 7-10 Animals array declared

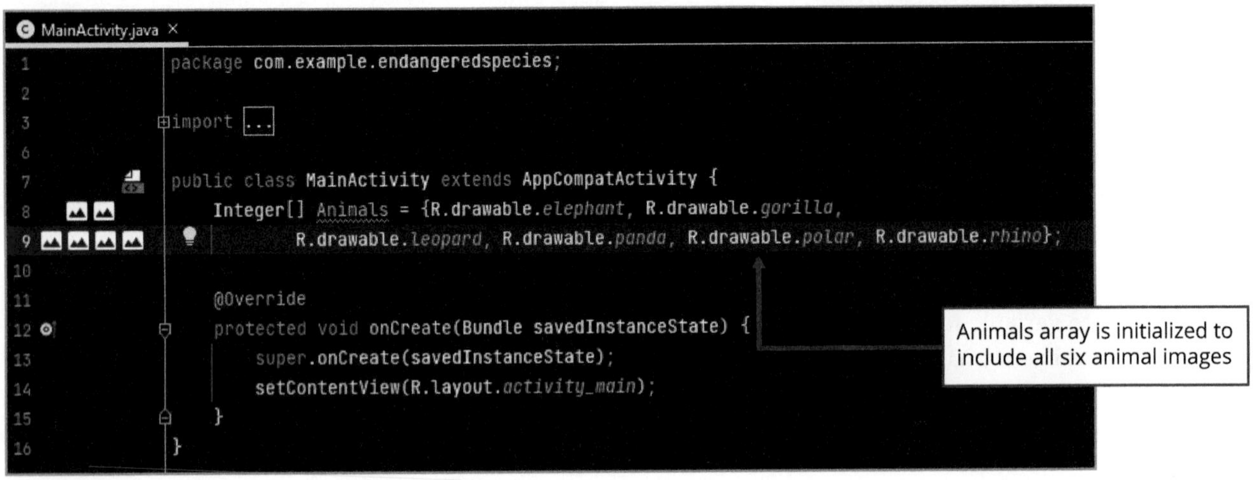

MainActivity.java

```
package com.example.endangeredspecies;

import ...

public class MainActivity extends AppCompatActivity {
    Integer[] Animals = {R.drawable.elephant, R.drawable.gorilla,
            R.drawable.leopard, R.drawable.panda, R.drawable.polar, R.drawable.rhino};

    @Override
    protected void onCreate(Bundle savedInstanceState) {
        super.onCreate(savedInstanceState);
        setContentView(R.layout.activity_main);
    }
}
```

Animals array is initialized to include all six animal images

Step 2

- Press the Enter key.
- To declare ImageView as a class variable, type **ImageView pic;**.
- Click ImageView (the red text) and then press Alt+Enter to import the ImageView component.

ImageView is referenced as a class variable (**Figure 7-11**).

Figure 7-11 ImageView referenced

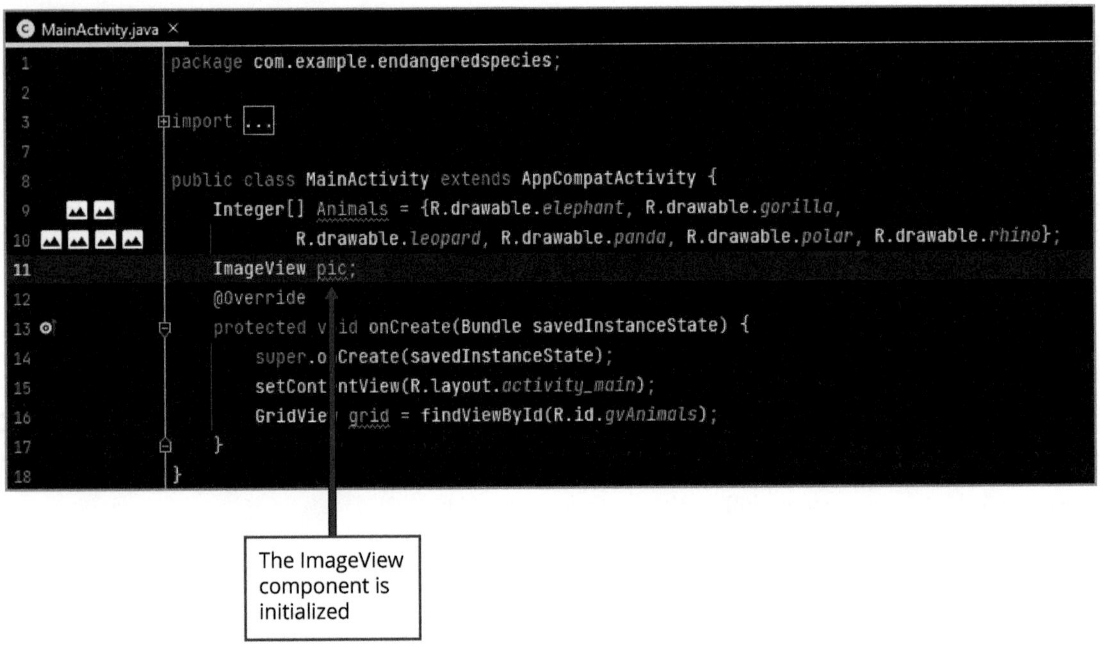

MainActivity.java

```
package com.example.endangeredspecies;

import ...

public class MainActivity extends AppCompatActivity {
    Integer[] Animals = {R.drawable.elephant, R.drawable.gorilla,
            R.drawable.leopard, R.drawable.panda, R.drawable.polar, R.drawable.rhino};
    ImageView pic;
    @Override
    protected void onCreate(Bundle savedInstanceState) {
        super.onCreate(savedInstanceState);
        setContentView(R.layout.activity_main);
        GridView grid = findViewById(R.id.gvAnimals);
    }
}
```

The ImageView component is initialized

Quick Check

Use Java code to create a string array named Seasons for four images named winter, spring, summer, and fall.

Answer: Integer[] Seasons = {R.drawable.winter, R.drawable.spring, R.drawable.summer, R.drawable.fall};

7.5 Instantiating the GridView and ImageView Components

The GridView and ImageView components in activity_main.xml must be instantiated in the onCreate( ) method of MainActivity.java. The first GridView component in the chapter project is named gvAnimals. The code to instantiate the GridView assigns the name gvAnimals to the component created in activity_main.xml, as shown in the following code syntax:

Code Syntax

```
GridView grid = findViewById(R.id.gvAnimals);
```

To instantiate the GridView and ImageView components, follow these steps.

Step 1

- To instantiate the GridView, go to the onCreate( ) method in MainActivity.java, click at the end of the setContentView(R.layout.*activity_main*); line, and then press the Enter key.
- In Line 16, type **GridView grid = findViewById(R.id.gvAnimals);**.
- If necessary, click GridView, press Alt+Enter, and then click Import Class.

The GridView component is instantiated (**Figure 7-12**).

Figure 7-12 GridView component is instantiated

```
12      @Override
13      protected void onCreate(Bundle savedInstanceState) {
14          super.onCreate(savedInstanceState);
15          setContentView(R.layout.activity_main);
16          GridView grid = findViewById(R.id.gvAnimals);
17      }
18  }
```

GridView is instantiated

Step 2

- Insert a new line. To instantiate the ImageView that is assigned as a class variable, type **final ImageView pic = findViewById(R.id.ivLarge);**.

The ImageView component is instantiated (**Figure 7-13**).

Figure 7-13 ImageView component is instantiated

```
    @Override
    protected void onCreate(Bundle savedInstanceState) {
        super.onCreate(savedInstanceState);
        setContentView(R.layout.activity_main);
        GridView grid = findViewById(R.id.gvAnimals);
        final ImageView pic = findViewById(R.id.ivLarge);
    }
}
```

ImageView component instantiated

Critical Thinking

What does it mean to set the ImageView variable pic to final?

The keyword final designates that the referenced variable cannot be changed. If you assign a new value to this variable later in the code, a compilation error will occur.

7.6 Using a setAdapter with an ImageAdapter

In Chapter 5, an adapter was used to display a ListView component. Similarly, a **setAdapter** provides a data model for the GridView layout. The GridView data model functions as a photo GridView in touch mode. This adapter helps to set the data from an array list or a database to the items of the grid. The following code syntax shows how to instantiate a custom BaseAdapter class called ImageAdapter and apply it to the GridView using setAdapter( ):

Code Syntax

```
grid.setAdapter(new ImageAdapter());
```

After the ImageAdapter is instantiated, the Android Java ImageAdapter class must be added to extend the custom BaseAdapter class. Using components such as the GridView, ListView, and Spinner, the adapter binds specific types of data and displays the data in a particular layout. To instantiate the ImageAdapter class for the GridView component, follow these steps.

Step 1

- Press the Enter key and type **grid.setAdapter(new ImageAdapter());**.
- Notice the red ImageAdapter text. Instead of automatically creating the class, a custom ImageAdapter class is added in the next step, so do not import the class now.

The ImageAdapter is coded for the GridView component. ImageAdapter appears in red text (**Figure 7-14**).

Figure 7-14 Instance of the ImageAdapter class

MainActivity.java ×

```
package com.example.endangeredspecies;

import ...

public class MainActivity extends AppCompatActivity {
    Integer[] Animals = {R.drawable.elephant, R.drawable.gorilla,
            R.drawable.leopard, R.drawable.panda, R.drawable.polar, R.drawable.rhino};
    ImageView pic;
    @Override
    protected void onCreate(Bundle savedInstanceState) {
        super.onCreate(savedInstanceState);
        setContentView(R.layout.activity_main);
        GridView grid = findViewById(R.id.gvAnimals);
        final ImageView pic = findViewById(R.id.ivLarge);
        grid.setAdapter(new ImageAdapter());
    }
}
```

In the next step, click after this brace

setAdapter to display images within the grid

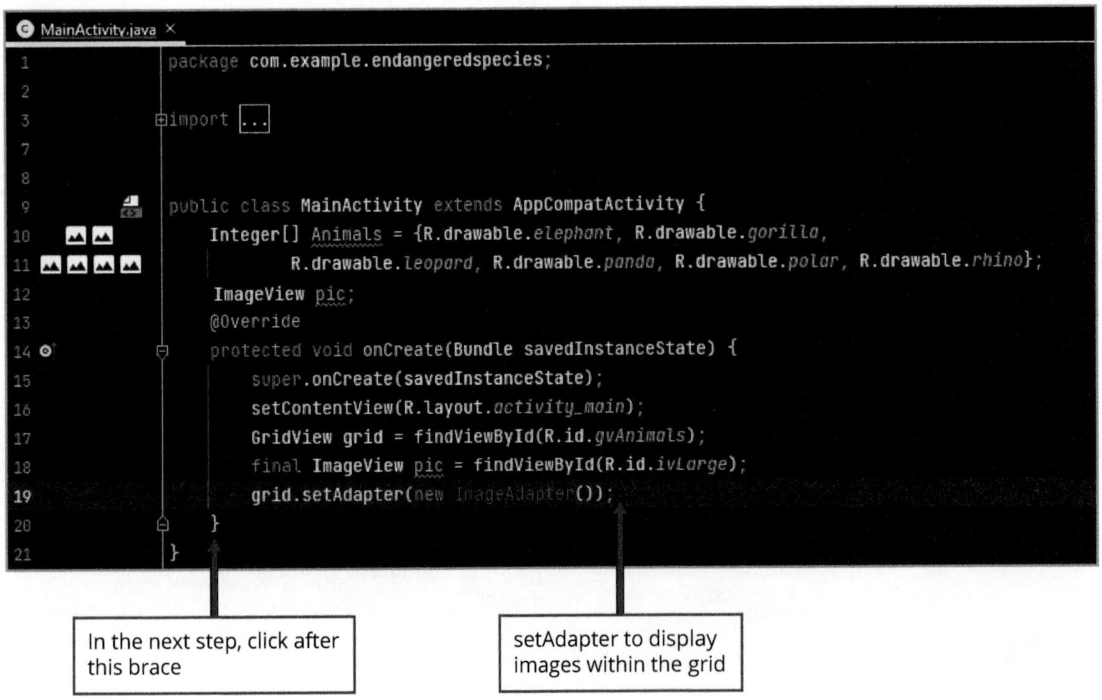

Step 2

- To add an ImageAdapter class that extends the BaseAdapter custom class, click after the first closing brace at the end of Line 20. Make sure you are typing between the two closing braces of this app in the next step because you are adding a new class.
- Press the Enter key and type **public class ImageAdapter extends BaseAdapter {**.
- Press the Enter key to display a closing brace.
- Click the red BaseAdapter text, click Alt+Enter, and then click Import Class.
- Click the red light bulb in the front of the same line and then click Implement Method. Click the OK button in the Select Methods to Implement dialog box.

The ImageAdapter class is coded to handle the image display (**Figure 7-15**). The methods within the ImageAdapter are auto-generated by Android Studio.

Figure 7-15 ImageAdapter class and auto-generated code

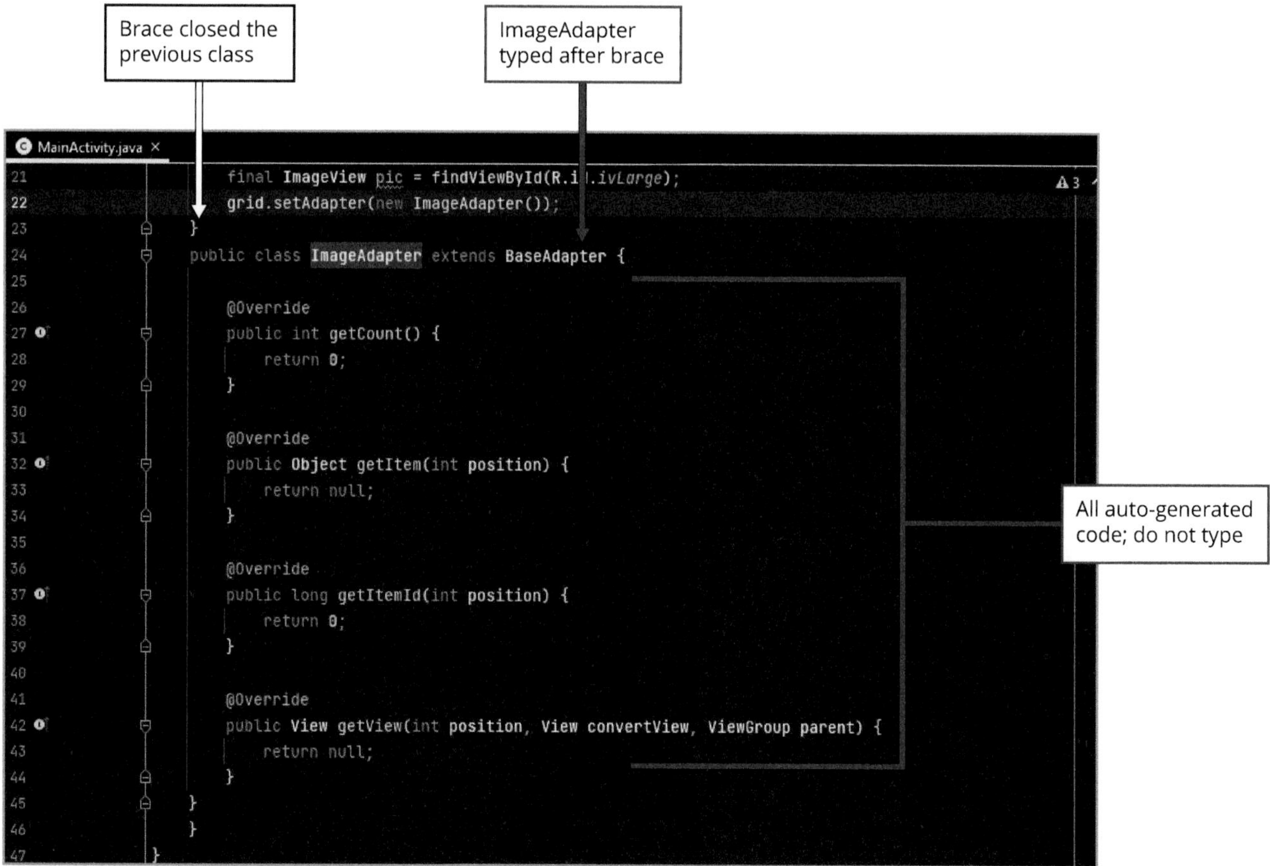


```
final ImageView pic = findViewById(R.id.ivLarge);
grid.setAdapter(new ImageAdapter());
}
public class ImageAdapter extends BaseAdapter {

    @Override
    public int getCount() {
        return 0;
    }

    @Override
    public Object getItem(int position) {
        return null;
    }

    @Override
    public long getItemId(int position) {
        return 0;
    }

    @Override
    public View getView(int position, View convertView, ViewGroup parent) {
        return null;
    }
}
}
}
```

7.7 Coding the OnItemClickListener

Like the OnClickListener used for a Button component in previous chapter projects, the OnItemClickListener awaits user interaction within the GridView component. When the user touches the GridView display layout, the OnItemClickListener processes an event called onItemClick. Just like a Button, the GridView awaits a user's interactions.

The **onItemClick( )** method defined by the OnItemClickListener provides a number of arguments, which are listed within the parentheses included in the code. The two components in the chapter project—ImageView and

GridView—enable the Android device to monitor for Click events using the OnItemClickListener and onItemClick commands. The following code syntax shows how to use onItemClick( ) in the chapter project.

Code Syntax

```
grid.setOnItemClickListener(new OnItemClickListener( ) {
  @Override
  public void onItemClick(AdapterView<?> arg0,
     View arg1, int arg2, long arg3) {
  }
}};
}
```

In this code syntax example, the grid variable is the instance of the GridView component. The OnItemClickListener executes the onItemClick( ) method as soon as the user touches any image within the GridView component. The onItemClick( ) method has four arguments. **Table 7-3** describes the role of the four arguments in the onItemClick( ) method.

Table 7-3 Arguments in the onItemClick( ) method

Argument	Purpose
AdapterView<?> parent	The AdapterView records "where" the user actually touched the screen in the argument variable parent. In other words, if the app has more than one View component, the AdapterView determines if the user touched the GridView component or another component in the application.
View view	The View parameter is the specific View within the item that the user touched. This is the View provided by the adapter.
int position	This is one of the most important portions of this statement in the chapter project. The position argument is an integer value that holds the position of the View in the adapter. For example, if the user taps the elephant picture, the integer value of 1 is stored in position because the elephant picture is the second image in the Animals array.
long id	The GridView component is displayed across multiple rows of the Android device. The argument id determines the row id of the item that was selected by the user. This is especially useful for a GridView component that has multiple rows in the layout.

Users can change their minds more than once when selecting picture images in the GridView. The onItemClick( ) method responds to an unlimited number of clicks throughout the life of the class based on the user's interaction with the GridView component. To code the OnItemClickListener and onItemClick( ) method, follow these steps.

Step 1

- In MainActivity.java, press the Enter key after the grid.setAdapter command in Line 22.
- To set up the OnItemClickListener, type **grid.setOnItemClickListener(new OnItemClickListener() {**.
- Press the Enter key to display a closing brace.
- A red error line appears under OnItemClickListener. Click OnItemClickListener, press Alt+Enter, and then select Implement Method. Click the OK button in the dialog box.
- After the closing brace on Line 31, type a closing parenthesis and a semicolon to complete the statement.

The GridView OnItemClickListener awaits user interaction (**Figure 7-16**). The onItemClick( ) method stub appears automatically.

Figure 7-16 GridView OnItemClickListener

MainActivity.java

```
protected void onCreate(Bundle savedInstanceState) {
    super.onCreate(savedInstanceState);
    setContentView(R.layout.activity_main);
    GridView grid = findViewById(R.id.gvAnimals);
    final ImageView pic = findViewById(R.id.ivLarge);
    grid.setAdapter(new ImageAdapter());
    grid.setOnItemClickListener(new OnItemClickListener( ) {

        @Override
        public void onItemClick(AdapterView<?> parent, View view, int position, long id) {

        }
    });
}

public class ImageAdapter extends BaseAdapter {

    @Override
    public int getCount() {
        return 0;
    }

    @Override
    public Object getItem(int position) {
```

setOnItemClickListener( ) method

Right parenthesis and a semicolon added to complete method

Auto-generated method

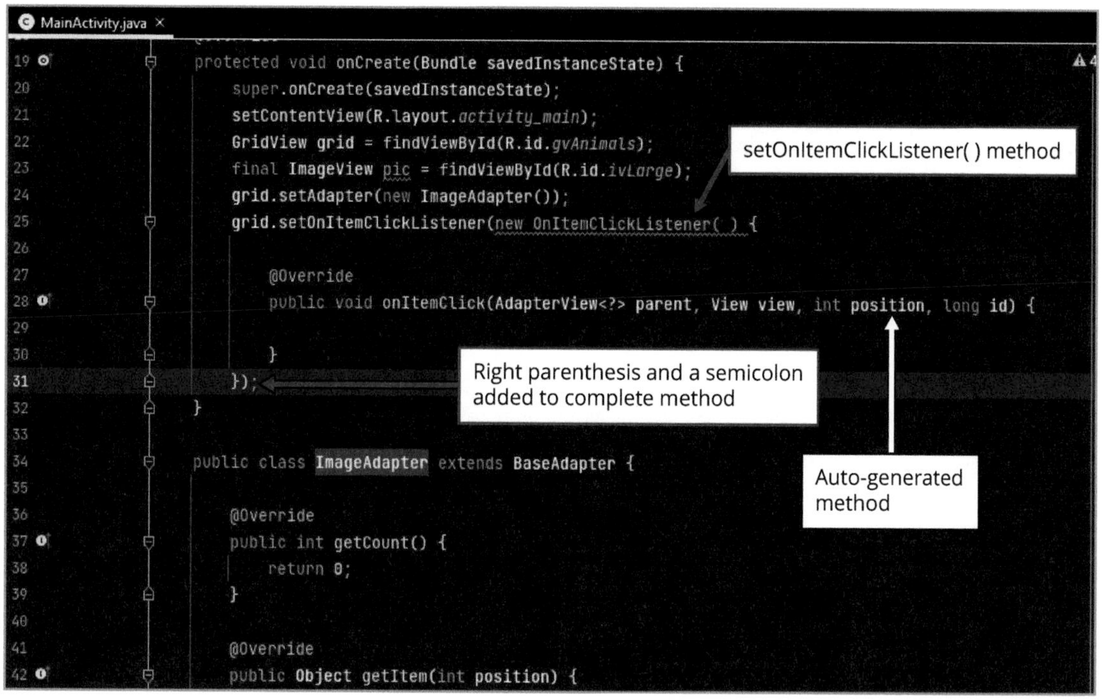

Step 2

- Save your work.

7.8 Coding a Custom Toast Notification

A toast notification in the Endangered Species program provides feedback for the selected animal image. When the toast message is shown to the user, it floats over the application and does not receive focus. In earlier chapters, you entered a toast notification to display a temporary message in the following form.

Code Syntax

```
Toast.makeText(MainActivity.this, "Typical Toast Message",
Toast.LENGTH_SHORT).show();
```

In the Endangered Species project, the toast notification message is different in two ways. First, the toast message in the GridView component appears in the onItemClick( ) method, which is executed only when the user makes a selection by tapping one of the six images. Because the toast notification is not used directly in the MainActivity, the reference to MainActivity.this in the toast statement creates an error. To use a toast message within an onItemClick( ) method, which is considered an AlertDialog class, you must replace MainActivity.this with a Context class called **getBaseContext( )**. In Android programs, you can place the getBaseContext( ) method in another method (such as onItemClick( )) that is triggered only when the user touches the GridView component. If you do, the getBaseContext( ) method obtains a Context instance.

A second difference is that the toast message includes a variable. The variable indicates which image number is selected in the Animals array. **Figure 7-17** shows the toast message when the user selects the leopard: Selected Species 3.

Notice that even though the leopard is in position Animals[2] in Table 7-2, the custom toast message is "Selected Species 3." Array position 2 is actually the third image because the array values begin with 0. The value of 1 is added to the integer position value in the toast message shown in the following code syntax. The position argument is an integer value that holds the position number of the View in the adapter, which is an argument of the onItemClick( ) method. The position identifies the image placement in the array.

Code Syntax

```
Toast.makeText(getBaseContext(),
"Selected Species " + (position +
1), Toast.LENGTH_SHORT).show();
```

To code the custom toast message that includes a getBaseContext( ) method and variables, follow this step.

Figure 7-17 Toast message displayed when the user selects the leopard image

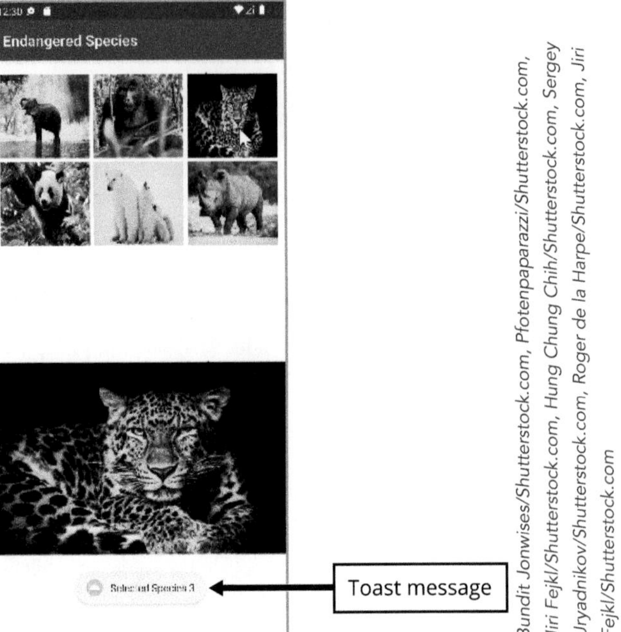

Step 1

- In MainActivity.java, click the blank line after the onItemClick statement in Line 29 to add the custom toast message.
- Use auto-completion to type **Toast.makeText(getBaseContext(), "Selected Species " + (position + 1), Toast.LENGTH_SHORT).show();**.
- Click Toast and press Alt+Enter. Click Import Class.

The custom toast message provides feedback to users of their picture selection from the GridView (**Figure 7-18**).

Figure 7-18 Custom toast message

```
MainActivity.java
20  protected void onCreate(Bundle savedInstanceState) {
21      super.onCreate(savedInstanceState);
22      setContentView(R.layout.activity_main);
23      GridView grid = findViewById(R.id.gvAnimals);
24      final ImageView pic = findViewById(R.id.ivLarge);
25      grid.setAdapter(new ImageAdapter());
26      grid.setOnItemClickListener(new OnItemClickListener( ) {
27
28          @Override
29          public void onItemClick(AdapterView<?> parent, View view, int position, long id) {
30              Toast.makeText(getBaseContext( ), text: "Selected Species " + (position + 1), Toast.LENGTH_SHORT).show( );
31          }
32      });
33  }
34
35  public class ImageAdapter extends BaseAdapter {
36
```

Toast message briefly appears to display the number of the image selected from the grid

7.9 Displaying the setImageResource Image

When the user touches an animal picture in the GridView, a toast message appears with an ImageView component that displays the selected image. The ImageView component was previously coded in activity_main. xml, though a specific image was not selected in the code. Instead, the full-sized picture in the ImageView component should be displayed dynamically to the user. An ImageView component is defined either by the android:src attribute in the XML element or by the setImageResource(int) method. The setImageResource( ) method indicates which image is selected, as shown in the following code syntax.

Code Syntax

```
pic.setImageResource(Animals[position]);
```

Animals is the name of the array and position represents the index of the array. The argument position is defined as the position of the selected image in the GridView. To assign a picture to the ImageView component, follow this step.

Step 1

- In MainActivity.java, click at the end of the Toast statement, if necessary, and press the Enter key.
- To display the selected image, type **pic.setImageResource(Animals[position]);**.

The selected image in the GridView component is displayed in the ImageView component with the use of setImage-Resource (**Figure 7-19**).

Figure 7-19 ImageView component displays selected GridView picture with setImageResource

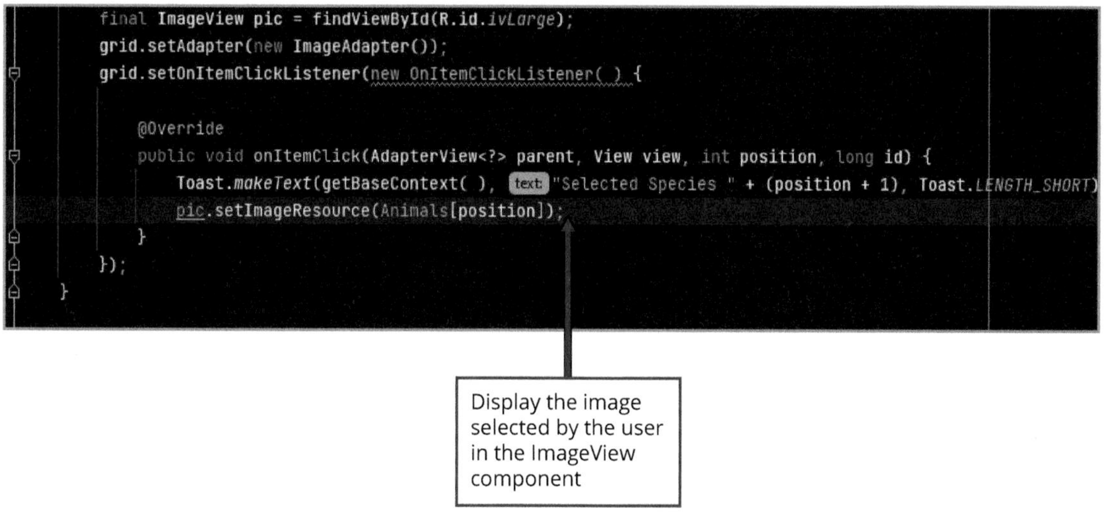

```
final ImageView pic = findViewById(R.id.ivLarge);
grid.setAdapter(new ImageAdapter());
grid.setOnItemClickListener(new OnItemClickListener( ) {

    @Override
    public void onItemClick(AdapterView<?> parent, View view, int position, long id) {
        Toast.makeText(getBaseContext( ), text: "Selected Species " + (position + 1), Toast.LENGTH_SHORT)
        pic.setImageResource(Animals[position]);
    }
});
}
```

Display the image selected by the user in the ImageView component

Good to Know An image can also be placed on the surface of a Button component using the android:src attribute in the XML code or using the setImageResource(int) method of a button.

Customizing the ImageAdapter Class

At this point in the chapter project code, the GridView and ImageView components are initialized, the onClickListener awaits interaction, and the toast message and ImageView are prepared for display, but the ImageAdapter class is simply a set of auto-generated method stubs. The ImageAdapter class is called with this line of code: gr.setAdapter(new ImageAdapter (this));.

Recall that the ImageAdapter class determines the layout of the GridView. The Context and images of the GridView need to be referenced within the ImageAdapter class. To complete the ImageAdapter class, you need to manage the layout of the GridView and connect the data sources from the array for display within the GridView component. These tasks are explained next.

7.10 Defining the Context of the ImageAdapter Class

The ImageAdapter class must provide information to set up the GridView with data and specifications necessary for the display. A Context variable is used to load and access resources for the application. In the following code syntax, the class variable named Context is initialized so it can hold each image in the GridView temporarily before it is displayed. The ImageAdapter constructor is changed from the MainActivity to handle the Context resources necessary for the GridView. **Constructors** are used to initialize the instance variables of an object. Constructors enable the programmer to set default values, limit instantiation, and write code that is flexible and easy to read. Constructors are so named because they construct the values of data members of the class.

Code Syntax

```
private Context context;
public ImageAdapter(Context c){
    context=c;
}
```

A constructor is quite similar to the methods we have written in this textbook thus far, but it is different from a method in two ways. First, a constructor always has the same name as the class whose instance members it initializes. Second, a constructor does not contain a return type such as void. The ImageAdapter class constructor is where the Context is defined for an ImageAdapter instance. The constructor is used to return the Context, which is linked to the Application, which holds all activities running inside it. The term *Context* is common in Java; to understand it better, imagine that you are awaiting a package from UPS. The UPS delivery person would be the Context in this activity. When we call a constructor, we often have to pass a Context, and often we use the Java command "this" to pass the activity Context to the application Context. This method is generally used at the application level and can be used to refer to all the activities. For example, if we want to access a variable throughout the Android app, it is done via getApplicationContext(). To define the Context for the ImageAdapter, follow these steps.

Step 1

- Save your work. Click the blank line after the public class ImageAdapter extends BaseAdapter { line.
- Initialize the Context variable by typing **private Context context;**.
- Click Context, press Alt+Enter, and select Import Class.

The Context variable named context is initialized (**Figure 7-20**).

Figure 7-20 ImageAdapter Context variable

```
        @Override
        public void onItemClick(AdapterView<?> parent, View view, int position, long id) {
            Toast.makeText(getBaseContext( ), text: "Selected Species " + (position + 1), Toast.LENGTH_SHORT).show( );
            pic.setImageResource(Animals[position]);
        }
    });
}

public class ImageAdapter extends BaseAdapter {
    private Context context;
    @Override
    public int getCount() {
        return 0;
    }
```

The Context variable named context is initialized within the ImageAdapter

Step 2

- To change the ImageAdapter constructor to define the Context in the next statement, type **public ImageAdapter (Context c) {**. Press the Enter key to insert a blank line.
- Type **context=c;**.

The ImageAdapter constructor for the ImageAdapter class holds the Context (**Figure 7-21**).

Figure 7-21 ImageAdapter constructor

```
public class ImageAdapter extends BaseAdapter {
    private Context context;
    public ImageAdapter (Context c) {
        context=c;
    }

    @Override
    public int getCount() {
        return 0;
    }
```

ImageAdapter is customized to hold Context resources

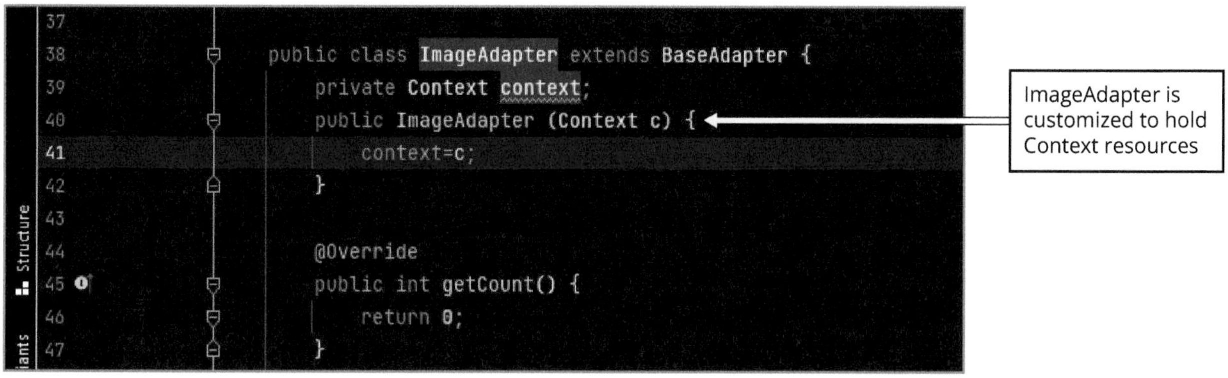

Step 3

- To pass the application Context, the ImageAdapter must be changed from an empty (or anonymous) method call. In Line 27, type **this** within the parentheses:

  grid.setAdapter(new ImageAdapter(this));

The ImageAdapter is updated to access the variable c throughout the Android app in order to pass the Context (**Figure 7-22**).

Figure 7-22 Passing the Context to the ImageAdapter Class

File Edit View Navigate Code Refactor Build Run Tools VCS Window Help Endangered Species - MainActivity.java [Endangered_Species.app.main]

angeredSpecies 〉 app 〉 src 〉 main 〉 java 〉 com 〉 example 〉 endangeredspecies 〉 MainActivity 〉 onCreate | app | Resizable (Experimental) API 33

MainActivity.java

```
21  @Override
22  protected void onCreate(Bundle savedInstanceState) {
23      super.onCreate(savedInstanceState);
24      setContentView(R.layout.activity_main);
25      GridView grid = findViewById(R.id.gvAnimals);
26      final ImageView pic = findViewById(R.id.ivLarge);
27      grid.setAdapter(new ImageAdapter( c: this));
28      grid.setOnItemClickListener(new OnItemClickListener( ) {
29
30          @Override
31          public void onItemClick(AdapterView<?> parent, View view, int position, long id) {
32              Toast.makeText(getBaseContext( ), text: "Selected Species " + (position + 1), Toast.LENGTH_SHORT).show( );
33              pic.setImageResource(Animals[position]);
34          }
35      });
36  }
37
38  public class ImageAdapter extends BaseAdapter {
39      private Context context;
40      public ImageAdapter (Context c) {
41          context=c;
42      }
```

this is added to pass the Context to the ImageAdapter Class

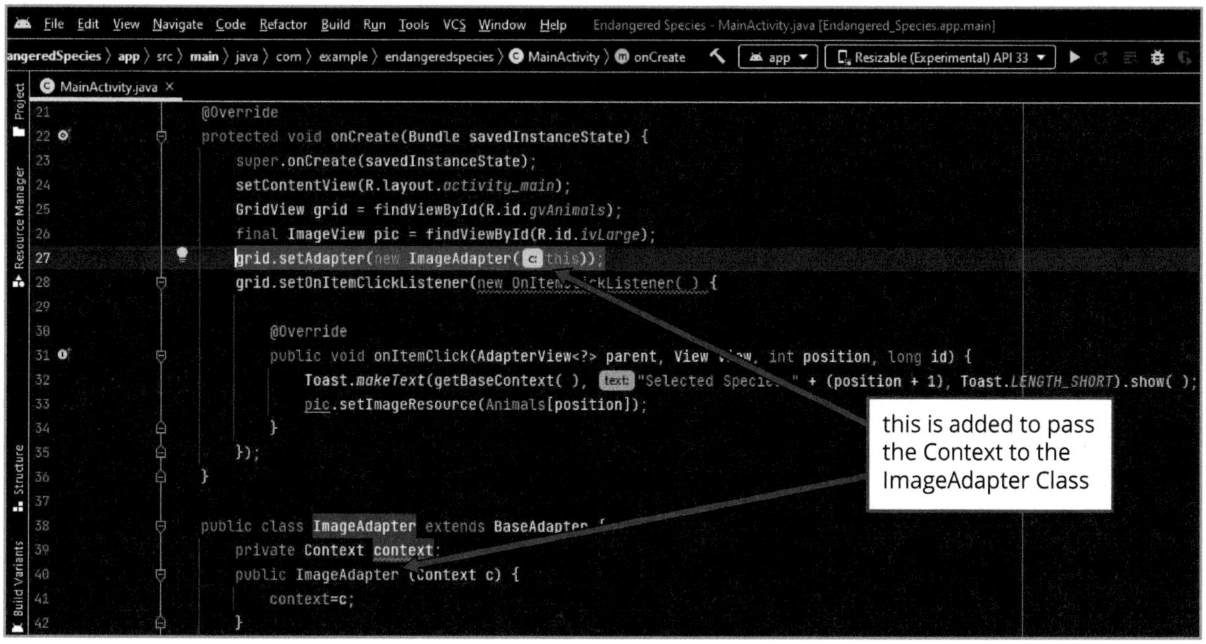

7.11 Calculating the Length of an Array

The next method in the ImageAdapter class is the getCount( ) method. When the ImageAdapter class is called, the getCount( ) method determines how many pictures should be displayed in the GridView component. It does so by finding the length of the Animals array, which references the pictures of the endangered species. To determine the length of an array, Java provides a method called length( ) that returns an integer value of any given string or array. For example, if a variable named phone is assigned the text "Android," the integer phoneLength is assigned the integer value of 7 to represent the length of the word "Android," which has seven letters.

Code Syntax

```
String phone = "Android";
int phoneLength = phone.length();
```

The length of an array is determined by the number of elements in the array. The length of the Animals array is an integer value of 6. The getCount( ) method must return the number of elements in the GridView in order to create the correct layout for the GridView component. To do so, include a return statement in the getCount( ) method, as shown in the following code syntax.

Code Syntax

```
return Animals.length;
```

A Java **method** is a series of statements that perform some repeated task. In the case of the chapter project, the getCount( ) method is called within the ImageAdapter class. The purpose of the method is to return the number of elements in the array. You declare a method's return type in its method declaration. In the following syntax, the declaration statement public int getCount( ) includes int. The data type int indicates that the return data type is an integer. Within the body of the method, you use the return statement to return the value. Any method declared void does not return a value because it returns to the method normally. Therefore, no return statement is necessary. Any method that is not declared void must contain a return statement with a corresponding return value, such as the length of an array.

Code Syntax

```
public int getCount() {
     return Animals.length;
}
```

To return the length of an array from the getCount( ) method, follow this step.

Step 1

- In the return statement for public int getCount( ) in Line 46, change the return type from return 0; to **return Animals.length;**.

The getCount( ) method returns the length of the Animals array (**Figure 7-23**).

Figure 7-23 Length of the Animals array

```
public class ImageAdapter extends BaseAdapter {
    private Context context;
    public ImageAdapter (Context c) {
        context=c;
    }

    @Override
    public int getCount() {
        return Animals.length;
    }

    @Override
    public Object getItem(int position) {
        return null;
    }

    @Override
    public long getItemId(int position) {
        return 0;
    }
```

Returns the length of the Animals array

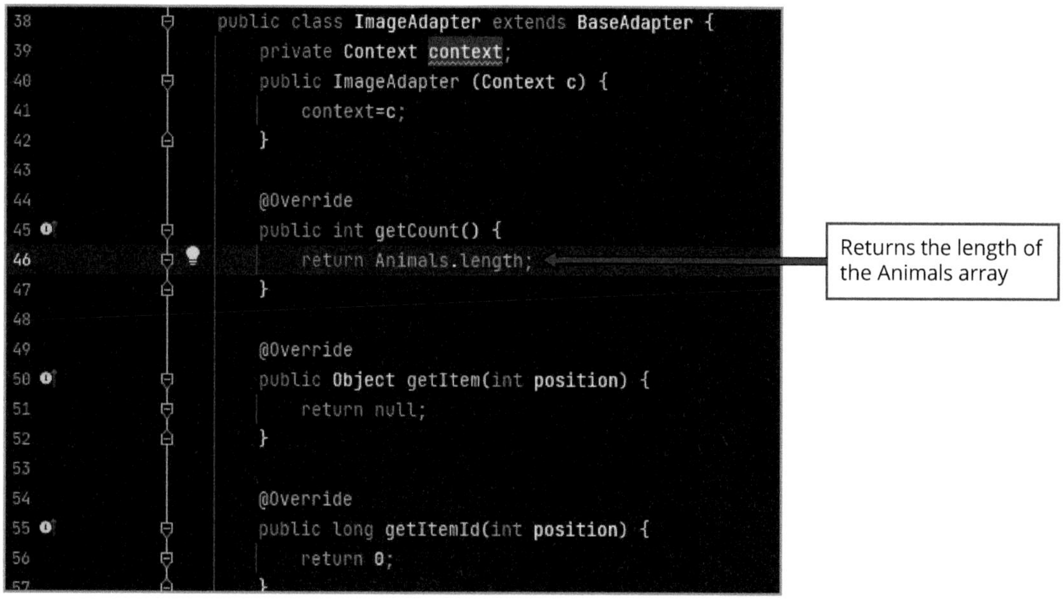

Critical Thinking

If I add more animal images to the Animals array, would the Animals.length command return the additional number of images?

Yes. Write your programs to be easily scalable to function well as they handle more information in order to meet the user's needs.

Good to Know

The length of an array is one more than the maximum subscript number. If the maximum subscript is 8, the length of the array is 9 because the array starts at subscript 0.

Quick Check

In the following code, what is the value of songLength?

```
String song = "While My Guitar Gently Weeps";
int songLength =song.length();
```

Answer: 28.

7.12 Coding the getView( ) Method

The most powerful method in the ImageAdapter class is the getView( ) method. The getView( ) method uses a Context to create a new ImageView instance that temporarily holds each image displayed in the GridView. In addition, the ImageView is scaled to fit the GridView component and sized according to a custom height and width. The following code syntax shows how the chapter project uses the getView( ) method.

Code Syntax

```
public View getView(int position, View convertView, ViewGroup parent){
        pic = new ImageView(context);
        pic.setImageResource(Animals[position]);
        pic.setScaleType(ImageView.ScaleType.FIT_XY);
        pic.setLayoutParams(new GridView.LayoutParams(330,300));
        return pic;
}
```

In the getView() method, notice that a return type of View is expected (in the View convertView argument). Recall that a View occupies a rectangular area on the screen and is responsible for drawing the GridView component. When pic is returned at the end of the method, it includes a scaled, resized image that is ready to display in the GridView component.

In the getView( ) method, an instance of an ImageView component named pic is established in the pic = new ImageView(context); Java code. On the next line, pic is given an image to display in the GridView, as defined by a position in the Animals array. As each position is passed to the getView( ) method, the ImageView component changes to hold each of the images referenced in the Animals array. The setImageResource( ) method assigns an image from the drawable folder to the ImageView component. After an animal picture is assigned to pic, the layout of the ImageView component needs to be established. In the next statement, setScaleType scales the image to the bounds of the ImageView. Scaling keeps or changes the aspect ratio of the image within the ImageView component. When an image is scaled, the aspect ratio is changed; for example, the picture may be stretched horizontally but not vertically. Notice that the ScaleType is set to the option FIT_XY. Several ScaleType options are available, but the most popular options are listed in **Table 7-4**.

Table 7-4 Popular ScaleType options

ScaleType Option	Meaning
ImageView.ScaleType.CENTER	This option centers the image within the View type but does not change the aspect ratio (no scaling).
ImageView.ScaleType.CENTER_CROP	This option centers the image within the View type and scales the image uniformly, maintaining the same aspect ratio.
ImageView.ScaleType.FIT_XY	This option scales the image to fit the View type. The aspect ratio is changed to fit within the component.

After the image is scaled, the GridView images are resized to fit the custom layout. The design of the Endangered Species app calls for small thumbnail-sized images, so the setLayoutParams are set to GridView.LayoutParams(330,300). The first value, 330, represents the number of pixels across the width of the image. The second value, 300, determines a height of 300 pixels. If you want to display a large GridView, the setLayoutParams can be changed to larger dimensions. The last statement in the getView() method, return pic;, must return the instance of the ImageView component named pic to display in the GridView component. To code the getView( ) method, follow these steps.

Step 1

- Scroll down to the statement beginning with public View getView in Line 60. Click at the end of the statement after the opening brace and press the Enter key to insert a blank line.
- To create an ImageView component that holds the images displayed in the GridView, type **pic = new ImageView(context);**.

An instance of ImageView named pic is created (**Figure 7-24**).

Figure 7-24 Code for the ImageView component

MainActivity.java ×

```
public class ImageAdapter extends BaseAdapter {
    private Context context;
    public ImageAdapter (Context c) {
        context=c;
    }

    @Override
    public int getCount() {
        return Animals.length;
    }

    @Override
    public Object getItem(int position) {
        return null;
    }

    @Override
    public long getItemId(int position) {
        return 0;
    }

    @Override
    public View getView(int position, View convertView, ViewGroup parent) {
        pic = new ImageView(context);
        return null;
    }
```

pic in this statement is an instance of ImageView

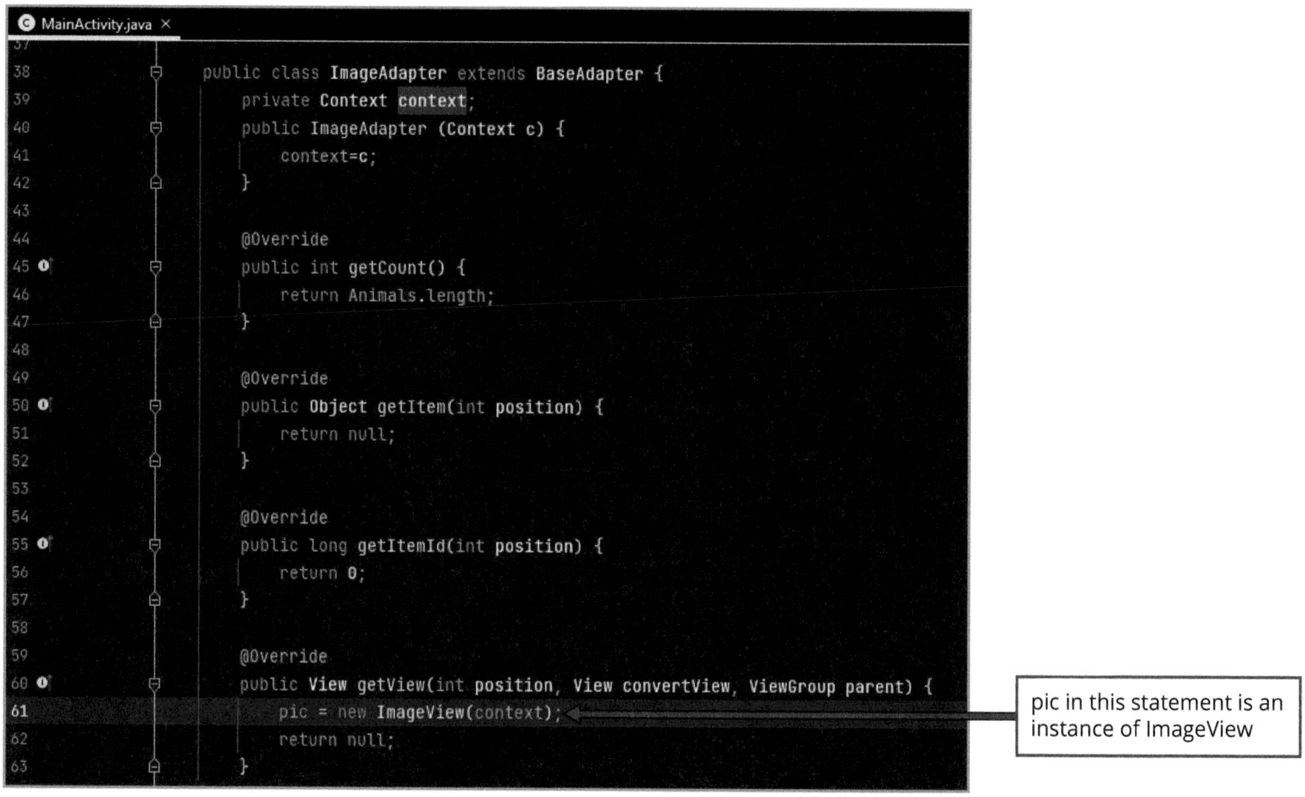

Step 2

- Press the Enter key.
- To assign each of the images and their positions referenced in the Animals array, type **pic.setImageResource(Animals[position]);**.

The instance of pic holds each of the images within the array (**Figure 7-25**).

Figure 7-25 Assigning images in the Animals array to the pic ImageView component

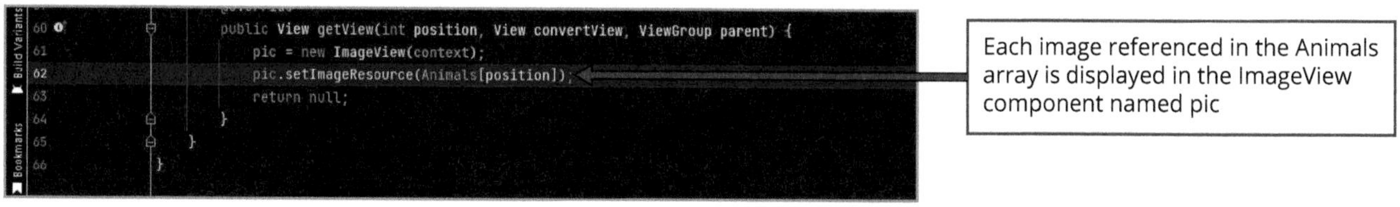

```
    public View getView(int position, View convertView, ViewGroup parent) {
        pic = new ImageView(context);
        pic.setImageResource(Animals[position]);
        return null;
    }
  }
}
```

Each image referenced in the Animals array is displayed in the ImageView component named pic

Step 3

- Press the Enter key.
- To set the scale type of the ImageView component, type **pic.setScaleType(ImageView.ScaleType.FIT_XY);**.

The scale type for the ImageView pic is set to FIT_XY (**Figure 7-26**).

Figure 7-26 Setting the scale type for the ImageView component

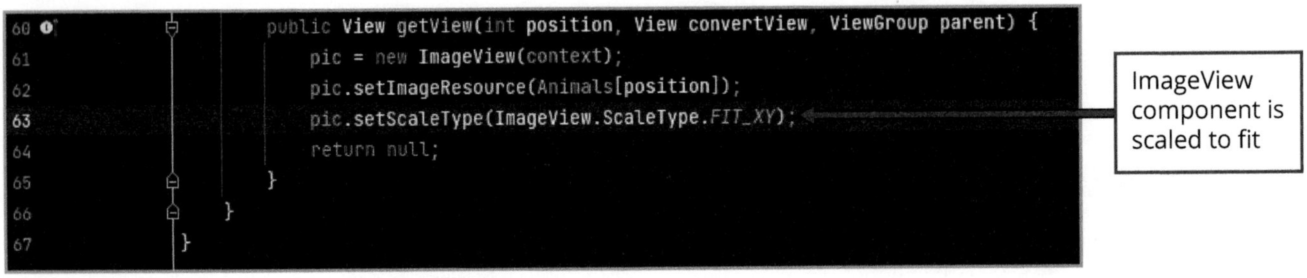

```
public View getView(int position, View convertView, ViewGroup parent) {
    pic = new ImageView(context);
    pic.setImageResource(Animals[position]);
    pic.setScaleType(ImageView.ScaleType.FIT_XY);
    return null;
  }
 }
}
```

ImageView component is scaled to fit

Step 4

- Press the Enter key.
- To resize the images displayed in the GridView component to 330 pixels wide and 300 pixels tall, type **pic.setLayoutParams(new GridView.LayoutParams(330,300));**.

The size of the images displayed in the GridView is set to 330 pixels wide by 300 pixels tall (**Figure 7-27**).

Figure 7-27 Resizing the GridView images

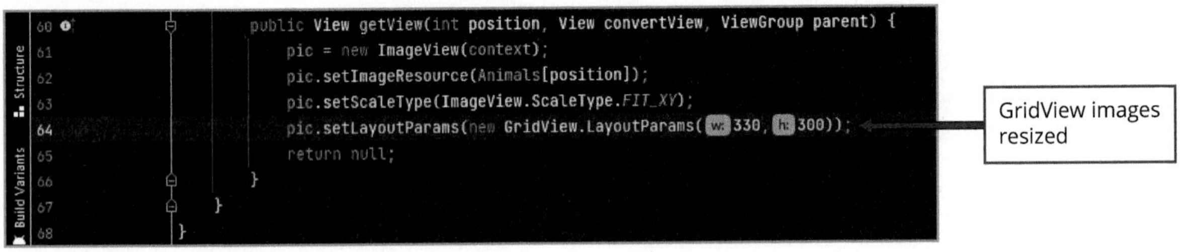

```
public View getView(int position, View convertView, ViewGroup parent) {
    pic = new ImageView(context);
    pic.setImageResource(Animals[position]);
    pic.setScaleType(ImageView.ScaleType.FIT_XY);
    pic.setLayoutParams(new GridView.LayoutParams( w: 330, h: 300));
    return null;
  }
 }
}
```

GridView images resized

Step 5

- To return pic to the MainActivity, change the return null; statement to **return pic;**.

The pic instance is returned to the MainActivity (**Figure 7-28**). The project code is complete.

On the Job

When displaying your company logo or other images, remember that the aspect ratio is the fractional relation of the width of an image compared with its height. The two most common aspect ratios are 4:3 and 16:9 in HDTV. "Keeping the aspect ratio" means that an image is not distorted from its original ratio of width to height.

Running and Testing the Application

It is time to see your finished product. Click Run app on the menu bar, select an emulator, and test the application in the emulator. Save all the files in the next dialog box, if necessary, and unlock the emulator. The application opens in the emulator window, where you can touch the GridView to view the images and select an image, as shown in Figures 7-1 and 7-2.

Figure 7-28 Complete code of MainActivity.java

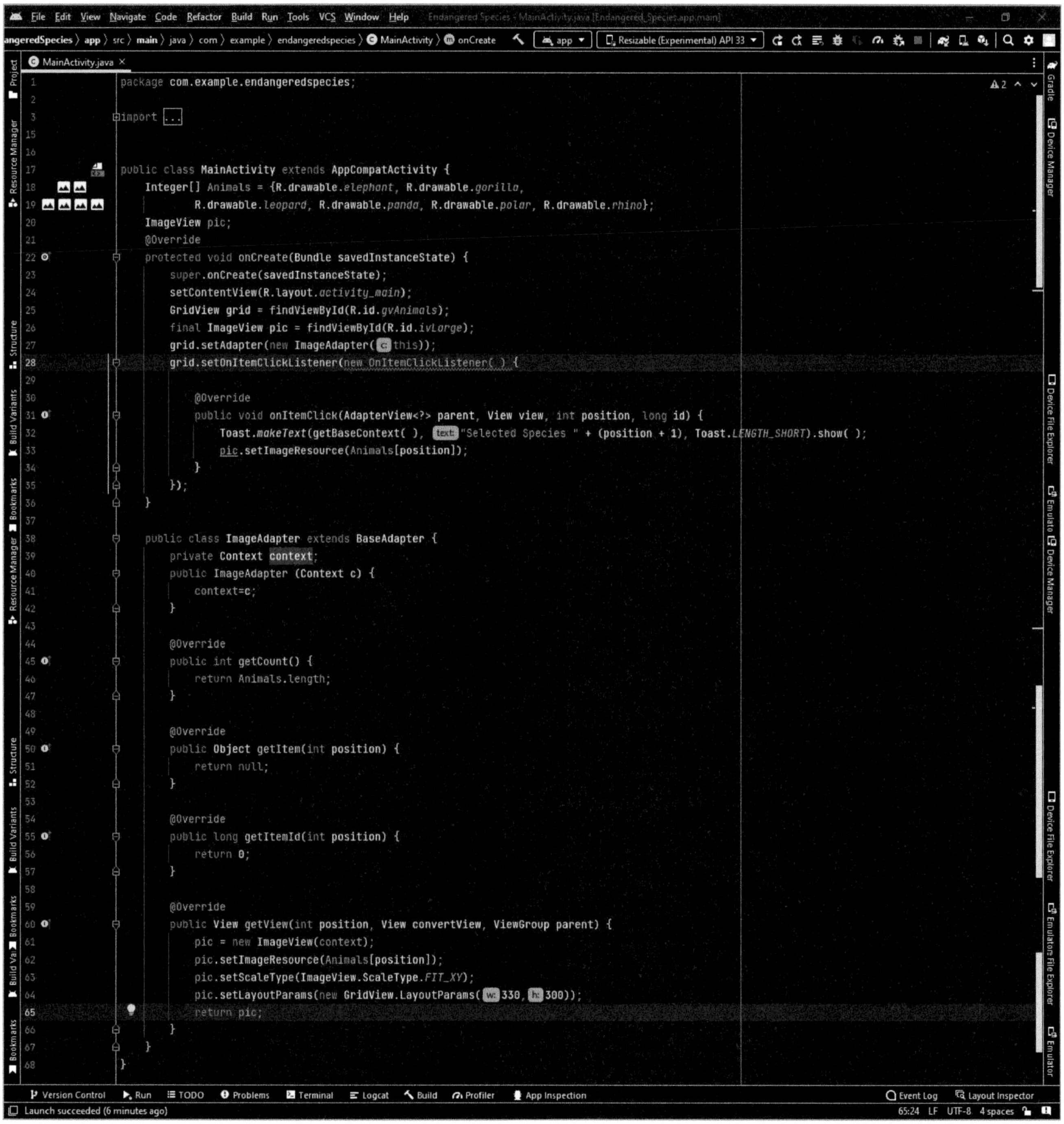

MainActivity.java
package com.example.endangeredspecies;
import ...
public class MainActivity extends AppCompatActivity {
Integer[] Animals = {R.drawable.elephant, R.drawable.gorilla,
R.drawable.leopard, R.drawable.panda, R.drawable.polar, R.drawable.rhino};
ImageView pic;
@Override
protected void onCreate(Bundle savedInstanceState) {
super.onCreate(savedInstanceState);
setContentView(R.layout.activity_main);
GridView grid = findViewById(R.id.gvAnimals);
final ImageView pic = findViewById(R.id.ivLarge);
grid.setAdapter(new ImageAdapter(c: this));
grid.setOnItemClickListener(new OnItemClickListener( ) {
@Override
public void onItemClick(AdapterView<?> parent, View view, int position, long id) {
Toast.makeText(getBaseContext( ), text: "Selected Species " + (position + 1), Toast.LENGTH_SHORT).show( );
pic.setImageResource(Animals[position]);
}
});
}
public class ImageAdapter extends BaseAdapter {
private Context context;
public ImageAdapter (Context c) {
context=c;
}
@Override
public int getCount() {
return Animals.length;
}
@Override
public Object getItem(int position) {
return null;
}
@Override
public long getItemId(int position) {
return 0;
}
@Override
public View getView(int position, View convertView, ViewGroup parent) {
pic = new ImageView(context);
pic.setImageResource(Animals[position]);
pic.setScaleType(ImageView.ScaleType.FIT_XY);
pic.setLayoutParams(new GridView.LayoutParams(w: 330, h: 300));
return pic;
}
}
}
Launch succeeded (6 minutes ago)

Wrap It Up—Chapter Summary

Many Android applications display a GridView to easily accommodate viewing a large amount of pictures. You created a GridView in this chapter to dynamically display images from an array, which provided experience with using a second class, a custom toast message, methods with return variables, and the length of an array. Creating a second class called the ImageAdapter class provided the customization for the GridView layout.

- A View container is a rectangular area of the screen that displays an image or text object. It can include various layouts, including a GridView layout, which displays a grid of objects such as images, songs, or text. Users can scroll the GridView list to select an object such as a photo and display it in another component, such as an ImageView component.
- To display an image in an ImageView component only if the user selects the image in the GridView, you must enter XML code for the ImageView component in activity_main.xml.
- An array variable can store more than one value. Arrays provide access to data by using a numeric index, or subscript, to identify each element in the array. For example, the first element in the array is assigned a subscript of 0. An array can assign more than one image to a GridView component, although it eventually displays only one image at a time.
- A setAdapter provides a data model for the GridView layout. With the GridView component, the adapter binds certain types of data and displays the data in a specified layout.
- Like the OnClickListener used for a Button component, the OnItemClickListener waits for user interaction in a GridView component. When the user selects an item in the GridView, the OnItemClickListener processes an onItemClick event, which includes four arguments. The position argument is an integer value that contains the position of the view in the adapter. For example, if the user taps the second image in the GridView, the integer value of 2 is stored in the position argument.
- By including a toast notification in the onItemClick( ) method, you can display a message indicating which image is selected in a GridView component. The message can include a variable to display the number of the image selected in the GridView. The toast message can float over the other components so that it does not receive focus.
- Because the toast notification in the chapter project is not used directly in the Main Activity, you must replace Main.this in the onItemClick( ) method with a Context class called getBaseContext( ). In Android programs, you use the getBaseContext( ) method to obtain a Context instance that is triggered only when the user touches the GridView component.
- To display an image in an ImageView component after the user selects the image in the GridView, you use the setImageResource( ) method with an int argument. The setImageResource command inserts an ImageView component and the int argument specifies which image is selected for display. If you are using an array to identify the images, you can use position as the int argument because it represents the position of the selected image in the GridView.
- The ImageAdapter class must provide information to set up the GridView so it can display the appropriate images. You use the Context class to load and access resources for the application. A class variable can hold each image in the GridView temporarily before it is displayed. To handle the Context resources necessary for the GridView, you use the ImageAdapter constructor. A constructor can initialize the instance variables of an object. In other words, it constructs the values of data members of the class. You define the Context for an ImageAdapter instance in the ImageAdapter class constructor.
- The chapter project uses the getCount( ) method to determine how many pictures to display in the GridView component. It does so by referencing the array that specifies the images for the GridView. To determine the length of an array, Java provides a method named length( ) that returns an integer value of any given string or array. The length of an array is determined by the number of its elements. The getCount( ) method uses length( ) to return the number of elements in the GridView.
- The declaration statement public int getCount( ) indicates that the return data type (int) is an integer. Because the getCount( ) method is not declared void, it must contain a return statement with a corresponding return value, such as the length of an array.
- In the chapter project, the getView( ) method uses a Context to create a new ImageView instance that temporarily holds each image displayed in the GridView. The getView( ) method also contains statements that scale the ImageView to fit the GridView component and contains a specified height and width.

Key Terms

constructor
getBaseContext( )
GridView
method
onItemClick( )
setAdapter
View

Developer FAQs

1. In the chapter example project, which Android component is used to display a vertical list of attractions? (7.1)
2. A ______ container is a rectangular area of the screen that displays an image or text object. (7.2)
3. Name three locations where photos that are used in the Android environment can be stored. (7.2)
4. Why was the ImageView component coded in the XML code of the chapter project instead of dragging the component onto the emulator? (7.3)
5. Name five View container layouts. (7.2)
6. Write a line of code that uses an instance of a GridView component named gridLayout in a new ImageAdapter class using setAdapter( ). (7.6)
7. Write a line of code that creates a reference array named Games for the images named spidermonkey, candycrush, halo, and titanfall. (7.4)
8. What are the array names and indexes of halo in question 7? (7.4)
9. What is the array length of the Games array in question 7? (7.11)
10. Write a line of code that determines the length of the Games array from question 7 and assigns the value to an int variable named numberOfGames. (7.11)
11. Write a line of code that assigns dentalLength to the length of a string named dental. (7.11)
12. What is the purpose of the position argument in the chapter project? (7.7)
13. In the chapter project, if the user selects panda, what is the value of position? (7.7)
14. Write a custom toast message that resides within an onItemClick( ) method and states "You have selected picture 4 of the political photos" when position is 4. (7.8)
15. What do the numbers in the following statement represent? (7.12)
    pic.setLayoutParams(new GridView.LayoutParams(300,325));
16. What does the aspect ratio 3:2 mean? (7.12)
17. In the following method, what does int (integer) represent? (7.11)

```
public int getCount( ) {
    return Soccer.length;
}
```

18. What would be returned in the method in question 17 if the Soccer array has the maximum index of 25? (7.11)
19. What term does the following define? "Constructs the values of data members of a class." (7.10)
20. Write a statement that sets the scale type to CENTER for an ImageView instance named tower. (7.12)

Beyond the Book

Search the web for answers to the following questions to further your Android knowledge.

1. Find GridView images from three websites and provide a URL and screenshot of each website.
2. Name five types of apps that were not discussed in this chapter and briefly explain how each would use a GridView component.
3. An excellent website that provides up-to-date information about the Android world can be found at *http://android.alltop.com*. Read an article that interests you and write at least a 100-word summary of the article.
4. One of the major issues in the Android world is the multiple operating systems currently running on Android devices. Write a one-page report about the issue of upgrading Android devices to the newest OS available.

Case Programming Projects

Complete one or more of the following case programming projects. Use the same steps and techniques taught within the chapter. Successful completion of these projects requires knowledge of all chapter learning objectives. Submit the program(s) you create to your instructor. The level of difficulty is indicated for each case programming project.

Case Project 7–1: Healthy Snacks App (Beginner)

Requirements Document

Application title:	Healthy Snacks App
Purpose:	Stocking your fridge with quick and healthy snacks helps you resist diet-damaging foods. The Healthy Snacks app displays five healthy snack options.
Algorithms:	**1.** The opening screen displays five snacks in a GridView component (**Figure 7-29**). **2.** When the user selects a thumbnail image of a healthy snack, a larger image appears below the GridView (**Figure 7-30**).
Conditions:	**1.** The pictures of the five healthy snacks are provided with your student files. The pictures are named snack1 through snack5. **2.** Display each image in the GridView using a layout height of 400dp, two columns, 2dp for horizontal and vertical spacing, and a column width of 150dp. Change the layout parameters to a width of 650 and a height of 450.

Figure 7-29 Healthy Snacks app

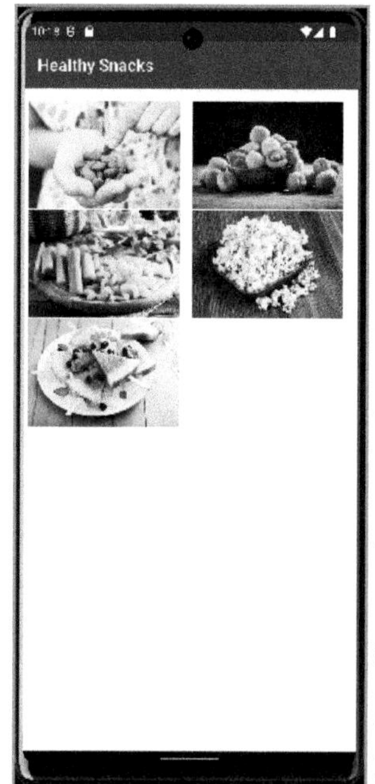

Daisy Daisy/Shutterstock.com, Nitr/Shutterstock.com, Ahanov Michael/Shutterstock.com, Andrey Starostin/Shutterstock.com, Elena Veselova/Shutterstock.com

Figure 7-30 Healthy Snacks app with snack selected

Daisy Daisy/Shutterstock.com, Nitr/Shutterstock.com, Ahanov Michael/Shutterstock.com, Andrey Starostin/Shutterstock.com, Elena Veselova/Shutterstock.com, Nitr/Shutterstock.com

Case Project 7–2: New Seven Wonders of the World App (Beginner)

Requirements Document

Application title: New Seven Wonders of the World (Monuments) App

Purpose: Wikipedia would like you to build an app to showcase the new seven wonders of the world and allow users to select a monument to see a larger picture of it.

Algorithms:

1. The opening screen should display a grid of seven images representing the new seven wonders of the world—the Great Wall of China, Petra, The Redeemer, Machu Picchu, Chichen Itza, the Colosseum, and the Taj Mahal (**Figure 7-31**).
2. When the user selects a monument image in the GridView component, a larger version of the image appears below the GridView. A toast message indicates which monument image the user selected (**Figure 7-32**).

Conditions:

1. The pictures of the seven wonders of the world are provided with your student files. The pictures have the names wonder1 through wonder7.
2. Display each image in the GridView component with up to three images across each row. Use a column width of 60dp, horizontal spacing of 3dp, and vertical spacing of 3dp.

Figure 7-31 New Seven Wonders app

Zhu Difeng/Shutterstock.com, Travelwild/Shutterstock.com, Marchello74/Shutterstock.com, Anton_Ivanov/Shutterstock.com, Jose Ignacio Soto/Shutterstock.com, Patryk Kosmider/Shutterstock.com, Yury Taranik/Shutterstock.com

Figure 7-32 New Seven Wonders app with a monument selected

Zhu Difeng/Shutterstock.com, Travelwild/Shutterstock.com, Marchello74/Shutterstock.com, Anton_Ivanov/Shutterstock.com, Jose Ignacio Soto/Shutterstock.com, Patryk Kosmider/Shutterstock.com, Yury Taranik/Shutterstock.com

Case Project 7–3: SPCA Rescue Shelter App (Intermediate)

Requirements Document

Application title:	SPCA Rescue Shelter App
Purpose:	Your local SPCA needs an app to display pictures of dogs in need of a home.
Algorithms:	**1.** The opening screen displays six dogs from the shelter in a large GridView component. **2.** When the user selects a thumbnail image of a dog, a full-size image appears below the GridView.
Conditions:	**1.** Online, find six pictures of dogs eligible for adoption. **2.** Display each image in the GridView with the size 300, 250.

Case Project 7–4: Car Rental App (Intermediate)

Requirements Document

Application title: Car Rental App

Purpose: A car rental company would like to display its car rental choices in a GridView.

Algorithms:

1. The opening screen displays images of six rental car models in a GridView component.
2. When the user selects a thumbnail image of a car, a full-size image appears below the GridView. Using an If statement, create a toast message that shows the type of car and the cost of each rental car.

Conditions:

1. Locate six rental car images on the Internet.
2. Create a custom layout using the CENTER scale type.

Case Project 7–5: Anthology Wedding Photography (Advanced)

Requirements Document

Application title: Anthology Wedding Photography App

Purpose: Anthology Wedding Photography would like to display a sample of its work with 10 wedding images in a GridView.

Algorithms:

1. Create a GridView that displays 10 wedding photos.
2. When the user selects a specific wedding image in the GridView, a larger image appears with a custom toast message that displays *Anthology Wedding Photo* and the image number.
3. A line of text appears at the bottom of the screen: *Contact us at anthology@wed.com.*

Conditions:

1. Select wedding images from the Internet.
2. Use a layout of your choice.

Case Project 7–6: Personal Photo App (Advanced)

Requirements Document

Application title: Personal Photo App

Purpose: Create your own photo app with eight images of your family and friends in a GridView component.

Algorithms:

1. Create a GridView that displays eight images of your friends and family.
2. When the user selects a specific thumbnail image in the GridView, a larger image appears with a custom toast message that displays the first name of the pictured person.

Conditions:

1. Select your own images.
2. Use a layout of your choice.

Chapter 8

Design! Using a DatePicker on a Tablet

Learning Objectives

At the completion of this chapter, you will be able to:

8.1 Create an Android app on a tablet

8.2 Design a tablet app with modern design principles

8.3 Add an Android virtual device for the tablet

8.4 Design a tablet table layout

8.5 Add date, time, and clock components

8.6 Create a Calendar class

8.7 Select the date from the DatePickerDialog

8.8 Add the onDateSet( ) method

8.9 Display the date using the getTime( ) method

8.10 Add an Android theme

The explosion of the Android market is not limited to the phone platform. Android tablet sales are successfully competing with the Apple iPad as well, proving that consumers are ready for a tablet environment. According to Statista, Android is the leading operating system worldwide for tablets, shipping a total of 19.2 million units in one quarter in 2022. Android's closest competitor was Apple's iOS, which was installed on 14.8 million iPads that were shipped worldwide in the same quarter. Now more than ever, mobile designers are being asked to create experiences for a variety of tablet devices. In today's post-PC world, the tablet market provides the mobility and simplicity users demand for connecting to the Internet, playing games, using Facebook, checking email, and more. Lower prices and a large app marketplace are driving growth in the Android tablet market. Android tablets come in various sizes, often ranging from 7.3 inches to 10.1 inches, comparable to the iPad Mini and the full-size iPad.

8.1 Creating an Android App on a Tablet

To understand the process of designing an application on the Android tablet, in this chapter you design a calendar program called Sailing Adventures on a 10.1-inch tablet. The app lets you book a reservation on a historic sailboat in Scotland. The Sailing Adventures application shown in **Figure 8-1** provides information about one of its historic sailing adventures in Edinburgh. This single-screen experience could be part of a larger app featuring sailing trips throughout the world.

Figure 8-1 Sailing Adventures Android tablet app

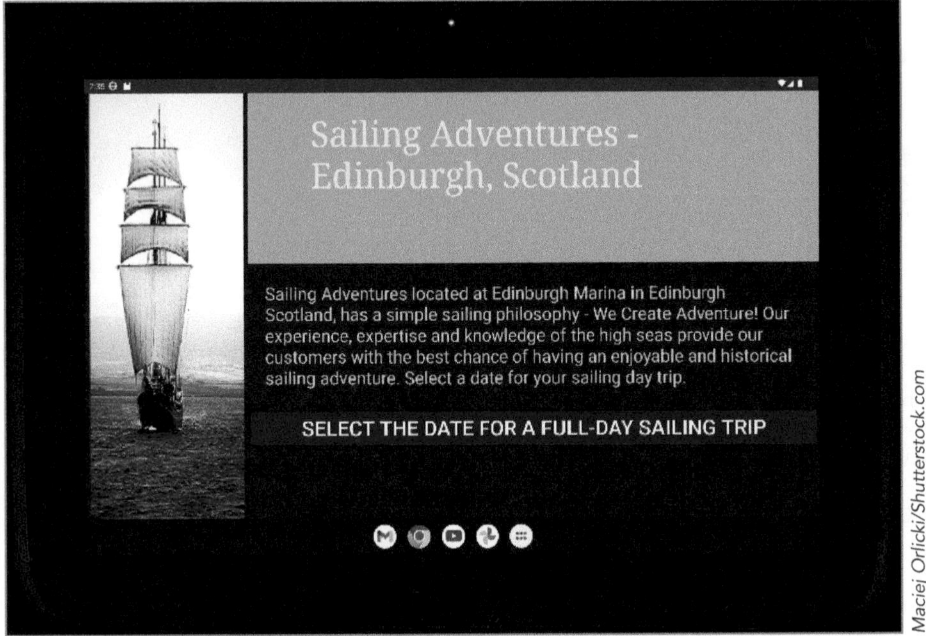

Maciej Orlicki/Shutterstock.com

The Android tablet app in Figure 8-1 appears on a 10.1-inch Nexus 10 display. When the user wants to make a reservation by touching the button component, a floating dialog box opens with a DatePicker calendar component, as shown in **Figure 8-2**. When the user sets the date, a TextView component confirms the reservation for the day trip, as shown in **Figure 8-3**.

Figure 8-2 DatePicker calendar component in a dialog box

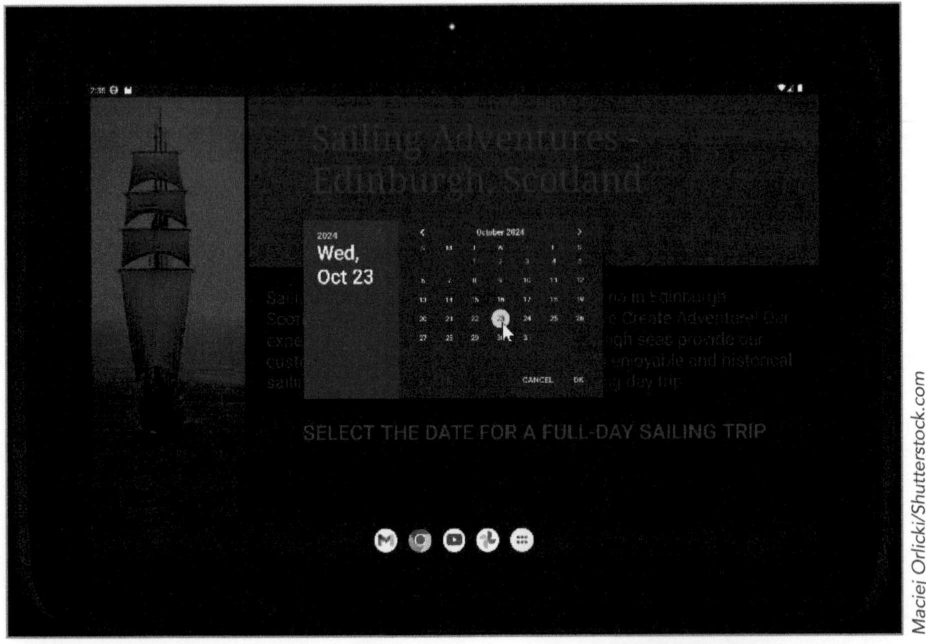

Maciej Orlicki/Shutterstock.com

Figure 8-3 TextView component displays reservation

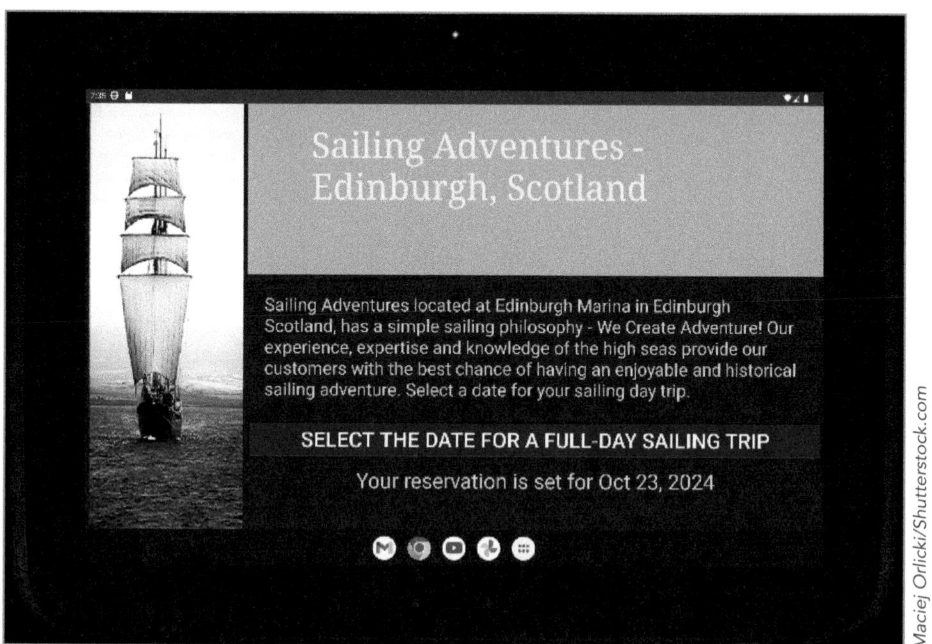

Good to Know The Android platform has been ported to many devices beyond phones and tablets in the IoT (Internet of Things). IoT devices include fingerprint sensors, televisions, microwaves, security home cameras, and automobiles.

To create this application, the developer must understand how to perform the following processes, among others:

1. Add an Android virtual device specifically designed for tablets.
2. Add the images used in this project.
3. Change the theme and icon for the tablet display.
4. Create a custom XML file with a table layout.
5. Add and initialize TextView components and the Button component.
6. Initialize a DatePickerDialog with the current date and listen for the user to select a date.
7. Return the selected date.
8. Display the selected reservation date in the TextView component.

8.2 Designing a Tablet App with Modern Design Principles

The Android market initially included only mobile phone devices, but the recent popularity of the tablet device provides a new platform for Android app programming. The growth of the Android tablet market goes hand in hand with dedicated applications designed especially for the tablet, not just enlarged versions of a phone app. **Native applications** are programs locally installed on a specific platform such as a phone or tablet. A native application is typically designed for a specific platform such as a phone on a 5-inch screen or a tablet on a 10.1-inch screen. In contrast, an **emulated application** is converted in real time to run on a variety of platforms—for example, a webpage—that can be displayed on various screen sizes through a browser. A native Android tablet app creates an optimal user experience based on the most common tablet screen sizes (between approximately 7.3 and 10.1 inches, as measured diagonally), a 2560 × 1600 pixel resolution, and a 16:10 screen ratio, as shown in the tablet in **Figure 8-4**. In comparison, an Apple iPad Air has a 9.7-inch screen, a 2048 × 1536 pixel resolution, and a screen ratio of 4:3. If you plan to create apps on multiple platforms, the different screen specifications will affect your design.

Figure 8-4 Android tablet

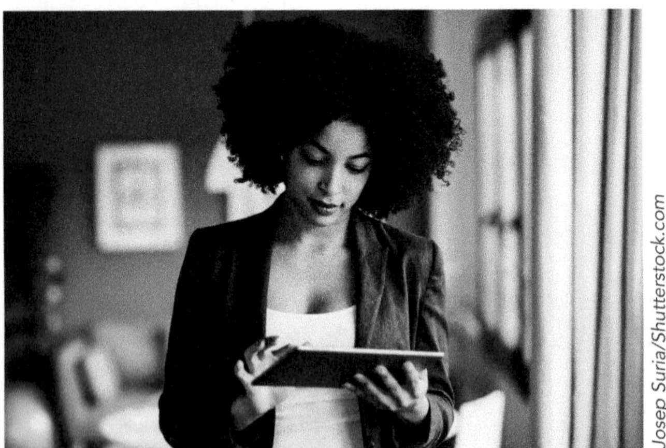

Josep Suria/Shutterstock.com

As you consider creating an Android tablet application, remember that tablets are not simply huge smartphones. Even the primary use of each device is different. A smartphone is most likely used on the go in a truly mobile fashion to quickly check email, update Facebook status, or send a text message while running errands. Tablets are typically used for longer periods of time. This prolonged interaction on tablets is more involved, with users sitting down at a table in Starbucks, riding a train, or relaxing with the tablet positioned in their laps while watching a movie. Whereas phone app design relies on simplicity, a tablet can handle the complexity of more graphics, more text, and more interaction during longer sessions.

On the Job | To gain some inspiration for your tablet design and for following best practices, download the most used business apps for the tablet, such as Zoom, Teams, Canva, Hootsuite, and Wave.

Design Best Practices for Tablets

As you begin designing an Android app, first consider how the user most likely will interact with your app. Will the tablet be in the user's lap, held with two hands (games often require this), or in a tablet stand? Will the user spend seconds, minutes, or hours using your app? Will the user be multitasking with your app and other apps? What is the optimal way to deliver the content? As you consider the answers to each of these questions, keep these design guidelines in mind:

- Understand the close relationship between users and their tablets; they are easy to pack and take everywhere. This creates use case scenarios with a screen that is larger than a phone's but not as large as a desktop or laptop computer monitor.
- Keep screens uncluttered and ensure that touch components such as buttons and radio buttons are of sufficient size for user interaction. Larger components are easier to find and enable simpler interaction for the user.
- Focus apps on the task at hand. Keep the design simple. Do not force the user to spend undue time figuring out how to use the application.
- Resist filling the large screen with "cool" interactions that distract the user without adding to the quality of the program. Buttons and components must be easily seen and accessed.
- Use flexible dimension values such as dp and sp instead of px or pt, which will allow you to display content perfectly on any device.
- Provide higher-resolution resources for screen densities (DPI) to ensure that your app looks great on any screen size.
- Create a unique experience for both the phone and tablet designs. If the apps have multiple screens, use a consistent theme and feel. Use a layout for screens and pages that users understand.
- Use larger fonts than you would with a phone app. Consider printing your user interface design to see how it looks. Do not make users double-tap or pinch your content to read it clearly. Instead, increase the font size to at least 16dp.

Good to Know

Consumers of all ages are spending more time playing games on tablets. This trend affects the retail market sales of console-based video games and traditional children's toys. The shift leaves retailers out of sales streams because most digital content is distributed within phone platform markets. Because tablets are affordable and easy to use, parents and guardians prefer tablets for their children. A reasonably priced tablet can be used to watch movies, play age-appropriate gaming apps, and access educational opportunities.

Quick Check

What is the minimum font size in dp for a tablet?

Answer: 16dp.

8.3 Adding an Android Virtual Device for the Tablet

To ensure that your Android tablet app deploys successfully to any Android device, an API platform and Android virtual devices (AVDs) are needed. The first API platform to ever support tablets was the Android Honeycomb 3.2 operating system (API 13). A particular Android virtual device is needed that is dedicated to tablet applications; you can add other AVDs in Android Studio for all your intended devices and platforms. Honeycomb was initially designed for the Xoom, the first Android tablet introduced, but newer SDKs support the full range of new Android tablet devices on the market. When you create an Android tablet app, the minimum required SDK should be set to API 13: Android 3.2 (Honeycomb) to cover the first generation of Android tablets; the target API is automatically set to cover the most recent versions of Android tablets. Each Android device configuration is stored in an AVD. This same technique can be used to cover earlier models of smartphone app development.

Creating a Tablet App

To begin creating an Android tablet application for the Sailing Adventures app and to change the emulator, follow these steps.

Step 1

- Open the Android Studio program.
- In the Welcome to Android Studio window, scroll down and click the New Project button in the Phone and Tablet templates to create a new Android Studio project.
- Click the Next button in the New Project window.
- Type **Sailing Adventures** in the Name text box.
- If necessary, select Java in the Language text box.
- If necessary, select API 23: Android 6.0 (Marshmallow) as the Minimum SDK. This is a later version than the first API (API 13), so it will work on most modern tablets.

A new Java Android project named Sailing Adventures is configured to save on your local computer (**Figure 8-5**). A different virtual tablet emulator will be added to display this app with a tablet design.

Figure 8-5 New Project window

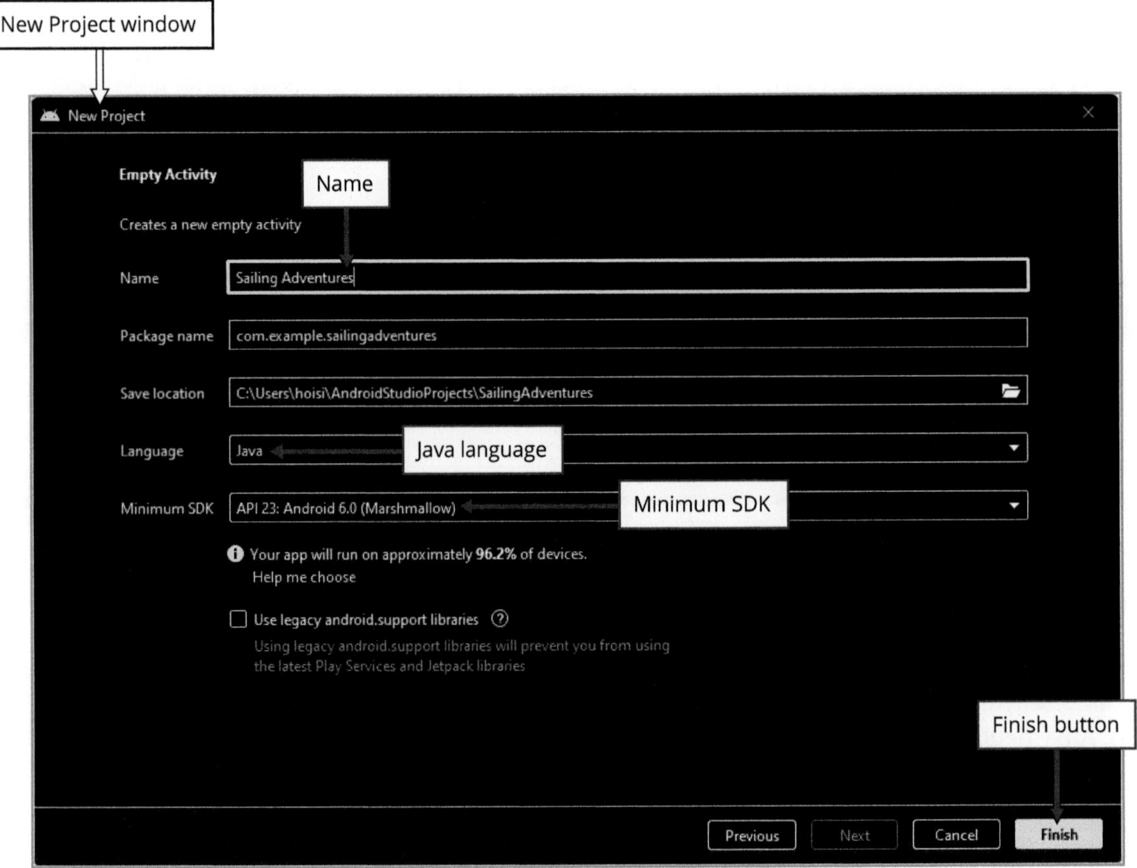

Step 2

- Click the Finish button in the New Project window.
- In activity_main.xml, click the Hello world! TextView component, which is displayed by default in the emulator. Press the Delete key.
- To change the emulator display for activity_main.xml, click the arrow on the Device for Preview (D) button.

The drop-down menu displays the various layouts for Android devices (**Figure 8-6**).

To use a recent tablet emulator, you first add the appropriate AVD configuration. The Nexus 10 works well on newer computers with high resolution, but if you are testing your project on an old physical tablet, select the WXGA 10.1-inch tablet with landscape orientation in the following steps. To select the Android development tools for a tablet emulator, follow these steps.

Step 1

- Click Tools on the Android Studio menu.
- Click Device Manager to open the Device Manager dialog box.
- Click the Create device button to open the Virtual Device Configuration dialog box.

The Android Virtual Device Configuration dialog box opens so you can select a tablet emulator (**Figure 8-7**).

Figure 8-6 The activity_main.xml file is displayed to select a tablet device

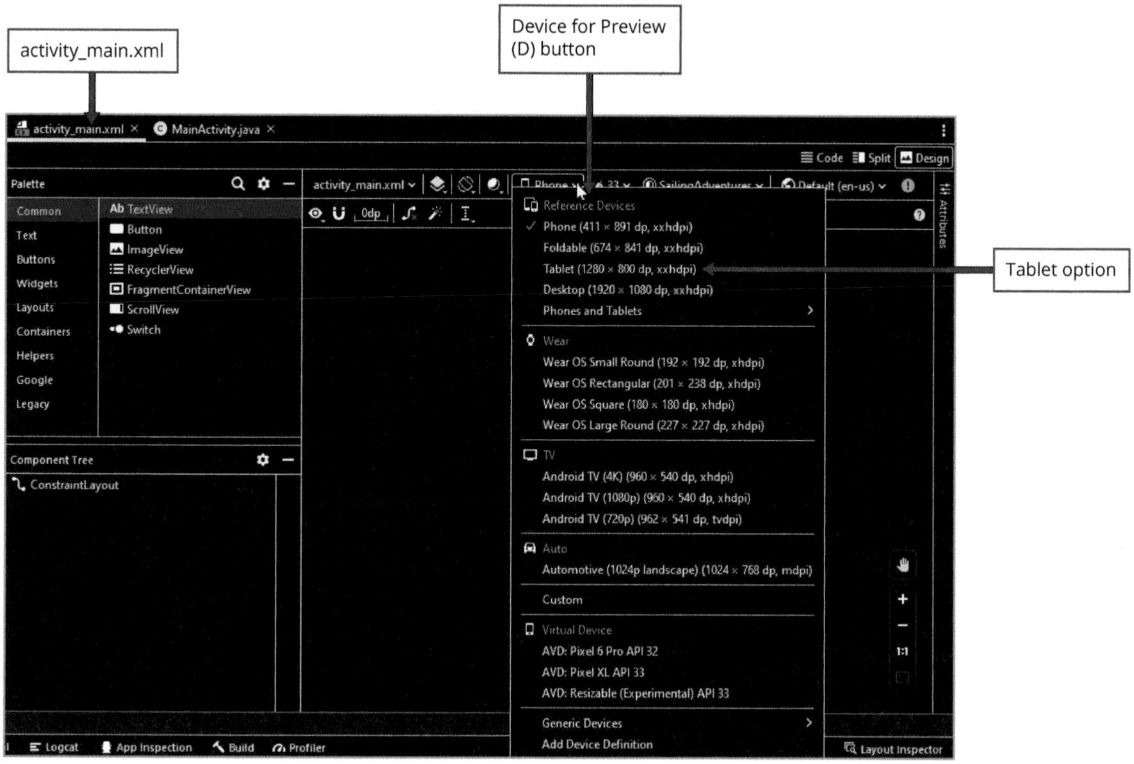

Figure 8-7 Adding a tablet emulator

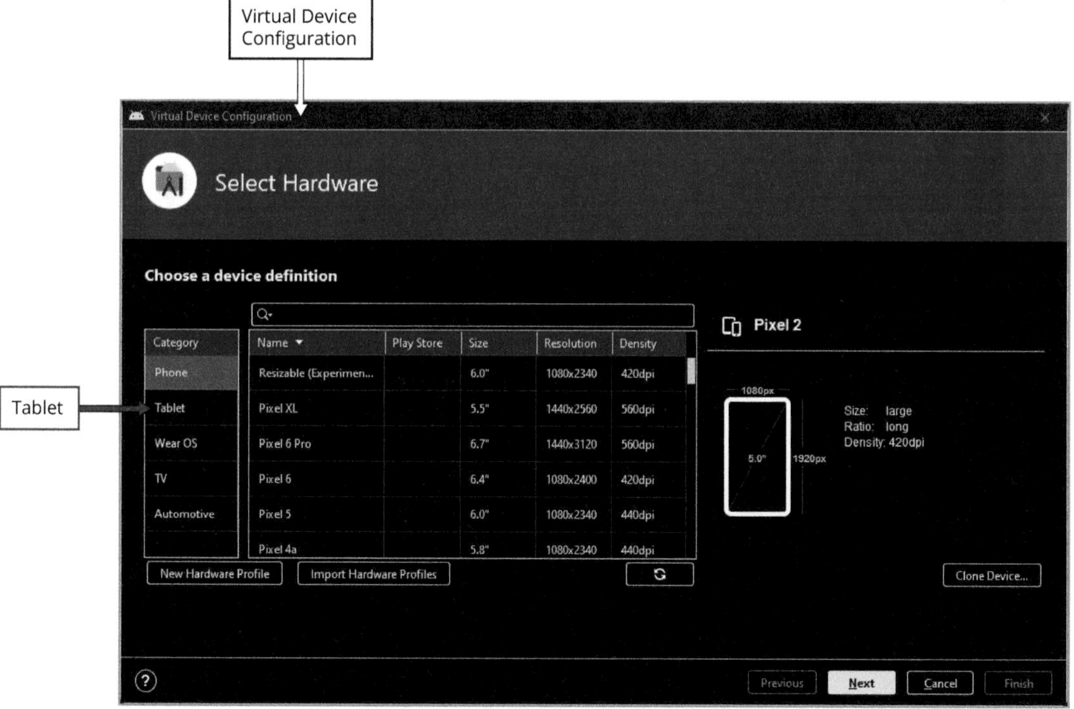

Step 2

- In the Virtual Device Configuration dialog box, click Tablet in the Category column.
- Click Nexus 10 in the second column to select the hardware emulator. (If you are testing your project on an older computer, select the 10.1-inch WXGA tablet with landscape orientation.)

The Nexus 10 tablet is selected in the Virtual Device Configuration dialog box (**Figure 8-8**).

Figure 8-8 Selecting a Nexus 10 virtual device

Step 3

- Click the Next button to open the System Image window.
- If necessary, select Tiramisu (or a recent build) in the Release Name column and then click the Next button.

The Virtual Device Configuration dialog box displays the Verify Configuration settings (**Figure 8-9**).

Figure 8-9 Verifying Android virtual device settings

Step 4

- Click the Finish button to add the Nexus 10 tablet to your virtual devices (emulators).
- Close the Android Virtual Device Manager dialog box.
- Click the Run button to launch the tablet emulator.
- After the tablet emulator runs, close the emulator.

Critical Thinking

When designing a tablet native app, should I copy an existing website layout and just reduce the size of the elements to fit within a smaller screen?

You should start from scratch and decide how a tablet user might use the information differently. Make the design an integrated experience and create an impression similar to that for the existing website and phone app.

Creating the String Table

The chapter project app contains four text strings, as shown in Figure 8-1: the content description for the image, the text title in the first TextView object, the description of the sailing trip, and the Button component text. To add the image to the drawable folder and text values to strings.xml, follow these steps.

Step 1

- In the Android Project view, expand the values folder within the res folder.
- Double-click the strings.xml file to display its contents.
- Click the Open editor link.
- Click the Add Key (plus) button.
- In the Key text box, type **ivSail** to name the string.
- In the Default Value text box, type **Sailing Image** to define the text that will be displayed as a content description for the ImageView component.
- Click the OK button.
- Click the Add Key (plus) button.
- In the Key text box, type **tvTitle** to name the string.
- In the Default Value text box, type **Sailing Adventures – Edinburgh, Scotland** to define the text that will be displayed in the first TextView component.
- Click the OK button.
- Click the Add Key (plus) button.
- In the Key text box, type **tvDescription** to name the string.
- In the Default Value text box, type the following text: **Sailing Adventures located at Edinburgh Marina in Edinburgh Scotland, has a simple sailing philosophy – We Create Adventure! Our experience, expertise and knowledge of the high seas provide our customers with the best chance of having an enjoyable and historical sailing adventure. Select a date for your sailing day trip.**
- Click the OK button.

- Click the Add Key (plus) button.
- In the Key text box, type **btDate** to name the string.
- In the Default Value text box, type **Select the Date for a Full-Day Sailing Trip** to define the text.
- Click the OK button and save your work.

The Keys and Default Values of the ImageView, TextView, and Button components are entered into the strings.xml file (**Figure 8-10**).

Figure 8-10 Strings added for the Sailing Adventures app

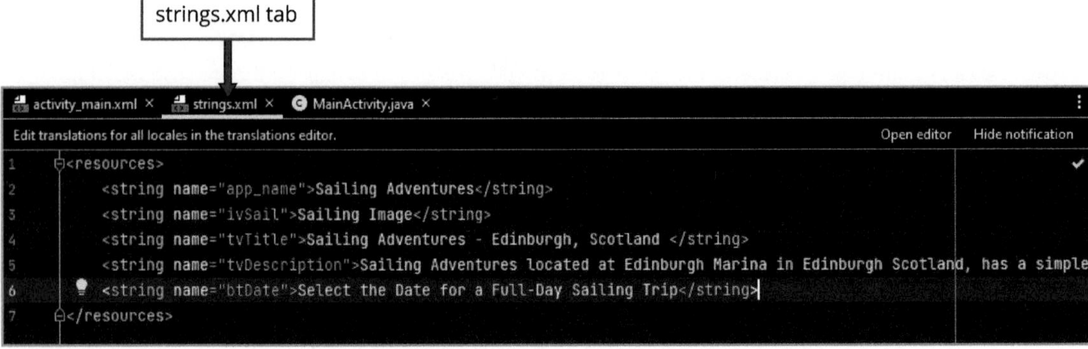

Step 2

- Close the Translations Editor and strings.xml tabs.
- Open the folder containing the student files from the textbook.
- Copy the sail.png file from the folder containing the student files and paste it in the drawable folder.
- Click the OK button in the Copy dialog box.

The sail.png image is placed in the drawable folder (**Figure 8-11**).

Figure 8-11 The sail.png image added to the drawable folder

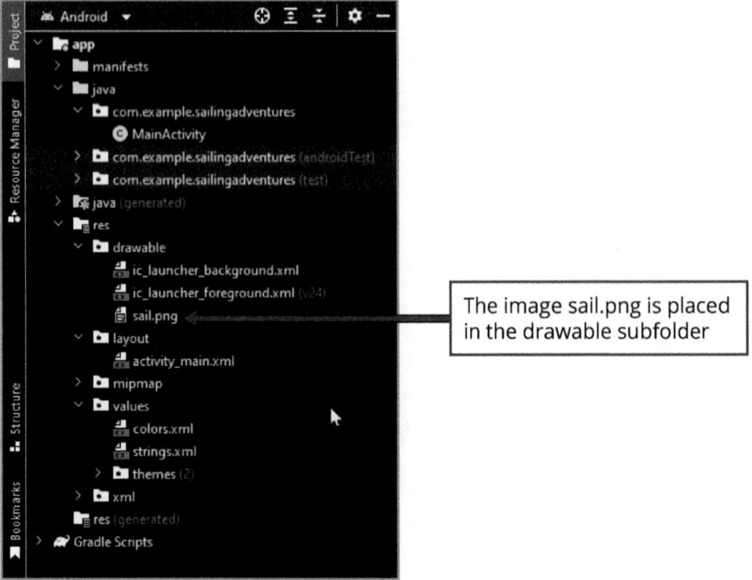

On the Job Google created an Android Design website *(http://developer.android.com/design)* to assist in best practices and to set a uniform look and feel across the various Android platforms when you are creating professional apps.

8.4 Designing a Tablet Table Layout

In the Sailing Adventures application, two layouts are combined in activity_main.xml to organize the tablet user interface components. The Linear layout and the Table layout create a simple, clean interface on the tablet that contains both rows and columns. The left column in **Table 8-1** uses the Linear layout to display the sail.png image. On the right side of Table 8-1, four rows are inserted in a Table layout to display the title, description, button, and reservation result. (Figure 8-3 shows this layout with all the design elements.)

Table 8-1 Table for Linear layout

sail.png	Title
	Day trip description
	Reservation button
	Reservation date after selection

A user interface design layout named **TableLayout** is composed of TableRow components—one for each row of the table in activity_main.xml. In Table 8-1, the layout consists of four rows and one column. The contents of each TableRow are the view components that will go in each cell of the table grid. The TableLayout shown in the following code has four TableRow components with either a TextView or Button component in each row within a LinearLayout:

Code Syntax

```
<?xml version="1.0" encoding="utf-8"?>
<LinearLayout xmlns:android="http://schemas.android.com/apk/res/android"
  <ImageView />
  <TableLayout
     <TableRow>
          <TextView />
     </TableRow>
     <TableRow>
          <TextView />
     </TableRow>
     <TableRow>
          <Button />
     </TableRow>
     <TableRow>
          <TextView />
     </TableRow>
  </TableLayout>
</LinearLayout>
```

To create additional columns, you add a view to a row. Adding a view in a row forms a cell, and the width of the largest view determines the width of the column.

Within the XML layout file, an Android property named *padding* is used to spread out the content displayed on the tablet. The **padding property** can be used to offset the content of the component by a specific number of pixels. For example, if you set a padding of 20 pixels, the content of a component is distanced from other components by 20 pixels. Another Android property named **typeface** sets the style of the text to a font family such as monospace, sans serif, or serif.

The Sailing Adventures app displays the table within a horizontal LinearLayout. By default, the Android layout is set to RelativeLayout, which allows you to place components anywhere on the emulator. Follow these steps to change the layout of activity_main.xml for the tablet to a LinearLayout.

Step 1

- Drag the LinearLayout (horizontal) widget from the Layouts category of the Palette to the emulator.
- Drag all four constraint handles to the edges of the tablet emulator.

The LinearLayout (horizontal) appears in the emulator (**Figure 8-12**).

Figure 8-12 LinearLayout (horizontal) in the emulator

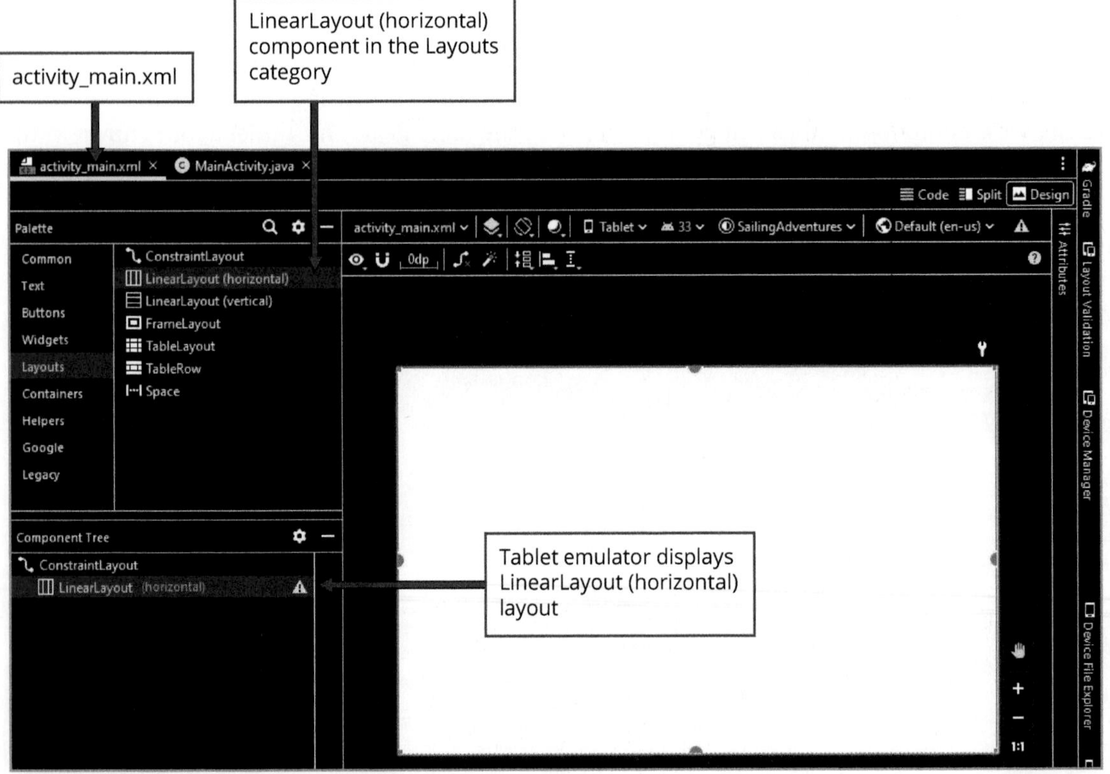

Step 2

- Click the Code button at the top right to display the XML code.

The activity_main.xml file displays the LinearLayout code, which will horizontally align the elements on the emulator (**Figure 8-13**).

Figure 8-13 LinearLayout in XML code

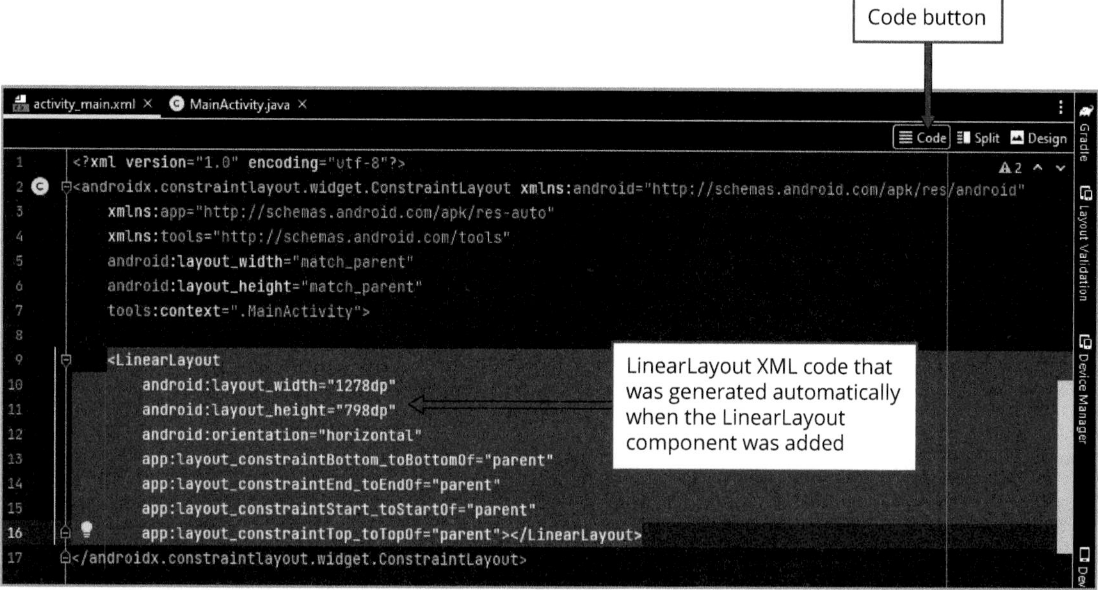

After the layout is set, the ImageView component and the table can be coded with four rows within the activity_main.xml file by following these steps.

Step 1

- Click to the left of the first bracket before </LinearLayout> in Line 16, press the Enter key twice to insert a blank line, and then type **<ImageView** in the blank line.
- Press the Enter key.
- Type the following code to add the ImageView component, using auto-completion as much as possible:

```
android:id="@+id/ivSail"
android:layout_width="280dp"
android:layout_height="800dp"
android:contentDescription="@string/ivSail"
android:src="@drawable/sail" />
```

The ImageView component is coded in activity_main.xml (**Figure 8-14**).

Figure 8-14 ImageView component in XML code

```
    android:orientation="horizontal"
    app:layout_constraintBottom_toBottomOf="parent"
    app:layout_constraintEnd_toEndOf="parent"
    app:layout_constraintHorizontal_bias="1.0"
    app:layout_constraintStart_toStartOf="parent"
    app:layout_constraintTop_toTopOf="parent"
    app:layout_constraintVertical_bias="1.0">

    <ImageView
        android:id="@+id/ivSail"
        android:layout_width="280dp"
        android:layout_height="800dp"
        android:contentDescription="@string/ivSail"
        android:src="@drawable/sail" />
</LinearLayout>
```

ImageView XML code to add the sail image to the left of the linear layout

Step 2

- To code the TableLayout for the first two table rows to display the title and description TextView components, press the Enter key.
- Type the following code, using auto-completion as much as possible:

```
<TableLayout
    android:layout_width="fill_parent"
    android:layout_height="800dp" >
    <TableRow android:layout_width="wrap_content">
        <View android:layout_height="100dp" />
        <TextView
            android:id="@+id/tvTitle"
            android:layout_width="wrap_content"
            android:background="#A49E99"
            android:gravity="fill_horizontal"
            android:padding="110dp"
            android:text="@string/tvTitle"
            android:textSize="60sp"
            android:typeface="serif" />
    </TableRow>
    <TableRow>
        <View android:layout_height="60dp" />
        <TextView
            android:id="@+id/tvDescription"
            android:layout_width="wrap_content"
            android:layout_gravity="left"
            android:padding="30dp"
            android:text="@string/tvDescription"
            android:textSize="30sp" />
    </TableRow>
</TableLayout>
```

The first two rows of the table display the title and description of Sailing Adventures in the emulator (**Figure 8-15**).

Figure 8-15 TableLayout XML code for first two TableRows

TableLayout XML code to create a table similar to Table 8-1

First TableRow

Second TableRow

```
<TableLayout
    android:layout_width="fill_parent"
    android:layout_height="800dp">

    <TableRow android:layout_width="wrap_content">

        <View android:layout_height="100dp" />

        <TextView
            android:id="@+id/tvTitle"
            android:layout_width="wrap_content"
            android:background="#A49E99"
            android:gravity="fill_horizontal"
            android:padding="110dp"
            android:text="Sailing Adventures - Edinburgh, Scotland"
            android:textSize="60sp"
            android:typeface="serif" />
    </TableRow>

    <TableRow>

        <View android:layout_height="60dp" />

        <TextView
            android:id="@+id/tvDescription"
            android:layout_width="wrap_content"
            android:layout_gravity="left"
            android:padding="30dp"
            android:text="Sailing Adventures located at Edinburgh Marina in Edinb..."
            android:textSize="30sp" />
    </TableRow>
```

Step 3

- Next, write the XML code for the third and fourth table rows, which display a navy-blue Button component and TextView component. Press the Enter key after the closing </TableRow> tag and then type the following code, using auto-completion as much as possible:

```
<TableRow>
   <View android:layout_height="50dp" />
   <Button
        android:id="@+id/btDate"
        android:layout_width="wrap_content"
        android:gravity="center_horizontal"
        android:backgroundTint="#000080"
        android:padding="10dp"
        android:text="@string/btDate"
        android:textSize="36sp" />
</TableRow>
```

```
<TableRow>
    <View android:layout_height="60dp" />
    <TextView
         android:id="@+id/tvReservation"
         android:layout_gravity="center"
         android:padding="10dp"
         android:textSize="36sp" />
</TableRow>
```

The last two rows of the table display the button and reservation date of Sailing Adventures (**Figure 8-16**). To view the finished design, click the Design tab at the bottom of the window (**Figure 8-17**). If you were to run the app at this point, the title bar would cover part of the app's title text. Later in the chapter, the title bar will be removed by changing the theme of the app.

Figure 8-16 TableLayout XML code for last two TableRows

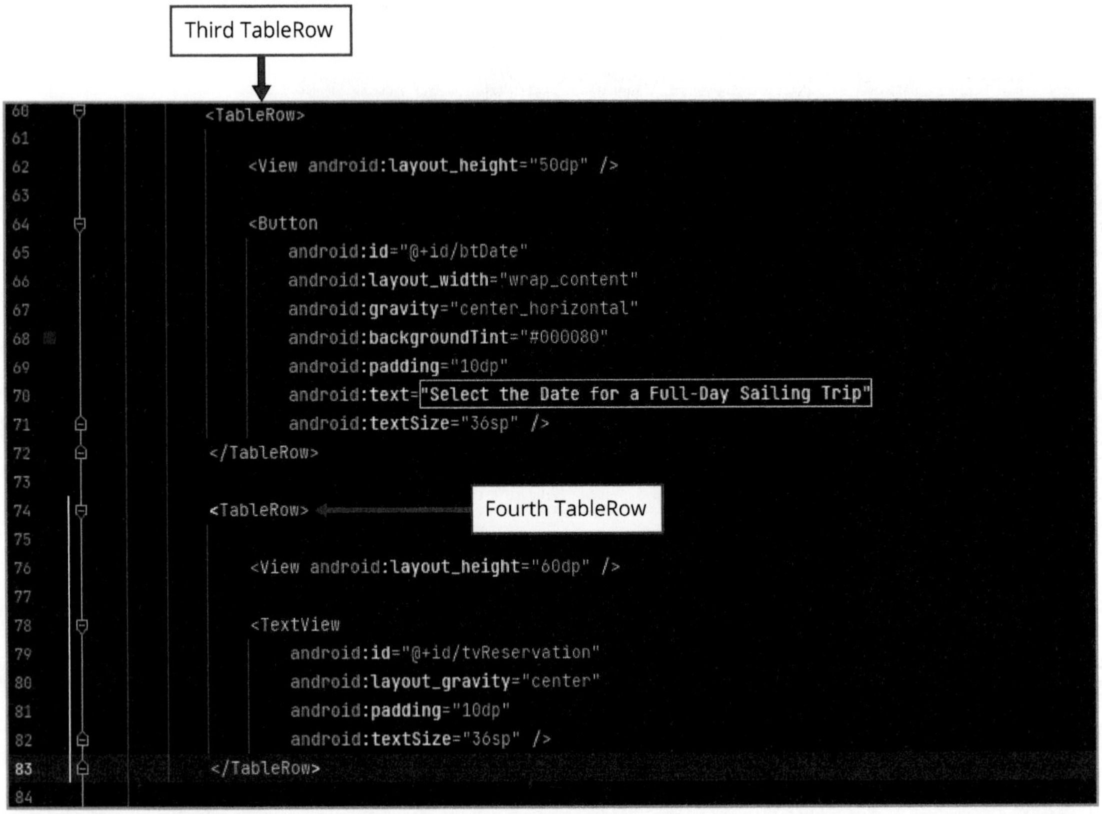

Third TableRow

```
<TableRow>

    <View android:layout_height="50dp" />

    <Button
        android:id="@+id/btDate"
        android:layout_width="wrap_content"
        android:gravity="center_horizontal"
        android:backgroundTint="#000080"
        android:padding="10dp"
        android:text="Select the Date for a Full-Day Sailing Trip"
        android:textSize="36sp" />
</TableRow>

<TableRow>

    <View android:layout_height="60dp" />

    <TextView
        android:id="@+id/tvReservation"
        android:layout_gravity="center"
        android:padding="10dp"
        android:textSize="36sp" />
</TableRow>
```

Fourth TableRow

Figure 8-17 Tablet layout Design in activity_main.xml

Maciej Orlicki/Shutterstock.com

Good to Know

If your app is rotated in the wrong direction, you need to tap the "six dots" button in the tablet emulator to open the app drawer, which contains all of your apps. Click Settings and search at the top for Auto-rotate screen. Click the slider to turn on the Auto-rotate screen.

Quick Check

Which type of Android layout was used to create a table on the tablet in the previous example?

Answer: LinearLayout.

8.5 Using Date, Time, and Clock Components

A common purpose of an Android application is to manage calendars and help the user select a date for a reservation or event. Whether you are a student or a businessperson, a solid scheduling app can remind you about an upcoming test or to pay a bill, and an alarm clock app can help you wake up each morning. Android provides ready-to-use components called **dialogs** or dialog boxes that enable the user to pick a valid time or date. In the chapter project, a calendar tool called a **DatePicker** component is displayed in a dialog box to help the user determine a preferred date for a full-day sailing trip. The DatePicker makes sure that the user selects a valid date. For example, the DatePicker will not allow the user to pick the thirty-second of March. In Java, many time and date components are available, including TimePicker, DatePicker, CalendarView, Chronometer, and AnalogClock. Each picker provides components for selecting each part of the time (hour, minute, AM/PM) or date (month, day, year).

All Android devices keep a numeric representation of the system's current date and time. These numbers can be displayed in multiple formats based on the cultural preferences of the user's location. For example, in the United States, the format of dates looks like this: March 17, 2024, or 03/17/2024. In Canada and Europe, the day value normally precedes the month, like this: 17 March 2024 or 17/03/2024. Similarly, some countries use the concept of AM and PM with a 12-hour clock, whereas others commonly use a 24-hour clock. For example, 7:30 PM is equal to 19:30 in countries that use a 24-hour clock. Developers often must program with cultural differences in mind, based on user preferences and geographical location.

Creating a component to enter the date is crucial because requiring users to type a date in a text box can lead to multiple errors, including incorrect formats or typos. To streamline the process, websites typically rely on some type of calendar component for input, in the same way that the Sailing Adventures app requests the reservation in a DatePicker. Initially, the Sailing Adventures app does not display a DatePicker dialog box. The user clicks the button to launch a dialog box that includes a coded DatePicker displaying today's date. Date and time components are often launched in dialog boxes to keep the user interface uncluttered.

On the Job | After an app is published, it is the developer's responsibility to monitor comments and reviews for the app at Google Play. Consider conducting user surveys and doing further usability testing to update new versions and create a popular application.

Instantiating the Components

In the Sailing Adventures app, the activity_main layout opens, displaying the btDate button. When the user interacts with the app and taps the btDate button, a DatePickerDialog box opens and displays today's date in the calendar. After the user selects the desired sailing date using the calendar and taps the OK button at the bottom of the calendar, the reservation date is displayed within the tvReservation TextView component. The component is referenced in multiple methods, so this instantiation must be declared as a class variable. To instantiate the TextView component, the Button component, and the Button OnClickListener, follow these steps.

Step 1

- Save your work and then close the activity_main.xml tab.
- In the Android Project view, double-click MainActivity to open it.
- In MainActivity, click after the public class MainActivity extends AppCompatActivity { statement and press the Enter key to insert a blank line.
- To initialize the class variable, type **private TextView reservation;**.
- Click TextView, press Alt+Enter, and then import the class.

A class variable that can be accessed by the rest of the program is initialized (**Figure 8-18**).

Figure 8-18 Date class variable for the reservation

MainActivity.java tab open

MainActivity.java ×

```
package com.example.sailingadventures;

import ...

public class MainActivity extends AppCompatActivity {
    private TextView reservation;
    @Override
    protected void onCreate(Bundle savedInstanceState) {
        super.onCreate(savedInstanceState);
        setContentView(R.layout.activity_main);
    }
}
```

Instantiation of the TextView component as a class variable

Step 2

- In the onCreate( ) method, click at the end of the setContentView(*R.layout.activity_main*); line and press the Enter key to insert a blank line.
- To reference the tvReservation id, type **reservation = findViewById(R.id.tvReservation);** and then press the Enter key.
- To create an instance of the Button component from the XML layout, type **Button btDate = findViewById (R.id.btDate);** and then press the Enter key.
- Click Button, press Alt+Enter, and then import the class.

The Button and TextView components named btDate and tvReservation are referenced in MainActivity.java (**Figure 8-19**).

Figure 8-19 Class variables for Button and TextView components

MainActivity.java ×

```
package com.example.sailingadventures;

import ...

public class MainActivity extends AppCompatActivity {
    private TextView reservation;
    @Override
    protected void onCreate(Bundle savedInstanceState) {
        super.onCreate(savedInstanceState);
        setContentView(R.layout.activity_main);
        reservation = findViewById(R.id.tvReservation);
        Button btDate = findViewById(R.id.btDate);
    }
}
```

TextView component

Button component instantiated

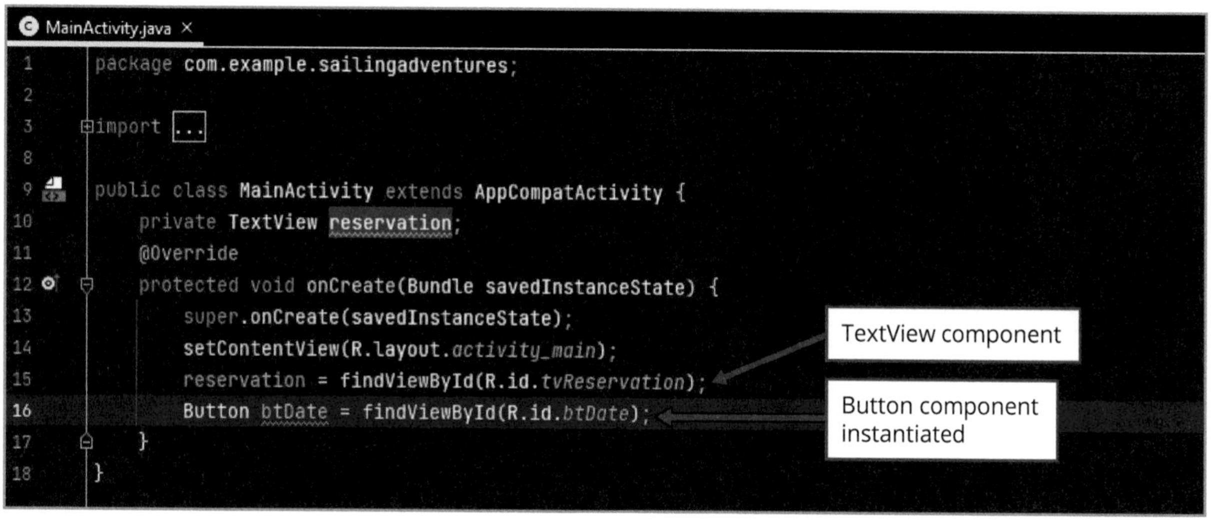

Step 3

- To create the btDate button's setOnClickListener( ) method necessary to wait for the user to click the button, type **btDate.setOnClickListener(new View.OnClickListener() {** and then press the Enter key to insert the closing brace.
- This onClickListener is designed for a Button component's variable. Click View, press Alt+Enter, and then import the class.
- Click the red error line below View.OnClickListener, press Alt+Enter, select Implement Method, and then click the OK button to add the quick fix.
- At the end of Line 23, type a right parenthesis and semicolon to complete the statement.

An onClick auto-generated stub appears in the code for the button (**Figure 8-20**).

Figure 8-20 The onClickListener( ) method for the button

MainActivity.java ×

```
package com.example.sailingadventures;

import ...

public class MainActivity extends AppCompatActivity {
    private TextView reservation;
    @Override
    protected void onCreate(Bundle savedInstanceState) {
        super.onCreate(savedInstanceState);
        setContentView(R.layout.activity_main);
        reservation = findViewById(R.id.tvReservation);
        Button btDate = findViewById(R.id.btDate);
        btDate.setOnClickListener(new View.OnClickListener() {
            @Override
            public void onClick(View v) {

            }
        });
    }
}
```

setOnClickListener( ) code stub awaiting interaction from the user

8.6 Creating a Calendar Class

The Android system date can be accessed by using the Java **Calendar class**, which is responsible for converting information between a Date object and a set of integer fields such as YEAR, MONTH, and DAY_OF_MONTH. Typically, an Android mobile device connects to a cell phone tower or wireless network, which automatically updates the time zone and date. When using the Calendar class, a method of the class called **getInstance( )** returns a calendar date or time based on the system settings. The date constants in this class are **YEAR**, **MONTH**, and **DAY_OF_MONTH**; they retrieve integer values of the system's current year, month, and day, respectively. Another Calendar constant is **DAY_OF_YEAR**, which displays the day number of the current year. For example, February 2 would be identified as the value 33 for the 33rd day of the year.

To request the local date from your computer, the following syntax creates an instance of the Calendar class named c. The Calendar class is part of the java.util.Calendar class.

Code Syntax

```
Calendar c = Calendar.getInstance( ) ;
```

Date Format

The DateFormat class in Java, as the name suggests, formats the date into a String value and is part of the java.text.DateFormat class. By default, the DateFormat class sets the date to the default long style for your country's format—for example, March 17, 2024, in the United States. If you were in France, the default format and country format for the same date would be 17 March 2024 because most countries list the day before the month.

Code Syntax

```
DateFormat fmtDate = DateFormat.getDateInstance();
```

DatePickerDialog Input

The Android platform has multiple dialog boxes that allow different types of user input. Each input dialog box has a specialized purpose; for example, the DatePickerDialog allows you to select a date from a DatePicker View, the TimePickerDialog allows you to select a time from the TimePicker View, and a ProgressDialog displays a progress bar below a message text box to show you how long a time-consuming operation is taking. In the Sailing Adventures app, a DatePickerDialog box opens when the user taps the Button object. The DatePickerDialog is launched in the onClick( ) method and must be passed the values for the current year, month, and day. The values for the current date must be set in order for the DatePicker to display today's date. When the DatePickerDialog opens, an OnDateSetListener is necessary to await the user's selection of the desired reservation date.

In the code syntax discussed earlier, notice that c is an instance of the Calendar class. The statement c.set(Calendar. YEAR, year) represents the device system's year; c.set(Calendar. MONTH, monthOfYear) represents the system's month; and c.set(Calendar.DAY_OF_MONTH, dayOfMonth) represents which day of the month is set on the system calendar. The field manipulation method called **get** accesses the system date or time, and **set** changes the current date or time.

Code Syntax

```
public void onClick(View v) {
// TODO Auto-generated method stub
 new DatePickerDialog(MainActivity.this, d,
     c.get(Calendar.YEAR), c.get(Calendar.MONTH),
     c.get(Calendar.DAY_OF_MONTH)).show();
}
```

The variable d in the code syntax is assigned later to the date selected by the user for the sailing reservation, when the OnDateSetListener is established. Just like the button listener that awaits user interaction, a second control is necessary to "listen" for the user to select a date after the dialog box displays a DatePicker component. To create an instance of the Calendar and DateFormat class and get the current date from the system calendar within the onClick( ) method, follow these steps.

Step 1

- In MainActivity.java, click to the right of the closing brace of the onCreate( ) method in Line 24 and press the Enter key.
- To create an instance of the Calendar class, type **Calendar c = Calendar.getInstance();**.
- Click Calendar, press Alt+Enter, and then import the class. If you are asked about a certain API, select the first one listed.

An instance of the Calendar class named c is created (**Figure 8-21**).

Figure 8-21 Instance of Calendar class

```
12  public class MainActivity extends AppCompatActivity {
13      private TextView reservation;
14      @Override
15      protected void onCreate(Bundle savedInstanceState) {
16          super.onCreate(savedInstanceState);
17          setContentView(R.layout.activity_main);
18          reservation = findViewById(R.id.tvReservation);
19          Button btDate = findViewById(R.id.btDate);
20          btDate.setOnClickListener(new View.OnClickListener() {
21              @Override
22              public void onClick(View v) {
23  
24              }
25          });
26      }
27      Calendar c = Calendar.getInstance( );
28  }
```

Creating an instance of the Calendar class

Step 2

- Press the Enter key and type **DateFormat Date = DateFormat.getDateInstance( );** to set the default format of the date.
- Click DateFormat, press Alt+Enter, and then import the DateFormat(java.text) class.

An instance of the DateFormat class named Date is created (**Figure 8-22**).

Figure 8-22 Format set with DateFormat

```
27      }
28      Calendar c = Calendar.getInstance( );
29      DateFormat Date = DateFormat.getDateInstance();
30  }
```

Instance of the DateFormat class

Step 3

- To display the DatePicker dialog box after the user selects the Button object, click inside the onClick(View v) { braces in Line 24.
- To show the device system's year, month, and day of the month in the DatePicker, type **new DatePickerDialog(MainActivity.this, d, c.get(Calendar.YEAR), c.get(Calendar.MONTH), c.get(Calendar.DAY_OF_MONTH)).show( );**. (Press Enter after a comma to place the code on two lines and improve visibility.)
- Import the DatePickerDialog class.

The calendar instance named c is assigned the current system date. The variable d is red. It will be assigned the date that the user selects for the sailing reservation in the next steps (**Figure 8-23**).

Figure 8-23 DatePickerDialog launched within the onClick( ) method

```
public class MainActivity extends AppCompatActivity {
    private TextView reservation;
    @Override
    protected void onCreate(Bundle savedInstanceState) {
        super.onCreate(savedInstanceState);
        setContentView(R.layout.activity_main);
        reservation = findViewById(R.id.tvReservation);
        Button btDate = findViewById(R.id.btDate);
        btDate.setOnClickListener(new View.OnClickListener() {
            @Override
            public void onClick(View v) {
                new DatePickerDialog( context: MainActivity.this, d, c.get(Calendar.YEAR),
                        c.get(Calendar.MONTH), c.get(Calendar.DAY_OF_MONTH)).show();
            }
        });
    }
    Calendar c = Calendar.getInstance( );
    DateFormat Date = DateFormat.getDateInstance();
}
```

DatePickerDialog code that opens the DatePicker dialog box; notice the d variable is red

Quick Check

What is the difference between get and set?

Answer: The field manipulation method called get accesses the system date or time, and set changes the current date or time.

8.7 Selecting the Date from the DatePickerDialog

When the app launches the DatePickerDialog component after the user taps the Button component, the Android system date is displayed, making it easier for the user to select a future date without having to move forward in a calendar from a date decades ago. To enable access to the system date, the variables are initialized and displayed for the current YEAR, MONTH, and DAY_OF_MONTH. Next, the DatePickerDialog component must await user interaction via an OnDateSetListener named d, which listens for a callback indicating that the user has filled in the reservation date.

Code Syntax

```
DatePickerDialog.OnDateSetListener d = new
DatePickerDialog.OnDateSetListener() {
}
```

8.8 Adding the onDateSet( ) Method

When the user selects a date from the DatePickerDialog, the **onDateSet( ) method** automatically obtains the date selected by the user. Three portions of the date must be set for the YEAR, MONTH, and DAY_OF_MONTH of the selected sailing reservation. The Sailing Adventures application calls the onDateSet( ) method in reaction to the user tapping the OK button at the bottom of the DatePickerDialog. Notice that earlier in the code, the get statement was used to display the current system date; set is now used to hold the selected date.

Code Syntax

```
public void onDateSet(DatePicker view, int year,
    int monthOfYear, int dayOfMonth) {
    c.set(Calendar.YEAR, year);
    c.set(Calendar.MONTH, month);
    c.set(Calendar.DAY_OF_MONTH, dayOfMonth);
}
```

The next set of steps help you code the onDateSetListener( ) and onDateSet( ) methods that respond to the user's selected date.

Step 1

- Save your work.
- At the end of the DateFormat statement (Line 32 in **Figure 8-24**), press the Enter key and type the following code on a new line:

  DatePickerDialog.OnDateSetListener d = new DatePickerDialog.OnDateSetListener( ) {
- Press the Enter key to display a closing brace.
- Type a semicolon after the closing brace to complete the statement.
- Click OnDateSetListener( ), press Alt+Enter, click Implement Method, and then click OK in the Select Methods to Implement dialog box.

The auto-generated stub for the onDateSet( ) method is displayed (Figure 8-24).

Figure 8-24 OnDateSetListener awaits the user's selection of a reservation date

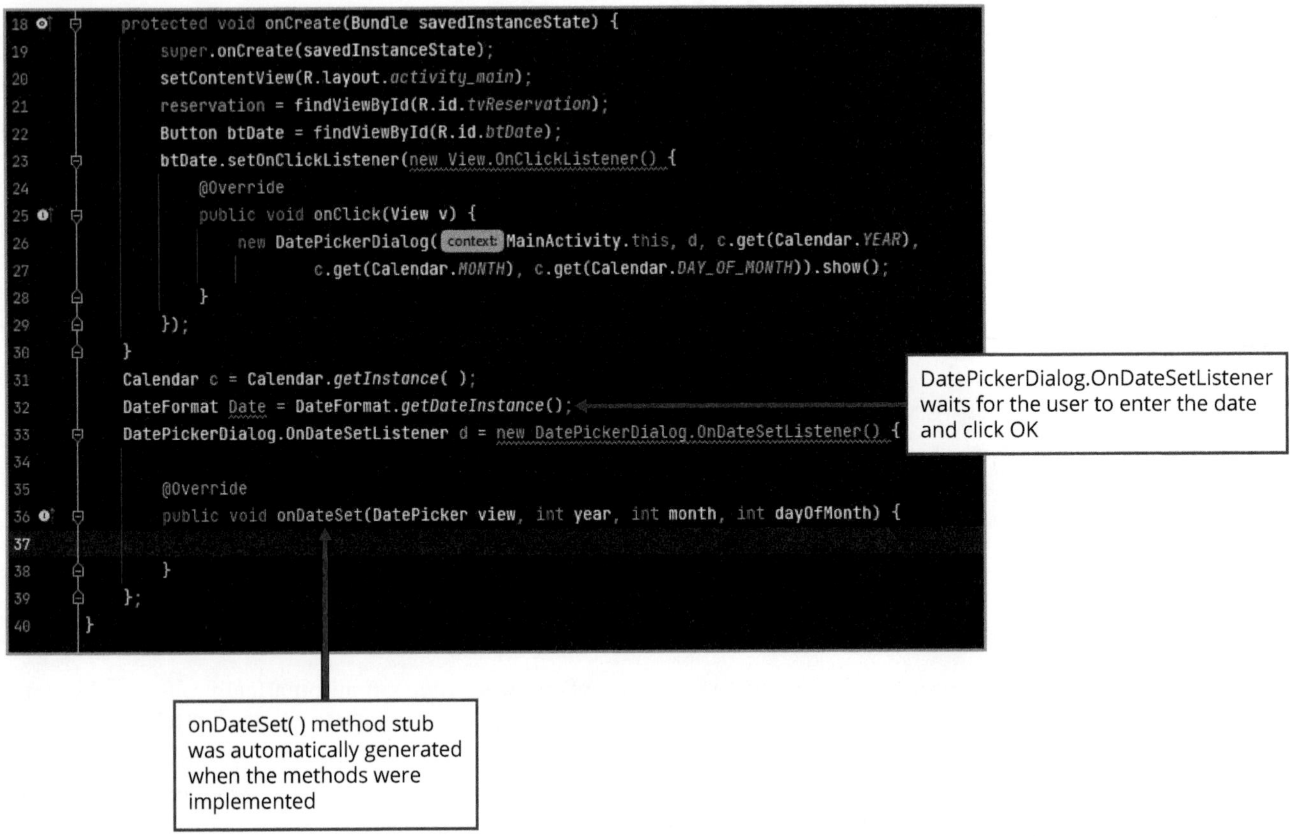

```
18    protected void onCreate(Bundle savedInstanceState) {
19        super.onCreate(savedInstanceState);
20        setContentView(R.layout.activity_main);
21        reservation = findViewById(R.id.tvReservation);
22        Button btDate = findViewById(R.id.btDate);
23        btDate.setOnClickListener(new View.OnClickListener() {
24            @Override
25            public void onClick(View v) {
26                new DatePickerDialog( context: MainActivity.this, d, c.get(Calendar.YEAR),
27                        c.get(Calendar.MONTH), c.get(Calendar.DAY_OF_MONTH)).show();
28            }
29        });
30    }
31    Calendar c = Calendar.getInstance( );
32    DateFormat Date = DateFormat.getDateInstance();
33    DatePickerDialog.OnDateSetListener d = new DatePickerDialog.OnDateSetListener() {
34
35        @Override
36        public void onDateSet(DatePicker view, int year, int month, int dayOfMonth) {
37
38        }
39    };
40 }
```

DatePickerDialog.OnDateSetListener waits for the user to enter the date and click OK

onDateSet( ) method stub was automatically generated when the methods were implemented

Step 2

- Click the blank line within the onDateSet( ) method stub, indent the line, and then type the following statements to set the desired date for the sailing reservation:

```
c.set(Calendar.YEAR, year);
c.set(Calendar.MONTH, month);
c.set(Calendar.DAY_OF_MONTH, dayOfMonth);
```

The calendar holds the selected reservation date consisting of the YEAR, MONTH, and DAY_OF_MONTH (**Figure 8-25**).

Figure 8-25 Setting the desired date for the sailing reservation

```
    Calendar c = Calendar.getInstance( );
    DateFormat Date = DateFormat.getDateInstance();
    DatePickerDialog.OnDateSetListener d = new DatePickerDialog.OnDateSetListener() {

        @Override
        public void onDateSet(DatePicker view, int year, int month, int dayOfMonth) {
            c.set(Calendar.YEAR, year);
            c.set(Calendar.MONTH, month);
            c.set(Calendar.DAY_OF_MONTH, dayOfMonth);
        }
    };
}
```

The selected date is assigned to the YEAR, MONTH, and DAY_OF_MONTH

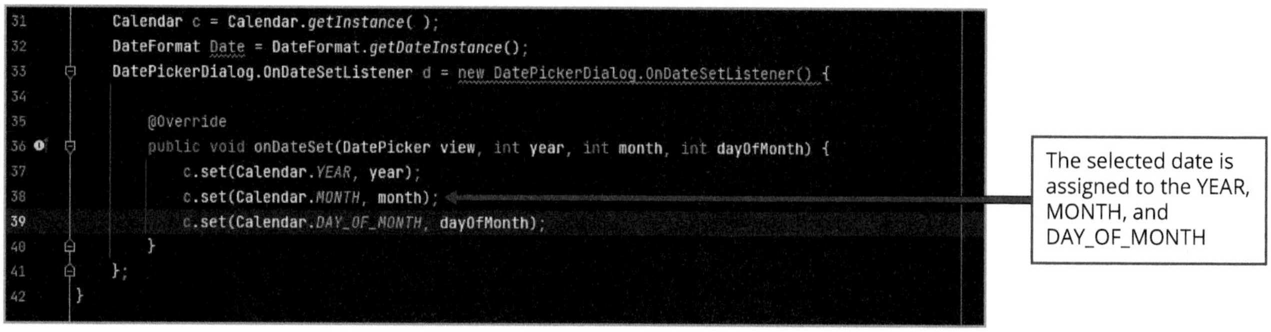

8.9 Displaying the Date Using the getTime( ) Method

After the user has selected a sailing date, the final step is to display the reservation date in the TextView object named tvReservation with the instance name of reservation. The reservation variable displays the sailing trip date in the default format named fmtDate. The **getTime( ) method** returns the time value in the Date object. The Sailing Adventures application at this point is one of many that might be part of a larger application. Typically, the application would either email the reserved date to the owners to make sure the date is available or verify the date in a connected database. The final step is to display the selected date in the TextView object.

Step 1

- Press Enter and type **reservation.setText("Your reservation is set for " + Date.format(c.getTime( )));** to display the date in the default local format of the device.
- Save your work.

The reservation is displayed in the TextView object (**Figure 8-26**).

Figure 8-26 Completed Java code for Sailing Adventures app

MainActivity.java ×

```
package com.example.sailingadventures;

import ...

public class MainActivity extends AppCompatActivity {
    private TextView reservation;
    @Override
    protected void onCreate(Bundle savedInstanceState) {
        super.onCreate(savedInstanceState);
        setContentView(R.layout.activity_main);
        reservation = findViewById(R.id.tvReservation);
        Button btDate = findViewById(R.id.btDate);
        btDate.setOnClickListener(new View.OnClickListener() {
            @Override
            public void onClick(View v) {
                new DatePickerDialog( context: MainActivity.this, d, c.get(Calendar.YEAR),
                        c.get(Calendar.MONTH), c.get(Calendar.DAY_OF_MONTH)).show();
            }
        });
    }
    Calendar c = Calendar.getInstance( );
    DateFormat Date = DateFormat.getDateInstance();
    DatePickerDialog.OnDateSetListener d = new DatePickerDialog.OnDateSetListener() {

        @Override
        public void onDateSet(DatePicker view, int year, int month, int dayOfMonth) {
            c.set(Calendar.YEAR, year);
            c.set(Calendar.MONTH, month);
            c.set(Calendar.DAY_OF_MONTH, dayOfMonth);
            reservation.setText("Your reservation is set for " + Date.format(c.getTime()));
        }
    };
}
```

Good to Know | This same program would function with a TimePicker component, Calendar.HOUR_OF_DAY and Calendar.MINUTE statements, and the TimePickerDialog method.

8.10 Adding an Android Theme

To prevent Android apps from looking too similar, the Android SDK includes multiple themes that can provide individual flair to an application. A **theme** is a style applied to an Activity or an entire application. Themes are Android's mechanism for applying a consistent style to an app or Activity on any device, including phones and tablets. The style specifies the visual properties of the elements that make up a user interface, such as color, height, padding, and font size. Some themes change the background wallpaper of the Activity, while others hide the title bar or display an action bar. Some themes display a background depending on the size of the mobile device. In the default theme for Nexus 10, the title bar shows the app name with a purple background and takes up part of the app's display. Themes can also be used for elements such as the app bar, status bar, and dialog boxes. Every user interface element in the application should follow the app's parent theme.

Figure 8-1 shows the Theme.Design.NoActionbar theme, which displays a light theme without a title bar on the tablet emulator. In **Figure 8-27**, the current Sailing Adventures app would display the default theme with a title bar that

Figure 8-27 Sailing Adventures app running in emulator

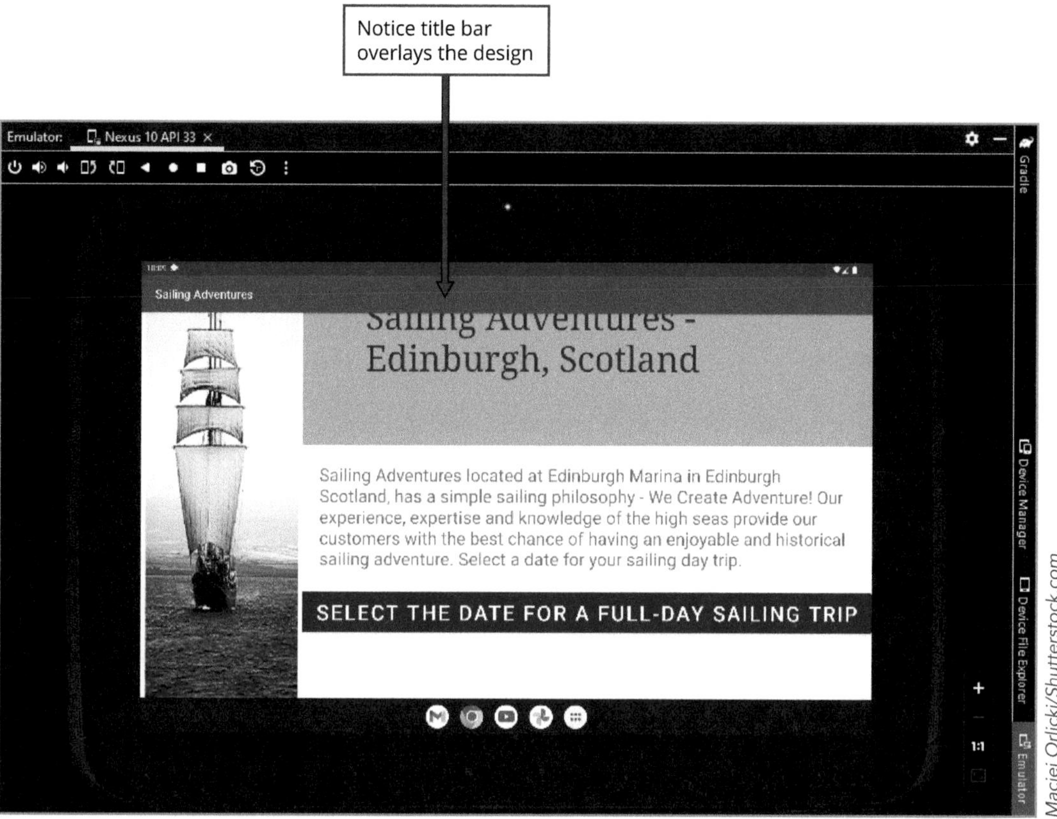

is too prominent at the top of the tablet app. Themes can be selected in the Design layout of themes.xml for viewing and then coded in XML, which in turn updates the AndroidManifest.xml file.

Popular themes for smartphones and tablets are light and transparent; their sheerness allows you to see the starting home screen through the background. **Figure 8-28** displays an AppCompat theme and the AppCompat.light theme, which appears in the title bar and dialog boxes.

Figure 8-28 Android theme examples

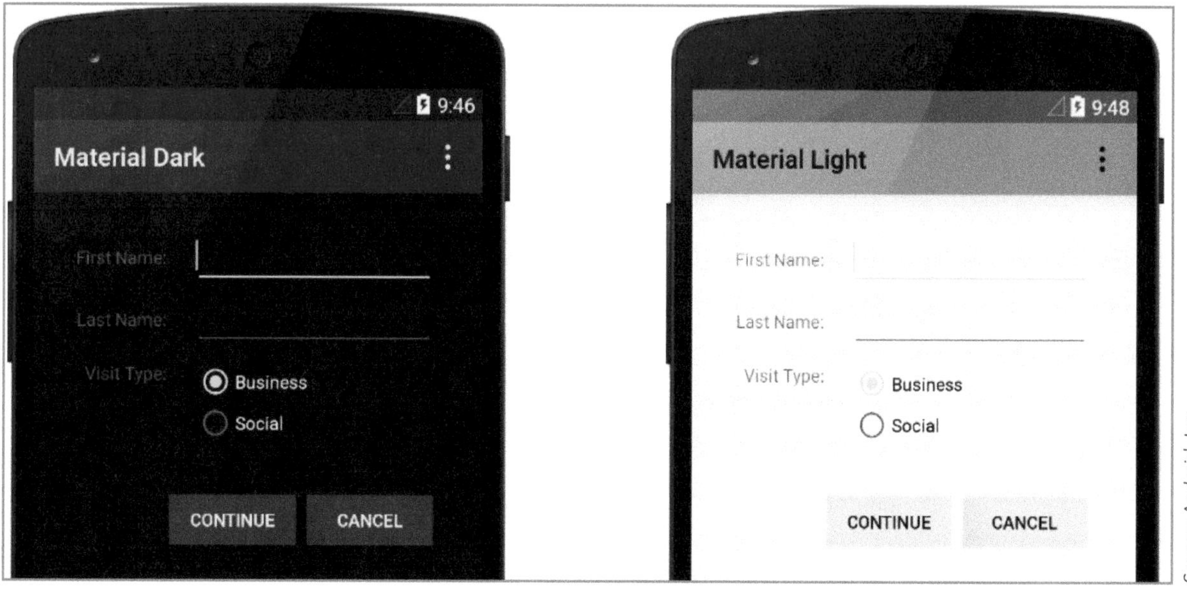

Changing a Theme

By changing the theme in the Design emulator in the activity_main.xml file, you can preview what the new theme looks like, but to change it permanently in the application, you must define themes in the themes.xml file, which is in the values subfolder for the Activity. After you place the theme in the styles.xml file, Android Studio updates the AndroidManifest.xml file to include the new theme. You can add a predefined system theme or a customized theme of your own design.

At this point, the theme appears only in the activity_main.xml graphical layout as a preview for design purposes. To display the theme in the finished application, you must update the styles.xml file in the res/values folders to include the change in the theme layout. A theme is a style applied to an entire app rather than to an individual layout file. **Table 8-2** displays a few samples of XML code for common themes.

Table 8-2 XML code for common themes

Theme Code in themes.xml	Description
<style name="AppTheme" parent="Base.Theme.AppCompat">	Black background, gray title bar
<style name="AppTheme" parent="Base.Theme.AppCompat.Light">	White background, gray title bar
<style name="AppTheme" parent="Theme.Design.NoActionBar">	White background, no title bar

After you add the new theme name to the XML code in the styles.xml file, Android Studio updates the AndroidManifest.xml file to include the new base application theme throughout all the Activities. To update the theme for the app within the themes.xml file, follow these steps.

Step 1

- In the Android project view, expand the values subfolder and themes subfolder and then double-click the first themes.xml file.
- Click after the first quotation mark following parent= " and delete the current theme within the quotes.
- After the first quotation mark, type **Theme.Design.NoActionBar**, allowing auto-complete to assist in spelling the theme name correctly.

The Android theme is updated within the Activity in the themes.xml file (**Figure 8-29**).

Figure 8-29 The themes.xml file

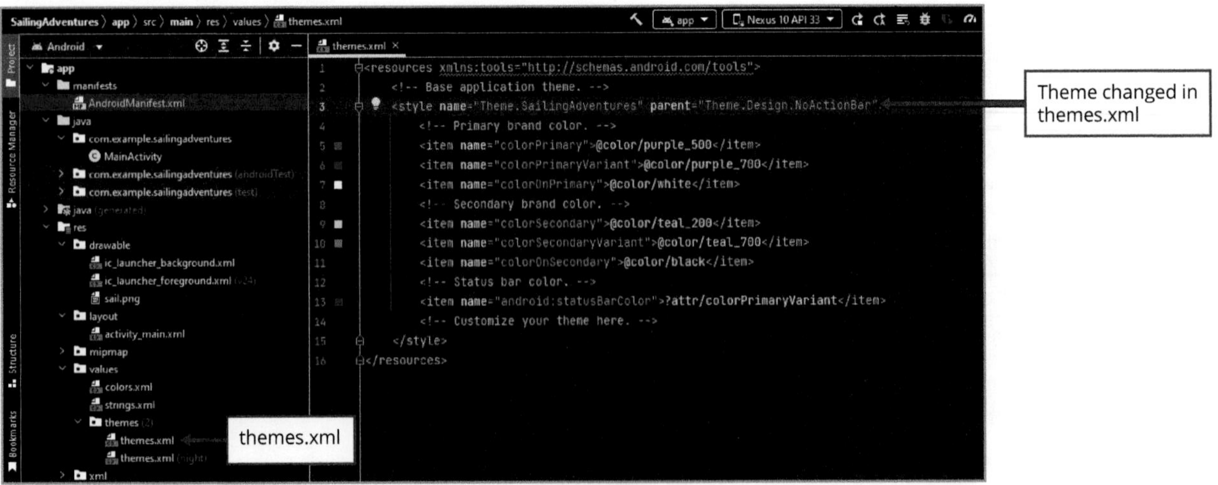

Step 2

- Close the themes.xml tab and click the Save All button on the Standard toolbar.

Quick Check

In which file do you change the theme of the app?

Answer: The themes.xml file.

Running and Testing the Application

It's time to reserve your day trip using the Sailing Adventures app. Click Run on the menu bar and then select Run to save and test the application in the tablet emulator. Choose the tablet AVD you set up earlier and then wait for the app to load. The application opens in the tablet 10.1-inch emulator window, where you can test the Button and DatePicker components in the Sailing Adventures app, as shown in Figures 8-1, 8-2, and 8-3.

Good to Know | Windows 11 now allows Android apps to be downloaded from the Microsoft Store. Mobile apps can now run on smartphones, tablets, laptops, and desktop computers.

Wrap It Up—Chapter Summary

This chapter described the steps to create a tablet application on a screen much larger than a phone screen. Creating a calendar component is a common specification on many Android applications. This same DatePicker application would also work with a smaller Android phone window using a different design. Your Android app, whether it is displayed on a phone or tablet, should strive to combine beauty, simplicity, and purpose to create a magical experience that is effortless to the end user.

- When designing apps for an Android tablet, keep your users' objectives and the size of the device in mind.
- To use an Android emulator designed for tablets, you first add an AVD configuration appropriate for a tablet.
- You can combine a Linear layout and a Table layout to create a simple, clean layout that takes advantage of a tablet's width. The TableLayout contains TableRow components—one for each row in your table in activity_main.xml. In each TableRow, you can insert a view component such as a Button or TextView.
- You can display a calendar tool called a DatePicker component in a dialog box so users can select a date from the component. The Time & Date category in the Palette contains many calendar components, including TimePicker, DatePicker, CalendarView, Chronometer, AnalogClock, and DigitalClock. In the chapter project, the user taps or clicks the button to launch a dialog box that includes a coded DatePicker widget displaying today's date.
- To access and display the current system date when the DatePicker component opens, you use the YEAR, MONTH, and DAY_OF_MONTH class variables.
- To create a DatePickerDialog instance, you must create an onDateSetListener( ) method to await user interaction. If you include a component such as a Button that users tap to display a calendar, use the setOnClickListener( ) method to implement the Button. The onClick( ) method responds to the user's action, so you place the code to launch the DatePicker dialog box in the onClick( ) method.
- When a dialog box containing a DatePicker appears, users can select a date and tap a Button component. Tapping the Button invokes an onDateSetListener in a DatePickerDialog, which passes integers representing the year, month, and day from the DatePicker into onDateSet( ). The selected date can then be displayed in a TextView component using the setText( ) and getTime( ) methods.

Key Terms

Calendar class
DatePicker
DAY_OF_MONTH
DAY_OF_YEAR
dialog
emulated application
get
getInstance( )
getTime( ) method
MONTH
native application
onDateSet( ) method
padding property
set
TableLayout
theme
typeface
YEAR

Developer FAQs

1. Explain the difference between a native app and a webpage. (8.2)
2. What is the range of the diagonal measurement of Android tablet screens? (8.2)
3. What is the diagonal size of the iPad screen? (8.2)
4. Describe the three most common activities for an Android phone that were mentioned in this chapter. (8.2)
5. How do the activities in question 4 differ from how one would typically use a tablet? (8.2)
6. Which Android AVD was first designed specifically for tablets? Identify the name and version. It is used for the minimum required SDK. (8.3)
7. What is IoT? (8.1)
8. In an XML table layout, what is the XML code name of each row? (8.4)
9. True or False: A LinearLayout and TableLayout cannot be used in the same XML layout file. (8.4)
10. Write the single line of XML code to set the padding to 32 density independent pixels. (8.4)
11. Write the single line of XML code to set text to the font family of sans serif. (8.4)
12. Name six calendar components. (8.5)
13. If a date is displayed as 9/30/2024 in the United States, how would that same date be displayed in Europe? (8.5)
14. Why is it best to use a dialog box for a DatePicker component? (8.5)
15. Which method retrieves the selected date of the DatePicker? (8.9)
16. In themes.xml, what would the XML parent code be if you wanted an AppCompat.Light theme? (8.10)
17. Write a line of code that, for the calendar instance named cal, assigns dueDay to the day of the month. (8.6)
18. Write the date for New Year's Eve before the year 2025 using the default format of your locale. (8.5)
19. Write a line of code that, for the calendar instance named c, assigns currentHour to the hour of the day. (8.6)
20. Write a line of code that, for the calendar instance named c, assigns currentMinute to the most recent minute. (8.6)

Beyond the Book

Search the web for answers to the following questions to further your Android knowledge.

1. Research Android tablet design. Find five design tips not mentioned in the chapter and describe them using complete sentences.
2. Research five popular Android calendar apps available in Google Play. Write a paragraph about the purpose of each one.
3. In the information technology field, Gartner, Inc., is considered one of the world's leading research and advisory companies. Research Gartner's opinion on the growth of the tablet. Locate a recent article by Gartner and write a summary of at least 150 words on the tablet trend.
4. The Android style guide at *http://developer.android.com/design* provides a foundation in Android best practices. Create a bulleted list of 15 best practices from this site.

Case Programming Projects

Complete one or more of the following case programming projects. Use the same steps and techniques taught within the chapter. Successful completion of these projects requires knowledge of all chapter learning objectives. Submit the program(s) you create to your instructor. The level of difficulty is indicated for each case programming project.

Case Project 8–1: Appalachian Trail Festival Tablet App (Beginner)

Requirements Document

Application title: Appalachian Trail Festival Tablet App

Purpose: The Appalachian Trail Festival would like an Android tablet app that displays a title and event description. When the user taps a button, a calendar appears and allows the user to reserve a ticket for the festival. The date is then shown as available for reservation.

Algorithms:

1. The opening tablet screen displays an image, a title, an event description, and a button to create a reservation for a day at the festival (**Figure 8-30**).
2. When the user taps the button, a DatePicker is displayed in a dialog box. The dialog box allows the user to select a date for attending the year-long festival. The selected date is shown on the opening screen (**Figure 8-31**).
3. Change the theme to Theme.AppCompat.NoActionBar.

Conditions:

1. The picture named hike.png is provided with your student files.
2. Write your own description of the festival.
3. Research the hexadecimal color for red.
4. Use the Theme.Black theme.
5. Use a Table layout with four rows within a Linear layout.

Figure 8-30 Appalachian Trail Festival tablet app

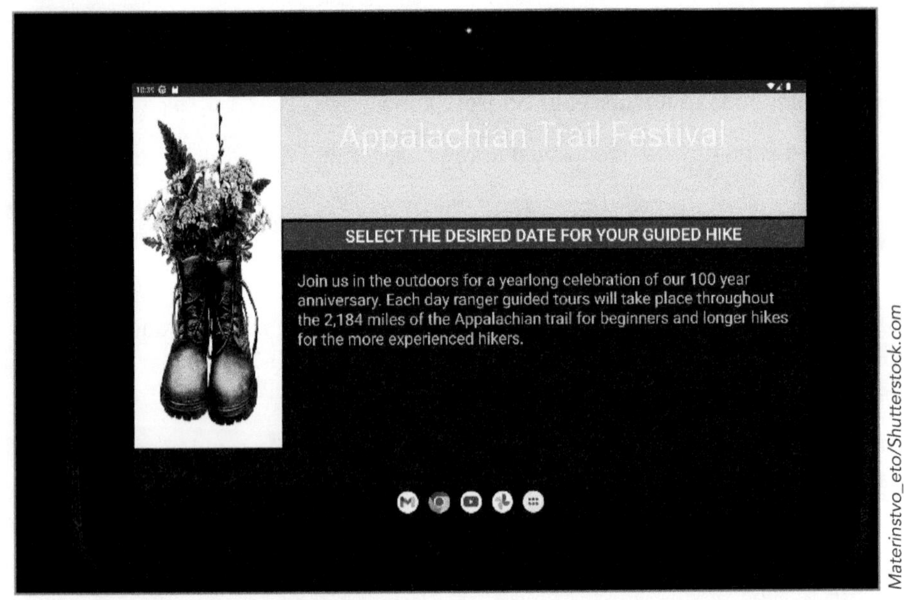

Materinstvo_eto/Shutterstock.com

Figure 8-31 App displays the reservation

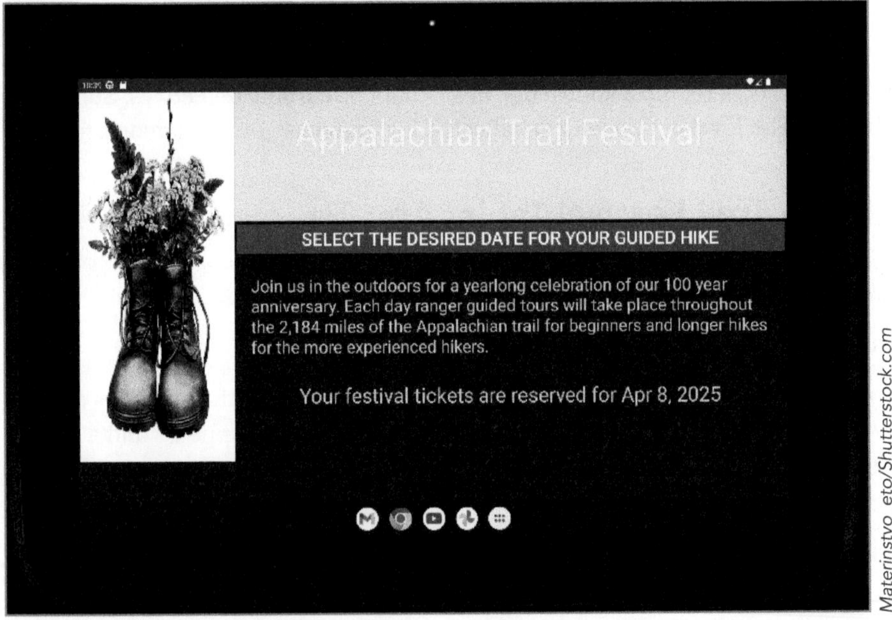

Materinstvo_eto/Shutterstock.com

Case Project 8–2: The Dog Sledding Experience Tablet App (Beginner)

Requirements Document

Application title:	The Dog Sledding Experience Tablet App
Purpose:	The Dog Sledding Experience tablet app provides a reservation button for selecting a date to sign up for the full-immersion experience of a one-day dog sledding trip in Alaska.
Algorithms:	**1.** The opening screen displays an image, a title, a trip description, and a button that launches a DatePicker dialog box (**Figure 8-32**). **2.** When the user taps the button, a DatePicker component is displayed in a dialog box (**Figure 8-33**). The dialog box sets and confirms the date of the reservation.

Figure 8-32 The Dog Sledding Experience tablet app

BlueOrange Studio/Shutterstock.com

Figure 8-33 Calendar confirms the date of the reservation

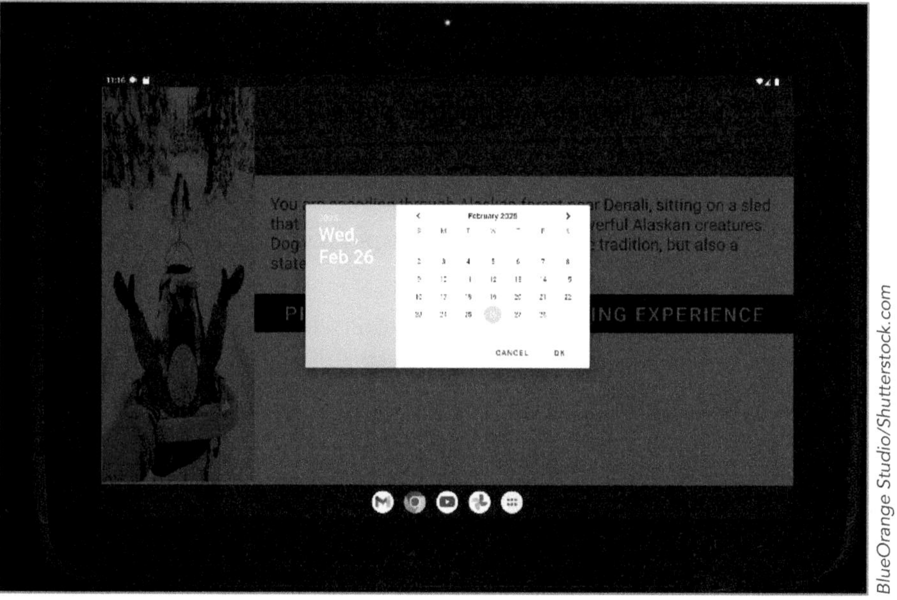

BlueOrange Studio/Shutterstock.com

Conditions:

1. A picture of the dog sledding experience, sled.png, is provided with your student files.
2. Write your own description of the sledding experience.
3. Select your own colors and font.
4. Use the theme Theme. MaterialComponents.Light.NoActionBar.

Case Project 8–3: Country Cabin Rental Tablet App (Intermediate)

Requirements Document

Application title:	Country Cabin Rental Tablet App
Purpose:	The Country Cabin Rental realty agency provides cabins for rental. Two cabins are available for a minimum three-night stay.
Algorithms:	**1.** The opening screen displays an image, cabin descriptions, two radio button components with different cabin names, and a button that launches a DatePicker dialog box. **2.** When the user taps the button, a DatePicker component is displayed in a dialog box. The user selects the first night of a three-night reservation. The dialog box displays the date range of the three-night reservation with the name of the selected cabin.
Conditions:	**1.** Find an appropriate picture on the web. **2.** Write your own descriptions of the cabins. **3.** Do not use the default theme. **4.** Only one radio button can be selected at a time. **5.** Use a Table layout.

Case Project 8–4: Final Touch Auto Detailing Tablet App (Intermediate)

Requirements Document

Application title:	Final Touch Auto Detailing Tablet App
Purpose:	Final Touch Auto Detailing provides a variety of detailing services. The company wants an app that lists each service and its price and then displays a calendar for making a service reservation.
Algorithms:	**1.** The opening screen displays an image, service descriptions, four check boxes offering different detailing services at different prices, and a button that launches a DatePicker dialog box for making a service reservation. **2.** When the user taps the button, a DatePicker component is displayed in a dialog box. The user selects the date for the reservation. The dialog box displays the date and final cost of the detailing services.
Conditions:	**1.** Select your own image(s). **2.** Write your own descriptions about the car detailing services. **3.** Do not use the default theme. **4.** More than one check box can be checked at once. **5.** Use a Table layout.

Case Project 8–5: Wild Ginger Dinner Delivery Tablet App (Advanced)

Requirements Document

Application title: Wild Ginger Dinner Delivery Tablet App with TimePicker

Purpose: The Wild Ginger Dinner Delivery service delivers dinners in the evening. The business wants an app that customers can use to select a dinner and reserve a delivery time.

Algorithms:

1. The opening screen displays an image, a Wild Ginger food description, and a button that launches a TimePicker dialog box so users can make a reservation for delivery tonight.
2. When the user taps the button, a TimePicker component is displayed in a dialog box. The user selects the time for delivery and the app confirms the delivery time, which is available only from 5:00 pm to 11:00 pm.

Conditions:

1. Select your own image(s).
2. Write your own description of the great food offered at Wild Ginger.
3. Do not use the default theme.
4. Use a Table layout.

Case Project 8–6: Create Your Own Tablet App (Advanced)

Requirements Document

Application title: Create Your Own Tablet App

Purpose: Create an app with a DatePicker and a TimePicker that allows a user to create a reservation.

Algorithms:

1. Create an app on a topic of your choice.
2. Use two buttons. The first button allows the user to select the reservation date and the second allows the user to select the time.

Conditions:

1. Select your own image(s).
2. Use a custom layout and icon.

Chapter 9

Customize! Navigating with a Primary/Detail Flow Activity on a Tablet

Learning Objectives

At the completion of this chapter, you will be able to:

- **9.1** Describe responsive design for Android apps
- **9.2** Create an Android tablet project using an application template
- **9.3** Use the Primary/Detail Flow template
- **9.4** Modify the Primary/Detail Flow template
- **9.5** Design an XML TableLayout
- **9.6** Add a WebView component
- **9.7** Customize the content of the sample template file
- **9.8** Display a custom layout in the detail pane

9.1 Understanding Responsive Design

Creating an attractive user interface that provides simple navigation can be challenging when programming an Android app for a tablet, phone, and other mobile devices. Fortunately, the Android platform provides a flexible way to simplify layout and navigation using built-in Android templates. To construct apps that automatically fit a device, you need design elements such as fluid grids and flexible images that can adapt to various screen sizes. Instead of creating a number of rigid XML layouts heavily optimized to a number of predefined screen sizes, built-in templates are available for using the best presentation mode based on the size of the device. Like multiple windows, multipane layouts can be used to show different topics within a single window in an intuitive interface.

In this chapter, you use an Android Studio template to create a multipane interface in an Android application that provides information about a European bike and barge cruise vacation. Bike and barge cruises combine two popular ways of exploring Europe—cycling and river cruising. On a bike and barge experience, you spend your days cycling through historic European sites and your nights cruising down scenic rivers through cities such as Amsterdam and Budapest. The Bike and Barge application shown in **Figure 9-1** features a three-item list containing Photos, Tour, and Website items. When the app first opens, the item list is displayed in the left pane and the right pane is blank.

Figure 9-1 Opening screen of the Bike and Barge tablet app

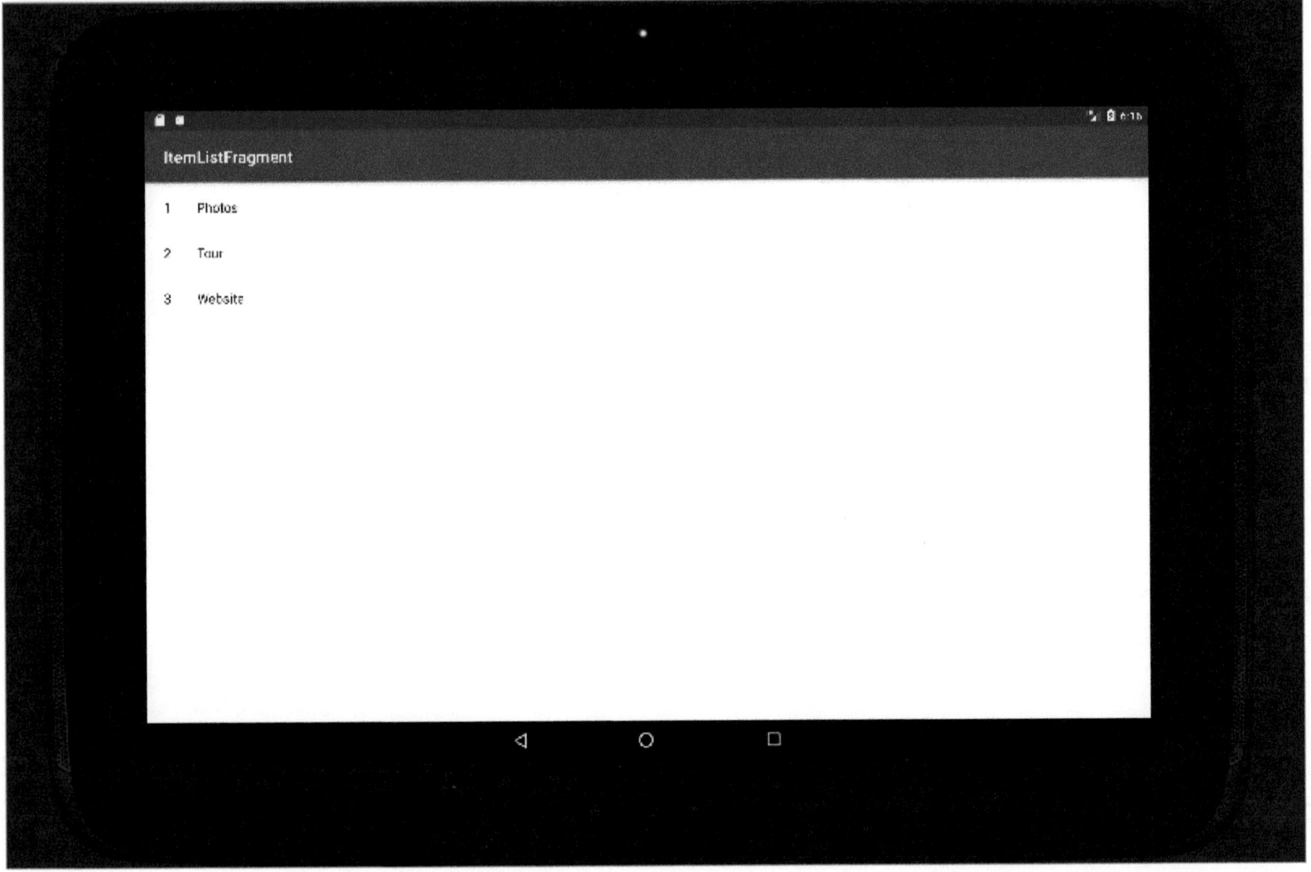

This Android tablet app provides images, text, and a link that opens a webpage within the Android browser. If the user selects Photos, which is the first item in the left pane, a TableLayout displays three images with text descriptions in the right pane, as shown in **Figure 9-2**. When the user taps Tour, the second list item on the left, the item details in the right pane change to display tour information, as shown in **Figure 9-3**. Website, the third list item, links to a browser that displays the full Bike and Barge website, including tour company contact information, as shown in **Figure 9-4**. The intuitive list items eliminate the need for additional navigation instructions.

Figure 9-2 Selecting Photos in the left pane

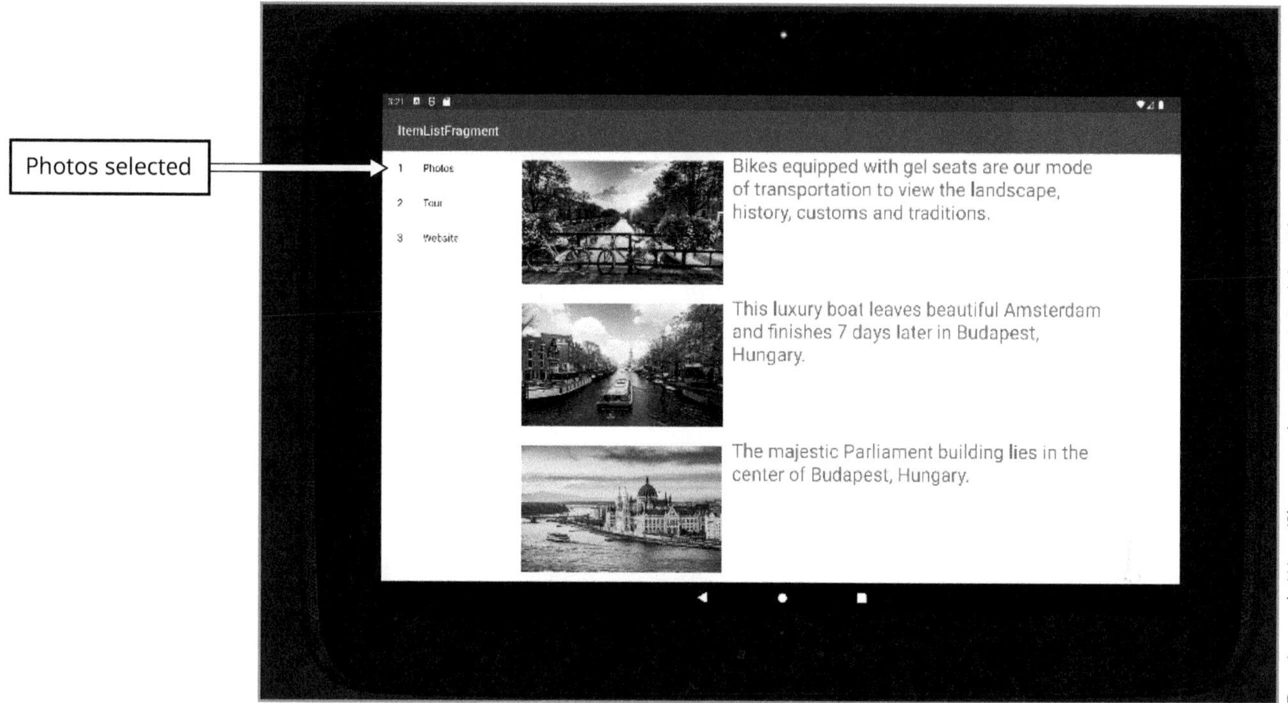

Dennis van de Water/Shutterstock.com, Prasit Rodphan/Shutterstock.com, Andrew Mayovskyy/Shutterstock.com

Figure 9-3 Selecting Tour in the left pane

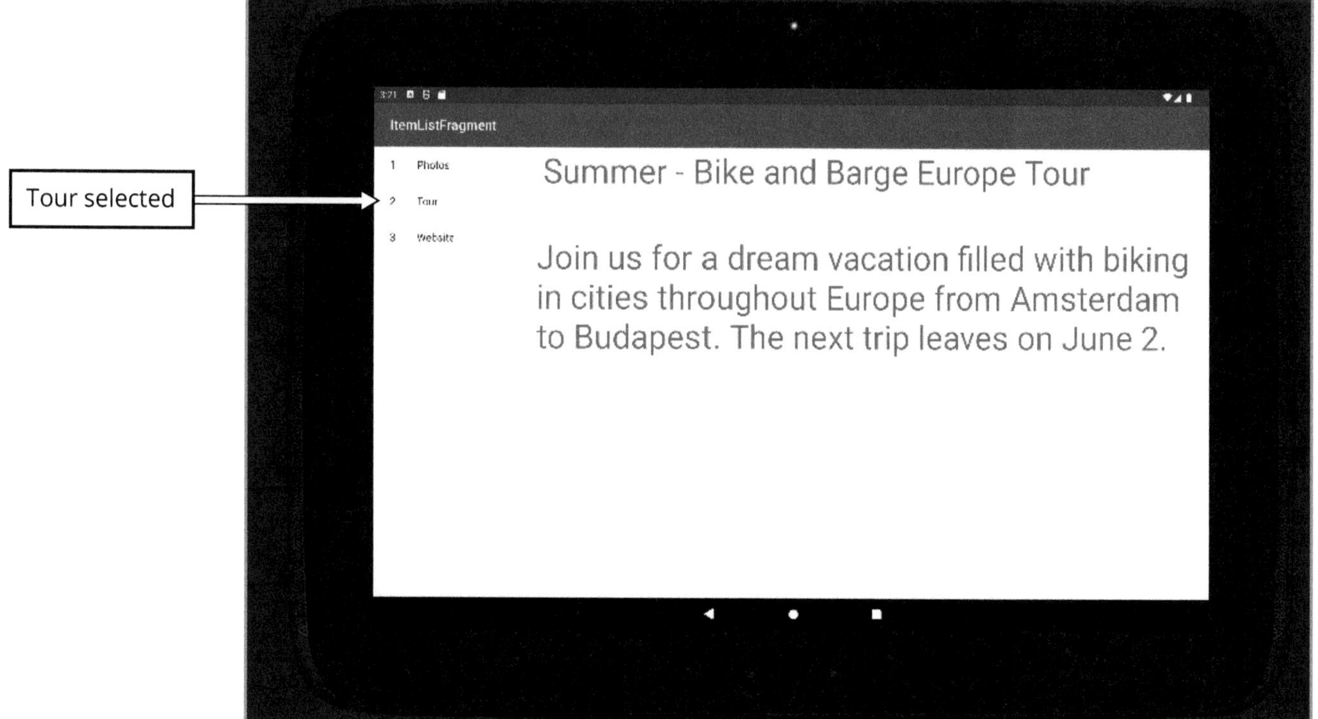

Figure 9-4 Selecting Website in the left pane

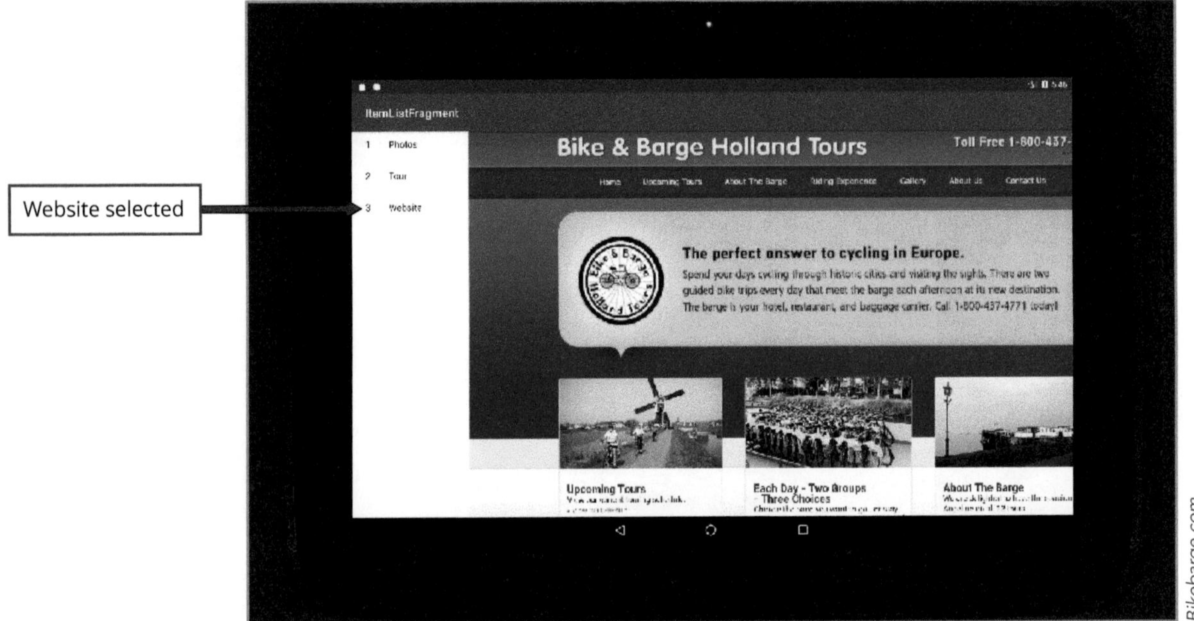

Bikebarge.com

> **Good to Know**
>
> Cycling apps already in Google Play include GPS-based biking routes, personal cycling logs, mountain biking trails, bike repair instructions, distance tracking, and cycling fitness tips to use on your trip. In addition, these apps can often be used on Android watches.

To create this application, the developer must understand how to perform the following processes, among others:

1. Create an application with a Primary/Detail Flow template.
2. Add the images to the drawable folder.
3. Add text to the String table.
4. Create the photos.xml file using a TableLayout for the detail pane of the first list item.
5. Create the tour.xml file for the detail pane of the second list item.
6. Change the default TextView component to a WebView component.
7. Update the AndroidManifest file to include an Internet permission.
8. Customize the PlaceholderContent class to display the item list.
9. Customize the PlaceholderContent class to connect the app to the website.
10. Modify the ItemDetailFragment.java class to:
    a. Display photos.xml in the detail pane.
    b. Display tour.xml in the detail pane.
    c. Display a website in a browser.

> **Good to Know**
>
> Watch out for that stretched-out look! On tablets, single-pane layouts lead to awkward white space and excessive line lengths. Use padding to reduce the width of user interface elements and consider using multipane layouts.

Creating Apps with Responsive Design

When mobile devices were first developed, the apps displayed simple text content designed for small screens, but the tablet and smartphone landscape can now handle complicated processes and full web access. This design approach is especially true for the Android platform. Instead of developers creating apps for multiple sizes of Android devices, apps and webpages should be developed once for a wide range of displays. **Responsive design** is an approach to designing apps and websites that provides an optimal viewing experience across as many devices as possible. Similarities between webpages and Android apps do not end with screen sizes. When building for the web, designers also have to take into account multiple browsers and multiple versions of each one. Responsive design uses code that automatically adjusts the design to different screens based on their sizes and resolutions. This approach allows you to have a smooth experience with a webpage regardless of whether you are viewing it on a wide desktop monitor or a small mobile screen.

Earlier in this book, you learned to use scalable pixels to change the size of text or margins as appropriate for the device resolution, but more tools are necessary for a complete approach to designing for all device sizes. To assist with responsive design in recent Android API versions, Android Studio has added responsive design templates, which allow you to build the app once but display it on multiple devices. You can run the Bike and Barge app on a smartphone emulator, as shown in **Figure 9-5**, without any change in code. The first screen shows the list of items. If you select Website, a separate Activity is displayed on the smartphone to show the Bike and Barge website.

Figure 9-5 The Bike and Barge app runs as two Activities on a smartphone

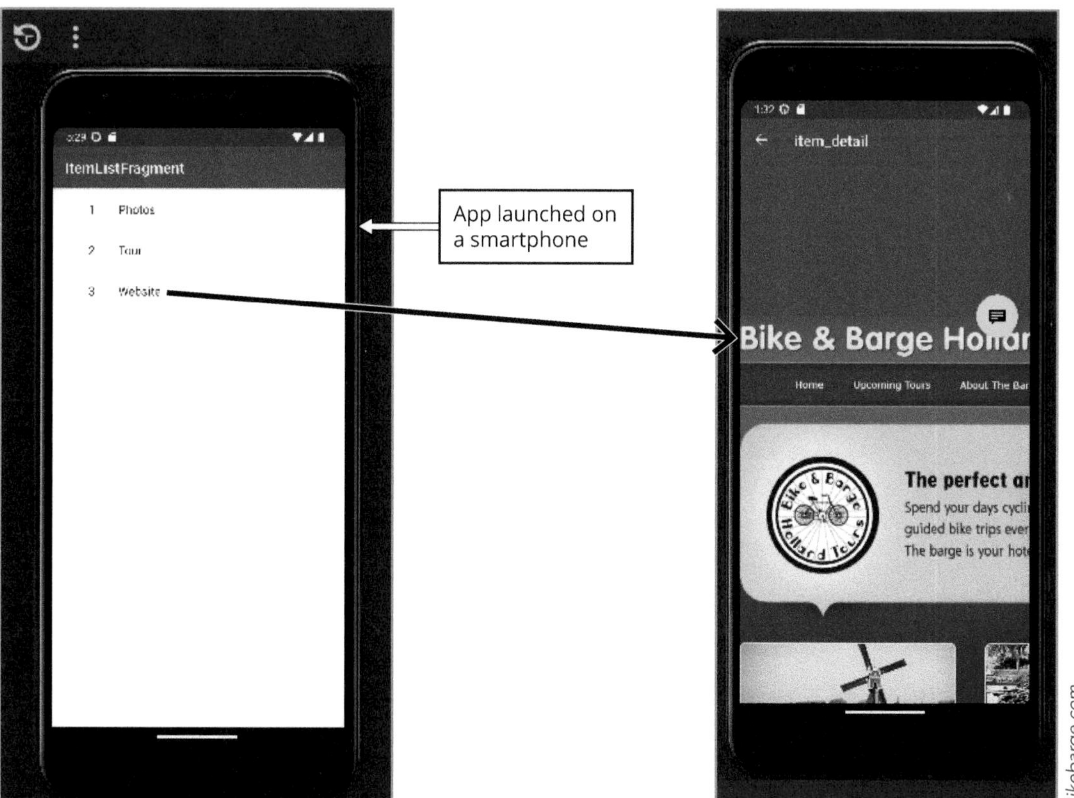

Good to Know Adobe Dreamweaver Creative Cloud is the most popular tool for building responsive-design websites.

9.2 Creating an Android Tablet Project Using an Application Template

The Android Studio software development kit provides tools for quickly creating apps that follow the Android design and development guidelines and include code that can be customized to the exact needs of your app. These tools are called **application templates**; you use them to create basic Android applications that you can immediately run and test on an Android device of any size. Android templates are available when you create a new Android project, as shown in **Figure 9-6**. Throughout this text, you have selected the Empty Activity, but in this chapter's project app, you use the Primary/Detail Flow application template.

Figure 9-6 Android application templates

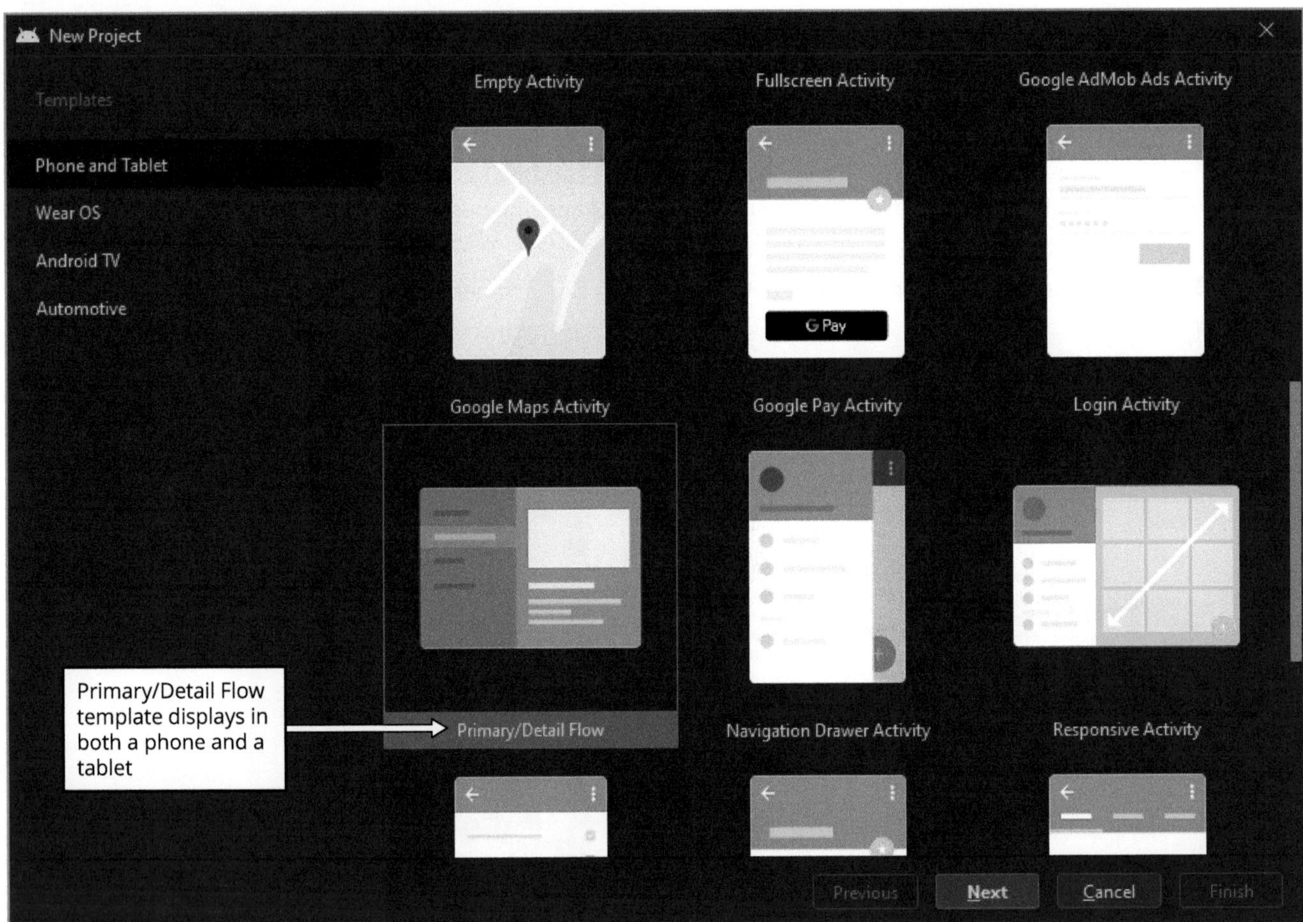

> **Good to Know**
>
> Another Android template that is similar to Primary/Detail Flow is the Navigation Drawer Activity. This template creates a Basic Activity with a navigation drawer menu. The floating navigation bar expands from the left or right side of your app and appears in addition to the regular app bar.

9.3 Using the Primary/Detail Flow Template

The Bike and Barge tablet app features an opening screen with three list items on the left, as shown in Figure 9-1. List items function as they do in a framed browser window. A menu of list items on the left side of a browser window displays webpage content for the selected item using intuitive navigation on the right side of the page. You can switch between items on the list to display new content without opening more browser windows. The **Primary/Detail Flow template** creates an adaptive, responsive layout for a set of list items and associated detail content. A Primary/Detail Flow is an interface design concept in which a list of items called the Primary list appears in a narrow vertical pane along the left edge of the screen. Without any customization, the Primary/Detail Flow template (**Figure 9-7**) can be displayed on a tablet or a smartphone. On a tablet, the Primary list appears in a narrow vertical pane along the left edge of the screen. The item details are displayed on the right side of the tablet screen in the wider detail pane. This arrangement is referred to as a two-pane layout. The Primary/Detail Flow template is considered a responsive screen design. On a smaller device, the list and details are displayed on separate screens when you select a list item. On a tablet device, the item list and item details are displayed on the same screen. This project will modify the default Primary/Detail Flow template with minimal coding.

Figure 9-7 Primary/Detail Flow template on a tablet and a smartphone

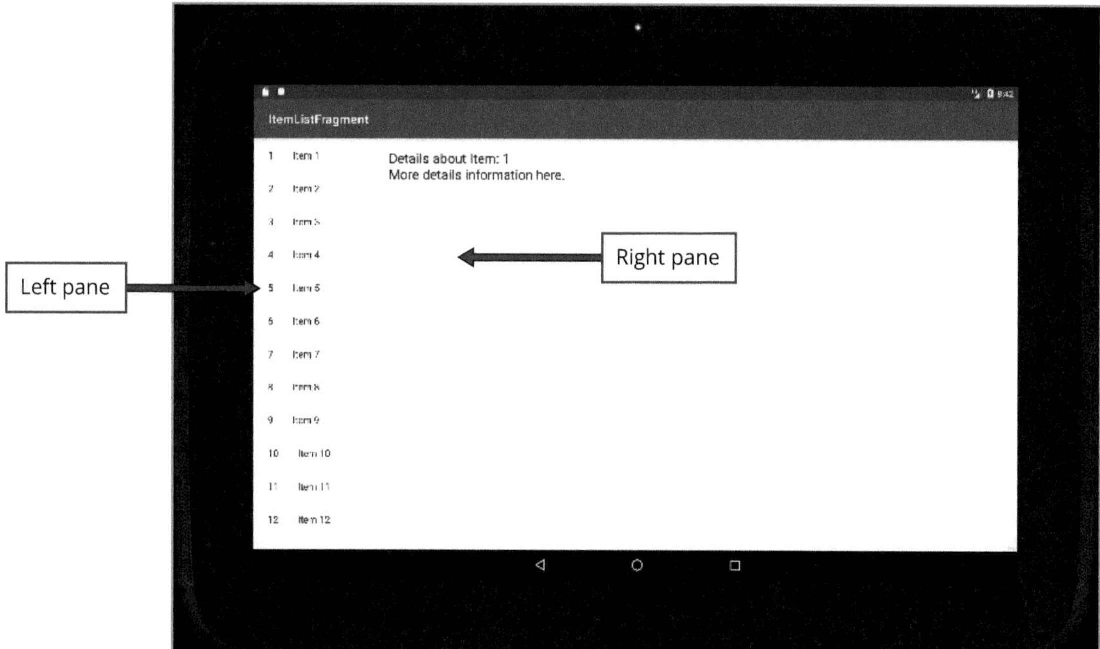

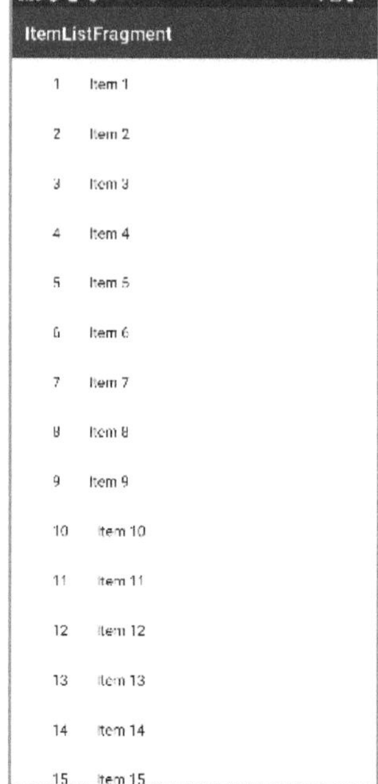

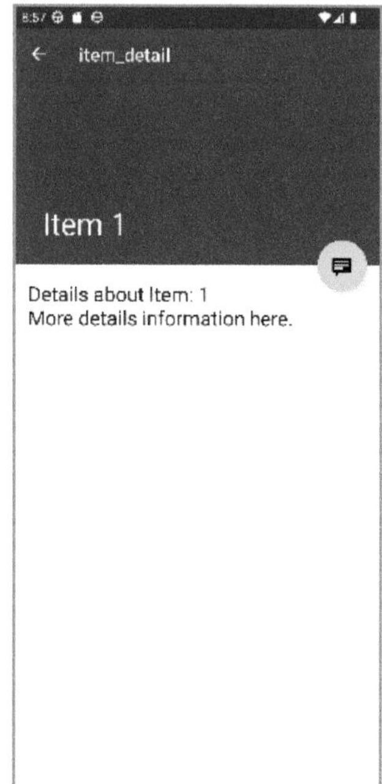

Critical Thinking

What are examples of other types of list items for the left pane of the Primary/Detail Flow template?

A list can include items such as news stories, songs, movies, pets, or homes for sale. When the list item is selected, the details for the specific item are displayed in the right pane.

To begin the application using the Primary/Detail Flow template on the tablet, follow these steps.

Step 1

- Open the Android Studio program.
- In the Welcome to Android Studio window, click the New Project button.
- Scroll down and select the Primary/Detail Flow template in the list of Activities.

The Primary/Detail Flow template is selected (**Figure 9-8**).

Figure 9-8 Selecting the Primary/Detail Flow template

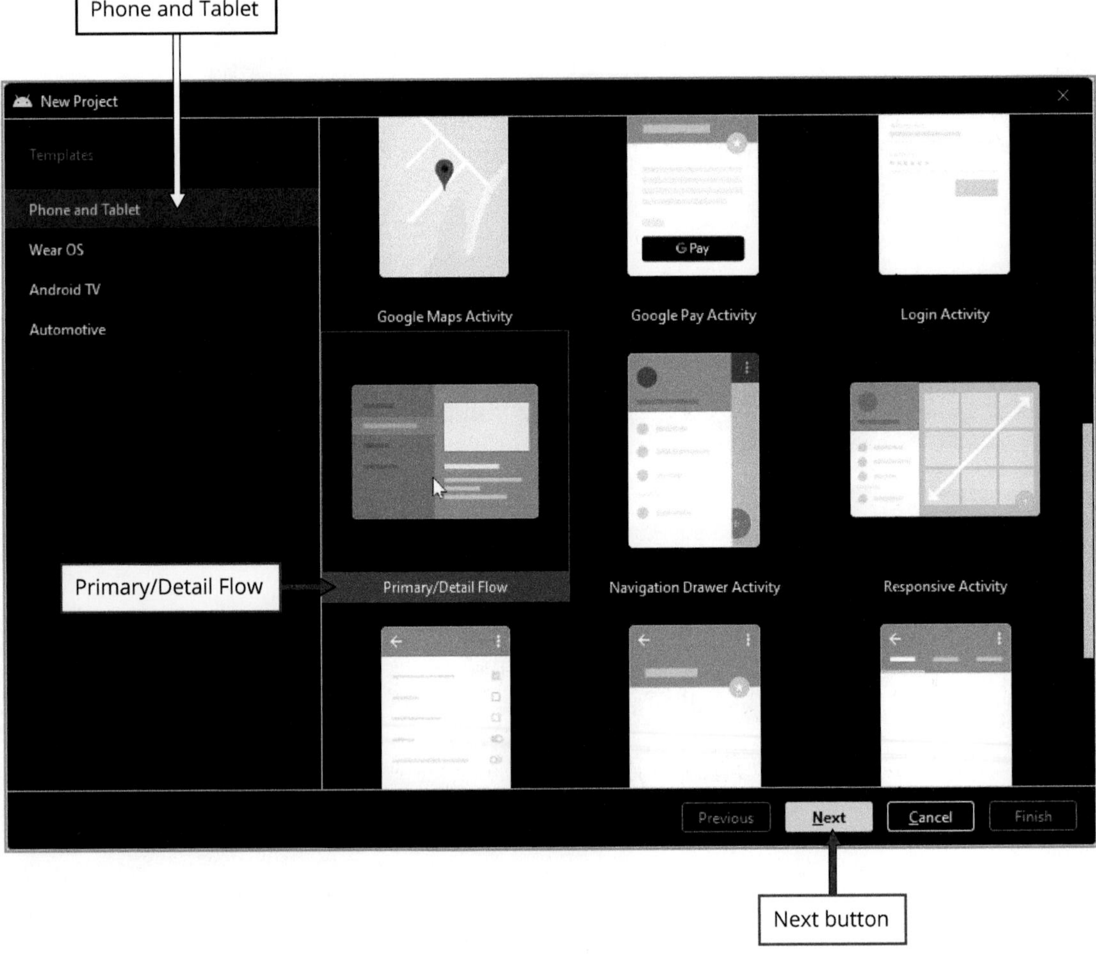

Step 2

- Click the Next button.
- Type **Bike and Barge** in the Name text box.
- If necessary, select Java in the Language text box.
- If necessary, select API 23: Android 6.0 (Marshmallow) in the Minimum SDK text box.

The new Bike and Barge project has a package name and a Primary/Detail Flow template (**Figure 9-9**).

Figure 9-9 Creating the Bike and Barge Android app

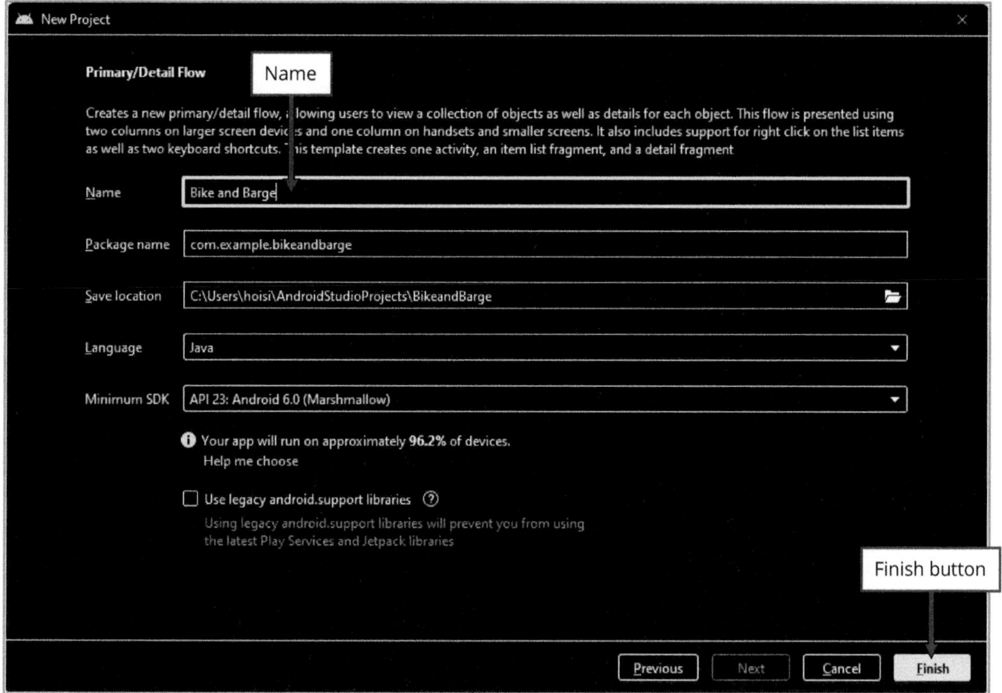

Step 3

- Click the Finish button to create the new application based on the Primary/Detail Flow template.
- Click the Device for Preview (D) arrow and then select Tablet.
- Expand the java folder in the left pane of the Android project and expand the com.example.bikeandbarge subfolder.

The new Bike and Barge project with a Primary/Detail Flow template is displayed for preview on a tablet (**Figure 9-10**).

Figure 9-10 Template code files in the java folder

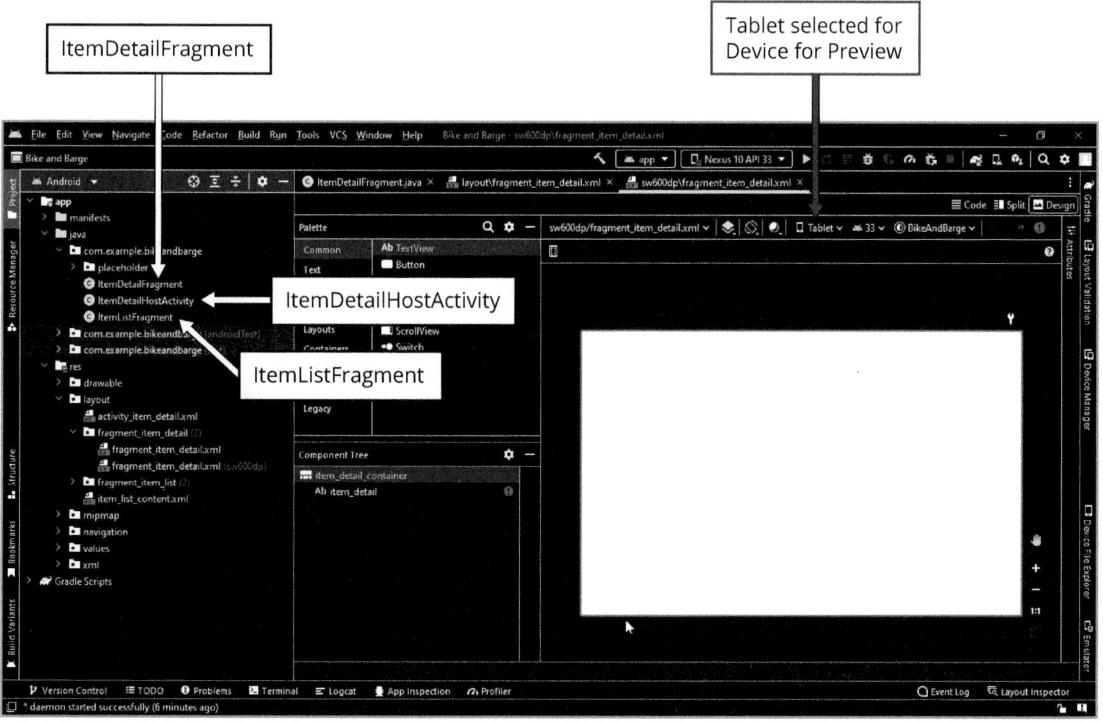

Quick Check

Typically, this book has used the Empty Activity template for its chapter projects. Which template is being used in this chapter project?

Answer: Primary/Detail Flow.

9.4 Modifying the Structure of the Primary/Detail Flow Template

When the Bike and Barge app is created, as shown in Figure 9-10, Android Studio adds a number of Java and XML layout resource files automatically. Each of the Java and layout files in the Primary/Detail Flow template has a specific purpose, as described in the following lists. Most of these files will not be altered in the development of the Bike and Barge app.

Java Files

- *ItemDetailFragment.java*: The purpose of this class is to display the fragment_item_detail.xml layout file. This class can be customized to determine which detailed items to display.
- *ItemDetailHostActivity.java*: The purpose of this class is to display the activity_item_detail.xml layout file if a smartphone is detected.
- *ItemListFragment.java*: The purpose of this class is to display the activity_item_list.xml layout file.

Layout Files

- *activity_item_detail.xml*: When a smartphone is detected, the app uses this layout to display the FrameLayout instance.
- *fragment_item_detail.xml*: This file is used when a smartphone is detected; the app uses this layout to display the Primary list fragment.
- *fragment_item_detail.xml (sw600dp)*: This file is used when a tablet is detected; the app is displayed in a two-pane layout containing both the Primary item list fragment and the item detail container.
- *item_list_content.xml*: When a smartphone or a tablet is detected, this layout file displays the detail pane using the onCreateView( ) method.

9.5 Designing an XML TableLayout

Before designing the XML layouts, first place three images in the drawable folder and then reference them in the photos.xml layout. To add the images for this project, follow this step.

Step 1

- Open the folder containing the student files.
- To add the three image files to the drawable resource folder, select bike.png, barge.png, and budapest.png, and then press Ctrl+C to copy the files.

- Right-click the drawable folder and then click Paste.
- Click the OK button in the Copy dialog box.

Copies of the three files appear in the drawable folder (**Figure 9-11**).

Figure 9-11 Image files for the Bike and Barge app

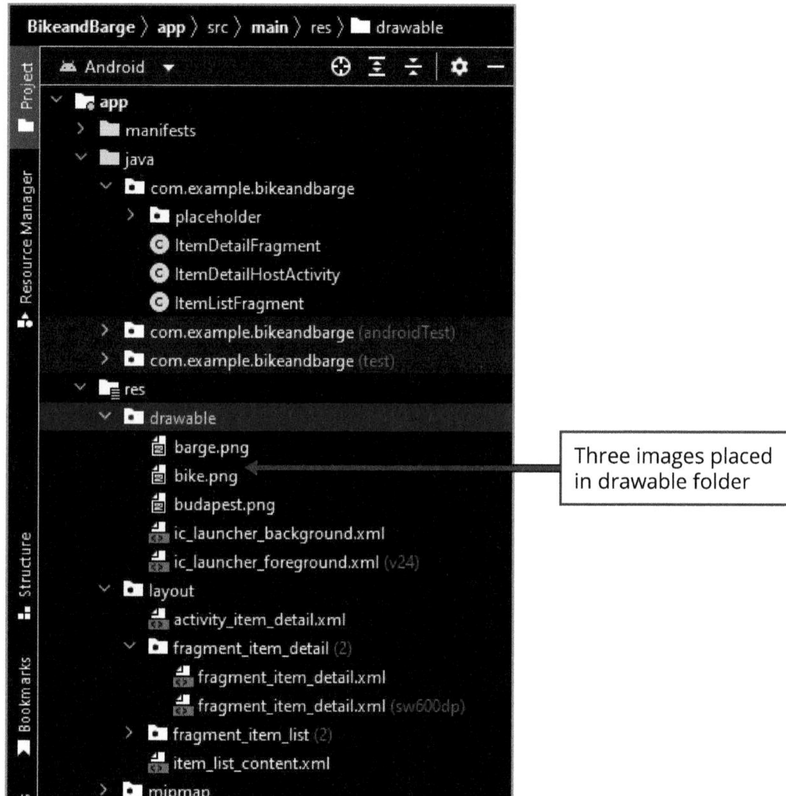

When the user selects the first list item in the Bike and Barge app, three images are displayed in a table: a bike in Amsterdam, a barge passenger boat on the Danube River, and the Parliament building in Budapest. Each image has a text description in an XML TableLayout, as shown in Figure 9-2. In Android Studio, a TableLayout can be used to arrange images and text in rows and columns, just like a table in Microsoft Word or Google Docs. Each row within a TableLayout is associated with a TableRow instance, which is divided into cells. In the chapter project, you create this layout in a new layout resource file named photos.xml.

Critical Thinking

How can I create a wider TableRow within a TableLayout?

The size of each TableRow is determined by the size of the text or image placed within the TableRow. If you want a TableRow to be wider, change the size of the text or image.

The String table, which is responsible for the text displayed in the app, has two initial strings in the template. The first string is named app_name and is displayed in the title bar of the tablet. By default, the string's value is set to Bike and Barge, the application name. The second string is named title_item_detail and is displayed in the title bar of a smaller device, such as a smartphone. By default, this string's value is set to Item Detail, but the text should be changed to Bike and Barge to create a consistent experience whether someone is using a tablet or smartphone. An image description appears for each of the three images in the app. To create a String table for the text descriptions necessary throughout the app and to code the XML layout for photos.xml, follow these steps.

Step 1

- In the Android Project view, expand the values folder within the res folder.
- Double-click the strings.xml file to display its contents.
- Click the Open editor link.
- Click title_item_detail in the String table and change the text in the Default Value text box to **Bike and Barge**.
- Click the Add Key button.
- In the Key text box, type **tvBike** to name the string.
- In the Default Value text box, type **Bikes equipped with gel seats are our mode of transportation to view the landscape, history, customs and traditions.**
- Click the OK button and then click the Add Key button.
- In the Key text box, type **tvBarge** to name the string.
- In the Default Value text box, type **This luxury boat leaves beautiful Amsterdam and finishes 7 days later in Budapest, Hungary.**
- Click the OK button and then click the Add Key button.
- In the Key text box, type **tvBudapest** to name the string.
- In the Default Value text box, type **The majestic Parliament building lies in the center of Budapest, Hungary.**
- Click the OK button and then click the Add Key button.
- In the Key text box, type **tvTitle** to name the string.
- In the Default Value text box, type **Summer - Bike and Barge Europe Tour**.
- Click the OK button and then click the Add Key button.
- In the Key text box, type **tvInfo** to name the string.
- In the Default Value text box, type **Join us for a dream vacation filled with biking in cities throughout Europe from Amsterdam to Budapest. The next trip leaves on June 2.**
- Click the OK button and then click the Add Key button.
- In the Key text box, type **description** to name the string.
- In the Default Value text box, type **Bike and Barge Image**.
- Click the OK button and then save your work.

The keys and default values of the TextView components are entered into the Translations Editor (**Figure 9-12**). Note that the Default Value column was expanded in the figure to show the text.

Figure 9-12 String table for the Bike and Barge app

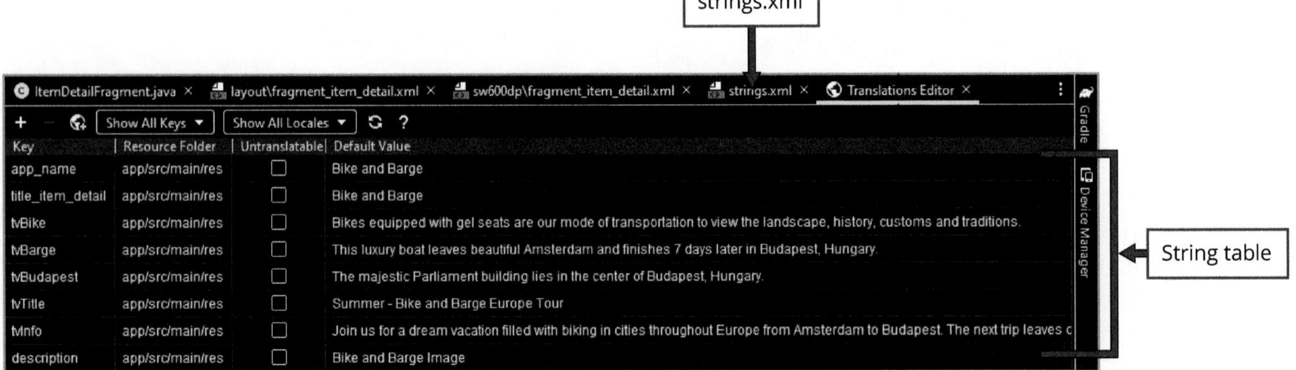

Step 2

- Close the Translations Editor and the strings.xml tabs.
- In the Android project view, collapse the drawable and values subfolders.
- Right-click the layout folder, click New on the shortcut menu, and then click Layout resource file to open the New Resource File dialog box.
- In the File name text box, type **photos.xml** to name the layout file.
- In the Root element text box, type **TableLayout**.

The XML file is named photos.xml and the layout is set to TableLayout (**Figure 9-13**).

Figure 9-13 The photos.xml TableLayout created

Step 3

- Click the OK button to create an XML layout file named photos.xml.
- Click the Orientation for Preview (O) button and then select Landscape to display the emulated tablet in landscape mode.
- Click the Code button of photos.xml to display the XML code.

The photos.xml code is displayed (**Figure 9-14**).

Figure 9-14 TableLayout in XML Code view

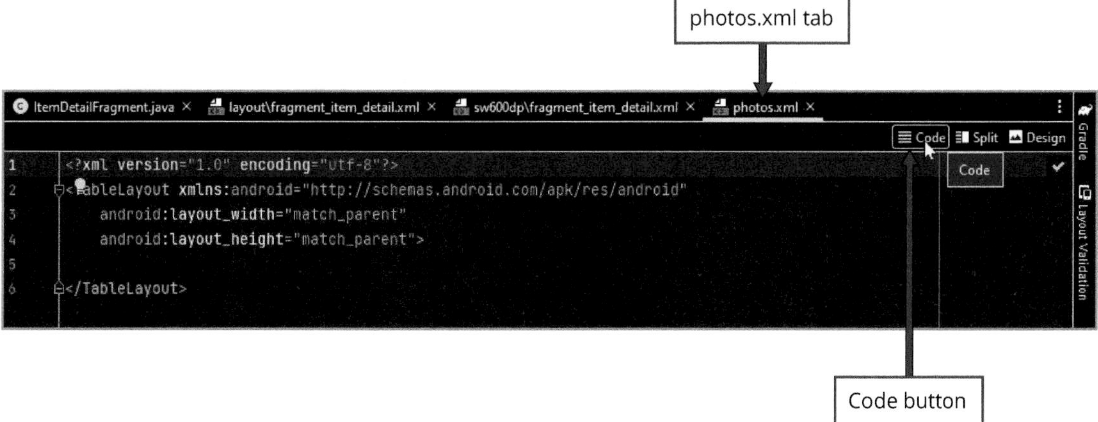

Step 4

- Starting on Line 5 of photos.xml, type the following code to add a table row that displays an image and text:

```
<TableRow>
<ImageView
    android:id="@+id/ivBike"
    android:contentDescription="@string/description"
    android:layout_width="wrap_content"
    android:layout_height="wrap_content"
    android:src="@drawable/bike"
    android:padding="15sp" />
<TextView
    android:layout_width="600dp"
    android:layout_height="wrap_content"
    android:text="@string/tvBike"
    android:textSize="30sp" />
</TableRow>
```

A table row displays an ImageView and TextView component in the TableLayout (**Figure 9-15**).

Figure 9-15 First row of the TableLayout

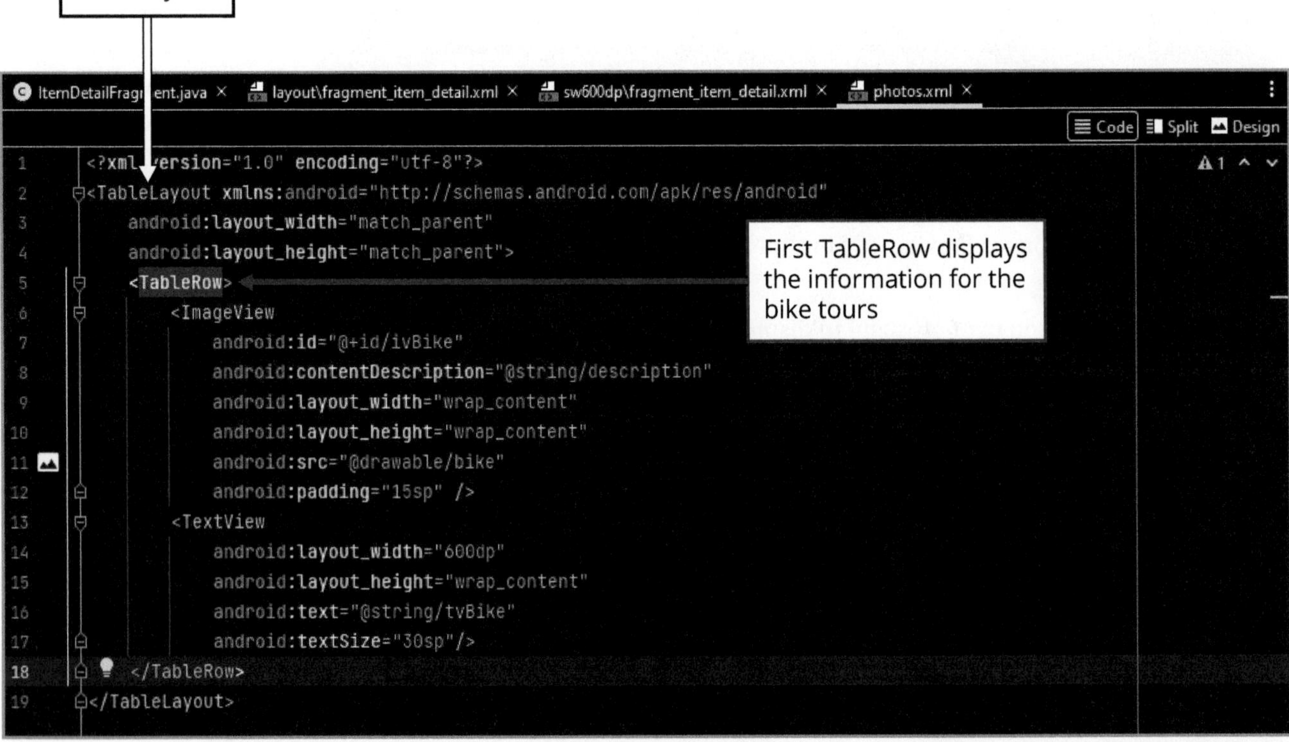

Step 5

- Copy the TableRow commands from Step 4, paste them two times in the photos.xml code, and then customize the new commands to match the following code:

```
<TableRow>
<ImageView
    android:id="@+id/ivBarge"
    android:contentDescription="@string/description"
    android:layout_width="wrap_content"
    android:layout_height="wrap_content"
    android:src="@drawable/barge"
    android:padding="15sp" />
<TextView
    android:layout_width="600dp"
    android:layout_height="wrap_content"
    android:text="@string/tvBarge"
    android:textSize="30sp" />
</TableRow>
<TableRow>
<ImageView
    android:id="@+id/ivBudapest"
    android:contentDescription="@string/description"
    android:layout_width="wrap_content"
    android:layout_height="wrap_content"
    android:src="@drawable/budapest"
    android:padding="15sp" />
<TextView
    android:layout_width="600dp"
    android:layout_height="wrap_content"
    android:text="@string/tvBudapest"
    android:textSize="30sp" />
</TableRow>
```

The second and third table rows display more ImageView and TextView components in the TableLayout (**Figure 9-16**).

Step 6

- Click the Design button in photos.xml.
- Click the Save All button on the Standard toolbar.

The TableLayout is displayed in the emulator for photos.xml (**Figure 9-17**).

Figure 9-16 Second and third rows of the TableLayout

```
    <TableRow>
        <ImageView
            android:id="@+id/ivBarge"
            android:contentDescription="@string/description"
            android:layout_width="wrap_content"
            android:layout_height="wrap_content"
            android:src="@drawable/barge"
            android:padding="15sp" />
        <TextView
            android:layout_width="600dp"
            android:layout_height="wrap_content"
            android:text="@string/tvBarge"
            android:textSize="30sp"/>
    </TableRow>
    <TableRow>
        <ImageView
            android:id="@+id/ivBudapest"
            android:contentDescription="@string/description"
            android:layout_width="wrap_content"
            android:layout_height="wrap_content"
            android:src="@drawable/budapest"
            android:padding="15sp" />
        <TextView
            android:layout_width="600dp"
            android:layout_height="wrap_content"
            android:text="@string/tvBudapest"
            android:textSize="30sp"/>
    </TableRow>
</TableLayout>
```

Second TableRow displays information about the barge

Third TableRow displays information about Budapest

Figure 9-17 Completed TableLayout in photos.xml in Design view

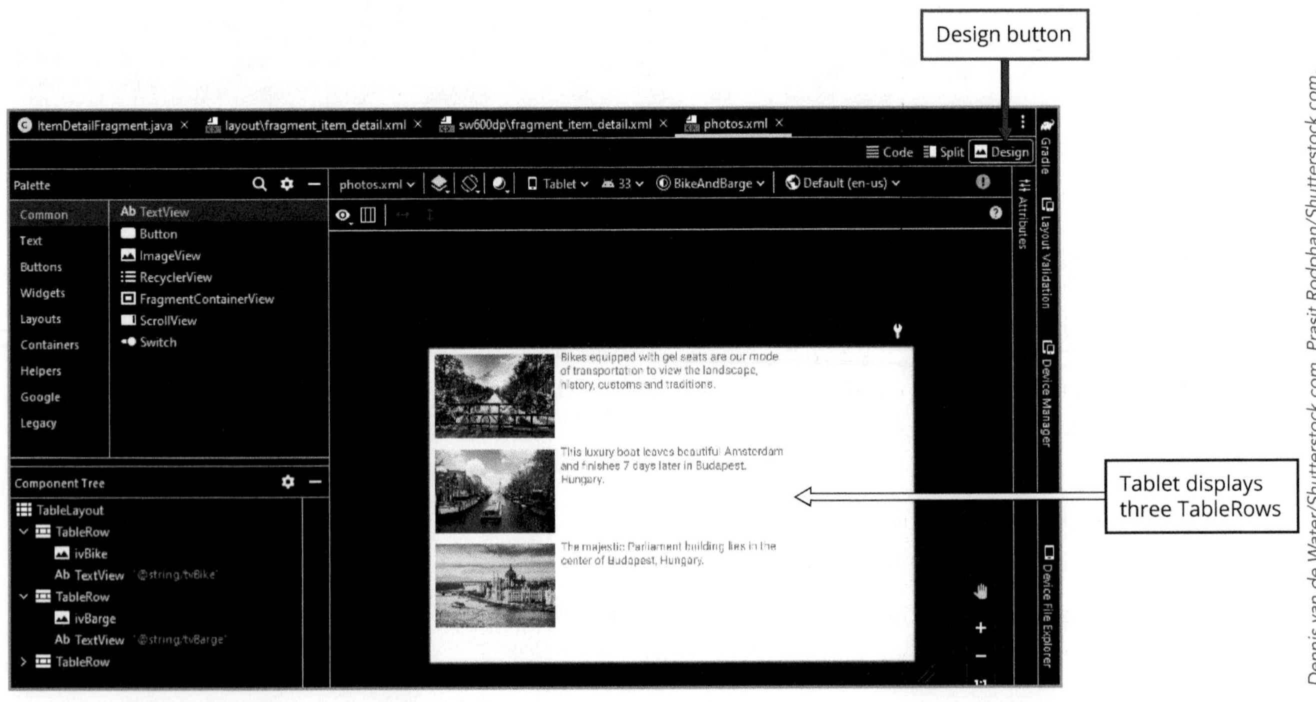

Dennis van de Water/Shutterstock.com, Prasit Rodphan/Shutterstock.com, Andrew Mayovskyy/Shutterstock.com

Creating a TextView XML Layout for the Second List Item

For the second list item of the Bike and Barge app, two TextView components display tour details within a LinearLayout. To create an XML layout file that displays two TextView components, follow these steps.

Step 1

- Close the photos.xml tab.
- In the Android project view, press and hold or right-click the layout folder, click New on the shortcut menu, and then click Android resource file to open the New Resource File dialog box.
- In the File name text box, type **tour.xml** to name the layout file.
- Click the OK button to create an XML layout with a default LinearLayout and open the emulator window.
- Click the Orientation for Preview (O) button and then select Landscape to display the emulated tablet in landscape mode.
- Click the Code button of tour.xml to display the XML code.
- Starting on Line 6, type the following XML code for the first TextView component, using auto-completion as much as possible:

```
<TextView
    android:id="@+id/tvTitle"
    android:layout_width="wrap_content"
    android:layout_height="wrap_content"
    android:text="@string/tvTitle"
    android:textSize="50sp"
    android:paddingStart="50sp"
    android:paddingBottom="60sp" />
```

The first TextView component is coded in tour.xml with a LinearLayout (**Figure 9-18**).

Figure 9-18 LinearLayout for tour.xml

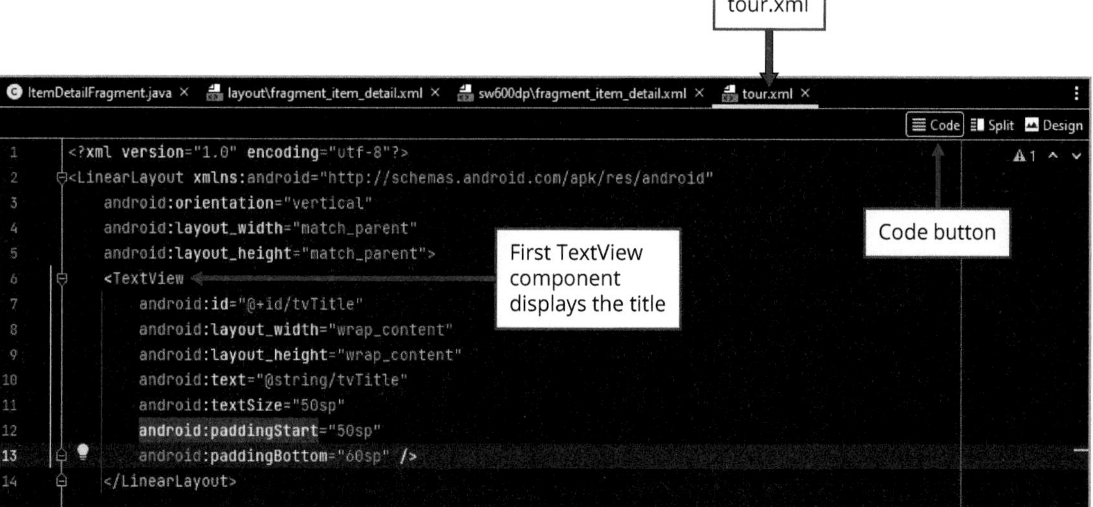

Step 2

- Press the Enter key and then type the following XML code for the second TextView component, using auto-completion as much as possible:

```
<TextView
    android:id="@+id/tvInfo"
    android:layout_width="1100dp"
    android:layout_height="wrap_content"
    android:paddingLeft="40sp"
    android:paddingRight="40sp"
    android:text="@string/tvInfo"
    android:textSize="50sp" />
```

- Save your work.

The second TextView component is coded in tour.xml (**Figure 9-19**).

Figure 9-19 Second TextView component in tour.xml

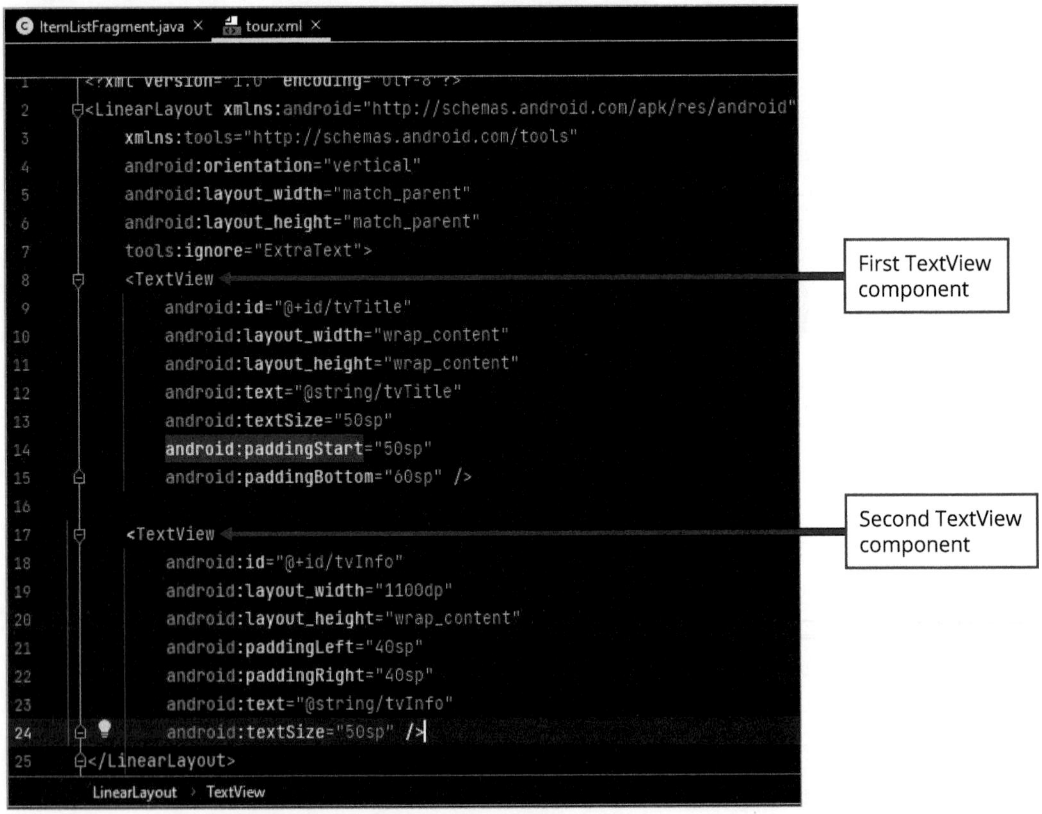

ItemListFragment.java × tour.xml ×

```
<?xml version="1.0" encoding="utf-8"?>
<LinearLayout xmlns:android="http://schemas.android.com/apk/res/android"
    xmlns:tools="http://schemas.android.com/tools"
    android:orientation="vertical"
    android:layout_width="match_parent"
    android:layout_height="match_parent"
    tools:ignore="ExtraText">
    <TextView
        android:id="@+id/tvTitle"
        android:layout_width="wrap_content"
        android:layout_height="wrap_content"
        android:text="@string/tvTitle"
        android:textSize="50sp"
        android:paddingStart="50sp"
        android:paddingBottom="60sp" />

    <TextView
        android:id="@+id/tvInfo"
        android:layout_width="1100dp"
        android:layout_height="wrap_content"
        android:paddingLeft="40sp"
        android:paddingRight="40sp"
        android:text="@string/tvInfo"
        android:textSize="50sp" />
</LinearLayout>
```

LinearLayout › TextView

First TextView component

Second TextView component

Step 3

- Click the Design button in tour.xml.
- Click the Save All button on the Standard toolbar.

The LinearLayout is displayed with two TextView components in the emulator for tour.xml (**Figure 9-20**).

Figure 9-20 Completed LinearLayout in tour.xml in Design view

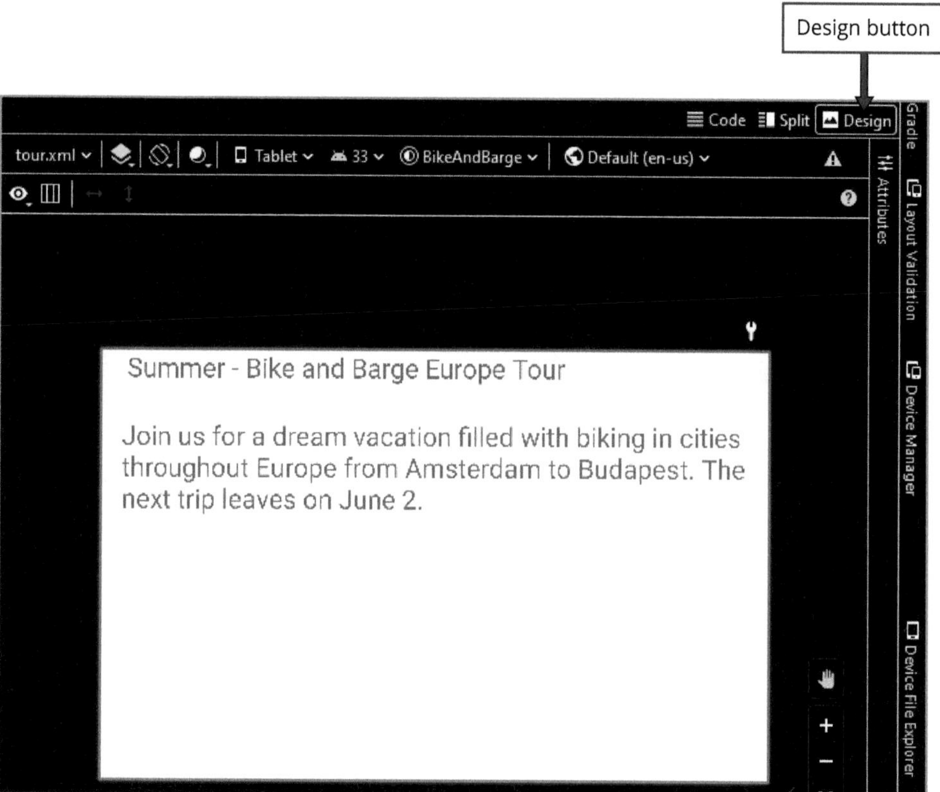

9.6 Creating a WebView XML Layout

The Primary/Detail Flow template initially displays each list item using the TextView object shown in the fragment_item_detail.xml layout file. In the Bike and Barge app, if the user selects the first list item, the photos.xml layout is displayed; if the user selects the second list item, the tour.xml layout is shown. The third list item in the Bike and Barge app uses the default fragment_item_detail.xml layout, but its TextView object cannot display a webpage. Instead, the TextView component must be changed to a **WebView** object, a View component that displays webpages. The WebView object allows you to place a web browser or simply display some online content within your Activity. The WebView object uses a built-in rendering engine to display webpages.

After placing the WebView object in the XML layout of the app, you must add Internet permissions to the Android Manifest file to enable your Activity to access the Internet and load webpages. A **permission** is a restriction that limits access to a part of the code or to data on the device. The permission protects critical data and code that could be misused to cause problems for your app and others. Permissions can be set in the Android Manifest file within an Android app to allow certain actions, such as to set the background wallpaper, check the device's power levels, read your contacts, write events to your calendar, and display a webpage. Every Android application must have an AndroidManifest.xml file in its app directory. The Android Manifest file presents essential information about an app to the Android system—information the system must have before it can run the code of the application. The AndroidManifest.xml file declares the app's theme, each Activity that is run within the application, and permissions necessary for the app to interact with other applications. Without the proper permission, attempts to access the Internet or to complete similar actions will fail. The general structure of AndroidManifest.xml is as follows:

```
<?xml version="1.0" encoding="utf-8"?>
<manifest>
    <uses-permission />
    <permission />
        <application>
          android:usesCleartextTraffic="true"
          icon
          label
          theme
        <activity>
          <intent-filter>
               <action />
               <category />
               <data />
          </intent-filter>
          <meta-data />
        </activity>
        </application>
</manifest>
```

Following is the code syntax for requesting permission to connect to the Internet within the AndroidManifest.xml file:

Code Syntax

```
<uses-permission android:name="android.permission.INTERNET" />
```

Notice that the general structure of the Android Manifest file includes a command line indicating that usesCleartextTraffic="true". When connecting to a website, it is recommended that you make connections over HTTPS to ensure that any web communication is secure. Hypertext Transfer Protocol Secure (HTTPS) is the secure version of HTTP, which is the primary protocol used to send data between a web browser and a website. HTTPS is encrypted in order to increase the security of data transfer. To enable viewing of remote documents from a URL, cleartext network traffic support is required. To keep your app more secure, cleartext is disabled by default on Android 9 (Pie, API 28) and later devices. Cleartext needs to be enabled for you to connect to a website. Place the following CleartextTraffic command within the application portion of the Android Manifest file.

Code Syntax

```
android:usesCleartextTraffic="true"
```

To change the TextView component to a WebView component in the fragment_item_detail.xml layout file and to add permissions to the Android Manifest file, which will allow the WebView component to use the Internet within the app, follow these steps.

Step 1

- Close the tour.xml tab.
- If necessary, expand the layout folder and double-click the fragment_item_detail.xml (sw600dp) layout file to open it. This file is designed to support tablet devices that are 600dp and larger.
- Click the Code button to display the default TextView component code.
- In Line 8, change TextView to **WebView**.
- Delete the rest of the TextView layout commands and replace them with the following code:

```
<WebView
    android:id="@+id/item_detail"
    android:layout_width="match_parent"
    android:layout_height="match_parent"
    tools:context= ".ItemDetailFragment" />
```

The WebView component replaces the TextView component, enabling the fragment_item_detail.xml tablet layout to display a webpage (**Figure 9-21**).

Figure 9-21 TextView component is changed to a WebView component for tablets

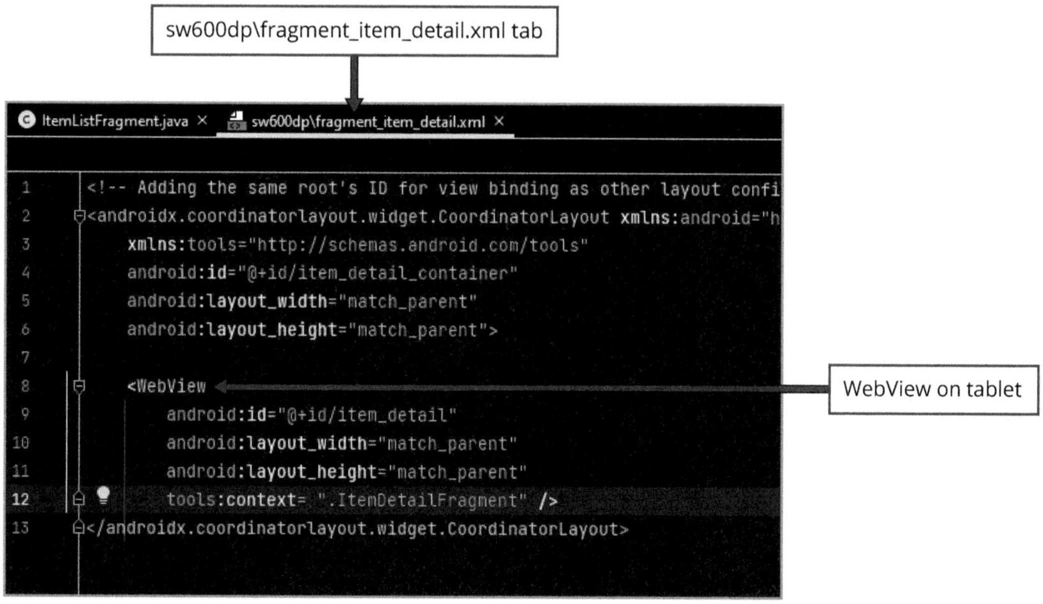

sw600dp\fragment_item_detail.xml tab

ItemListFragment.java × sw600dp\fragment_item_detail.xml ×

```
1  <!-- Adding the same root's ID for view binding as other layout confi
2  <androidx.coordinatorlayout.widget.CoordinatorLayout xmlns:android="h
3      xmlns:tools="http://schemas.android.com/tools"
4      android:id="@+id/item_detail_container"
5      android:layout_width="match_parent"
6      android:layout_height="match_parent">
7
8      <WebView
9          android:id="@+id/item_detail"
10         android:layout_width="match_parent"
11         android:layout_height="match_parent"
12         tools:context= ".ItemDetailFragment" />
13 </androidx.coordinatorlayout.widget.CoordinatorLayout>
```

WebView on tablet

Step 2

- If necessary, expand the layout folder and double-click the fragment_item_detail.xml layout file to open it. This file is designed to support smartphone devices that are smaller than 600dp.
- Click the Code button to display the default TextView component code.
- In Line 42, change TextView to **WebView**.

- Delete the rest of the TextView layout commands and replace them with the following code:

```
<WebView
    android:id="@+id/website_detail"
    android:layout_width="match_parent"
    android:layout_height="match_parent"
    tools:context= ".ItemDetailFragment" />
```

The WebView component replaces the TextView component, enabling the fragment_item_detail.xml smartphone layout to display a webpage (**Figure 9-22**).

Figure 9-22 TextView component is changed to a WebView component for phones

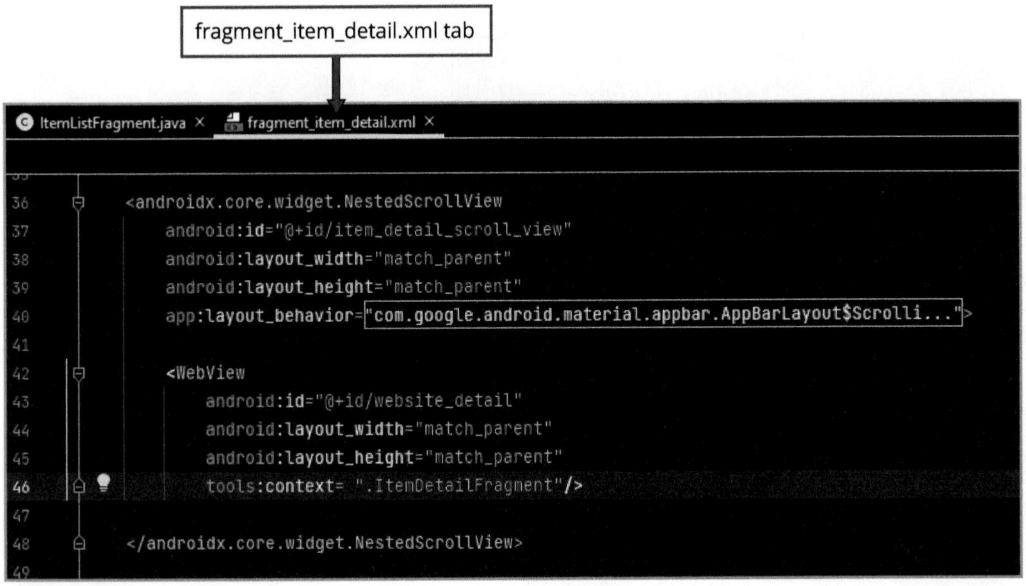

fragment_item_detail.xml tab

ItemListFragment.java × fragment_item_detail.xml ×

```
<androidx.core.widget.NestedScrollView
    android:id="@+id/item_detail_scroll_view"
    android:layout_width="match_parent"
    android:layout_height="match_parent"
    app:layout_behavior="com.google.android.material.appbar.AppBarLayout$Scrolli...">

    <WebView
        android:id="@+id/website_detail"
        android:layout_width="match_parent"
        android:layout_height="match_parent"
        tools:context= ".ItemDetailFragment"/>

</androidx.core.widget.NestedScrollView>
```

Step 3

- Save your work and close both fragment_item_detail.xml files.
- To set the permissions that allow the webpage to open in the app, expand the manifests folder in the Android project view.
- Double-click the AndroidManifest.xml file.
- Click Line 4 and then type **<uses-permission android:name="android.permission.INTERNET" />** to add the permission to connect the WebView component to the Internet.
- Click at the end of Line 5 and press Enter to add a new line.
- Type **android:usesCleartextTraffic="true"** to allow a URL to be opened in the app.

The permission to connect to the Internet is set within the AndroidManifest.xml file before the application code begins (**Figure 9-23**).

Figure 9-23 Setting permission for the WebView component to connect to the Internet in the AndroidManifest file

Good to Know If you run the app without the Internet permission, the error "The webpage at the site could not be loaded because: net::ERR_CACHE_MISS" appears when you click the website list item.

Quick Check

What is the purpose of the two lines of code that were added to the AndroidManifest.xml file in this project?

Answer: The code provides permission to open a webpage in the app.

9.7 Customizing the Content of the Sample Template File

The Primary/Detail Flow template provides a folder named placeholder in the com.example.bikeandbarge folder, which contains a Java class file named PlaceholderContent.java. The purpose of this class is to provide sample content to display in the user interface of the template. This class can be customized or replaced by classes that are created from scratch. In Lines 30–32 of PlaceholderContent.java, three items are added to replace a for loop that simply filled the app with placeholder numbers from 1 to 25:

Code Syntax

```
    // Add some sample items.
        addItem(new PlaceholderItem("1", "Photos", ""));
        addItem(new PlaceholderItem("2", "Tour", ""));
        addItem(new PlaceholderItem("3", "Website", "https://bikebarge.com"));
```

The addItem command displays list items in the left pane of the tablet display or in the first Activity display of a smartphone. You can add more addItem commands if your app has more than three list items. In the Bike and Barge app, the list items should display the text Photos (Item 1), Tour (Item 2), and Website (Item 3). The third item is different from the first two items because selecting it displays the bikebarge.com website in the right pane of the tablet screen. Also, because the Bike and Barge app displays the website within its detail pane, it is different from the Chicago City Guide app designed in Chapter 5, which launched the phone's built-in browser to display city websites.

By default, the PlaceholderContent.java file is displayed in a two-pane layout on a tablet with a component displayed in the detail pane. Because the TextView component cannot display a website, you specify the WebView component in the fragment_item_detail.xml page, which can display webpages. To specify the home page of the Bike and Barge website as the content to display in the WebView component, you add code to the addItem statement in the PlaceholderContent.java file.

To customize the display of the list items in the PlaceholderContent.java file within the template, follow these steps.

Step 1

- Save your work and close the AndroidManifest.xml tab.
- If necessary, expand the java folder and the first net.androidbootcamp.bikeandbarge folder in the Android Project view.
- Expand the placeholder folder.
- Double-click the PlaceholderContent.java class.
- Delete Lines 28–30 to delete the sample items of numbers 1–25 in the loop.
- On Line 28, type **addItem(new PlaceholderItem("1", "Photos", ""));**
- On Line 29, type **addItem(new PlaceholderItem("2", "Tour", ""));**
- On Line 30, type **addItem(new PlaceholderItem("3", "Website", "https://bikebarge.com"));**

The PlaceholderContent.java file is customized with the item list shown in the left pane of the tablet (**Figure 9-24**).

Step 2

- Save your work and close the PlaceholderContent.java tab.

Figure 9-24 Customizing the PlaceholderItem class in the PlaceholderContent.java content file

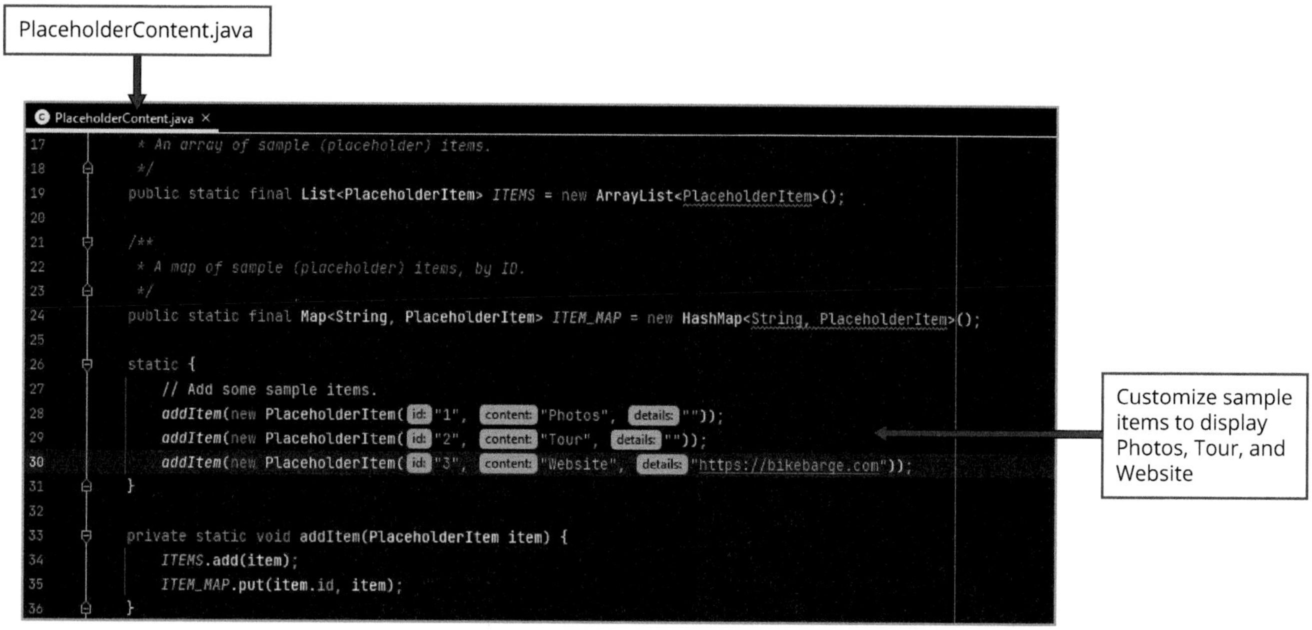

PlaceholderContent.java

PlaceholderContent.java ×

```
     * An array of sample (placeholder) items.
     */
    public static final List<PlaceholderItem> ITEMS = new ArrayList<PlaceholderItem>();

    /**
     * A map of sample (placeholder) items, by ID.
     */
    public static final Map<String, PlaceholderItem> ITEM_MAP = new HashMap<String, PlaceholderItem>();

    static {
        // Add some sample items.
        addItem(new PlaceholderItem( id: "1", content: "Photos", details: ""));
        addItem(new PlaceholderItem( id: "2", content: "Tour", details: ""));
        addItem(new PlaceholderItem( id: "3", content: "Website", details: "https://bikebarge.com"));
    }

    private static void addItem(PlaceholderItem item) {
        ITEMS.add(item);
        ITEM_MAP.put(item.id, item);
    }
```

Customize sample items to display Photos, Tour, and Website

9.8 Displaying the Custom Layout in the Detail Pane

A Primary/Detail Flow interface for a tablet consists of a primary list of items that, when selected, displays additional information about that selection within the detail pane. According to the design of the Bike and Barge app, if the user selects the first item, the photos.xml layout is displayed in the detail pane. If the user selects the second item, the tour.xml layout is displayed in the detail pane. If the user selects the third item, the WebView in the template fragment_item_detail.xml file displays the home page of the Bike and Barge website. To display the correct details in the right pane, the ItemDetailFragment.java file works with a **fragment**, which is a piece of an application's user interface or behavior that can be placed in an Activity. A fragment is essentially a sub-Activity hosted inside another Activity. By dividing components of the user interface and displaying them in fragments, it is easier for developers to reuse these components across various Activities. For example, in the chapter project, a fragment is displayed in the right pane while the left pane remains unchanged. Android introduced fragments in Android 3.2, API level 13, primarily to support more dynamic and flexible user interface designs on large screens.

Three conditional If statements are necessary in the ItemDetailFragment.java file. In the PlaceholderContent.java file, the variable id was set to the string value of the user's selection of the three list items. To determine if two String objects match exactly, you should use the **.equals( ) method**, not the == operator. The == operator compares two objects to determine whether they are exactly the same object. Two strings may be different objects but have the same exact characters. The .equals() method is used to compare strings for equality. The first If statement determines whether the user has selected one of the items—in other words, if the user's selection is not null (nothing). When you compare the value of a string, the following syntax is necessary in Java:

Code Syntax

```
if (mItem != null) {
  if (mItem.id.equals("1"))
}
```

Within the ItemDetailFragment.java file, the following code displays a custom XML layout file named photos.xml in the detail pane:

Code Syntax

```
rootView = inflater.inflate(R.layout.photos, container, false);
```

The inflate( ) method has three arguments: The first part displays the XML layout, the second part applies the layout parameters to the container, and the third part is false, a Boolean type declaring that the layout was already passed to the container.

WebView is a component with which you can display webpages. To display the webpage URL with the variable named item_*url* within the WebView component, the following syntax is necessary:

Code Syntax

```
((WebView) rootView.findViewById(R.id.item_detail)).loadUrl(mItem.content);
```

By default, the browser that opens in Android Studio is the Google Chrome browser, but we want the page to load in the right pane, not in a separate screen in the Chrome browser. An instance of the WebViewClient class is created and assigned the shouldOverrideUrlLoading( ) callback method. This forces the Android device to use the WebView instance to load the page instead of the Chrome browser. The WebView class is an extension of Android's View class that allows you to display webpages as a part of your activity layout. The command shouldOverrideUrlLoading gives the application a chance to take over the device when a new website is about to be loaded in the current WebView component. When your WebView component overrides URL loading, it automatically accumulates a history of visited webpages on your device.

Code Syntax

```
WebView webView = rootView.findViewById(R.id.item_detail);
  webView.setWebViewClient(new WebViewClient() {
  @Override
public boolean shouldOverrideUrlLoading(WebView view, WebResourceRequest
  request) {
   return super.shouldOverrideUrlLoading(view, request);
           }
});
webView.loadUrl(mItem.details);
```

To code the four conditional If statements to display the XML layout and the webpage within the detail pane, complete the following steps.

Step 1

- Save your work and close the PlaceholderContent.java tab.
- If necessary, open the ItemDetailFragment.java file, which displays the layout files for the detail list in the right pane of the tablet.
- Scroll down and delete Lines 76–80, which originally displayed the detail list in a TextView component.
- Starting on Line 76, type the following code to confirm when the user selects one of the three options:

```
if (mItem != null) {
}
```

The TextView component is deleted and an If statement awaits the user's action of clicking one of the three items (**Figure 9-25**).

Figure 9-25 ItemDetailFragment.java class customized with an If statement to check whether the user has selected an item

ItemDetailFragment.java

ItemDetailFragment.java ×

```
66      }
67
68      @Override
69      public View onCreateView(LayoutInflater inflater, ViewGroup container,
70                               Bundle savedInstanceState) {
71
72          binding = FragmentItemDetailBinding.inflate(inflater, container, attachToParent: false);
73          View rootView = binding.getRoot();
74
75          mToolbarLayout = rootView.findViewById(R.id.toolbar_layout);
76          if (mItem != null) {
77
78          }
79          return rootView;
80      }
81
82      @Override
83      public void onDestroyView() {
84          super.onDestroyView();
85          binding = null;
86      }
87
88      private void updateContent() {
89          if (mItem != null) {
90              mTextView.setText(mItem.details);
91              if (mToolbarLayout != null) {
```

This If statement determines if the user has selected an item

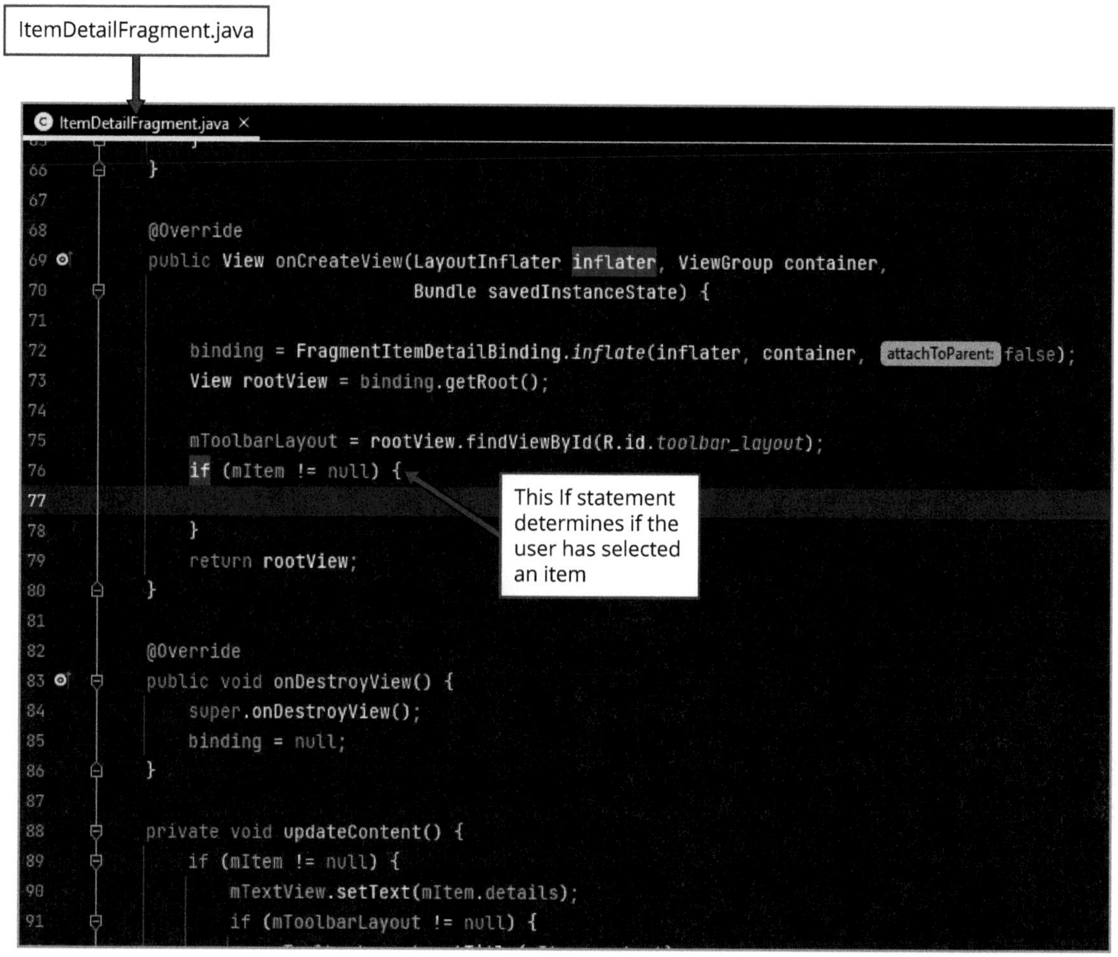

Step 2

- Type the following code between the braces in Line 77 and Line 78 to display the XML layout if the first list item is selected. The braces are not needed here because the If statement only includes one line:

```
if (mItem.id.equals("1"))
    rootView = inflater.inflate(R.layout.photos, container, false);
```

- Starting on the next line, type the following code to display the XML layout if the second list item is selected:

```
if (mItem.id.equals("2"))
    rootView = inflater.inflate(R.layout.tour, container, false);
```

The first and second list items are displayed in the detail pane with their corresponding XML layout when the user selects one of the three options (**Figure 9-26**).

Figure 9-26 ItemDetailFragment.java class customized for the first and second list items

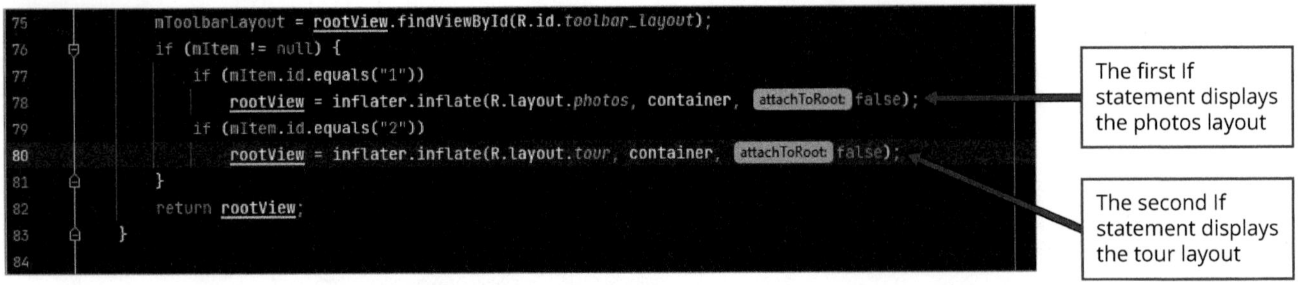

```
        mToolbarLayout = rootView.findViewById(R.id.toolbar_layout);
        if (mItem != null) {
            if (mItem.id.equals("1"))
                rootView = inflater.inflate(R.layout.photos, container, attachToRoot: false);
            if (mItem.id.equals("2"))
                rootView = inflater.inflate(R.layout.tour, container, attachToRoot: false);
        }
        return rootView;
    }
```

The first If statement displays the photos layout

The second If statement displays the tour layout

Step 3

- On the next line, type the following code to display the Bike and Barge home page if the third list item is selected:

```
if (mItem.id.equals("3")) {
    ((WebView) rootView.findViewById(R.id.item_detail)).loadUrl(mItem.content);
}
```

- Click WebView and press Alt+Enter to import the class.

The third list item displays the Bike and Barge URL in a WebView component (**Figure 9-27**).

Figure 9-27 ItemDetailFragment.java class customized for the third list item

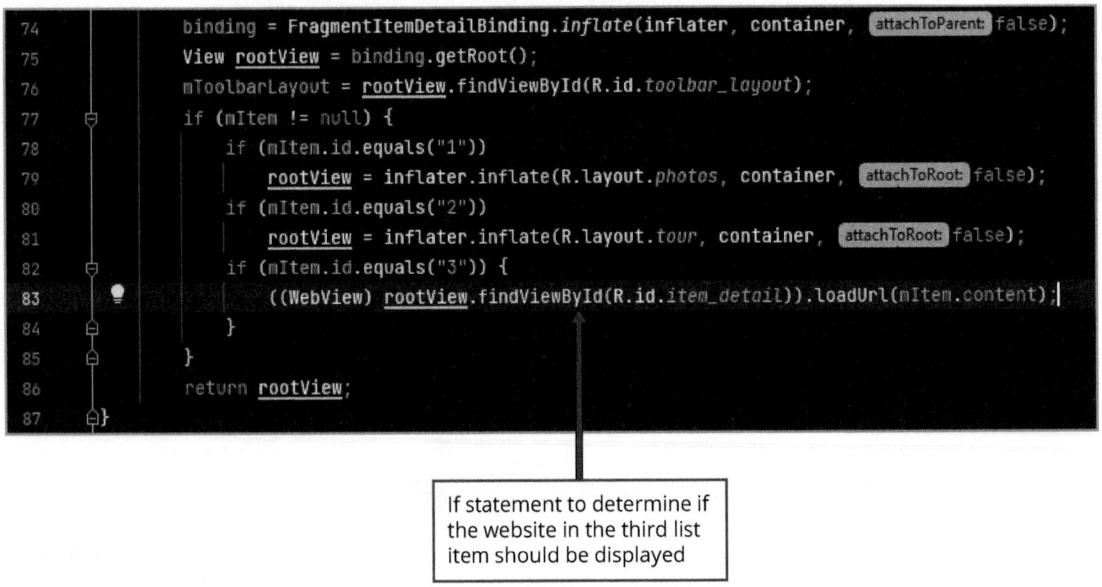

```
        binding = FragmentItemDetailBinding.inflate(inflater, container, attachToParent: false);
        View rootView = binding.getRoot();
        mToolbarLayout = rootView.findViewById(R.id.toolbar_layout);
        if (mItem != null) {
            if (mItem.id.equals("1"))
                rootView = inflater.inflate(R.layout.photos, container, attachToRoot: false);
            if (mItem.id.equals("2"))
                rootView = inflater.inflate(R.layout.tour, container, attachToRoot: false);
            if (mItem.id.equals("3")) {
                ((WebView) rootView.findViewById(R.id.item_detail)).loadUrl(mItem.content);
            }
        }
        return rootView;
}
```

If statement to determine if the website in the third list item should be displayed

Step 4

- On the next line, type the following code to force the website to load within the app instead of opening in the Google Chrome browser (**Figure 9-28**):

```
WebView webView = rootView.findViewById(R.id.item_detail);
webView.setWebViewClient(new WebViewClient() {
```

```
                @Override
                  public boolean shouldOverrideUrlLoading(WebView view,
                    WebResourceRequest request) {
                    return super.shouldOverrideUrlLoading(view, request);
                  }
            });
            webView.loadUrl(mItem.details);
    }
```

- Press Alt+Enter to import the needed classes.
- Delete the lines following Line 96 and fix your braces to match the configuration of the braces in the figure.
- Delete Line 46, updateContent( );.
- Save your work.

Figure 9-28 Forcing the website to open within the app

```
77          if (mItem != null) {
78              if (mItem.id.equals("1"))
79                  rootView = inflater.inflate(R.layout.photos, container, attachToRoot: fals
80              if (mItem.id.equals("2"))
81                  rootView = inflater.inflate(R.layout.tour, container, attachToRoot: false)
82              if (mItem.id.equals("3")) {
83                  ((WebView) rootView.findViewById(R.id.item_detail)).loadUrl(mItem.conte
84                  WebView webView = rootView.findViewById(R.id.item_detail);
85                  webView.setWebViewClient(new WebViewClient() {
86                      @Override
87                      public boolean shouldOverrideUrlLoading(WebView view, WebResourceRe
88                          return super.shouldOverrideUrlLoading(view, request);
89                      }
90                  });
91                  webView.loadUrl(mItem.details);
92              }
93          }
94          return rootView;
95      }
96  }
97
98
```

Makes website load in app instead of default Google Chrome browser

Loads the website in the right pane

Critical Thinking

How would this app differ if all the list items in the left pane of the tablet opened a website within the right pane?

Each list item would use code similar to the code of list item 3 in this chapter project.

Quick Check

What is the .equals( ) method used for?

Answer: The .equals( ) method compares strings for equality.

Running and Testing the Application

The Android Primary/Detail Flow template provides easy-to-use navigation for displaying multiple windows within the tablet interface or two separate Activities on a smartphone device. To test the Bike and Barge Android app, click the Run app button on the Standard toolbar, select the Nexus 10 emulator to test the application, and then click the OK button. After unlocking the emulator, run the application and test the list items in the Bike and Barge app, as shown in Figures 9-1, 9-2, 9-3, and 9-4. You must have Internet connectivity to open the webpage and enough memory available to handle the app's connection to the web. If you have trouble using the Nexus 10 emulator on an older computer with low resolution, add the 10.1-inch WXGA tablet emulator to use instead.

Good to Know | Because a tablet's screen is much larger than a smartphone's, it provides more room to combine and interchange user interface components.

Wrap It Up—Chapter Summary

Using responsive design helps you meet the challenges of creating apps for the wide range of Android devices. The wide screen of a tablet allows for easy navigation; you can use list items in the left pane and display details in the right pane. The chapter provided steps to use a custom Primary/Detail Flow template that created a simple structure to display three screens of content. The WebView component was introduced; it allows you to open Internet content directly within an app using AndroidManifest Internet permissions.

- Responsive design is an approach to designing apps and websites that provides an optimal viewing experience across as many devices as possible.
- Android templates are available when you create a new Android project. You use them to create basic Android applications that you can run and test on an Android device of any size.
- A tablet app created with the Primary/Detail Flow template displays a Primary list of items in a narrow vertical pane along the left side of the screen. When the user selects an item in the list, associated content appears in the detail pane on the right. On a smaller device, such as a smartphone, the Primary list and detail content are displayed on separate screens.
- To display the detail content for the first list item in the Bike and Barge app, you provide images and text descriptions in an XML TableLayout. Each row in the TableLayout displays an ImageView and TextView component.
- To display the detail content for the second list item, you code two TextView components in a Linear layout that includes the tour details.
- To display the detail content for the third list item, you customize the default fragment_item_detail.xml layout to use a WebView object instead of a TextView object. A WebView object allows you to place a web browser within your Activity or simply display online content there. A WebView object uses a built-in rendering engine to display webpages.
- After including a WebView object in the XML layout of an app, you must add Internet permissions to the Android Manifest file so the app can access the Internet and load webpages.
- To associate the content displayed in the detail pane with each list item in the left pane, you customize the PlaceholderContent.java class file by adding code to the addItem statements so they reference three String objects: the id, the item list string, and the website URL.
- To handle responses to user selections, you add conditional statements to the ItemDetailFragment.java file.

Key Terms

application template
.equals( ) method
fragment
permission
Primary/Detail Flow template
responsive design
WebView

Developer FAQs

1. In the chapter project, the Primary/Detail Flow template was selected when creating the app. Which Activity has been used in the first eight chapters of this book? (9.2)
2. Which template XML layout file displays the item list fragment and the item detail container for a tablet? (9.4)
3. How many list items are in the Primary/Detail Flow template by default? (9.7)
4. What is the name of the sample Java file that contains content in the Primary/Detail Flow template? (9.7)
5. True or False: Each list item in the Primary/Detail Flow template launches a separate Activity using the full screen on a smartphone. (9.7)
6. Which layout was used in the photos.xml file in the chapter project? (9.5)
7. Write a line of code starting with addItem to display an app's first list item named Soccer Location. (9.7)
8. Write a line of code starting with addItem to display an app's second list item named View News Site, which connects to the site *cnn.com*. (9.7)
9. In which file would the lines in Questions 7 and 8 be written? (9.7)
10. When a smartphone is detected, the app uses which XML layout to display the FrameLayout instance? (9.4)
11. Which XML code creates rows within a TableLayout? (9.5)
12. True or False: You cannot add more list items to the Primary/Detail Flow template. (9.7)
13. By default, does the WebView component open a full-screen browser on the tablet? (9.8)
14. Which XML file in the chapter project was switched from a TextView component to a WebView component? (9.6)
15. Give four examples of Android device permissions mentioned in this chapter. (9.6)
16. What types of code permissions are necessary when using the WebView component? (9.6)
17. In which file are permissions set? (9.6)
18. What do fragments make it easier for developers to code? (9.8)
19. Write an If structure to compare whether mItem is equal to 7. The value 7 has been assigned to an Integer value. (9.8)
20. Write an If structure to compare whether mItem is equal to 5. The value 5 has been assigned to a String value. (9.8)

Beyond the Book

Search the web for answers to the following questions to further your Android knowledge.

1. Research three Android tablet devices. Write a paragraph about the cost, usage, dimensions, and posted reviews for each of these three tablets.
2. Using *cnet.com* (a popular review site), compare the newest Android, iPad, and Windows tablets and summarize their recommendations in a one-page paper.
3. Using *developer.android.com*, research the topic of permissions. After writing many Android projects, the Android help files should be easier for you to understand now. Explain the use of permissions in your own words (at least 100 words).
4. A common user complaint is that it is difficult to use an onscreen keyboard to type long documents. Discuss three alternatives to using a traditional onscreen keyboard layout for input. Write a paragraph about each.

Case Programming Projects

Complete one or more of the following case programming projects. Use the same steps and techniques taught within the chapter. Successful completion of these projects requires knowledge of all chapter learning objectives. Submit the program(s) you create to your instructor. The level of difficulty is indicated for each case programming project.

Case Project 9–1: Oasis Spa Tablet App (Beginner)

Requirements Document

Application title:	Oasis Spa Tablet App
Purpose:	This tablet app describes a full-service spa named Oasis Spa.
Algorithms:	**1.** The opening screen displays three list items titled Spa Services, Spa Address, and Spa Website. The first list item displays two table rows within a table layout, with an image in each row (spa1.png and spa2.png) and the text shown in **Figure 9-29**. **2.** The second item displays the address and phone number of Oasis Spa at 1268 Andrew Lane, Pond, OK 43277, 555-332-3366. **3.** The third list item opens *https://www.theluxuriousspa.com* in a browser (**Figure 9-30**).
Conditions:	**1.** The pictures are provided with your student files. **2.** Use the Primary/Detail Flow template.

Figure 9-29 Opening screen of the Oasis Spa tablet app

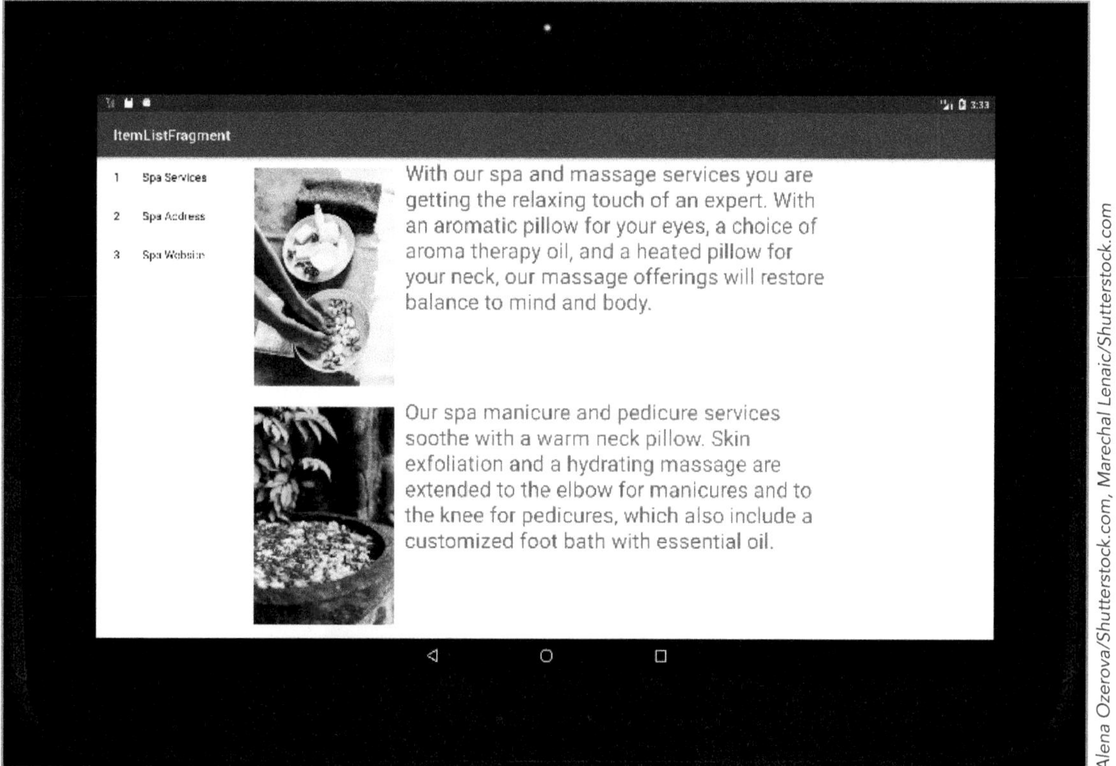

Alena Ozerova/Shutterstock.com, Marechal Lenaic/Shutterstock.com

Figure 9-30 Selecting the third list item in the left pane

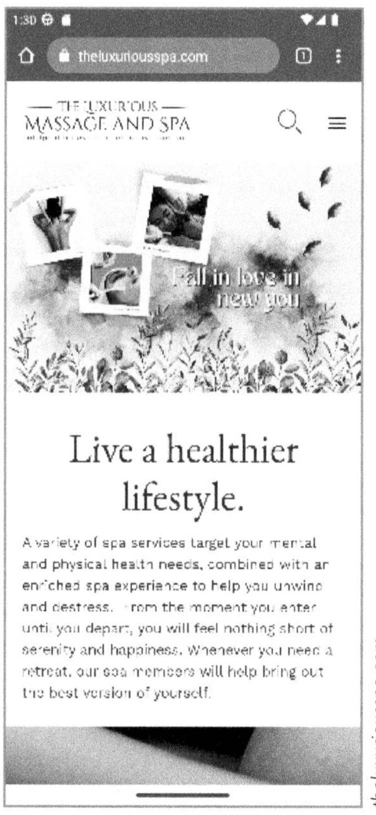

theluxuriousspa.com

Case Project 9–2: Modern Art Museums (Beginner)

Requirements Document

Application title:	Modern Art Museums Tablet App
Purpose:	The app shows three of the world's famous art museum websites.
Algorithms:	1. The opening screen displays three list items (**Figure 9-31**): Barnes Museum (*www.barnesfoundation.org*), Tate Modern (*www.tate.org.uk*), and Van Gogh Museum (*www.vangoghmuseum.nl/en*). 2. Selecting the first list item displays the Barnes Museum website in the detail pane. 3. Selecting the second list item displays the Tate Modern Museum website in the detail pane. 4. Selecting the third list item displays the Van Gogh Museum website in the detail pane.

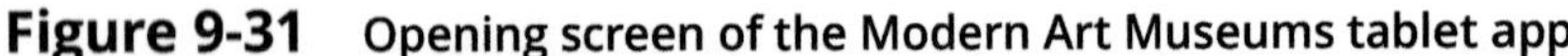

Figure 9-31 Opening screen of the Modern Art Museums tablet app

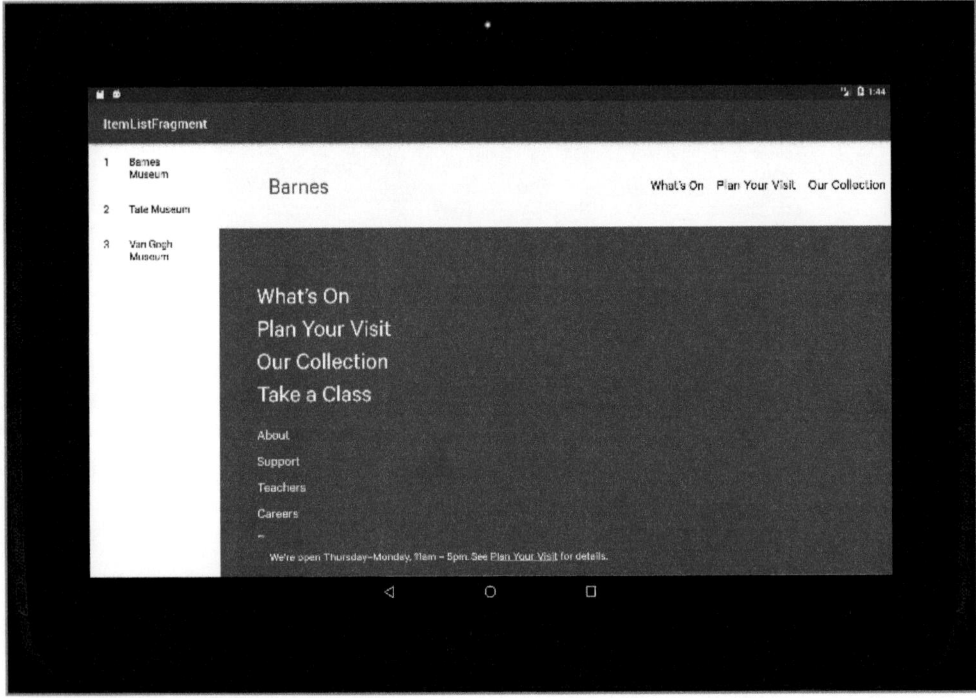

Case Project 9–3: Famous Athlete Tablet App (Intermediate)

Requirements Document

Application title:	Famous Athlete Tablet App
Purpose:	Create a tablet screen for a large app that features information about the famous athletes of the world. You can select your favorite athlete to feature.
Algorithms:	1. The first list item uses a TableLayout to display the name of the athlete. The second row should have an image of the athlete and text about the athlete. 2. The second list item displays the athlete's birth date, hometown, and statistics. Research the information needed. 3. The third list item opens a link about the featured athlete.

Case Project 9–4: Snap Fitness Tablet App (Intermediate)

Requirements Document

Application title: Snap Fitness Tablet App

Purpose: The local fitness gym in your area wants an app that provides information about the gym's activities and memberships.

Algorithms:

1. The app's list items are labeled Site, Info, and Photos. The first list item links to the gym's website.
2. The second list item displays the costs for the gym:
   Youth (ages 14–17): $25
   Adult (18 and over): $50
   Family/Household: $75
   Active Senior: $50
3. The third list item displays four photos in four rows, with information about the gym next to each photo.

Case Project 9–5: Top Tablet Apps (Advanced)

Requirements Document

Application title: Top Tablet Apps

Purpose: The app displays six of your favorite web technology sites.

Algorithms:

1. An opening screen displays the names of six top technology sites.
2. Each list item includes a link to open the corresponding tech site.

Case Project 9–6: Pick Your Topic Tablet App (Advanced)

Requirements Document

Application title: Pick Your Topic Tablet App

Purpose: Get creative! Create an app with four list items on a topic of your choice.

Algorithms:

1. Create four list items on the opening screen.
2. The four list items should link to a TableLayout with three rows, one TextView layout, one large ImageView layout, and a webpage.

Conditions: Select your own images.

Chapter 10

Move! Creating Animation

Learning Objectives

At the completion of this chapter, you will be able to:

10.1 Create an Android application with Frame and Tween animation

10.2 Create frame-by-frame animation

10.3 Set the background resource

10.4 Use the start( ) and stop( ) methods

10.5 Move with Tween animation

10.6 Launch Tween animation

10.7 Add the layout for the Tween image

10.8 Set Tween animation attributes

10.9 Code the startAnimation( ) method

10.10 Change the orientation of the emulator

Computer animation is widely used by television, the video game industry (as on Xbox, Vita, and Wii), and gaming applications on mobile devices. Animation displays many images in rapid succession or displays many changes to one image to create an illusion of movement. Animation is an integral part of many of the most popular Android apps on Google Play, including Dragon Ball Legends, Baldur's Gate, Word Link, Minecraft, and Candy Crush. Android developers see the value in using 3D graphics to create more graphical apps and in-demand games.

10.1 Creating an Android Application with Frame and Tween Animation

Using Android animation, the chapter project named Northern Lights Animation displays multiple photos of the Iceland Aurora Borealis, also called the Northern Lights, during a single night in Iceland. The Northern Lights are one of Mother Nature's greatest light shows; they draw thousands of visitors to the northern polar regions each year, inspiring myth, legend, and an incomparable sense of awe. The Northern Lights most commonly occur within the geographic area beneath the auroral oval. They encompass latitudes between 60 and 75 degrees and take in Iceland, northern parts of Sweden, Finland, Norway, Russia, Canada, and Alaska.

The app includes a START FRAME ANIMATION button that reveals the animated images frame by frame. When the user taps the START TWEEN ANIMATION button, the frame-by-frame animation stops and the last image of the lights rotates several times using Tween animation. A **motion tween** specifies a start state of an object and then animates it using a uniform transition type, such as rotating a predetermined number of times or an infinite number of times. The Northern Lights Animation smartphone app shown in **Figure 10-1** allows the user to start and stop the animated images at different moments in a frame-by-frame sequence and then launches a second Activity that plays a rotation of the last image spiraling through the sky six times.

Figure 10-1 Northern Lights Animation app using Frame animation

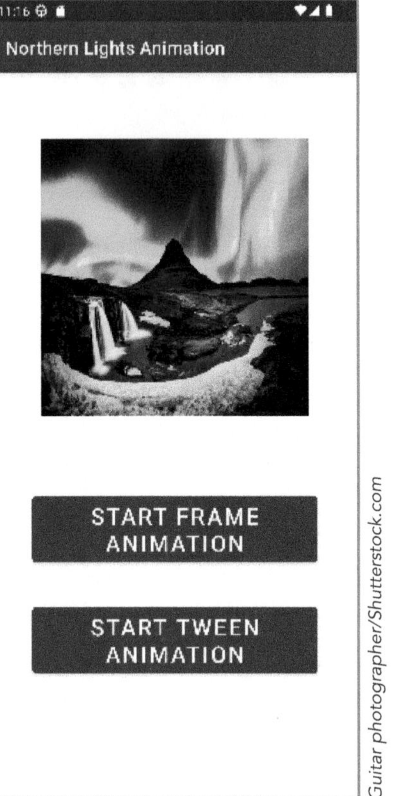

The Android app in Figure 10-1 displays frame-by-frame animation in which the time between each photo is measured in 100-millisecond intervals. Tapping the START FRAME ANIMATION button begins displaying the Northern Lights images; tapping the START TWEEN ANIMATION button stops the continuous Frame animation and begins the Tween animation of rotating the last Northern Lights image, as shown in **Figure 10-2**. The Tween animation rotates the image six times in a perfect circle. The orientation of the emulator is switched to landscape in Figure 10-2.

Good to Know

Professional Android animation can be created by using complex programs such as Maya, 4D Launcher, Adobe Animate, and Cinema 4D. A freeware program named Blender develops 3D animated content in the gaming environment.

To create this application, the developer must understand how to perform the following processes:

1. Add the layout for the image and button objects in activity_main.xml.
2. Add five images to the drawable folder.
3. Add a Frame animation XML file to the project.
4. Set the duration between frames in the frame-by-frame animation.
5. Declare and instantiate the ImageView, Button, and AnimationDrawable controls.
6. Code the OnClickListeners for the Button controls.
7. Run the Frame animation application.
8. Add a Tween animation XML file to rotate the last image.
9. Create a second Activity named Tween.java to launch the rotation Tween animation with an XML layout.
10. When the application executes, change the orientation of the emulator.

Figure 10-2 Northern Lights Animation app using Tween animation

Using Animation in Android

Android provides two types of animation: Frame and Tween animation. **Frame animation**, also called frame-by-frame animation, assigns a sequence of photos to play with a predefined interval between images. Frame-by-frame animation is like a slide show and is typically created to show steps in a process, such as how to fly-fish or play a fast-paced sequence. To create the illusion of movement, a cartoon image can be displayed on the screen and repeatedly replaced by a new image that is similar but slightly advanced in the time sequence.

Instead of using a sequence of images, **Tween animation** creates an animation on a single image or the contents of a View object by performing a series of transformations that alter position, size, rotation, and transparency. Text can fly across the screen, an image of an engine can be rotated to display different angles, or the transparency of an image can change from transparent to solid. A sequence of animation instructions defines the Tween animation using either XML or Android code. In this chapter project, the application first displays a frame-by-frame animation. Code is added to the same application to display a second type of animation called a Tween rotation effect.

Adding the Layout for the Frame Image and Button Controls

The layout specifications for the chapter project reside within the activity_main.xml file in a ConstraintLayout. A single ImageView control named ivLights displays the Northern Lights images in a frame-by-frame animation. The two Button controls named btStart and btStop start and stop the Frame animation, respectively. In the Relative layout, an ImageView control displays the animation images. You insert this control and its properties in the activity_main.xml file to specify precise settings for the control. Below the ImageView control, two Button controls are added and centered in the emulator. Later in the chapter, a Tween animation is added to the application and launched when the Frame animation ends.

This application is coded to display a modern smartphone platform from Lollipop to Tiramisu and beyond. As shown in **Figure 10-3**, when you create an app, a link named "Help me choose" is available when selecting a form factor to show the distribution of active devices running each version of Android, based on the number of devices that visit

Figure 10-3 Setting up the project in the New Project window

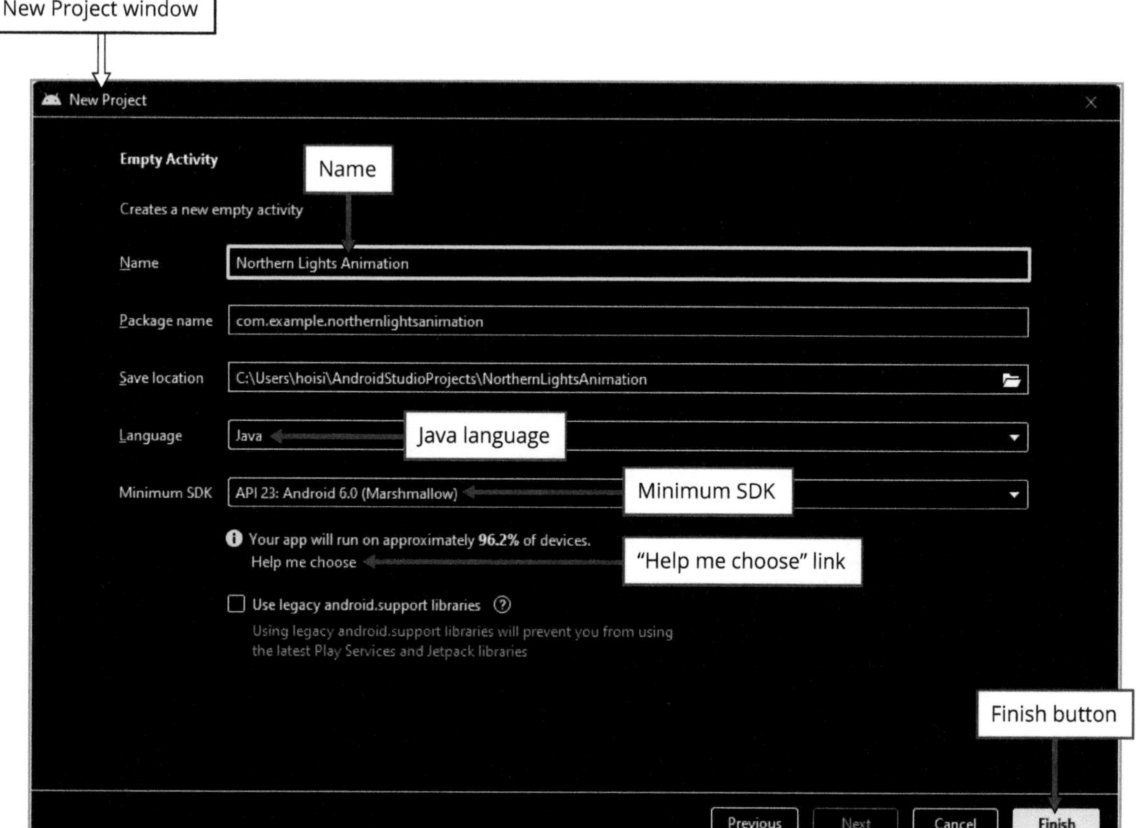

the Google Play Store. The versions with high APIs have more features but fewer users than versions with low APIs. You want to balance features and users. Generally, it is best to support about 90 percent of the active devices in the present market. To begin the application, set up the String table, and code the activity_main.xml layout, follow these steps.

Step 1

- Open the Android Studio program.
- In the Welcome to Android Studio window, scroll down and click the New Project button in the Phone and Tablet templates to create a new Android Studio project.
- Click the Next button in the New Project window.
- Type **Northern Lights Animation** in the Name text box.
- If necessary, select Java in the Language text box.
- If necessary, select API 23: Android 6.0 (Marshmallow) as the Minimum SDK.

The new Northern Lights Animation project has an application name (Figure 10-3).

Critical Thinking

What is the benefit of only targeting an app to the most recent Android platform?

When a new platform of Android arrives, few devices initially upgrade, but if you are building an app based on a brand-new feature, you must target the latest platform.

Step 2

- Click the Finish button in the New Project window.
- Click the Hello world! TextView widget displayed by default in the emulator and press the Delete key.
- Click the Next button on the Configure your new project page of the Create New Project dialog box.
- Change the available virtual device to a smartphone emulator.
- In the Android project view, expand the res\values folder and then double-click the strings.xml file to display its contents.
- Click the Open editor link.
- Click the Add Key (plus sign) button in the Translations Editor.
- In the Key text box, type **description** to name the string.
- In the Default Value text box, type **Northern Lights Image** to define the description text and then click the OK button.
- Click the Add Key button.
- In the Key text box, type **btStart** to name the string.
- In the Default Value text box, type **Start Frame Animation** to define the text and then click the OK button.
- Click the Add Key button.
- In the Key text box, type **btStop** to name the string.
- In the Default Value text box, type **Start Tween Animation** to define the text and then click the OK button.

The String table includes an image description and two Button control text strings (**Figure 10-4**).

Step 3

- Save your work. Close the Translations Editor and the strings.xml tabs.
- In the res/layout folder, double-click activity_main.xml to display the graphical layout.

Figure 10-4 String table

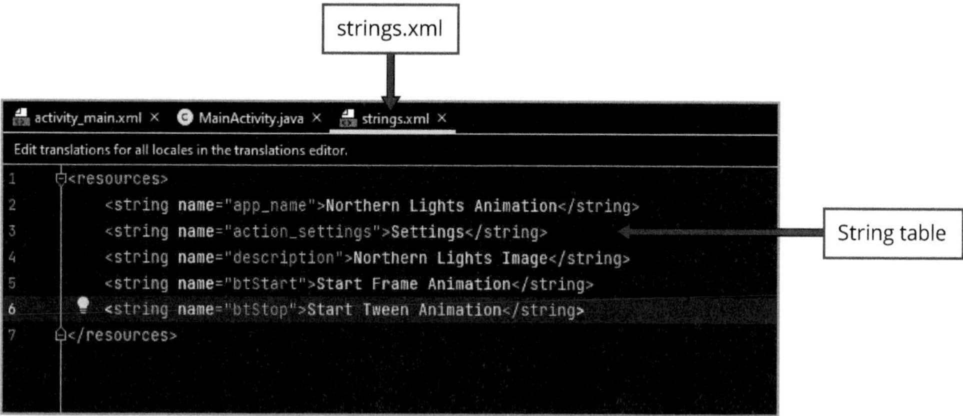

- Click the Code button in the upper-right part of the window. By default, a ConstraintLayout is set.
- Click at the end of Line 7, press the Enter key, and then add the ImageView control within the ConstraintLayout by typing the following custom XML code, using auto-completion as much as possible:

```
<ImageView
    android:id="@+id/ivLights"
    android:layout_width="300dp"
    android:layout_height="300dp"
    android:layout_alignParentTop="true"
    android:layout_centerHorizontal="true"
    android:contentDescription="@string/description" />
```

The ImageView control is coded in activity_main.xml (**Figure 10-5**).

Figure 10-5 ImageView XML code

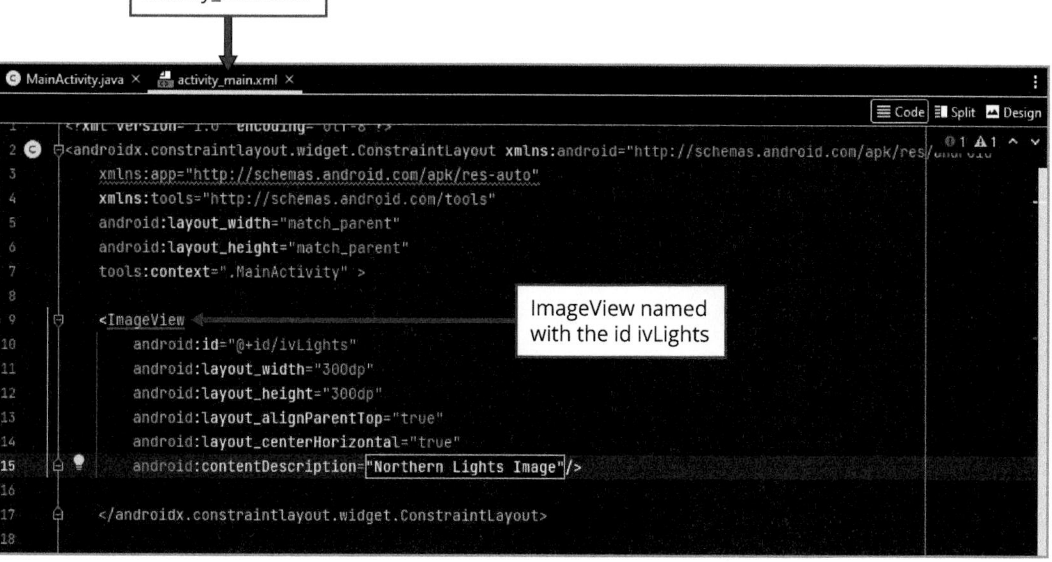

Step 4

- Press the Enter key and then add the two Button controls by typing the following custom XML code, using auto-completion as much as possible:

```
<Button
    android:id="@+id/btStart"
    android:layout_width="wrap_content"
    android:layout_height="wrap_content"
    android:layout_below="@+id/ivLights"
    android:layout_centerHorizontal="true"
    android:text="@string/btStart"
    android:textSize="25sp" />
<Button
    android:id="@+id/btStop"
    android:layout_width="wrap_content"
    android:layout_height="wrap_content"
    android:layout_below="@+id/btStart"
    android:layout_alignParentStart="true"
    android:layout_alignParentLeft="true"
    android:text="@string/btStop"
    android:textSize="25sp" />
```

- Click the Design button in the upper-right part of the window.
- Drag all four Constraint handles of the ImageView component to the top, bottom, left, and right edges of the emulator screen. Repeat this process with the two Button components.

The two Button controls are coded in activity_main.xml and shown in the emulator (**Figure 10-6**).

Figure 10-6 Two Button controls in the XML code (*continues*)

Figure 10-6 *(Continued)*

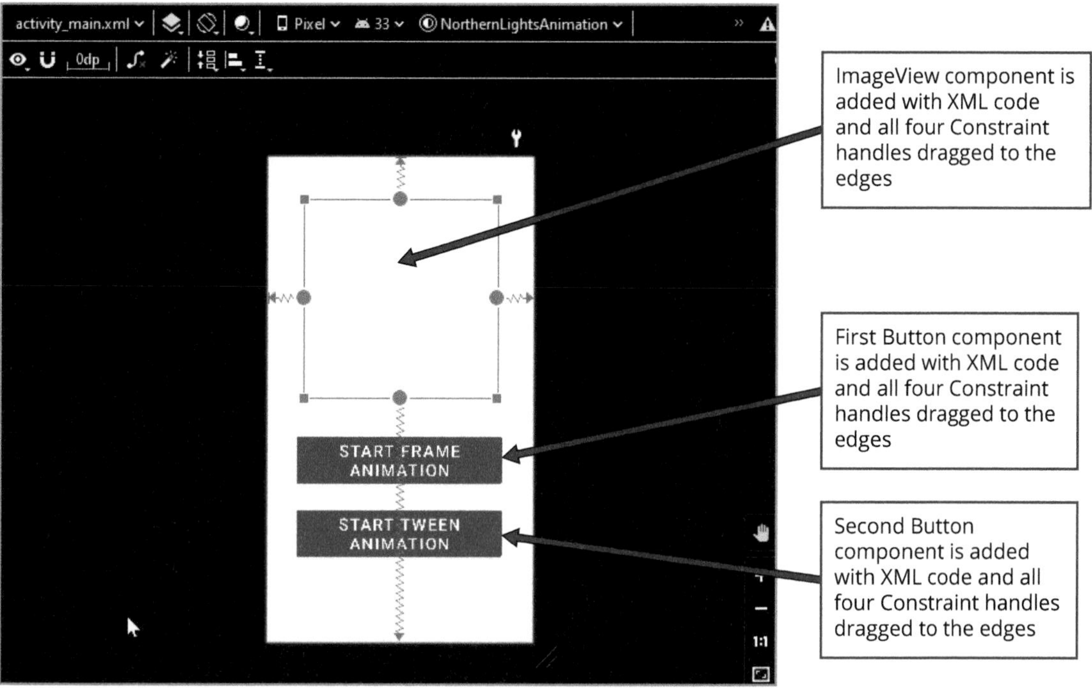

10.2 Creating Frame-by-Frame Animation

In the Northern Lights Animation app, the frame-by-frame animation loads and displays a sequence of Northern Lights images from the drawable folder. A single XML file named animation.xml lists the frames that constitute the animation. You create animation.xml in the res\drawable folder. Frame-by-frame animations are also known as drawable animations. In the XML code, an **animation-list** root element references five Northern Lights images stored in the drawable folder. Each item in the animation-list code specifies how many milliseconds to display each image. In the chapter project, each image is displayed for one-tenth of a second. The animation-list code includes the oneshot property, which is set to true by default. By setting the **android:oneshot** attribute of the animation-list element to false, as shown in the following code, the animation plays repeatedly like a film until the START TWEEN ANIMATION button is tapped. If the oneshot attribute is set to true, the animation plays once and then stops and displays the last frame. Note that you add the oneshot attribute to the code in the opening animation-list tag.

Code Syntax for animation.xml

```
<?xml version="1.0" encoding="utf-8"?>
<animation-list xmlns:android="http://schemas.android.com/apk/res/android"
android:oneshot="false" >
<item android:drawable="@drawable/lights1" android:duration= "100"/>
<item android:drawable="@drawable/lights2" android:duration= "100"/>
<item android:drawable="@drawable/lights3" android:duration= "100"/>
<item android:drawable="@drawable/lights4" android:duration= "100"/>
<item android:drawable="@drawable/lights5" android:duration= "100"/>
</animation-list>
```

When the XML file is added to the Android project, the Android resource type is selected and animation-list is specified as the root element of the XML code. The animation-list code displays a listing of the images in the preferred order. Store the animation.xml file in the drawable folder. To copy the images into the drawable folder and create the animation-list XML code for the frame-by-frame animation, follow these steps.

Step 1

- Save and close the activity_main.xml file.
- If necessary, copy the student files to your USB drive. Open the USB folder containing the student files.
- To add the five image files to the drawable resource folder, copy the lights1.png, lights2.png, lights3.png, lights4.png, and lights5.png files (press Ctrl+C) and then paste them in the drawable folder.
- Click the OK button in the Copy dialog box.

Copies of the five files appear in the drawable folder (**Figure 10-7**).

Figure 10-7 Copied images in the drawable folder

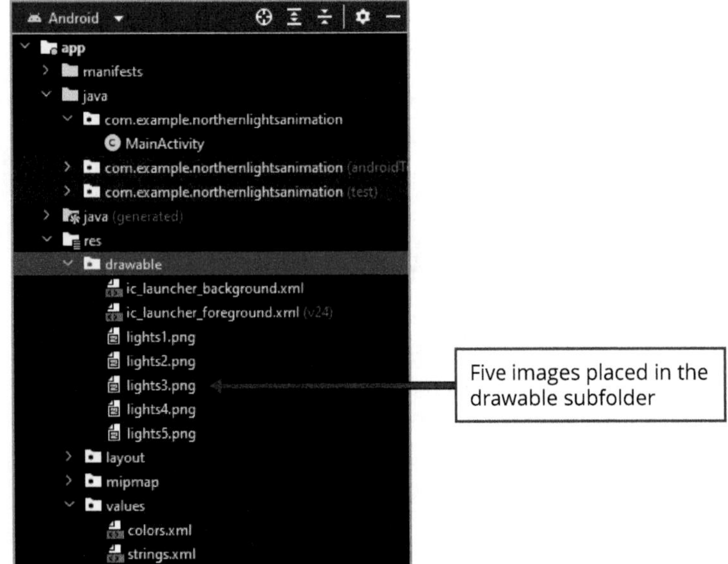

Step 2

- Right-click the res folder to select the folder where the animation folder will reside.
- Click New on the shortcut menu and then click Android resource file to open the New Resource File dialog box.
- In the File name text box, type **animation**.
- In the Resource type list box, select **Animator**.
- In the Root element text box, type **animation-list** as the type of element to add to the XML file.
- In the Directory name text box, type **drawable** as the name of the folder for storing animation.xml.

An XML file named animation is created in a folder named drawable with the animation-list root element and a resource type of Animator (**Figure 10-8**).

Figure 10-8 Creating the animation.xml file

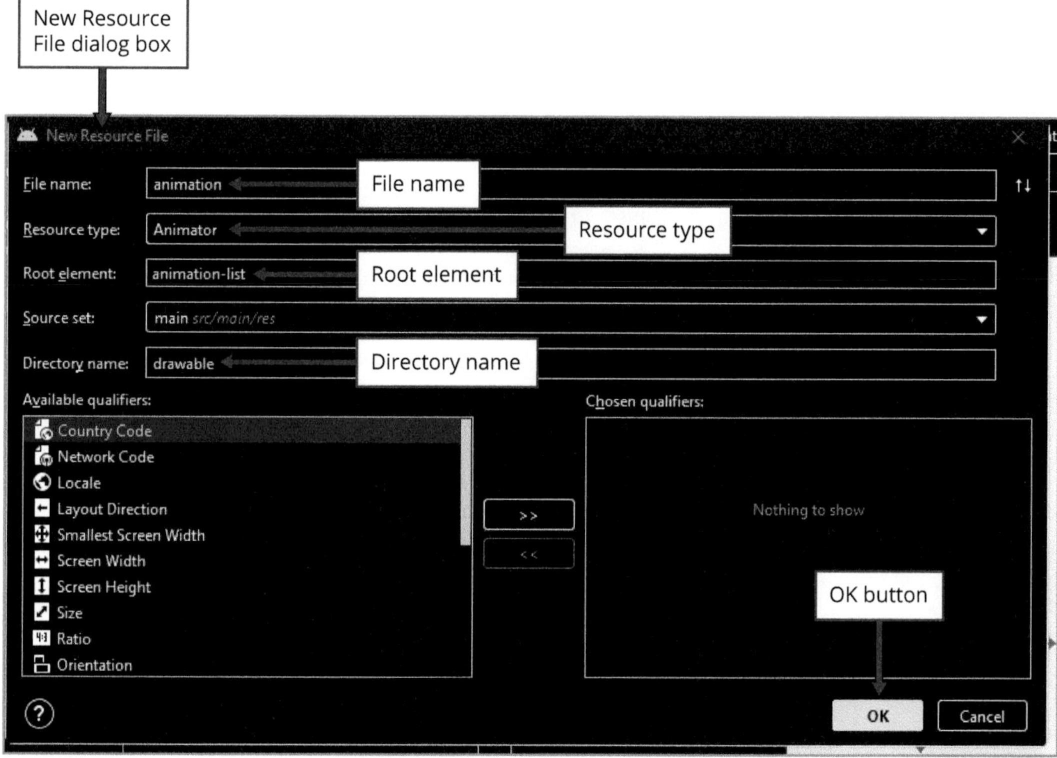

Step 3

- Click the OK button. When the animation.xml file opens, the animation-list element is already coded.
- Click the animation-list source tag, click before the closing tag (>) in Line 2, and then press the spacebar to insert a space.
- To add the oneshot attribute to create a continuous loop of animation, type **android:oneshot="false"**. The auto-completion feature assists in typing this command.

In animation.xml, the oneshot attribute is set to false in the animation-list code to animate the frames continuously (**Figure 10-9**).

Figure 10-9 Setting the oneshot attribute

Step 4

- Click Line 3 within the animation-list element to add the five list items that are displayed within the frame-by-frame animation. Type the following five lines to reference the images and millisecond durations:

```
<item android:drawable="@drawable/lights1" android:duration="100"/>
<item android:drawable="@drawable/lights2" android:duration="100"/>
<item android:drawable="@drawable/lights3" android:duration="100"/>
<item android:drawable="@drawable/lights4" android:duration="100"/>
<item android:drawable="@drawable/lights5" android:duration="100"/>
```

In animation.xml, the five frames of the animation are entered as items in the animation-list element, including the time in milliseconds that each frame should be displayed (**Figure 10-10**). A value of 1000 would indicate a full second; the value 100 indicates one-tenth of a second.

Figure 10-10 Entering the animation-list items with image names and duration

```
MainActivity.java ×   animation.xml ×
1 <?xml version="1.0" encoding="utf-8"?>
2 <animation-list xmlns:android="http://schemas.android.com/apk/res/android" android:oneshot="false">
3     <item android:drawable="@drawable/lights1" android:duration="100"/>
4     <item android:drawable="@drawable/lights2" android:duration="100"/>
5     <item android:drawable="@drawable/lights3" android:duration="100"/>
6     <item android:drawable="@drawable/lights4" android:duration="100"/>
7     <item android:drawable="@drawable/lights5" android:duration= "100"/>
8 </animation-list>
```

Each image lasts one-tenth of a second on the screen

Quick Check

If you coded android:oneshot="true", how many times would the animation take place?

Answer: One time.

Good to Know | Android includes support for high-performance 2D and 3D graphics with the Open Graphics Library named OpenGL. OpenGL is a cross-platform graphics API that specifies a standard software interface for 3D graphics processing hardware and uses a coordinate system to map the image to the screen.

Coding the AnimationDrawable Object

The **AnimationDrawable class** provides the methods for drawable animations to create a sequence of frame-by-frame images played in order, like a roll of film. In Android development, frame-based animations and image transitions are defined as drawables. The instance of AnimationDrawable is instantiated as a class variable because it is used in multiple methods within the MainActivity class. To instantiate the AnimationDrawable object in MainActivity.java as a class variable, follow this step.

Step 1

- Save your work and then close the animation.xml tab.
- If necessary, open the MainActivity.java tab.
- On Line 9 within the MainActivity class, type **AnimationDrawable lightsAnimation;** to instantiate the object.
- Click AnimationDrawable and press Alt+Enter to import AnimationDrawable, which moves the line down to add the library.

The AnimationDrawable instance named lightsAnimation is coded within MainActivity.java (**Figure 10-11**).

Figure 10-11 Instantiating the AnimationDrawable class variable

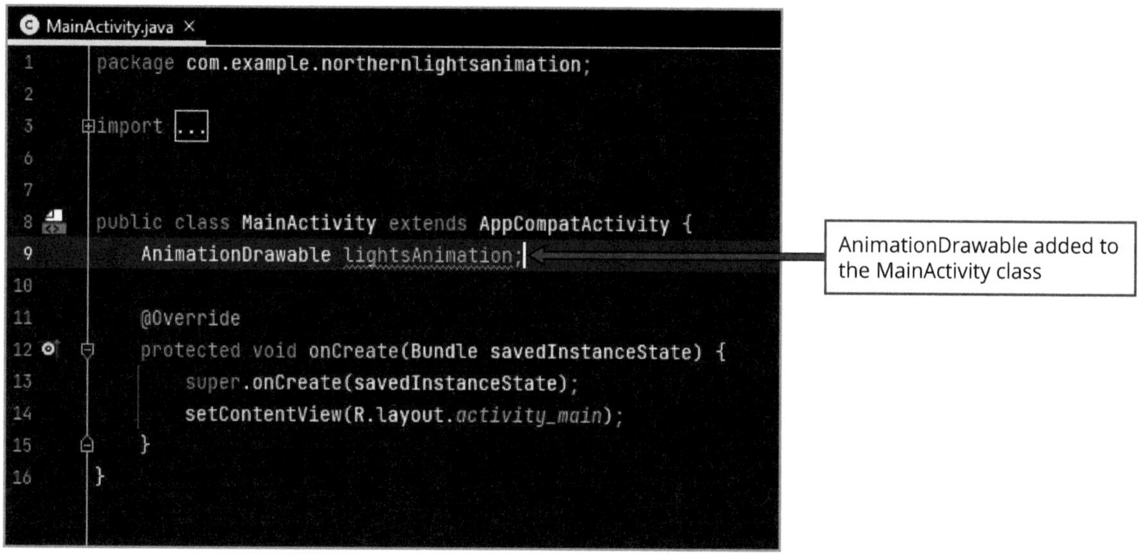

MainActivity.java ×

```
1   package com.example.northernlightsanimation;
2
3   import ...
6
7
8   public class MainActivity extends AppCompatActivity {
9       AnimationDrawable lightsAnimation;
10
11      @Override
12      protected void onCreate(Bundle savedInstanceState) {
13          super.onCreate(savedInstanceState);
14          setContentView(R.layout.activity_main);
15      }
16  }
```

AnimationDrawable added to the MainActivity class

10.3 Setting the Background Resource

The ImageView control named ivLights that was coded in activity_main.xml must also be coded in MainActivity.java to bind the drawable resource files to the Background property. The Background property of an image can be set to any full drawable resource, such as a .png file, a 9-patch image file, or a solid color designated with hexadecimal code—for example, #FF0000 for red. A special image called a **9-patch image** has predefined "stretching" areas that maintain the same look on different screen sizes. These 9-patch graphics are named for their nine areas, called patches, that scale separately. For example, a button may change sizes when it is stretched across different form factors.

The images used in the Northern Lights Animation application are .png files and are referenced in animation.xml as items in the animation-list code. In the following code, a new instance of ImageView named ivFrame is assigned to the ImageView control named ivLights, which was defined in the activity_main.xml layout. The list of drawable images in the animation-list code is connected to the ivFrame instance by the ivFrame.setBackgroundResource( ) method. The **setBackgroundResource( )** method shown in the following code places the five Northern Lights images in a frame-by-frame display that resembles a slide show. Each frame points to one of the Northern Lights images that were assembled in the XML resource file. The ivFrame instance is the image that you want to animate; the image is set to the animation drawable as its background.

Code Syntax

```
ImageView ivFrame=findViewById(R.id.ivLights);
ivFrame.setBackgroundResource(R.drawable.animation);
lightsAnimation=(AnimationDrawable) ivFrame.getBackground( );
```

In the third line of the code syntax, the instance of AnimationDrawable called lightsAnimation is assigned as the background of the five images to display in the animation. Android constructs an AnimationDrawable Java object before setting it as the background. At this point, the animation is ready to display the five images but must wait for you to code the start( ) method, which actually begins the movement in the Frame animation. To instantiate the ImageView control and assign the five images to the Background property, follow these steps.

Step 1

- Click at the end of the setContentView(R.layout.*activity_main*); line and press the Enter key.
- Instantiate the ImageView that accesses ivLights in the XML layout file by typing **ImageView ivFrame= findViewById(R.id.ivLights);**.
- Click ImageView and press Alt+Enter to import the ImageView control.

The ImageView control that displays the frame animation is instantiated (**Figure 10-12**).

Figure 10-12 Instantiating the ImageView control

```
MainActivity.java ×
package com.example.northernlightsanimation;

import ...

public class MainActivity extends AppCompatActivity {
    AnimationDrawable lightsAnimation;
    @Override
    protected void onCreate(Bundle savedInstanceState) {
        super.onCreate(savedInstanceState);
        setContentView(R.layout.activity_main);
        ImageView ivFrame= findViewById(R.id.ivLights);
    }
}
```

ImageView is instantiated

Step 2

- Press the Enter key to insert a blank line and then set the background resource image (the instance of the ImageView control) for the animation-list code in animation.xml by typing **ivFrame.setBackgroundResource(R.drawable.animation);**.

The animation-list code within animation.xml is set as the Background property of the ivFrame ImageView (**Figure 10-13**).

Step 3

- Next, access the AnimationDrawable object by "getting" the view object. Press the Enter key and then type **lightsAnimation=(AnimationDrawable)ivFrame.getBackground();**.

The AnimationDrawable object is ready to display the five images (**Figure 10-14**).

Figure 10-13 Setting setBackgroundResource( ) for the ImageView control

```
MainActivity.java ×
package com.example.northernlightsanimation;

import ...

public class MainActivity extends AppCompatActivity {
    AnimationDrawable lightsAnimation;
    @Override
    protected void onCreate(Bundle savedInstanceState) {
        super.onCreate(savedInstanceState);
        setContentView(R.layout.activity_main);
        ImageView ivFrame= findViewById(R.id.ivLights);
        ivFrame.setBackgroundResource(R.drawable.animation);
    }
}
```

setBackgroundResource( ) assigned to the animation file

Figure 10-14 The getBackground( ) method prepares the AnimationDrawable object

```
MainActivity.java ×
package com.example.northernlightsanimation;

import ...

public class MainActivity extends AppCompatActivity {
    AnimationDrawable lightsAnimation;
    @Override
    protected void onCreate(Bundle savedInstanceState) {
        super.onCreate(savedInstanceState);
        setContentView(R.layout.activity_main);
        ImageView ivFrame= findViewById(R.id.ivLights);
        ivFrame.setBackgroundResource(R.drawable.animation);
        lightsAnimation=(AnimationDrawable)ivFrame.getBackground();
    }
}
```

The AnimationDrawable object gets the view object ready

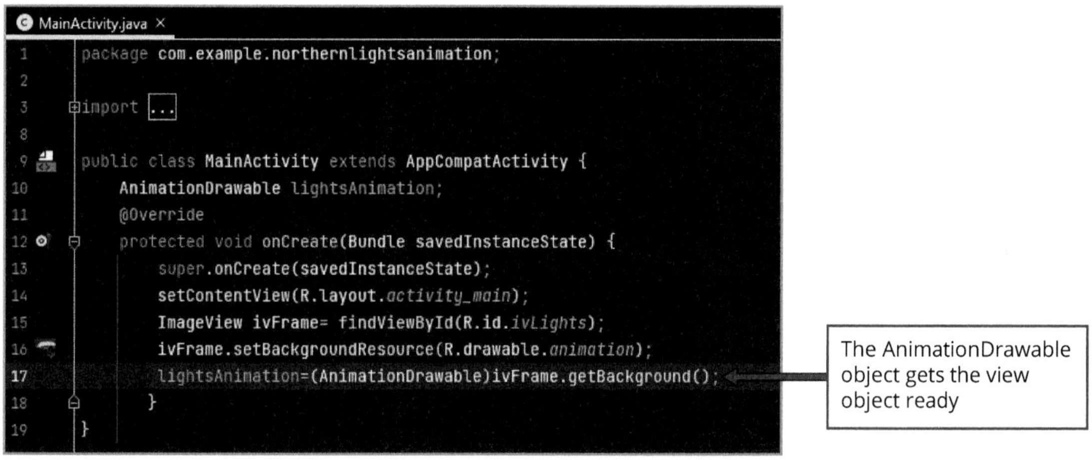

On the Job

Common frame-by-frame animations in professional apps include rotating timers, email symbols, activity icons, page-loading animations, cartoons, sequenced timelines, and other useful user interface elements.

Adding Two Button Controls

The Button controls in the Northern Lights Animation project turn the frame-by-frame animation on and off. Both buttons use a setOnClickListener to await user interaction. To instantiate the two Button controls and add the setOnClickListener, follow these steps.

Step 1

- To code the first button, press the Enter key and then type **Button button1 = findViewById(R.id.btStart);**.
- Click Button, import the Button object, and then click at the end of the line.

The first Button control that begins the animation is instantiated (**Figure 10-15**).

Figure 10-15 Coding the button for the Frame animation

```
MainActivity.java ×
1   package com.example.northernlightsanimation;
2
3   import ...
9
10  public class MainActivity extends AppCompatActivity {
11      AnimationDrawable lightsAnimation;
12      @Override
13      protected void onCreate(Bundle savedInstanceState) {
14          super.onCreate(savedInstanceState);
15          setContentView(R.layout.activity_main);
16          ImageView ivFrame= findViewById(R.id.ivLights);
17          ivFrame.setBackgroundResource(R.drawable.animation);
18          lightsAnimation=(AnimationDrawable)ivFrame.getBackground();
19          Button button1 = findViewById(R.id.btStart);
20      }
21  }
```

Instantiate first Button component btStart as button1

Step 2

- To code the second button, press the Enter key and type **Button button2 = findViewById(R.id.btStop);**.

The second Button control that stops the animation and begins the Tween animation is instantiated (**Figure 10-16**).

Figure 10-16 Coding the button to start the Tween animation

```
MainActivity.java ×
1   package com.example.northernlightsanimation;
2
3   import ...
9
10  public class MainActivity extends AppCompatActivity {
11      AnimationDrawable lightsAnimation;
12      @Override
13      protected void onCreate(Bundle savedInstanceState) {
14          super.onCreate(savedInstanceState);
15          setContentView(R.layout.activity_main);
16          ImageView ivFrame= findViewById(R.id.ivLights);
17          ivFrame.setBackgroundResource(R.drawable.animation);
18          lightsAnimation=(AnimationDrawable)ivFrame.getBackground();
19          Button button1 = findViewById(R.id.btStart);
20          Button button2 = findViewById(R.id.btStop);
21      }
22  }
```

Instantiate second Button component btStop as button2

Step 3

- To code the first Button listener, press the Enter key and type **button1** followed by a period (.) to open a code listing.
- Double-click the first **setOnClickListener** displayed in the auto-completion list.
- Inside the parentheses, type **new On** and then press the Ctrl+spacebar keys to display the auto-completion list.
- Double-click the first choice, which is a **View.OnClickListener** for the auto-generated onClick stub (the button1.setOnClickListener statement).

The first button OnClickListener awaits user interaction for button1 (**Figure 10-17**).

Step 4

- Press the Enter key after the semicolon in Line 27 to code the second Button listener.
- Type **button2** followed by a period (.) to open a code listing.

Figure 10-17 OnClickListener for the first button

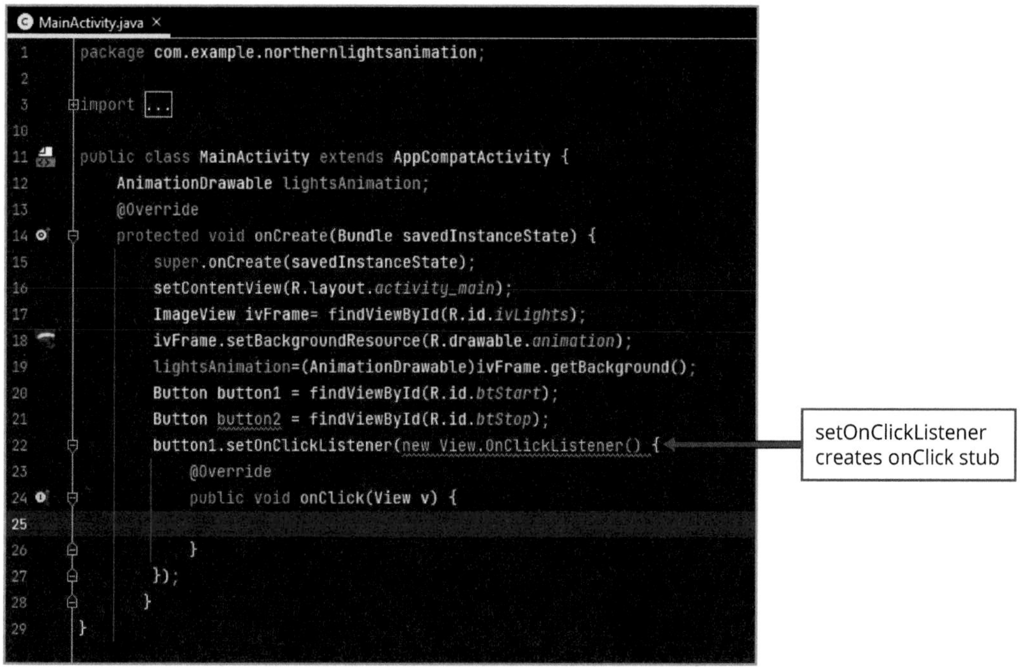

MainActivity.java ×

```
package com.example.northernlightsanimation;

import ...

public class MainActivity extends AppCompatActivity {
    AnimationDrawable lightsAnimation;
    @Override
    protected void onCreate(Bundle savedInstanceState) {
        super.onCreate(savedInstanceState);
        setContentView(R.layout.activity_main);
        ImageView ivFrame= findViewById(R.id.ivLights);
        ivFrame.setBackgroundResource(R.drawable.animation);
        lightsAnimation=(AnimationDrawable)ivFrame.getBackground();
        Button button1 = findViewById(R.id.btStart);
        Button button2 = findViewById(R.id.btStop);
        button1.setOnClickListener(new View.OnClickListener() {
            @Override
            public void onClick(View v) {

            }
        });
    }
}
```

setOnClickListener creates onClick stub

- Double-click the first **setOnClickListener** displayed in the auto-completion list.
- Inside the parentheses, type **new On** and then press the Ctrl+spacebar keys to display the auto-completion list.
- Scroll down and double-click the first choice, which is a **View.OnClickListener** with an Anonymous Inner Type event handler.

The second button OnClickListener awaits user interaction for button2 (**Figure 10-18**).

Figure 10-18 OnClickListener for the second button

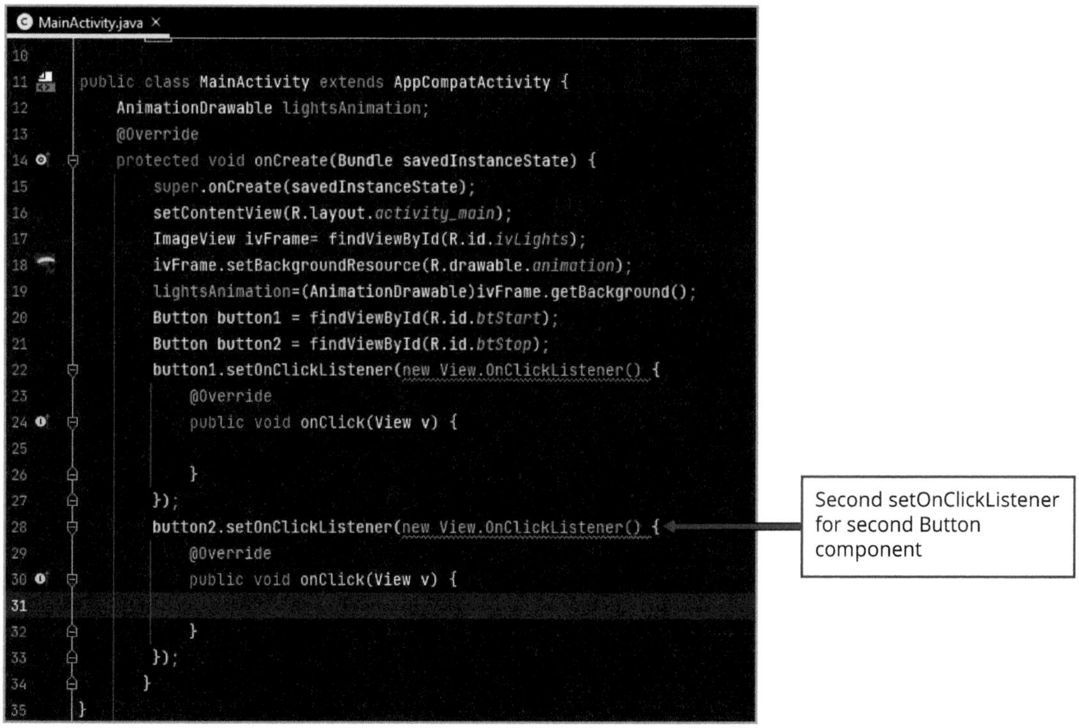

MainActivity.java ×

```
public class MainActivity extends AppCompatActivity {
    AnimationDrawable lightsAnimation;
    @Override
    protected void onCreate(Bundle savedInstanceState) {
        super.onCreate(savedInstanceState);
        setContentView(R.layout.activity_main);
        ImageView ivFrame= findViewById(R.id.ivLights);
        ivFrame.setBackgroundResource(R.drawable.animation);
        lightsAnimation=(AnimationDrawable)ivFrame.getBackground();
        Button button1 = findViewById(R.id.btStart);
        Button button2 = findViewById(R.id.btStop);
        button1.setOnClickListener(new View.OnClickListener() {
            @Override
            public void onClick(View v) {

            }
        });
        button2.setOnClickListener(new View.OnClickListener() {
            @Override
            public void onClick(View v) {

            }
        });
    }
}
```

Second setOnClickListener for second Button component

10.4 Using the start( ) and stop( ) Methods

After associating AnimationDrawable with the animation images and coding the buttons, you can use the start( ) and stop( ) methods of the drawable objects to control the Frame animation. When the user taps the START FRAME ANIMATION button, the start( ) method begins the Frame animation to run continuously because oneshot is set to false. By setting the android:oneshot attribute of the list to true, the animation will cycle just once, then stop and hold on the last frame. The Frame animation stops only when the user taps the START TWEEN ANIMATION button, which launches the stop( ) method and then initiates the startActivity. The second Activity is named Tween.java. In the following code, the start( ) method is placed within the onClick( ) method for the START FRAME ANIMATION button and the stop( ) method is placed within the onClick( ) method for the START TWEEN ANIMATION button.

Code Syntax

```
lightsAnimation.start( );
lightsAnimation.stop( );
```

The start( ) method launches the lightsAnimation.xml file and displays the animation-list items; the stop( ) method ends the display of the animation-list items. To add the start( ) and stop( ) methods, follow these steps.

Step 1

- Click the blank line within the first onClick( ) method for the first button and then type **lightsAnimation.start();** in Line 25.

The START FRAME ANIMATION button is coded to start lightsAnimation.xml (**Figure 10-19**).

Figure 10-19 Entering the start( ) method

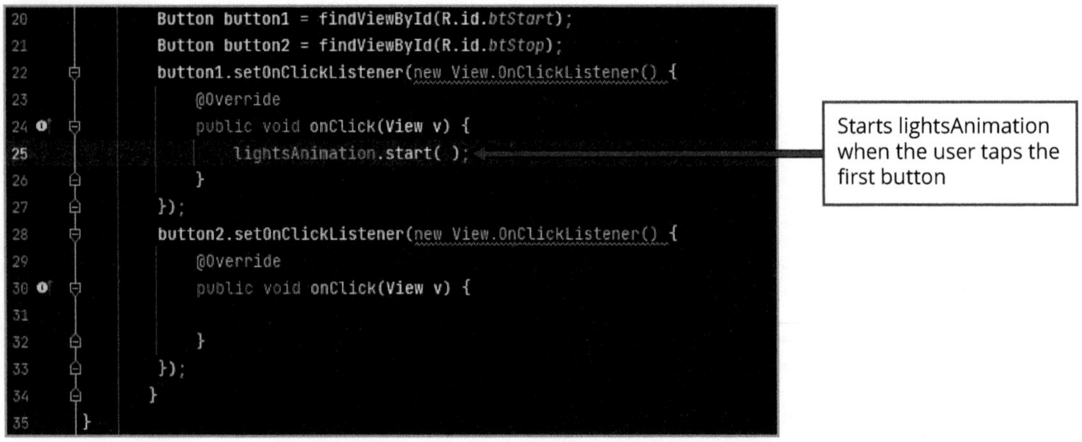

```
20            Button button1 = findViewById(R.id.btStart);
21            Button button2 = findViewById(R.id.btStop);
22            button1.setOnClickListener(new View.OnClickListener() {
23                @Override
24                public void onClick(View v) {
25                    lightsAnimation.start( );
26                }
27            });
28            button2.setOnClickListener(new View.OnClickListener() {
29                @Override
30                public void onClick(View v) {
31
32                }
33            });
34        }
35    }
```

Starts lightsAnimation when the user taps the first button

Step 2

- Click the blank line within the second onClick( ) method for the second button and then type **lightsAnimation.stop();** in Line 31.

The START TWEEN ANIMATION button is coded to stop the Frame animation within lightsAnimation.xml and then begin the Tween animation (**Figure 10-20**).

Figure 10-20 Entering the stop( ) method

```
MainActivity.java ×

public class MainActivity extends AppCompatActivity {
    AnimationDrawable lightsAnimation;
    @Override
    protected void onCreate(Bundle savedInstanceState) {
        super.onCreate(savedInstanceState);
        setContentView(R.layout.activity_main);
        ImageView ivFrame= findViewById(R.id.ivLights);
        ivFrame.setBackgroundResource(R.drawable.animation);
        lightsAnimation=(AnimationDrawable)ivFrame.getBackground();
        Button button1 = findViewById(R.id.btStart);
        Button button2 = findViewById(R.id.btStop);
        button1.setOnClickListener(new View.OnClickListener() {
            @Override
            public void onClick(View v) {
                lightsAnimation.start( );
            }
        });
        button2.setOnClickListener(new View.OnClickListener() {
            @Override
            public void onClick(View v) {
                lightsAnimation.stop( );
            }
        });
    }
}
```

When the user taps the second button, the lightsAnimation stops

Step 3

- To test the Frame animation, click the Run app button on the Standard toolbar and then select the smartphone emulator to launch the emulator.
- Click the START FRAME ANIMATION button to view the Northern Lights animation.

The emulator displays the frame-by-frame animation (**Figure 10-21**).

Figure 10-21 Frame-by-frame animation displayed in the emulator

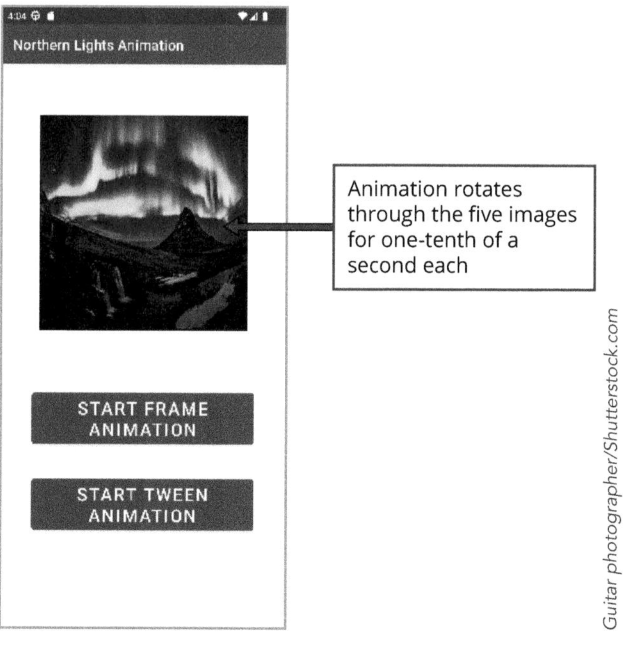

Critical Thinking

To make an object move across the screen, I can either use Frame animation to redraw the object or Tween animation to move the object. Which is easier?

Using Tween animations to move an object's position, change the size of the object, or make opacity changes is less labor-intensive than manually redrawing the image over and over again like a cartoon to show movement.

10.5 Moving with Tween Animation

Instead of rendering several images in a sequence in Frame animation, Tween animation manipulates a drawable image by adding tween effects. Defined in an XML file, **tween effects** are transitions that change objects from one state to another. An ImageView or TextView object can move, rotate, grow, or shrink. As shown in **Table 10-1**, Tween animations include a built-in library of tween effects. These effects are saved within an animation XML file that belongs in the res/anim folder of your Android project. With Tween animation, an Android game could show an avatar hero moving toward a treasure chest, change the opacity of the chest so you can see inside, and spin a clock to indicate the passing of time.

Table 10-1 Tween animation effects

Tween Effect	Purpose
Alpha	Transitions an object from one level of transparency to another, where 0.0 is transparent and 1.0 is opaque
Rotate	Spins an object from one angular position to another. To rotate an object completely around, start at 0 degrees and rotate to 359 degrees (a full circle). A pivotX and pivotY percentage shows the amount of pivot based on the object's left edge.
Scale	Transitions the size of an object (grow or shrink) on an X/Y scale
Translate	Moves the object vertically or horizontally by a percentage relative to the element width (for example, deltaX="100%" would move the image one image width away)

The Tween animation effects in Table 10-1 can be coded in an XML file and individually configured or nested together to animate an object in any possible direction or size.

Good to Know

Android requires that your animated image stay within the original bounds of the View object. Rotations, movement, and scaling transformations that extend beyond the original boundaries clip the image.

Quick Check

What would happen to an image if you used the Translate Tween code deltaY="200%"?

Answer: The image would move down the screen two image widths.

10.6 Launching Tween Animation

When the user taps the START TWEEN ANIMATION button in the Northern Lights Animation app, two actions are triggered within the second onClick( ) method. The Frame animation is concluded with the stop( ) method and a startActivity intent launches a second Activity named Tween.java. To code a second Activity and launch the startActivity, follow these steps.

Step 1

- Minimize the emulator.
- To create a second class and XML layout file, right-click the first com.example.northernlightsanimation folder in the java folder, click New on the shortcut menu, click Activity, and then click Blank Activity.
- In the New Android Activity dialog box, type **Tween** in the Activity Name text box to create a second class that defines the Tween Activity.

A new class named Tween.java and a second XML layout file named activity_tween is created (**Figure 10-22**).

Figure 10-22 Creating the Tween.java class and activity_tween layout

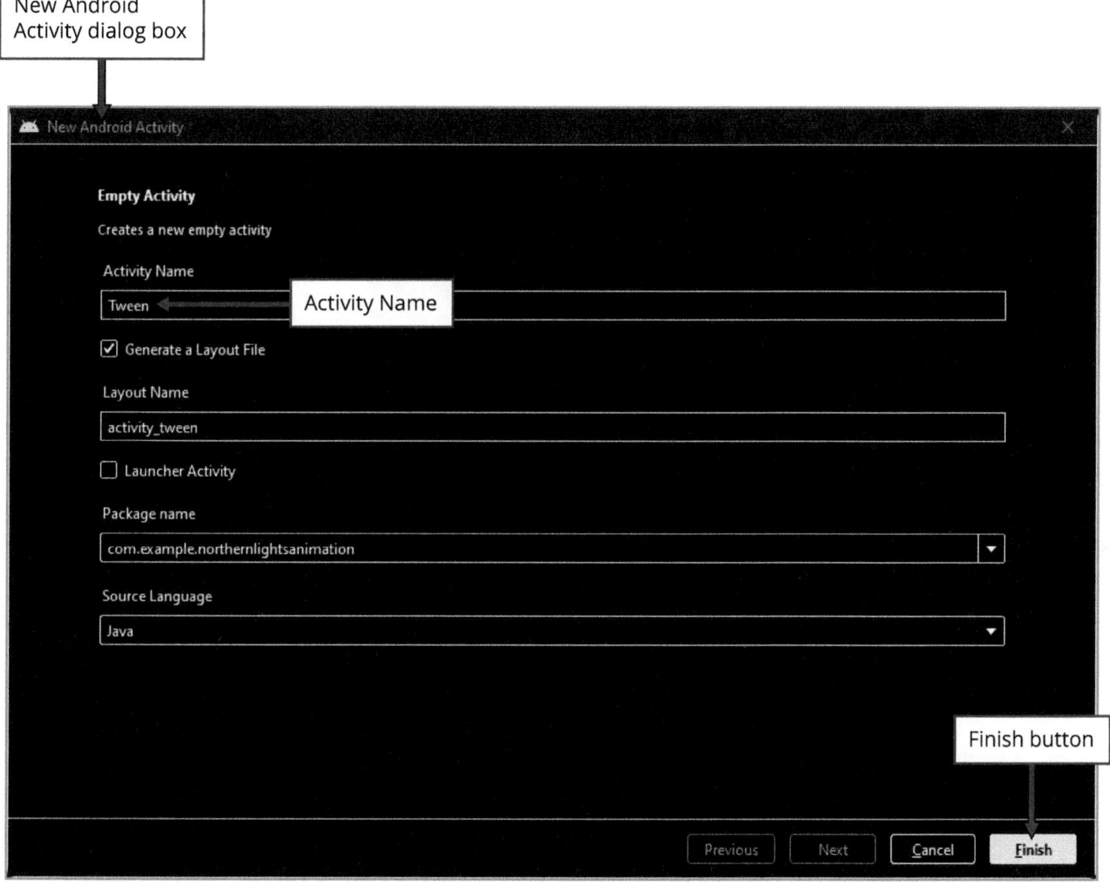

Step 2

- Click the Finish button to finish creating the Tween class and the associated XML layout file.
- To launch the Tween Activity class from the MainActivity.java class, open MainActivity.java.
- Scroll down to the statement lightsAnimation.stop( ) in Line 31.
- Click at the end of the statement and press the Enter key.
- To launch an intent that starts the second Activity, type **startActivity (new Intent (MainActivity.this, Tween.class));**.
- Click the red text "intent" and then press Alt+Enter to import the intent and launch the second class.

A startActivity launches the Tween.java class (**Figure 10-23**).

Figure 10-23 The startActivity launches the Tween class

```
public class MainActivity extends AppCompatActivity {
    AnimationDrawable lightsAnimation;
    @Override
    protected void onCreate(Bundle savedInstanceState) {
        super.onCreate(savedInstanceState);
        setContentView(R.layout.activity_main);
        ImageView ivFrame= findViewById(R.id.ivLights);
        ivFrame.setBackgroundResource(R.drawable.animation);
        lightsAnimation=(AnimationDrawable)ivFrame.getBackground();
        Button button1 = findViewById(R.id.btStart);
        Button button2 = findViewById(R.id.btStop);
        button1.setOnClickListener(new View.OnClickListener() {
            @Override
            public void onClick(View v) {
                lightsAnimation.start( );
            }
        });
        button2.setOnClickListener(new View.OnClickListener() {
            @Override
            public void onClick(View v) {
                lightsAnimation.stop( );
                startActivity (new Intent( packageContext: MainActivity.this, Tween.class));
            }
        });
    }
}
```

startActivity launches Tween class

10.7 Adding the Layout for the Tween Image

After the user taps the START TWEEN ANIMATION button, the Frame animation ends and a second Activity is launched. This second Activity is named Tween.java, and it defines a second layout named activity_tween.xml with a single ImageView control identified as ivTween, which references the fifth image named lights5 that will be rotated with Tween animation. To code the activity_tween.xml file layout to display an ImageView control, follow this step.

Step 1

- Open the activity_tween.xml tab. Click the Design tab at the bottom of the window, if necessary, and then delete the Hello World! TextView object.
- Click the Text tab at the bottom of the activity_tween.xml tab.
- Click Line 8 and press the Enter key to insert a new blank line.
- Add the ImageView control by typing the following custom XML code beginning on Line 9, using auto-completion as much as possible:

```
<ImageView
    android:id="@+id/ivTween"
    android:layout_width="398dp"
    android:layout_height="299dp"
    android:layout_gravity="center"
    android:contentDescription="@string/description"
    android:src="@drawable/lights5" />
```

- Click the Design button to display the emulator.

- Drag all four Constraint handles of the ImageView component to the top, bottom, left, and right edges of the emulator screen.

A second XML layout named activity_tween.xml displays an ImageView control (**Figure 10-24**).

Figure 10-24 ImageView control coded in activity_tween.xml

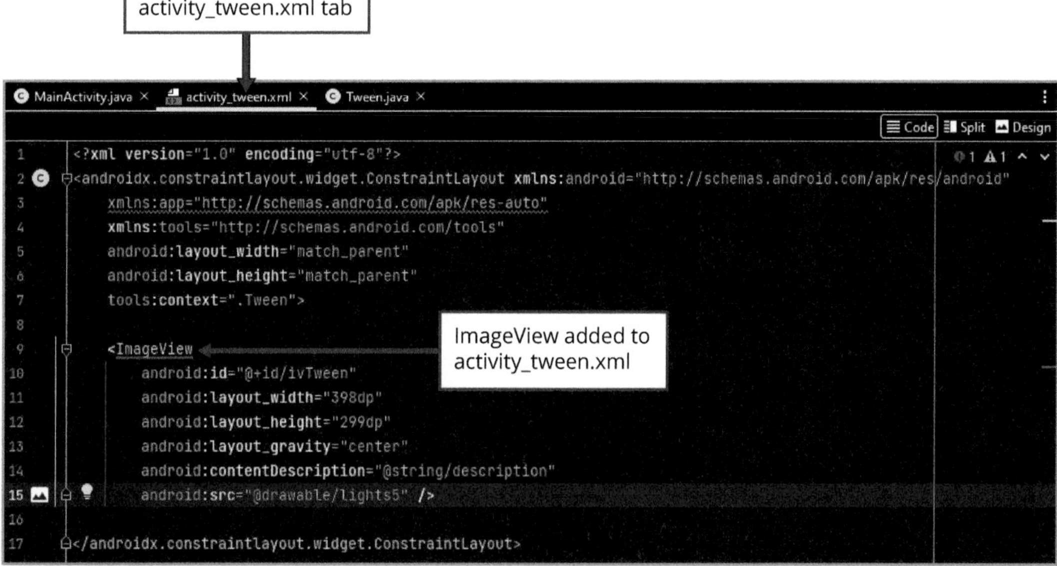

Good to Know | According to *themanifest.com*, 21 percent of millennials say they open an app more than 50 times a day, compared with only 2 percent of baby boomers.

10.8 Setting Tween Animation Attributes

In the Northern Lights Animation application, the last image (lights5.png) is rotated when the user taps the START TWEEN ANIMATION button. Android uses an XML file-creator utility that supports 10 different resource types that can be set as attributes. The default resource type is Layout, but in the chapter project, you select Tween animation. After entering the XML filename as rotation.xml, click the root element of rotate to store the rotation.xml code for a Tween animation in the /res/anim folder. Recall that the XML file for a Frame animation is stored in the /res/drawable folder. The rotation.xml statements are shown in the following code.

Code Syntax

```
<?xml version="1.0" encoding="utf-8"?>
<rotate
xmlns:android="http://schemas.android.com/apk/res/android"
android:fromDegrees="0"
android:toDegrees="359"
android:pivotX="50%"
android:pivotY="50%"
android:duration="2000"
android:repeatCount="5"
```

The rotation.xml code defines the attributes of the Tween animation. Notice that the tween effect is set to rotate in the second line. The fromDegrees and toDegrees rotate attributes spin the object from 0 to 359 degrees, which equals 360 degrees for a full circle. The image in the chapter project completes several clockwise rotations. The pivotX and pivotY attributes pivot an object from its center by setting the pivot point, which can be a fixed coordinate or a percentage. By default, the object pivots around the (0,0) coordinate, or the upper-left corner of the object. Notice that pivotX and pivotY are set to 50 percent in the code example, which determines that the pivot location is from the center of the object.

The duration for each rotation is set for 2000 milliseconds. Tween movement is necessary to convey a sense of fluid movement with still images. The repeatCount represents how many times the object rotates after the initial rotation. You can set repeatCount to an integer or to "infinite" if you do not want the rotation to stop. Remember that the number of rotations is always one greater than the repeat value, so if you set the repeatCount to the integer 5, the object rotates six times. By creating an XML file, it is easier to make simple changes to fine-tune the animation. You might want to try different values in the rotation.xml file to see how the animation changes. To code the Tween animation to rotate an image, follow these steps.

Step 1

- Save and close the activity_tween.xml layout file.
- To create a new rotation XML file, right-click the res folder.
- Click New on the shortcut menu and then click Android resource file. The New Resource File dialog box opens.
- In the File name text box, type the XML filename **rotation**.
- In the Resource type list box, select **Animator**, which is a type of Tween animation.
- In the Root element text box, type **rotate** as the type of element that is added to the XML file.
- In the Directory name text box, type **anim** as the name of the folder in which the Tween animation file is stored.

The New Resource File dialog box displays the specified File name, Resource type, Root element, and Directory name settings (**Figure 10-25**).

Figure 10-25 New Resource File dialog box

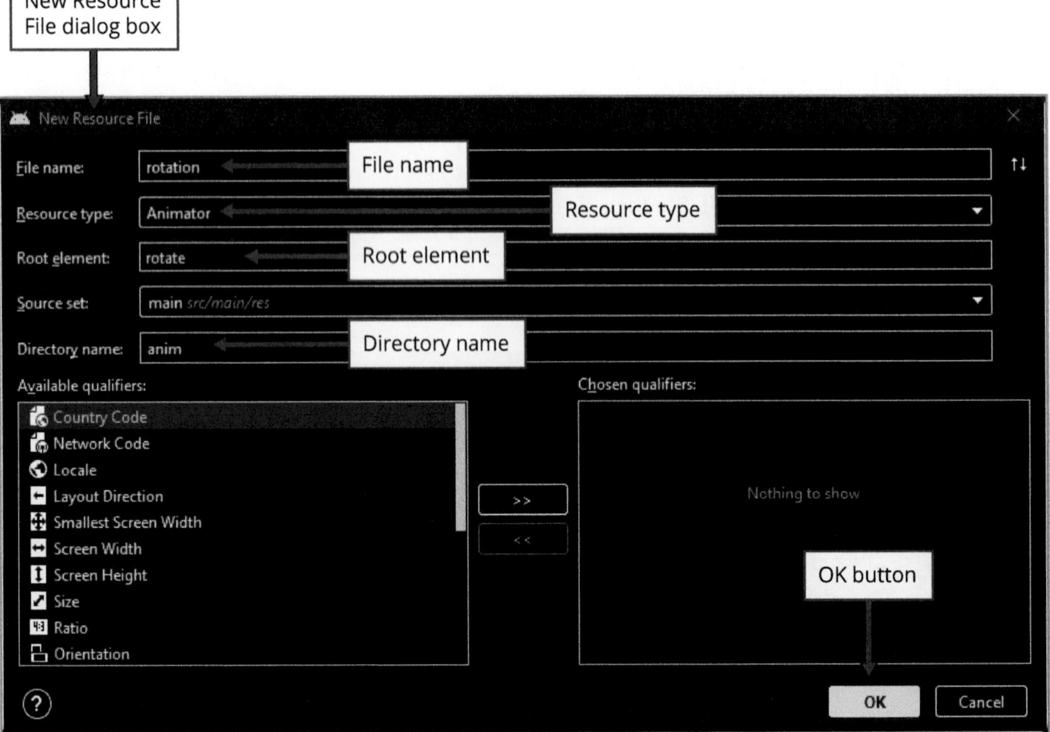

Step 2

- Click the OK button.
- Expand the anim folder in the Android project view. The rotation.xml file opens with the rotate element already coded.
- Delete the closing rotate code on Line 4 and the right angle bracket (>) on Line 2.
- Click Line 3 and type the following code after the opening rotate root element:

```
android:fromDegrees="0"
android:toDegrees="359"
android:pivotX="50%"
android:pivotY="50%"
android:duration="2000"
android:repeatCount="5" />
```

In rotation.xml, the Tween animation attributes are coded to rotate the still image (**Figure 10-26**).

Figure 10-26 The rotate attributes in rotation.xml within the anim folder

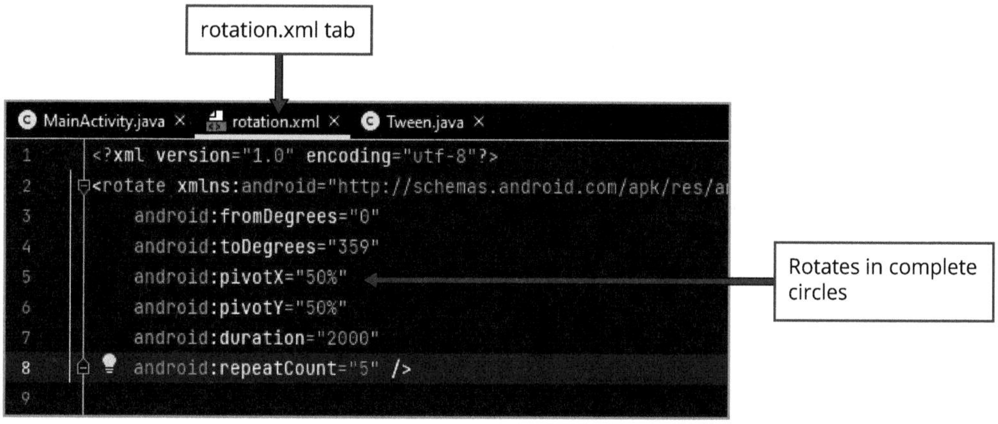

rotation.xml tab

MainActivity.java × rotation.xml × Tween.java ×

```
1 <?xml version="1.0" encoding="utf-8"?>
2 <rotate xmlns:android="http://schemas.android.com/apk/res/a
3     android:fromDegrees="0"
4     android:toDegrees="359"
5     android:pivotX="50%"
6     android:pivotY="50%"
7     android:duration="2000"
8     android:repeatCount="5" />
9
```

Rotates in complete circles

Good to Know To change an image from transparent to opaque, code an alpha statement in an XML file, such as <alpha xmlns:android = http://schemas.android.com/apk/res/android android:fromAlpha="0.0" android:toAlpha="1.0" android:duration="100">.

10.9 Coding the startAnimation( ) Method

Now that the layout, rotation XML file, and second Activity are ready, the Tween animation can be launched using the startAnimation() method. To apply the Tween rotation animation, the **startAnimation( )** method begins animating a View object by calling the AnimationUtils class utilities to access the resources necessary to load the animation. A Tween animation can perform a series of simple transformations with startAnimation( ), changing position, size, rotation, and/or transparency on the contents of a View object. To code the startAnimation( ) method to launch the rotation, follow these steps.

Step 1

- Save and close rotation.xml.
- Open Tween.java from the first java com.example.northernlightsanimation folder.

- Click at the end of Line 13 and press Enter. To instantiate the ImageView control named ivTween, type **ImageView ivRotate = findViewById(R.id.ivTween);**.
- Click ImageView, press Alt+Enter to import the control into this class, and then click at the end of the line.

An instance of the ImageView control named ivRotate is instantiated (**Figure 10-27**).

Figure 10-27 Instantiating the ImageView control

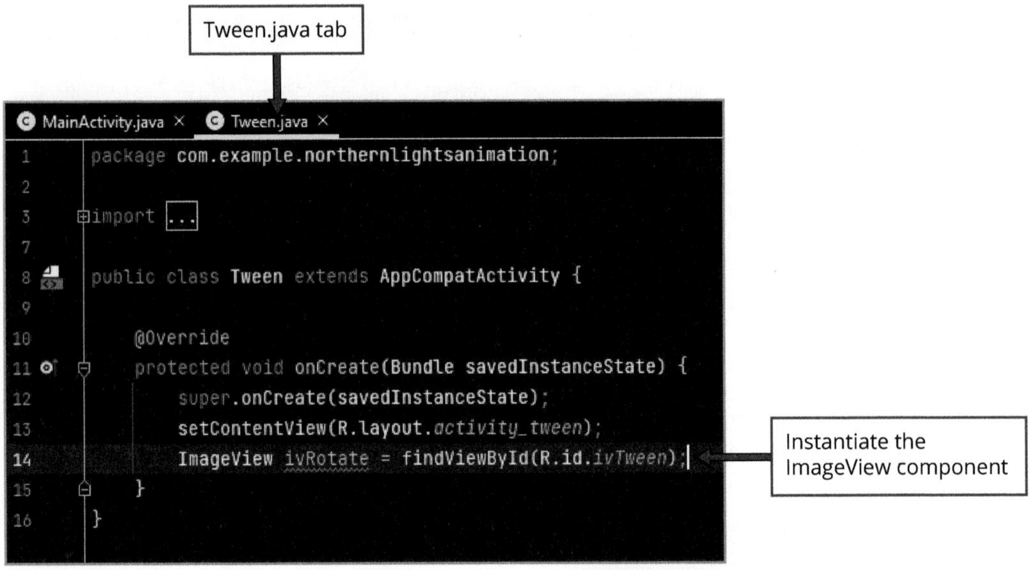

Tween.java tab

MainActivity.java × Tween.java ×

```
1    package com.example.northernlightsanimation;
2
3    import ...
7
8    public class Tween extends AppCompatActivity {
9
10       @Override
11       protected void onCreate(Bundle savedInstanceState) {
12           super.onCreate(savedInstanceState);
13           setContentView(R.layout.activity_tween);
14           ImageView ivRotate = findViewById(R.id.ivTween);
15       }
16   }
```

Instantiate the ImageView component

Step 2

- To begin the Tween rotation animation, press the Enter key and type the following: **ivRotate.startAnimation(AnimationUtils.loadAnimation(this, R.anim.rotation));**.
- Click AnimationUtils and then press Alt+Enter to import the animation utilities into the app.

The Tween animation begins. The fifth image rotates six times and stops (**Figure 10-28**).

Figure 10-28 Image rotates using Tween animation (completed code for Tween.java)

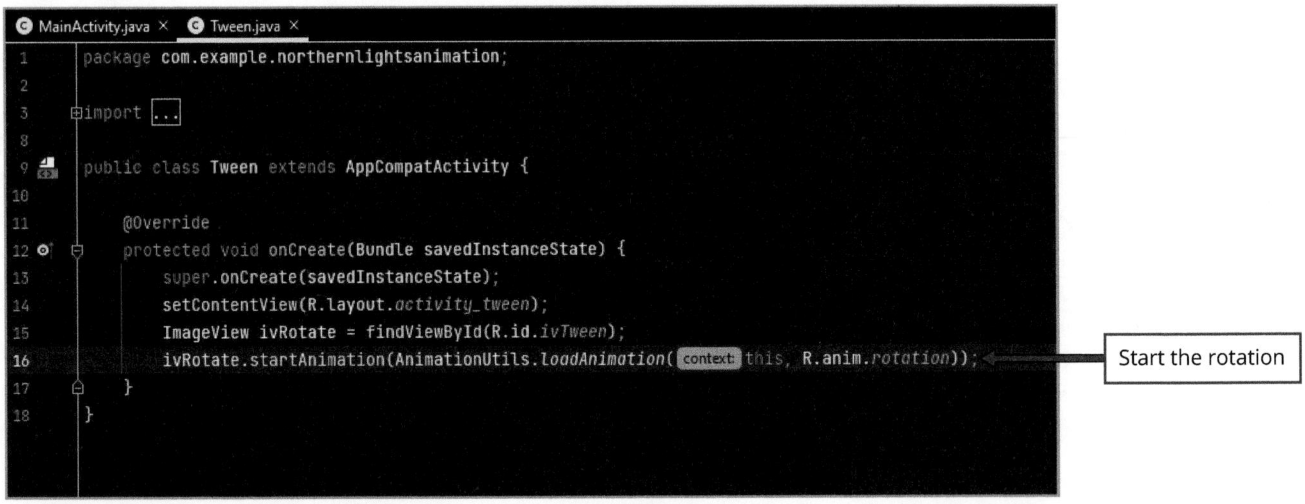

MainActivity.java × Tween.java ×

```
1    package com.example.northernlightsanimation;
2
3    import ...
8
9    public class Tween extends AppCompatActivity {
10
11       @Override
12       protected void onCreate(Bundle savedInstanceState) {
13           super.onCreate(savedInstanceState);
14           setContentView(R.layout.activity_tween);
15           ImageView ivRotate = findViewById(R.id.ivTween);
16           ivRotate.startAnimation(AnimationUtils.loadAnimation( context: this, R.anim.rotation));
17       }
18   }
```

Start the rotation

Critical Thinking

What is the purpose of using AnimationUtils?

The AnimationUtils class launches the animation file from the anim folder by using the loadAnimation( ) method to begin the rotation.

Quick Check

What is the difference between Frame and Tween animation?

Answer: Frame-by-frame animation involves displaying a new image for each frame. Tween animation means transforming or moving a single image over a period of time.

10.10 Changing the Emulator to Landscape Orientation

Most Android phones and tablets automatically rotate the display from portrait to landscape orientation when the user turns the device 90 degrees. In most chapters, the emulator has been shown in a portrait orientation because when you first install the Android emulator, the default screen orientation layout is vertical. To switch the emulator to a landscape orientation on a PC, press the Fn+left Ctrl+F12 keys simultaneously when the emulator is displayed during execution, as shown in Figure 10-2. (You can also press the 7 key on the keypad when Num Lock is turned off.) To rotate the phone emulator back to the initial portrait position, press the Fn+left Ctrl+F12 keys again. Mac users can press the Fn+Ctrl+F12 keys to change the orientation.

Running and Testing the Application

It is time to see both types of animation running in the Android emulator. Click the Run app button on the Standard toolbar and display the app in the Nexus 5 emulator. Click the START FRAME ANIMATION button to begin the Frame animation of the five Northern Lights images, as shown in Figure 10-1. To end the Frame animation and begin the rotation shown in Figure 10-2, click the START TWEEN ANIMATION button. The Tween animation rotates the image six times in a complete circle and ends. Practice changing the orientation of your emulator.

Wrap It Up—Chapter Summary

Android supports two types of animations, frame-by-frame and Tween animations, as shown in the Northern Lights Animation application in this chapter. Frame-by-frame animation shows different drawable images in a view in the opening window. The second Activity displays a Tween animation that rotates an image. Using the animation methods provided in the Android environment, developers can explore the user interface layouts that provide more usability and interest.

- Frame animation assigns a sequence of images to play, similar to a slide show, with a specified interval between images. Tween animation performs a series of transformations on a single image to change its position, size, rotation, and transparency.
- To create a Frame animation, you write code in an XML file to load a sequence of images from the drawable folder. In the XML code, an animation-list root element references these images. Each item in the animation-list code specifies how many milliseconds to display the image.

- In the animation-list code, you can include the oneshot property to determine how many times to play the animation. The oneshot property is set to true by default, meaning the animation plays once and then stops. Set the oneshot property to false to have the animation repeatedly play through to the end and then play again from the beginning.
- When you add the XML file with the animation-list code to the Android project, select Animator as the resource type and select animation-list as the root element so that Android stores the XML file in the res/drawable folder.
- The AnimationDrawable class provides the methods for drawable animations to create a sequence of frame-by-frame images. In Android development, frame-based animations and image transitions are defined as drawables.
- You can set the Background property of an image to any full drawable resource, such as a .png file. In MainActivity.java, you must specify the ImageView control that contains the animation images so you can bind the drawable resource files to the Background property. Assign a new instance of ImageView to the ImageView control that was originally defined in the activity_main.xml layout. Use the setBackgroundResource( ) method to connect the images in the animation-list code to the instance of ImageView.
- In MainActivity.java, also include an instance of AnimationDrawable and assign it as the background of the animation images. Android constructs an AnimationDrawable Java object before setting it as the background. The animation is now ready to display the images, though it does not actually start playing them until the start( ) method is triggered.
- You can use the start( ) and stop( ) methods of the drawable objects to control a Frame animation. When the user taps one button, the start( ) method begins playing the animation continuously if the oneshot property is set to false. The animation stops only when the user taps another button to execute the stop( ) method. The code can then initiate a startActivity that launches another Activity.
- A Tween animation manipulates a drawable image by adding tween effects, which are predefined transitions that change an object from one state to another. Save a tween effect within an animation XML file. Specify the resource type of this XML file as Tween animation so that Android stores the file in the res/anim folder of your Android project.
- The XML file for a Tween animation defines rotate attributes such as the number of degrees to spin, the pivot location, the rotation duration, and the number of times to repeat the rotation.
- To launch a Tween animation, use the startAnimation( ) method, which begins animating a View object by calling the AnimationUtils class utilities to access the resources it needs in order to play.
- To switch the emulator to use a landscape orientation on a PC, press the Fn+left Ctrl+F12 keys. To rotate the emulator to the original portrait position, press the Fn+left Ctrl+F12 keys again. Mac users can press the Fn+Ctrl+F12 keys to change the orientation.

Key Terms

9-patch image
android:oneshot
AnimationDrawable class
animation-list
Frame animation
motion tween
setBackgroundResource( )
startAnimation( )
Tween animation
tween effect

Developer FAQs

1. What are the two types of built-in Android animation? (10.1)
2. Which type of animation displays a slide-show type of presentation? (10.1)
3. Which type of animation is applied to a single image? (10.1)
4. What is the root element of a Frame animation within the XML file? (10.2)
5. Write the code that sets an attribute to play a Frame animation until the app ends. (10.2)
6. Write the code that sets an attribute to play a Frame animation for eight-tenths of a second. (10.2)
7. Would the oneshot property be set to true or false in Question 6? (10.2)
8. Which type of drawable image stretches across different screen sizes? (10.3)
9. Name three types of drawable objects that can be set as a Background drawable. (10.3)
10. Which method launches a Frame animation? (10.4)
11. Which method ends a Frame animation? (10.4)
12. Name four tween effects. (10.5)
13. Which tween effect shrinks an image? (10.5)
14. Which tween effect changes the transparency of an image? (10.5)
15. When you create a Tween XML file, which folder is the file automatically saved in? (10.5)
16. To turn an image one-quarter of a circle starting at 0 degrees, write two lines of the code necessary to make the rotation. (10.8)
17. Write the attribute for a rotation that repeats 11 times. (10.8)
18. When an emulator launches, which orientation type is displayed? (10.10)
19. Which keys change the orientation of the emulator on a PC? (10.10)
20. What happens to an image if you animate an object past the edges of the View object? (10.5)

Beyond the Book

Search the web for answers to the following questions to further your Android knowledge.

1. Research how smartphone animation games have changed the sales of console games in the gaming industry. Write at least 200 words on this topic.
2. Research OpenGL graphic development. Write at least 150 words on this topic.
3. A relatively new player on the mobile platform is the Google Pixel Fold phone. Research why this phone might or might not be successful in the long term. How do apps for this phone need to be developed differently? Write at least 150 words on this topic.
4. On the Google Play site, determine the top four grossing apps. Write a paragraph about each.

Case Programming Projects

Complete one or more of the following case programming projects. Use the same steps and techniques taught within the chapter. Successful completion of these projects requires knowledge of all chapter learning objectives. Submit the program(s) you create to your instructor. The level of difficulty is indicated for each case programming project.

Case Project 10–1: Four Seasons Animation App (Beginner)

Requirements Document

Application title:	Four Seasons Animation App
Purpose:	A series of images uses Frame animation to demonstrate the four seasons.
Algorithms:	**1.** The opening screen displays the first image of the Spring season (**Figure 10-29**). **2.** When the user taps the CHANGE SEASONS button, the four seasons are each displayed for two seconds. After each image is shown once, the animation ends.
Conditions:	**1.** The pictures of the four seasons are provided with your student files; the picture files have the names season1 through season4.

Figure 10-29 Four Seasons Animations app

Case Project 10–2: Flower Growth App (Beginner)

Requirements Document

Application title:	Flower Growth App
Purpose:	A series of images uses Frame animation to demonstrate the life cycle stages of a hibiscus flower.
Algorithms:	**1.** The screen displays five images, each a different stage of the life cycle of a hibiscus flower. Display the images in a Frame animation with 0.5 seconds between each image. Each image should only be displayed once when the user taps the LIFE OF A FLOWER button (**Figure 10-30**). **2.** When the user taps the ROTATE THE FLOWER button, rotate the fifth image 270 degrees nine times with an interval of three seconds.
Conditions:	**1.** Five pictures of a hibiscus flower at different stages are provided with your student files; the picture files have the names flower1 through flower5. **2.** Display each image with the size 500, 600.

Figure 10-30 Flower Growth app

Case Project 10–3: Android Rotation App (Intermediate)

Requirements Document

Application title:	Android Rotation App
Purpose:	As an advertisement at the end of a television commercial, an Android phone rotates in a perfect circle four times.
Algorithms:	**1.** The opening screen displays an Android phone in the center and automatically begins rotating the image four times in a perfect circle with an interval of 1.5 seconds.
Conditions:	**1.** Find a picture online of an Android phone. **2.** Display the image with the size 100, 170. **3.** Code a theme with no title bar.

Case Project 10–4: Cartoon Animation App (Intermediate)

Requirements Document

Application title:	Cartoon Animation App
Purpose:	A sequence of cartoon images is displayed to create the sense of motion.
Algorithms:	**1.** The opening screen displays one of four cartoon images of a man with an idea. When the user taps the START CARTOON button, each image is displayed for 0.15 seconds. **2.** When the user taps the STOP CARTOON button, the current image rotates once and then stops.
Conditions:	**1.** Find cartoons online to create a moving animation. **2.** Display each image with the size 300, 400.

Case Project 10–5: Flags of the World App (Advanced)

Requirements Document

Application title:	Flags of the World App
Purpose:	A sequence of flag images appears when the app starts.
Algorithms:	**1.** The opening screen displays images of seven world flags. When the user taps a START FLAGS button, a Frame animation displays each flag for 0.75 seconds until the app ends. **2.** When the user taps the STOP FLAGS button, the Frame animation stops. The last flag image fades away for 10 seconds until it is no longer visible.
Conditions:	**1.** Find pictures of the seven world flags online. **2.** Display each image with the size 170, 100. **3.** Code a theme with no title bar.

Case Project 10–6: Frame and Tween Animation Game App (Advanced)

Requirements Document

Application title:	Frame and Tween Animation Game App
Purpose:	Display images of your favorite game in action.
Algorithms:	**1.** Locate at least four images of your favorite game character (such as one in Angry Birds) and create a custom Frame animation of your choice. **2.** Create a Tween animation with one of the images that uses at least two tween effects.
Conditions:	**1.** Select your own images. **2.** Use a layout of your choice.

Chapter 11

Discover! Persistent Data

Learning Objectives

At the completion of this chapter, you will be able to:

11.1 Create an Android project using persistent data

11.2 Use different types of shared preferences

11.3 Use internal and external storage

11.4 Save to a database connection

11.5 Save data using a network connection

11.6 Write persistent data using a SharedPreferences object

11.7 Retrieve data using the getString( ) method

11.1 Creating an Android Project Using Persistent Data

An Android app typically requests data and then modifies that data to produce a result throughout multiple activities. To demonstrate the usefulness of storing data across classes, this chapter's Electric Car Financing project requests the number of years for a loan, the loan amount, and an interest rate. A government program provides subsidized electric car loans starting at an interest rate of 1.9 percent if you are approved for a three-, four-, or five-year loan. The opening screen (**Figure 11-1a**) provides three EditText components to accept user input for the term of the loan (three, four, or five years), the amount of the loan, and the interest rate. The user's entries of the three variables are stored in a local variable on the computer (**Figure 11-1b**). These values will persist throughout the life of the app and after the program stops execution. After the user taps the button on the opening screen, a second Activity opens (**Figure 11-2**) and the monthly payment for the loan can be calculated. A unique image is displayed in an ImageView component based on whether the user selected a three-, four-, or five-year loan.

Figure 11-1 Electric Car Financing app

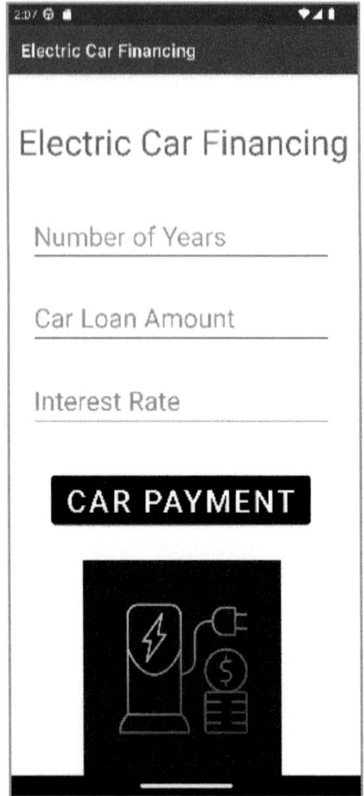

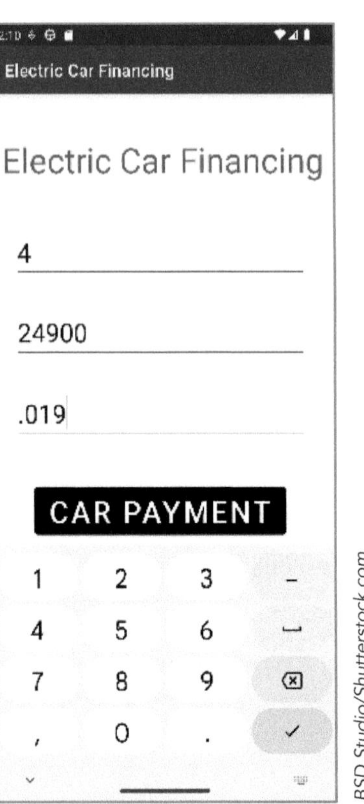

BSD Studio/Shutterstock.com

Figure 11-2 Car payment computed using persistent data in second Activity

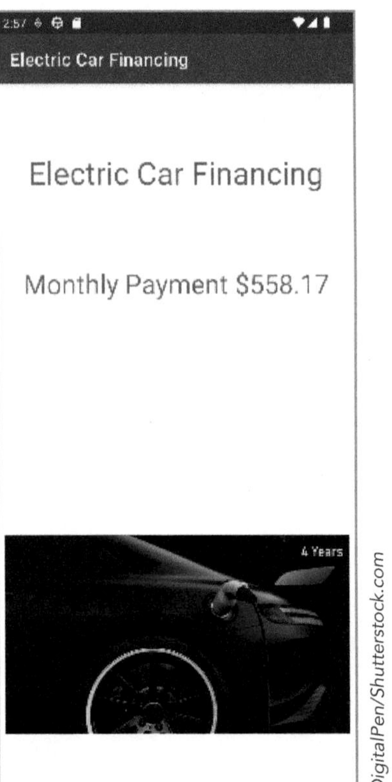

DigitalPen/Shutterstock.com

Good to Know The persistent data structure is available in some form in every programming language.

To create this application, the developer must understand how to perform the following processes, among others:

1. Add strings to the String table.
2. Add images to the drawable folder.
3. Design two XML layouts for the first and second Activity.
4. Instantiate the XML components in the first Activity.
5. Establish a SharedPreferences object to store the data entered.
6. Write data to the SharedPreferences object.
7. Launch a second Activity.
8. Initialize the XML components on the second Activity.
9. Retrieve the data from the SharedPreferences object.
10. Calculate the monthly payment for the car loan and display the appropriate image for the number of loan years using an If structure.
11. Display the monthly payment on the second Activity.

The Electric Car Financing app opens with a window that requests user input. Unlike the Easy Recipes project in Chapter 2, this program allows input that is stored within the device. That data is then used in the second Activity class. With the programs that you have written so far, the values entered did not persist beyond the Activity in which they were created. The data was lost because it was stored in RAM (random access memory), which is cleared when the app or the device stops running. Android applications can save data on the device's drive or other storage media, such as a memory card or cloud service, so that the data can be retrieved later within the app or after the program is ended. **Persistent data** stores values permanently by placing the information in a file.

Android provides several options for saving persistent application data. Persistent data can be saved within a variable or within a database, based on the specific need of the app. Some apps may require private storage, while others should be accessible to other applications. Persistent data can be stored in five ways in Android applications:

- Shared preferences—Stores private data in key-value pairs
- Internal storage—Stores private data in the memory of the device
- External storage—Stores data that can be available to other apps on shared external storage
- SQLite database—Stores structured data in a private database
- Network connection—Stores data on a web server

11.2 Using Different Types of Shared Preferences

While developing a mobile application, you may want to save information for later use—for example, you can save a user's information when the application uses multiple activities or use the information when the app is opened later. If you want the app to welcome users the next time they open it, the app can save the user's name. The SharedPreferences class provides one of the easiest ways to save and load primitive data, whether you are looking to save the user's name or a particular setting, such as the font size the user prefers. In the Electric Car Financing app, the SharedPreferences object stores user data even if the user closes the application. Shared preferences can save any data, including user preferences, such as the wallpaper a user chose or individual values entered by the user in an EditText component.

Shared preferences can be used to save any primitive data: Boolean, floats, ints, longs, and strings. In the chapter project app, this data includes the number of years for the electric car loan (int), the amount of the loan (int), and the interest rate (float). In the first Activity, these values are saved using shared preferences, and in the second Activity, they are retrieved to determine which of three images to display depending on the number of years in the loan. Shared preferences are best when your app needs to save small chunks of data such as a name/value pair. The two-part pair specifies a name for the data you want to save and the actual value. The pair is saved to an XML file that can be retrieved later in the app or after the app closes. To save persistent data in a SharedPreferences file, you must complete the following steps:

- Obtain an instance of the SharedPreferences file.
- Create a SharedPreferences.Editor object.
- Assign values to SharedPreferences objects using the putString( ) method.
- Save the values to the preferences file using the commit( ) method.

11.3 Using Internal and External Storage

Another option when saving persistent data is to store the information directly on the device's internal drive. Persistent storage is any data storage device that retains data after power to the device is shut off. The saved files on the device are available only to the app that created the files. Other applications cannot access files saved with the internal storage method. Use caution when storing internal files; insufficient internal storage space can drastically affect the speed of an Android device and battery life.

Android apps can also save persistent data to external storage—for example, to the device's SD (Secure Digital) card. All applications can read and write files placed on external storage, and the owner of the Android smartphone or tablet can remove them. To use external storage, the following permissions are necessary in the Android Manifest file:

```
<uses-permission android:name="android.permission.WRITE_EXTERNAL_STORAGE"/>
<uses-permission android:name="android.permission.READ_EXTERNAL_STORAGE"/>
```

Quick Check

When an app is saved to the external storage of a smartphone, where is the data typically saved?

Answer: The external data is saved to the SD card.

11.4 Saving to a Database Connection

If you have a large amount of data to store as persistent data, a database is the perfect choice. The default database engine for Android is SQLite. **SQLite** (SQL stands for Structured Query Language) is a lightweight, preloaded mobile database engine that has been available since the Cupcake 1.5 version of Android and occupies a small amount of disk memory. Data is stored within the SQLite database so that it persists even after the app is terminated. Unlike a traditional database, SQLite is embedded into the user's program or browser. Using an SQLite database, Android apps model data items in tables and columns, with optional relationships between the entities within the database. The tables can be queried using SQL statements.

Critical Thinking

Does Android SQLite store the information in a managed interface on a smartphone?

No. Android SQLite is created within the app through a class that handles all the operations required to deal with the database, such as creating the database, adding tables, and updating records.

11.5 Saving Data Using a Network Connection

If your device is connected to the Internet, persistent data can be stored and retrieved using a web service. Before an app attempts to connect to a network, it should check to see whether an Internet connection is available. The device may be out of range of a 4G/5G network or the user may have disabled both Wi-Fi and mobile data access. If a connection is not available, the user cannot save or retrieve the app's persistent data.

Creating XML Layout Files

The Electric Car Financing app begins with the activity_main.xml layout, which displays a title, three EditText Number components, and a Button component. A second XML layout named activity_payment.xml displays an ImageView component with an image of the number of years in the loan and a TextView component to show the monthly payment. To start the application by adding images, a String table, and the first XML layout file, complete the following steps.

Step 1

- Open the Android Studio program.
- In the Welcome to Android Studio window, scroll down and click the New Project button in the Phone and Tablet templates to create a new Android Studio project.
- Click the Next button in the New Project window.
- Type **Electric Car Financing** in the Name text box.
- If necessary, select Java in the Language text box.
- If necessary, select API 23: Android 6.0 (Marshmallow) as the Minimum SDK.

The new Android project has an application name (**Figure 11-3**).

Figure 11-3 Setting up the Electric Car Financing project

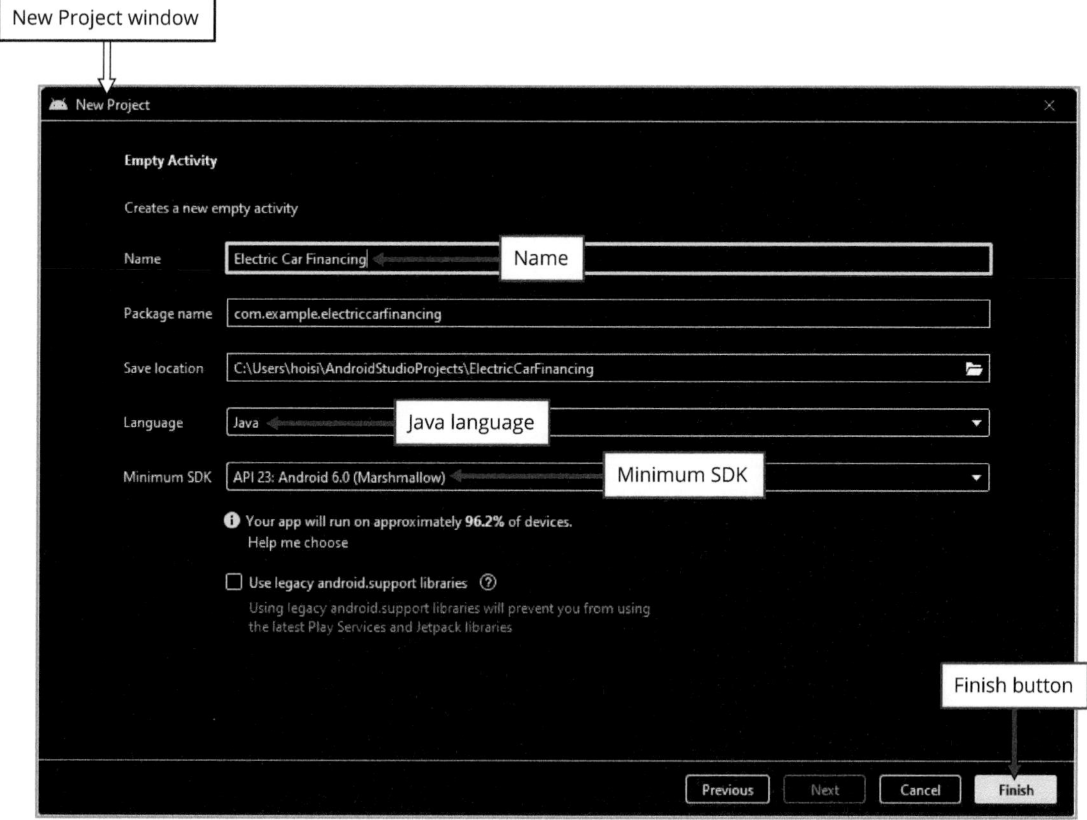

Step 2

- Click the Finish button in the New Project window.
- Click the Hello world! TextView widget displayed by default in the emulator and press the Delete key.
- To add the four image files to the drawable resource folder, copy opening.png, three.png, four.png, and five.png from the student folder on the USB drive and paste the files in the drawable folder.
- Click the OK button in the Copy dialog box.

Copies of the four image files appear in the drawable folder (**Figure 11-4**).

Figure 11-4 Image files in the drawable folder

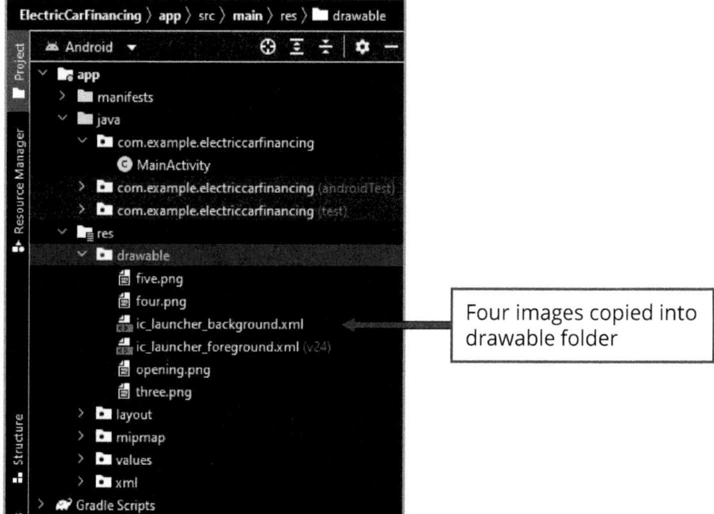

Step 3

- Expand the res\values folder and then double-click the strings.xml file.
- Click the Open editor link and then click the Add Key button.
- Type **btPayment** in the Key text box and type **Car Payment** in the Default Value text box.
- Repeat the process of adding the strings shown in **Table 11-1** to the Translations Editor.
- Save your work.

Table 11-1 String table

Key	Default Value
hint1	Number of Years
hint2	Car Loan Amount
hint3	Interest Rate
ivDescription	Number of Years Image
tvPayment	Monthly Payment
tvTitle	Electric Car Financing

The strings.xml file contains the string values needed for this app (**Figure 11-5**).

Figure 11-5 String values for the app

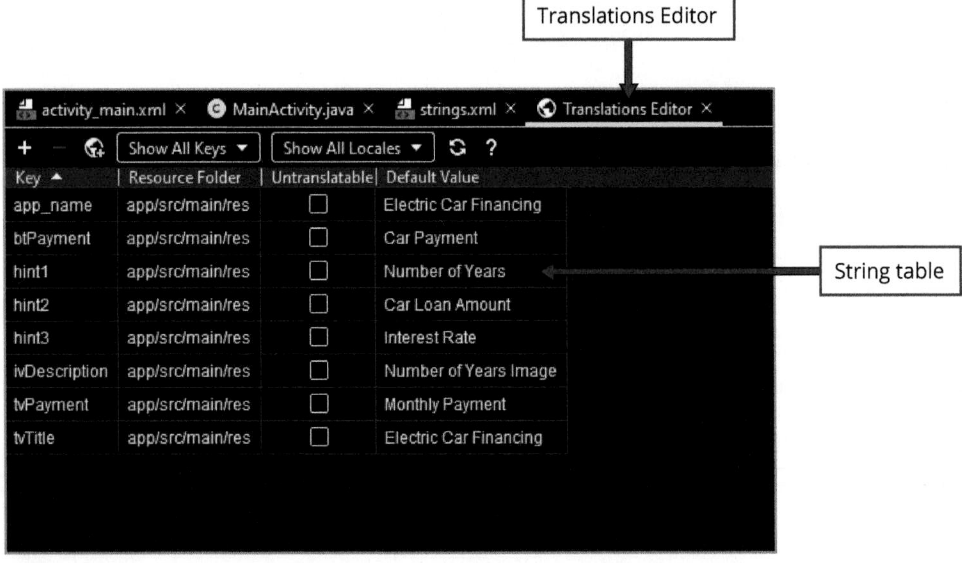

Step 4

- Close the Translations Editor and strings.xml tab.
- If necessary, open the activity_main.xml layout file.
- Drag a TextView component to the top-center part of the emulator.
- Drag a Number component from the Text Fields category of the Palette, and then center the component below the TextView component. This new component represents the number of years of the loan.
- Drag another EditText Number component to the emulator and center it below the first Number component. This new component represents the loan amount.
- Drag an EditText Number (Decimal) component to the emulator and center it below the second Number component. This new component represents the interest rate.

- Drag a Button component from the Form Widgets category and center it below the third Number component.
- Drag an ImageView component from the Widgets category and center it below the Button component.
- Double-click the image placeholder, click the src ellipsis button, and then select “opening” from the Resource Chooser dialog box.
- Click the OK button.
- Drag all four constraint handles of each component to the four edges of the emulator.
- Click the Text tab at the bottom of the window to view the XML code.
- Alter the XML code to match the following customized code.

```
<TextView
        android:id="@+id/tvTitle"
        android:layout_width="wrap_content"
        android:layout_height="wrap_content"
        android:layout_alignParentTop="true"
        android:layout_centerHorizontal="true"
        android:text="@string/tvTitle"
        android:textSize="40sp"
        app:layout_constraintBottom_toBottomOf="@+id/ivOpening"
        app:layout_constraintEnd_toEndOf="parent"
        app:layout_constraintHorizontal_bias="0.0"
        app:layout_constraintStart_toStartOf="parent"
        app:layout_constraintTop_toTopOf="parent"
        app:layout_constraintVertical_bias="0.067" />

<EditText
        android:id="@+id/tvYears"
        android:layout_width="wrap_content"
        android:layout_height="wrap_content"
        android:layout_below="@+id/tvTitle"
        android:layout_centerHorizontal="true"
        android:ems="10"
        android:hint="@string/hint1"
        android:inputType="number"
        android:textSize="30sp"
        app:layout_constraintBottom_toBottomOf="parent"
        app:layout_constraintEnd_toEndOf="parent"
        app:layout_constraintHorizontal_bias="0.423"
        app:layout_constraintStart_toStartOf="parent"
        app:layout_constraintTop_toTopOf="parent"
        app:layout_constraintVertical_bias="0.208" />

<EditText
        android:id="@+id/tvLoan"
        android:layout_width="wrap_content"
        android:layout_height="wrap_content"
```

```
        android:layout_below="@+id/tvYears"
        android:layout_centerHorizontal="true"
        android:ems="10"
        android:hint="@string/hint2"
        android:inputType="number"
        android:textSize="30sp"
        app:layout_constraintBottom_toBottomOf="@+id/ivOpening"
        app:layout_constraintEnd_toEndOf="parent"
        app:layout_constraintHorizontal_bias="0.423"
        app:layout_constraintStart_toStartOf="parent"
        app:layout_constraintTop_toTopOf="parent"
        app:layout_constraintVertical_bias="0.334" />

    <EditText
        android:id="@+id/tvInterest"
        android:layout_width="wrap_content"
        android:layout_height="wrap_content"
        android:layout_below="@+id/tvLoan"
        android:layout_centerHorizontal="true"
        android:ems="10"
        android:hint="@string/hint3"
        android:inputType="numberDecimal"
        android:textSize="30sp"
        app:layout_constraintBottom_toBottomOf="parent"
        app:layout_constraintEnd_toEndOf="parent"
        app:layout_constraintHorizontal_bias="0.423"
        app:layout_constraintStart_toStartOf="parent"
        app:layout_constraintTop_toTopOf="parent"
        app:layout_constraintVertical_bias="0.463" />

    <Button
        android:id="@+id/btPayment"
        android:layout_width="wrap_content"
        android:layout_height="wrap_content"
        android:layout_below="@+id/tvInterest"
        android:layout_centerHorizontal="true"
        android:layout_marginBottom="276dp"
        android:backgroundTint="#000000"
        android:text="@string/btPayment"
        android:textSize="35sp"
        app:layout_constraintBottom_toBottomOf="parent"
        app:layout_constraintEnd_toEndOf="parent"
        app:layout_constraintHorizontal_bias="0.458"
        app:layout_constraintStart_toStartOf="parent" />
```

```
    <ImageView
            android:id="@+id/ivOpening"
            android:layout_width="346dp"
            android:layout_height="242dp"
            android:layout_below="@+id/btPayment"
            android:layout_centerHorizontal="true"
            android:contentDescription="@string/ivDescription"
            android:src="@drawable/opening"
            app:layout_constraintBottom_toBottomOf="parent"
            app:layout_constraintEnd_toEndOf="parent"
            app:layout_constraintHorizontal_bias="0.441"
            app:layout_constraintStart_toStartOf="parent"
            app:layout_constraintTop_toTopOf="parent"
            app:layout_constraintVertical_bias="1.0" />
    </androidx.constraintlayout.widget.ConstraintLayout>
```

The activity_main.xml file contains TextView, EditText, Button, and ImageView components (**Figure 11-6**).

Figure 11-6 First XML layout (*continues*)

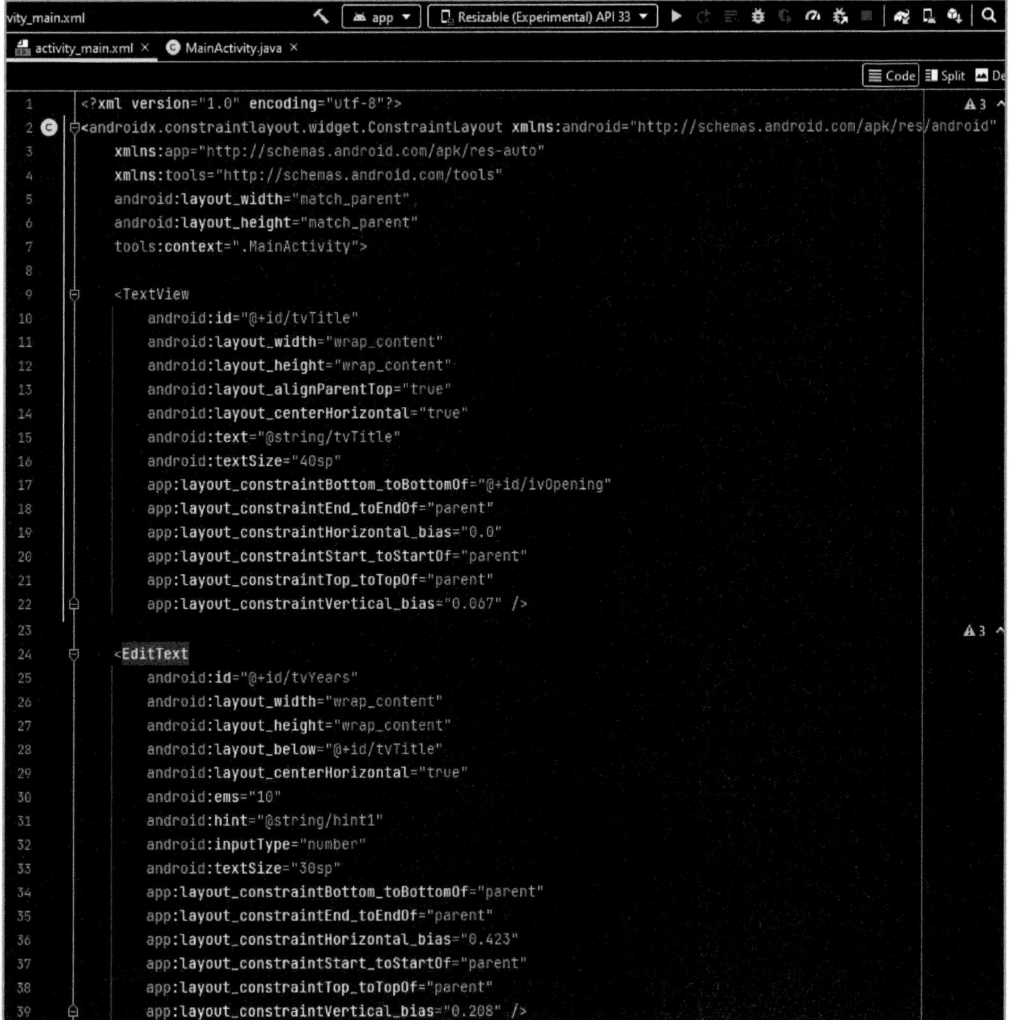

Figure 11-6 (*Continues*)

```
    <EditText
        android:id="@+id/tvLoan"
        android:layout_width="wrap_content"
        android:layout_height="wrap_content"
        android:layout_below="@+id/tvYears"
        android:layout_centerHorizontal="true"
        android:ems="10"
        android:hint="@string/hint2"
        android:inputType="number"
        android:textSize="30sp"
        app:layout_constraintBottom_toBottomOf="@+id/ivOpening"
        app:layout_constraintEnd_toEndOf="parent"
        app:layout_constraintHorizontal_bias="0.423"
        app:layout_constraintStart_toStartOf="parent"
        app:layout_constraintTop_toTopOf="parent"
        app:layout_constraintVertical_bias="0.334" />

    <EditText
        android:id="@+id/tvInterest"
        android:layout_width="wrap_content"
        android:layout_height="wrap_content"
        android:layout_below="@+id/tvLoan"
        android:layout_centerHorizontal="true"
        android:ems="10"
        android:hint="@string/hint3"
        android:inputType="numberDecimal"
        android:textSize="30sp"
        app:layout_constraintBottom_toBottomOf="parent"
        app:layout_constraintEnd_toEndOf="parent"
        app:layout_constraintHorizontal_bias="0.423"
        app:layout_constraintStart_toStartOf="parent"
        app:layout_constraintTop_toTopOf="parent"
        app:layout_constraintVertical_bias="0.463" />

    <Button
        android:id="@+id/btPayment"
        android:layout_width="wrap_content"
        android:layout_height="wrap_content"
        android:layout_below="@+id/tvInterest"
        android:layout_centerHorizontal="true"
        android:layout_marginBottom="276dp"
        android:backgroundTint="#000000"
        android:text="@string/btPayment"
        android:textSize="35sp"
        app:layout_constraintBottom_toBottomOf="parent"
        app:layout_constraintEnd_toEndOf="parent"
        app:layout_constraintHorizontal_bias="0.458"
        app:layout_constraintStart_toStartOf="parent" />

    <ImageView
        android:id="@+id/ivOpening"
        android:layout_width="346dp"
        android:layout_height="242dp"
        android:layout_below="@+id/btPayment"
        android:layout_centerHorizontal="true"
        android:contentDescription="@string/ivDescription"
        android:src="@drawable/opening"
        app:layout_constraintBottom_toBottomOf="parent"
        app:layout_constraintEnd_toEndOf="parent"
        app:layout_constraintHorizontal_bias="0.441"
        app:layout_constraintStart_toStartOf="parent"
        app:layout_constraintTop_toTopOf="parent"
        app:layout_constraintVertical_bias="1.0" />
</androidx.constraintlayout.widget.ConstraintLayout>
```

Figure 11-6 (*Continued*)

BSD Studio/Shutterstock.com

Step 5

- Close the activity_main.xml tab and save your work.

Creating a Second Activity and XML Layout

When the user taps the CAR PAYMENT button in the Electric Car Financing application, a startActivity intent launches a second Activity named Payment.java, which opens a second XML layout named activity_payment.xml to display the monthly car payment and an image that indicates whether the loan is for three, four, or five years. To create a second class and second XML layout and then design the second layout, follow these steps.

Step 1

- Save and close the activity_main.xml tab.
- To create a second class and XML layout file, right-click the first java/com.example.electriccarfinancing folder, click New on the shortcut menu, click Activity, and then click Blank Activity.
- Type **Payment** in the Activity Name text box of the New Android Activity dialog box to create a second class that defines the Payment Activity.

A new class named Payment.java and a second XML layout file named activity_payment is created (**Figure 11-7**).

Figure 11-7 Creating a second class named Payment and a second XML layout named activity_payment

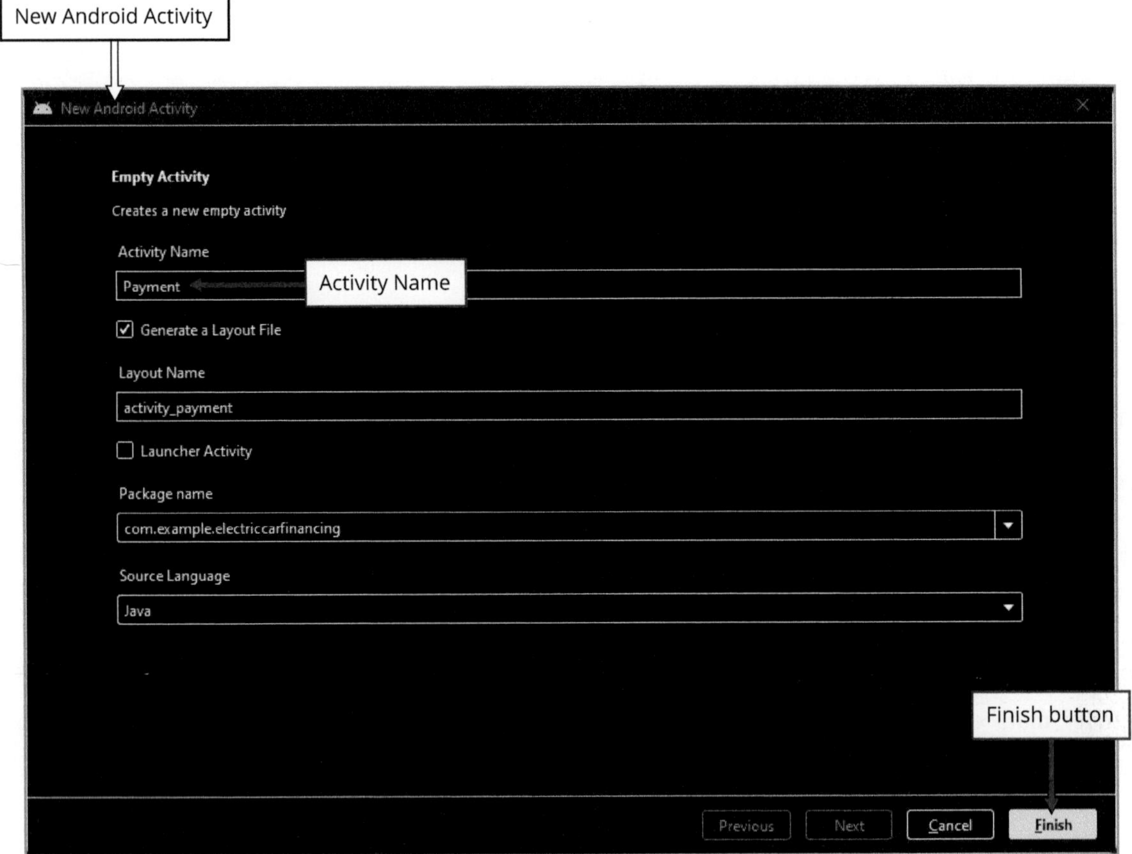

Step 2

- Click the Finish button to finish creating the Payment class and the associated XML layout file.
- Click the Design tab in activity_payment.xml.
- Drag a TextView component from the Palette to the top-center part of the activity_payment emulator.
- Drag a second TextView component to the emulator and center it below the first one.
- Drag an ImageView component below the two TextView components and center it horizontally.
- Drag all four constraint handles of each component to the edges of the emulator.
- Click the Text tab at the bottom of the window to display the XML code for this layout.
- Alter the XML code to match the following customized code and then save your work.

```
<TextView
    android:id="@+id/tvTitle2"
    android:layout_width="wrap_content"
    android:layout_height="wrap_content"
    android:layout_alignParentTop="true"
```

```
        android:layout_centerHorizontal="true"
        android:text="@string/tvTitle"
        android:textSize="35sp"
        app:layout_constraintBottom_toBottomOf="parent"
        app:layout_constraintEnd_toEndOf="parent"
        app:layout_constraintStart_toStartOf="parent"
        app:layout_constraintTop_toTopOf="parent"
        app:layout_constraintVertical_bias="0.101" />

    <TextView
        android:id="@+id/tvMonthlyPayment"
        android:layout_width="wrap_content"
        android:layout_height="wrap_content"
        android:layout_below="@+id/tvTitle2"
        android:layout_centerHorizontal="true"
        android:textSize="30sp"
        app:layout_constraintBottom_toBottomOf="parent"
        app:layout_constraintEnd_toEndOf="parent"
        app:layout_constraintHorizontal_bias="0.498"
        app:layout_constraintStart_toStartOf="parent"
        app:layout_constraintTop_toTopOf="parent"
        app:layout_constraintVertical_bias="0.27" />

    <ImageView
        android:id="@+id/ivYears"
        android:layout_width="396dp"
        android:layout_height="285dp"
        android:layout_alignParentBottom="true"
        android:layout_centerHorizontal="true"
        android:contentDescription="@string/ivDescription"
        app:layout_constraintBottom_toBottomOf="parent"
        app:layout_constraintEnd_toEndOf="parent"
        app:layout_constraintStart_toStartOf="parent"
        app:layout_constraintTop_toTopOf="parent"
        app:layout_constraintVertical_bias="0.935" />
</androidx.constraintlayout.widget.ConstraintLayout>
```

The activity_payment.xml file contains two TextView components and an ImageView component (**Figure 11-8**). The figure also shows the app screen in progress.

Figure 11-8 TextView and ImageView components for activity_payment.xml

```
<androidx.constraintlayout.widget.ConstraintLayout xmlns:android="http://schemas.android.com/apk/res/android"
    xmlns:app="http://schemas.android.com/apk/res-auto"
    xmlns:tools="http://schemas.android.com/tools"
    android:layout_width="match_parent"
    android:layout_height="match_parent"
    tools:context=".Payment">

    <TextView
        android:id="@+id/tvTitle2"
        android:layout_width="wrap_content"
        android:layout_height="wrap_content"
        android:layout_alignParentTop="true"
        android:layout_centerHorizontal="true"
        android:text="@string/tvTitle"
        android:textSize="35sp"
        app:layout_constraintBottom_toBottomOf="parent"
        app:layout_constraintEnd_toEndOf="parent"
        app:layout_constraintStart_toStartOf="parent"
        app:layout_constraintTop_toTopOf="parent"
        app:layout_constraintVertical_bias="0.101" />

    <TextView
        android:id="@+id/tvMonthlyPayment"
        android:layout_width="wrap_content"
        android:layout_height="wrap_content"
        android:layout_below="@+id/tvTitle2"
        android:layout_centerHorizontal="true"
        android:textSize="30sp"
        app:layout_constraintBottom_toBottomOf="parent"
        app:layout_constraintEnd_toEndOf="parent"
        app:layout_constraintHorizontal_bias="0.498"
        app:layout_constraintStart_toStartOf="parent"
        app:layout_constraintTop_toTopOf="parent"
        app:layout_constraintVertical_bias="0.27" />

    <ImageView
        android:id="@+id/ivYears"
        android:layout_width="396dp"
        android:layout_height="285dp"
        android:layout_alignParentBottom="true"
        android:layout_centerHorizontal="true"
        android:contentDescription="@string/ivDescription"
        app:layout_constraintBottom_toBottomOf="parent"
        app:layout_constraintEnd_toEndOf="parent"
        app:layout_constraintStart_toStartOf="parent"
        app:layout_constraintTop_toTopOf="parent"
        app:layout_constraintVertical_bias="0.935" />
</androidx.constraintlayout.widget.ConstraintLayout>
```

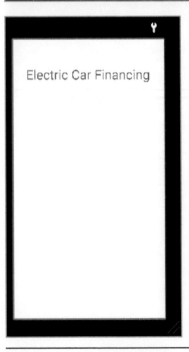

Instantiating the XML Components

When the Electric Car Financing app starts, the activity_main.xml layout opens, displays the TextView component title, and asks the user to enter the number of years for financing the loan, the loan amount, and the interest rate as a decimal value. When the user taps the Button component, the values are assigned to the variables in the MainActivity class. To instantiate the XML components from the first Activity, follow these steps.

Step 1

- Close the activity_payment.xml tab.
- Open the MainActivity.java code window.
- Press the Enter key to insert a new line after Line 13, type **final EditText years = (EditText)findViewById(R.id.tvYears);** to instantiate the first EditText component, and then press the Enter key.
- Click EditText and import the class by pressing Alt+Enter.
- Type **final EditText loan = (EditText)findViewById(R.id.tvLoan);** to instantiate the second EditText component, and then press the Enter key.
- Type **final EditText interest = (EditText)findViewById(R.id.tvInterest);** to instantiate the third EditText component.

The three EditText components are instantiated (**Figure 11-9**).

Figure 11-9 EditText components instantiated

MainActivity.java

MainActivity.java × Payment.java ×

```
1   package com.example.electriccarfinancing;
2
3   import ...
7
8   public class MainActivity extends AppCompatActivity {
9
10      @Override
11      protected void onCreate(Bundle savedInstanceState) {
12          super.onCreate(savedInstanceState);
13          setContentView(R.layout.activity_main);
14          final EditText years = (EditText) findViewById(R.id.tvYears);
15          final EditText loan = (EditText)findViewById(R.id.tvLoan);
16          final EditText interest = (EditText)findViewById(R.id.tvInterest);
17      }
18  }
```

Three EditText components instantiated

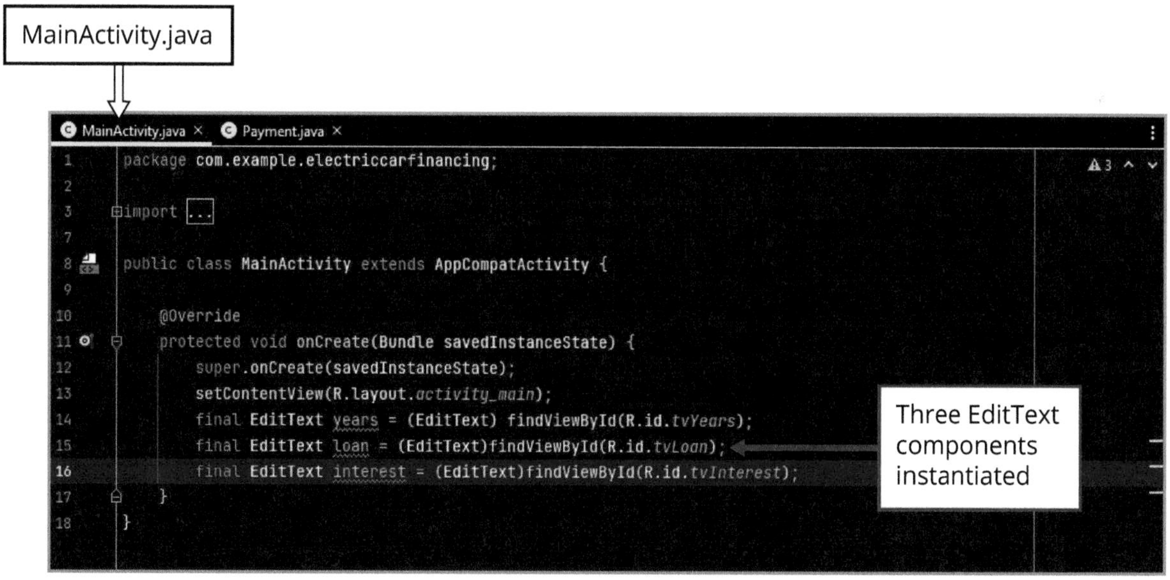

Step 2

- On the next line, type **Button button = (Button)findViewById(R.id.btPayment);** to instantiate the Button component, and then press the Enter key twice.
- Click the red Button text and press Alt+Enter to import the Button library.
- Click the next line (Line 20). To create a setOnClickListener( ) method so the Button component waits for the user's click, type **button.setOn** and wait for the auto-complete listing to appear.
- Double-click setOnClickListener to select it from the auto-complete listing.
- In the parentheses, type **new On** and wait for the auto-complete listing to appear.
- Double-click the first choice, which lists a View.OnClickListener.

An OnClickListener auto-generated stub appears in the code (**Figure 11-10**).

Figure 11-10 Button OnClickListener stub

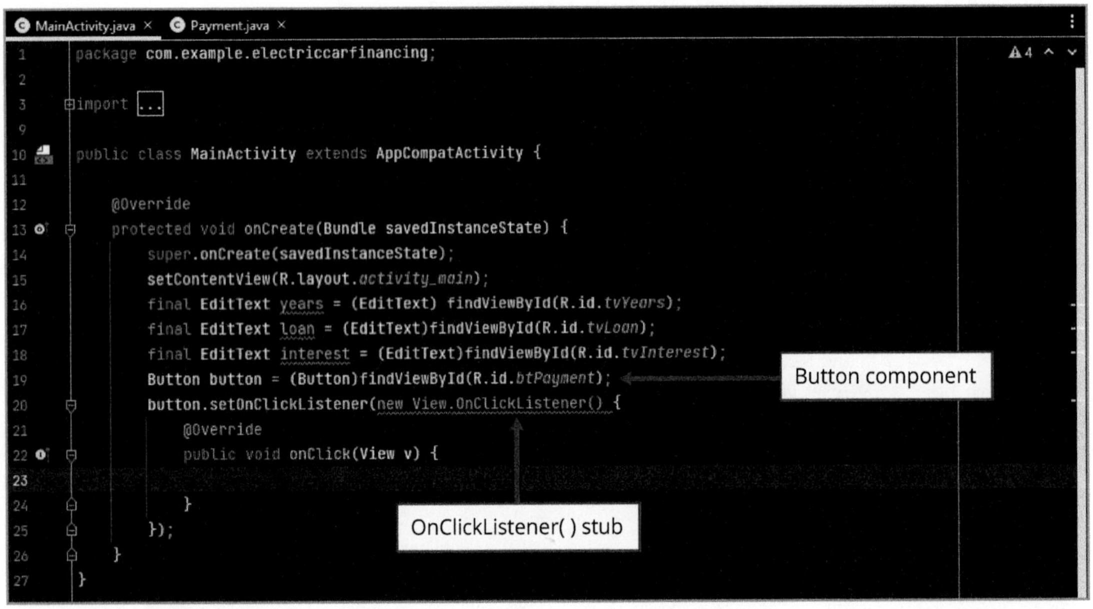
MainActivity.java ×
Payment.java ×
1 package com.example.electriccarfinancing;
2
3 import ...
9
10 public class MainActivity extends AppCompatActivity {
11
12 @Override
13 protected void onCreate(Bundle savedInstanceState) {
14 super.onCreate(savedInstanceState);
15 setContentView(R.layout.activity_main);
16 final EditText years = (EditText) findViewById(R.id.tvYears);
17 final EditText loan = (EditText)findViewById(R.id.tvLoan);
18 final EditText interest = (EditText)findViewById(R.id.tvInterest);
19 Button button = (Button)findViewById(R.id.btPayment);
20 button.setOnClickListener(new View.OnClickListener() {
21 @Override
22 public void onClick(View v) {
23
24 }
25 });
26 }
27 }
Button component
OnClickListener( ) stub

Step 3

- On Line 11, begin to initialize the variables by typing **int intYears;** and pressing Enter.
- On the next line, type **int intLoan;** and then press Enter.
- On the next line, type **float decInterest;** and press Enter.
- Click within the onClick( ) method on Line 25 and assign the number of years for the term of the loan by typing **intYears = Integer.parseInt(years.getText().toString());** and then pressing Enter.
- On the next line, assign the amount of the requested loan to an integer value by typing **intLoan = Integer.parseInt(loan.getText().toString());** and then pressing Enter.
- On the next line, assign the interest rate to a float value by typing **decInterest = Float.parseFloat(interest.getText().toString());**.

The variables intYears, intLoan, and decInterest are assigned to the entered number of years, the loan amount, and the decimal interest rate (**Figure 11-11**).

Figure 11-11 Variables intYears, intLoan, and decInterest assigned

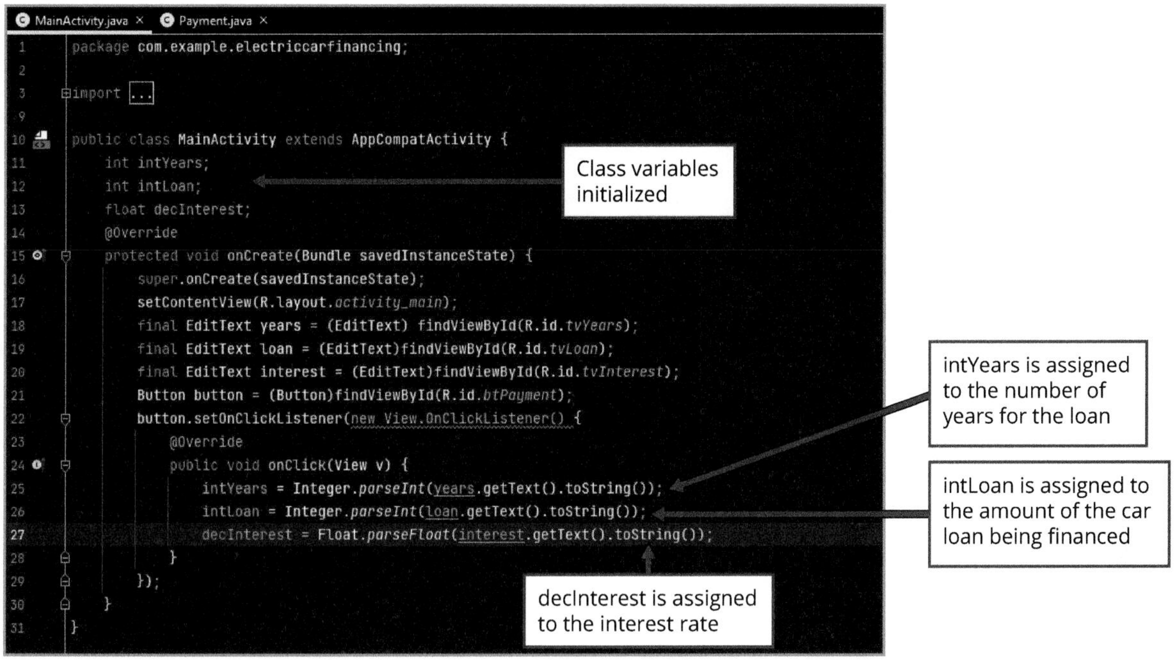
MainActivity.java ×
Payment.java ×
package com.example.electriccarfinancing;
import ...
public class MainActivity extends AppCompatActivity {
int intYears;
int intLoan;
float decInterest;
@Override
protected void onCreate(Bundle savedInstanceState) {
super.onCreate(savedInstanceState);
setContentView(R.layout.activity_main);
final EditText years = (EditText) findViewById(R.id.tvYears);
final EditText loan = (EditText)findViewById(R.id.tvLoan);
final EditText interest = (EditText)findViewById(R.id.tvInterest);
Button button = (Button)findViewById(R.id.btPayment);
button.setOnClickListener(new View.OnClickListener() {
@Override
public void onClick(View v) {
intYears = Integer.parseInt(years.getText().toString());
intLoan = Integer.parseInt(loan.getText().toString());
decInterest = Float.parseFloat(interest.getText().toString());
}
});
}
}
Class variables initialized
intYears is assigned to the number of years for the loan
intLoan is assigned to the amount of the car loan being financed
decInterest is assigned to the interest rate

Good to Know When you write data using SharedPreferences, you can make changes to the data by using the SharedPreferences Editor.

11.6 Writing Persistent Data with SharedPreferences

One of the most effective ways to save simple application data to an Android device is by using the SharedPreferences object. The data is saved to an XML file as a key-value pair. The **key** is a string such as "key1" that uniquely identifies the preference, and the **value** is the data represented as a string, int, long, float, or Boolean value. Android SharedPreferences store data that can be used in different Activities of your application or by another application. A common example of using SharedPreferences is in a game like Angry Birds. The Angry Birds app needs to save the high score from game to game, the username, and the current level achieved. Preferences can be stored at the Activity or application level.

In the chapter project app, the first data to be stored is the number of years in the term of the car loan. The SharedPreference for this data is a set of values: key1 uniquely identifies the preference and intYears represents the actual value of the integer. A preference can be any of a number of different data types. The following data types are supported by the SharedPreferences class:

- putString( )—Stores string values
- putInt( )—Stores integer values
- putLong( )—Stores long values
- putFloat( )—Stores float values
- putBoolean( )—Stores Boolean values

To create an instance of the SharedPreferences object from an Activity, you use the following code syntax.

Code Syntax

```
final SharedPreferences sharedPref =
    PreferenceManager.getDefaultSharedPreferences(this);
SharedPreferences.Editor editor = sharedPref.edit();
editor.putInt("key1", intYears);
editor.putInt("key2", intLoan);
editor.putFloat("key3", decInterest);
editor.commit();
```

In the first line, a valid SharedPreferences object is instantiated. Next, a SharedPreferences.Editor provides a method to add, modify, or delete preference content. Within the editor, you can also remove a specific preference by name using the remove( ) method or remove all preferences within the set by using the clear( ) method. The putInt( ) and putFloat( ) methods are not called immediately. The commit( ) method must be called to actually write the values to the XML file. Save values as persistent data using SharedPreferences by following these steps.

Step 1

- In the code on the MainActivity.java tab, after the Button is instantiated in Line 21, type **final SharedPreferences sharedPref = PreferenceManager.getDefaultSharedPreferences(this);**.
- Click SharedPreferences and press Alt+Enter to import SharedPreferences.
- Click PreferenceManager and press Alt+Enter to import the library.

An instance of the SharedPreferences class named sharedPref is created in the MainActivity class (**Figure 11-12**).

Figure 11-12 SharedPreferences class

```
11
12  public class MainActivity extends AppCompatActivity {
13      int intYears;
14      int intLoan;
15      float decInterest;
16      @Override
17      protected void onCreate(Bundle savedInstanceState) {
18          super.onCreate(savedInstanceState);
19          setContentView(R.layout.activity_main);
20          final EditText years = (EditText) findViewById(R.id.tvYears);
21          final EditText loan = (EditText)findViewById(R.id.tvLoan);
22          final EditText interest = (EditText)findViewById(R.id.tvInterest);
23          Button button = (Button)findViewById(R.id.btPayment);
24          final SharedPreferences sharedPref = PreferenceManager.getDefaultSharedPreferences( context: this);
25          button.setOnClickListener(new View.OnClickListener() {
26              @Override
27              public void onClick(View v) {
28                  intYears = Integer.parseInt(years.getText().toString());
29                  intLoan = Integer.parseInt(loan.getText().toString());
30                  decInterest = Float.parseFloat(interest.getText().toString());
31              }
32          });
33      }
34  }
```

Instantiate the SharedPreferences object

Step 2

- Click at the end of Line 30 (the assignment of decInterest) and then press Enter to add a new line within the OnClick( ) method.
- To store data using the editor, type **SharedPreferences.Editor editor = sharedPref.edit();** and then press Enter.
- On the next line, assign the first key-value pair by typing **editor.putInt("key1", intYears);** and pressing Enter.
- On the next line, assign the second key-value pair by typing **editor.putInt("key2", intLoan);** and pressing Enter.
- On the next line, assign the third key-value pair by typing **editor.putFloat("key3", decInterest);** and pressing Enter.
- To write the values to the XML data file, type **editor.commit();** on the next line.

Three values are saved to the SharedPreferences XML data file (**Figure 11-13**).

Figure 11-13 Three values (persistent data) written in an XML data file

```
17      protected void onCreate(Bundle savedInstanceState) {
18          super.onCreate(savedInstanceState);
19          setContentView(R.layout.activity_main);
20          final EditText years = (EditText) findViewById(R.id.tvYears);
21          final EditText loan = (EditText)findViewById(R.id.tvLoan);
22          final EditText interest = (EditText)findViewById(R.id.tvInterest);
23          Button button = (Button)findViewById(R.id.btPayment);
24          final SharedPreferences sharedPref = PreferenceManager.getDefaultSharedPreferences( context: this);
25          button.setOnClickListener(new View.OnClickListener() {
26              @Override
27              public void onClick(View v) {
28                  intYears = Integer.parseInt(years.getText().toString());
29                  intLoan = Integer.parseInt(loan.getText().toString());
30                  decInterest = Float.parseFloat(interest.getText().toString());
31                  SharedPreferences.Editor editor = sharedPref.edit();
32                  editor.putInt("key1", intYears);
33                  editor.putInt("key2", intLoan);
34                  editor.putFloat("key3", decInterest);
35                  editor.commit();
36              }
37          });
38      }
39  }
```


Good to Know | There is no limit to the number of shared preferences you can create.

Quick Check

Given the following information, how would you code the first line of data to be stored to represent the value of tire pressure as a float?

The SharedPreference for this data is a set of values: key1 uniquely identifies the preference and decPressure represents the actual value of the float.

Answer: editor.putFloat("key1", decPressure);

Launching the Second Activity

After the persistent data is saved to a local XML file, MainActivity starts a second Activity named Payment.java. The second Activity is responsible for retrieving the persistent data, which is tested using a conditional If statement to determine the payment amount based on the number of years in the loan. To launch the second class, follow this step.

Step 1

- To launch the Payment class from the first Activity, insert a new line in the onClick(View v) auto-generated method stub after the editor.commit(); statement.
- Type **startActivity(new Intent(MainActivity.this, Payment.class));** to launch the second Activity.
- Click Intent and then press Alt+Enter. Save your work.

The second Activity named Payment is launched with an Intent statement (**Figure 11-14**).

Figure 11-14 A startActivity Intent launches the Payment class

```
protected void onCreate(Bundle savedInstanceState) {
    super.onCreate(savedInstanceState);
    setContentView(R.layout.activity_main);
    final EditText years = (EditText) findViewById(R.id.tvYears);
    final EditText loan = (EditText)findViewById(R.id.tvLoan);
    final EditText interest = (EditText)findViewById(R.id.tvInterest);
    Button button = (Button)findViewById(R.id.btPayment);
    final SharedPreferences sharedPref = PreferenceManager.getDefaultSharedPreferences( context: this);
    button.setOnClickListener(new View.OnClickListener() {
        @Override
        public void onClick(View v) {
            intYears = Integer.parseInt(years.getText().toString());
            intLoan = Integer.parseInt(loan.getText().toString());
            decInterest = Float.parseFloat(interest.getText().toString());
            SharedPreferences.Editor editor = sharedPref.edit();
            editor.putInt("key1", intYears);
            editor.putInt("key2", intLoan);
            editor.putFloat("key3", decInterest);
            editor.commit();
            startActivity(new Intent( packageContext: MainActivity.this, Payment.class));
        }
    });
}
}
```

Launch second Activity

Instantiating the Second Activity Components

As soon as the second Activity launches, the activity_payment.xml layout file is displayed. Next, the Payment class must instantiate the TextView component that displays the monthly payment for the car loan and an ImageView component that displays the number of years in the loan. To set the layout and instantiate the TextView and ImageView components in the second Activity, follow this step.

Step 1

- Close the MainActivity.java tab.
- Click at the end of Line 14 and press Enter in the Payment.java tab.
- To create an instance of the TextView component, type **TextView monthlyPayment = (TextView)findViewById(R.id.tvMonthlyPayment);** and press Enter.
- Click TextView and press Alt+Enter to import the class.

- To create an instance of the ImageView component, go to the next line and type **ImageView image = (ImageView)findViewById(R.id.ivYears);**. Import the ImageView class.

The TextView and ImageView components named monthlyPayment and image are referenced in Payment.java (**Figure 11-15**).

Figure 11-15 Instantiating the TextView and ImageView components in Payment.java

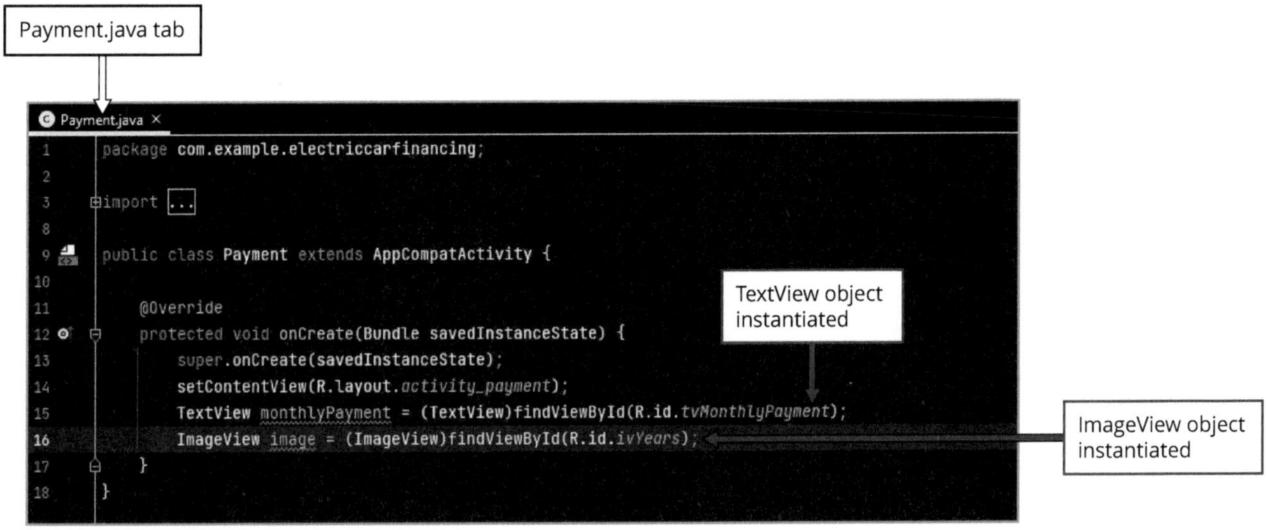

Payment.java tab

TextView object instantiated

ImageView object instantiated

```
Payment.java ×
package com.example.electriccarfinancing;

import ...

public class Payment extends AppCompatActivity {

    @Override
    protected void onCreate(Bundle savedInstanceState) {
        super.onCreate(savedInstanceState);
        setContentView(R.layout.activity_payment);
        TextView monthlyPayment = (TextView)findViewById(R.id.tvMonthlyPayment);
        ImageView image = (ImageView)findViewById(R.id.ivYears);
    }
}
```

11.7 Retrieving Data Using getString( ) Methods

Retrieving Android data is just as easy as saving it when you are working with SharedPreferences. Loading data saved in the SharedPreferences XML file begins in the second Activity by instantiating the SharedPreferences object. You do not need an editor to read saved data in SharedPreferences. Instead, retrieve the SharedPreferences object and use the appropriate method to retrieve a key's value by name:

- getString( )—Retrieves string values
- getInt( )—Retrieves integer values
- getLong( )—Retrieves long values
- getFloat( )—Retrieves float values
- getBoolean( )—Retrieves Boolean values

Each of these methods has two parameters: the preference key string and a default value to return if the preference is undefined. If a string value is undefined, it is set to a null value, which is represented by empty quotes. If a numeric value is undefined, the variable is assigned the value of zero. If the key is not found, the default value is given in response. To create an instance of the SharedPreferences object and to load the data from the persistent data XML file, use the following code syntax.

Code Syntax

```
SharedPreferences sharedPref =
PreferenceManager.getDefaultSharedPreferences(this);
int intYears = sharedPref.getInt("key1", 0);
int intLoan = sharedPref.getInt("key2", 0);
float decInterest = sharedPref.getFloat("key3", 0);
```

In this code, intYears is assigned the number of years in the term of the loan. The value for the loan amount is assigned to intLoan, which is stored in the XML persistent data file. The variable decInterest is assigned the float value of the loan's interest rate. To retrieve the data from the SharedPreferences object, follow these steps.

Step 1

- In Payment.java, press Enter at the end of Line 16 to insert a new line.
- On the new line, create an instance of the SharedPreferences object within the Status class by typing **SharedPreferences sharedPref = PreferenceManager.getDefaultSharedPreferences(this);**.
- Click SharedPreferences and press Alt+Enter, and then click PreferenceManager and press Alt+Enter again to import both libraries.

An instance of the SharedPreferences class named sharedPref is created in the Payment class (**Figure 11-16**).

Figure 11-16 SharedPreferences instance in the Payment class

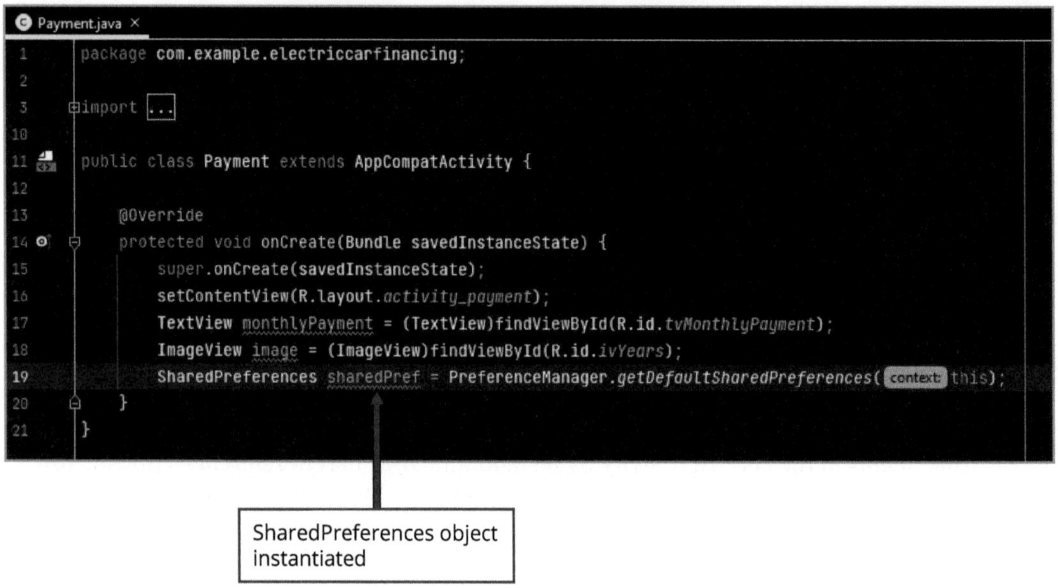

```
Payment.java
1   package com.example.electriccarfinancing;
2
3   import ...
10
11  public class Payment extends AppCompatActivity {
12
13      @Override
14      protected void onCreate(Bundle savedInstanceState) {
15          super.onCreate(savedInstanceState);
16          setContentView(R.layout.activity_payment);
17          TextView monthlyPayment = (TextView)findViewById(R.id.tvMonthlyPayment);
18          ImageView image = (ImageView)findViewById(R.id.ivYears);
19          SharedPreferences sharedPref = PreferenceManager.getDefaultSharedPreferences( context: this);
20      }
21  }
```

SharedPreferences object instantiated

Step 2

- To read the first value written in the XML file and assign the integer value to intYears, go to the next line, type **int intYears = sharedPref.getInt ("key1", 0);**, and press Enter.
- On the next line, read the second value saved as persistent data and assign the integer value to intLoan by typing **int intLoan = sharedPref.getInt("key2", 0);** and pressing Enter.
- On the next line, read the third value retrieved from the SharedPreferences object and assign the float value to **float decInterest = sharedPref.getFloat("key3", 0);**.
- Save your work.

The three values are retrieved from the SharedPreferences object from the first Activity (**Figure 11-17**).

Figure 11-17 SharedPreferences values are retrieved

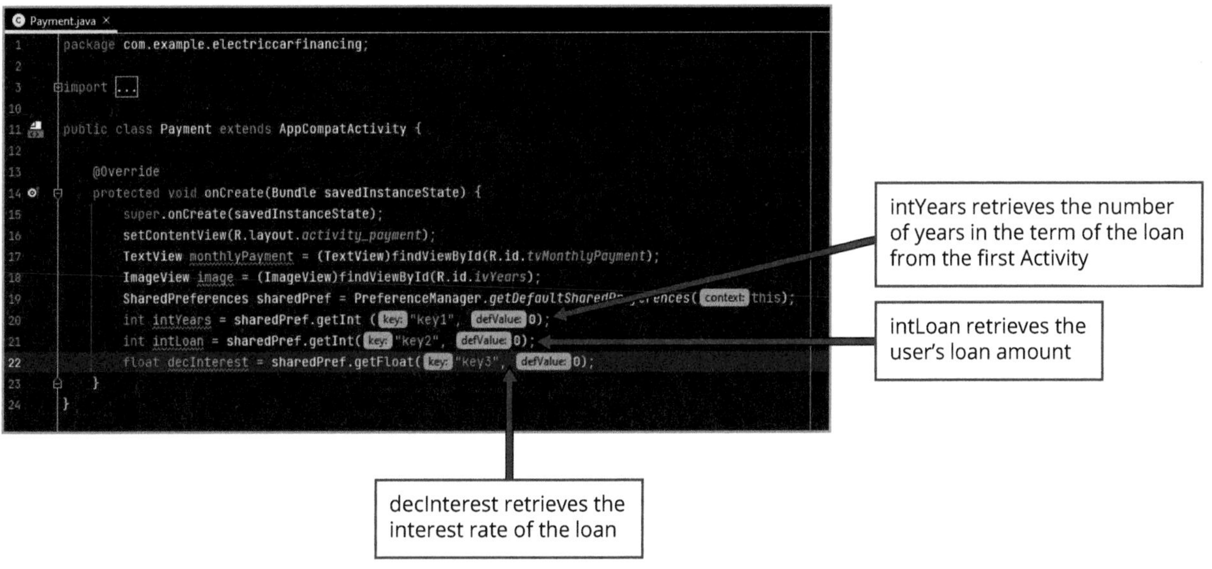

intYears retrieves the number of years in the term of the loan from the first Activity
intLoan retrieves the user's loan amount
decInterest retrieves the interest rate of the loan

Good to Know

You can assign literal text to the SharedPreferences object by coding the following line:

```
editor.putString("key", "literal text");
```

Quick Check

How would you save an integer named intTravelTime as persistent data?

Answer: int intTravelTime = sharedPref.getInt ("key1", 0);

Displaying the Correct ImageView Component

In an Android project, an ImageView component can display an image if you assign a source path (android:src="drawable/filename") in the XML layout file or dynamically assign the image within the Java code.

Code Syntax

```
image.setImageResource(R.drawable.three);
```

In the Electric Car Financing app, the image displayed in Payment.java depends on the number of years of the loan: three, four, or five years. The three values retrieved from the SharedPreferences object stored in memory are used in an equation that calculates the monthly payments based on a simple interest loan and are assigned to the variable named decMonthlyPayment. Calculating monthly costs allows you to budget accordingly and figure out the total price of the car—not just the sticker price. The formula to calculate the monthly payment is:

```
decMonthlyPayment = (intLoan + (intLoan * decInterest * intYears)) / (12 *
   intYears)
```

After the monthly payment is computed, the number of years in the loan is compared in the nested If structure. If the car loan is paid over three years, the three.png image is displayed. If the loan is paid over four years, the four.png image is shown, and if the loan is paid over five years, the five.png file image is shown. A nested If decision structure is used to determine which image is displayed. If the user does not enter three, four, or five years as the term of the loan, then no image is displayed and a text response indicates that the user has not selected an appropriate number of years. To code the nested Else If decision structure and display the TextView result and ImageView components, follow these steps.

Step 1

- At the end of Line 22, press Enter to insert a new line. To declare the variable assigned the monthly payment, type **float decMonthlyPayment;**.
- Press Enter. To compute the monthly payments for the simple interest car loan, type **decMonthlyPayment = (intLoan+ (intLoan * decInterest * intYears)) / (12 * intYears);** and press Enter.
- To format the monthly payment as currency and display the value two places past the decimal place, type **DecimalFormat currency = new DecimalFormat("$###,###.##");**.
- Click DecimalFormat and press Alt+Enter to import DecimalFormat.

The monthly payment is computed based on the values entered in the first Activity and is formatted as currency (**Figure 11-18**).

Figure 11-18 Computing the monthly loan payment and formatting the result

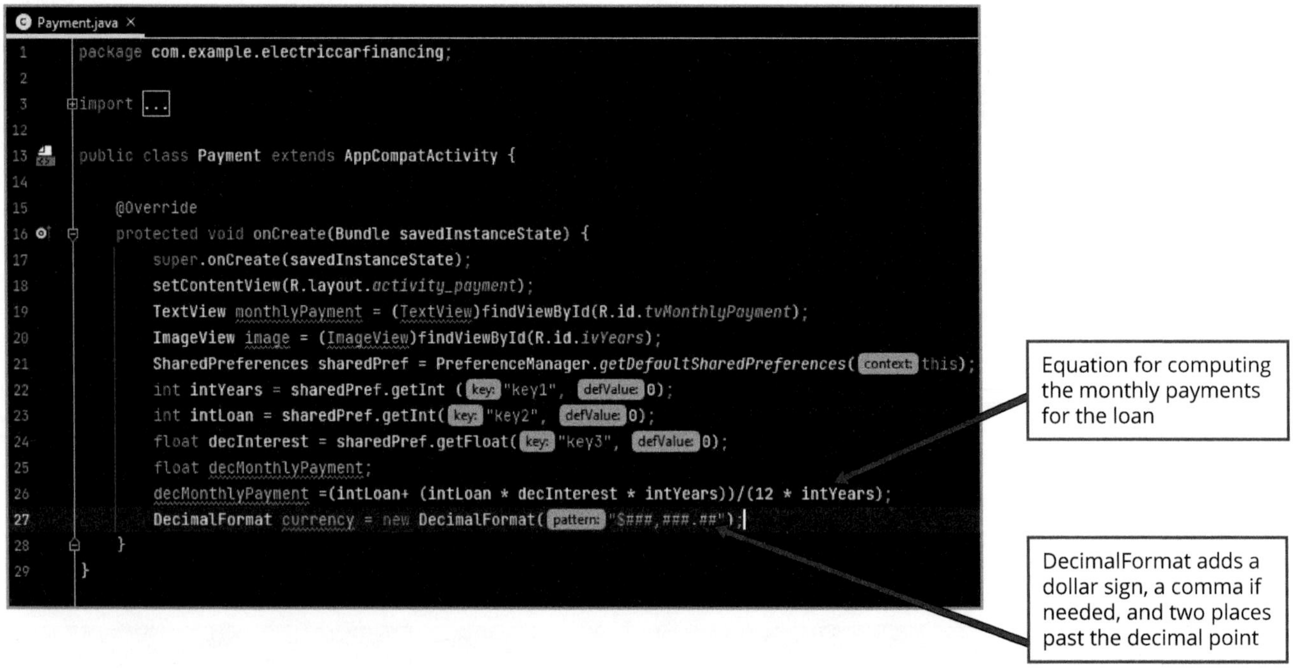

Payment.java ×

```
1   package com.example.electriccarfinancing;
2
3   import ...
12
13  public class Payment extends AppCompatActivity {
14
15      @Override
16      protected void onCreate(Bundle savedInstanceState) {
17          super.onCreate(savedInstanceState);
18          setContentView(R.layout.activity_payment);
19          TextView monthlyPayment = (TextView)findViewById(R.id.tvMonthlyPayment);
20          ImageView image = (ImageView)findViewById(R.id.ivYears);
21          SharedPreferences sharedPref = PreferenceManager.getDefaultSharedPreferences( context: this);
22          int intYears = sharedPref.getInt ( key: "key1",  defValue: 0);
23          int intLoan = sharedPref.getInt( key: "key2",  defValue: 0);
24          float decInterest = sharedPref.getFloat( key: "key3",  defValue: 0);
25          float decMonthlyPayment;
26          decMonthlyPayment =(intLoan+ (intLoan * decInterest * intYears))/(12 * intYears);
27          DecimalFormat currency = new DecimalFormat( pattern: "$###,###.##");
28      }
29  }
```

Equation for computing the monthly payments for the loan

DecimalFormat adds a dollar sign, a comma if needed, and two places past the decimal point

Step 2

- At the end of Line 27, press Enter to insert a new line. To display the monthly payment amount, type **monthlyPayment.setText("Monthly Payment " + currency.format(decMonthlyPayment));**.

The monthly payment text is displayed (**Figure 11-19**).

Figure 11-19 The monthly payment is displayed in the second Activity

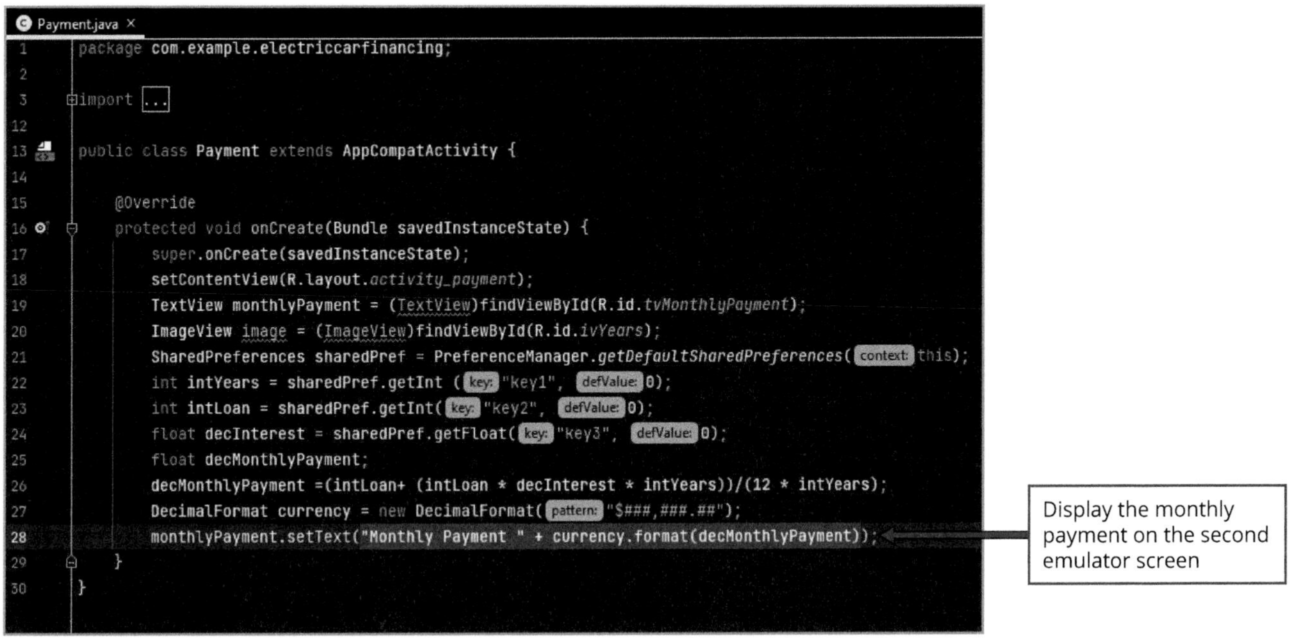

```
Payment.java
1   package com.example.electriccarfinancing;
2
3   import ...
12
13  public class Payment extends AppCompatActivity {
14
15      @Override
16      protected void onCreate(Bundle savedInstanceState) {
17          super.onCreate(savedInstanceState);
18          setContentView(R.layout.activity_payment);
19          TextView monthlyPayment = (TextView)findViewById(R.id.tvMonthlyPayment);
20          ImageView image = (ImageView)findViewById(R.id.ivYears);
21          SharedPreferences sharedPref = PreferenceManager.getDefaultSharedPreferences( context: this);
22          int intYears = sharedPref.getInt ( key: "key1",  defValue: 0);
23          int intLoan = sharedPref.getInt( key: "key2",  defValue: 0);
24          float decInterest = sharedPref.getFloat( key: "key3",  defValue: 0);
25          float decMonthlyPayment;
26          decMonthlyPayment =(intLoan+ (intLoan * decInterest * intYears))/(12 * intYears);
27          DecimalFormat currency = new DecimalFormat( pattern: "$###,###.##");
28          monthlyPayment.setText("Monthly Payment " + currency.format(decMonthlyPayment));
29      }
30  }
```

Display the monthly payment on the second emulator screen

Step 3

- To determine if the car loan is paid over three, four, or five years and display the associated image, type the following If structure on the next line:

```
if (intYears == 3) {
    image.setImageResource(R.drawable.three);
    }
```

Good to Know

In Java, two equal signs are used to compare the references of the objects, not to assign a value to a variable.

- To display the four-year image, place your cursor after the closing curly brace on Line 31, type **else if (intYears == 4)** {, and press the Enter key to insert the closing brace for the Else If statement.
- To complete the code for displaying the four.png image, type the following code:

```
image.setImageResource(R.drawable.four);
```

- To display the five-year image, place your cursor after the closing curly brace on Line 34, type **else if (intYears == 5) {**, and press the Enter key to insert the closing brace for the Else If statement.
- To complete the code for displaying the five.png image, type the following code:

  image.setImageResource(R.drawable.five);

The appropriate image appears for the corresponding loan years (**Figure 11-20**).

Figure 11-20 Else If structure for three-, four-, and five-year loans

```
18  setContentView(R.layout.activity_payment);
19  TextView monthlyPayment = (TextView)findViewById(R.id.tvMonthlyPayment);
20  ImageView image = (ImageView)findViewById(R.id.ivYears);
21  SharedPreferences sharedPref = PreferenceManager.getDefaultSharedPreferences( context: this);
22  int intYears = sharedPref.getInt ( key: "key1",  defValue: 0);
23  int intLoan = sharedPref.getInt( key: "key2",  defValue: 0);
24  float decInterest = sharedPref.getFloat( key: "key3",  defValue: 0);
25  float decMonthlyPayment;
26  decMonthlyPayment =(intLoan+ (intLoan * decInterest * intYears))/(12 * intYears);
27  DecimalFormat currency = new DecimalFormat( pattern: "$###,###.##");
28  monthlyPayment.setText("Monthly Payment " + currency.format(decMonthlyPayment));
29  if (intYears == 3) {
30      image.setImageResource(R.drawable.three);
31  }
32  else if (intYears == 4) {
33      image.setImageResource(R.drawable.four);
34  }
35  else if (intYears == 5) {
36      image.setImageResource(R.drawable.five);
37  }
38  }
39  }
```

If structure for 3-year loan and Else If structure for 4- and 5-year loans

Step 4

- If the number of years for the loan is not valid based on the three-, four-, or five-year loans that are available, display a message by typing the following code after the closing curly brace on Line 37:

  else {

  monthlyPayment.setText("Enter 3, 4, or 5 years");

  }

A closing Else statement displays a message if the user has not entered an appropriate number of years (**Figure 11-21**).

Figure 11-21 Closing Else statement

```
        super.onCreate(savedInstanceState);
        setContentView(R.layout.activity_payment);
        TextView monthlyPayment = (TextView)findViewById(R.id.tvMonthlyPayment);
        ImageView image = (ImageView)findViewById(R.id.ivYears);
        SharedPreferences sharedPref = PreferenceManager.getDefaultSharedPreferences( context: this);
        int intYears = sharedPref.getInt ( key: "key1", defValue: 0);
        int intLoan = sharedPref.getInt( key: "key2", defValue: 0);
        float decInterest = sharedPref.getFloat( key: "key3", defValue: 0);
        float decMonthlyPayment;
        decMonthlyPayment =(intLoan+ (intLoan * decInterest * intYears))/(12 * intYears);
        DecimalFormat currency = new DecimalFormat( pattern: "$###,###.##");
        monthlyPayment.setText("Monthly Payment " + currency.format(decMonthlyPayment));
        if (intYears == 3) {
            image.setImageResource(R.drawable.three);
        }
        else if (intYears == 4) {
            image.setImageResource(R.drawable.four);
        }
        else if (intYears == 5) {
            image.setImageResource(R.drawable.five);
        }
        else {
            monthlyPayment.setText("Enter 3, 4, or 5 years");
        }
    }
}
```

Closing Else statement for users who did not enter 3, 4, or 5 years

Running and Testing the Application

Your first experience with persistent saved data in an Android application is complete. Click the Run app button on the Standard toolbar and then select the Nexus 5 emulator. The application opens in the emulator window, as shown in Figures 11-1 and 11-2. The first Activity requests the number of years of the loan, the loan amount, and the interest rate; this data is saved to an XML file using the SharedPreferences object. The second Activity launches the Payment.java file, which retrieves the stored data and calculates the monthly payment for the car loan. The monthly payment is shown, and a decision structure determines which image should be displayed to indicate the loan term.

Wrap It Up—Chapter Summary

In this chapter, the Android SharedPreferences object was used to easily store application-persistent data. Application preferences are stored as key-value pairs and can be many different data types, including numbers, strings, and Boolean values. Different sets of preferences can be stored in named preference sets. Use shared preferences to store simple data such as the user's name or numeric information in a persistent manner.

- When data that users enter in an Android app is stored in RAM, it is lost when the app or the device stops running. Persistent data, on the other hand, is stored on the device's drive or another storage medium, such as a memory card or cloud service, so that the data can be retrieved later within the app or after the program is terminated.
- Persistent data can be stored using shared preferences, internal storage, external storage, an SQLite database, or a network connection. Use the SharedPreferences object to save any primitive data, including Boolean data, floats, ints, longs, and strings.

- When you save application data using the SharedPreferences object, the data is saved to an XML file as a key-value pair. The key is a string such as "key1" that uniquely identifies the preference, and the value is the data represented as a string, int, long, float, or Boolean value.
- You can use the key-value pairs stored in SharedPreferences in different Activities of your application or in another application.
- Use a put*DataType*( ) method to store the data in a SharedPreferences object, and use a get*DataType*( ) method to retrieve the data. The names of the methods depend on the data types you are using.

Key Terms

key
persistent data
SQLite
value

Developer FAQs

1. What is the general name of the type of data that is saved after an app is executed? (11.1)
2. Name five ways to store data in an app. (11.1)
3. When is it best to use SharedPreferences to save persistent data? (11.2)
4. What does each part of the SharedPreferences data pair represent? Explain each part of the pair. (11.2)
5. True or False: When you save persistent data with internal storage, other apps cannot access and use the data. (11.3)
6. Why should an app not store massive amounts of data using internal storage? (11.3)
7. You can save data using external storage to your SD card. What does SD stand for? (11.3)
8. What does SQL stand for? (11.4)
9. If you decide to use a network to save an app's persistent data, what is the limitation? (11.5)
10. In what kind of file is persistent data saved when using the SharedPreferences object? (11.6)
11. Which method stores a string value using the SharedPreferences object? (11.6)
12. Write a statement that assigns the variable decShoeSize with the key of key1 to the SharedPreferences object. (11.6)
13. The preference values are not saved until which method is executed? (11.6)
14. What is the maximum number of preferences that can be saved to a SharedPreferences object? (11.6)
15. Write a line of Java code that displays an image named flight. (11.7)
16. Which method retrieves an integer value? (11.7)
17. If a float value is retrieved from the SharedPreferences object and the value does not exist, which value is retrieved? (11.7)
18. Write a line of Java code to retrieve an integer value that is referenced by the key named key1 and save the value to intAudienceCount. (11.7)

19. Write a line of Java code to retrieve a string value that is referenced by the key named key3 and save the value to strPolitician. (11.7)

20. In a single line of Java code, assign a string value of "App Developer" to a SharedPreferences object with a key value named key5. (11.6)

Beyond the Book

Search the web for answers to the following questions to further your Android knowledge.

1. Research the SD cards that are available for Android devices. Write 100 words about your findings.
2. Find five apps in the Google Play store that use mobile databases to save the data used in the app. Identify and describe the reason the database connection is necessary.
3. Google Maps now requires a paid account to access map features as an Android developer. Write a summary of at least 100 words to describe some of the latest Google mapping features.
4. Find more information about saving to an SQLite database. Write a 200-word paragraph and show sample code for saving information to a local mobile database.

Case Programming Projects

Complete one or more of the following case programming projects. Use the same steps and techniques taught within the chapter. Successful completion of these projects requires knowledge of all chapter learning objectives. Submit the program(s) you create to your instructor. The level of difficulty is indicated for each case programming project.

Case Project 11–1: BMI Calculator App (Beginner)

Requirements Document

Application title: BMI Calculator App

Purpose: An app computes your body mass index (BMI) using a formula.

Algorithms:

1. The first Activity opens and displays the bmi.png image with the title "BMI Calculator."
2. The first screen requests your weight in pounds and your height in inches; each value must be entered to the nearest whole integer (**Figure 11-22**). These values are saved as persistent data using SharedPreferences.
3. The second Activity opens and retrieves the saved values.
4. The BMI formula needed is:

$$\frac{\text{Weight in pounds} * 703}{\text{Height in inches}^2}$$

5. The BMI is displayed to one-tenth of a decimal place and the image bmi2.png is displayed (**Figure 11-23**).

Conditions:

1. The two image files are provided with your student files.

Figure 11-22 First Activity of BMI Calculator app

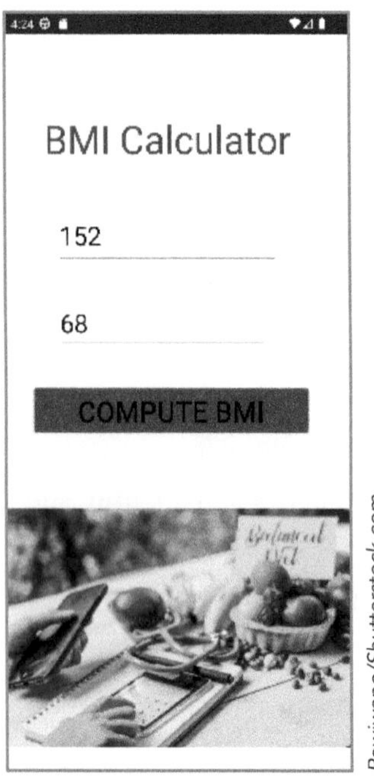

Rawiwano/Shutterstock.com

Figure 11-23 Second Activity of BMI Calculator app

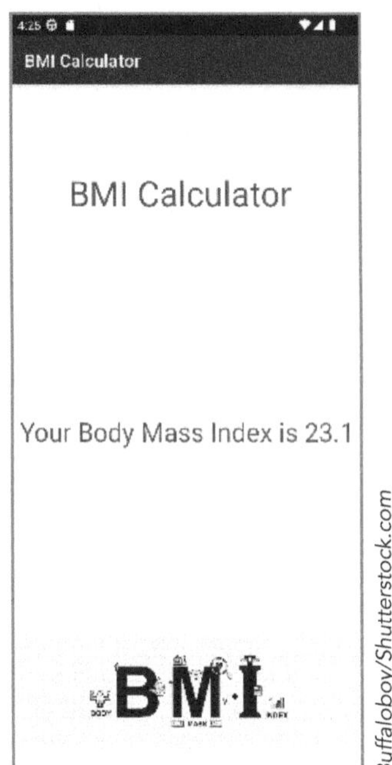

Buffaloboy/Shutterstock.com

Case Project 11–2: Home Mortgage Interest App (Beginner)

Requirements Document

Application title:	Home Mortgage Interest App
Purpose:	The Home Mortgage Interest app computes the total interest paid for the life of a home mortgage loan.
Algorithms:	**1.** The opening screen displays an image (house.png) and the title "Mortgage Loan Interest." **2.** The user enters the amount of their monthly mortgage payment, the number of years (10, 20, or 30) of the loan, which must be converted to months, and the initial principal of the loan. Save these values using the SharedPreferences object (**Figure 11-24**). **3.** In the second Activity, retrieve the three values and compute the total interest paid over the life of the loan with this formula: **Total Interest = (Monthly Payment * Number of Months) – Initial Principal** **4.** The second screen displays the interest paid with an appropriate image for a 10-, 20-, or 30-year loan (**Figure 11-25**).
Conditions:	**1.** Four images are provided with your student files. Three of the images are named ten.png, twenty.png, and thirty.png for the various terms of the loan. **2.** The interest result should appear in currency format.

Figure 11-24 First Activity of Home Mortgage Interest app

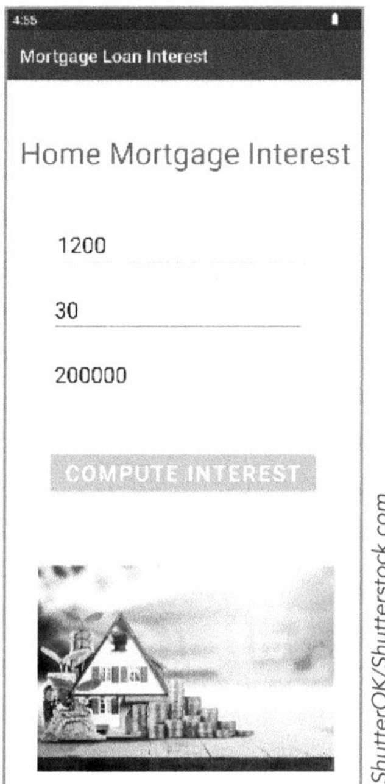

ShutterOK/Shutterstock.com

Figure 11-25 Second Activity of Home Mortgage Interest app

Ai.user/Shutterstock.com

Case Project 11–3: Relocation Moving Truck Rental App (Intermediate)

Requirements Document

Application title: Relocation Moving Truck Rental App

Purpose: A relocation app provides the costs of renting a truck.

Algorithms:

1. An opening screen displays an image of a moving truck and a title.
2. The first Activity asks whether you are renting a 10-foot truck ($19.95), a 17-foot truck ($29.95), or a 26-foot truck ($39.95) for one day. The number of miles is also requested (99 cents per mile). This data is saved to the SharedPreferences object.
3. The second screen displays a picture of a rental truck that matches the size you are renting. The screen also shows the full cost of the rental for one day with the cost of mileage included.

Conditions:

1. Locate images for this app online.
2. The moving costs should be displayed as currency.

Case Project 11–4: Marathon Race App (Intermediate)

Requirements Document

Application title: Marathon Race App

Purpose: Your city is planning a full 26-mile marathon. Each runner's finishing time is ranked in the top, middle, or bottom third of all participating runners.

Algorithms:

1. The opening screen displays the text "Marathon Race" and an image of a marathon.
2. The total time needed to run the race is requested in two TextView components that save the hour and the minutes (for example, 3 hours and 27 minutes).
3. A second screen displays the average time required to run one mile.
4. If the average time to run each mile is under 11 minutes, display a gold-medal image to indicate that the runner was among the top one-third of all participants.
5. If the average time to run each mile is under 15 minutes, display a silver-medal image.
6. If the average time to run each mile is equal to or more than 15 minutes, display a bronze-medal image.

Conditions:

1. The completion time for the marathon cannot be more than 10 hours.
2. The number of minutes entered cannot be more than 59.
3. Locate images for this app online.

Case Project 11–5: Amtrak Train App (Advanced)

Requirements Document

Application title: Amtrak Train App

Purpose: The Amtrak Train app determines your arrival time after you enter the boarding time and trip length.

Algorithms:

1. Create an app that opens with a picture of the Amtrak logo and a title. This activity should request:
   a. The boarding time with separate inputs for hours and minutes on a 24-hour clock. (For example, 9:30 p.m. would be represented as 21 hours and 30 minutes.)
   b. The length of the entire train trip in minutes only.

   The three values are saved using SharedPreferences.
2. The second screen shows the arrival time of the train using hours and minutes based on a 24-hour clock.
3. If the scheduled arrival time is past midnight, display the message "Red-Eye Arrival" in addition to an appropriate image.

Conditions:

1. Locate images for this app online.
2. The maximum hour a user can enter for the boarding time is 23, and the maximum number of minutes is 59.
3. The maximum number of minutes that a user can enter for the length of travel is 1500.

Case Project 11–6: Your Personal Limerick App (Advanced)

Requirements Document

Application title:	Your Personal Limerick App
Purpose:	Get creative! Request a city, an occupation, a number, and an action verb and then create a happy limerick with the text entered.
Algorithms:	**1.** Create an app that opens with an image and title and requests a city, occupation, number, and action verb. Save these four items to an XML file using SharedPreferences. **2.** The second screen should display an image and a limerick using the four requested items.
Conditions:	**1.** Select your own images and limerick wording.

Chapter 12

Finale! Publishing Your Android App

Learning Objectives

At the completion of this chapter, you will be able to:

12.1 Describe Google Play

12.2 Target various device configurations and languages

12.3 Test your app before publishing

12.4 Create an Android App Bundle

12.5 Prepare promotional materials to upload to Google Play

12.6 Publish your app on Google Play

After all the work of designing your Android app, the time to publish it has arrived. Your Android app can be published to a variety of application distribution networks that make the app available to users on their devices. As an Android developer, you can publish your app to Google Play and to many other online Android app stores, such as Amazon Appstore, Huawei AppGallery, Xiaomi Mi GetApps, and Aurora. Because Google Play is the largest marketplace, this chapter uses it as an example to describe how to publish apps.

12.1 Using Google Play

The process of publishing an app consists of preparing it for publication, registering, configuring, and uploading it, and then finally publishing it in an online repository or app store. Before publishing an application, the developer must understand how to perform the following processes, among others:

1. Test the app.
2. Prepare the app for publication.
3. Create an AAB package and digitally sign the application.
4. Prepare promotional materials.
5. Publish the app to Google Play.

Google Play (*https://play.google.com*) is a digital repository that serves as the storefront for Android devices and apps. It includes an online store for paid and free Android apps as well as music, movies, books, and games. Android phones, tablets, and Google TV can all access the Google Play services. The Google Play website, shown in **Figure 12-1**, includes the features and services of Android apps, Google Music, and Google e-books. In addition, Google Play provides free cloud storage services, which save space on an Android device. Google Play is entirely cloud based, so you can store all your music, movies, books, and apps online and have them available to you at all times. More than 190 countries around the world currently use Google Play. Competing companies such as the Apple App Store and Microsoft Store for Windows also market their applications within a similar structure. When you select an app on Google Play, the app installs directly to your Android device. Google Play is part of the default setup on new Android devices.

Figure 12-1 Google Play

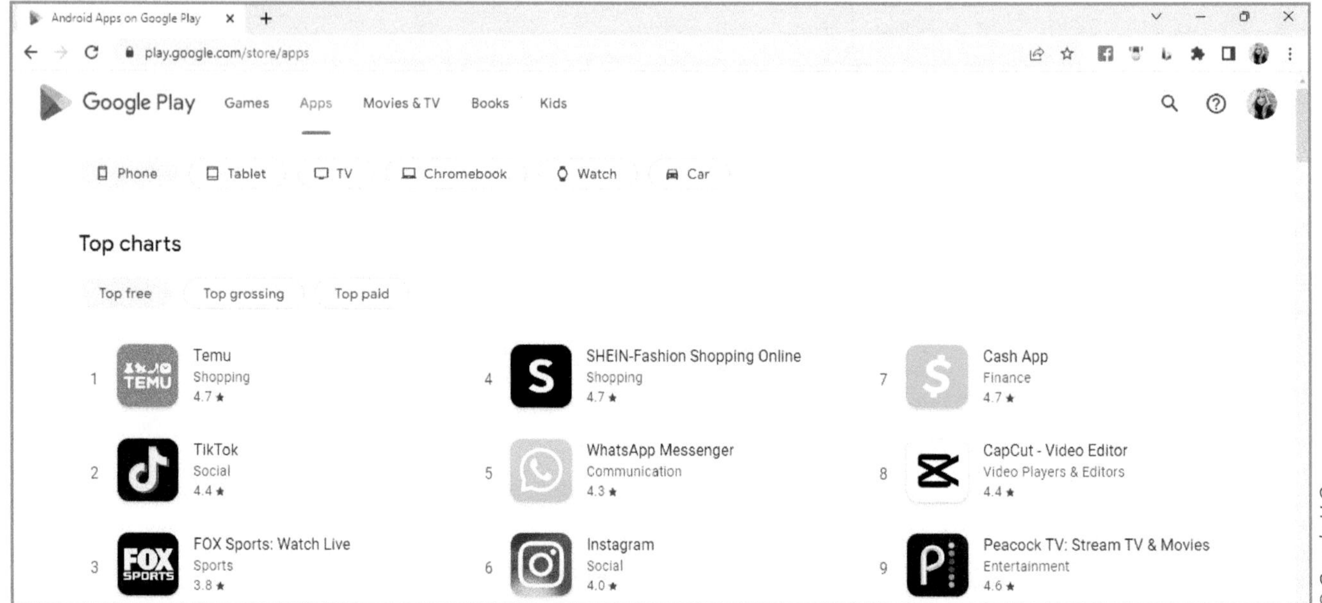

12.2 Targeting Device Configurations and Languages

To reach a larger audience within the Google Play market, consider targeting multiple Android devices and translating your app into multiple languages. The Android platform runs on a variety of devices that offer different screen sizes and pixel densities. Thousands of Android handheld devices are available, so the use of flexible design layouts that work on many screen sizes and resolutions ensures that your app operates well with a wide range of Android phones and tablets. Creating a custom experience for different screen sizes, foldable phones, pixel densities, orientations, and resolutions makes users feel that the app was designed specifically for their phone or tablet.

Android users live in every corner of the world and speak hundreds of languages. As you design an Android app, you can provide alternate resources such as app text translated into multiple languages; the language changes depending on the default locale detected on the device. For example, if your home country is Spain, your phone's locale for the dialect selection is most likely set to Spanish (Spain). If you want your application to support both English and Spanish text, you can create two resource directories in the strings directory (the strings.xml file) using the Translations Editor. By customizing these resource files, you can write one application that recognizes many languages. When creating your app in English, remember that the majority of the world does not speak English and consider extending your app's reach to the worldwide pool of Android users.

Good to Know | To translate the languages used in your app, you can use Google Translate (*https://translate.google.com*), a free service that provides instant translations among over 100 languages.

Good to Know | Only 5.1 percent of the world's population speaks English as their first language. Research shows that to reach 90 percent of Internet users, app developers need to support 21 languages.

Adding Localization Using the Translations Editor

The Translations Editor within Android Studio supports multiple languages. Based on the default language of a device, you can add translated text as you develop an app and have the Translations Editor display the appropriate translation strings when the app runs. **Localization** is the process of adapting an app or webpage to a language while considering cultural differences, such as whether the language is read from left to right or right to left, calendar layout, measurements, currency, date and time formats, and traditions of your target audience. For example, the language and the date formats of Spain are different from those of the United States. If an app promises to deliver goods on 8/10/2025, Spanish users expect this date to be October 8, 2025, while American users read the delivery date as August 10, 2025. Within the Translations Editor, the globe-shaped Add Locale icon provides access to a list of locales around the world. To add localization for another country, follow these steps.

Step 1

- In Android Studio, create an Android project named Locale with an Empty Activity.
- Expand the values folder in the Android Project view, open strings.xml, and then click the Open editor link.
- Click the Add Locale button (the globe icon) in the Translations Editor.

A list of languages and countries is displayed to add localization to your app (**Figure 12-2**).

Figure 12-2 Locale listing in the Translations Editor

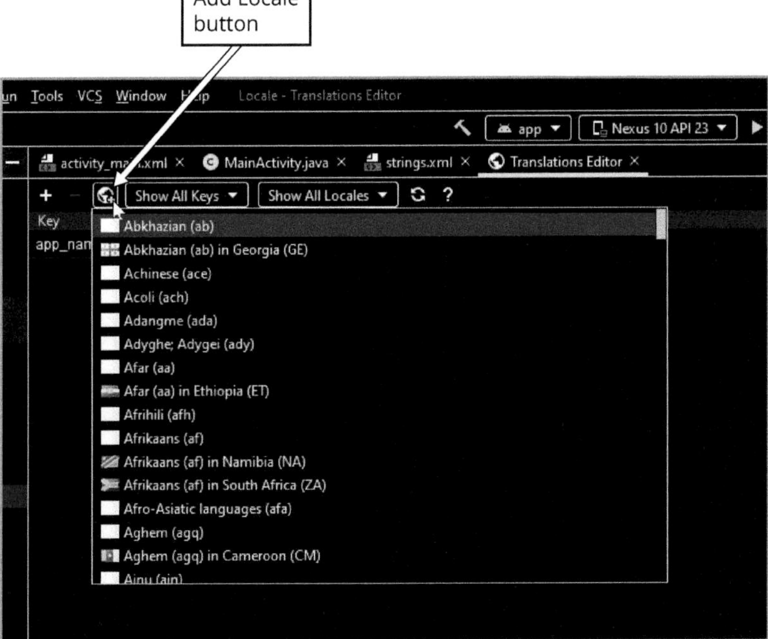

Step 2

- Scroll down and click Spanish (es).

A new column appears in the Translations Editor for the Spanish (es) locale (**Figure 12-3**).

Figure 12-3 Spanish (es) added as another locale

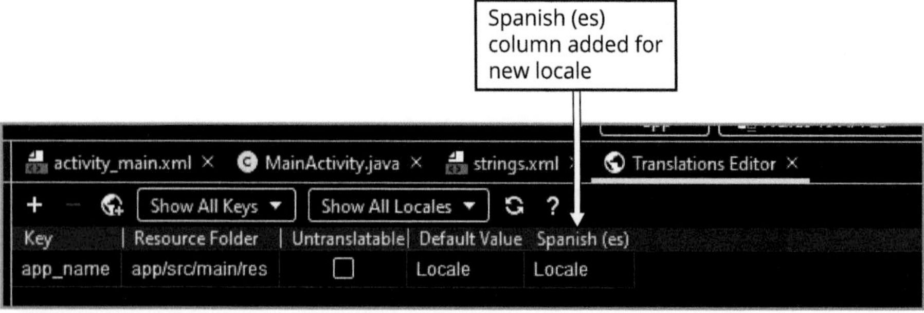

Step 3

- Click the Add Key button (the plus sign).
- Type **tvOpen** in the Key text box.
- Type **Hello World** in the Default Value text box.
- Click the OK button.

The translation for Hello world! is entered into the Translation text box. The tvOpen text appears in red to indicate that the Spanish translation has not been added (**Figure 12-4**).

Figure 12-4 Red text on key designates missing translation

Step 4

- Click the tvOpen row in the Spanish (es) column.
- At the bottom of the Translations Editor window, click the Translation text box.
- Type **Hola Mundo**, the Spanish translation for Hello World from *translate.google.com*.

The translation for Hello World is entered into the Translation text box (**Figure 12-5**). If the app is run on a device with the Spanish locale setting, Hola Mundo is displayed instead of Hello World.

Figure 12-5 Spanish translation of Locale app text

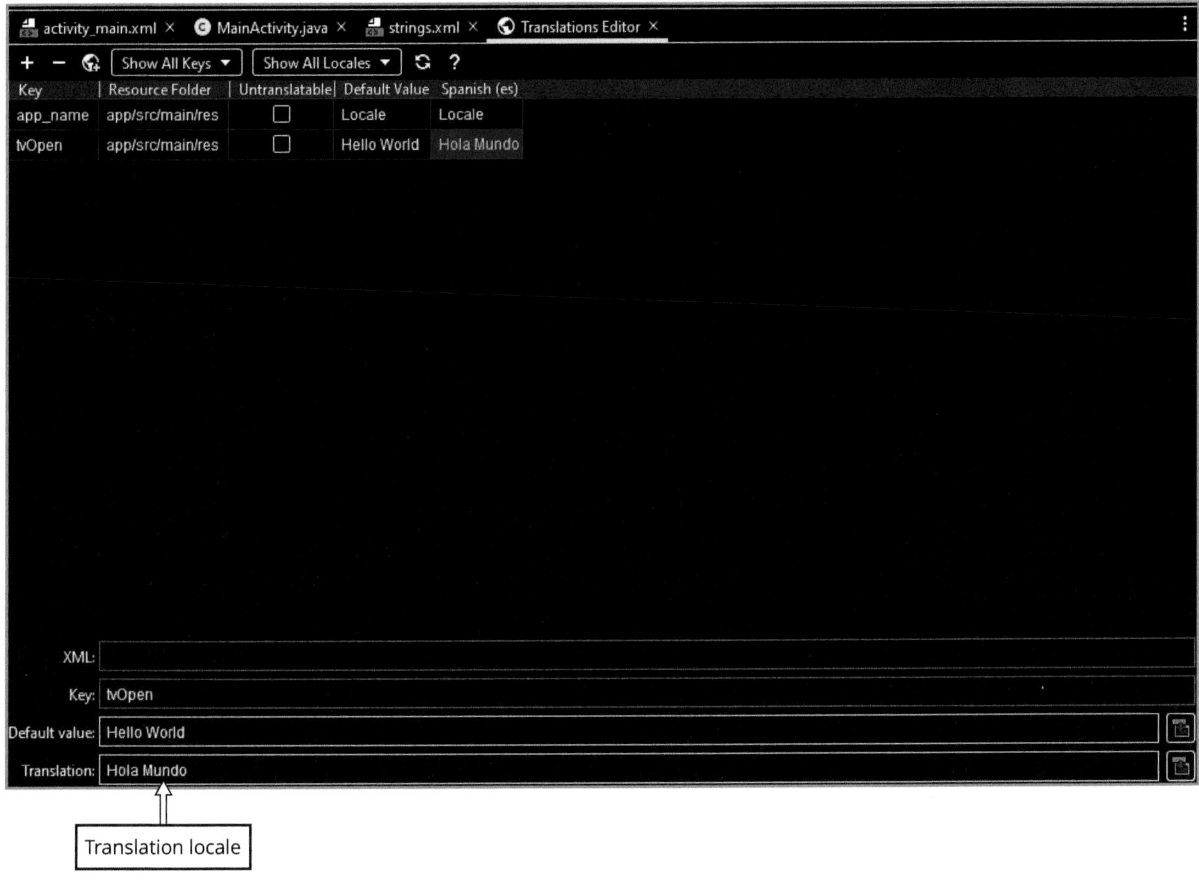

Good to Know If your app includes proper nouns such as first and last names, check Untranslatable in the Translations Editor to display them "as is" in other languages.

Critical Thinking **Can I add multiple locales to an app?**

Yes. Repeat the process illustrated in Figure 12-2 to add as many locales as you need to target.

Good to Know Sites such as Google Translate are helpful, but before you publish your app to Google Play, have a natural speaker of the target language check the translation for correctness, formality, cultural cues, and grammar.

Quick Check

If you sell your app, why would adding localization be an excellent idea?

Answer: You want your app to grow and be used beyond your local community, to reach across continents, and ultimately to be used globally, increasing your profit greatly.

12.3 Testing Your App before Publication

After completing your Android app and adding locales to it, you must test the app on various devices before publication. Using the built-in emulators in Android Studio, you can test the design and functionality of your app on a wide range of devices. You can also see how your application will perform in a real-world environment by using Android Studio to install and test the app directly on an Android phone. With an Android-powered device, you can develop and debug your Android applications just as you would on the emulator. You can connect your device either with a cable or by using Wi-Fi. After you change the settings on your Android phone or tablet, you can use a versatile tool called the **Android Debug Bridge (ADB)** to communicate with a connected Android device. To set up a device for testing your app, follow these steps.

Step 1

- On the home screen of an Android device such as your smartphone or tablet, tap the **Settings** app to display the device settings.
- The Developer options command is hidden by default. To make it available, select Settings, select About device (or About phone) in the Software Information category, and then tap **Build number** seven times. A message indicates that you are now a developer.
- Go back to Settings and tap **Developer options**. Check the USB debugging option and then tap the OK button.

The Android device changes the settings to enable USB debugging.

Step 2

- To set up your computer to detect your Android device, first install a USB driver for Android Debug Bridge on a Windows computer by following the steps at *http://developer.android.com/sdk/oem-usb.html.*
- Each Android phone brand, such as Pixel and Samsung, has its own drivers that must be downloaded and installed on your Windows computer. Be sure to install the drivers for the appropriate device brand. If you are using a Mac, you do not need to install a driver.

The USB drivers are installed on a Windows computer.

Step 3

- Attach an Android device to a USB cable.
- Run your application from Android Studio as usual (i.e., using the Run app button).
- When the Choose Device dialog box lists the available emulator(s) and connected device(s), select the running device you want to use to install and run the application, and then click the OK button.

The Android application is tested on your Android device.

12.4 Creating an Android App Bundle

After testing and refining your Android application, you must create a release-ready app bundle that users can install and run on their Android phones and tablets. **Android App Bundle (AAB)** was developed in 2021 as a new format to package your Android apps; it is published in Google Play Store. (The format replaced the previous .apk format called Android Package Kit.) AAB is a mandatory requirement for Google Play Store. The AAB packaging feature saves an app package to an AAB format in Android Studio 3.2 and later versions. As a developer, you can create a package in AAB format within Android Studio and upload your app package in AAB format to Google Play Store.

The release-ready package is called an **.aab file**, which is a compressed archive similar to a .zip file that contains the application, the manifest file, and all associated resources, such as image files, music, and other required content.

Google developed the .aab format to create smaller compressed files of all code and app resources; on average, the files are about 15 percent smaller. After upload, Google Play uses a process called Dynamic Delivery to deliver optimized versions of app bundles to user devices so they contain only the specific portions of the app that each device needs to run. Using the Android Studio Build menu, you can build a release-ready .aab file that is signed with your private key and optimized for publication. A private key digitally signs your application with information from your local system. All Android applications must be digitally signed with a certificate before the system can create an .aab bundle of your app for distribution in the Google Play Store. The Android system uses the certificate as a means of identifying the author of an application and establishing trust relationships between applications.

To create an .aab bundle that generates a private key for your local system, follow these steps.

Step 1

- In Android Studio, open a completed project that has been tested and runs properly.
- To create an .aab bundle, click Build on the menu bar.

The Build menu displays an option called Generate Signed Bundle/APK (**Figure 12-6**).

Figure 12-6 Using the Build menu in Android Studio

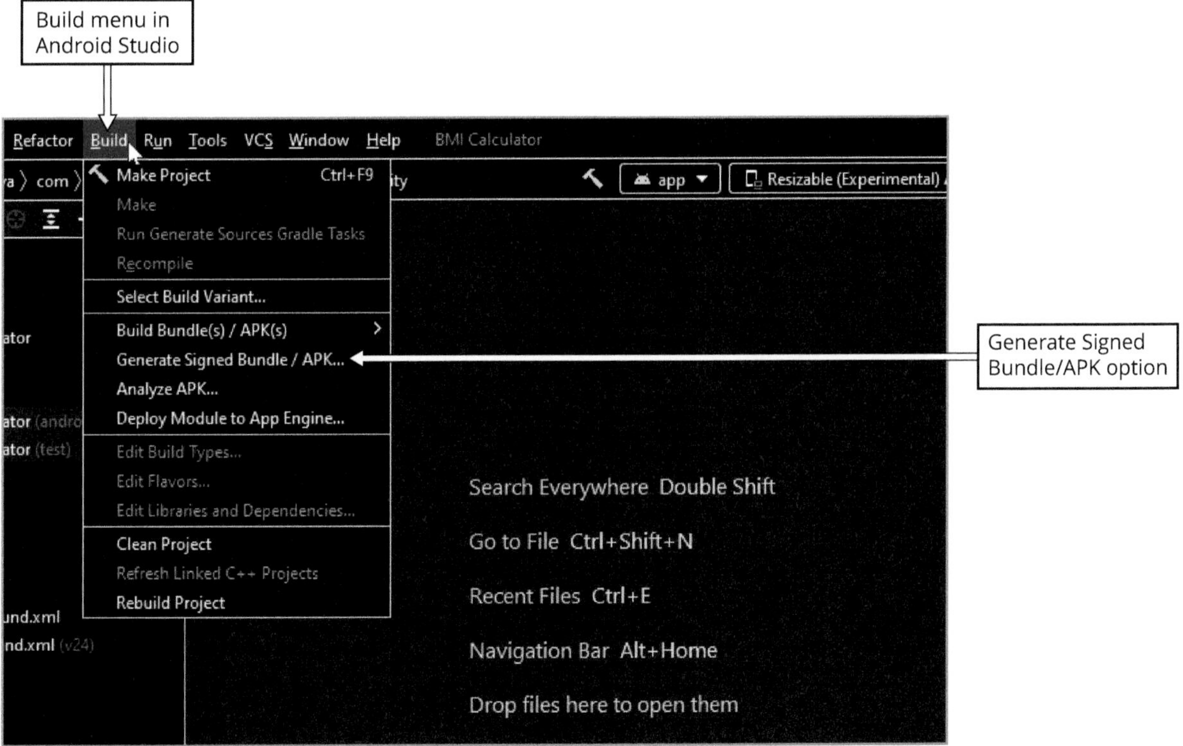

Step 2

- Click Generate Signed Bundle/APK.

The Generate Signed Bundle or APK dialog box opens (**Figure 12-7**).

Step 3

- Click the Next button to create a new signed key.
- A signed key file can be placed in any location on your computer or USB drive. Type a path similar to the one shown in **Figure 12-8** or ask your instructor for a specified path to enter in the Key store path text box. (Replace "Corinne" with your actual PC user name.)

Figure 12-7 Generate Signed Bundle or APK dialog box

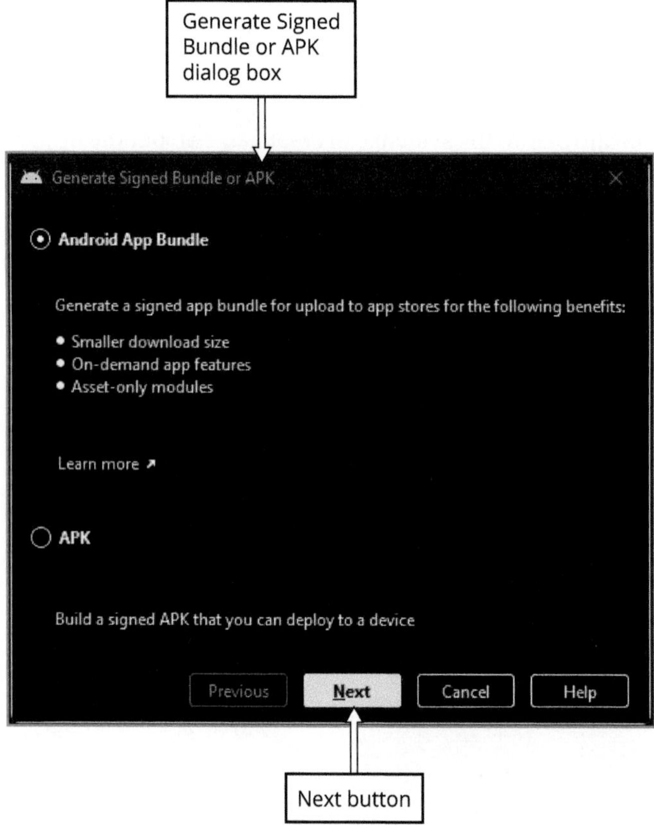

Figure 12-8 Creating a key in the Generate Signed Bundle or APK dialog box

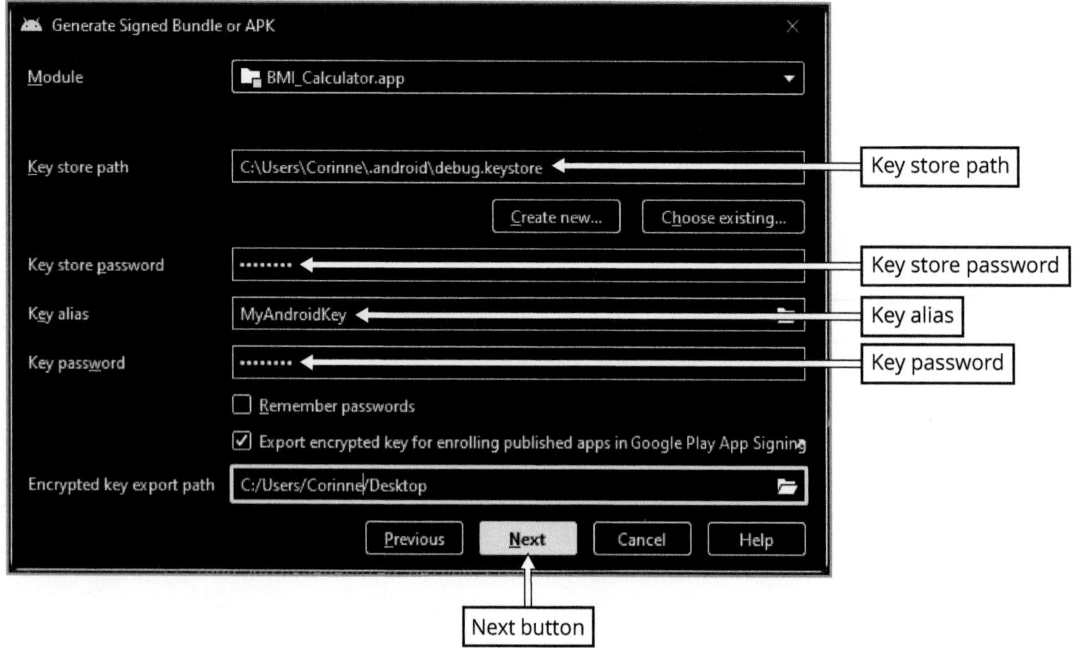

- Enter a password of your own choosing in the Key store password text box. You use this password for your Google Play developers account.
- In the Key alias text box, enter **MyAndroidKey**.
- Type the same password again in the Key password text box.

The information needed to create a new key is entered in the Generate Signed Bundle or APK dialog box (Figure 12-8).

Step 4

- Click the Next button.
- Click the debug option below the Destination Folder field.

The Generate Signed Bundle or APK dialog box displays the Destination Folder needed to create a signed key (**Figure 12-9**).

Figure 12-9 Selecting the debug option

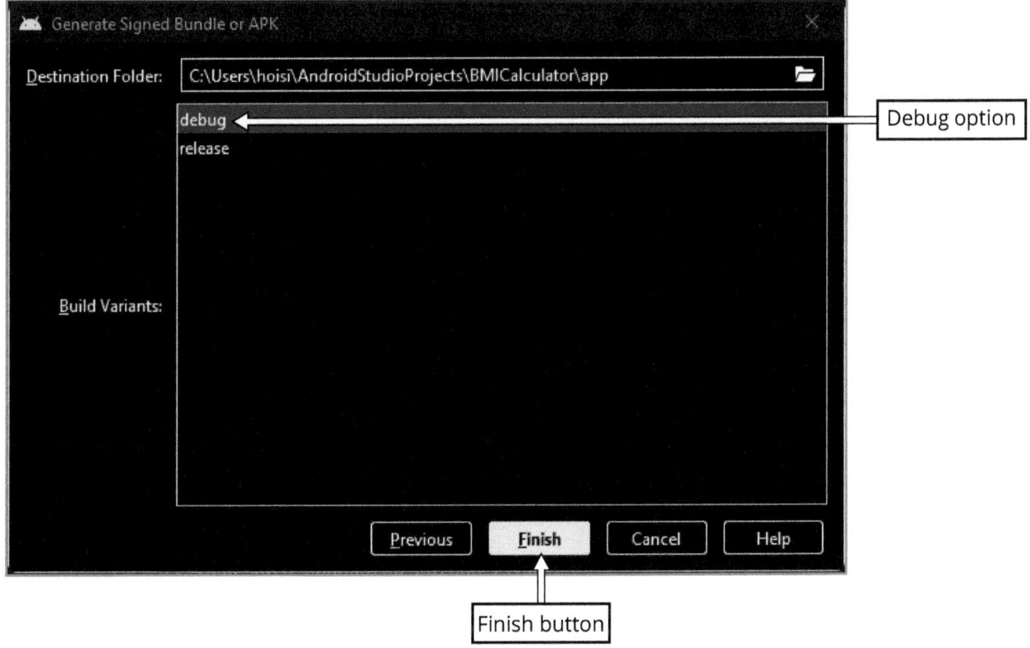

Step 5

- Click the Finish button to open the Master Password dialog box.
- If necessary, type your password again in the New Password and Confirm New Password text boxes.
- If necessary, click the Set Password button.

Your password is entered twice in the Master Password dialog box. To view the saved location of your .aab file, click the Show in Explorer button.

Good to Know | Android .aab files can be installed and run directly on an Android device. You can email the .aab files to others so that they can install the file attachment directly on their devices.

On the Job | The key creates your private key for Android deployment. It is best to back up your key in a safe file location. If you lose your key file, you will not be able to upgrade your Android Google Play app.

12.5 Preparing Promotional Materials to Upload

When you publish your app to Google Play, you are required to post several images that accompany the app and assist with marketing. There are hundreds of thousands of apps in the Google Play Store, so you must publicize your app to make it stand out and be noticed by casual visitors. To leverage your app in the store, you can upload the app with screenshots, a video link, promotional graphics, and descriptive text, as shown on the National Geographic app page at Google Play (see **Figure 12-10**).

Figure 12-10 National Geographic Android app from Google Play

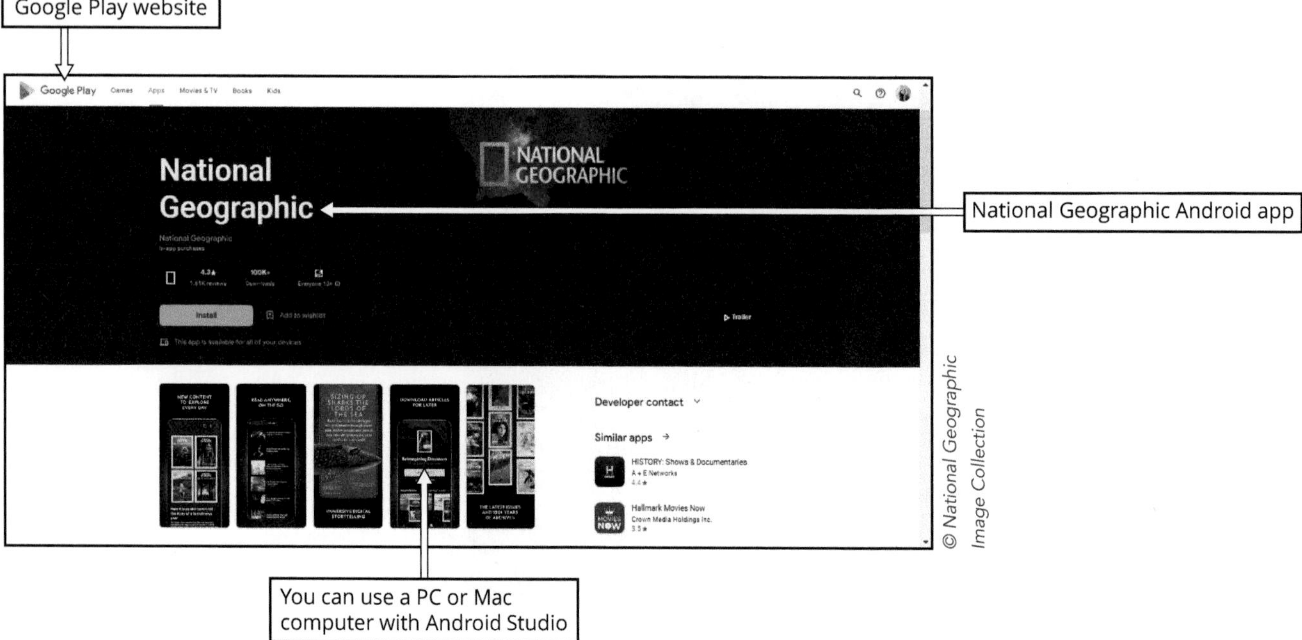

Providing Images

By adding preview assets on the store listing page to showcase your app's features and functionality, you can help the app attract new users on Google Play. Assets are categorized by required assets and highly recommended assets in the Google Play Store. In the National Geographic Android app, a high-resolution application icon is displayed near the top of the page. The application icon does not replace your launcher icon but serves to identify and brand your app. The size of the application icon should be 512 × 512 pixels, and the icon should be stored in a 32-bit .png file. In addition, you must provide at least two screenshots of the app to display in the Details section of your app page on the Google Play site. Large .png images such as those in the National Geographic app (**Figure 12-11**) are displayed in any of the following dimensions: 480 × 320, 800 × 480, or 854 × 480 pixels. You can upload up to eight screenshots for the app page. The screenshots appear before a written description.

You can also display a preview video to demonstrate your app, though Google Play does not require one. As an alternative when publishing your app, you can upload it with a video link to a demo video on YouTube.com. The video should highlight the top features of your app and last between 30 seconds and 2 minutes. These visual elements are the first impression that potential users will have of your app. Creating high-quality media helps improve an app's marketability.

Figure 12-11 Preview images and description of National Geographic Android app

Preview images of the National Geographic app

Google Play Games Apps Movies & TV Books Kids

NEW CONTENT TO EXPLORE EVERY DAY

READ ANYWHERE, ON THE GO

SIZING UP SHARKS, THE LORDS OF THE SEA

IMMERSIVE DIGITAL STORYTELLING

DOWNLOAD ARTICLES FOR LATER

THE LATEST ISSUES AND 130+ YEARS OF ARCHIVES

About this app →

About this app description

From the deepest depths of the ocean to the peak of Mt. Everest, National Geographic allows you to see and experience the world in new ways. The new National Geographic app now provides online and offline access to stories that reveal insights into cultures, ideas and discoveries.

App features:
• Downloadable articles for offline reading..

Updated on
Jan 6, 2023

News & Magazines

Data safety →

Safety starts with understanding how developers collect and share your data. Data privacy and security practices may vary based on your use, region, and age. The developer provided this information and may update it over time.

Good to Know Google Play has more than 2.68 million published apps and more than 110 billion downloads.

Providing a Description

In addition to the promotional material, an app description provides a quick overview of the app's purpose and what it does. To intrigue your readers, you can include some of the app's features in the description and explain why your app is unique in comparison with competitors without mentioning their names. The description needs to sell your app to the widest audience possible. For example, the description of the National Geographic app in Figure 12-11 appeals to an audience searching for a cultural discovery. Notice that the description highlights the features and benefits of the app using direct and concise language. A good description can motivate users to download the app. Revise the description with each update of your app, adding information such as new features and user reviews.

In **Figure 12-12**, notice the Review section and the ratings. If you scroll down, you can also display the date of the app's last update, its current version, Android platform requirements, and the app's category, size, price, and content rating. Users search for the most popular apps, as measured by their ratings. Prospective app buyers read user reviews to determine if your app is worth their time and money. When a visitor writes a good review about your application, you can quote the review within your description. Customers value good reviews and are more likely to download your app if it is well recommended.

The National Geographic app on Google Play is free, although it has optional in-app purchases. So, how do the developers make money? At the bottom of the National Geographic page on Google Play is a list of other products

Figure 12-12 National Geographic reviews

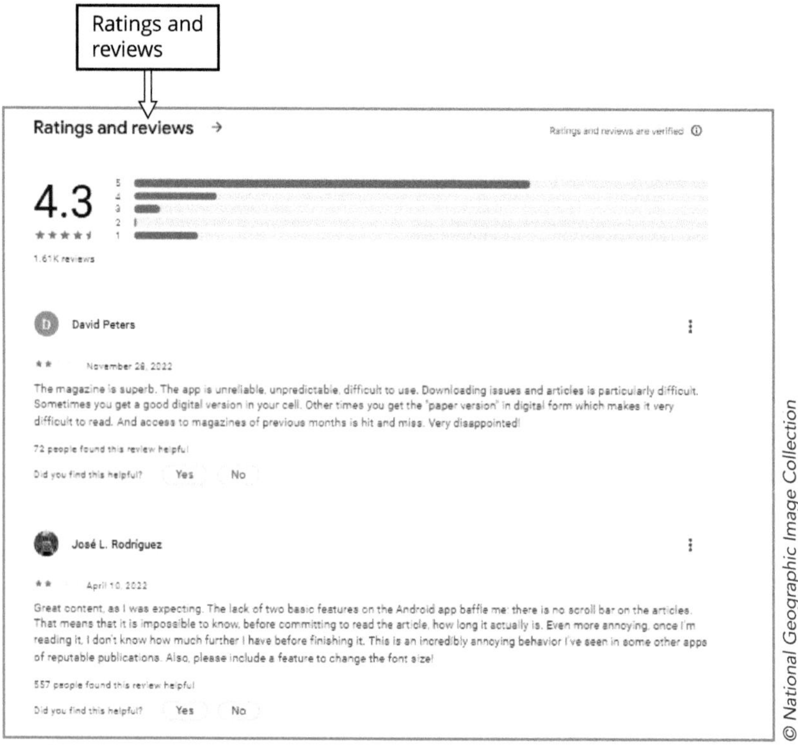

created by the developer. Gaming apps sometimes use a similar approach: Upon mastering a free game, users are often motivated to buy the full version of a product or to buy additional features, including in-app purchases such as extra lives or more levels. As you price your app, consider that some users never want to pay for an average app, but many will pay for a great one. Consider also adding Facebook, Twitter, and other social networking links on your app's page at Google Play so users can market your app within their friend networks.

When you upload your app to Google Play, you select one of the application categories shown in **Table 12-1**. If your app fits into more than one category, be sure to include each one to attract visitors in each category searched.

Table 12-1 App category types on Google Play

Category	Example Types of Apps
Books & Reference	Book readers, reference books, textbooks, dictionaries, thesauruses, wikis
Business	Document editors/readers, package tracking, remote desktops, email management, job searches
Comics	Comic players, comic titles
Communications	Messaging, chat/IM, dialers, address books, browsers, call management
Education	Exam preparations, study aids, vocabulary, educational games, language learning
Finance	Banking, payment, ATM finders, financial news, insurance, taxes, portfolio/trading, tip calculators
Health & Fitness	Personal fitness, workout tracking, diet and nutritional tips, health and safety
Libraries & Demo	Software libraries
Lifestyle	Recipes, style guides
Media & Video	Subscription movie services, remote controls, media/video players
Medical	Drug and clinical references, calculators, handbooks for healthcare providers, medical journals and news

(continues)

Table 12-1 App category types on Google Play (*continued*)

Category	Example Types of Apps
Music & Audio	Music services, radios, music players
News & Magazines	Newspapers, news aggregators, magazines, blogging
Personalization	Wallpapers, live wallpapers, home screens, lock screens, ring tones
Photography	Cameras, photo-editing tools, photo management and sharing
Productivity	Notepads, to-do lists, keyboards, printing, calendars, backup, calculators, conversion
Shopping	Online shopping, auctions, coupons, price comparison, grocery lists, product reviews
Social	Social networking, check-in, blogging
Sports	Sports news and commentary, score tracking, fantasy team management, game coverage
Tools	System utility tools
Travel & Local	City guides, local business information, trip management tools
Weather	Weather reports

Including Contact and Social Networks

On the National Geographic app page, a Developer contact button provides links to their website, email, and possible social networks. Using links to social networks in the app's promotional materials, people can become fans of National Geographic on Facebook (**Figure 12-13**) or follow National Geographic on Instagram. Having a social networking presence for your app enables you to build relationships among customers who share common interests, backgrounds, or hobbies. Through your Facebook and Instagram pages, you can communicate with your fans in a more entertaining manner. Customers might suggest additions for future versions of the app.

Figure 12-13 National Geographic's Facebook account helps create a social media presence

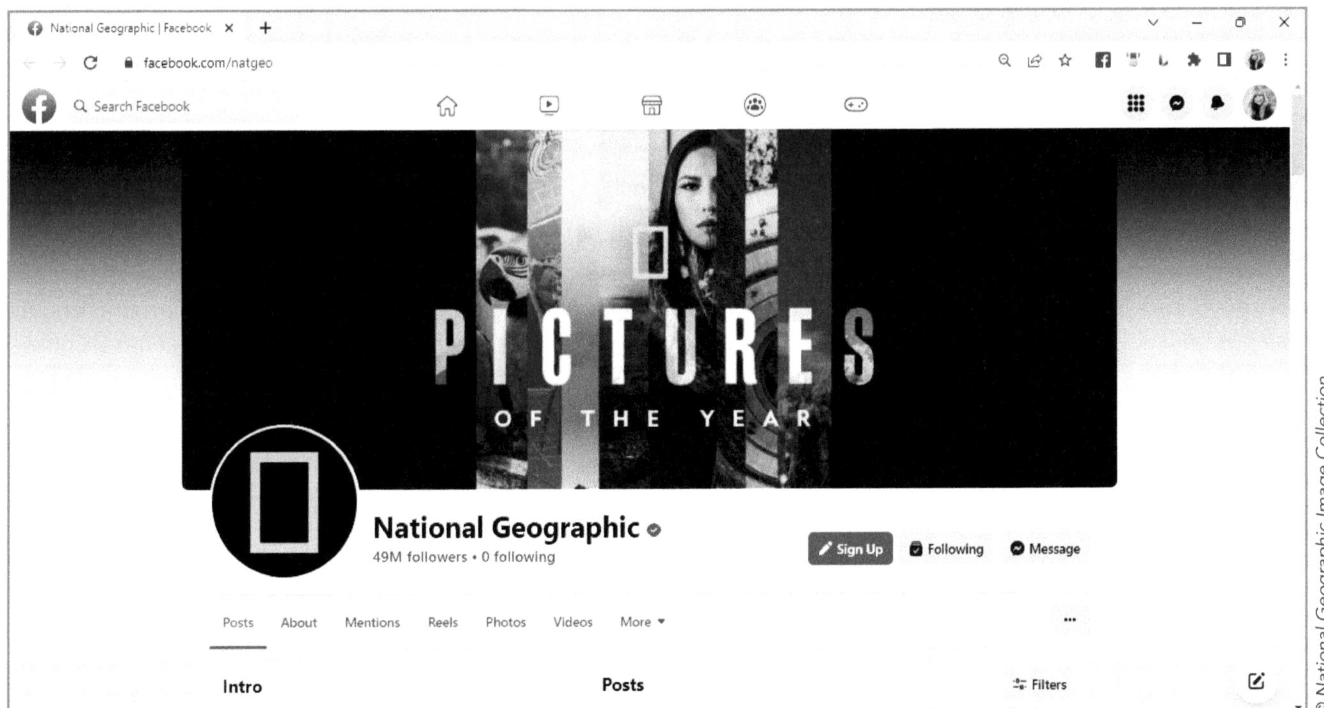

Setting Versions for your App

After your app has been published to Google Play, you will continue to update the app with new features and new SDK platforms. You can set the version of code and the version name number within the AndroidManifest.xml file in the following format, which allows the Android OS to check whether a newer version of the app is available from the Google Play Store and then prompt the user to upgrade the app, if necessary.

```
<?xml version="1.0" encoding="utf-8"?>
<manifest xmlns:android="http://schemas.android.com/apk/res/android"
    xmlns:tools="http://schemas.android.com/tools"
    android:versionCode="1"
    android:versionName="1.0">
```

Critical Thinking

How much does it cost to create a fan page for my app on Facebook or Instagram?

You can create a fan page on Facebook or Instagram for free.

Registering for a Google Play Account

Google Play is a publishing platform that helps you distribute your Android apps to users around the world. Before you can publish apps through Google Play, you must register as an Android application developer using your Gmail account username and password at *https://play.google.com/apps/publish*. Registering at Google Play requires a one-time-only payment of $25, which enrolls you in a Google Merchant account. Google charges the one-time fee to encourage higher-quality products on Google Play. To receive payment for purchased apps, you must first specify a bank account. Bank account information is not added or updated within your Google Checkout account but in the Google Wallet Merchant Center. You can allow an unlimited number of people to access your Google Play developer's account. You will remain the owner of the account and will be the only person who can grant or revoke access to other users.

The registration process requires you to have a Google account, agree to the legal terms, and pay the fee via your Google Merchant account. If you charge for your app, Google Merchant disperses revenue for application sales. If you register to sell applications, you must also be registered as a Google Merchant with a Google Wallet account. As a developer, you have access to view your app ratings, comments, and number of downloads.

If you charge for your application, note that Google Play has a service fee. The fee for the first $1 million of revenue is 15 percent of the app payment. You will receive 85 percent of the application price, with the remaining 15 percent distributed among the phone carriers affiliated with Google Play. If you earn more than $1 million in profits, Google Play's service fee is 30 percent. The profit from your first sale will arrive in your Google Merchant account 24 hours later. Purchasers who buy and install an app have their credit cards charged 24 hours later. If the user uninstalls the app within 24 hours of buying it, Google issues a full refund of the purchase price.

To register as a Google Play Android developer, follow these steps.

Step 1

- To register at Google Play, open a browser and go to **https://play.google.com/apps/publish**.
- If necessary, enter your Gmail account information. Enter the password for your Gmail account.

Your Gmail account username and password are entered in the Google Play Developer Console (**Figure 12-14**).

Figure 12-14 Signing in to a Google developer's account

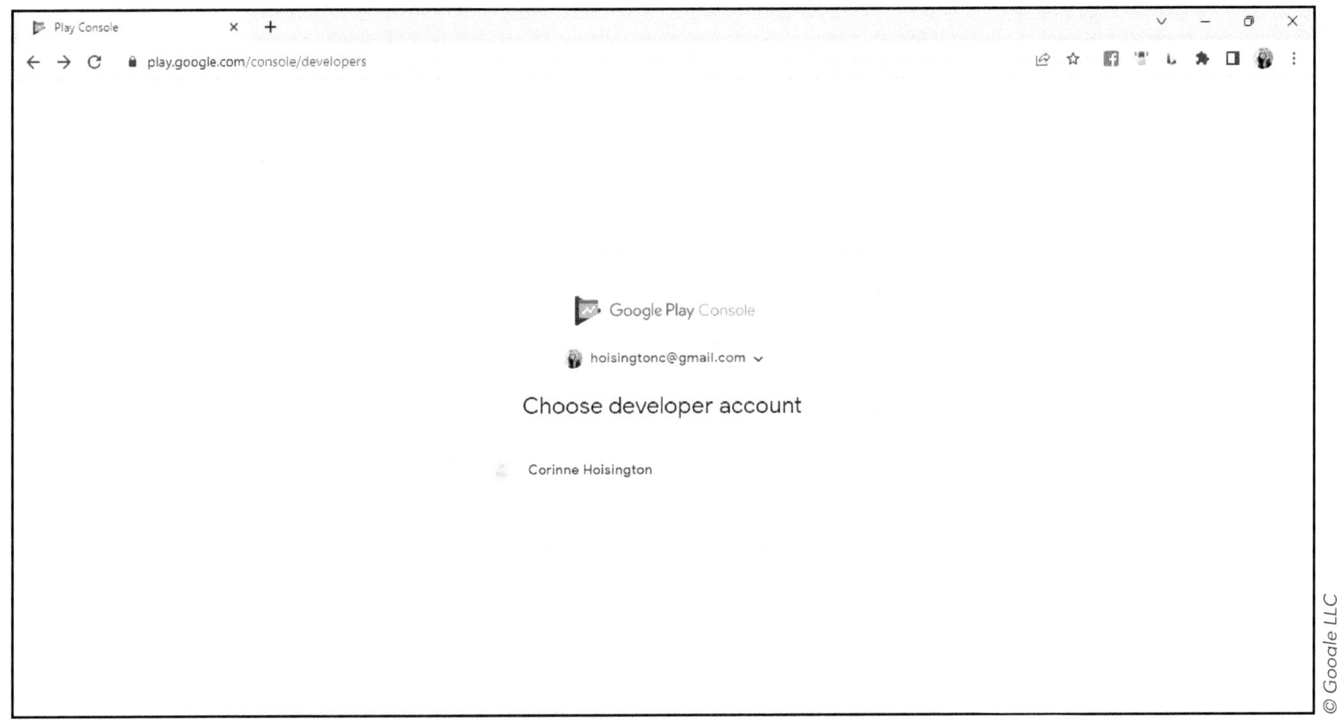

Step 2

- Click the Sign in button to sign in with your Google account information.
- Click the check box acknowledging that you read the Google Play Developer distribution agreement, and then click the Continue to payment button.
- Complete the payment process.
- To complete your account details and register for a developer's Google Play account, type your name in the Developer name text box. The email address is added based on your Google account.
- In the Phone Number text box, type your phone number. Follow the steps to complete your registration.

On the Developer Console page of the Google Play Developer Console, your name and details are entered.

Good to Know After creating your account in Google Play, it may take up to 48 hours for the account to be approved for publishing Android apps.

Quick Check

If you sell your app for $1.99 and make $30,000 in sales, how much of that amount would you earn as the developer?

Answer: $25,500.

12.6 Publishing Your App to Google Play

As you upload your app to Google Play, you will be prompted to enter information about your application. Once you create an account, the Developer Console pages take you through the steps to upload your unlocked application .aab file and the promotional assets. The maximum supported file size for an .aab file at Google Play is 150 MB. After your app is posted and rises in popularity, Google Play gives you higher placement in weekly "top" lists and promotional slots in collections such as Top Free Apps. Before submitting an app to Google Play, ensure that it complies with their content policies and with local laws that restrict gambling, illegal activities, unapproved substances, and content that could endanger a child. If you have created a Google Play Developer's account, take the following steps to upload an Android application to Google Play.

Step 1

- To upload your app to Google Play, click All Apps to open the Developer's Console.

The All apps page opens and displays a list of any apps that have been uploaded previously (**Figure 12-15**).

Figure 12-15 All apps page on Google Play Console

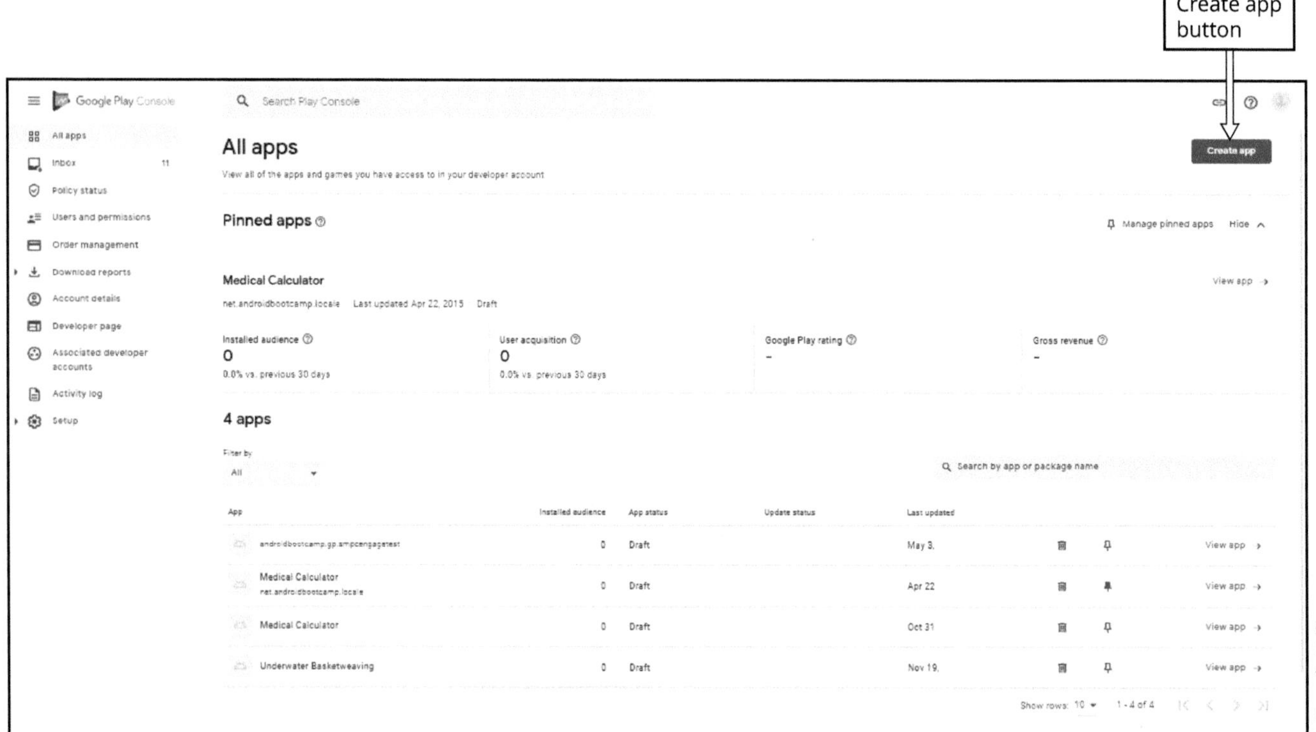

Step 2

- Click the **Create app** button to upload the .aab file.

The Create app website opens (**Figure 12-16**).

Step 3

- Type the name of the app in the App name text box.
- Select the Default language of your app.
- Click the appropriate radio button to classify your program as an app or a game.

Figure 12-16 Create app website

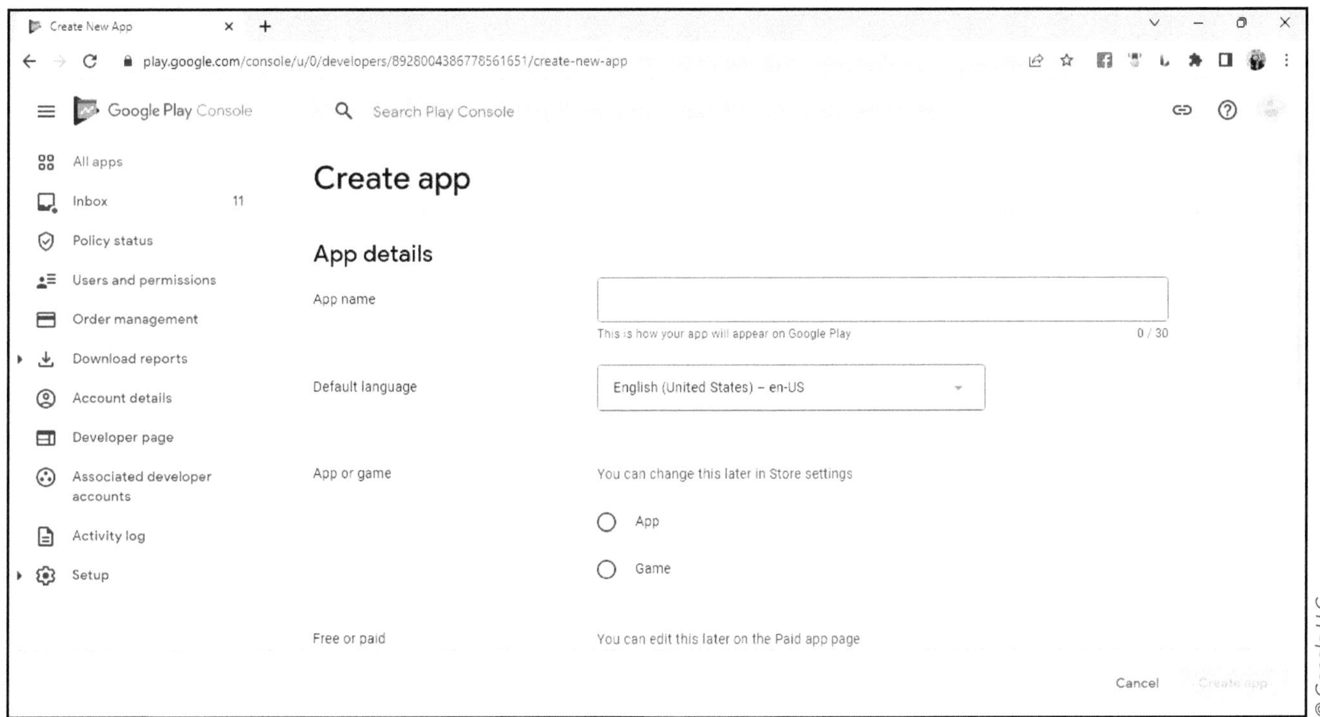

- Click the appropriate radio button for whether your app is free or not.
- Check the boxes for the declarations to agree to the Developer Program Policies.
- Click the **Create app** button.

Clicking the Create app button opens the Dashboard website within the browser (**Figure 12-17**).

Figure 12-17 Google Play developers Dashboard

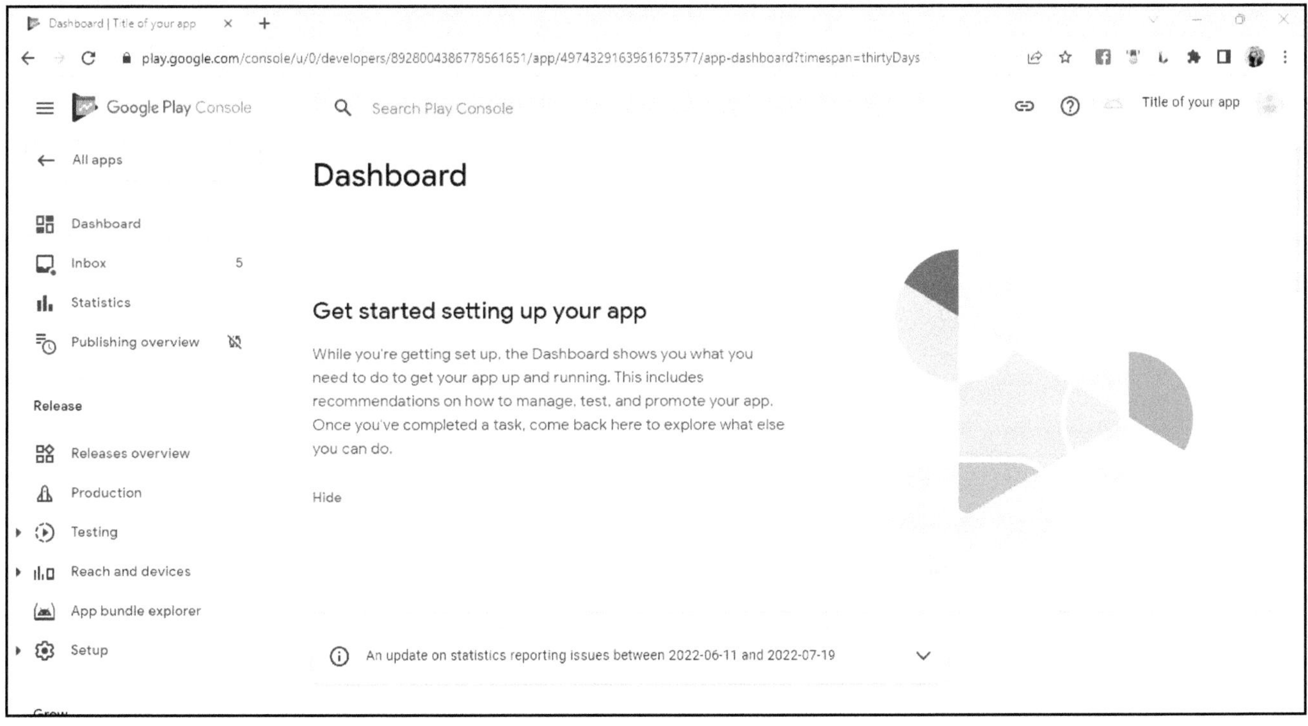

Step 4

- On the Dashboard page, follow the directions for the different categories and tasks related to app setup and release. You must complete the mandatory tasks before you can launch your app on Google Play.
- When you complete a task, you'll see a green tick mark and strikethrough text. The progress bar at the top of the section will also be updated. As you complete more tasks, your dashboard will populate with performance data and key insights by set time periods.
- After launching your app, you can visit your dashboard to get an overview of the app's key metrics, trends, and insights. If you want to learn more about these metrics, go to View app statistics. Scroll down the page to display additional details.

You can see your app's latest publishing status under the name and package name when you select the app in Dashboard.

Critical Thinking

Can I upload separate apps for the form factors of different devices?

Yes. If you cannot support all devices with a single .aab file, you can upload multiple AABs using the same app listing to target different device configurations, each with a maximum size of 150 MB.

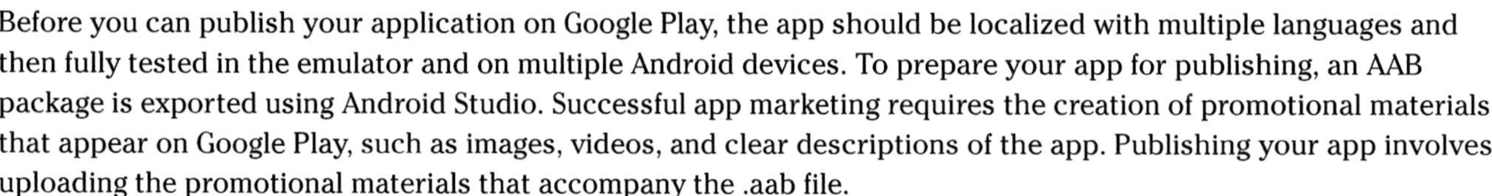

Wrap It Up—Chapter Summary

Before you can publish your application on Google Play, the app should be localized with multiple languages and then fully tested in the emulator and on multiple Android devices. To prepare your app for publishing, an AAB package is exported using Android Studio. Successful app marketing requires the creation of promotional materials that appear on Google Play, such as images, videos, and clear descriptions of the app. Publishing your app involves uploading the promotional materials that accompany the .aab file.

- Google Play is the storefront for Android devices and apps. It provides access to Android apps, Google Music, and Google e-books. It also includes an online store for paid and free Android apps, music, movies, books, and games. Android phones, tablets, and Google TV can access the Google Play services.
- To reach a larger audience within the Google Play market, you should target multiple Android devices and translate your app into multiple languages using the Translations Editor and Locale features. Create a custom experience for devices with different screen sizes, pixel densities, orientations, and resolutions so that users feel the app was designed specifically for their phone or tablet.
- As you design an Android app, you can provide alternate resources such as strings of text translated into multiple languages; the language changes depending on the default locale detected on the device.
- Before publishing an Android app, test it on various devices. Using different built-in emulators in Android Studio, you can test the design and functionality of your application on a wide range of devices and see how it performs in a real-world environment. Using the Android Debug Bridge (ADB) tool in Android Studio, you can develop and debug an Android application on an Android device.
- After testing an Android app, you must create an .aab file (Android App Bundle), which is a release-ready package that users can install and run on their Android phones and tablets. An .aab file is a compressed archive that contains the application, the manifest file, and all associated resources, such as image files, music, and other required content. Using the Generate Signed Bundle or APK dialog box in Android Studio, you can build a release-ready .aab file that is signed with your private key and optimized for publication.

- When you publish your app in Google Play, you must post several images, including an application icon and screenshots. You can also post a video or link to a video that demonstrates your app. You must include a description that provides an overview of the app's purpose and features. Finally, include app information such as ratings, Android platform requirements, category, and price.
- To publish apps through Google Play, you must register as a developer using your Gmail account username and password at *https://play.google.com/apps/publish*. The registration process requires you to have a Google account, agree to the legal terms, and pay a $25 fee via your Google Merchant account.
- After you create a Google Play account, the Developer Console Dashboard pages at the Google Play website step you through uploading your unlocked application .aab file and its promotional assets.

Key Terms

.aab file
Android App Bundle (AAB)
Android Debug Bridge (ADB)
Google Play
localization

Developer FAQs

1. What is the URL of Google Play? (12.1)
2. Approximately how many countries use Google Play? (12.1)
3. Name four services of Google Play. (12.1)
4. What are the names of other Android app stores similar to Google Play? (12.1)
5. To increase your target audience on Google Play, what two considerations should you make? (12.2)
6. How do you change your app to multiple languages? (12.2)
7. What is the address of the Google website that assists with language translation? (12.2)
8. What does .aab stand for? (12.4)
9. What does APK stand for? (12.4)
10. Can you deploy your app to your Android phone directly? (12.3)
11. Do you have to install ADB drivers on a Mac computer? (12.3)
12. Name four promotional assets that you can upload with your app at Google Play. (12.5)
13. What is the maximum number of screenshots of your app in action that you can post on Google Play? (12.5)
14. Where must you post your promotional video? (12.5)
15. What are the minimum and maximum lengths of the promotional video? (12.5)
16. On which two social networking sites should you create a marketing presence? (12.5)
17. Which category would you select on Google Play for a calendar app? (12.5)
18. Which category would you select for a recipe app? (12.5)
19. How much is the registration fee to publish Android apps on Google Play? (12.5)
20. What is the maximum size of an .aab file on Google Play? (12.6)

Beyond the Book

To answer the following questions, create an idea for an app that you think would sell well on Google Play.

1. Write about 200 words describing your Google Play app idea, beginning with a catchy title for the app.
2. Locate an image link that could work as the application icon for your Android app idea. (If you plan to use the icon, you will need to properly obtain the image following copyright guidelines.)
3. Consider the price for selling your Android app. Write at least 150 words explaining why you selected this price after researching the Internet for price points.
4. Create a short YouTube video to market your app idea, and provide the link to your instructor.

Case Programming Projects

Note that this chapter has no case programming projects.

Glossary

A

.aab file A release-ready package of an Android app stored in a compressed archive similar to a .zip file that contains the application, the manifest file, and all associated resources, such as image files, music, and other required content.

Action bar icon An icon that appears in the upper-left corner on the Action bar of an Activity.

ACTION_VIEW A generic action you can use to send any request to get the most reasonable action to occur.

Activity An Android component that represents a single screen with a user interface.

adapter An Android tool that provides a data model for the layout of a list and for converting the data from the array into list items.

Android App Bundle (AAB) A format for packaging your Android apps; it is published in Google Play Store.

Android Debug Bridge (ADB) An Android tool you use to communicate with a connected Android device.

Android Manifest A file named AndroidManifest.xml that is required in every Android application. This file provides essential information to the Android device, such as the name of your Java application and a listing of each Activity.

Android project view A pane on the left side of the Android Studio program window that contains the folders for the current project.

Android Studio The recommended IDE for writing Java programs and for building and integrating application development tools and open-source projects for Android.

Android Virtual Device (AVD) An emulator configuration for design and layout purposes.

android:oneshot An attribute of the animation-list element that determines whether an animation plays once and then stops or continues to play until the Stop Animation button is tapped.

AnimationDrawable class A class that provides the methods for drawable animations to create a sequence of frame-by-frame images.

animation-list An XML root element that references images stored in the drawable folder and is used in an animation.

API version The version of an Android on which to preview your layout.

app A mobile application.

application template A design you can use to create basic Android applications and then customize them.

array A container object that holds a fixed number of values of a single type.

ArrayAdapter<String> A ListAdapter that supplies string array data to a ListView object.

array variable A variable that can store more than one value.

attribute A characteristic of a project or object that describes what it can do.

Attributes pane A display of the attributes and controls for the selected view's attributes.

B

backgroundTint A Button attribute that can change the color of the background.

Boolean operators When comparing expressions, these operators return a true (1) or false (0) value.

break A statement that ends a case within a Switch statement and continues with the statement following the Switch decision structure.

C

Calendar class A class you can use to access the Android system date. The Calendar class is also responsible for conversions between a Date object and a set of integer fields such as YEAR, MONTH, and DAY_OF_MONTH.

case A keyword used in a Switch statement to indicate a condition. In a Switch statement, the case keyword is followed by a value and a colon.

class A group of objects that establishes an introduction to each object's properties.

class variable A variable with global scope; it can be accessed by multiple methods throughout a program.

codec A computer technology used to compress and decompress audio and video files.

Component Tree A pane in the Android Studio project window that displays the ordered hierarchy of the emulator layout's structure.

compound condition More than one condition included in an If statement.

ConstraintLayout A layout option in the Component Tree that organizes how components appear on the app's various screens using the Layout Editor's visual tools.

constraints The building blocks in an Android layout that attach or align a component to the screen, either by attaching it vertically and horizontally to the edges of the screen or aligning it with another component (or parent) on the screen.

constructor A part of the Java code used to initialize the instance variables of an object.

D

data validation Checking the integrity, accuracy, and structure of an app.

DatePicker A component within a dialog box that ensures a user selects a valid date.

DAY_OF_MONTH A date constant of the Calendar class that retrieves an integer value of the system's current day.

DAY_OF_YEAR A date constant of the Calendar class that retrieves the day of the current year as an integer. For example, February 1 is day 32 of the year.

DecimalFormat A class that provides patterns for formatting numbers in program output.

decision structure A fundamental component structure used in computer programming that deals with the different conditions that occur based on the values entered into an application.

descriptions Additions to user interface components that can be read out loud to users by a speech-based accessibility service such as a screen reader. Descriptions are useful in applications that are accessible to people with visual disabilities.

Design editor An editor that displays the emulator in Design view, Blueprint view, or both.

dialog A dialog box; in this chapter, a user can select a valid date from a dialog box.

E

element An individual item that contains a value in an array.

emulated application An application that is converted in real time to run on a variety of platforms—for example, a webpage—and that can be displayed on various screen sizes through a browser.

emulator Software that duplicates how an app looks and feels on a particular device.

entries A Spinner attribute that connects a string array to the Spinner component for display.

equals( ) method A method of the String class that Java uses to compare strings for equality.

event handler A part of a program coded to respond to a specific event.

F

final A type of variable that can only be initialized once; any attempt to reassign the value results in a compile error when the application is executed.

form factor The screen size, configuration, or physical layout of a technology device.

fragment A piece of an application's user interface or behavior that can be placed in an Activity.

Frame animation A type of animation, also called frame-by-frame animation, that plays a sequence of images as in a slide show, with a specified interval between images.

G

get The field manipulation method that accesses the system date or time.

getBaseContext( ) A Context class method used in Android programs to obtain a Context instance. Use getBaseContext( ) in a method that is triggered only when the user touches the GridView component.

getInstance( ) method A method of the Calendar class that returns a calendar date or time based on the system settings.

getSelectedItem( ) A method that returns the text of the selected Spinner item.

getText( ) A method that reads text stored in an EditText component.

getTime( ) method A method of the Calendar class that returns the time value in the Date object.

global scope A property of a variable that makes it accessible from anywhere in a class.

Google Play A digital repository that serves the Android market and includes an online store for paid and free Android apps as well as music, movies, books, and games.

Gravity A tool that changes the linear alignment of a component so that it is aligned to the left, center, right, top, or bottom of an object or the screen.

GridView A View container that displays a grid of objects with rows and columns.

H

hexadecimal color code A triplet of three colors using hexadecimal numbers, where colors are specified by a pound sign followed by the amount of red, green, and blue contained in the final color. Each of the three colors in the code is represented by two characters on the hexadecimal scale of 00 to FF.

hint A short description of a Text component that appears as light text in the component.

I

id attribute The name of a component. An id attribute is also called a key. Every string is composed of an id attribute and a default value, which is the text associated with the component.

If statement A statement that executes one set of instructions if a specified condition is true and takes no action if the condition is not true.

If Else statement A statement that executes one set of instructions if a specified condition is true and another set of instructions if the condition is false.

Image Asset Studio A feature of Android Studio that places generated icons in density-specific folders under the res/ directory in your project. At runtime, Android uses the appropriate resource based on the screen density of the device your app is running on.

ImageView component A component that displays an icon or a graphic from a picture file.

import To make the classes from a particular Android package available throughout the application.

import statement A statement that makes more Java functions available to a program.

instantiate To create an object of a specific class.

IntelliSense A general term for automated code-editing features that are sometimes known by other names, such as code completion, content assist, and code hinting.

intent Code in the Android Manifest file that allows an Android application with more than one Activity to navigate among Activities.

isChecked( ) method A method that tests a checked attribute to determine if a RadioButton object has been selected.

item In a Spinner component, a string of text that appears in a list for user selection.

J

Java An object-oriented programming language and a platform originated by Sun Microsystems.

java folder The folder that includes the Java code source files for a project.

K

key The name of a component. A key is also called the id attribute. Every string is composed of a key and a default value, which is the text associated with the component.

L

launcher icon An icon that appears on the home screen to represent the application.

layout A container that can hold widgets and other graphical components to help you design an interface for an application.

Layout Editor A feature in Android Studio that enables you to build layouts by dragging components into a visual design editor instead of writing XML layout code.

layout:margin A set of attributes that allow you to change the spacing around an object. You can change all the margins equally or change the left, top, right, and bottom margins individually.

layout_height An attribute that sets the height of a Spinner component.

layout_width An attribute that sets the width of a Spinner component.

life cycle The series of actions from the beginning, or birth, of an Activity to its end, or destruction.

local variable A variable declared by a variable declaration statement within a method.

localization The process of adapting an app or webpage to a language while considering cultural differences.

logo A graphic symbol that identifies an organization or one of its products.

M

manifests folder The folder that includes the AndroidManifest.xml file, which contains all the information about the application that Android needs to run.

MediaPlayer class The Java class that provides the methods for component audio playback on an Android device.

method In Java, a series of statements that perform some repeated task.

method body The part of a method containing a collection of statements that defines what the method does.

MONTH A date constant of the Calendar class that retrieves an integer value of the system's current month.

motion tween A type of animation that specifies the start state of an object and then animates it a predetermined number of times or an infinite number of times using a transition.

N

native application A program locally installed on a specific platform such as a phone or tablet.

nested A term for the placement of one statement, such as an If statement, within another statement.

9-patch image A special image with predefined stretching areas that maintain the same look on different screen sizes.

O

object A specific, concrete instance of a class.

object-oriented programming language A type of programming language that allows good software engineering practices such as code reuse.

onDateSet( ) method A method that automatically obtains the date selected by the user.

onDestroy( ) method A method used to end an Activity. The onCreate( ) method sets up required resources and the onDestroy( ) method releases those resources to free up memory.

onItemClick( ) An event the OnItemClickListener processes when the user touches the GridView display layout. The onItemClick( ) method is defined by OnItemClickListener and sends a number of arguments within the parentheses included in the line of code.

Open Handset Alliance An open-source business alliance of 80 firms that develop open standards for mobile devices.

open-source operating system An operating system that organizations and developers can use to extract and modify source code free of charge and copyright restrictions.

P

padding property A property that you can use to offset the content of a component by a specific number of pixels.

Palette A collection of widgets and view groups that you can drag into your layout.

Parse A class that converts a string into a number data type.

Pascal case Text that begins with an uppercase letter and uses an uppercase letter to start each new word.

permission A restriction limiting access to a part of the code or to data on the device.

persistent data The type of data that stores values permanently by placing the information in a file.

Phone Link A Microsoft app that integrates your Android phone with your PC, giving you access to the phone's notifications, text messages, and photos on your PC.

playback state The state of the MediaPlayer that determines whether an audio file is playing.

position The placement of an item in a list. When an item in a list is selected, the position of the item is passed from the onListItemClick( ) method and evaluated with a decision structure. The first item is assigned the position of 0, the second item is assigned the position of 1, and so forth.

Primary/Detail Flow template A template that Android Studio provides for creating an Android app with an adaptive, responsive layout; it displays a set of list items on the left and the associated details on the right.

prompt Text that displays instructions at the top of the Spinner component.

R

RadioGroup A group of RadioButton components; only one RadioButton component can be selected at a time.

res folder A project folder that contains all the resources, such as images, music, and video files, that an application may need.

responsive design An approach to designing apps and websites that provides an optimal viewing experience across as many devices as possible.

Responsive Design UI A design approach that is based on the size of your screen, platform, and orientation. If you use a ConstraintLayout, for example, your app can work on a phone of any size and automatically adjust, whether the phone has a vertical or horizontal orientation.

return type The data type for any value a method returns. Every method in Java is declared with a return type; it is mandatory for all Java methods.

S

scope A reference to a variable's visibility within a class.

set The field manipulation method that changes the system date or time.

setAdapter A command that provides a data model for the GridView layout, similar to an adapter that displays a ListView component.

setBackgroundResource( ) A method that places images in a frame-by-frame display for an animation, with each frame pointing to an image referenced in the XML resource file.

setContentView The Java code necessary to display the content of a specific screen.

setOnItemClick( ) A method called when an item in a list is selected.

soft keyboard An on-screen keyboard positioned over the lower part of an application's window.

Software Development Kit (SDK) A package containing development tools for creating applications.

sp A unit of measurement that stands for "scaled-independent pixels."

Spinner component A component similar to a drop-down list for selecting a single item from a fixed listing.

spinnerMode An attribute that sets a Spinner component either to dialog mode, which uses a pop-up dialog box for selecting Spinner items, or to drop-down mode, which displays the items in a list box.

SQLite A lightweight, preloaded mobile database engine that has been available since the Cupcake 1.5 version of Android and occupies a small amount of disk memory.

startAnimation( ) A method that begins the animation process of a View object by calling the AnimationUtils class utilities to access the resources necessary to load the animation.

state A stage in an Activity's life cycle that determines whether the Activity is active, paused, stopped, or dead.

string A series of alphanumeric characters that can include spaces.

string array Two or more text strings.

String table A location in Android Studio where all the text used in an app is stored. The text in the String table can be translated to multiple languages for different worldwide users.

strings.xml A default file that is part of every Android application and contains commonly used strings for an application. When you add strings to strings.xml, you can easily translate your entire app into other languages.

stub A piece of code that serves as a placeholder to declare itself; it contains just enough code to link to the rest of the program.

Switch A type of decision statement that allows you to choose from many statements based on an integer or single-character (char) input.

T

TableLayout A user interface design layout that includes TableRow components to form a grid.

text attribute An attribute that references a string resource to display text within a component.

textColor An attribute that sets the color of text in a component.

textColorHint An attribute that sets the color of a hint.

textSize attribute An attribute that sets the size of text in a component.

theme A style applied to an Activity or an entire application.

thread A single sequential flow of components within a program.

Timer A Java class that creates a timed event when the schedule( ) method is called.

timer A tool that performs a one-time task, such as displaying an opening splash screen, or that performs a continuous process, such as a morning wake-up call set to run at regular intervals.

TimerTask A Java class that invokes a scheduled timer.

toast notification A message that appears as an overlay on a user's screen, often displaying a validation warning.

Translations editor An area in Android Studio that can display text in the language in which it was programmed as well as in the language of the current locale.

Tween animation A type of animation that, instead of using a sequence of images, creates an animation on a single image or the contents of a View object by performing a series of transformations that alter position, size, rotation, and transparency.

tween effect A transition that changes objects from one state to another, such as by moving, rotating, growing, or shrinking.

typeface A property that you can use to set the style of component text to a font family such as monospace, sans serif, or serif.

U

URI An acronym for Uniform Resource Identifier; a string that identifies the resources of the web. Similar to a URL, a URI includes additional information necessary for gaining access to the resources required for posting a webpage.

URL An acronym for Uniform Resource Locator; a website address.

user experience The interactions that occur between people and an app.

V

value The data part of a key-value pair that represents a string, int, long, float, or Boolean value.

variable A name used in a Java program to contain data that changes during the execution of the program.

View A rectangular container that displays a drawing or text object.

visibility attribute The Java attribute that determines whether a component is displayed on the emulator.

W

WebView A View component that displays webpages.

widget A single element such as a TextView, Button, or CheckBox component; also called an object or control.

X

XML An acronym for Extensible Markup Language, a widely used system for defining data formats; assists in the layout of the Android emulator.

Y

YEAR A date constant of the Calendar class that retrieves an integer value of the system's current year.

Index

Note: Page numbers in **bold** indicate where keywords are defined

S

T

U

V